Augusta Cooks for Company

A COLLECTION of RECIPES

Collected and Compiled

by

Jeanette Steed

for

THE AUGUSTA COUNCIL of the

GEORGIA ASSOCIATION
FOR CHILDREN AND ADULTS

with

LEARNING DISABILITIES

Featuring

HISTORICAL AUGUSTA
and
FAVORITE RECIPES of FAMILIES and FRIENDS
TREASURED RECIPES of YESTERDAY and TODAY

THIS BOOK IS DEDICATED TO LIGHTEN THE LOAD
of
CHILDREN and ADULTS
WITH LEARNING DISABILITIES
by
PROVIDING FUNDS for a SCHOLARSHIP FUND
to
BUILD A BRIDGE "BETWEEN"
for LEARNING DISABLED STUDENTS and TEACHERS

ISBN: 0-9639524-0-4
Library of Congress Catalog Card Number: 93-74846

COPYRIGHT © 1990
Jeanette Steed

Additional copies of "AUGUSTA COOKS for COMPANY" may be obtained by sending $15.95 per book plus $2.00 per book for postage and handling (Georgia residents add $ .96 per book for sales tax).

August Cooks For Company
P.O. Box 3231
Hill Station
Augusta, Georgia 30914-3231

| First Printing | 1990 | 3,000 copies |
| Second Printing | 1994 | 3,000 copies |

Printed in the USA by

WIMMER
The Wimmer Companies, Inc.
Memphis • Dallas

ACKNOWLEDGEMENTS

This book contains a collection of favorite recipes of friends and families of Learning Disabled youths. We wish to acknowledge the fine spirit of cooperation of all who shared their special and treasured recipes with us for this project. For:

"Where there is joy in sharing,
Where there is love to impart,
Never bare is the cupboard,
Never empty, the heart."
Laura Baker Haynes

A recipe that is not shared will soon be forgotten, but when it's shared, it will be enjoyed by future generations. It will also help some very fine young people to realize a dream that otherwise might never have been possible.

We do not claim that all the recipes are originals, only that they are our favorites. We regret that we were unable to include many recipes which were submitted due to space or similarity.

We have no reason to doubt that these recipes, ingredients and instructions will work successfully if followed correctly. The recipes in this book have been collected from various sources and neither the organization nor any contributor, publisher, printer or seller of this book is responsible for errors or omissions.

Add to them or subtract from them according to your own taste. Make them your favorites too and in doing so pass them on to your friends and families.

THANKS

Thank you for purchasing our cookbook. Your generosity allows us a chance to help build a "Bridge between school and a successful life for the Learning Disabled youth. The monetary gifts, made possible through your purchase, will benefit all. We will be able to offer scholarships to colleges and technical schools for Learning Disabled youth and to LD teachers seeking help to acquire more knowledge. It is to this involvement we dedicate this book.

We offer to you a sampling of our hearts, our past and present dreams, our lifestyles, our pride, our traditions and our tastes. Most importantly we offer you our thanks for giving us a chance to help build a bridge between school and a successful life for Learning Disabled children and youth by providing them help when needed. The investment you have made in these youths will be returned to our community, state and nation many times over, perhaps even to the world.

Cover Watercolor by Lucy Hargrove Weigle

Lucy Weigle is one of Augusta's most active, involved, visual artists. She has made a name for herself as an accomplished painter, teacher and leaded of the art community. A Birmingham, Alabama native, Mrs. Weigle is currently president of the Georgia Watercolor Society, a post which puts her in touch with painters across the nation. Mrs. Weigle works primarily in watercolor, painting everything from endearing portraits to complex but free-flowing abstractions of nature. She loves color, and her paintings often vibrate with exotic, intense shades from her palate. She likes to do close-ups of things and develop patterns.

Lucy Weigle received her BS in Art from Auburn University. She said, "I have always been in love with art". She continued her art studies during her travels with her husband who was in the Navy. In San Francisco, she studied watercolor at Alameda College and portraiture with Cedric Elegy in Annapolis, Maryland. In Athens, Greece she was an apprentice to noted contemporary artist Nikos Krideras.

Mrs. Weigle's travels have had a great influence on her work. Her favorite subjects are people, having encountered many interesting characters. Others include flowers, animate and inanimate subjects and abstractions of nature done in an impressionist style with strong use of color and design.

An award-winner on the national level, as well as locally, Lucy has been honored by Augusta as the recipient of the Woman of Excellence Award in arts. Her work is included in corporate collections locally and regionally and in private collections internationally.

Lucy is the mother of three sons. One of which is a very special, gifted and talented learning disabled young adult.

Inside Artwork by Ray Baird

Special thanks to Mr. Ray Baird who so generously gave his permission for use of his historical sketches of Augusta.

Mr. Baird is a talented and versatile artist working primarily in pen and ink. For his subject matter, he most often turns to old buildings and outdoor scenes that lend themselves to the powerful drama of black lines on white paper. Ray's drawings capture the charm and mystique of an era and its buildings that have largely gone by. His extensive travels throughout America, Europe and the world have given him a vast and fascinating repertoire of subject matter. Ray is a native of the hills and lakes of East Tennessee. He studied art and architecture at Ohio State University, graduating with a Bachelor of Architecture. He also has a Masters degree from the University of Southern California. His studio is in Martinez, Georgia. His works hang in private and corporate collections in most all states and in numerous foreign countries. His collection of Augusta Masters are excellent and are in many, many homes and offices. They are prized collector items for fans of the Masters. Ray now calls Martinez home.

Our thanks would not be complete without a word of thanks to Miss Sheryn Jones of Wimmer Press. We would like to extend our heartfelt thanks to Sheryn for her help, encouragement, patience and moral support. Without her efforts this book could never have become a reality.

Prints available by writing to Ray Baird, Baird Prints, Inc., P.O. Box 11229, 323 Fair Oaks Ct., Martinez, Georgia 30907 or call 404-860-6570.

PURPOSE

The purpose of this book is to raise funds to establish a scholarship fund for learning disabled youth, providing a bridge between secondary school and college and technical schools so that they may develop their lives to their fullest potential, as others have done in the past. All of us hope for a life that contains meaning and self respect. Learning Disabled youth are no exception. They have the same need to be successful productive citizens, to be proud of their accomplishments and rewarded for their efforts.

Despite the bleak history of learning disabled youth and adults, today the future is bright for them. They can lead useful, normal lives. They can go to college. They can become respected leaders of their community, if their problem is correctly diagnosed. If they are provided with special educational attention and they are treated with compassion and understanding. They must be given the tools to help themselves instead of pity.

Years ago, most children with learning problems left school at an early age, after only one or two years of failure. Later in life many of these school failures have become successful and respected members of the community by completing a job training program successfully or through PERSEVERANCE and hard work. Today, the youth with learning problems may be a failure even in our public vocational schools, so great are the additional skills, talents and job knowledge required. To avoid the loss of these gifted and talented youth from the job field and to provide for them some degree of self-sufficiency and self-respect during their lifetime, we must provide "Bridges Between" so they can develop their lives to their fullest potential, as others in the past have done. Some who have made it in our lifetime that you know are:

Nelson Rockefeller

He memorized whole speeches, used large type with words broken into syllables and sentences broken into segments. He became Governor and then Vice-President of our nation.

Bruce Jenner

He became an Olympic winner. He had a Learning Disability called Dyslexia.

Luci Johnson Nugent

She told the Kansas Association for Learning Disabilities, "By labeling myself as stupid and incompetent I no longer had to try to succeed. I could give up and find some peace." Her problem ended when a doctor discovered she had a visual disability.

5

Marilyn VanDebeur

A Learning Disabled person who went on to become Miss America.

Whoopi Goldberg

A well-known comedienne and actress who received the Hans Christian Anderson Award for outstanding achievement by a person with Dyslexia. Whoopi said, "After years of being considered retarded, I'm doing pretty good."

Tom Cruise

A lonely kid with serious learning problems who has become one of Hollywood's leading actors. His mother, a special education teacher, recognized his symptoms and tutored him in ways to overcome the disability. He did not run away from them — he discovered a passion for acting at 16 years of age. He was on his way to success.

Greg Louganis

He had perceptual and reading problems as well as stuttering. He was called a "dummy" by his peers in school yet he became an Olympic Diver. When he enrolled at the university of California, he looked up Dyslexia and found out about himself. He learned to compensate. When it came to physical activities, he took a back seat to no one. He took dancing, gymnastics and diving and excelled in all. He has 3 Olympic medals and 35 national titles-the most ever earned by a diver.

Stephen J. Cannell

Stephen, TV WHIZ, is the hottest writer/producer in Hollywood today. He has done it all despite a lifelong struggle with severe reading and writing disability. He has made fame and fortune from the written and spoken word while suffering from dyslexia, a learning disability which has impeded his reading and spelling throughout his life. He has become a Story Teller and a Master of Comedy. As a child, he was considered a slow learner, a "dumb kid". He wrote backwards, couldn't spell and couldn't trust anything he wrote because of his reversals. His professors in college said his writing was very interesting, but he got an F because of spelling. He developed a staggering visual imagination. He has given us *Riptide*, *"A" Team*, *Rockford Files*, *Hardcastle and McCormick* and *Baretta*, just to name a few.

Judge Jeffrey Gallet

A highly respected New York Judge who's written two law books, can't tell right from left or read, write or spell very well. He suffers from dyslexia and dysgraphia. He did not let his disabilities defeat him. With determination and persistence, today he is a Family Court Judge. He uses Dictaphone and still cannot spell, types slowly, reads slowly and can't write longhand. Today he is one of the brightest on the bench; a truly dedicated, committed individual; a successful judge, book author, teacher at Columbia University Medical School.

Helen Brooke Taussig

A M.D., who founded pediatric cardiology and co-developed the first successful "blue baby" operation was a dyslexic. Her father helped her to learn to compensate for her learning problems. She was admitted to Harvard Medical School as a "special student" to study medicine. Her grandfather was an immigrant Missouri physician who was dyslexic. He helped with problems in learning. She went to Boston University and finally graduated from Johns Hopkins. Her heart defect research produced the "blue baby" operation saving tens of thousands of children who suffered from a congenital heart defect causing their skin to turn blue.

Dr. Charles Drake

Founder of Landmark School for the Learning Disabled. He learned early that Learning Disabilities had nothing to do with intelligence. He grew up a bad speller, illegible in handwriting, with difficulty in reading and reversals of letters in words. While at the University of Georgia, he wrote of his aspiration to become a writer, a statement that provoked a cruel reaction from his teacher, who laughed, saying that he would never become a writer. He went on to earn a degree in journalism from the University of Georgia. He then went to the New York Theological Seminary. Teaching had an allure for him that he could not resist, so he went to Berea in Kentucky. While there, he won a Fulbright Scholarship and went to Denmark to study. In class for only 30 minutes, he learned from Edith Norrie what had been his problem all these years. The boy who had been humiliated in that Georgia classroom, discovered he was not stupid. He was learning disabled. It changed his life. He went on to earn a doctorate in education from Harvard. He then borrowed money and established the Landmark school to help Learning Disabled youth.

Pat Buckley Moss

An artist who was called "dummy" for most of her life until she was diagnosed as being dyslexic, overcame her inability to read. The world of art gave her an outlet to express herself like nothing else could. She has shared this with the world. Pat has given her paintings to worthy causes worldwide. Her latest Gift to Learning Disabilities of America is called "We Love Them All." Her gifts of "Reading Lessons for Brighter Tomorrows and Mother's Story" were to the Orton Society. She has also given to other worthy causes worldwide.

These are but a few of modern day "Learning Disabled" people who have found friends along the way that helped. There are many successful, talented, creative and gifted persons in every profession in life who, with hard work, determination and the right help at the right time in their lives, have made and are making contributions to our society.

LEARNING DISABILITIES

Who are these children and youths? Children and adults with learning disabilities are difficult to recognize because their handicaps are often invisible to the untrained eye. They are often mislabeled as being "lazy, dumb or uncooperative" by their teachers, parents and friends. They have average or above average intelligence. Some are geniuses. They are unable to cope with the demands of the average classrooms.

The hidden handicap which we term learning disabilities (LD) has been evident ever since people have been required to process information and learn. It has become more noticeable throughout the ages as societies continue to put greater emphasis on learning and education.

Learning disabilities occur in many forms...visual, auditory, motor control, logic and communication. Effective correction must include a total approach to the educational, physiological, psychological and medical needs of the individual. The term "specific learning disability" means a disorder in one or more of the basic psychological processes involved in understanding or in using language, spoken or written, which may manifest itself in an imperfect ability to listen, think, speak, read, write, spell or to do mathematical calculations. The term includes such conditions as perceptual handicaps, brain injury, minimal brain dysfunction, dyslexia and developmental aphasia. The term does not include children who have learning problems which are primarily the result of visual, hearing or motor handicaps, of the mental retardation, of the emotional disturbance or of environmental, cultural or economic disadvantaged.

Each child, adolescent or adult with a learning disability is

UNIQUE. Each shows a different combination and severity of problems. A learning disabled person is an individual who has one or more significant deficits in the essential learning processes. With the proper training and guidance their learning disabilities, in most cases, can be overcome. It is imperative they have an accurate professional diagnosis. Only then will they be given their rightful chance to participate fully and fruitfully in society.

Perception is the process of understanding experience, of comprehending and organizing the information our senses give us. Without perception, our world seems fragmentary and distorted.

To the Learning Disabled, life is a distortion. For them, it is difficult — often impossible to separate ideas, words, or sounds; to discriminate between the important and the irrelevant; to coordinate and use information effectively. They may experience one or more difficulties:

Visual

They may have difficulty in remembering what words look like even after much exposure to them; or they may transpose words (was for saw) or they may have trouble focusing on a word. They may be called "word blind."

Auditory

They may confuse similar words, such as "lecture" for "electric" or will transpose sounds or syllables, such as "plasket" for "plastic," "aminal" for "animal." Also background noises disorganize his learning ability.

Thinking

Their ideas are often out of order, characterized by poor sequencing. They have trouble following directions.

Language

Their usage of words may be confused or poorly organized. Their self-expression may be poor and vocabulary only rudimentary.

Movement

They may be awkward in coordinating their arms and legs. They may be slow in writing or have an illegible handwriting. They usually have poor integration of vision and movement and very often cannot determine the consequences of a particular movement.

It must be emphasized that these examples constitute but a few learning disability difficulties. Because the symptoms of learning disabilities are exhibited occasionally (but not continuously) by all children, identification of the learning disabled is difficult. The learning disabled person has a cluster of these symptoms which do not disappear with the advancement in age. Close scrutiny is required before physicians, parents, teachers and psychologists can recognize him as one whose failures to achieve are not due to emotional or motivational factors. A plan of positive action and seeing that the plan is implemented at school, home and the community is essential to success. It should include a competent diagnosis, sound educational planning and treatment of the individual with regard to their strengths and weaknesses.

It is only recently that the various fields of education, psychology, medicine, rehabilitation and others are beginning to emphasize the fact that learning disability youth grow up and become adults with a learning disability. The old notion that the LD child will "grow out of it" is no longer acceptable.

Easily distracted, their attention span is short. He is often hyperactive, restless and easily confused. He lacks continuity of effort and perseverance. Changes in established routine upset them easily. They may be stubborn and uncooperative, overly apprehensive and illogical, explosive and erratic, more often unhappy than his peers and often unmanageable in group situations.

The symptoms are, of course, numerous and will not all be evident in any one learning disabled child. Misinterpretation often results in erroneously diagnosing the symptoms as the problem. Hence, the child is falsely labeled "retarded" or "delinquent" or as a "trouble maker." Frequently, society's false evaluation of them is adopted as their own low self esteem, a most unfortunate result.

Life offers the LD child little satisfaction. At school he meets with constant failure, frustration and censure in reading, writing, listening and understanding. Unless his parents are aware of his real difficulty and are taking measures to deal with constructively with it, he receives neither the special attention nor the education he requires. We have come to realize that children with learning disabilities are children with a problem and are not problem children! They need help, not condemnation or punishment. They become problem children and adolescents only when their needs are ignored and they do not receive proper recognition and help. They can learn; they can adjust. They can realize their full potential. They can grow into well adjusted and successful individuals. All of us hope for a life that contains meaning and self-respect. They are no exception. History has taught us this.

Did you know that Thomas Edison was sent home from school

because the teacher said that he was "addled." He said, "I was never able to get along at school. I was always at the foot of the class. My father thought I was stupid. I thought I was a dunce." Where would we be without light? What if he had given up? Harvey Cushing was a very poor speller. His father gave him a dictionary to keep by his side at all times because it was the words he should know that he misspelled. George S. Patton never went to school until he was 12 year of age because he couldn't read. His father tutored him. He got through West Point by memorizing whole lectures and texts, then parroting them verbatim. Paul Ehrlich could not write. His written exams were so poor he almost didn't get his degree in medicine. His thesis was entirely written in the handwriting of someone else. Einstein was considered backward. Teachers told his father he was mentally slow, unsociable and adrift forever in his foolish dreams. He couldn't do simple arithmetic, yet without his Theory of Relativity, we couldn't have put a man into outer space and bring him back. Despite his learning disability, Edison was still able to see the LIGHT.

These children and youth have the same need to be successful learners, to be proud of their accomplishments and to be rewarded for their efforts. There is no cookbook recipe or easy solution to the multiple problems facing them. Let us help them, as Edison did to see the light at the end of their tunnel of disabilities.

COMPANY'S COMING...

Augusta has long been known for hospitality both to visitors and among residents. Founded in 1736 by James Oglethorpe to protect fur trappers who congregated on the banks of the Savannah River to ship the skins to the coast, the fort-trading post town soon attracted farmers, land speculators, and shop keepers. During the colonial period Augusta evolved from a frontier environment where backcountry trappers came to conduct their business and seek relaxation in the local taverns to a settled family community with a church (St. Paul's), school, and elements of "genteel" society. The letters of Mary Chilcott Mackay, the wife of Robert Mackay, a trading post owner, tell of social gatherings, neighborly visits, and even the need for more dishes, for ". . . I find it difficult to make them go around for the present family, and you know two dozen and a half will by no means do when we have company."

After the Revolution famous guests who enjoyed Augusta's hospitality included President George Washington in 1791, President James Monroe in 1819, and the Marquis de Lafayette in 1825. During his three day visit, President Washington was the guest of honor at two banquets, a ball, a reception, and an afternoon dinner. He toured the town and was present for examinations at the Academy of Richmond County. On his last evening in Augusta the President was allowed a much deserved rest. Although President Monroe's purpose in visiting the city was to inspect the arsenal being constructed on the river, he was entertained for dinner at a private home on the Hill and was given a ball at the Planters Hotel. Lafayette's visit in 1825 was even more hectic than Washington's. On his arrival at the river bank, he was greeted by six volunteer militia companies and a welcoming address. The following day, he received an address from the French community of the city, attended a reception and speech at City Hall, was guest of honor at an outdoor banquet at the Courthouse, and heard the third speech of the day later that evening before attending a grand ball.

When Henry Clay visited Augusta in 1844, he was the guest of his former ward Emily Tubman and was entertained at a festive banquet. Clay came to the city as the Whig presidential candidate and his renown as an orator was exhibited in a splendid speech delivered at the Courthouse. Another famous orator Daniel Webster arrived in Augusta three years later. Again Augustans prepared to fete the visiting dignitary, but Webster was ill for four days and left the city without receiving the honors that the citizens wished to publicly extend. In view of the city's past exhibitions of hospitality, this turn of events was particularly disappointing.

Even in the tense days following Georgia's secession from the Union, Augustans displayed their cordial feelings to old friends. In 1861, the contingent at the U.S. Arsenal surrendered the facility but before the men left the city, a farewell banquet was held and political divisiveness was set aside as residents toasted their departing Union friends.

Following the war, Augustans resumed their sociability. When company came to Montrose (the current Alan Fuqua Center), Mrs. Charles C. Jones offered an evening of music, poetry, readings, and good food. In the late 1870's, Mrs. Jones wrote, "We have been taken up with friends and visitors all day, and every evening nearly we (have) company or are invited out . . . the callers and the called upon, the dinners and teas to go to and, par consequence, the luncheons and dinners to be given in exchange." In 1877, she described a party for her daughter Ruth, "There never had been so grand a party before. We had a fiddler, and three or four cotillions were formed at a time." After a gathering at Mrs. Joseph Cumming's the following year, Mrs. Jones noted, "We spend a charming evening . . . reading, recitation and sweet music . . . until 1 o'clock when we had a charming supper." In recent years, the Augusta Symphony, the Summerville Neighborhood Association, and Augusta College have renewed this tradition at the Fuqua Center with musical programs and Antebellum and Victorian presentations.

By the late 1800's and 1900's, the Augusta area — particularly Summerville — welcomed many winter visitors including former Presidents U.S. Grant and Rutherford Hayes, John D. Rockefeller, Alexander Graham Bell, and during their terms in office Presidents William Howard Taft and Warren Harding. Many of these famous people stayed at the Bon Air Hotel, which opened in 1889 with a gala banquet:

THE MENU

Blue Points on Half Shell

LATOUR BLANCHE

Celery   Olives   Cream of Chicken, alla Reine

AMONTILLADO SHERRY

Philadelphia Capon, Oyster Sauce
Duchess Potatoes

LATROSE

Diamond Back Terrapin, a la Maryland

PAHLTINHO

Wild Turkey Croquettes, Castronom
Fillet of Beef, a la Periqueux

PONTET CANET

French Peas   Asparagus   Orange Portugaise
Harve (sic) de Cras Canvas Back Duck
Fried Hominy
Partridges, with Currant Jelly

POMMERY SEC

Chicken Salad, Mayonnaise d'Homard
Boned Turkey, with Truffles
Patties of Game, a la Bon Air
Omelette Souffle, au Maraschino
Charlotte Parisienne
Petite Fours   Assorted Cakes   Ornamental Ice Cream
Fruits   Raisins   Nuts
Stilton and Adam Cheese   Bent's Crackers
Black Coffee   Brandy

Although the advent of easier transportation to Florida channeled the winter colony further South, a new attraction was being born. The Masters Golf Tournament first played in 1934 has brought thousands of visitors each year to Augusta not only to enjoy the greatest golfing event in the world, but also, to engage in the week-long social whirl.

President and Mrs. Dwight David Eisenhower made a number of visits always staying at the Augusta National Golf Club while the White House staff and reporters were lodged at the Richmond Hotel on Broad Street. President and Mrs. Ronald Reagan and Secretary of State George Schultz have been more recent visitors to our city and they, too, stayed at the Augusta National.

From the beginning Augusta has been a military town — Fort Augusta, the U.S. Arsenal, Camp Hancock, Camp Wheeless, and Camp (now Fort) Gordon. Many of the men stationed at these installations married Augusta young women and remained here to build their future and that of the city. Others who were stationed here chose to make Augusta their home after retirement.

Local hospitality has been a major factor in attracting people to Augusta, which has the reputation of offering various social and cultural amenities while maintaining the easy, open atmosphere usually attributed to smaller cities and towns. "Company is coming" is an Augusta way of life. May we continue to enjoy good friends and good food!

We wish to express our thanks to Dr. Helen Callahan for her excellent and informative article on Augusta and Entertaining in Augusta and her articles for Mr. Ray Baird's Historical Sketches. Dr. Callahan, professor of history at Augusta College, is among the best known writer-historians. Dr. Callahan didn't set out to go into writing or to become a historian. In fact, she was a drop-out from Augusta College when she simply got tired of her work at the Speech and Hearing Center. There she came to know several of our Learning Disabled students, even though they were not called LD then.

On the way home from work one day, she stopped by the registrar's office and asked what she had to do to get back into school. The secretary told her it was registration time at the school and asked if she wanted to register. Without thinking, she told her she wanted to major in "History." She had never actually considered studying the subject before. History was something she liked to read. She earned her Bachelor's degree in history, to be followed by a Master's and finally the Doctor of Philosophy degree in History from the University of Georgia. She simply took off like a "steam engine."

On returning to Augusta, she got a job teaching at Augusta College. She started on a few articles on history when asked by Dr. Cashin. One article led to another. She followed it up with research for Dr. Cashin's Book, History of Augusta College. Dr. Callahan has written books on Augusta History and on "Augusta, Key to the Back Countrey," (General Oglethorpe's spelling). When we asked her to do this for us, she came through with flying colors. Many thanks to a very special "Lady."

Table of Contents

Sᴀᴄʀᴇᴅ Hᴇᴀʀᴛ
Aᴜɢᴜsᴛᴀ, Gᴇᴏʀɢɪᴀ

SACRED HEART

The original Sacred Heart Church was built in 1874, but within twenty-four years the structure was too small for the growing population, and a new building was begun on the corner of Greene and Twelfth Street. In 1900, James Cardinal Gibbons of Baltimore dedicated the church. The unique masonry, turrets, dome, and arches of this victorian Romanesque building make it one of the most interesting architectural achievements in the Southeast.

Due to the decline in the innercity population, three Roman Catholic parishes merged in 1971, and Sacred Heart was closed. The building was purchased by a private corporation and is used periodically for dramatic and dance performances and craft fairs.

Appetizers

ANCHOVY DIP

1 cup mayonnaise	salt and pepper to taste
1 (8-ounce) package cream	3 Tablespoons chives (frozen)
cheese, softened	1 clove garlic (pressed)
3 Tablespoons anchovy paste	1 Tablespoon lemon juice
1/3 cup parsley leaves minced	3 Tablespoons Tarragon vinegar

Blend all ingredients well. Should be taken out of refrigerator at least 45 minutes to 1 hour to soften before serving.

ARTICHOKE DIP

1 can artichoke hearts	2 to 3 slices crisp bacon
1/2 cup mayonnaise	red pepper
1 teaspoon Worcestershire sauce	paprika
1 to 2 teaspoons grated onion	
(optional)	

For a dip that's a little different, mash artichoke hearts. Blend with mayonnaise and onion and Worcestershire sauce. Refrigerate until serving time. Put dip into serving dish. Crumble bacon over top. Sprinkle with red pepper and/or paprika. Serve with unflavored Melba Rounds or crackers.

CHIPPED BEEF AND BREAD

1 loaf unsliced rye bread	4 minced green onions
8 ounces cream cheese	2 teaspoons Worcestershire sauce
5 ounces dried chipped beef	1 cup sour cream
1 cup Cheddar cheese	

Hollow out round loaf rye or other bread (similar to cutting a pumpkin with a lid) and set aside the bite-size pieces removed from the bread. Fill loaf with mixture of the other ingredients; place bread lid back on and bake at 350 degrees for 1-1/2 hours. During the last 1/2 hour, place the bite size pieces on a cookie sheet and leave in oven until they become sort of hard. To serve, place toasted bite size pieces around loaf on a tray to be used to dip hot mixture from the loaf.

OUTRAGEOUS ARTICHOKE DIP

2 (14-ounce) cans artichoke
hearts, drained
2 cups (8 ounces) grated
Parmesan cheese
1 cup mayonnaise
1 cup sour cream
1 teaspoon red pepper sauce
2 pounds corn chips

6 medium (2 pounds) zucchini,
cut into strips
4 large cucumbers, peeled and
cut into strips
6 medium carrots, peeled and cut
into strips
2 bunches green onions, trimmed

Preheat oven to 300 degrees. Finely chop artichokes. Place in large bowl with remaining ingredients; stir until well mixed. Pour into a 4-cup souffle dish or casserole. (May be made ahead and refrigerated up to 24 hours.) Bake 45 minutes or until golden brown and bubbly. Serve warm with vegetables and chips. Makes 4 cups, about 45 calories per tablespoon.

UNBEATABLE CRAB DIP

1 (6-1/2 ounce) can crab meat,
drained
1 (3-ounce) package cream cheese
with chives
1 (3-ounce) package cream cheese
2 Tablespoons mayonnaise

1 teaspoon Dijon mustard or 1
teaspoon prepared horseradish
2 teaspoons fresh lemon juice
1/8 teaspoon red pepper sauce
1/4 teaspoon salt
2 Tablespoons dry white wine, if
desired

Preheat oven to 350 degrees. Combine cream cheese, horseradish, mayonnaise, mustard, lemon juice, red pepper and salt in the top of double boiler. Over simmering water stir until smooth and well blended. Add wine gradually, then crab meat; check seasonings. Spoon into an oven-proof baking dish and bake for 15 minutes or until hot and bubbly. Serve with crackers or chips. Makes about 1-1/4 cups of dip.

THE BIG DIPPER

2 Tablespoons butter/margarine
1 pound lean ground beef
1 clove garlic, crushed
1/4 teaspoon oregano
1/4 teaspoon basil
1/4 teaspoon fennel
1/4 teaspoon rosemary
1 envelope dry onion soup mix

1 (6-ounce) can tomato paste
1/2 cup red cooking wine
1 cup sharp Cheddar cheese,
shredded
1 (8-ounce) package cream
cheese, softened
assorted chips and crackers

Melt butter/margarine in a large skillet and brown beef lightly. Drain well and blend in garlic, seasonings and soup mix. Add tomato paste and wine. Simmer covered for 15 minutes. Add cheeses and stir until completely melted. Serve warm as a dip with chips or crackers. Makes 6 servings.

HORSERADISH SAUCE OR DIP

1 cup sour cream
1/2 cup hot prepared horseradish
2 Tablespoons finely chopped chives or green onions
1 Tablespoon Worcestershire sauce
1/2 teaspoon salt
1/4 teaspoon garlic powder
1/8 teaspoon cumin
1/4 teaspoon white pepper
1/4 teaspoon fresh lemon juice

Combine all ingredients and mix gently until well blended. Serve with potato chips, crackers or crisp fresh vegetables such as carrots, celery, broccoli, cauliflower. Makes an excellent spread for meat sandwiches and is excellent served with roast beef, pork or ham.

BEST RECIPE — SHRIMP-ARTICHOKE DIP

2 (8-1/2 ounce) cans artichoke hearts, drained and chopped
1 pound small shrimp, cooked and cleaned
1 bunch green onions, chopped
1 cup mayonnaise
1 cup sour cream
Jane's Krazy Mixed-Up Salt to taste

Mix all ingredients. Serve with Hearty Wheat crackers. Serves 20 and improves with overnight refrigeration.

POLYNESIAN DIP FOR VEGETABLES

1 cup sour cream
1 cup mayonnaise
1/4 pound tiny cooked shrimp, chopped
1/4 cup minced green onions and tops
1/4 cup minced fresh parsley
2 cloves garlic, minced
1/4 cup finely chopped water chestnuts
1 teaspoon grated fresh ginger root
1 red cabbage
Assortment of crudites such as carrot sticks, cauliflower-ettes, cucumber sticks, celery sticks, green pepper wedges, broccoli flowerettes

In a bowl, combine sour cream, mayonnaise, shrimp, onions, parsley, garlic and water chestnuts. Add grated ginger root, stir well, and refrigerate for at least 1 hour. Taste for seasoning; add more ginger root, if desired. Slice a lid off the top of the red cabbage. Trim stem end so cabbage will stand upright. With a sharp knife, hollow interior of cabbage, being careful not to puncture the sides of the shell. Discard center of cabbage, or reserve for another use. Fill cabbage with chilled dip. Place on a platter and surround with crudites.

PIZZA DIP

8 ounces cream cheese, softened	1 cup peeled, seeded and
1 cup catsup	chopped tomatoes
1 small can shrimp, diced	1/2 cup black olives, chopped
2 Tablespoons horseradish	1 cup chopped green pepper
5 scallions, chopped	1 cup Monterey Jack cheese,
	grated

Spread cream cheese in a shallow serving dish. Combine catsup, shrimp and horseradish; spread over cream cheese. Layer each of the remaining ingredients, ending with grated cheese on top. Chill before serving. Serve with crackers or taco chips.

Called PIZZA DIP because it looks like a pizza, not because it tastes like one.

CLASSIC SPINACH DIP

1 cup mayonnaise	1 (8-ounce) can water chestnuts,
1-1/2 cups sour cream	drained and chopped
1 (10-ounce) package frozen	3 or 4 green onions, chopped
chopped spinach, drained	1 round loaf bread, unsliced or 1
and squeezed dry	head cabbage (red), hollowed
1 package Knorr dry vegetable	out
soup mix	

Combine mayonnaise and sour cream in a medium-size mixing bowl, mixing until smooth. Thaw and drain the spinach, squeezing out all liquid. Add spinach and soup mix, water chestnuts and onions. Refrigerate overnight, covered (or for at least 2 hours). Serve in a bowl or make an attractive serving bowl by cutting the top off a round loaf of French or pumpernickel bread. Hollow out the loaf and bake at 250 degrees for 20 minutes or until slightly toasted. Spoon chilled dip into hollow loaf. Surround loaf with toasted torn bread, king-sized Fritos or raw vegetables for dipping. This dip makes a very good filling for hollowed-out cherry tomatoes to be used as appetizers or in large red, ripe tomatoes to be used as a salad.

SHRIMP DIP

1 can tomato soup	1 cup mayonnaise
2 teaspoons plain gelatin	2 cans small shrimp, washed
1/4 cup cold water	1/2 onion, chopped
1 (8-ounce) package cream cheese	1/2 cup chopped celery

Heat tomato soup and dissolve gelatin in the cold water. Add remaining ingredients to soup. Serve with Ritz crackers or Waverly Wafers.

CHAFING DISH SEAFOOD DIP

3 cans mushroom soup
2 cans shrimp soup
1 (8-ounce) package cream cheese
3 pounds raw shelled shrimp
2 cans water chestnuts, sliced and
  drained
1 pound lump crab meat
1 teaspoon Tabasco sauce
2 teaspoons dry mustard
4 Tablespoons Worcestershire
  sauce

1/2 stick butter
1 cup finely chopped celery
1/2 cup finely chopped green
  onion (including tops)
1 cup fresh parsley, chopped
1/4 cup chopped green pepper
chopped pimiento for color
  (optional)
small wine glass of cream sherry
  (optional)

Cook in double boiler. Melt butter, saute all raw vegetables until tender. Add dry mustard and chopped raw shrimp. Cook until shrimp turn pink. Add cream cheese and stir until cheese melts. Add cream soups and water chestnuts. Season to taste with salt and pepper, Tabasco and Worcestershire sauce. Just before serving from a chafing dish, stir in lump crab meat, pimiento and cream sherry to suit taste. Will serve 75 to 80 as a cocktail canape with Melba rounds or can be served in patty shells for luncheons or buffets.

TEX-MEX DIP

2 (10-1/2 ounce) cans jalapeno
  bean dip
3 medium avocados, ripe
2 Tablespoons lemon juice
1/2 teaspoon salt
1 clove garlic, minced
1/4 teaspoon white pepper to taste
1 cup sour cream
1/2 cup mayonnaise
1 (1-1/4 ounce) package taco
  seasoning mix

1 bunch green onions with tops,
  chopped
3 medium tomatoes, peeled and
  chopped
2 (3-1/2 ounce) cans pitted ripe
  olives, chopped
8 ounces Cheddar cheese,
  shredded or 8 ounces
  Monterey Jack cheese,
  shredded

Spread bean dip in large shallow serving dish. Mash avocados with lemon juice, garlic, salt and pepper, then spread over bean dip. Mix sour cream, mayonnaise and taco seasoning and spread over avocado layer. Sprinkle with onions, tomatoes and olives. Cover with shredded cheese and refrigerate. Serve chilled with round tortilla chips.

DEVILED CHEESE

1-1/2 cups grated cheese
2 Tablespoons olive oil
2 Tablespoons vinegar
1 level teaspoon dry mustard

1 teaspoon Worcestershire sauce
salt and pepper to taste
crackers

Mix the cheese, mustard, salt and pepper, add the oil, beat until creamy and then mix in the vinegar and sauce. Spread on hot toasted crackers, or on ordinary crackers or toast, and heat for five minutes in a quick oven.

CHEESE TIDBITS

1 cup butter, softened
2 small jars English cheese
3 cups flour, sifted

1 teaspoon salt
80 stuffed olives, drained

Pre-heat oven to 400 degrees. Grease baking sheet. Cream butter, English cheese, flour and salt together. Roll into walnut sized balls and stuff olive into each center. Chill overnight. Bake 15 to 20 minutes in 400-degree oven and serve warm. (These may also be frozen and baked on the day they are to be served.)

TEA AND PARTY PICK-UPS

1-1/2 cups flour
1/2 teaspoon salt
1/2 teaspoon red pepper
1/2 pound grated sharp Cheddar
    cheese

1/2 cup butter
24 pecan halves
24 dates

Cream butter and grated cheese to velvet-like consistency. Add flour, salt and pepper. Knead until easy to work with (dough will not roll). Pinch off generous tablespoon and form in palm of hand to wrap around pecan half which has been wrapped with a date. Bake at 400 degrees for 15 to 20 minutes until done. Will keep fresh in tins for several days. Also good with plain pecans half wrapped in dough.

CHEESE COOKIES

2 sticks oleo
2 cups grated sharp cheese
2 teaspoons salt

dash of red pepper
1 cup finely chopped nuts
3 cups plain flour

Cream butter with grated cheese. Add flour, salt, red pepper, nuts and form 2 large rolls or several small ones. Wrap in wax paper. Chill, then slice and cook at 350 degrees for 10 minutes.

LORRAINE'S CHEESE COOKIES

1 pound sharp Cheddar cheese, grated
1 pound butter or margarine, softened at room temperature
4-1/2 cups plain flour
1 (3-ounce) can grated Parmesan cheese

Mix all ingredients and form into balls about the size of a marble. Flatten to desired size (these do not rise). Bake on cookie sheet for 30 minutes at 325 degrees. Makes about 250 small cheese bits.

GRANDMA'S SAND DOLLARS

2/3 cup yellow cornmeal
2 Tablespoons butter
3/4 cup boiling water
1 teaspoon garlic salt
1 teaspoon parsley flakes
Parmesan cheese

While oven preheats to 400 degrees, line large baking sheet with aluminum foil. Spray foil with non-stick spray and set aside. Pour cornmeal into a medium-sized bowl and keep it handy. In a small bowl, cut butter into small pieces and pour boiling water over them. Stir to melt. Add this to cornmeal and mix. Add garlic salt, parsley flakes; stir and let mixture stand for 10 minutes. It will look thin. Drop batter by teaspoon onto baking sheet, stirring after each spoonful. (These spread, so drop 3 to a row.) Sprinkle with Parmesan cheese and bake 7 to 10 minutes or until dry and lightly browned at the edges. Carefully lift off baking sheet with spatula and cool on a wire rack.

LUCILLE'S CHEESE BITS

1/2 pound margarine
1/2 pound grated sharp New York State cheese
2-2/3 cups flour
pecan halves
dash cayenne pepper

Grate cheese. Cream together with margarine. Add dash of cayenne pepper. Work in flour to form stiff dough. Shape into ball and chill for 2 hours. Pinch off bits of mixture. Mold over pecan half and arrange cheese bits on cookie sheet. Bake at 350 degrees about 20 minutes.

SHERRIED CHEESE CROCK

Favorite cheeses in a festive blend

1 cup grated Cheddar cheese
3/4 cup crumbled bleu cheese
2 (3-ounce) packages cream cheese
1 Tablespoon prepared mustard
1 Tablespoon Worcestershire sauce
1/2 cup Buena Vista ultra-dry sherry
1/2 cup finely chopped pistachios or walnuts

Combine Cheddar, bleu and cream cheeses and allow to stand at room temperature until softened. Blend in mustard, Worcestershire and sherry. Stir in nuts. Pack into crock or bowl (will fill two 1-1/4 cups crocks), cover and refrigerate at least 24 hours. Serve with thin crackers, toast or celery sticks.

TRIED IT, LIKED IT

1-1/2 cups (6 to 8 ounces) minced black olives

3 ounces shredded Parmesan cheese or 1-1/2 cups grated sharp Cheddar cheese

1/2 cup green onions, thinly sliced

1/2 cup good quality mayonnaise

1/4 teaspoon curry powder (optional)

sliced party rye bread or 6 English muffins, quartered

NOTE: A combination of ripe and green olives may be used.

Drain and finely chop black olives; combine with grated cheese and minced onion. Moisten mixture with mayonnaise and add curry powder if desired.

For a small group, spread the mixture on party rye or quartered English muffins. Place under broiler until bubbly and golden brown (about 3 to 4 minutes).

For a large group, place mixture in an oven to warm using low heat setting. Transfer to a chafing dish and serve with crackers.

NOTE: The party rye or English muffin wedges spread with mixture, may be frozen on a cookie sheet until hard and stored in a plastic bag. Bake when needed in a 350 degree oven for 10 to 15 minutes. Great to have on hand for unexpected company.

CHEESE AND FRUIT DELIGHT

1 (12-ounce) package cream cheese

1 stick butter

1/2 cup sour cream

1/2 cup sugar

1 package plain gelatin

1/4 cup cold water

1/2 cup white raisins

1/2 to 1 cup toasted slivered almonds

rind of two lemons, grated

juice of two lemons

strawberries for garnish or maraschino cherries and green leaves

Soften cream cheese, butter and sour cream; beat together well. Add sugar. Soften gelatin in cold water; heat to dissolve. Fold into cream cheese mixture. Add white raisins and toasted almonds, grated lemon rind and juice. Pour into 1 quart ring mold and chill until firm and set. Unmold and decorate with maraschino cherries and green leaves. May be used as dessert or with cheese crackers as an appetizer.

NOTE: Raisins may be soaked overnight in enough brandy to cover if desired. Drain and blot dry with paper towel and add.

PIMIENTO CHEESE

1 pound sharp Cheddar cheese, grated
1 Tablespoon finely grated onion
1 (4-ounce) jar sliced pimiento, diced
6 to 8 drops Tabasco sauce

1 Tablespoon Worcestershire sauce
1/4 teaspoon garlic salt (optional)
1 Tablespoon prepared mustard
1/2 teaspoon salt
mayonnaise to make mixture spreadable (about 1/2 cup)

Combine all ingredients. Let stand at least 1 hour. Taste and add more seasonings if needed to suit your taste. May be used for sandwiches or to stuff celery.

CHEESE RAISIN SPREAD

1 cup dark raisins
1/3 cup rum

8 ounces sharp Cheddar cheese, grated (room temperature)
6 ounces cream cheese

Soak raisins in rum for 1 hour. Remove raisins from rum and set aside. Beat cheese in a blender or cuisinart until smooth. Add rum. Fold in raisins. Serve with Waverly Wafers.

FRUITED CHEESE RING

1/2 cup dried chopped apricots
1/4 cup chopped dates
1/4 cup golden raisins
3/4 cup quality bourbon
16 ounces sharp Cheddar cheese, grated fine
8 ounces cream cheese, softened

1/2 cup finely chopped almonds
2/3 cup toasted almonds, ground
whole dried apricots for garnish
white raisins for garnish
crackers
ginger snaps

Soak fruit in bourbon for 1 hour (may be soaked overnight). Using the metal blade in a food processor, combine cheese, bourbon-marinated fruits and 1/2 cup ground almonds. Do not over process! Cover and refrigerate to chill thoroughly, preferably overnight. Shape into a log and roll in toasted almonds. Form into a ring on a serving platter. Garnish on top with flowers, made of the dried apricots as the center and petals made of the raisins. Holly leaves, washed and cleaned can be used as leaves. Serve with crackers and gourmet ginger snap cookies.

TOMATO CHEESE WREATH

2 cups grated sharp Cheddar
  cheese
1 cup fresh tomatoes, peeled,
  seeded and chopped
1 (8-ounce) package cream
  cheese, softened
1/2 cup real butter, softened

1/3 cup chopped green onions
1 teaspoon salt
1/8 teaspoon cayenne pepper
1/8 teaspoon garlic powder
1-1/2 cups toasted chopped pecans
crackers

Combine cheeses, butter and seasonings, mixing well. Add tomatoes and onions. Mix well. Chill. Roll into a log and roll in pecans. Form into a ring on a serving platter. Chill. Fill the center with assorted crackers.

CHUTNEY CREAM CHEESE BALL

11 ounces cream cheese, softened
3 Tablespoons golden raisins
3 Tablespoons sour cream
3 teaspoons curry powder
3/4 cup chopped toasted almonds
1/2 cup Major Gray Chutney
  (home-made chutney best)

4 Tablespoons crisp cooked
  crumbled bacon
1 Tablespoon green onion,
  minced
1/4 cup toasted coconut
green onion brushes

Mix all ingredients except coconut together well. Chill for 1 hour or until firm enough to shape into a ball. Refrigerate and when ready to serve, roll in toasted coconut. Place on serving dish and garnish with brushes made of green onions. May be made 1 day ahead without coconut. Roll in coconut when ready to serve. Serve with assorted crackers. To create green onion "brushes" for garnish, make thin lengthwise cuts on both ends of onions; soak in ice water until ends "fan."

CHRISTMAS CHEESE BALL

3 (5-ounce) packages bleu or
  Roquefort cheese,
  softened
8 ounces cream cheese, softened
1/4 teaspoon garlic salt

1 Tablespoon chopped green
  pepper
1 Tablespoon chopped pimiento
1/2 cup fresh finely chopped
  parsley

Blend all ingredients together until smooth. Wrap in wax paper and chill until firm. Shape as desired. While cheese mixture is being chilled, toast 1/2 cup finely chopped nut meats in 350 degree oven until brown (about 8 to 10 minutes), stirring occasionally. Chop 1/2 cup fresh parsley finely. Allow nuts to cool, then mix with parsley. Roll shaped cheese in nuts and parsley until well coated. Chill until serving time. Serve with assorted crackers or Ritz crackers.

CHEESE BALL #1

1/2 pound grated New York
  sharp cheese
2 (8-ounce) packages cream
  cheese
1 Tablespoon grated onion

1/2 cup parsley, chopped
1/2 cup chopped pecans
salt to taste
red pepper to taste

Let cream cheese soften; mix with remaining ingredients. Roll in chopped nuts and chill. Makes one large ball. Serve with Ritz crackers.

BLACK OLIVE CHEESE BALL

It's Delicious

12 ounces cream cheese, softened
4 ounces blue cheese, softened
1/2 cup real butter, softened
8 to 10 green onions, chopped
  (some tops)

1 3-1/2 ounces chopped black
  olives
1/2 cup slivered toasted almonds
assorted crackers or toasted party
  rye bread

Cream cheese and butter together, mixing well. Add onions and chopped olives; mix well. Chill until firm. Form into a ball. Roll in slivered almonds. Serve with crackers or toasted rye bread. This freezes well.

CHEESE PATE PINEAPPLE

2 (3-ounce) packages cream
  cheese
2/3 cup prepared brown mustard
2-1/2 pounds natural sharp
  Cheddar cheese

1 (2-ounce) jar small pimiento
  olives, drained
1 fresh green pineapple frond

Combine cream cheese and mustard; beat with mixer until blended. At low speed, gradually beat in grated cheese. Turn onto board and knead until smooth and pliable. Refrigerate for 45 minutes. Roll into a cylinder and stand on cookie sheet. Shape like a pineapple. Cut olives crosswise and carefully place halves on cheese in straight horizontal rows, arranging them so vertical rows run on the diagonal. With a wooden pick, make diagonal lines 1/8" deep between rows of olives. Cover with plastic film and refrigerate overnight. To serve, place on serving platter and arrange pineapple frond on top. Surround with small crackers. Let stand at room temperature about 30 minutes before serving.

CHEESE BALL #2

2 (3-ounce) packages bleu cheese
4 (3-ounce) packages cream
   cheese
2 (10-ounce) packages soft sharp
   cheese (Wispride)

2 teaspoons Worcestershire sauce
2 Tablespoons grated onion
1/2 cup ground pecans
2 Tablespoons dried parsley

Allow cheeses to soften, blend with mixer. Add Worcestershire sauce and onion. Form into one large ball or two small ones. Wrap in waxed paper overnight. Remove paper and roll in mixture of nuts and parsley. Serve with crackers.

TINY DARLING MEATBALLS

1 pound lean ground meat
1/2 cup bread crumbs
2 eggs, beaten
1/2 cup grated Parmesan cheese
1 teaspoon chopped parsley

1/2 teaspoon garlic salt
1/2 teaspoon salt
1/4 teaspoon black pepper
oil

Combine meat, bread crumbs, beaten eggs, cheese and seasonings; mix well and shape into tiny balls. Saute in oil in skillet until thoroughly browned and cooked throughout. Set in chafing dish.

Sauce:

1/2 cup A-1 Sauce
1/4 cup catsup
2 Tablespoons brown sugar
2 Tablespoons Dijon mustard

1/2 teaspoon grated onion
1/4 cup sour cream
1/4 cup butter

Combine A-1 Sauce, catsup, sugar, grated onion and mustard with butter in a saucepan; heat over low flame for 15 minutes. Remove and add sour cream; mix gently. Pour sauce over the meatballs and serve.

CHOPPED LIVER (LIVER PATE)

1 pound chicken livers
7 hardboiled eggs
2 large onions

2 Tablespoons chicken fat
salt and pepper to taste

Saute livers in chicken fat with diced onions until done. Grind or chop livers, onions and eggs; add salt and pepper to taste. Mix thoroughly until smooth. If needed, add more melted chicken fat to hold together. Refrigerate until 30 minutes before serving. Serve with crackers or party rye. Serves 10 to 12 people.

COCKTAIL PARTY MEATBALLS

2 pounds round ground steak
1 cup bread crumbs (seasoned)
Pepperidge Farm croutons, finely
   crushed
1/2 cup green onions, finely
   chopped

2 teaspoons salt
1 teaspoon prepared horseradish
1/4 teaspoon pepper
1 large egg, beaten
1/3 cup milk
1/2 cup Crisco

Mix beef, crumbs, onion, salt, pepper, horseradish, eggs and milk. Form into balls, about 1" in diameter. Brown in Crisco and drain. Makes about 75 to 90 balls. Add meat balls to one of the following sauces; simmer for about 30 minutes and serve in a chafing dish.

Sauce #1:
Sweet and Sour
2 cups pineapple juice
2 teaspoons ginger
1/4 cup cornstarch
1/4 cup soy sauce

1 cup brown sugar (light)
1 teaspoon salt
1 cup vinegar

Combine all ingredients in a sauce pan, cooking sauce until thick. Serve the sauce in a chafing dish and use toothpicks for getting the balls from the chafing dish. Serve hot. This sauce can be made ahead of time and reheated for serving.

Sauce #2:
1 clove garlic, crushed
1 Tablespoon Crisco oil
1/4 teaspoon dry mustard
1 Tablespoon soy sauce

1/8 teaspoon black pepper
2 Tablespoons catsup
1 Tablespoon vinegar
1 small Dr. Pepper

Combine all sauce ingredients in a sauce pan. Bring to a boil. Add meat balls to the sauce. Cook over low heat for 1 hour. Simmer to keep hot. Serve hot in a chafing dish. Eat on toothpicks.

Sauce #3:
1/2 cup butter
2 medium onions, chopped
1/4 cup flour
3 cups beef broth
1 cup red wine
1/4 cup brown sugar

1/4 cup catsup
2 Tablespoons lemon juice
6 ginger snaps, crumbled
   (optional)
2 teaspoons salt

In a heavy sauce pan, melt butter. Saute onions until golden. Blend in flour. Add broth, stirring until smooth. Stir in the remaining ingredients and simmer over low heat for 15 minutes. Add meatballs to hot sauce. Serve in chafing dish. Eat on toothpicks.

SNAPPY CHICKEN CURRY BALLS

2 cups cooked chicken, finely chopped (white chicken)
1-1/2 cups almonds, finely chopped
1 Tablespoon green onions, finely chopped
4 Tablespoons Major Grey's Chutney, chopped (home made chutney best)

1 (8-ounce) package cream cheese, softened
1/4 cup mayonnaise
1 teaspoon Durkees sauce
2 teaspoons curry powder
salt to taste
1 cup fresh frozen coconut, thawed or fresh minced parsley, if desired

Combine chicken, almonds, green onions and chutney. In a separate bowl, blend cream cheese, mayonnaise, Durkees sauce and curry powder. Combine chicken mixture and cream cheese mixture; blending well. Chill. Shape into bite-size balls (1"). Roll each ball in grated coconut. Refrigerate, covered, until ready to serve. When ready to serve, place balls in the center of a round glass serving dish, mounding high. Surround this mound with angel endive petals to form a daisy. May also be garnished with tiny yellow and white flowers. Makes 80 to 90 balls and will keep for 3 to 4 days.

Option:

Ring with washed seedless white and red grapes off stems, and surround grapes with seedless raisins. Core a tart apple into even slices. Dip slices in lemon juice and place slices, peel side up, evenly spaced between raisins at opposite sides of platter.

NOTE: Can be made into 2 chicken balls and served with assorted crackers.

SHRIMP BALLS

1-1/2 pounds cooked shrimp, finely minced
1 Tablespoon cocktail sauce
1/4 cup celery, finely minced
2 Tablespoons water chestnuts, finely minced
2 Tablespoons grated onion
1 hard-cooked egg, sieved

1 (3-ounce) package cream cheese, softened
1/2 teaspoon salt
1/4 teaspoon white pepper
dash cayenne pepper
1 teaspoon lemon juice (fresh)
3 Tablespoons mayonnaise
1/2 teaspoon Durkees sauce
minced parsley, fresh

Combine all ingredients, except parsley, in a mixing bowl. Blend well. Adjust seasonings. Chill. Mold into 1" balls; roll in minced parsley. Makes about 50 to 75 balls. Serve with very fresh sliced mushrooms, jicama roots or assorted crackers.

SAUSAGE PINWHEELS

3 Tablespoons Crisco
2 cups self-rising flour

2/3 cup sweet milk
1/2 to 1 pound hot ground sausage

Mix shortening with flour; gradually add milk. Knead a minute or so, then roll out on floured board in rectangular shape. Roll thinly, approximately 1/8" thick. Spread sausage on dough and roll as for jelly roll. Refrigerate several hours. When ready to bake, preheat oven to 350 degrees. Slice dough in thin slices and place on ungreased baking sheet. Bake 15-20 minutes or until lightly browned. Remove from sheet and place on paper towel to drain. Makes about 24.

NOTE: These may be placed in the refrigerator or freezer for several days before baking.

ELEGANT CHICKEN PATE

1 cup minced onion
4 Tablespoons chicken fat or
  Crisco
1/2 pound chicken livers
1-1/2 pounds boned cooked
  chicken meat

1/2 cup unsalted butter, softened
2 to 3 Tablespoons brandy or
  cognac
1-1/2 Tablespoons Pate Spice

Saute onion in hot fat until limp and golden. Add livers; saute until last trace of pink disappeared. Cool. Place livers and onions in a food processor and puree. Add rest of meat and process until the mixture is smooth. Blend in butter 1 tablespoon at a time; process until fluffy. Add brandy and Pate Spice mixture. Mix well. Adjust seasonings to taste. Turn into waxed paper-lined 9x5" loaf pan. Chill until firm (may be made a day or two ahead). To serve, turn onto platter and slice. Accompany with small dill pickles and crusty bread.

NOTE: Cooked turkey, pork or veal may be used in place of chicken.

Pate Spice:
1 Tablespoon crushed bay leaf
1 Tablespoon dried thyme
1 teaspoon powdered mace
1 Tablespoon rosemary
1 Tablespoon dried basil
2 Tablespoons ground cinnamon

1/2 teaspoon cloves
1/2 teaspoon allspice
1 teaspoon ground white pepper
2 teaspoons hot paprika
1/2 cup fine table salt

Combine all ingredients, except salt, in a food processor. Blend for several minutes until all are fine and well combined. Add salt and process 2 to 3 minutes longer. Store in a cool place in tightly covered jar. Makes 1-1/2 cups.

COCKTAIL HAM BISCUITS

2/3 cup flour	2 to 3 Tablespoons sweet milk
6 Tablespoons grated cheese	deviled ham or marble size,
1/2 teaspoon salt	cooked sausage balls
2 Tablespoons butter	1 egg, beaten

Mix flour, cheese, and salt; chop in butter and add enough milk to form stiff dough. Roll very thinly and cut with a small round cutter. Moisten edges with slightly beaten egg. Spread half of the rounds with ham or the sausage balls. Cover with remaining rounds and press edges together. Brush with melted butter and bake 12 to 15 minutes in hot oven (400 degrees). Makes approximately 40 small biscuits and can be made ahead of time and frozen.

MARINATED SHRIMP

1 pound shrimp, cooked in	1/2 cup catsup
lemon juice and peeled	1 Tablespoon lemon juice
2 onions, sliced	1 Tablespoon capers
mushroom pieces	horseradish and Worcestershire
1/2 cup French dressing	to taste

Layer shrimp, onions and mushrooms 48 hours ahead and refrigerate; 24 hours before serving, make marinate and pour over shrimp, onions and mushrooms; refrigerate until time to serve.

MOLDED SHRIMP FISH

8 ounces cream cheese	3 Tablespoons grated onion
1-1/2 packages plain gelatin	2 cups chopped cooked shrimp
3/4 cup celery, finely chopped	salt and pepper to taste
1 cup mayonnaise	dash of Tabasco

Soften cream cheese and whip. Soften gelatin to 1/2 cup cold water; place in small saucepan and dissolve over low heat. Fold gelatin into whipped cream cheese. Fold into this mixture all remaining ingredients. Pour into 3-1/2 cup fish mold. Chill and serve with plain crackers. May be doubled for larger mold.

SHRIMP HORS D'OEUVRES

1 pound fresh shrimp, cleaned	1/2 teaspoon grated lemon rind
and cooked	1/4 teaspoon salt
1 Tablespoon minced onions	3 to 4 drops Tabasco sauce
1 teaspoon minced green pepper	dash of pepper
1 teaspoon minced celery	3/4 cups mayonnaise
2 teaspoons lemon juice	

Cut shrimp into very fine pieces. Mix together all ingredients. Add more seasoning if desired. Cut 36 rounds about the size of a half dollar from bread sliced 1/4" thick. Pile a heaping teaspoon of shrimp mixture on each round. Garnish with parsley. Yield: 3 dozen.

SPICY BOURBON COCKTAIL FRANKS

1 pound cocktail-size beef
    frankfurters
1/2 cup firmly packed light
    brown sugar
1/4 cup green onions, finely chopped

1/2 teaspoon dry mustard
1/4 cup bourbon
3 Tablespoons ketchup
1 Tablespoon Worcestershire sauce

Pan-broil the frankfurters with the chopped onions. In the top pan (the blazer) of a chafing dish, stir together the sugar and mustard; add the bourbon, ketchup and Worcestershire sauce. On the rangetop, over low heat, stir constantly until sugar is melted and mixture is hot; boil gently, stirring often, until it is reduced to 1/2 cup (about 5 minutes). Add the frankfurters, stirring to coat. Place the blazer over boiling water in the water pan and light heat unit. Keep hot while serving from the chafing dish. Makes 8 to 10 servings.

CHEESE BISCUITS WITH HAM

2 cups sifted all-purpose flour
2 teaspoons baking powder
1 teaspoon salt
1/4 teaspoon cayenne pepper

1/3 cup vegetable shortening
1 cup shredded sharp cheese
1/2 cup ice water
12 slices cooked ham (1/4" thick)

Cheese biscuits are an old Southern specialty. The best ham to use is, of course, Virginia or country ham. Leftover baked ham sliced cold and fairly thick also works well. A nip of red pepper and ice water instead of milk is what makes this recipe different.

Sift flour, baking powder, salt and cayenne into a large mixing bowl. Cut in shortening with a pastry blender until mixture resembles coarse cornmeal. Add cheese and toss to mix. Drizzle ice water over the dry ingredients, mixing lightly with a fork just until dough holds together. Turn dough out onto a lightly floured surface and knead lightly 7 or 8 times. Roll dough to 1/2" thickness, then cut with a floured 2" biscuit cutter. Place rounds 1/2" apart on ungreased cookie sheet. Bake at 425 degrees for 20 minutes. Yield: 1 dozen.

SAUCY COCKTAIL MEATBALLS

1 pound ground beef
2 Tablespoons bread crumbs
1 egg, slightly beaten
1/2 teaspoon salt
1/3 cup finely chopped onion
1/3 cup finely chopped green
    pepper

2 Tablespoons brown sugar
4 teaspoons Worcestershire sauce
1 Tablespoon prepared mustard
1 Tablespoon vinegar
2 Tablespoons butter/margarine
1 can Campbell's tomato soup

Mix beef, crumbs, egg and salt. Shape into small balls (50). Place in shallow baking dish (13x9x2). Broil until browned, turning once. Spoon off fat. In a saucepan, cook pepper and onion in butter until tender. Stir in remaining ingredients and pour over meatballs. Cover and bake at 350 degrees for 20 minutes.

SHRIMP MOUSSE

3 cups shrimp, cooked and chopped (2 pounds raw)
1 cup sour cream
8 ounces cream cheese, softened
1/2 cup mayonnaise
1/4 cup finely chopped green pepper
1/2 cup minced celery
1/4 cup chopped shallots or green onion
juice of 1 lemon
1/2 cup boiling water
1-1/2 envelopes unflavored gelatin
1/4 teaspoon Tabasco
1/2 teaspoon salt
1/2 Tablespoon Worcestershire sauce
red food coloring

Cook raw shrimp in crab boil following package directions. Peel and chop shrimp. Mix sour cream, cream cheese and mayonnaise. Add green pepper, celery, onions and lemon juice. Dissolve gelatin in water; add Tabasco, salt and Worcestershire sauce. Add this mixture and shrimp to sour cream mixture, adding enough food coloring to give a pink color. Pour into mold immediately. Chill 6 to 8 hours to set well. May be served with crackers or put in individual molds and served on sliced avocados. Serves 10 to 15 as an appetizer or 6 for luncheon. May be doubled.

SALMON PARTY LOG

2 cups red salmon (16 ounce can)
8 ounces cream cheese, softened
1 Tablespoon lemon juice
2 teaspoons grated onion
1 teaspoon prepared horseradish
1/4 teaspoon salt
1/4 teaspoon liquid smoke
1/2 cup chopped pecans
3 Tablespoons snipped parsley

Drain and flake salmon, removing skin and bones. Combine salmon with next six ingredients, mixing thoroughly. Chill several hours. Combine pecans and parsley. Shape salmon mixture into 8x2" log; roll in nut mixture; chill well and serve with crackers.

SPICY SHRIMP HORS D'OEUVRES

5 pounds medium or large shrimp, cooked, peeled and deveined
1/2 cup Durkee Famous Sauce
1/2 cup ketchup
1-1/2 cups mayonnaise
1/2 cup horseradish sauce
1/2 cup Dijon mustard (Grey Poupon)
1 cup finely chopped celery
1/2 cup finely chopped green onions
1/2 cup finely chopped dill pickle
4 teaspoons Worcestershire sauce
juice of 3 lemons

Combine all ingredients. Refrigerate overnight. Serve with toothpicks. Makes about 20 good-size servings. May be served in lettuce cups as a salad for a luncheon.

SPICY HOT MARINATED SHRIMP

2 large red onions, sliced
1 quart vinegar
1 cup salad oil
1 cup catsup
1/3 cup lemon juice
3 to 5 garlic cloves, pressed
1/2 cup sugar
1 Tablespoon salt
1 teaspoon pepper
1/4 teaspoon cayenne pepper

1 teaspoon paprika
1/2 teaspoon Tabasco sauce
2 Tablespoons Worcestershire
  sauce
1 bay leaf
1/2 teaspoon chili powder
capers to taste
5 pounds large shrimp, cooked
  and peeled

Must be prepared ahead. Mix onions, vinegar, oil, catsup, lemon juice, garlic, sugar, salt, pepper, cayenne pepper, paprika, Tabasco and Worcestershire sauces, bay leaf, chili powder and capers. Add shrimp and stir well. Cover and marinate in refrigerator for 3 days. Drain and serve in clear glass bowl. Serves 8.

PICKLED SHRIMP

4 cups water
1 bay leaf
6 whole cloves
12 peppercorns
1 thick lemon slice
1 teaspoon salt divided
1-1/2 pounds shrimp, shelled and
  deveined

1 cup vegetable oil
1/4 cup red wine vinegar
1/4 cup green onions, finely sliced
  or 1 small onion, chopped fine
1/4 teaspoon hot pepper sauce
  (more if desired)
2 Tablespoons chopped parsley
1 clove garlic, minced

In a large saucepan, bring to a boil the water, bay leaf, cloves, peppercorns, lemon and 1/2 teaspoon salt. Add shrimp, return to a boil, stirring frequently; remove from heat. Cover and let stand 5 minutes or until the shrimp are pink. Drain and discard the bay leaf, cloves, peppercorns and lemon. In a small bowl, combine oil, vinegar, onion, hot pepper sauce, parsley, garlic and remaining 1/2 teaspoon salt. Add shrimp; toss. Cover and chill for 2 to 3 hours, or overnight. This recipe may be doubled.

CORNED BEEF RING

3 ounce package lemon jello
1-1/2 cups boiling water
3 eggs, hard boiled and finely
  chopped
1 cup mayonnaise

1 cup sour cream
1-1/2 cups finely diced celery
1 Tablespoon minced onion
12 ounce can of corned beef,
  crumbled

Combine jello and water, stirring until dissolved. Set aside to partially set (do not let it get too firm). Add remaining ingredients and stir gently. Pour into lightly oiled ring mold. Serve with assorted crackers as appetizers. (May also be made in 9x5" dish and cut into squares. Garnish each square with sprig of parsley, a dollop of mayonnaise, or a sliced olive and use as a salad.)

CRAB FONDUE TARTS

7-1/2 ounces canned Alaska King
crab or 6 ounces frozen
Alaska King crab
1/4 cup butter
1-1/2 Tablespoons flour
1 cup milk
2 egg yolks

1-1/2 Tablespoons sherry wine
1 Tablespoon lemon juice
2/3 cup grated Swiss cheese
1/4 teaspoon salt
1-1/2 teaspoons finely chopped
green onion

Drain canned crab and slice (or thaw frozen crab, drain and slice). Melt butter in saucepan over low heat. Blend in flour; add milk and cook, stirring constantly, until thick and smooth. Beat egg yolks. Add small amount of hot mixture to egg yolks and return to saucepan. Cook gently until thickened. Blend in sherry, lemon juice, Swiss cheese, salt, green onion and crab. Heat gently until cheese melts and crab is hot. Spoon crab mixture in baked tart shells. Serve immediately, or reheat tarts in 450 degree oven 5 to 6 minutes. Makes 2 dozen cocktail tarts.

Cream Cheese Pastry:
1/2 cup butter
3 ounces cream cheese

1 cup flour
dash of salt

Cream butter and cheese, beating until smooth. Blend flour and salt into creamed mixture and mix thoroughly. Wrap pastry in waxed paper and refrigerate 1/2 hour. Press small portions of pastry into small tart pans. Top with another tart pan the same shape and press firmly. Bake at 400 degrees for 8 minutes. Remove top tart pan and bake 2 minutes longer. Remove pastry from tart pans and cool thoroughly before filling. Makes 24 tart shells.

KING CRAB SNACK SQUARES

7-1/2 ounces canned Alaska King
crab or 1/2 pound frozen
Alaska King crab
1-1/2 cups grated Cheddar cheese
3 Tablespoons minced green
onion
3 Tablespoons finely sliced black
or green olives

1 egg, slightly beaten
1/4 cup mayonnaise
2 cups buttermilk biscuit mix
1/2 cup cornmeal
2/3 cup water
3 Tablespoons melted butter

Drain and slice crab. Toss with cheese, onion and olives. Stir in egg and mayonnaise. Combine biscuit mix with remaining ingredients. Spread into a greased 9x13" baking pan. Spread crab mixture evenly over dough. Bake at 375 degrees 20 to 25 minutes or until golden. Serve hot, cut into squares. Makes 3 to 4 dozen small appetizer squares or 15 larger snack-size squares.

BUFFALO CHICKEN-WING DISH

30 chicken wings (about 5 pounds)
1/4 cup all-purpose flour
1 teaspoon salt
1/2 teaspoon black pepper
vegetable oil

6 Tablespoons butter
6 Tablespoons Louisiana Red Hot Sauce (not Tabasco)
bleu cheese dressing
celery and carrot sticks

Cut off small tip from each wing and discard. Cut each wing into 2 pieces. Wash and pat dry. Combine flour, salt and pepper and place in a paper bag. Dredge chicken wings, a few at a time, in the flour mixture. Place oil in a heavy skillet to the depth of 1". Heat oil to 350 degrees and fry wings, about 1/3 at a time, until they are golden brown and crisp. Drain well.

In a small saucepan melt butter and stir in hot sauce. Pour mixture over chicken wings, cover, and shake until wings are evenly coated. Place on a serving platter along with celery and carrot sticks. Serve Bleu Cheese Dressing alongside. Makes 6 servings.

Bleu Cheese Dressing:

1/4 cup crumbled bleu cheese
2 Tablespoons chopped onion
1 garlic clove, crushed
1/4 cup chopped fresh parsley
1 cup mayonnaise

1/2 cup sour cream
1 Tablespoon lemon juice
1 Tablespoon vinegar
salt, black pepper and cayenne pepper to taste

Combine all ingredients, adding seasonings to taste. Chill. Makes 2-1/2 cups.

CHINESE EGG ROLLS

3 eggs
1 cup all-purpose flour
2 Tablespoons cornstarch
2 cups water
1/2 teaspoon salt
1/2 cup of shrimp
1/2 cup of crab meat
1/2 cup finely diced celery

1/4 cup minced ham
1/4 cup water chestnuts
1/4 cup bamboo shoots
1 Tablespoon soy sauce
2 Tablespoons minced green onion
fat for frying

Beat 2 eggs slightly. Beat in flour, cornstarch, water and salt. Heat greased 7" or 8" skillet on very low temperature. Add 1 Tablespoon of batter and tip and tilt pan so that batter runs evenly over bottom of pan. Fry one side only. Mix 1 egg and remaining ingredients except fat. Shape into finger-size rolls. Lay on cooked sides of pancakes and roll up, tucking in edges to seal in filling. A little uncooked batter can be used for sealing. Chill. Just before serving, brown in 2" of hot fat. Makes about 30.

ELEGANT STUFFED MUSHROOMS

36 very large mushrooms (2-1/2"
to 3" across)
water
1/2 Tablespoon salt
juice of 1/2 lemon (2 Tablespoons; reserve squeezed
half)
5 slices prosciutto, chopped finely
4 slices Genoa salami 1/8" thick,
chopped finely
3 slices boiled ham, chopped
finely

2 Tablespoons minced parsley
dash of thyme
dash of oregano
1/2 teaspoon crumbled leaf sage
1/2 teaspoon dried basil or 2
leaves basil, minced coarsely
5 generous twists fresh-ground
pepper
1-1/2 cups grated Parmesan
cheese, divided
2/3 cup chicken broth

Carefully remove mushroom stems without damaging caps. Chop stems finely; set aside. Bring large kettle of water to boil; add salt, lemon juice and squeezed half. Add mushroom caps; cook 10 minutes or until tender. Drain.

Filling:

Mix well reserved chopped mushroom stems, prosciutto, salami, ham, parsley, thyme, oregano, sage, basil, pepper and 1 cup Parmesan. Stuff mushroom caps, packing in firmly and heaping generously. Pour broth into 15x10x1" or other large baking pan; add mushrooms, filled sides up. Bake in preheated 350 degree oven 15 minutes or until filling is hot. Sprinkle remaining 1/2 cup Parmesan over mushrooms; broil about 6" from heat source about 3 minutes or until Parmesan melts and tops are lightly browned. Arrange on warm large serving platter. Serve hot. Reserve broth for sauce or as desired. Makes 6 main-dish servings. Any leftover filling may be baked in foil packet alongside mushrooms.

PRE-PARTY MUSHROOMS

12 to 16 large mushrooms
12 to 16 cubes sharp Cheddar
cheese

butter/margarine
salt and pepper to taste

Rinse mushrooms under running water. Break stems off and place caps on a cookie sheet, bottom up. Place a pat of butter and a cube of cheese in each mushroom. Salt and pepper to taste and bake at 325 degrees for 15 to 20 minutes. Serve hot. Serves 4 to 6 people.

CRAB-STUFFED MUSHROOM CAPS

3 pounds large fresh mushrooms
1 cup finely chopped onion, green
1/4 cup butter/margarine, melted
1 pound fresh crab meat, drained
    and flaked
juice of 1 lemon
1/4 cup chopped fresh parsley
dash of Tabasco
1 teaspoon Worcestershire sauce
1/2 teaspoon salt
1/4 teaspoon pepper
1/2 cup mayonnaise
1/4 cup dry sherry (optional)
grated Parmesan cheese
1 cup butter/margarine, melted

Clean mushrooms with damp paper towels. Remove stems and chop; set aside. Place mushroom caps in a shallow baking pan. Saute mushroom stems and onion in 1/2 cup butter in a skillet until tender. Remove from heat and set aside. Sprinkle crab meat with lemon juice. Add sauteed mushrooms and next 5 ingredients; mix well. Stir in mayonnaise and sherry. Spoon mushroom mixture into mushroom caps; sprinkle with cheese. Drizzle remaining butter over mushrooms and bake at 350 degrees for 20 minutes. Yields about 4 dozen appetizers.

MUSHROOM MARINADE

1 pound mushrooms
2-1/2 cups salad oil
1 cup white vinegar
1 bunch chives, chopped
1 bunch green onions, finely
    chopped
2-1/2 Tablespoons sugar
1-1/2 Tablespoon salt
1 Tablespoon fresh lemon juice
1 Tablespoon finely minced garlic
2 teaspoons Worcestershire sauce
2 teaspoons bottled browning
    sauce
1/8 teaspoon prepared mustard

Whisk all ingredients except mushrooms in deep bowl until well combined. Add mushrooms. Cover and marinate in refrigerator 4 hours or, preferably, overnight. This marinade also works well with sliced zucchini, cauliflower or broccoli.

ARTICHOKE NIBBLES

1 clove garlic, minced
1/2 cup chopped onions
1 Tablespoon olive oil
4 well-beaten eggs
1/4 cup dry bread crumbs
1/2 teaspoon salt
1/2 teaspoon pepper
2 Tablespoons minced parsley
1/8 teaspoon dried oregano
2 or 3 drops bottled hot pepper
    sauce (Tabasco)
2 cups shredded Cheddar cheese
12 ounces marinated artichoke
    hearts drained and finely
    chopped

Saute onions and garlic until tender (about 5 minutes); drain. Combine eggs, bread crumbs, salt and pepper, oregano and hot pepper sauce in a bowl. Stir in onion, garlic, parsley, cheese and artichokes. Spread in greased 7x11" pan. Bake at 350 degrees for 17 to 18 minutes. Cut in 1" squares. Serve hot.

STUFFED MUSHROOM APPETIZERS

1 pound fresh mushrooms, cleaned and stemmed
French or Italian dressing
8 ounces cream cheese, softened
1 Tablespoon milk

2 Tablespoons snipped parsley
1/4 cup minced green onion with tops or chives
chilled cooked small shrimp
fresh dill, optional

Marinate mushrooms overnight in dressing. 1 hour before serving, combine cream cheese and milk. Stir in parsley and onion. Drain mushrooms and fill with cheese mixture. Top with shrimp and sprig of fresh dill.

NOTE: Use leftover filling as a spread on crackers or as a topping on baked potatoes. Reserve stems to use in your favorite vegetable casserole or to make duxelles.

Variation:

Substitute 1/4 cup each finely chopped toasted almonds and chopped green pepper and 1/2 teaspoon seasoned salt for the milk, parsley, chives, shrimp and dill. Garnish stuffed caps with shredded carrot, snipped parsley, toasted slivered almonds or paprika.

ZUCCHINI APPETIZERS
"A Tasty Hit"

3 cups thinly sliced unpared zucchini
1 cup Bisquick baking mix
1/2 cup finely chopped onion
1/2 cup Parmesan
2 Tablespoons snipped parsley
1/2 teaspoon salt

1/2 teaspoon seasoned salt
1/2 teaspoon ground oregano
1/2 teaspoon basil leaves
1/4 teaspoon garlic powder
dash of pepper
1/2 cup vegetable oil
4 eggs, slightly beaten

Heat oven to 350 degrees. Grease and flour an oblong pan (13x9x2"). Mix all ingredients thoroughly and pour into pan. Bake until golden brown (about 30 minutes). Cut into pieces, about 2x1".

Serve warm. Makes about 4 dozen.

STUFFED CHERRY TOMATOES

36 cherry tomatoes
1-1/2 cups ground ham or chicken
1 (3-ounce) package cream
  cheese, softened

2 Tablespoons commercial sour
  cream
salt and pepper to taste
grated Parmesan cheese
fresh parsley sprigs

Wash tomatoes thoroughly. Cut a thin slice from top of each tomato; carefully scoop out pulp, reserving pulp for other uses. Invert the shells on paper towels to drain. Combine next 4 ingredients in a mixing bowl; beat at low speed with an electric mixer until smooth. Spoon about 2 teaspoons meat mixture into tomato shells. Sprinkle with cheese, and garnish with parsley sprigs. Chill. Yields about 36 appetizer servings.

Cherry tomatoes may also be stuffed with one of the following:

Bacon Filling:
1-1/2 pounds bacon, finely
  chopped

8 green onions, finely chopped
1/3 cup mayonnaise

Fry bacon until crisp and drain well. Mix with green onions and mayonnaise. Stuff tomatoes and chill.

Crab Meat Cheese Filling:
1 cup shredded crab meat
1/4 cup fresh lemon juice
3 ounces cream cheese, softened
1/4 cup cream
2 Tablespoons mayonnaise

1 Tablespoon minced green onion
1/2 teaspoon garlic, minced
1 teaspoon Worcestershire sauce
2 drops Tabasco
salt and pepper to taste

Marinate crab meat in lemon juice for 1 hour. Drain well. Combine cream cheese, cream and mayonnaise until smooth. Mix together with crab meat and remaining ingredients. Fill tomatoes and chill.

PICKLED EGGS

1-1/2 dozen hardboiled eggs,
  peeled
1 medium onion, sliced
1-3/4 cups white vinegar
3/4 cup water
3 Tablespoons brown sugar

1/2 teaspoon salt
1/4 teaspoon garlic salt
5 peppercorns
1 whole clove
1/4 teaspoon dill seed
piece of ginger root

Combine onion and remaining ingredients in a saucepan; bring to boiling and simmer about 5 minutes. Put eggs into two quart jars; pour half the vinegar mixture over eggs in each jar. Cover jars, cool, and refrigerate at least overnight to develop flavor (may be kept in refrigerator up to 2 weeks). Cut pickled eggs into halves lengthwise and serve with a platter of sliced ham; or cut into crosswise slices and use to garnish appetizers, salads, and main dishes; or finely chop and sprinkle over salad greens which have been tossed with an oil-vinegar dressing; or tuck a jar into the picnic basket.

ORANGE PECANS

4 cups pecan halves
1/2 cup evaporated milk
1/2 cup orange juice
butter (size of walnut)

2 cups sugar
orange peel from 1 orange
pinch of salt

Mix sugar, orange juice, milk, butter and salt; cook until it forms a hard ball. Cut rind of orange in strips and boil in water until tender. Drain and dry thoroughly, then add to mixture and cook. When the sugar mixture begins to cool, mix nuts in and pour onto slab of marble or waxed paper. Separate nuts with two forks.

"IT"

1 (6-ounce) package small cheese crackers
2 (6-1/4 ounce) packages king-size corn chips
8 ounces toasted coconut chips
8 ounces walnuts
12 ounces pecans
1 quart fresh popped corn

1 cup butter
1/2 teaspoon garlic salt
1 clove garlic, crushed
1 teaspoon salt
1 teaspoon curry powder
2 to 3 dashes hot pepper sauce
1 Tablespoon Worcestershire sauce

Mix crackers, corn chips, coconut chips, walnuts, pecans and popped corn together in a big shallow pan. Melt butter and add garlic salt, crushed garlic, salt, curry, hot pepper sauce and Worcestershire. Sprinkle over dry mixture, tossing as additions are made. Bake in 250 degree oven for about 1 hour, stirring occasionally. Drain on paper towels. Yields about 6 quarts.

CHOCOLATE-COVERED PECANS

1 pound milk chocolate
1/2 pound moist coconut

120 pecan halves

Melt chocolate slowly in top of double boiler. Make pecan "sandwiches" using 2 pecan halves with moist coconut between. When chocolate has melted, use 2 forks to dip pecans in the chocolate, covering pecans well. Remove and place on waxed paper until thoroughly dry. Makes about 60.

WHEAT SNACKS

1 large box bite-size shredded
    wheat
1 package ranch-style buttermilk
    dressing mix

1 teaspoon dill weed
1/4 teaspoon garlic powder
1/4 teaspoon lemon
1/2 cup cooking oil

Mix seasonings well with oil. Put shredded wheat in large bowl and cover with oil mixture. Keep turning and tossing until all of the oil mixture is absorbed. Keep in covered container or put back into box.

OYSTER CRACKER SNACKS

1 (12-ounce) box oyster crackers
1 package original ranch-style
    buttermilk dressing mix

2 teaspoons dill weed
dash of garlic powder
1/2 cup cooking oil

Pour crackers in a large pan and mix with dressing mix, dill weed and garlic powder. Pour oil over all and stir thoroughly until well coated. Put in plastic bag and tie securely. Shake contents. May be eaten anytime and flavor enhances after sitting for a couple of hours. Store in a covered container. This is a delicious, low calorie snack.

PARTY SNACK MIX

3 cups small pretzels
2 cups shoestring potatoes
2 cups Spanish peanuts
1-1/2 cups seasoned croutons

1 (3-ounce) can french fried
    onion rings
1/2 cup butter, melted
1/2 cup grated Parmesan cheese

In a large bowl, mix pretzels, shoestring potatoes, peanuts, croutons and onion rings. Pour butter over mixture, sprinkle with Parmesan cheese and mix well. Spread on 15x10" jelly-roll pan or shallow roasting pan. Bake at 250 degrees for 1 hour, stirring twice during cooking. May be prepared ahead; keeps well.

Old First Baptist Church — Augusta   c.1903

THE FORMER FIRST BAPTIST CHURCH

On March 25, 1817, the Baptist Praying Society of Augusta was formed. Their first church was dedicated four years later at Greene and Eighth Streets. As the tensions heightened between the North and South over slavery, economic and political issues, the strains of the controversies affected many denominations throughout the nation. In May 1845, 327 delegates representing eight Southern states and the District of Columbia gathered in Augusta at the First Baptist Church. At that historic conference, it was decided to form the Southern Baptist Convention.

The congregation of First Baptist built a new church on the site in 1903. By the early 1970's, most of the members lived on the west side of Augusta. Therefore, property was acquired at the end of Walton Way to construct a new, and much needed, larger church. The downtown building for a time was the home of the Landmark Baptist Congregation.

Beverages

BLOODY MARY'S
FOR THE MULTITUDES

1 gallon tomato juice
1 can frozen lemon juice
4 Tablespoons Worcestershire
   sauce
1/2 cup confectioner's sugar

1 Tablespoon celery salt
1 to 2 teaspoons black pepper
salt to taste (2 to 3 teaspoons)
Tabasco sauce (optional)
2 fifths cold vodka

Mix all ingredients except vodka. Add vodka at serving time. Makes 48 four-ounce servings or 32 six-ounce servings.

EGGNOG

12 eggs, separated
1 cup sugar
3 cups bourbon
2 cups brandy
1/2 cup sherry or Madiera wine

2-1/2 cups milk
2-1/2 cups cream
1-1/2 cups heavy cream, whipped
grated fresh nutmeg

Beat egg yolks with 1/2 cup sugar until thick and pale yellow. Beat in brandy, bourbon, and milk and cream. Beat egg whites and, as they begin to stiffen, gradually add remaining 1/2 cup sugar, beating well with each addition. When whites are stiff enough to form peaks, add them to yolk mixture along with the whipped cream. Fold together gently but thoroughly using a rubber spatula. Serve from a well-chilled punch bowl set in ice. Sprinkle with grated fresh nutmeg. Serves 18 to 20 people who are braced for the best!

WASSAIL PUNCH

The word Wassail is derived from the old Anglo-Saxon drinking pledge "Wass-Hael" which meant "be in health". It was the custom to toast the lord of the manor, and the practice was easily assimilated into the Christmas tradition. This recipe is a direct import from England.

1 gallon apple cider/apple juice
1 (12-ounce) can frozen orange
   juice concentrate
1-1/2 cups water
1 (6-ounce) can lemonade
   concentrate
16 whole cloves

4 cinnamon sticks
1 teaspoon nutmeg
1 teaspoon ground cinnamon
1 teaspoon ground cloves
2 cups bourbon
1 orange, sliced
1 lemon, sliced

Combine all ingredients except orange and lemon slices in a large pot. Heat mixture to boiling, then reduce heat to simmer. Simmer for 10 minutes to blend flavors. Serve hot with orange and lemon slices floated on top. Serves 40 people.

MINT JULEP

This gentlemanly beverage (the rite, that is) should not be entrusted to the novice — duplicate player or damn Yankee. The mint julep is a heritage of the Old South, a true emblem of hospitality.

"Go to a spring where cool, crystal clear water bubbles from under a bank of dew-washed ferns and, in a consecrated vessel, dip up a little water at the source. Follow the stream until it broadens and trickles through beds of a mint growing in aromatic profusion and waving softly in the summer breeze. Gather the sweetest and tenderest shoots and gently carry them home. Go to the sideboard and select a decanter of Kentucky bourbon, distilled by a master's hand and mellowed with age, yet still vigorous and inspiring. An ancestral sugar bowl, a row of silver goblets, some spoons and ice and you are ready to start. In a canvas bag, pound twice as much ice as you think you will need. Make it fine as snow; keep it dry and do not allow it to degenerate into slush.

In each goblet, put a slightly heaping teaspoonful of granulated sugar; barely cover this with spring water and slightly bruise one mint leaf into this, leaving the spoon in the goblet. Then pour elixir from decanter until the goblets are one fourth full. fill goblets with snowy ice, sprinkling in a small amount of sugar as you fill. Wipe the outside of the goblets dry and embellish copiously with mint.

Now comes the important and delicate operation of frosting. By proper manipulation of the spoon, the ingredients are circulated and blended until nature, wishing to take a further hand and add another of its beautiful phenomena, crusts the whole in a glistening coat of white frost.

When all is ready, assemble your guests on the porch or in the garden where the aroma of the Juleps will rise heavenward and make the birds sing. Propose a worthy toast, raise the goblet to your lips, bury your nose in the mint, inhale a deep breath of its fragrance and sip the nectar of the gods."

There, now, doesn't that make you thirsty!

PINK WINE PUNCH
(Must do ahead; serves 30)

48 ounces frozen, sliced
  strawberries
1 cup sugar
4 bottles rose wine, chilled

24 ounces frozen lemonade
  concentrate
2 large bottles club soda

This is a delicious punch for an afternoon party or a cocktail party! Thaw strawberries, mix with sugar and a bottle of wine in a large container. Allow to stand, covered, for 1 hour. Strain into punch bowl, add frozen lemonade and stir until thawed. Add remaining wine and club soda. Stir gently. If desired, float ice ring.

HOT BUTTERED RUM

Hot Buttered Rum Batter:
1 pound brown sugar
1 pound butter, softened (no
   substitutes)
1 quart vanilla ice cream, softened

1 teaspoon ground nutmeg
1 teaspoon ground cinnamon
1 teaspoon ground cloves
1 pound powdered sugar

Prepare hot buttered rum batter by beating butter in a bowl until creamy. Gradually beat in brown sugar until smooth like cake batter. Add ice cream, nutmeg, cinnamon, and cloves. If a sweeter mix is desired, add powdered sugar. Store in freezer. May be stored in refrigerator up to 3 weeks.

Hot Buttered Rum:
1 Tablespoon of rum batter
1 jigger of light Puerto Rican

1 jigger of brandy
boiling water

Preheat mug with boiling water. Put batter into heated mug. Add 1 jigger of rum and 1 jigger of brandy. Fill mug with hot water and stir well. Hit top surface with a hot spoon or poker so that butter will not stay on top. Garnish with a sprinkle of freshly grated nutmeg. Add a cinnamon stick to stir.

NOTE: A jar of this Hot Buttered Rum mix, in a decorative jar, and a bottle of rum makes a nice hostess gift when you have been invited for a winter weekend or to give as a gift. Be sure to include a card with serving instructions.

IRISH COFFEE

The most delectable drink that ever crosses the palate.
The one word for it is divine.

Irish Whiskey..."smooth as the wit of the land"
Coffee..."strong as a friendly hand"
Sugar..."sweet as the tongue of a rogue"
Cream..."rich as an Irish brogue"

Heat a stemmed whiskey goblet (6 to 8 ounces); pour in 1/3 glass Irish whiskey (a generous jigger); add 1 teaspoon sugar (confectioner's sugar preferred) or more according to taste. Fill goblet with strong black coffee to within an inch of the brim. Stir to dissolve sugar and top with slightly whipped cream, so that it floats on top. Do not stir, but sip through cream to enjoy the true flavor of the drink.

Although good Irish whiskey is one of the most important ingredients, Irish coffee probably was not concocted in Ireland. Legend has it that this potent pleasing drink was invented by a bartender working on a pier somewhere in California.

SUNSHINE PUNCH

3 cups water
2/3 cup sugar
6 ounces frozen orange juice
concentrate
6 ounces frozen lemonade
concentrate

2 ripe medium-sized bananas,
cut up
3 cups unsweetened pineapple
juice
2 Tablespoons lemon juice
2 750-ml. bottles champagne,
chilled

In large saucepan, combine water and sugar and bring to a boil. Stir until sugar is dissolved and boil gently, uncovered, for 3 minutes. Remove from heat; stir in orange juice and lemonade concentrates. Meanwhile, combine bananas and half of the pineapple juice in a blender. Cover and blend until smooth. Stir into sugar mixture. Add remaining pineapple juice and lemon juice. Turn into shallow freezer container. Seal, label and freeze overnight or up to two months.

To serve, scrape spoon across frozen mixture and spoon about 2/3 cup into each chilled glass. Slowly pour in champagne and stir gently. If desired, garnish with orange slice and orange leaves. Makes about 15 eight-ounce servings.

SWEDISH GLUG

3 cups sugar
3 cups water
15 prunes
1/2 cup raisins
1 teaspoon whole cloves
3 sticks cinnamon

peel of 1 orange
15 cardamons
1/4 cup walnuts
1/2 gallon port wine
1/2 gallon muscatel wine
3 jiggers pure alcohol (190 proof)

Combine all ingredients except wines and alcohol in large pot and cook for 10 to 15 minutes. Let set overnight. Next day, add alcohol and wines. Heat to just boiling but do not allow to boil. Remove from heat and light with a match to burn off alcohol, quickly put lid on pot to smother fire. Let sit overnight before pouring into jug. Keeps for months or years, if it lasts that long. As it ages, it gets clearer.

SCUPPERNONG WINE

2 gallons scuppernongs
3 cups sugar

water to cover

Fill earthenware with scuppernongs (they should be crushed, but they do not have to be). Cover grapes with water and allow to sit and ferment for about a week. Check daily to see that grapes are not rotting. In about 5 days to a week, strain and sweeten to taste; juice will ferment and work off again in about 3 days; restrain and place in airtight bottles.

CRANBERRY-GRAPE SPRITZER

12 ounces Welch's frozen
cranberry juice cocktail
concentrate, thawed
4-1/2 cups club soda, chilled

50.8 ounces Welch's sparkling
red or white grape juice
chilled orange slices

Gently stir cranberry juice cocktail concentrate and club soda together in a punch bowl; add sparkling grape juice. Garnish with orange slices and serve immediately in ice-filled glasses. Makes about 15 servings (3/4 cup each).

ORANGE TEACO

This recipe is reprinted from "Treasure Chest of Recipes" (November 1956), sponsored by the Moriet Reid class of Associate Reformed Presbyterian Church, formerly on 957 N. Highland Avenue, Atlanta.

1-1/2 pints whipping cream
6 ounces frozen orange juice
1 cup sweet milk

1 teaspoon vanilla
sugar to taste

Make frozen orange juice according to directions on can. Whip cream and combine with other ingredients. (Orange flavor and thickness desired may be obtained by varying amounts of juice and cream.) Serve in punch bowl with very small amount of crushed ice or in individual glasses topped with vanilla ice cream and garnished with a cherry.

FROSTED MINT TEA

3 quarts boiling water
24 regular tea bags
1/4 cup mint jelly
1/4 cup sugar
lemon juice

sugar
3 quarts lemon-lime carbonated
beverage or gingerale, chilled
lemon or lime slices (optional)
fresh mint sprigs (optional)

Pour boiling water over tea bags; cover and allow to stand 5 minutes. Remove tea bags; add mint jelly and 1/4 cup sugar, stirring until dissolved. Chill. Dip rims of glasses in lemon juice and then in sugar; freeze glasses. To serve, combine tea and lemon-lime carbonated beverage; pour over ice in glasses. Garnish each glass with a lemon slice and mint sprig. Yields 6 quarts.

FRIENDSHIP TEA MIX
Russian Tea

18 ounces orange-flavored
instant breakfast drink
1 cup sugar
1/2 cup pre-sweetened lemonade
mix
1/2 cup instant tea

3 ounces apricot-flavored gelatin
mix (optional)
2-1/2 teaspoons ground cinnamon
1 teaspoon ground cloves
boiling water

Combine first 7 ingredients in a large bowl, stirring well. Store mix in airtight container. To serve, place 1-1/2 Tablespoons mix in a cup. Add 1 cup boiling water and stir well. Yields about 50 servings.

FROSTY SHERBET FLIP

1 pint lime or orange sherbet
2 cups dry white wine

2 cups gingerale
mint leaves (optional)

Place a scoop of sherbet into 4 chilled glasses; fill with equal parts of wine and gingerale. If desired, garnish with mint leaves. Makes 6 six-ounce servings. NOTE: Another time, try this delightful-tasting drink with peach sorbet and rose wine!

WEDDING PUNCH

3 Tablespoons tea
1 quart boiling water
2 cups sugar
1 orange peel
1 lemon peel
8 whole cloves
1-1/2 cups water
12 ounces orange concentrate

12 ounces lemonade or 1 small
  can lemonade and 1 small
  can limeade
46 ounces pineapple juice
  (unsweetened)
1 teaspoon almond flavoring
3 quarts gingerale
1 small bottle maraschino cherry
  juice (optional)

Pour boiling water over tea leaves. Steep for 5 minutes, strain and allow to cool. Put sugar, peelings, cloves, and 1-1/2 cups water in saucepan and allow to boil for 5 minutes. Cool tea and sugar mixture. Mix with other ingredients except gingerale. Chill until serving time. To serve, add cold gingerale, garnish with ice ring made with fruit. This punch base freezes well before gingerale has been added.

AUNT FANNY'S PARTY PUNCH

1 (46-ounce) can pineapple juice
1 (46-ounce) can apricot nectar
1 quart orange juice
2 quarts orange sherbet
2 pints vanilla ice cream

1 (10-ounce) package frozen
  strawberries, thawed
2 quarts gingerale, chilled
pineapple cubes
mint sprigs
whole fresh strawberries

Combine all fruit juices in a large punch bowl. Mix sherbet and ice cream in with a whisk, leaving them in small chunks. Add strawberries. When ready to serve, gently stir in gingerale, add a large piece of ice (an ice ring or ice cubes), and garnish with pineapple cubes, mint sprigs and fresh strawberries (enough so that will scoop up a bit with each serving). Serves 70 punch cups.

RUBY RED FROST

1 pint bottle cranberry juice
  cocktail
1-1/2 cups fresh lemon juice
1 cup sugar

2 (28-ounce) bottles chilled
  gingerale
1 pint raspberry sherbet
lemon slices

Combine cranberry juice cocktail, fresh lemon juice and sugar, blending well. Chill. To serve, pour over ice in punch bowl. Add chilled gingerale and sherbet. Garnish with lemon slices. Serve at once. Yields 24 cups.

ICE RINGS FOR PUNCHES

Basic Ring:

Use a metal round salad mold with a hole in the middle, or you may use a plastic salad mold. Put a small amount of water or fruit juice in the bottom of the bowl (just enough liquid to cover bottom of pan). Let it freeze. Add decoration to make it pretty and add flavor to the punch. Add fillings and liquid at different intervals or layers. This will take most of the day, as the addition of the liquid must be made in small amounts. The more frozen ice you have, the more liquid can be added.

Grape Ice Ring:

4 small bunches white seedless grapes, washed with stems attached

4 small bunches red seedless grapes, washed with stems attached
bunch of mint sprigs (amount depends on your arrangement)

Alternate grapes according to color, with mint leaves placed so that the ring has appearance of grape branches surrounded by leaves.

Wedding Ice Ring:

bunch of leather-leaf fern, washed well and cleaned
bunch of maiden-hair fern, washed well and cleaned
daisy blossoms, washed well and cleaned (amount depends on you)

miniature roses (color of your choice) washed well and cleaned (amount depends on you); buds as well as flowers
violet blossoms, washed well and cleaned

Arrange blossoms and ferns to resemble small bouquets. When ring is unmolded, it will make a beautiful addition to your punch bowl.

NOTE: Ice rings may be made using lemonade in place of water and arranging assorted melon balls and strawberries in groups.

CITRIC ACID PUNCH

2 quarts heated water
6-1/2 cups sugar
2 ounces citric acid (from pharmacy)
4 quarts cold water

1 large can unsweetened pineapple juice
1 large can unsweetened orange juice
2 quarts gingerale
coloring, if desired

Heat 2 quarts of water, add sugar, and pour into glass or tupperware container (such as a large cake taker). Add 2 ounces citric acid (from pharmacy), cold water, pineapple juice and orange juice. May be colored at this time. Freeze in tupperware container or new milk cartons. To serve, thaw 4 hours at room temperature or 24 hours in refrigerator. Add 2 quarts gingerale just before serving. Punch base may be refrozen providing gingerale has not been added. Serves approximately 50 people.

FRENCH CHOCOLATE

Base for about 6 cups of French Chocolate:

3 squares unsweetened chocolate	1/2 cup heavy cream
1/2 cup water	1 teaspoon vanilla
3/4 cup sugar	hot milk
1/8 teaspoon salt	

Combine chocolate and water in a saucepan and stir over moderate heat until chocolate melts. Take off heat and stir until smooth. Stir in sugar and salt and cook 4 minutes over low heat, stirring constantly. Remove from heat and cool. Whip cream and fold into cooled chocolate with vanilla. Refrigerate. To serve, place 1 rounded tablespoon of chocolate cream in a mug and stir in a cup of hot milk. Top with whipped cream or a marshmallow, if desired.

NOTE: This rich chocolate base may be prepared in quantity and kept in the refrigerator, ready to mix with milk and heat up. Good to have on hand in the winter.

HOT MULLED CIDER

A great hot non-alcoholic drink for after skiing...
children love it.

1/2 cup brown sugar	3" stick cinnamon
1/4 teaspoon salt	dash of nutmeg
2 quarts apple cider	a cinnamon stick for each mug
1 teaspoon whole allspice	an orange slice for each mug
1 teaspoon whole cloves	(optional)

The history of cider may be as old as the history of man, for it is thought cider has been made whenever man had apples. Supposedly, it was an apple that caused Adam and Eve's downfall (although the Bible never specifically names the Forbidden Fruit), and that takes us all the way back to the beginning.

Historians believe the name "cider" is derived from the Hebrew name for strong drink, "cekar", and it is the hard, alcoholic cider that has continuously caught man's fancy. Through the ages its popularity has ebbed and flowed, rising perhaps to its highest peak during American Colonial days when it was expedient because it was simple and inexpensive to make. Now its popularity is on the increase again in perhaps its true place of origin, France, and in England and America.

Combine the first 7 ingredients and bring to a boil. Simmer for 20 minutes. Remove spices and serve in mugs with cinnamon sticks and orange slice floaters, if desired. Makes 10 servings.

COCOA MIX

Make a jar of homemade cocoa mix to keep in the cupboard. Your family will love the convenience of adding a scoop to some boiling water and having a cup of hot cocoa whenever they want it. Makes 20 3/4-cup servings.

3 cups dry non-dairy coffee creamer
2 cups sugar

1 cup unsweetened cocoa
1/4 teaspoon salt
1 vanilla bean

Combine milk, sugar, cocoa and salt in a blender or food processor. Split vanilla bean and scrape as much as possible of the inside of the bean into blender/processor. Cut remaining bean parts and place a piece in each storage jar (store a week or more before using to allow vanilla flavor to be absorbed). Process mixture until well combined; store in tight jar in a cool, dry place. To use, combine 1/4 cup mix and 3/4 cup boiling water for each serving and top with marshmallows or whipped cream for added flavor.

For HOT MOCHA mix, add 1/2 cup instant coffee to above mixture. Both mixes are excellent to have on hand.

FROSTY LEMONADE

What's more American than lemonade stands with enterprising children behind them, trying to make extra money! This simple drink, made from fresh lemons, is a real thirst quencher.

1 Tablespoon freshly grated lemon rind
1-1/2 cups granulated sugar
1/2 cup boiling water

1-1/2 cups freshly squeezed lemon juice
lemon slices for garnish

In a jar with a tight-fitting cover, combine lemon peel, sugar and boiling water; cover and shake until sugar dissolves. Add lemon juice (5 to 6 medium sized lemons will yield a cup of juice). Store syrup base in refrigerator, tightly covered, until ready to use. 2-2/3 cups syrup base makes 8 to 10 servings.

To make lemonade by the glass, pour about 1/4 cup syrup base into a tall glass; add 3/4 cup cold water and ice cubes. Stir quickly, garnish with a lemon slice, and serve.

To make a 2-quart pitcher of lemonade, pour entire recipe of syrup base into pitcher, add 6 cups cold water, stir briskly; add ice cubes and stir again.

St. Paul's Episcopal Church

ST. PAUL'S CHURCH

St. Paul's Church was established in 1750 beside Fort Augusta on the Savannah River bank. During the colonial period the church and nearby parsonage served as temporary living quarters for refugees who had fled from Indian uprisings west of the town. The buildings were destroyed in the Revolutionary Battle for Augusta in 1871.

After the war, a new interdenominational church was constructed on the same site. By 1819 the building could no longer accommodate the growing congregations of the various groups using the facility. While the other denominations chose to build elsewhere in the town, the Episcopalians remained to construct a larger church on the site of the first St. Paul's Anglican Church.

For nearly a hundred years, the congregation worshipped in this third edifice. Then, in 1916, the church was destroyed in Augusta's Great Fire. Following the previous design but on a larger scale, construction of the present building began soon after the tragedy. The grave of Signer of the Constitution William Few is located in the historic church cemetery.

Soups

SENATE BEAN SOUP

Served daily in the U.S. Senate since 1904

1 pound dry navy beans
10 cups water
1-1/2 pound ham hock, pork
  shoulder, or spare ribs
1 bay leaf
1 teaspoon pepper
2 Tablespoons butter, preferably
  bacon drippings
1 large onion, chopped

2 large ribs celery, finely
  chopped (about 1 cup)
1/4 cup parsley
2 cloves garlic, minced
1 teaspoon salt
1 teaspoon oregano
1 teaspoon basil
1/4 teaspoon dry mustard
black pepper to taste

Sort and wash beans well; place in large saucepan or Dutch oven. Cover beans with water (6 cups), add 1 teaspoon salt, and soak overnight covered. Add remaining water, ham hock, bay leaf and pepper. Bring to a boil, reduce heat, cover, and allow to simmer 1-1/4 hours or until beans are almost tender. Saute onion and celery in butter until transparent. Add to beans and ham, then stir in remaining ingredients; reduce heat and simmer, covered, for 30 to 40 minutes or until beans are tender. Discard bay leaf, remove ham hock from soup; separate meat from bone and return meat to soup. Makes 6 servings. Serve with crusty French or Garlic bread.

NOTE: 2 cups of finely diced potatoes may be added with the beans and ham to simmer the last 30 to 40 minutes.

TIFFANY BEAN POT SOUP

2 cups dried pinto beans
1 pound ham, cubed
1 quart water
1 (22-ounce) can tomato juice
4 cups chicken stock or broth
3 onions, chopped
3 cloves garlic, minced
3 Tablespoons chopped parsley
1/4 cup chopped green pepper
4 Tablespoons brown sugar
1 Tablespoon chili powder
1 teaspoon salt

1 teaspoon crushed bay leaves
1 teaspoon oregano
1/2 teaspoon cumin
1/2 teaspoon rosemary leaves,
  crushed
1/2 teaspoon celery seed
1/2 teaspoon ground thyme
1/2 teaspoon ground marjoram
1/2 teaspoon sweet basil
1/4 teaspoon hot curry powder
4 whole cloves
1 cup sherry

Soak cleaned beans in water overnight in large Dutch oven. Drain and add remaining ingredients (except sherry). Bring to boil, cover, and cook slowly until beans are tender (about 3 hours). Remove whole cloves, add sherry, and serve in generous soup bowls topped with chopped green onions.

(Continued)

This soup is said to have been served at Tiffany's Saloon in New Mexico. Operated in the Territorial West, Tiffany's was one block east of the hotel where Lew Wallace completed writing "Ben Hur." The saloon burned to the ground in March, 1977. The recipe was made public by the restaurant at that time. The seasons are what makes it so delicious.

BLACK BEAN SOUP

1 pound beans
1/2 cup olive oil
1 cup chopped onions
1 cup chopped green pepper
1 clove garlic, minced
1 diced fresh tomato
1 bay leaf
1 teaspoon crushed oregano
1/4 teaspoon cumin
2 Tablespoons wine vinegar
1 Tablespoon salt
1/2 teaspoon Tabasco
1 Tablespoon sherry

1 smoked ham bone
1 slice minced bacon or lean salt
  pork
Garnishes:
sour cream
1 cup minced bell pepper, green
1 cup minced red bell pepper
1 cup minced green onion
1 cup chopped hardboiled egg
1 cup chopped ham
2 lemons, sliced thinly
sprigs of parsley
chopped dill pickles

Wash and soak beans overnight in water to cover. Next morning, add water to make 6 cups of liquid. Place beans in 4-quart kettle, adding water to 1" above beans. Add 2 tablespoons olive oil, tomato, bay leaf, 1/2 cup of onions, green pepper, and crushed garlic. Cook for an hour, adding more water if necessary. In a skillet, saute remaining onion and minced garlic until transparent in 1/2 cup of olive oil. Add oregano and cumin; add to beans along with smoked ham bone and minced bacon or lean salt pork. Add Tabasco; cover; allow to cook slowly for about 1 hour or until beans begin to fall apart, adding more water if necessary. Add Tabasco, sherry, and wine vinegar. Allow to simmer for about 30 minutes longer. Serve over a mound of hot cooked rice topped with a slice of lemon and desired garnishes. Excellent with hop crisp corn sticks or fresh bread and a salad.

CREAM OF BROCCOLI SOUP

"A beautiful soup, so rich and green,
waiting in a hot tureen to be served."

7 Tablespoons butter/margarine
1 cup chopped onions
2/3 cup thinly sliced celery
2/3 cup thinly sliced leeks (white part only)
1 large clove garlic, crushed
1-3/4 pounds broccoli, heads and tender stalks

1 quart chicken stock or canned broth
5 Tablespoons flour
2 cups half and half or light cream
salt and pepper
Garnishes:
Chopped scallions, hot paprika, sour cream, croutons

Melt 3 Tablespoons butter in medium saucepan. Add celery, onions, leeks, and garlic and cook until tender. Wash and trim broccoli, slicing stalks into 1" slices and discarding the rough stems. Separate tops into small florets. In a large saucepan, bring broccoli and chicken broth to a boil, cover, and simmer for 20 minutes over medium heat. Add celery and onion mixture. Place in blender and blend quickly, leaving small pieces of broccoli. Return to a clean pot. Make a roux of 5 tablespoons flour and 4 tablespoons butter; cook 3 to 4 minutes, stirring constantly. Add broccoli and stock to roux. To avoid lumps, stir constantly until mixture is thickened. Thin to preferred consistency with half and half. Add salt and pepper to taste. Ladle into bowls and garnish with sour cream or scallions or both. Have plenty of croutons available. This soup can be made ahead of time and reheated just before serving.

NOTE: A cup of florets may be reserved and added before serving. This makes a very attractive soup.

KENTUCKY BURGOO

2-1/2 pound chicken
2 pounds lean beef
1 pound veal or 1 pound boneless pork
4 quarts water
6 ears fresh corn
2 cups diced raw Irish potatoes
2 cups diced onions
1 pint fresh butterbeans
3 carrots, diced
1 cup shredded cabbage

2 cups okra, sliced
1 cup whole kernel corn
2 green peppers, diced
1 button garlic
1 small pod hot pepper or 1 teaspoon hot sauce
1 cup minced parsley
1 quart tomatoes
1 stalk celery, diced
4 teaspoons salt
3/4 teaspoon black pepper

A native Kentucky dish, the original was cooked by Gus Jaubert who made a stew of what was handy to serve to Confederate General John Hunt Morgan and his calvary men during the Civil War. This chunky meat and vegetable stew became popular long after the war ended; it is always served on Derby Day. Genuine burgoo need three kinds of meat and a combination of vegetables.

(Continued)

Boil beef, veal or pork and chicken until very tender, using water in a heavy aluminum or iron kettle with a tight lid. Remove meat and separate from bones. Replace meat in the pot. Fry onions in bacon fat until yellow; add to stock and meat mixture. Add potatoes, carrots, and celery; cook for 15 minutes; add butterbeans and cook about two hours, simmering slowly. Mixture should be very thick; to prevent sticking, add a small amount of water from time to time. Add okra, cabbage, tomatoes, garlic, and a red pepper pod (or 1-1/2 teaspoons Tabasco sauce) and simmer for another hour. Add corn and cook for thirty minutes. When ready to remove from the stove, remove pepper pod, stir in parsley; serve with corn pones or hush puppies, a green salad, and a fruit pie for dessert.

SPRINGTIME ASPARAGUS SOUP

1 meaty ham hock	2 teaspoons sugar
1 quart fresh cut asparagus	1/2 stick soft butter/margarine
1 cup green onions with tops	1/4 cup flour
2 Tablespoons fresh parsley,	1/2 gallon whole milk
chopped	salt and pepper to taste

Cover ham hock with water and boil until meat falls from bone (pressure cooking speeds this process). Tear meat into small pieces and return to stock. Add cut asparagus, onions, parsley, and cook until tender. Season with salt, pepper, and sugar. Heat milk in separate pot. Mix flour and butter together until it forms a smooth ball; drop into vegetables and stir until soup begins to thicken. Gradually stir in hot milk. Serve soup hot with lemon slices in each bowl. Be sure to pass Ritz crackers.

CIOPPINO

Cioppino is one of California's gifts to cooks. It is said to be the invention of the Italian fishermen in San Francisco. Supposedly, they put the leftovers of the day's catch in a big pot, stewed it with tomatoes, oil, garlic, and seasonings and came up with what we call CIOPPINO. Others claim the first savory pot was concocted by an Italian, Guiseppe Buzzaro, who owned a restaurant on a boat anchored off the famed Fisherman's Wharf. Cioppino is a free style dish with the main ingredients being whatever you like best of available seafood.

2 large onions	1 (15-ounce) can tomato sauce
2 bunches scallions, chopped	1 (28-ounce) can Italian pear
2 green peppers, seeded and	tomatoes
chopped	1 bay leaf
2 cloves garlic, minced	1 teaspoon oregano
2 Tablespoons olive oil	1 Tablespoon chopped fresh
4 Tablespoons butter	basil or 1 teaspoon dried
1/2 pound fresh, medium	3 dashes Tabasco
mushrooms sliced	juice of one lemon
1 cup dry white wine	salt and pepper to taste
1 cup water	

(Continued)

2 dozen fresh clams, scrubbed well, or one can clams
2 pounds red snapper or any firm-flesh fish, cut in chunks
2 dozen large shrimp, shelled and deveined
1/2 pound raw scallops (optional)
2 Dungeness crabs, cooked, cleaned and picked or one small can crab meat or 1 lobster

In a large kettle, saute onions, scallions, green peppers and garlic in oil and butter for 5 minutes or until tender, stirring often. Add mushrooms and saute 4 to 5 minutes more. Add wine, water, tomato sauce, tomatoes, herbs, and Tabasco. Cover and simmer 1 hour or more.

If the sauce has been made ahead of time, reheat 15 minutes before serving time. Add the lemon juice and salt and pepper to taste.

To the heated sauce, add the clams and simmer 3 minutes. Add snapper, shrimp and scallops and simmer 3 more minutes or until clams open and shrimp is pink. Do not over cook. Add crab or lobster at very last, just to heat thoroughly. (You may add cooked live lobster in CIOPPINO, but add it 5 minutes before the clams. Also, instead of live lobster, you may use 2 frozen lobster tails but cut them in half lengthwise and add them at the same time as the snapper.) As soon as the crab is heated thoroughly, remove the bay leaf, check the seasonings, and serve in large warmed bowls with chunks of sourdough bread, a green salad and a bottle of hearty red wine.

NOTE: The sauce may be made a day or two in advance.

CORN CHOWDER

The Indian word for corn meant "our life." Corn was so much a part of pre-colonial Indian tribes that it was intricately intertwined with religion. Mayans believed that Hunab-Ky, the supreme god who created the world, made the first men out of corn. The Aztecs believed that Quetzalcoatl, the god of life and fertility, brought the gift of corn to man. Florida's Seminole Indian tribe worshiped Mother Corn, and Green Corn Dance - a six day ceremony that culminates in the first harvesting of the new crop. It is still an important ritual. Corn chowder is a Pennsylvania Dutch specialty and normally served hot.

2 medium potatoes, diced
1/2 cup chopped scallions or 1 medium onion, diced
1 small green pepper, diced
2 cups water
6 ears fresh corn or substitute 1 (10-ounce) frozen corn nibblets, defrosted and 1 (10-ounce) frozen creamed corn, defrosted
1 pint heavy cream
2 cups milk
2 chicken-flavored bouillon cubes
1 teaspoon white pepper
salt to taste
4 Tablespoons flour
6 to 8 slices lean bacon

(Continued)

In a Dutch oven, fry bacon over medium heat until crisp. Remove bacon strips; reserve 2 tablespoons drippings. Add potatoes, onions and green peppers to the reserved drippings and stir over medium heat for 5 minutes or until onion is transparent and potatoes are lightly browned. Blend in flour and salt and pepper. Add water and bouillon cubes; over medium heat, cook, stirring constantly, until mixture is smooth and thickened, about 5 minutes.

Cut corn from cobs and scrape cobs to remove all the corn milk. Add to the pot along with milk and half and half. Cook, stirring frequently, until corn is tender and mixture is heated through, smooth and slightly thickened, about 5 minutes. Do not allow to boil (or over cook)! Adjust seasonings. Serve in bowls with bacon and chopped green onions or minced fresh parsley.

OYSTER SOUP
One of the best!

1/2 cup butter
1 cup minced celery (rib and leaves)
1/2 cup minced green onions
1/2 cup flour
1 clove garlic, minced
2 dozen shucked oysters or 1
   quart stew size with liquid

2 cups half and half
2 cups water
1 small bay leaf (optional)
1 teaspoon salt
1/2 teaspoon white pepper
dash of Worcestershire sauce

Melt butter in a 4-quart saucepan. Add celery and green onions and saute until tender. Stir in flour and cook until smooth and a pale golden color, about 5 minutes. Drain oysters, reserving liquid. Add enough water to liquid to make 4 cups. Gradually stir into flour mixture. Add garlic, oysters, bay leaf, salt, white pepper and half and half. Bring to simmering point and simmer for about 20 minutes, or until oysters are ruffled on the edges. Remove bay leaf and add the seasonings. Serve hot with a dash of paprika on top. Makes about 6 to 8 servings.

CRAB BISQUE

1 cup onion, chopped fine
1 medium carrot, chopped fine
1/2 cup celery, chopped fine
1/2 cup fresh mushrooms,
   chopped fine
3/4 cup butter (1-1/2 sticks)
1 Tablespoon flour
1 teaspoon fresh parsley
1 teaspoon seafood seasoning
1/4 teaspoon celery salt
1/2 teaspoon ground white pepper

1 teaspoon salt
1 quart (4 cups) milk, heated
3 drops Tabasco
1 teaspoon Worcestershire sauce
1 Tablespoon freshly squeezed
   lemon juice
2 cups half and half
1 pound lump crab meat
3 Tablespoons dry sherry
paprika as garnish

(Continued)

Melt butter in a heavy saucepan over medium-high heat. Add vegetables and saute until soft. Reduce heat to medium and add flour. Cook over low heat until mixture is smooth and bubbly, stirring constantly. Remove from heat and stir in 1 cup of milk. Return to heat and bring to a boil, stirring constantly for 1 minute. Stir in parsley and seasonings and 1 cup of milk. Gradually add lemon juice, stirring constantly to prevent curdling. Stir in half and half and remaining 2 cups milk. Add crab meat and sherry. Simmer 15 to 20 minutes; don't boil. Serve hot. Garnish with lemon slices and paprika. Makes 6 to 8 servings. If bisque is thicker than desired, stir in a little more half and half.

SPLIT PEA AND LENTIL SOUP

2-1/2 pounds smoked picnic ham, trimmed
5 cups water
1 cup split peas
1 cup lentils
4 cups chicken broth
1 onion, chopped
1 medium carrot, chopped
1 medium celery stalk, chopped
1 large garlic clove, minced
1 small bay leaf
1/2 teaspoon sugar
1/8 teaspoon dried thyme, crushed
1 (28-ounce) can tomatoes, chopped
salt and pepper to taste

Combine ham, water, peas and lentils in stockpot. Bring to boil over high heat; reduce to low heat; cover; simmer 1 hour, stirring occasionally. Add chicken broth, onion, carrot, celery, tomatoes, garlic, bay leaf, sugar and thyme; simmer uncovered over low heat for 1 hour, stirring occasionally. Cool soup slightly. Remove ham from bone; cut in 1/2" cubes; discard bay leaf and remove vegetables with slotted spoon. Push vegetables through coarse sieve to mash; return to soup with ham. Simmer over low heat until thick, about 30 minutes. Season.

MANHATTAN CLAM CHOWDER

36 large clams or 2 (7 or 8-ounce) cans minced clams
1/4 cup (1/2 stick) butter
1 large onion, diced
1-1/2 cups diced potatoes
1 cup diced celery
3/4 cup diced carrots
1/4 cup diced green pepper
1 (35-ounce) can Italian style plum tomatoes
1-1/2 teaspoons leaf thyme, crumbled
1/4 teaspoon white pepper
1/8 teaspoon curry powder

Shuck fresh clams (or use canned clams), reserving broth. Chop clams coarsely. Measure broth and add water or bottled clam broth if needed to bring measure to two cups. Melt butter in a large saucepan, then saute onions until lightly browned. Add remaining ingredients and extra water to cover vegetables (if needed). Bring to a boil, then lower heat. Cover and simmer 30 minutes or just until vegetables are tender. Add fresh or canned clams and turn heat off; cover and let stand 2 minutes or until clams are thoroughly hot. Serve with warm buttered French bread or corn sticks or crackers.

GEORGIA GUMBO

1/2 pound bacon
1/2 cup chopped scallions and tops
2 large onions, chopped
1 large clove garlic, minced
1 bell pepper, minced
4 to 5 Tablespoons plain flour
2 bay leaves
2 Tablespoons fresh parsley
5 cups water
2 teaspoons salt
1 teaspoon dried thyme

1/4 teaspoon coarse ground black pepper
2 (16-ounce) cans tomatoes and liquid
2 packages frozen okra
2 cups diced ham
1 teaspoon creole seasoning (opt)
3 or 4 drops Tabasco
2 pounds cooked shelled shrimp
1 pound fresh/frozen crab meat
1 teaspoon gumbo file powder (optional)

In a large Dutch oven, saute bacon until crisp; remove bacon, crumble and reserve. In bacon drippings, saute onions, scallions, garlic and bell pepper. Add flour. Brown to make "roux." Gradually add water, salt, thyme, pepper, tomatoes, bay leaves and parsley. Cover pot and simmer slowly for 2 hours. Add okra, diced ham, creole seasoning and Tabasco and simmer 15 minutes. Add shrimp and crab meat and simmer uncovered 10 minutes. Just before serving, add 1 tablespoon file powder. Spoon hot fluffy rice in serving bowls. Ladle gumbo over rice. Sprinkle with bacon bits and serve.

CHICKEN GUMBO

Gumbo is an African word for the okra that was brought to America by slaves. File powder, added before serving, is used as a thickener and seasoning in many Creole recipes. File powder is made by finely grinding dried sassafras leaves.

3 to 4-pounds broiler-fryer chicken, cut up
1 cup chopped celery tops
1 medium onion, sliced
1 clove garlic, crushed (optional)
1 bay leaf, crumbled
2 teaspoons salt
2 cups chicken broth or water
2 Tablespoons margarine or butter
2/3 cup chopped onion

1/2 cup chopped green pepper
1 can (28-ounce) tomatoes
1/4 cup snipped parsley
1/2 teaspoon red pepper sauce
1-1/2 cups fresh or frozen okra, chopped
2/3 cup uncooked long-grain rice
dash pepper
1-1/2 teaspoons file powder
2 Tablespoons sugar
salt and pepper to taste

Remove any excess fat from chicken. Heat chicken, giblets, neck, celery tops, sliced onions, garlic, bay leaf, salt and water to boiling; reduce heat. Cover and simmer until thickest pieces of chicken are done, about 45 minutes. Strain broth. Refrigerate chicken and broth separately.

Remove chicken from bones; cut into pieces. Skim fat from broth. Place broth and chicken in a sauce pan.

(Continued)

Cook and stir margarine, chopped onion and green pepper until onion is tender but not brown. Stir green pepper mixture, tomatoes (with liquid), parsley and pepper sauce into chicken and broth. Heat to boiling; reduce heat. Simmer uncovered 15 minutes. Stir in okra, rice and pepper; simmer 20 minutes. Stir frequently until rice floats to top and is done. Remove from heat; stir in file powder. (To prepare soup ahead; stir in file powder after reheating.)

SHRIMP GAZPACHO

2 (28-ounce) cans whole
 tomatoes, chopped
1 (8-ounce) can tomato sauce
2 cloves garlic, minced
1 medium red onion, finely
 chopped
1 green pepper, finely chopped
1 (4-ounce) can chopped green
 chilies
2 Tablespoons Worcestershire
 sauce
1 teaspoon seasoned salt
1 teaspoons oregano
1 Tablespoon unflavored gelatin
1 beef bouillon cube
1/2 cup boiling water
3/4 pound small shrimp, cooked,
 shelled, deveined
1/2 cup sliced green olives with
 pimiento
1 cucumber, peeled, seeded, diced
croutons

Mix tomatoes, tomato sauce, garlic, onion, green chilies, Worcestershire, seasoned salt and oregano together and bring to a boil. Simmer for 10 minutes, then chill overnight. About 1 hour before serving, dissolve gelatin and bouillon cube in boiling water; stir into chilled mixture. Add shrimp, green olives and cucumber. Refrigerate until serving time. Garnish with croutons.

MINESTRONE SOUP

1/2 pound bacon
1 cup dried beans (navy or red
 kidney), rinsed and drained
2 cans (10-3/4-ounce) chicken
 broth (condensed)
salt to taste
4 cups water
1 small head of cabbage (1-1/2
 pounds), shredded
1 cup sliced carrots
2 medium Irish potatoes (3/4
 pound), diced
1 cup coarsely chopped onions
1 cup coarsely chopped celery
1 cup broken-up vermicelli
1-1/2 cups sliced zucchini
1/2 pound sliced mushrooms
1/4 cup olive oil
1 pound can Italian tomatoes
1 large fresh tomato
1 clove garlic
1/4 teaspoon black pepper
1/4 cup chopped parsley
1/4 cup Parmesan cheese

Fry bacon in large Dutch oven; drain on paper towel. Pour off all except 2 tablespoons of drippings; add 3 tablespoons flour to drippings and stir until smooth. Cook mixture to light brown color, then add beans, broth, water and seasonings. Slowly bring to a boil and boil for 5 minutes. Remove from heat and let stand covered for 45 minutes (beans may be covered with cold water and allowed to sit overnight).

(Continued)

Return to heat and bring to boiling point, stirring occasionally. Reduce heat and simmer uncovered for 1 hour or until tender. Wash and slice cabbage in thin slivers. Cut carrots on diagonal 1/4" thick. Slice potatoes 1/2" thick, then cut into 1/2" cubes. Add cabbage, potatoes and carrots to soup along with canned tomatoes. Peel onions; slice thinly. Saute onion, stirring, in 1/4 cup hot oil about 5 minutes. Set aside. Slice celery 1/8" thick. Wash zucchini and slice into rounds 1/4" thick. Peel tomato and slice 1/2" thick; cut in cubes. Press or mince garlic. Add vegetables to onion with salt and pepper; cook slowly, uncovered, for about 20 minutes, stirring occasionally. Add to bean mixture with parsley and vermicelli. Cook slowly, uncovered, additional 30 minutes, stirring. Serve hot, topped with Pesto sauce if desired. Cheese bread is excellent served with the soup.

Pesto Sauce:

1/4 cup butter, softened
1/4 cup grated Parmesan cheese
1/2 cup finely chopped parsley
1 clove garlic, crushed
1 teaspoon dried basil leaves

1/2 teaspoon dried marjoram
  leaves
1/4 cup olive oil or salad oil
1/4 cup finely chopped walnuts

Blend butter with Parmesan cheese, parsley, crushed garlic and herbs; gradually add oil, beating constantly, then add nuts.

DO NOT OMIT pesto sauce as it contains ALL the good seasonings!!!!

CHILI BEAN SOUP

4 Tablespoons salad oil, divided
4 cups chopped onions
2 large bell peppers, diced
1 cup chopped celery
2 medium potatoes, diced
1 medium carrot, diced
2 pounds lean ground beef
4 garlic cloves, chopped
6 Tablespoons chili powder
1 Tablespoon ground cumin
1 (32-ounce) can tomatoes,
  chopped
13 to 14 ounces beef broth
2 teaspoons oregano
2 teaspoons hot paprika

1 teaspoon sugar
1 teaspoon salt
1 Tablespoon lemon juice or
  cider vinegar
1 (12-ounce) can tomato paste
1 teaspoon black pepper
1 (16-ounce) can kidney beans,
  drained
1 (16-ounce) can green beans,
  drained
Garnishes:
avocados
shredded Cheddar cheese
green onions, chopped
sour cream

(Continued)

In Dutch oven, heat 3 tablespoons oil. Add onions, celery, bell peppers and saute until golden brown. Remove with slotted spoon and set aside. In same pot, heat remaining tablespoon of oil; add meat and brown. Pour off fat; add garlic, chili powder and cumin; cook, stirring frequently, for 2 minutes. Add tomatoes, tomato paste, potatoes, beef broth, seasonings and sauteed vegetables. Bring to a boil. Reduce heat and simmer, covered, for 3 hours, stirring occasionally. Add beans and cook 10 to 15 minutes more. Skim off fat and season to taste. Serve with garnishes. Corn sticks or French bread are excellent with this soup.

NOTE: 1 cup vermicelli may be added if desired. Also 1/8 teaspoon cinnamon.

NEW ENGLAND CLAM CHOWDER

The custom of making a hearty fish soup from the catch of the day was brought to New England by French Canadian settlers, who called it "La Chaudier"; an Americanized version was with clams dug on the beach, salt pork and cream sauce. The tomato-based version, once considered absolute heresy by New Englanders, came into existence as chowder making moved southward along the east coast. Tomatoes replaced the milk of the New England chowder, and diced green pepper and carrots were added for color and texture.

12 large hardshell clams or 1 (13-ounce) can minced clams	3 medium potatoes, peeled and diced
1/4 pound salt pork	1/8 teaspoon thyme leaves, crushed
1 medium onion, diced	
1 Tablespoon all-purpose flour	4 cups half and half
1/2 teaspoon salt	1 Tablespoon butter/margarine
1/4 teaspoon pepper	hot paprika

If using fresh clams: Scrub clams with stiff brush under cold running water until free of sand. Using a 4-quart saucepan, bring 1 cup of water to boiling. Add clams and allow to return to boiling point; reduce to low heat, cover, and simmer just until clams open (about 5 minutes). Remove clams from shells and allow to cool; reserve broth and discard shells. Allow broth to stand until any sand it may contain settles, then CAREFULLY pour clear broth into measuring cup. If using fresh clams: Drain clams, reserving liquid.

Measure liquid and add enough water or bottled clam broth to make 2 cups. Cook salt pork or bacon in saucepan until lightly browned (you may use the same pan you cooked the fresh clams in). Meanwhile, chop clams coarsely. Add onion and cook until tender, stirring occasionally. Stir in flour, salt and pepper until blended; cook 1 minute. Gradually stir in clam liquid until smooth, then add potatoes and heat to boiling. Reduce to low heat, cover and simmer 15 minutes or until potatoes are tender. Stir in the half and half and the clams, heat thoroughly, and serve. Sprinkle top of soup with hot paprika.

VIRGINIA PEANUT SOUP

Peanuts were known in South America over 2000 years ago and are believed to be native to Brazil. The ancient pre-Incan tribes buried their dead with peanuts to give them strength on their long voyage through eternity. These tribes also depicted the peanut on their pottery. The Spanish later took peanuts to Europe, and thence they spread to Asia and Africa. Early Virginians fed them to their hogs, producing particularly delicious pork products. Although Thomas Jefferson recorded peanut crops in his plantation ledger in the eighteenth century, peanut cultivation was not widespread until the next century. Peanut soup, a specialty of Southern cooks, is presented here in a modern interpretation.

3 Tablespoons finely chopped
   onion
1/2 cup finely chopped celery
2 Tablespoons butter
3 Tablespoons flour
4 cups chicken stock

1-1/3 cups creamy peanut butter
2 cups half and half
1 Tablespoon lemon juice
1/2 cup chopped salted peanuts
watercress or parsley sprigs
   (optional)

Saute onion and celery in butter in a heavy saucepan until tender but not brown. Stir in flour and cook until bubbly. Add chicken stock, stirring constantly, until thickened. Add peanut butter and lemon juice; stir until smooth. Stir in half and half and heat through. Serve hot or chill thoroughly and set in crushed ice. Garnish with watercress or parsley and chopped, salted peanuts. For a thinner, smoother soup, mix briefly in a blender before serving.

CREAM OF SQUASH SOUP

1/4 cup butter/margarine, melted
2 Tablespoons vegetable oil
1 large onion, minced
2 cloves garlic, minced
3 pounds yellow squash, thinly
   sliced
3-1/2 to 4 cups chicken broth
1 cup half and half

1-1/2 teaspoons salt
1/2 teaspoon white pepper
chopped fresh parsley
Garnish:
dollop of sour cream
strip of pimiento
parsley

Combine butter and oil in a large Dutch oven. Add onion and garlic; saute until tender. Stir in squash and chicken broth; cover and simmer 15 to 20 minutes or until squash is tender. Spoon 1/3 of squash mixture into container of electric blender and process until smooth. (Be very careful of heat!) Repeat with remaining squash mixture. Return squash mixture to Dutch oven; stir in half and half, salt and pepper. Cook over low heat, stirring constantly, until well heated. Serve hot or chilled. Garnish with parsley or other items listed. Yields 10 cups.

SHRIMP-TOMATO BISQUE

1-1/2 to 2 pounds medium shrimp
water
salt
4 Tablespoons butter or margarine
1 small onion, diced
2 ribs celery, finely diced
2 Tablespoons all-purpose flour
2 teaspoons hot paprika

1 teaspoon salt
1 can (8-ounce) tomatoes
2 cups half and half
2 Tablespoons sherry (optional)
1 Tablespoon Worcestershire sauce
1/4 teaspoon white pepper
2 limes or lemons, cut into 5
   wedges each for garnish

Shell and devein shrimp, leaving tail part on 10 shrimp for garnish later. In a 3-quart saucepan, over high heat, heat 2 cups water and 1-1/2 teaspoons salt to boiling; add shrimp; heat to boiling. Reduce heat to medium-low; cook 1 minute or until shrimp are tender and pink. With a slotted spoon, remove shrimp to plate. Strain shrimp broth into medium bowl to remove skim, and reserve. Wipe saucepan dry.

In same saucepan over medium heat, melt butter or margarine; add onion and celery and cook until tender, stirring occasionally. Stir in flour, paprika, and 1 teaspoon salt until blended. Cook 1 minute. Gradually stir in shrimp broth; cook, stirring constantly, until thickened and smooth. Remove.

Set aside shrimp with tails left on. Chop remaining shrimp finely and add to the shrimp broth mixture. In blender or food processor with knife blade attached, blend tomatoes and juice. Add to shrimp mixture. Return all to same pan; stir in half and half, sherry, Worcestershire sauce and pepper. Over medium heat, heat until hot, stirring occasionally.

To serve, pour into bowls and garnish with a reserved shrimp and a wedge of lime or lemon, if desired. Makes about 6 cups or 10 first-course servings.

STEP LADDER SOUP

1 large meaty hambone or bag of
   beef bone plus small chuck
   roast
3 to 4 large onions, chopped
1 bunch celery, chopped
1 quart butter beans
1 quart snap beans
6 to 8 ears of corn, cut from cob or
   approximately 1 quart
1 dozen carrots, sliced
1 gallon tomatoes, peeled and
   quartered

1/2 small head of cabbage,
   shredded
2 quarts okra, sliced
3 to 4 bay leaves
4 Tablespoons parsley
2 teaspoons basil
1/2 cup sugar
salt and pepper to taste
1 dozen potatoes, peeled and
   cubed
1 extra large stockpot
1 step ladder

Put meat and bones in stockpot with enough water to cover well. Boil with lid on pot until meat falls off bone. Remove meat and bones, tear meat into small pieces, and return meat to stockpot. Add fresh vegetables (except tomatoes and potatoes) and cook until tender.

(Continued)

Add tomatoes, potatoes, and seasonings, and simmer in open pot for at least 1 hour. Add water if soup becomes too thick. OOPS, don't add the step ladder! You just climb up every now and then to stir and taste the simmering soup. Be sure to make a large pone of crackling bread to go with this soup.
NOTE: This is especially good in the summertime when vegetables are fresh.

GALVESTON GUMBO

2 pounds raw shrimp (fresh or
   frozen)
2 (10-ounce) cans fresh oysters
1 can crabmeat
1 can minced clams
6 lobster tails
1-1/2 cups chopped onions
1-1/2 cups chopped celery
1 cup chopped green pepper
1 (10-ounce) package frozen
   sliced okra
1 clove garlic, minced

1/3 cup cooking oil
1/3 cup flour
1 can (28-ounce) tomatoes,
   undrained
1 can (13-ounce) chicken broth
1 Tablespoon Worcestershire
   sauce
2 dashes Tabasco
2-1/2 teaspoons salt
1/4 teaspoon black pepper
1 bay leaf
6 to 8 servings hot cooked rice

Peel shrimp, thaw oysters (if frozen). In a large Dutch oven, saute onion, celery, green pepper and garlic until tender. Blend in flour; add tomatoes, chicken broth, Worcestershire sauce, salt, pepper and bay leaf. Mix and heat. Add Tabasco; cover, simmer 30 minutes, stirring occasionally. Uncover; add shrimp, oysters, clams, lobster tails and okra. Simmer 15 to 20 minutes or until tender and mixture is of consistency desired. Serve over hot rice. Serves 6 to 8.

BRUNSWICK STEW

4-1/2 or 5-1/2 pound chicken
2/3 cups okra (cut in 1/2" rounds)
1 cup canned tomatoes
1 cup frozen butter beans
1 cup corn
1 cup raw Irish potatoes, diced in
   1/2" pieces
1 onion, finely chopped
3 Tablespoons butter

1 Tablespoon flour
1 Tablespoon sugar
dash of pepper
dash of thyme
1 teaspoon curry powder
   (optional)
1-1/2 teaspoons Worcestershire
   sauce
1/2 teaspoon salt

Simmer whole chicken (covered) in 2-1/2 quarts water with 1 tablespoon salt. Cook chicken slowly for about 1-1/2 hours. Remove chicken from broth; allow to cool. To the chicken broth (should be about 1-3/4 to 2 quarts), add okra, tomatoes, corn, lima beans, potatoes, and salt. Cook for 15 minutes. Saute onions in butter; stir in flour; mix some hot broth to make a thickened sauce. Stir sauce into broth mixture. Remove chicken from bones; cut in 1" pieces; add to broth mixture. Add sugar, pepper, curry powder, thyme, and Worcestershire sauce. Simmer for 10 minutes, then serve hot. Makes a meal when served with cornbread and a tossed salad. The American Indians introduced succotash to the colonists, who in turn added meat and named the dish after a county in Virginia.

First Presbyterian Church · Augusta, Georgia   ©1991 Ray Baird

FIRST PRESBYTERIAN CHURCH

The cornerstone of the First Presbyterian Church was laid in 1809. Five years earlier, the Reverend Washington McKnight had formed a Presbyterian congregation which assembled for worship at the then non-denominational St. Paul's Church. In 1808, the Trustees of Richmond Academy granted a lot on Telfair Street, and plans for the church were designed by Robert Mills, who also was the architect of both the South Carolina State Capitol in Columbia and the Washington Monument in the District of Columbia. First Presbyterian was dedicated in 1812 with the spire added six years later.

The Reverend Joseph R. Wilson, father of Woodrow Wilson, served as pastor from 1858 to 1870. During his tenure, the General Assembly of the Presbyterian Church in the United States was organized here in 1861. The church was one of several downtown buildings and churches used as medical facilities during the Civil War. Reverend Wilson, a staunch Confederate, was active enlisting the aid of the female members of his congregation in nursing, rolling bandages, sewing, and even making bullets.

First Presbyterian Church was renovated in 1892. The Sunday School building, which was constructed in 1881, was enlarged in 1951; then in the 1970's, an even larger, modern Sunday School was completed with the architectural design in keeping with that of the church.

Salads and
Salad Dressings

Salad

Apple Salad, 75
Autumn Apple Ring, 75
Waldorf Salad, 76
Fresh Cranberry Salad, 77
Apricot Congealed Salad, 77
Berry-Cherry Ring, 78
Blueberry Salad, 78
Sinful Salad, 79
Bing Cherry Mold, 79
Cranberry Cream Salad Ring, 80
Pickled Peach Salad Mold, 80
Berry Duet Salad, 81
Red, White and Blue Fruit Salad, 81
Sunshine Salad, 82
Rosy Wassail Salad Mold, 82
Grapefruit-Cream Cheese Salad, 83
White Grape and Wine Salad Mold, 83
Mandarin Orange Salad, 84
Georgia Peaches
   and Cream Gelatin Salad, 84
Russian Salad, 84

Meat Salads

Baked Chicken Salad Supreme, 85
Corned Beef Molded Salad, 85
Beef Salad, 85
Chicken Salad Mold, 86
Red, White and Green Ribbon Salad, 86
Tarragon Chicken Salad, 87
Seafood Tomato Aspic Supreme, 87
Spicy Shrimp Salad, 88
Party Shrimp Salad, 88
Cobb Salad, 88
Ocean Bay Salad, 90
Seaside Salmon Salad, 90
Tuna-Potato Stack-up Salad, 91

Vegetable Salads

Asparagus Salad, 91
Molded Gazpacho Salad, 91
Calico Bean Salad, 92
Mediterranean Bean Salad, 92
Caesar Salad, 93
Mean Bean Salad, 93
Marinated Broccoli Salad, 94
Cole Slaw, 94
Italian Slaw, 95
Rainbow Cole Slaw
   with Cooked Dressing, 95
Sour Cream Potato Salad, 96
French Vegetable Salad, 96
German Potato Salad, 96
Leseur Pea Salad, 97
Classic Spinach Salad, 97
Cliff's Spinach Salad, 98
Sweet Potato Salad, 99
Seven Layer Salad, 99
Wilted Lettuce Salad, 99
Zippy Horseradish Ring, 100

Salad Dressings

Bea's Cheese Salad Dressing, 100
Parmesan Cheese Dressing, 100
Deluxe French Dressing, 101
Williamsburg Dressing, 101
Honey Fruit Salad Dressing, 101
Poppy Seed Dressing, 101
Green Goddess Salad Dressing, 102
Red Dog Saloon (Arizona)
   Salad Dressing, 102
Guacamole Dressing, 102
Thousand Island Dressing, 103
Shrimp Vinaigrette Salad Dressing, 103
"Better Than Store-Bought" Croutons, 104
Spicy Salad Seasoning Mix, 104

APPLE SALAD

Dressing:
1/3 cup flour
3/4 cup sugar
1 cup heavy whipping cream

1 large can crushed pineapple
(drained)
1/2 stick butter or margarine

Sift flour and sugar together. Stir into the unwhipped cream; add pineapple. Cook in double boiler or heavy aluminum boiler. Remove from heat, add butter and cool.

Salad:
4 large tasty apples
1 cup chopped nuts

1/2 cup sliced maraschino cherries

Peel and dice apples, add nuts and cooled dressing. Add cherries and mix or sprinkle the cherries on top. Salad dressing can be made a few days in advance and refrigerated.

AUTUMN APPLE RING

1/3 cup sugar
4 envelopes unflavored gelatin
5 cups white grape juice
3 medium-size ribs celery, finely
   chopped
1 pound seedless red grapes

3 medium Granny Smith apples
   (1 pound)
3/4 cup mayonnaise
1/4 cup whipping cream
   (unwhipped)
1 cup California walnuts,
   coarsely chopped

In a 4-quart saucepan, stir sugar and gelatin. Stir in 2 cups white grape juice. Cook over medium heat, stirring frequently, until gelatin is completely dissolved. Remove saucepan from heat. Stir in remaining grape juice. Refrigerate until mixture mounds when dropped from a spoon, about 45 minutes. Meanwhile, chop celery; cut each grape in half. When gelatin mixture almost comes to mounding consistency, quickly shred apples. (Apples will turn brown if shredded too early.) You may sprinkle apples with Fresh Fruit, if you desire, before adding to gelatin mixture. Fold celery, grapes and apples into thickened gelatin mixture. Pour into a 10" bundt pan or 10-cup mold. Cover and refrigerate until set, about 3 hours. This salad is best made the day before serving.

To serve:

In a small bowl, mix mayonnaise and whipping cream until well blended; fold in chopped walnuts. Unmold salad onto a chilled lettuce-covered serving platter. Serve with walnut dressing. Makes about 12 servings. This may be halved for a smaller family.

WALDORF SALAD

Waldorf Salad was conceived by the maitre d' Oscar Tschirky for the first Public Charity Ball given by Mrs. William K. Vanderbilt for the St. Mary's Free Hospital for Children in 1893. Oscar, also known as "Oscar of the Waldorf," evidently was more of a snob than a cook. He developed his salad in defiance of the heavy, overblown cuisine at that time. As it turned out, it was the only dish he ever created. The Waldorf Salad was a revolutionary combination of foods in 1893, because people didn't eat fruit salads as they do today. It was a light, different touch to a great heavy meal and was thought to have started the fruit salad vogue. Unfortunately, there existed no original recipe. 20 years later, walnuts were added. From supper tables to picnics in the park, the Waldorf Salad has been present ever since. But it has been changed a bit—more substituting and creating in the family kitchens to individual tastes.

Walnut Oil Mayonnaise:
1 egg, room temperature
1 egg yolk, room temperature
1/4 teaspoon Dijon mustard
1/8 teaspoon curry powder
3/4 teaspoon salt
1 Tablespoon fresh lemon juice
1/4 cup walnut oil (if walnut oil
  not available, use a cup of
  safflower oil)
3/4 cup safflower oil
1/4 cup heavy cream, whipped to
  soft peaks
dash of red pepper

Salad:
1-1/2 cups coarsely chopped walnuts
2 medium red Delicious apples,
  unpeeled, cored, and cut into
  1/2" diced pieces
2 medium Granny Smith apples,
  unpeeled, cored, and cut into
  1/2" diced pieces
1 Tablespoon fresh lemon juice
1 Tablespoon orange juice
4 medium ribs of celery, cut into
  1/2" pieces
3 Tablespoons raisins, cut into
  Bibb or Boston lettuce
3 teaspoons lemon zest for garnish
red grapes, for garnish

In a blender, blend egg, egg yolk, mustard, curry powder, salt, dash of red pepper and 1 Tablespoon lemon juice for about 10 seconds. Add oils in a steady stream with blender running, about 60 seconds. Or, whisk until smooth all ingredients but oils and creams. Add oils in a very slow steady stream, continuing to whisk, until all oils are incorporated and mayonnaise is smooth. Fold whipped cream into mayonnaise and reserve. You may store mayonnaise, covered and refrigerated, for up to 3 days.

Spread walnuts on a baking sheet in a single layer and toast in a preheated oven (350 degrees) until lightly brown, about 8 minutes. This may also be done the day before. In a large bowl, toss diced apples with lemon juice and orange juice. Add chopped raisins, celery and walnuts. Toss mayonnaise with salad to combine thoroughly.

Form lettuce cups on 6 to 8 individual salad plates. Spoon salad onto the lettuce cups, sprinkle with zest and garnish with grapes.

(Continued)

Dressing #2:
1 egg
2 Tablespoons lemon juice, fresh
1 Tablespoon honey
1 Tablespoon grated fresh ginger
2 teaspoons grated lemon peel
1/2 teaspoon salt
1 cup vegetable oil
milk as needed

In a blender, combine egg, lemon juice, honey, ginger peel, salt and 1/4 cup of oil. Blend 5 seconds. With motor on high, add remaining oil in a slow stream, turning motor off and scraping sides as needed. Thin to a pourable consistency with about 2 Tablespoons of milk.

Toss Waldorf salad with dressing to combine thoroughly. Just before serving, sprinkle with a few extra toasted chopped walnuts.

FRESH CRANBERRY SALAD

1 (3-ounce) package cherry or red
   raspberry jello
1 envelope unflavored gelatin
1 cup hot water
1 cup sugar
1 Tablespoon lemon juice
1 (8-ounce) can crushed
   pineapple with juice
2 cups fresh cranberries, ground
1 orange, seeded and ground
1/2 cup minced celery
1-1/2 cups chopped pecans

Grind or process cranberries and orange. Mix with sugar and let stand at room temperature for about 2 hours. Soften gelatin in 1/4 cup cold water. Dissolve jello in hot water, add to softened gelatin, stirring to dissolve. Combine cranberry mixture, gelatin, jello, pineapple, pecans and celery. Pour into a 6-cup mold that has been slightly oiled with salad oil. Refrigerate for several hours or overnight. Unmold on a bed of lettuce. Garnish with slices of orange and mayonnaise.

NOTE: To unmold, loosen edge of mold with a small spatula, shake. Dip mold in warm water for 5 seconds. Invert serving plate over mold; invert mold and plate; remove mold. Garnish plate with lettuce and slices of orange.

APRICOT CONGEALED SALAD

1 package apricot jello
17 ounces whole canned apricots
1 package cream cheese
juice of 1 lemon
juice of 1 orange
3/4 cup chopped pecans
3 to 4 Tablespoons coffee cream

Use 1 cup hot apricot juice instead of water for dissolving jello. Add cold orange juice, lemon juice and 1 cup cold apricot juice (if juices are insufficient, add water to make correct amount of liquid). Mix cream cheese with cream to soften; add chopped nuts and form into small balls. Remove pits from apricots; place cream cheese balls into apricots to replace pits and press together. When jello mixture has thickened; add stuffed apricots. Chill and serve.

BERRY-CHERRY RING

Perfect for either Thanksgiving or Christmas dinner

2 (3-ounce) packages jello (cherry, blackberry or black cherry)
2 cups of boiling water
2 (16-ounce) cans dark pitted cherries, drained, reserve juice
1 (16-ounce) can orange-cranberry relish

1 (16-ounce) can whole cranberries, drained
1 (8-ounce) can chunk pineapple, drained
1 cup chopped walnuts or pecans
mint leaves or watercress to garnish
fresh cranberries or fresh black cherries to garnish

Dissolve jello in boiling water; add reserved juice from cherries for the other two cups of liquid. Pour into a medium sized bowl and chill until soft set. Add cherries, orange-cranberry relish, whole cranberries, pineapple and walnuts. Mix gently, pour into a 10-ounce ring mold. Chill until firm. Unmold onto a chilled platter and garnish as desired.

Dressing:

1/2 cup sour cream
1 cup mayonnaise

2 Tablespoons powdered sugar

Mix sour cream, mayonnaise and powdered sugar thoroughly. Serve in the middle of a ring mold or in a side dish if a ring mold is not used.

BLUEBERRY SALAD

2 (3-ounce) packages black raspberry jello
1 (15-ounce) can blueberries or 1-1/2 cups fresh blueberries
8-1/4 ounces canned crushed pineapple
2 cups boiling water

1/2 pint sour cream
8 ounces cream cheese, softened
1/2 cup sugar
1/2 teaspoon vanilla
chopped pecans (optional)

Dissolve gelatin in 2 cups boiling water. Drain blueberries and pineapple; measure liquid and add water to make a cup of liquid. Stir liquid into gelatin mixture. Add drained blueberries and pineapple. Turn into a 2-quart flat pan, cover, and refrigerate until firm. Cream sour cream, cream cheese, sugar and vanilla together. Spread over salad and sprinkle with chopped pecans.

SINFUL SALAD

2 (3-ounce) packages strawberry
jello
1 cup boiling water
2 (10-ounce) packages frozen
strawberries, thawed (do not
drain)
1 medium can crushed
pineapple, drained

3 medium bananas, mashed
(approximately 1 cup)
1 cup chopped walnuts or pecans
1 cup finely chopped celery
(optional)
1 pint (2 cups) sour cream

Combine gelatin and boiling water in a medium-size bowl. Stir until gelatin is completely dissolved. Cool. Add strawberries with juice, bananas, nuts and pineapple to gelatin and stir to combine; divide in half. Pour half of the mixture into a mold or bowl (a bundt pan works beautifully) which has been oiled. Refrigerate until set (about 1 hour). Keep remaining gelatin at room temperature. Place sour cream in center, being careful to leave a ridge on inside and outside edge of partially set gelatin in pan. Pour on remaining gelatin. Cover and refrigerate until set (about 1-1/2 hours). This salad makes a delightful dessert or may be served with your holiday turkey.

BING CHERRY MOLD

2 packages black cherry jello
2 cups cherry juice
1-1/2 cups orange juice
1 (#2-1/2) can black cherries
1/2 cup dry sherry wine

1 small package cream cheese
3 Tablespoons mayonnaise
3 Tablespoons heavy cream
1 cup pecans
1 envelope plain gelatin

Soften gelatin in 1/4 cup cherry juice. Dissolve jello in cherry juice that has been brought to a boil, then add softened gelatin. Add orange juice and wine. Place in refrigerator until slightly thickened. Blend cream cheese, mayonnaise and cream. Line bottom of lightly oiled 2-quart ring mold with cheese mixture. Add cooled gelatin mixture. Stuff each cherry with pecans, add to mixture when it begins to thicken. Serves 8.

Dressing:
3 ounces cream cheese, softened
1 cup heavy cream, whipped
1/2 cup mayonnaise

1 cup minced pecans
1/2 cup minced celery

Mash cream cheese; combine with whipped cream. Add remaining ingredients and mix well.

CRANBERRY CREAM SALAD RING

Cranberry Layer:

2 envelopes unflavored gelatin
3/4 cup sugar, divided
1-1/2 cups boiling water

1-1/2 cups cranberry juice cocktail
2 teaspoons grated orange peel
2 cups chopped cranberries

In a medium bowl combine gelatin with 1/4 cup sugar. Add boiling water and stir until gelatin is completely dissolved. Add remaining sugar; stir to dissolve. Add cranberry juice and orange peel. Refrigerate, stirring occasionally, until mixture is the consistency of unbeaten egg whites, about 1 hour. Fold in chopped cranberries. Spoon into a greased 7-cup ring mold. Refrigerate until almost firm.

Cream Layer:

1 envelope unflavored gelatin
1/3 cup sugar
2/3 cup orange juice
1 egg, beaten
1 cup sour cream

1 cup half and half
1/2 cup chopped walnuts or
   pecans
frosted cranberries for garnish

Meanwhile, in a small saucepan combine gelatin with sugar. Add orange juice beaten with egg. Let stand for 1 minute. Stir over low heat until gelatin is completely dissolved, about 5 minutes. Remove from heat. Whisk in sour cream and half and half. Refrigerate, stirring occasionally, until mixture mounds slightly when dropped from a spoon, about 1 hour. Fold in nuts. Spoon gently onto almost-set cranberry layer. Cover and refrigerate overnight. Cover a serving platter with crisp lettuce leaves and unmold onto platter. Garnish with frosted cranberries. Makes 12 servings.

Frosted Cranberries:

Roll 1/2 cup cranberries, a few at a time in 2 beaten egg whites, then in 1/2 cup sugar. Set on a wire rack to dry.

NOTE: If desired, a Tablespoon of port wine may be added with the cranberry juice and orange peel.

PICKLED PEACH SALAD MOLD

1 (29-ounce) jar peach pickles
1 (3-ounce) package lemon jello
1-1/2 cups boiling water

1/2 cup peach pickle juice
1 (3-ounce) package cream cheese
pecans, chopped finely

Dissolve gelatin in hot water and peach juice. Cool. Remove seeds from peaches. Roll cream cheese into tiny balls, then roll in chopped nuts. Stuff whole peaches with cheese balls and place one in each individual mold. Pour gelatin mixture over each and congeal. Good with turkey, chicken, pork or ham.

BERRY DUET SALAD

1/2 cup sugar	2 cups cold water
1-1/2 cups water	1 cup sour cream
1-1/2 cups fresh cranberries	1/2 cup chopped pecans
3 (3-ounce) packages raspberry jello	lettuce leaves for garnish

Combine sugar and water in medium saucepan; to boiling over medium heat. Add cranberries; reduce heat and cook until skins pop, about 7 to 10 minutes. Drain cranberries, reserving liquid; set cranberries aside. Add enough water to cranberry liquid to equal 2 cups. Return to saucepan and heat to boiling. Remove from heat and pour over gelatin in a large bowl. Stir constantly until gelatin mixture is completely dissolved. Stir in cold water. Pour half of gelatin mixture into another bowl; refrigerate both until consistency of unbeaten egg whites. In a small mixer bowl, beat sour cream. Fold into 6-cup mold. Add cranberries and pecans to remaining gelatin. Refrigerate both mixtures (sour cream gelatin and cranberry-pecan gelatin) until thickened but not set (about 30 minutes). Carefully spoon cranberry-nut mixture into sour cream mold, cover, refrigerate until set (about 3 hours). Unmold onto serving platter and garnish with lettuce leaves. Makes 6 to 8 servings. Good enough to be dessert!

RED, WHITE AND BLUE FRUIT SALAD

1 (3-ounce) package of wild strawberry jello	1 cup sugar
1 pint fresh ripe strawberries, washed and sliced (save a few for garnish)	1 envelope unflavored gelatin
	1 cup half and half
	3 Tablespoons lemon juice
water	1 teaspoon vanilla
1 pint blueberries (save a few for garnish)	dash salt
	1 (8-ounce) package cream cheese, softened
1 (3-ounce) package black raspberry jello	1/2 cup black walnuts or pecans, chopped

Red layer:

Slice enough strawberries to make 3/4 cup; reserve remaining strawberries for garnish. In a medium bowl, stir strawberry gelatin with 3/4 cup boiling water until gelatin is completely dissolved. Stir in 3/4 cup of cold water, add sliced strawberries and pour into a 6-cup mold. Refrigerate until set.

White layer:

Meanwhile, in a 2-quart saucepan, mix sugar and unflavored gelatin with 1/2 cup cold water to soften. Combine half and half in a small saucepan. Heat but do not boil. Add gelatin and sugar mixture along with lemon juice, vanilla, salt, cream cheese and walnuts. Blend until cream cheese is smooth. Pour over set strawberry layer. Return to refrigerator to set.

(Continued)

Blue layer:

Make the blue layer by preparing the black raspberry jello as directed on package. Add blueberries, pour over the cream cheese layer and refrigerate to set.

To serve:

Unmold salad onto a serving platter, surround with lettuce leaves. Garnish with mint leaves, whole strawberries and blueberries.

SUNSHINE SALAD

1 (3-ounce) package lemon gelatin
1 (12-ounce) can apricot nectar
1 (6-ounce) can frozen orange juice, thawed

1 (3-ounce) package cream cheese
1/2 cup finely chopped pecans
1 (11-ounce) small can mandarin oranges, drained

Heat apricot nectar to a boiling point. Dissolve lemon gelatin in this. Do not dilute. Add can of orange juice undiluted. Combine cream cheese and pecans. Make small balls and place 3 balls in each mold (6 individual) or in groups of three if using a round ring mold. Add orange segments to gelatin mixture and pour into molds. Refrigerate until jelled. This is good with fowl, pork or ham. It may be also used at holiday time in place of cranberry sauce.

ROSY WASSAIL SALAD MOLD

2 (3-ounce) packages raspberry jello
2 cups boiling water
1/2 of a 20-ounce bag of dry-pack frozen tart red cherries (2 cups)

1 (10-ounce) package frozen red raspberries
1 cup Basic Wassail Mix
1/2 cup chopped nuts (pecans and walnuts)

Basic Wassail Mix:

1 (32-ounce) bottle cranberry juice cocktail
2 cups apple juice
1 cup sugar

6" stick cinnamon
12 whole allspice
1 lemon, sliced thinly
6-1/2 cups (2 fifths) dry red wine

Make Basic Wassail Mix by combining cranberry juice, apple juice and sugar in a large saucepan. Tie spices in cheesecloth and add to juices along with sliced lemon. Bring to a boil, stirring until sugar dissolves. Simmer (covered) for 30 minutes. Remove cheesecloth bag and discard. Stir in wine. To serve as a beverage, heat thoroughly but do not boil. Serve hot in mugs or cups. Refrigerate remaining wassail to use in other recipes. Makes 12-1/2 cups.

For the salad mold, dissolve jello in boiling water, using a large bowl. Stir in cherries and raspberries. Stir in wassail mix and nuts. Chill until partially set, then pour into 6-cup ring mold. Chill until set, 12 hours or overnight. Unmold and garnish with spiced crabapples. Good with turkey and ham.

GRAPEFRUIT-CREAM CHEESE SALAD

4 envelopes unflavored gelatin
1 cup cold water
1 cup boiling water
1 cup sugar
4 cups fresh grapefruit sections
    sprinkled with lemon juice

8 ounces cream cheese
2 Tablespoons cream
1 teaspoon lemon juice
2 Tablespoons mayonnaise
1 cup chopped pecans

Dissolve unflavored gelatin in cold water, then add 1 cup boiling water and 1 cup sugar. When dissolved, add grapefruit sections. Place half the mixture in a 6-quart greased mold in refrigerator. Leave the other half outside the refrigerator. When refrigerated mixture is congealed, cover with finely chopped nuts. Cover nuts with a layer of cream cheese softened with cream, lemon juice and mayonnaise. Add another layer of nuts. Press nuts into cream cheese, then fill mold with other half of grapefruit mixture. Put mold back into refrigerator until set. Serve on lettuce with a small amount of mayonnaise. May be made in a rectangular pan and cut into squares. Good with seafood or chicken.

WHITE GRAPE AND WINE SALAD MOLD

Mold:
3/4 cup sugar
2 envelopes unflavored gelatin
1 cup water
2 cups white wine

3/4 cup sweet sherry
1-1/2 pounds (4 cups) white
    seedless grapes

In a large saucepan, mix sugar and gelatin. Add water and cook over low heat until sugar and gelatin are dissolved, stirring constantly. Stir in white wine and sherry. Place grapes in a 6-cup ring mold; pour in gelatin mixture. Refrigerate until set, about 4 to 5 hours.

Sauce:
3/4 cup half and half
3 egg yolks, slightly beaten
2 Tablespoons sugar

1 teaspoon vanilla extract
2/3 cup heavy cream whipped

Make a sauce by heating half and half in a heavy saucepan until bubbles form at the edge. In a small bowl, heat egg yolks and sugar. Gradually add some hot cream to egg mixture, stirring constantly. Pour warmed egg mixture gradually back into heated cream, stirring constantly to prevent lumping. Cook over low heat, stirring constantly with wooden spoon, until thick (about 15 minutes). Cover surface of custard with wax paper; refrigerate until well chilled. Stir in vanilla and fold in whipped cream. Makes 2 cups.

Quickly dip grape mold into warm water and invert onto platter; remove mold. Serve with custard sauce. Makes 8 to 10 servings.

MANDARIN ORANGE SALAD

1 large package orange jello
2 cups boiling water
1 pint orange sherbet
1 small can mandarin oranges
(drained)

1 (#2) can crushed pineapple
(drained)
1/2 cup nuts

Mix the jello and boiling water in a large bowl. Stir in orange sherbet until melted. Refrigerate until slightly thickened, then add oranges, pineapple and nuts. Pour into a large rectangular cake pan and chill until serving time. Cut into squares and serve on lettuce.

GEORGIA PEACHES AND CREAM GELATIN SALAD

Layer 1:

1 (3-ounce) package peach jello
1 cup boiling water
3/4 cup cold water

3 cups fresh peaches, sliced
1 banana, sliced

Dissolve peach gelatin in boiling water. Stir in cold water and chill until partially set. Fold in fresh peaches and bananas. Pour into a 6-cup gelatin mold. Chill until nearly firm.

Layer 2:

1 envelope plain gelatin
3 Tablespoons cold water
1/2 cup light cream, scalded
1 cup whipping cream (not
whipped)

8 ounces cream cheese, softened
1/2 cup sugar
1 cup pureed fresh peaches
2 Tablespoons sugar

Soften plain gelatin in 3 tablespoons cold water. Stir in scalded cream and mix until gelatin is dissolved. Cream softened cream cheese and whipping cream together. Add the 1/2 cup sugar and mix thoroughly. Sweeten pureed fresh peaches with 2 tablespoons sugar and add to cream cheese/whipping cream mixture. Combine with dissolved gelatin and mix well. Pour over fruit gelatin layer in the mold and chill until firm. Unmold and garnish with fresh peach slices to serve.

RUSSIAN SALAD

1 (8-ounce) package cream cheese
1 large package lime jello
3/4 cup water
15 large marshmallows
2 Tablespoons mayonnaise

1 small can crushed pineapple
1 cup diced bananas
1 small can evaporated milk
3 Tablespoons sugar
small amount of lemon juice

Mix cream cheese, jello, water and marshmallows; cook over low heat until dissolved. Mix mayonnaise, pineapple, bananas, milk, sugar and 1 to 1-1/2 teaspoons lemon juice; add to cream cheese mixture. Pour into greased mold and set until firm. Good enough for a dessert.

BAKED CHICKEN SALAD SUPREME

2 hardboiled eggs
3 cups cooked chicken, cubed (all white meat is best)
1-1/2 cups celery, chopped
3/4 cup slivered almonds
1 (6-ounce) can sliced water chestnuts
1/2 teaspoon salt

2 teaspoons grated onion
2 Tablespoons lemon juice
1-1/2 cups mayonnaise
1 (11-ounce) can cream of chicken soup
3/4 cup grated sharp Cheddar cheese
1-1/2 cups crushed potato chips

Combine everything but the cheese and potato chips. Place in a greased casserole dish. Combine the cheese and crushed potato chips and sprinkle on top of chicken mixture. Bake at 325 degrees for 45 minutes or until browned. Serves 8.

CORNED BEEF MOLDED SALAD

1 (3-ounce) package lemon jello
1 cup boiling water
1 (12-ounce) can corned beef, diced
1 can beef consomme
1-1/2 Tablespoons lemon juice
1 cup minced onions (scallions better)
1 cup finely chopped cucumbers
1 cup finely chopped celery
2 hardboiled eggs, diced

1/2 cup finely chopped green pepper
1 cup mayonnaise
1 teaspoon salt
1 teaspoon horseradish (optional)
Dressing:
1 carton sour cream
1 teaspoon prepared horseradish
2 Tablespoons mayonnaise
1 teaspoon lemon juice

Dissolve gelatin in water and cool until thickened. Stir in mayonnaise, corned beef, celery, cucumbers, onions, green peppers, eggs and horseradish. Pour into greased mold, decorate with olives and refrigerate overnight. Combine dressing ingredients and serve. May be used as a main course salad or with crackers as an appetizer.

BEEF SALAD

This is a perfect way to use leftover roast beef on a hot day.
A good hearty salad.

1/4 cup red wine vinegar
1/4 cup water
2 Tablespoons lemon juice
2 Tablespoons sugar
1/4 teaspoon dill weed
1/2 teaspoon salt
freshly ground pepper to taste

3 cups (about 12 ounces) cold roast beef cut in strips
1 small onion, thinly sliced
1 head romaine lettuce
1 cup sour cream
artichoke hearts
tomato wedges

Simmer the first 7 ingredients for 15 minutes. Cool. Combine with beef and onion, and chill several hours or overnight. Drain, saving the marinade. Break up lettuce and place in large bowl. Top with beef and onion. Combine sour cream with reserved marinade. Toss with lettuce and beef. Garnish with artichoke hearts and tomato wedges. Serves 6.

CHICKEN SALAD MOLD

2 envelopes plain gelatin
1 cup cold chicken stock
1 Tablespoon salt (or to taste)
2 Tablespoons lemon juice
1 cup mayonnaise
1-1/2 Tablespoons grated onion
1/2 cup finely chopped green
   peppers
black pepper to taste

4 hardboiled eggs, chopped
1-1/4 cups hot chicken stock
2 Tablespoons French's mustard
2 Tablespoons Durkee's
1 cup diced celery
1/2 cup dill pickle, finely diced
1/4 cup sweet pickle, finely diced
4 to 5 pound hen, cooked, boned
   and diced

Soften gelatin in cold chicken stock. Dissolve softened gelatin in hot chicken stock. Add lemon juice and salt; cool. Add chicken, eggs, chopped vegetables and seasonings. Spoon into oiled 1-1/2 quart ring mold. Refrigerate. May be used as main course for luncheon.

RED, WHITE AND GREEN RIBBON SALAD

A delicious cheese, crab and vegetable salad.

Avocado Layer:
1 envelope unflavored gelatin
1/2 cup water, divided
1 teaspoon salt
3 Tablespoons fresh lemon juice

4 to 5 drops Tabasco
1-1/2 cups avocado, mashed
few drops green food coloring if
   desired

Soften gelatin in 1/4 cup cold water; add 1/4 cup boiling water. Add salt, lemon juice and Tabasco. Cool until mixture thickens. Add avocado and the green food coloring. Pour into a 5x9" loaf pan lightly oiled with salad oil. Chill until almost firm.

Cheese-Crab Layer:
1 envelope unflavored gelatin
1/4 cup cold water
1 (8-ounce) package cream
   cheese, softened
1/4 cup milk
1/4 cup sour cream
1 teaspoon salt

2/3 cup mayonnaise
1/4 teaspoon Worcestershire sauce
1/4 teaspoon chopped green onion
2 Tablespoons chopped ripe
   olives
juice of lemon

Soften gelatin in cold water and dissolve over boiling water. Beat together the cheese, milk and sour cream. Stir in remaining ingredients. Stir in gelatin. Pour over the avocado layer. Chill this mixture until almost firm.

(Continued)

Tomato Layer:

1-1/2 envelopes unflavored gelatin
1/4 cup cold water
6 to 8 fresh tomatoes (3 cups)
1/2 cup chopped celery
1 green pepper (small), chopped

1 Tablespoon grated onion
1/2 (3-ounce) package cream cheese, broken into pieces
1/4 cup mayonnaise
salt and pepper to taste

Cut tomatoes into small pieces over a bowl, using all juice. Add celery, green pepper, onion and cream cheese, broken into small pieces. Soften gelatin in cold water and add to it sufficient hot water (1/4 cup) to dissolve the gelatin. Add to tomato mixture. Add mayonnaise, seasoning to taste with salt and pepper. Pour over the Cheese-Crab layer and chill until set. Makes a delicious luncheon salad.

TARRAGON CHICKEN SALAD

4 quarts water
3 pounds chicken breasts
1/2 cup sour cream
1/2 cup mayonnaise
2 ribs celery, chopped

2 green onions, thinly sliced
1/2 cup chopped pecans
2 teaspoons dried tarragon flakes
salt and pepper to taste

Cook chicken breasts in boiling water for 20 minutes, until done. Remove from water; cool and bone. Cut meat into bite-size chunks and put in a large mixing bowl. In another bowl, whisk together sour cream and mayonnaise. Pour over chicken. Add celery, onions, pecans, tarragon, salt and pepper. Toss well. Cover and refrigerate at least 4 hours. Serves 4 to 6.

SEAFOOD TOMATO ASPIC SUPREME

1 (10-3/4 ounce) can tomato soup
12 ounces V-8 juice
8 ounces cream cheese
4 Tablespoons gelatin
1/2 cup water
salt to taste
1 Tablespoon Tabasco sauce
1 cup mayonnaise
3/4 cup chopped celery
1/4 cup chopped green onion tops

1/4 cup chopped green pepper
2 avocados, mashed
1 medium onion, chopped
squeeze of lemon
1 Tablespoon parsley flakes
1 pound cooked, peeled shrimp (cleaned), cut into bite-sized pieces
6 ounces crab meat, flaked

Heat soup, juice and cream cheese. Strain to remove any remaining lumps of cheese. Dissolve gelatin in water and add to mixture. Add remaining ingredients and chill. This salad is pretty garnished with artichoke hearts, pickled cucumbers and ripe olives. Serve with thin bacon-flavored crackers or finger sandwiches. Serves 12 persons.

SPICY SHRIMP SALAD

3 pounds large shrimp, cooked
  and peeled
2/3 cup celery, finely chopped
1/2 cup green onions, thinly sliced
2 Tablespoons chives, finely
  chopped
1/2 cup chopped pickle, sweet or
  dill
2 cups salad oil
1/2 cup chili sauce

3 Tablespoons fresh lemon juice
2 Tablespoons horseradish
  (prepared)
1 Tablespoon Dijon mustard
1 Tablespoon Durkee's sauce
1/2 teaspoon paprika
1/2 teaspoon salt
1 or 2 dashes Tabasco
lettuce

Refrigerate cooked shrimp until well chilled. Add celery, onions, chives and pickle. Combine salad oil, chili sauce, lemon juice, Durkee's, horseradish, mustard, paprika, salt and Tabasco. Mix well and pour over shrimp. Stir gently. Cover and refrigerate for 12 hours, stirring 2 or 3 times. Serve in lettuce cups or on a bed of shredded lettuce. Crusty French bread or crackers are excellent with it.

PARTY SHRIMP SALAD

2 pounds shrimp
1/2 cup chopped celery
1/4 cup chopped olives
2 Tablespoons chopped dill pickle
1 Tablespoon grated onion
2 Tablespoons chopped sweet
  pickle
dash of garlic salt

1 medium boiled white potato,
  diced
2 hardboiled eggs, diced
1/2 cup mayonnaise
1 Tablespoon Durkee's
2 teaspoons lemon juice
salt and pepper to taste
1 Tablespoon French's mustard

Clean shrimp and cook, boiling about 3 minutes only. Dice shrimp in large pieces. Dice eggs and potato into medium-sized pieces. Add all remaining ingredients and chill. More mayonnaise may be added if needed. Serve on bed of lettuce with tomato wedges.

COBB SALAD

Cobb salad is a cross between a chef's salad and a club sandwich. It was created by Robert Cobb, proprietor of Hollywood's fabled Brown Derby Restaurant, late one night when he went into the restaurant kitchen to fix something to eat for himself and a friend. From a number of ingredients in the refrigerator, including avocado, tomato, salad greens, Roquefort cheese, chicken, hard cooked eggs and crisp bacon, he prepared a salad of sorts. The next time the friend came in, he ordered the "Cobb salad". It has been changed a little in both salad ingredients and dressing ingredients to individual tastes. It still remains a favorite.

(Continued)

Vinaigrette Dressing:

1/3 cup white wine vinegar
1 teaspoon lemon juice
1/4 teaspoon freshly ground
  pepper
1/2 teaspoon salt
1 teaspoon Dijon mustard
1 small clove garlic, finely minced

2 teaspoons minced green onions
1/2 teaspoon minced fresh
  tarragon or 1/4 teaspoon
  dried tarragon
1/4 cup high-quality olive oil
3/4 cup safflower oil

To make the vinaigrette, whisk together all ingredients listed except oils. Slowly whisk in oils until dressing is well mixed. Set aside.

Salad:

1 whole chicken breast, skinned
  and halved (about 12 ounces)
1/3 cup dry white wine
1/2 teaspoon lemon juice
1/2 rib celery, coarsely chopped

2 sprigs parsley
1/2 small onion, coarsely chopped
1 sprig fresh tarragon or pinch
  dried
1/2 teaspoon salt

To poach chicken, place in a lightly buttered deep skillet to hold in a single layer. Add wine and lemon juice and enough water to cover chicken. Add remaining ingredients and bring to a simmer over medium heat. Lower heat, cover and simmer until chicken is firm and springy (7 to 10 minutes). Remove from heat and let chicken cool in broth (about 20 minutes). Place chicken in a bowl with 2 to 3 tablespoons of broth to keep moist. Cover and set aside.

Salad Ingredients:

1/2 medium-size head of iceberg
  lettuce
1 small head chicory
1 small bunch watercress, leaves
  only
2 medium ripe tomatoes, peeled,
  seeded and cut into 1/2"
  diced pieces
salt and fresh ground pepper
3 hard-cooked eggs, coarsely
  chopped

6 slices bacon, cooked crisp,
  drained and crumbled
2 scallions, white part and 2" of
  green, sliced thin
1 teaspoon minced shallot
3 ounces blue cheese, crumbled
1 medium ripe avocado, peeled
  and cut into 1/2" dice, tossed
  with juice of 1/2 lemon
1 small stalk of endive, separated
  into spears

To assemble salad:

Finely slice lettuce and chicory. Cut slices crosswise to chop them fine. Place in a large shallow bowl with minced watercress leaves and toss gently to combine. Lightly season diced tomatoes with salt and pepper. Arrange in two rows at either end of salad bowl on top of greens.

(Continued)

Working inward, make two rows of chopped eggs, then two rows of crumbled bacon. Drain reserved chicken, pat dry, and cut into 1/4 to 1/2" pieces. Make two rows of chicken over greens inside rows of bacon. Combine scallions and shallot and sprinkle over chicken. Make two rows of blue cheese. You may assemble salad up to 1 hour before serving and keep it chilled. To serve at table, drizzle salad with vinaigrette and toss gently to combine all ingredients. Divide onto 6 to 8 individual salad plates and garnish with endive spears. Pass remaining vinaigrette dressing. This salad makes a good meal with lots of buttered French bread.

OCEAN BAY SALAD

1-1/2 cup flaked crab meat
(6-1/2 ounces)
1 cup chopped, cooked shrimp
3/4 cup mayonnaise
1/2 cup chopped green peppers
2 cups finely chopped pimiento

2 Tablespoons finely chopped
onion
1 teaspoon Worcestershire sauce
1/2 teaspoon salt
1/2 cup chow mein noodles
lime twists

Combine crab meat, shrimp, mayonnaise, peppers, onion, pimiento, Worcestershire and salt. Mix well, then place in 1-quart casserole dish. Sprinkle with chow mein noodles. Bake at 350 degrees for 25 minutes. Garnish with lime twists. Serves 4.

SEASIDE SALMON SALAD

2 cups uncooked shell macaroni
1/4 cup French dressing
1 tall can red salmon
1/2 cup diced celery
2 Tablespoons sweet pickle relish
2 hard-cooked eggs, diced
1/3 cup chopped green onion
3 Tablespoons minced parsley
2/3 cup mayonnaise

1/4 teaspoon salt
1/8 teaspoon pepper
1/4 teaspoon garlic salt
1 teaspoon prepared mustard
lettuce
parsley sprigs
tomato wedges
cucumber slices

Cook macaroni in boiling, salted water until tender. Drain; add French dressing to hot macaroni and toss. Chill. Add flaked salmon, celery, pickle relish, eggs, green onion, parsley, mayonnaise and seasonings to macaroni. Chill to blend flavors. To serve, spoon into lettuce-lined bowl; or spoon into individual custard cups (serves 6), chill, and put on lettuce-lined plates. Garnish with sprigs of parsley, tomato wedges and cucumber slices.

TUNA-POTATO STACK-UP SALAD

A gorgeous "layered-look" salad with a tasty dill dressing

1 quart chopped cooked potatoes	1/2 teaspoon dill weed
2 cups cooked peas	3 cups shredded iceberg lettuce
2 (6-1/2 ounce) cans tuna,	2 cups chopped tomato
drained, flaked	2 cups chopped cucumber

Combine potato and peas. Toss tuna with dill weed. Layer lettuce, potato mixture, tomato, tuna mixture and cucumber in 3-1/2 quart salad bowl. Top with 1-1/2 cups Dill Sauce. Cover and chill. Serve with remaining Dill Sauce.

Dill Sauce:	1/2 cup milk
1 cup Miracle Whip salad	1/4 cup chopped dill pickle
dressing	1/4 cup green onion slices
1 cup dairy sour cream	1/2 teaspoon dry mustard

Combine ingredients, mixing well. Makes 10 to 12 servings.

ASPARAGUS SALAD

1 cup liquid (drain canned	1/2 teaspoon salt
asparagus and add water to	1 cup chopped celery
make a cup of liquid)	chopped pimentos
3/4 cup sugar	1 small can asparagus tips
1/2 cup white vinegar	juice of 1/2 lemon
2 envelopes gelatin	2 Tablespoons grated onion

Mix sugar, asparagus liquid and vinegar and bring to a boil. Dissolve gelatin in 1/2 cup water and add to mixture. When cool, add other ingredients. Pour into a square pan and cut into squares to serve. Yield: 6 servings.

MOLDED GAZPACHO SALAD

2 envelopes unflavored gelatin	dash of cayenne pepper
1 cup + 2 cups tomato juice	3/4 cup chopped cucumber
(divided)	1/4 cup chopped pimientos
1/4 cup wine vinegar	2 large tomatoes, chopped
1 clove garlic, crushed	1/2 cup chopped green onion
1/4 teaspoon pepper	3/4 cup chopped green pepper
2 teaspoons salt	

Soften gelatin in 1 cup tomato juice for 5 minutes. Heat until mixture simmers and gelatin dissolves. Remove from heat; add remaining tomato juice, vinegar, garlic, salt, pepper and cayenne. Chill until mixture begins to set. Fold in tomatoes, onion, green pepper, cucumber and pimiento. Pour into a greased 6-cup ring mold or bundt cake pan. Chill about 3 hours or until firm. Unmold salad, garnish with parsley, and serve with Avocado Cream or Horseradish Sour Cream.

(Continued)

Avocado Cream:

1/3 cup mashed avocado   1/2 teaspoon salt
1/2 cup sour cream   dash of cayenne pepper

Combine ingredients and blend well. Men especially find this recipe appetizing.

Horseradish Sour Cream:

1/4 cup sour cream   1/2 teaspoon salt
1/4 cup mayonnaise   1 teaspoon horseradish

Mix all ingredients and serve over salad. Serves 10 to 12 persons.

NOTE: Mayonnaise may be used to grease molds.

CALICO BEAN SALAD
(A Summertime Favorite)

3/4 cups green beans   1/2 bell pepper, sliced
1 can garbanzos (chick peas)   1/4 of a small red cabbage,
1 cucumber, sliced   shredded
1/2 cup sliced celery   3 to 4 medium tomatoes, cut in
1/4 cup green onions, chopped   wedges
   with tops or 1 medium onion   1/2 cup mayonnaise
   sliced into rings   salt and pepper to taste

Green beans from the can are alright, but leftover beans that have been cooked with meat grease are better. If using leftover beans, heat just until cold grease is melted, then drain. Drain garbanzos and combine all vegetables in a bowl. Sprinkle with salt and pepper to taste and toss with desired amount of mayonnaise. Line salad bowl or platter with torn lettuce and pile bean salad in center.

MEDITERRANEAN BEAN SALAD

1 (9-ounce) package frozen   1 (3-ounce) can boiled
   French-cut green beans or 1   mushrooms, sliced (drained)
   (15-ounce) can French-cut   1/3 cup Italian salad dressing
   green beans   1/4 teaspoon salt
1 medium onion, thinly sliced   dash of freshly ground pepper
   into rings   2 medium tomatoes, cut into
      wedges

If using frozen beans, thaw before using. Pour boiling water over beans to cover and let stand about 5 minutes; drain thoroughly and place in salad bowl with onion rings and mushrooms. Combine salad dressing, salt and pepper; add to bean mixture and toss. Marinate in refrigerator for at least 2 hours, tossing occasionally. Arrange tomato wedges on top just before serving and top with bacon bits if desired. Serves 4 to 6 persons.

CAESAR SALAD

Caesar or California Salad is said to have been created in Tijuana, Mexico, during the 1920's. The original salad (romaine lettuce mixed with grated cheese, coddled eggs, and bread cubes fried in olive oil) started a trend. Caesar Salad quickly crossed the border and became the last word in sophisticated American restaurants. Diners managed to extricate the secret of the coddled eggs from chefs, and Caesar Salad finally became a classic of the American home kitchen.

2 cloves garlic, cut in half	coddled eggs
4 slices white bread	1 lemon
2/3 cup olive oil	1/2 cup grated Parmesan or
1 teaspoon salt	Romano cheese
1/2 teaspoon pepper	1 (2-ounce) can anchovy fillets,
2 large bunches romaine	drained and chopped

Rub large salad bowl with garlic. Trim crusts from bread and cut bread into cubes. Heat 1/3 cup of oil in 10" skillet. Add garlic and bread cubes. Cook over medium heat, stirring constantly, until bread cubes are brown. Remove from heat and discard garlic. Mix remaining 1/3 cup oil, salt and pepper in salad bowl. Tear romaine into bite-size pieces and toss until leaves glisten. Break coddled eggs onto romaine; squeeze juice from lemon over romaine. Toss until leaves are well coated. Add cheese, anchovies and bread cubes; toss. Makes 8 servings.

Coddled Eggs:

Place 2 eggs in warm water. Heat to boiling enough water to completely cover eggs. Immerse eggs in boiling water and remove from heat; cover and let stand 30 seconds. Immediately cool eggs in cold water and refrigerate.

MEAN BEAN SALAD

1 can cut green beans	1/2 cup sugar
1 can cut wax beans	1 teaspoon salt
1 can kidney beans	1 teaspoon pepper
1 small can lima beans	1/2 cup salad oil
1 can garbanzo beans	1 cup wine vinegar
1 green bell pepper, finely	6 to 10 green onions, finely
chopped	chopped (use part of green
1 cup celery, finely chopped	tops)

Drain all beans and combine with green pepper and celery. Mix sugar, salt, pepper, oil, vinegar and onions. Combine both mixtures, cover and refrigerate for 12 to 24 hours, stirring often. Serves 10 to 12 persons.

MARINATED BROCCOLI SALAD

1 bunch fresh broccoli (use
flowerettes only)
6 green onions
3 hardboiled eggs
1 small bottle green stuffed
olives (about 1/4 cup),
chopped

1/3 pound bacon, cooked crisp
and crumbled
1 (7-ounce) bottle Italian dressing
1/2 cup mayonnaise
1/4 cup Parmesan cheese

Wash and cut broccoli into flowerettes, drain well. Chop eggs; slice onions, using a small amount of green tops. Cook, drain and crumble bacon. Combine broccoli, onions and olives. Make a dressing by adding Parmesan cheese to mayonnaise and Italian dressing. Toss dressing thoroughly with all ingredients except eggs and bacon. Top salad with eggs and bacon and refrigerate for several hours. Serve either as a salad or as a vegetable.

COLE SLAW

In the 1700's, Dutch settlers were firmly established on the banks of the Hudson River. From their kitchens came such specialties as oliebollen (later called dumplings), koekje (cookies), pannekoeken (now called pancakes) and cool sla (literally cabbage salad, but corrupted in spelling and pronunciation to cole slaw).

1 medium cabbage, shredded
2 carrots, cut in julienne
1 green bell pepper, cored,
seeded, and cut in julienne
5 green onions, minced
(including green portion)
1/2 cup dry-roasted peanuts

Dressing:
3/4 cup mayonnaise
1/4 cup sour cream
juice of 1 large lemon (about 1/4
cup)
1/4 cup sugar
1/2 teaspoon salt

Mix dressing ingredients together thoroughly. In a separate bowl, combine slaw ingredients. Pour dressing over salad and toss well to coat. Cover and refrigerate for several hours. Drain off most of the dressing before serving. Serve chilled. Serves 8.

NOTE: The dressing is also delicious served over cold blanched asparagus.

ITALIAN SLAW

4 cups finely shredded cabbage	1/3 cup sugar
1 medium onion, chopped	1/4 teaspoon mustard seed
1/2 green pepper, chopped	1/2 teaspoon celery seed
1 Tablespoon salt	dash of cayenne pepper
1/2 cup vinegar	2 pimentos, chopped

Combine vegetables and salt and let stand for 1 hour. Add remaining ingredients and mix well. Let stand for at least 4 hours before serving.

RAINBOW COLE SLAW
WITH COOKED DRESSING

"Cole slaw" may have been derived from the term "kool sla" used by early Dutch settlers to mean cabbage salad. Since cabbage was inexpensive and easily grown almost anywhere, cole slaw became a common dish in all parts of the U.S. The first dressings for cole slaw were made from heavy cream sweetened with sugar and thinned with vinegar. Later a cooked dressing was used.

3 cups finely sliced green cabbage	1 teaspoon dry mustard
3 cups finely sliced red cabbage	pinch of cayenne
2 cups finely sliced savoy cabbage	1 teaspoon salt
1 cup thinly sliced green pepper	2 Tablespoons sugar
1/2 cup thinly sliced radishes	1 cup milk
2 Tablespoons finely chopped red onion	3 Tablespoons cider vinegar
	2 Tablespoons lemon juice
1 cup finely julienned carrots	2 egg yolks
salt and freshly ground pepper	1/2 teaspoon celery seed
Cooked Dressing:	salt and freshly ground pepper
1 Tablespoon flour	1/2 cup sour cream

In a large bowl, combine all slaw ingredients and toss to mix. Set aside. Make dressing by combining flour, mustard, cayenne, salt and sugar in a heavy 2-quart saucepan. Whisk in about 4 Tablespoons milk to make a paste. Over medium-low heat, gradually whisk in remaining milk and cook, stirring, until thickened and smooth (about 5 minutes). In a small bowl, whisk vinegar, lemon juice and egg yolks together. Whisk about half the hot milk mixture into vinegar mixture, and return to saucepan. Cook, stirring, over low heat until smooth and thickened to consistency of thin mayonnaise (about 3 minutes). Do not boil. Stir in celery seed and remove from heat to cool. Season with salt and pepper to taste. When cool, stir in creme fraiche or sour cream. Toss dressing with slaw, cover, and chill for 2 to 4 hours. To serve, spoon directly from bowl or put into hollowed-out pepper shells or large cabbage leaves. Yield: 8 to 10 servings.

SOUR CREAM POTATO SALAD

4 cups cubed cooked potatoes	2 Tablespoons chopped parsley
1/4 cup creamy French dressing	2 Tablespoons chopped dill pickle
1 cup chopped celery	2 Tablespoons chopped pimiento
3 hardboiled eggs, chopped	1 Tablespoon prepared mustard
1 cup sour cream	1 teaspoon salt
2 Tablespoons grated onion	1/4 teaspoon pepper

Combine potatoes and dressing; mix lightly. Chill 1 hour. Add celery and eggs. Mix sour cream, onion, parsley, pickle, pimiento, mustard, salt and pepper. Combine with other ingredients and mix lightly. Chill. Yields 6 to 8 servings.

FRENCH VEGETABLE SALAD

A tasty combination of bacon, beans and potatoes

1 pound bacon, cooked and crumbled	1/2 cup green onions, thinly sliced
	1/4 cup fresh minced parsley
3 pounds small red new potatoes, unpeeled	1 clove garlic, crushed
	1 teaspoon salt
1 pound fresh Blue Lake green beans	2 teaspoons Dijon mustard
	1 teaspoon Durkee Sauce
Dressing:	1/2 teaspoon sweet basil, crushed
1/2 cup light olive oil	1/2 teaspoon tarragon, crushed
1/4 cup tarragon vinegar	freshly ground pepper
1/4 cup canned beef broth consomme, undiluted	

Boil potatoes until tender, but not crumbly. Cool and slice into 1/4" thick slices and set aside. Snap green beans and cook until tender-crisp. Drain and set aside. Cook bacon until crisp, drain and crumble.

Combine all dressing ingredients, mixing well. To serve, combine potatoes and beans in a large bowl, add dressing and toss. Sprinkle with bacon. Serve at room temperature. Serves 6 to 8.

NOTE: Beans may be left unsnapped and cooked full length if you desire. This may be served hot by heating dressing before tossing.

GERMAN POTATO SALAD

2-1/2 pounds red potatoes, cooked, peeled and sliced 1/2" thick	1 teaspoon finely chopped pimiento
	1 teaspoon celery seed
2 celery stalks, finely chopped	1 teaspoon coarsely ground pepper
1/2 medium onion, finely grated or 1 cup minced scallions	1/2 pound smoked bacon, finely chopped

(Continued)

1 Tablespoon all-purpose flour
1 cup cold water
1/4 cup cider vinegar

2 Tablespoons sugar
1 teaspoon salt

Combine sliced potatoes, celery, onion, pimento, celery seed and pepper in bowl. Cook bacon in heavy medium skillet over medium-high heat until crisp. Drain, reserving 1/4 cup drippings. Add bacon to salad. Heat reserved drippings in heavy saucepan over low heat. Stir in flour until smooth. Stir in water. Continue stirring until mixture is hot and glossy. Add vinegar, sugar and salt. Increase heat to high and bring to boil. Cook 3 minutes. Pour over salad and toss well. Serve immediately.

LESEUR PEA SALAD

1 head lettuce
1 (15-ounce) can Leseur peas
1 medium onion, thinly sliced
1 stalk celery, sliced
1/2 to 3/4 cup Polish pickles,
    drained and thinly sliced

1 cup Parmesan cheese or grated
    Cheddar cheese
salt and pepper to taste
1 pint mayonnaise

Break lettuce and arrange in the bottom of a large casserole dish. Add a layer of peas, then make a layer of celery, then a layer of onions and pickles, and top with another layer of peas. Sprinkle each layer with salt and pepper, and sprinkle Parmesan or Cheddar cheese on top. Spoon mayonnaise over all, cover and refrigerate overnight. Mayonnaise will seep down through the vegetables and hold them together. DO NOT STIR.

CLASSIC SPINACH SALAD

26 ounces fresh spinach
4 green onions and tops, thinly
    sliced
8 to 10 fresh mushrooms, sliced
2 hardboiled eggs, chopped,
    sliced or quartered

4 slices bacon, fried crisp and
    crumbled
Interesting additions:
1 (8-ounce) can sliced water
    chestnuts, drained
1 cup fresh sprouts
2 small Belgian endives

Combine prepared spinach and onions (and additions of your choice) in a large bowl. Sprinkle with sliced mushrooms (water chestnuts, if desired), egg and bacon on top. Just before serving, add the dressing of your choice and toss.

Dressing #1: Dijon Salad Dressing
1 Tablespoon sugar
1-1/2 Tablespoons minced onion
4 Tablespoons Dijon mustard

1-1/2 teaspoons salt
2/3 cup cider vinegar
2/3 cup warm water

(Continued)

1 teaspoon Worcestershire sauce 2 cups vegetable oil
Tabasco sauce

Mix sugar, onion, salt, mustard, vinegar and water. Add remaining ingredients and mix well. Serve with this spinach salad or any other green salad. Makes about 12 to 15 servings.

Dressing #2: Sour Cream Spinach Dressing
1 cup vegetable oil   1 teaspoon Durkee Sauce
5 Tablespoons red wine vinegar   (optional)
5 Tablespoons sour cream   2 cloves garlic, pressed or minced
1-1/2 teaspoons salt   2 teaspoons minced parsley
2 Tablespoons sugar   coarsely ground black pepper
                                    2 teaspoons mustard

Mix all ingredients well. Chill at least 6 hours before using. Makes about 6 to 12 servings.

CLIFF'S SPINACH SALAD

6 ounces fresh mushrooms   1/4 cup wine vinegar
fresh spinach   1 hard-cooked egg yolk
3 green onions, thinly sliced   3/4 cup salad oil
1 teaspoon sugar   1 teaspoon salt
1 small garlic bud, minced   1 teaspoon Dijon mustard
1 Tablespoon Burgundy red wine
   (optional)

Remove stems from spinach and wash well; drain on paper towel, then tear into bite-sized pieces. Rinse mushrooms in cold water, drain and slice thinly. Slice onion into thin rings. Combine egg yolk, garlic, vinegar, mustard, Burgundy, oil, salt and pepper in blender; blend well. Combine spinach, mushrooms and onion rings in small bowl, toss gently with dressing and serve. For a more colorful salad, use red onions.

Dressing #2:
1 hard-cooked egg, chopped fine   1 heaping Tablespoon
2 Tablespoons vinegar   horseradish
2 Tablespoons mayonnaise   dash of Tabasco
2 Tablespoons Durkee Famous   salt and pepper to taste
   Sauce

Mix all ingredients, chill and serve over spinach salad.

SWEET POTATO SALAD

3 large sweet potatoes or yams,
  cooked in skins
1 cup diced celery
1 cup chopped tart apples
1/2 cup chopped walnuts
1 cup pineapple tidbits

1/2 cup miniature marshmallows
1/2 cup raisins
1/2 cup mayonnaise
3 Tablespoons fresh lemon juice
3 Tablespoons sugar
1/2 teaspoon salt

Combine mayonnaise, lemon juice, sugar and salt in large bowl, whisking to blend. Peel potatoes and cut into 1/2" cubes. Add potatoes, celery, apple, nuts, marshmallows and raisins to mayonnaise mixture and toss to coat. Cover and refrigerate. Serve chilled salad on lettuce leaves. Excellent with chicken, pork, turkey or ham.

SEVEN LAYER SALAD

The peanuts make it different and special

6 cups iceberg lettuce, torn in
  bite-size pieces
1 cup sliced green onions
salt and pepper
1 Tablespoon sugar
6 hardboiled eggs, sliced
1 (10-ounce) package Leseur peas,
  cooked and drained

4 ounces peanuts
4 ounces sliced water chestnuts
1 pound bacon, cooked crisp, and
  crumbled
2 cups shredded Swiss cheese
1-1/2 cups mayonnaise
1/2 cup shredded Cheddar cheese

Place 3 cups lettuce in bottom of a large salad bowl (a clear glass bowl makes a very pretty salad). Add a layer of green onions. Sprinkle with salt, pepper and sugar. Add layer of eggs and season again. Add layers in the following order: peas, peanuts, water chestnuts, remaining lettuce, bacon and Swiss cheese. Cover and seal with mayonnaise. Cover and refrigerate 24 hours. Before serving, garnish with Cheddar cheese. Salad may be served layered or tossed. Serves 20 as an accompaniment, or 8 to 12 as a main luncheon dish. Recipe may be halved.

WILTED LETTUCE SALAD

First sign of Spring

4 strips lean bacon
2 heads leaf lettuce, torn into
  bite-size pieces
4 green onions, thinly sliced
1/4 cup sugar

1/4 cup water
1/4 cup cider vinegar
2 hard-cooked eggs, finely
  chopped

Fry bacon until crisp. Drain and set aside, reserving the drippings. Combine the lettuce and onions. Heat reserved bacon drippings, sugar, water and vinegar to boiling. Immediately pour over lettuce and onions. Add eggs. Crumble bacon and add. Toss well. Serve immediately. Best made with the first lettuce of spring or leaf lettuce.

ZIPPY HORSERADISH RING

1 envelope unflavored gelatin
1/4 cup cold water
1 (3-ounce) package lemon jello
1 cup boiling water
1 (5-ounce) jar prepared
  horseradish

1 cup mayonnaise
1 cup sour cream
1 teaspoon Durkee Sauce
dash of Tabasco

Dissolve unflavored gelatin in cold water. Dissolve lemon jello in the cup of boiling water, add together, stirring to completely dissolve. Let cool. Fold in horseradish, mayonnaise, Durkee Sauce, sour cream and Tabasco. Pour into a ring mold that has been lightly oiled. Refrigerate and chill until firm. Unmold onto a chilled lettuce-lined serving platter. Garnish with cherry tomatoes. Serve with meat as a side dish or fill the ring with marinated shrimp and serve as an appetizer. It is very good with roast beef or steak.

BEA'S CHEESE SALAD DRESSING

1 pint French dressing
1 pint salad oil
1/2 teaspoon Tabasco
1 Tablespoon Worcestershire
  sauce
1/2 cup cider vinegar

juice of 2 lemons
1 small garlic clove, crushed
1 teaspoon white pepper
1 pint mayonnaise
1 pound bleu or Roquefort cheese

Mix all ingredients, except cheese, together. Blend well, then add crumbled cheese and allow to "ripen" in refrigerator for a day or two. Remove garlic clove and serve. Will keep in refrigerator for weeks. Yield: 2 quarts.

PARMESAN CHEESE DRESSING

1/2 cup salad oil
1/4 cup vinegar or lemon juice
1 teaspoon Dijon mustard
1 teaspoon salt
1 teaspoon freshly ground pepper

2 Tablespoons freshly grated
  Parmesan cheese
1 clove garlic, crushed
1/4 teaspoon sugar

Combine all the ingredients in a small mixing bowl and beat for 2 to 3 minutes with a wire whisk, blending well. Pour into a pint jar or cruet, cover and refrigerate for at least 2 hours before using. Shake well before serving.

NOTE: This is especially refreshing on fresh tomato slices, tossed vegetable salad or chilled spinach greens.

DELUXE FRENCH DRESSING

1 Tablespoon sugar
1 teaspoon salt
1-1/2 teaspoons dry mustard
1 teaspoon paprika
1 (10-1/2 ounce) can condensed
   tomato soup
1 Tablespoon horseradish
1 cup vinegar

1-1/2 Tablespoons Worcestershire
   sauce
1 cup salad oil
1 clove garlic, grated
1 small onion, grated
2 Tablespoons lemon juice
1/4 teaspoon Tabasco

Combine all ingredients in bottle or jar; cover and shake thoroughly. Makes 1 quart.

WILLIAMSBURG DRESSING

1 (10-3/4 ounce) can condensed
   tomato soup
1/2 cup sugar
1-1/2 cup salad oil
1 Tablespoon Worcestershire
   sauce
3/4 cup vinegar

1 teaspoon grated onion
1 teaspoon dry mustard
1 teaspoon salt
1 teaspoon pepper
1 Tablespoon catsup
1 clove garlic, peeled

Mix all ingredients except garlic. Place in jar. Add garlic and allow to remain for 24 hours. Remove.

HONEY FRUIT SALAD DRESSING

2/3 cup sugar
1 teaspoon dry mustard
1 teaspoon paprika
1 teaspoon celery seed
1/4 teaspoon salt

5 Tablespoons vinegar
1 Tablespoon lemon juice
2/3 cup honey
1 teaspoon grated onion
1 cup salad oil

Mix dry ingredients in a blender. Add remaining ingredients and blend.

POPPY SEED DRESSING

2/3 cup honey
1 teaspoon salt
1/8 teaspoon white pepper
3/4 cup vinegar (cider)
2 teaspoons paprika

6 Tablespoons prepared mustard
2 cups vegetable oil
3/4 Tablespoon poppy seeds
2 Tablespoons grated onion

Mix first 6 ingredients and blend in a blender or electric mixer until thickened and oil has disappeared. Add poppy seeds and onion and stir. Good dressing for a fruit salad. Yield: 3-1/2 cups.

GREEN GODDESS
SALAD DRESSING

Invented by the chef of the Palace Hotel in San Francisco especially for George Arliss on the opening night of his famous play, "The Green Goddess."

4 anchovy fillets, finely chopped	1 Tablespoon lemon juice
1/4 cup finely chopped green onion	2 Tablespoons tarragon vinegar
	2 Tablespoons garlic vinegar
1 cup mayonnaise	1 Tablespoon chopped chives
1/2 cup sour cream	1/3 cup chopped or dried parsley

Add lemon juice to sour cream, then mix other ingredients and blend well. Refrigerate until well chilled. Serve on crisp salad greens, asparagus or broccoli. Keeps refrigerated for about 2 weeks.

NOTE: To make garlic vinegar, place 2 to 3 peeled garlic cloves in a pint of white vinegar and allow to sit (leave garlic in).

RED DOG SALOON
(ARIZONA) SALAD DRESSING

2 cups mayonnaise	1 Tablespoon tarragon vinegar
1 cup sour cream	1 mashed avocado
2 cups buttermilk	1/2 cup chives, minced
2 cloves garlic, minced	1/2 cup parsley, minced
4 anchovies, minced	1/2 teaspoon salt
1 Tablespoon white vinegar	

Blend all ingredients together in a mixer and let stand at least 15 minutes to "ripen" before serving. Serve on tossed salad greens.

GUACAMOLE DRESSING

1-1/3 cups sour cream	1/4 teaspoon prepared mustard
1 cup mayonnaise	1/4 teaspoon celery salt
1 green onion, thinly sliced	1/4 teaspoon freshly ground white pepper
1 Tablespoon finely minced fresh parsley	dash of hot pepper sauce
1 small garlic clove, finely minced	1 to 2 drops green food coloring (optional)
2 teaspoons wine vinegar	1 very large or 2 medium ripe avocados, peeled, pitted and finely chopped
2 teaspoons Worcestershire sauce	
1 teaspoon anchovy paste	
1 teaspoon fresh lemon juice	
1/2 teaspoon honey	

Combine all ingredients except avocado in medium bowl and blend well. Gently stir in avocado. Cover and chill before serving.

THOUSAND ISLAND DRESSING

Thousand Island Dressing is believed to have been first served in 1910 at the Blackstone Hotel in Chicago. Some believe it was named after the Thousand Islands in the St. Lawrence River where the dressing may have been first concocted. It is a mayonnaise-based dressing containing onions, pickles and hard-cooked eggs based on Russian Dressing. It makes a wedge of iceberg lettuce a pleasure, and it is a perfect topping for open-faced sandwiches layered with lettuce, slices of ham, turkey, cheese and tomatoes. A must for Reúben sandwiches! Just be sure to butter the bread to keep it from getting soggy.

3/4 cup mayonnaise
1/2 cup ketchup
1/4 cup salad oil
2 Tablespoons prepared mustard
    (Dijon good)
1 teaspoon garlic salt

2 Tablespoons minced onion
    (green onions extra good)
3 hard-cooked eggs, finely
    chopped
1/2 cup pickle relish

Combine all ingredients in a mixing bowl. Stir, mixing well. Pour into a quart jar. Store in refrigerator. Makes 2 cups.

SHRIMP VINAIGRETTE SALAD DRESSING

1 (8-ounce) package frozen tiny
    uncooked shrimp, thawed
1 bay leaf
1/3 cup olive oil
2 teaspoons fresh lemon juice
4 Tablespoons white wine
    vinegar
1 clove garlic, minced
3 Tablespoons Dijon-style
    mustard

1 Tablespoon green onions,
    finely sliced
1 Tablespoon fresh dill weed,
    finely snipped
1 Tablespoon fresh parsley,
    finely chopped
1/2 teaspoon salt ·
1/4 teaspoon white pepper (may
    use black)
1/2 teaspoon sugar

Rinse and devein shrimp. Add bay leaf to 2 quarts water in a 3-quart saucepan. Bring to a boil. Stir in shrimp. Cook and stir until shrimp are cooked (2 to 3 minutes). Drain shrimp in a colander. Cool under running cold water to stop cooking. Mix the remaining ingredients and shake well in dressing bottle or a covered jar. Pour over shrimp in a bowl. Cover and refrigerate at least several hours, preferably overnight. Makes about 1 cup dressing. So very good over tossed salad or a fresh spinach salad.

"BETTER THAN STORE-BOUGHT" CROUTONS

A delightful addition to vegetable salads, soups or crushed into crumbs for a special topping.

Butter slices of bread and sprinkle with Parmesan cheese, then seasoned salt, then Italian seasoning. Freeze slightly to make cutting easier. Cut into cubes. Put bread cubes (single layer) in a pan and put into an oven preheated to 350 degrees. Turn oven off and allow cubes to remain overnight. Croutons keep indefinitely in an airtight container.

SPICY SALAD SEASONING MIX

A great seasoning mix for vegetables, salads and baked potatoes!

2 cups grated Parmesan cheese	1 Tablespoon instant minced
2 teaspoons salt	onion
1/2 cup sesame seeds	2 Tablespoons parsley flakes
2 teaspoons paprika	1/2 teaspoon dried dill weed
1/2 teaspoon pepper	2 Tablespoons poppy seeds
1/2 teaspoon garlic salt	3 Tablespoons celery seeds

Mix all ingredients thoroughly. Seal in a glass jar and store in a cool dry place.

Serving Suggestions:

1. Mix 3 tablespoons with 1 cup sour cream and a dash of seasoned salt. Mix well and use with vegetable sticks (carrot, cucumber, green pepper or squash).

2. For croutons: Cut buttered bread slices into cubes and sprinkle with mix. Place on ungreased cookie sheet in 225 degree oven for 2 to 3 hours or until crisp. Store in an airtight container. Great with salads and soups. Freezes beautifully.

3. For appetizers: Dip vegetables (cauliflower, broccoli, zucchini or yellow squash sticks) in butter and then dip in a mixture of bread crumbs and mix. Microwave until tender.

4. Sprinkle on cooked vegetables or on salads. Very good sprinkled on baked potatoes.

Golf in Augusta

©1991 Ray Baird

THE AUGUSTA NATIONAL

The clubhouse of the world famous Augusta National Golf Club, home of The Masters, originally was constructed by Dennis Redmond in the 1850's. Shortly after, Fruitland Nurseries was established on the property. Redmond, editor of The Southern Cultivator, sold both the house and the 200 acre nursery to Louis E. Berckmans. His son Prosper J.A. Berckmans, an internationally known horticulturist, developed one of the largest nurseries in the South and also became a successful landscape architect.

In 1931, the recently established Augusta National Golf Club purchased Fruitland for a course to be designed by Bobby Jones and Alister Mackenzie. The Augusta National Invitational, which began in 1934, grew into golf's most prestigious tournament, The Masters.

Breads

BUTTERMILK BISCUITS
(old-fashion way)

2 cups plus 2 Tablespoons
all-purpose flour
1-1/2 teaspoons baking powder
1/2 teaspoon salt

1/2 teaspoon baking soda
4 Tablespoons shortening
1 cup buttermilk

Preheat oven to 400 degrees. Generously grease a cookie sheet or baking pan. Mix dry ingredients together in a mixing bowl. Cut in shortening until mixture is crumbly. (Can be made ahead. Spoon mixture into container, cover and refrigerate up to 1 month.) Pour in buttermilk and mix lightly. Roll dough on lightly floured surface 3/4" thick adding as little extra flour as possible. Cut out biscuits, using floured rim of a juice glass or biscuit cutter. Place at least 1" apart in prepared pan. Bake until golden brown. Serve hot. Makes about 15 2" biscuits.

Any time biscuits without the fuss:
Prepare your biscuit mix up to the buttermilk addition and it will keep in the refrigerator for a month. Want to make just a few at a time? Take some of the dry mix and add enough buttermilk to form a soft dough, roll, cut and bake any time.

PUTTING the "RISE" in BREADS (Leavening)

Legend says that bread wasn't leavened until an ancient Egyptian baker set some dough aside and discovered much later that it had expanded and soured from wild yeast plants in the air; he baked it anyway and created the first leavened bread. Breadmaking has come a long way since that time and even since colonial bakers depended on home-made "starters". Today's homemakers can take advantage of packaged active dry yeast to make plump loaves of fine-textured breads.

With Frontier families, after the Bible, Sourdough was their most important possession. It was used to make bread, flapjacks and biscuits. It was also used to fill cracks in the log cabin, treat wounds, brew hooch and feed their dogs. The word "sourdough" became a part of the American language during the 1897 Yukon gold strike. Prospectors carried their starter buried in flour or pots strapped to their backs.

In the 19th century, Austrian chemists developed a system for mass-producing yeast. It later was called dried or German yeast. In 1863, an immigrant named Charles Fleichmann returned to Austria to search for a good quality baker's yeast. He came back to America with the yeast cells in a test tube in his vest pocket. Five years later, he had made and sold compressed yeast wrapped in tinfoil.

Cooks got a substitute for sour milk in cream of tartar. This is a by-product of winemaking. Used with baking soda, it produces excellent results in leavening bread. A Harvard professor added cornstarch to this mixture and made our baking powder that we use today.

SWEET POTATO BISCUITS
(An old Georgia recipe)

1 cup sifted all-purpose flour
3 teaspoons baking powder
1/2 teaspoon salt
1/3 cup Crisco

1 cup mashed baked sweet
  potatoes
about 3 Tablespoons milk

Sift dry ingredients together. Cut in Crisco with 2 knives or a pastry blender. Add sweet potatoes and enough milk to make a soft dough. Knead lightly and roll to 1/2" thickness. Cut and place on baking sheet. Bake at 425 degrees for 15 to 20 minutes.

TARA BUTTERMILK BISCUITS

2 cups all-purpose flour
1/2 teaspoon soda
1 teaspoon sugar
2/3 cup buttermilk

2 teaspoons baking powder
1/2 teaspoon salt
8 Tablespoons shortening

Tara Biscuits show shades of "Gone With The Wind" and Margaret Mitchell. These are a necessary biscuit to serve with fried country ham and red-eye gravy.

Measure flour before sifting, then sift with all dry ingredients. Add shortening and mix with pastry blender until mixture resembles coarse cornmeal. Add buttermilk and mix well. Dough will be rather soft. Place dough on lightly floured board, sprinkle with a little flour, and (with lightly floured hands) knead gently about 7 times. Roll dough to 1/3" thickness with floured pin and cut with floured biscuit cutter, dipping the cutter into the flour before cutting each biscuit. Place biscuits in pan with space between biscuits and bake at 375 degrees for about 15 to 20 minutes until golden brown.

NUT MUFFINS

3 Tablespoons butter
1 cup sugar
1 egg
1/2 cup pecans, chopped
1/2 teaspoon salt

1 teaspoon soda
2 teaspoons cream of tartar
1 cup sweet milk
2 cups plain flour
3 teaspoons ground cinnamon

Cream butter until light; continue to beat while gradually adding first sugar then beaten egg yolk. Sift dry ingredients together and alternately add dry ingredients and milk to butter mixture. Stir in chopped nuts. Beat egg white until stiff, then fold into butter mixture. Bake in greased small muffin tins at 400 degrees for 20 minutes. Makes 24 small muffins.

SOUR CREAM BISCUITS

Not only are these biscuits cloud-like, they are versatile and may be made hours ahead of time, covered and refrigerated until baking.

2 cups unbleached flour	2 teaspoons sugar
4 teaspoons baking powder	1/2 cup vegetable shortening
1/2 teaspoon salt	1/3 cup sour cream
1/2 teaspoon cream of tartar	1/3 cup milk

Increase sugar to 1-1/2 teaspoons, and the dough will make one great, big, beautiful shortcake. Make herb biscuits to top a stew such as ragout of pork by adding 2 teaspoons chopped parsley and 1/2 teaspoon dried summer savory to dry ingredients.

Sift dry ingredients together into a large bowl. Cut in shortening until mixture resembles coarse crumbs. Add sour cream and milk all at once. Stir with fork only until dough follows fork around bowl. Turn dough out onto floured board. Lightly knead for only a few seconds, handling dough as gently as you would a baby. Pat or roll dough out to 1/2" thickness. Cut with biscuit cutter and place on ungreased cookie sheet. May be refrigerated at this point until baking time. Bake at 450 degrees for 10 to 12 minutes.

ST. TIMOTHY'S COFFEE CAKE

A great Winston-Salem favorite named for
St. Timothy's Episcopal Church

1 cup butter or margarine	1/2 cup golden seedless raisins
2 cups sugar	1 cup sour cream
1/2 teaspoon vanilla extract	1 to 2 teaspoons cinnamon sugar
2 eggs	Topping:
2 cups unsifted all-purpose flour	1/3 cup firmly packed brown
1 teaspoon double-acting baking	sugar
powder	1/4 cup sugar
1 teaspoon cinnamon	1 teaspoon ground cinnamon
1/4 teaspoon salt	1 cup chopped pecans
1 cup chopped nuts	

Preheat oven to 350 degrees; grease and flour a 12-cup Bundt pan or 10" tube pan and set aside. Mix butter/margarine in a large bowl until soft; add sugar gradually and continue to beat until light and fluffy. Mix in vanilla. Add eggs one at a time, beating well after each addition. Combine flour, baking powder, cinnamon and salt; add nuts and raisins, mix to coat well. Alternately add flour/nut mixture and sour cream to creamed ingredients. Blend well until batter looks like whipped cream tinged with honey. Spoon into pan and sprinkle with cinnamon sugar. Bake 60 minutes or until toothpick inserted in center comes out clean. Cool on wire rack in pan for at least an hour. Remove from pan and sprinkle with additional cinnamon sugar, if desired. Makes 16 servings (about 365 calories per serving).

ALL AMERICAN PANCAKES

Griddle cakes or pancakes, are the oldest form of bread. Originally made of pounded grain mixed with water and spread on a hot rock to dry. There are now many known versions. From appetizers to dessert pancakes. They have become a delightful part of any meal. In England, they are traditionally served on Shrove Tuesday, the day before Lent. Great sport is made of this preparation. The person who prepares the pancakes must flip them in front of family and friends. Flipping pancakes has become a popular sport in some places.

1-1/3 cups sifted flour	1-3/4 cups whole milk
3 Tablespoons sugar	1/2 teaspoon vanilla
2-1/2 teaspoons baking powder	1/4 cup melted butter or
1 teaspoon salt	margarine
2 eggs, beaten slightly	

Sift flour, sugar, baking powder, and salt together into a mixing bowl. Combine eggs, milk, and vanilla and add to dry ingredients, beating just until dry ingredients are moistened. Stir in butter or margarine.

Pour 1/4 cup batter onto a hot lightly greased griddle. Turn pancakes when puffed, full of bubbles, and the edges are cooked.

Variations – Buttermilk Pancakes:

Reduce baking powder to 1-1/2 teaspoons. Add 1 teaspoon baking soda. Substitute 2 cups buttermilk for the 1-3/4 cups milk.

Blueberry or Huckleberry Pancakes:

Omit vanilla and fold in 1 cup washed fresh blueberries or huckleberries and 1/2 teaspoon grated lemon peel into the batter before baking. Serve with plenty of butter, syrup, or preserves.

REFRIGERATOR RAISIN BRAN MUFFINS

5 cups sifted flour	4 eggs, well beaten
4 teaspoons baking soda	1 quart buttermilk
3 cups sugar	1 cup melted shortening
2 teaspoons salt	1 cup raisins (optional)
1 box (15 ounces) raisin bran	

Preheat oven to 400 degrees. Grease muffin pans (do not use paper liners). Mix raisin bran, flour, soda, salt, and extra raisins (if desired) in large bowl. Combine the beaten eggs, oil and buttermilk; mix thoroughly with dry ingredients. Spoon batter into desired number of muffin pans, filling about half full. Bake for 15 to 20 minutes. Store leftover batter in airtight container in refrigerator; batter will keep for up to six weeks for freshly baked muffins in minutes. Do not stir batter after it has been refrigerated, just scoop from the top. Yields 4 dozen muffins.

WAFFLES

Kitchens of Southern plantations were well known for their waffles during the Colonial and Antebellum days. A typical Southern waffle was made with baking soda and buttermilk.

4 eggs, separated
2 cups whole milk or half and
   half
3 cups sifted flour

5 teaspoons baking powder
1 teaspoon salt
2 teaspoons sugar
2/3 cup butter, melted

Beat egg whites until very stiff; set aside. Beat egg yolks until pale yellow; add milk and beat 1 minute longer. Sift flour, baking powder, salt, and sugar together; add to egg yolk mixture. Beat 1 minute. Add melted butter and beat until blended well. Gently fold in egg whites. Cook in preheated waffle iron until steaming stops, about 5 minutes. Makes about 12 single waffles.

Excellent served with syrup and fruit for breakfast or for lunch with a side of seafood or chicken.

CORNBREAD

Corn was an important part of the diet of the Colonial Americans and Indians. Pounded into meal, it was used for breads, porridges, cakes, and other foods. Numerous cornbread recipes have been developed, some with whimsical names such as "hoecake", "ashcake", and "Johnny cake."

"Hoecake" was actually baked over an open fire on a hoe; ashcakes were wrapped in palm or cabbage leaves and baked in hot ashes. The name "Johnny cake" is an alteration of "Shawnee cake," a type of bread made by the Shawnee Indians.

Yankee and Southern cornbreads differ because of the type of cornmeal used in each locale. Yellow corn was mostly grown in New England, while white was predominant in the South. Southern cornbread is richer because plantation cooks used more buttermilk and shortening in their recipes.

HARLEM, GEORGIA
CORNBREAD

Delicious hot or cold, this recipe has a light and fluffy cake-like texture when baked in a shallow dish or baked in an iron corn stick pan.

2 eggs, beaten
1 teaspoon sugar
1 cup self-rising cornmeal

1 cup cream style corn
1 cup sour cream
1/2 cup corn oil

Mix all ingredients. Pour into shallow 1-1/2 quart baking dish sprayed with Pam or Cooking Ease. Bake at 400 degrees for 25 to 30 minutes.

CRACKLIN' CORNBREAD

Cracklings used to be made at hog-killing time. They can be bought in some stores, but they are usually hard and not very good for making cracklin' cornbread. To make your own, ask your favorite meat counter for some of their pork scraps (a good time to ask is when they have a special on pork.)

Cut away all skin and any lean meat which may be left on pork scraps. Cut fat into cubes about 1/2" in size. Place fat cubes in thick iron pot and cook on medium heat until all grease cooks out. Cubes will be light brown and will float on top of grease when done. Skim off fat cubes (cracklings) and drain dry on paper towels. Place cooled cracklings in a tight can or jar and save until ready for use. Strain rendered lard into a can and use for cooking purposes.

To make cracklin' cornbread, use the basic cornbread recipe, adding 1 cup of fine cracklings into cornmeal before mixing in the other ingredients. Follow directions for the basic cornbread recipe.

NOTE: Bacon also makes good cracklings, but don't cook it too hard.

CORNBREAD

2 cups self-rising cornmeal
1/2 teaspoon soda
1 egg

1 cup buttermilk
3 Tablespoons melted lard or
    bacon fat

Beat egg in mixing bowl; add buttermilk. Mix soda and cornmeal together well, then add to egg/buttermilk mixture. Stir until well mixed, adding enough water to make a thin batter. Melt lard or bacon grease into a 10" iron skillet, turning skillet so that melting grease will grease all sides. Pour excess grease into batter, stirring as you add. Pour batter into hot skillet and place in 400 degree oven. Bake for one hour or until golden brown.

Crackling Cornbread:

Mix one cup fine crackling into meal before adding to egg and buttermilk. Bake the same as regular cornbread.

CHEESY CORNBREAD

Cornbread served warm from the oven is redolent of country suppers from America's rural past. As this type of bread does not reheat well, plan to eat it all at one meal.

1 medium onion, finely chopped
3 Tablespoons butter
2/3 cup (2-1/2 ounces) grated
    sharp Cheddar cheese
1/2 cup sour cream
1 cup all-purpose flour
2 Tablespoons sugar

4 teaspoons baking powder
3/4 teaspoon salt
1 cup yellow cornmeal
2 eggs
1 cup milk
1/4 cup melted butter or
    vegetable oil

(Continued)

Preheat oven to 400 degrees and butter an 8x8" baking pan. In a small skillet, saute onion in butter until soft and barely golden. While onion is still warm, stir in grated cheese until it melts, then stir in sour cream. Set aside. Combine flour, sugar, baking powder, salt, and cornmeal in a mixing bowl. Make a well in the center and add milk, and melted butter/oil all at once. Mix with wooden spoon until ingredients are barely moistened (batter will be lumpy). Pour batter into prepared pan and dot top with onion mixture. Swirl onion mixture deep into batter with a knife. Bake 20 to 25 minutes, or until top is golden. Cut in squares and serve promptly.

HUSH PUPPIES

2 cups cornmeal

1/3 cup chopped onion

1 Tablespoon flour

1 teaspoon baking powder

1 teaspoon baking soda

1 teaspoon salt

1 egg, well beaten

1-1/2 cups buttermilk

Legend tells us that "hush puppies" originated at a fish fry. To quiet the hungry dogs, they dropped cornbread batter into the kettle of heated fat and tossed the fried cakes to the dogs. The cakes looked and smelled so tempting that folks, not dogs, have eaten them ever since. A poem has even been written about this:

"Hound puppies howls in Georgia,
Hound puppies howls at home,
I 'spect dey cries in Paris
An' I heer dey squeeks in Rome;
But de hunters an' de hounds,
Dey don't make a soun'
After y'all passes
Dese yere pones aroun'!"

Heat grease in an automatic deep fryer or deep saucepan to 375 degrees. Mix cornmeal, onion, flour, baking powder, baking soda, and salt, blending thoroughly. Blend well-beaten egg and buttermilk. Make a well in center of dry ingredients and pour liquid mixture into well. Mix until well blended. Form into small cakes (about 1 tablespoon for each). Fry 3 to 4 minutes or until well browned. Turn cakes with tongs or a fork as they rise to the surface and several times during cooking. Be careful not to pierce the cakes. Remove hush puppies with a slotted spoon and drain over fat for a few seconds before transferring to absorbent paper. Serve hot with fried fish. Makes about 2 dozen.

NOTE: For a change try adding 1/2 cup grated sharp cheese and dash of Cayenne pepper.

PLANTATION CORNBREAD

2 cups white cornmeal
1/2 cup sifted flour
2 teaspoons baking powder
1 teaspoon salt
1/2 teaspoon baking soda

1 cup buttermilk
1 cup milk
1/4 cup shortening, melted and
  cooled
2 eggs, beaten

Preheat oven to 450 degrees. Five minutes before mixing, place a well-greased 9x9x2" pan on bottom shelf of oven. Sift first 5 ingredients together in a bowl. Add milk, shortening, and eggs; stir just until dry ingredients are moistened. Pour batter into prepared pan. Bake **at once** in top half of very hot oven (450 degrees) for 25 to 30 minutes, or until done. Serve hot.

TENNESSEE "BATTY" CAKES WITH LACY EDGES

An adaptation of two recipes dating from the late 1800's, this recipe makes a very tasty batter cake. The batter should not be so thin that it will run, or thick it will have to be spread with a spoon. Excellent for Sunday or Holiday brunches.

2 cups yellow cornmeal
1/2 teaspoon baking soda
1/2 teaspoon salt

2-1/2 cups buttermilk
2 eggs
2 Tablespoons melted shortening

Sift dry ingredients together. Beat egg well, mix in buttermilk, and add to dry ingredients. Beat mixture until very smooth, then drop by teaspoons onto well-greased iron skillet (allow 1 teaspoon of oil for every 4 cakes). When cake is browned on one side, turn with pancake turner and brown on other side. Batter has a tendency to get too thick; add a bit more buttermilk, a tablespoon at a time. These are small, thin cakes. Count on 4 to 6 per serving. Serve hot with butter, honey, applesauce, syrup, sorghum, or preserves.

NOTE: Water-ground cornmeal is better. The bagged meal is not as good as the sifted country meal. Recipe works well when halved for smaller numbers.

APPLE RAISIN BREAD

1 cup butter, softened
2 cups sugar
4 eggs, beaten
4 cups all-purpose flour
2 teaspoons baking powder
1-1/2 teaspoons baking soda
1 teaspoon ground cinnamon

1/8 teaspoon ground allspice
1/8 teaspoon ground nutmeg
2 cups golden raisins
2 cups applesauce
1/4 teaspoon salt
1 teaspoon lemon juice
1 teaspoon vanilla extract

Preheat oven to 350 degrees. Cream butter and sugar together until fluffy. Add beaten eggs. Sift together flour, baking powder, baking soda, nutmeg, and allspice. Add to the creamed mixture. Add raisins that have been plumped in hot water for about 5 minutes, after draining and patting dry. Add lemon juice, salt and vanilla. Mix well. Spoon into 2 lightly greased loaf pans. Bake 50 minutes, or until done. Cool. Serve warm with butter or cream cheese if desired. Good for tea sandwiches or lightly toasted for breakfast. These loaves freeze well.

AMERICAN CHRISTMAS BREAD

1-1/4 cups sifted flour
2 teaspoons baking powder
3/4 teaspoon salt
1/2 cup seedless raisins
3/4 cup chopped pecans
1 egg, beaten

1 cup sugar
1 teaspoon soda
1 medium orange
1 cup applesauce
3/4 cup wheat germ
3 Tablespoons melted butter

Heat oven to 350 degrees; grease 8-1/2x4-1/2x2-1/2" loaf pan. Sift flour, sugar, baking powder, soda, and salt together. Peel and slice orange; put slices, half of the peel, and raisins through food grinder, using fine blade. Add applesauce and remaining ingredients. Beat at medium speed for 1 minute or until batter gets thinner. Bake 70 minutes or until toothpick comes out clean. Store for 12 hours before serving. This bread freezes well.

BISHOP'S BREAD

Two traditions exist regarding the way Bishop's Bread got its name.

Hundreds of years ago in Germany, the monks at one monastery were not permitted by the Bishop to eat sweets, so the baker devised this dark cake recipe and baked it to resemble loaves of bread. It was called Bishop's Bread for the Bishop who forbade the sweets. The second story relates that in Colonial times the Bishop made his visits on horseback, which at times resulted in a very uncertain schedule. The good wives of his parish wanted something special to serve and came up with this recipe which had wonderful lasting qualities and could be made ahead in preparation for the Bishop's visit, yet kept on hand until he actually arrived.

BISHOP'S BREAD #1

(Monk's Recipe)

1/2 cup butter/margarine
1 cup brown sugar
2-1/2 cups all-purpose flour
1/2 teaspoon salt
1 teaspoon cinnamon

1 cup buttermilk or sour milk
1 egg, slightly beaten
1/2 teaspoon baking powder
1/2 teaspoon baking soda

Mix butter, brown sugar, flour, salt, and cinnamon together as you would make a pie crust until crumbly; set aside 1/2 cup for topping. Add buttermilk, egg, baking soda and baking powder to remaining butter mixture. Mix and pour into 10" greased utility pan. Sprinkle evenly with reserved crumbs and bake at 325 degrees for 45 minutes or until done.

BISHOP'S BREAD #2

(Colonial Recipe)

1-1/2 cups sifted flour	1 cup dates, finely chopped
1/2 teaspoon baking powder	1 cup candied cherries, chopped
1/4 teaspoon salt	3 eggs
2/3 cup chocolate chips	1 cup sugar
2 cups walnuts, chopped	

Preheat oven to 325 degrees. Line bottom of loaf pan with wax paper, greasing paper and sides of pan. Sift flour, baking powder and salt together; stir in chocolate chips, walnuts, dates, and cherries until well coated with flour. In a large bowl, beat eggs well; gradually beat in all sugar. Fold in flour mixture and pour into loaf pan. Bake 1-1/2 hours or until well done. Cool in pan. Remove when cool and wrap in foil to store. Even people who hate fruit cake will love this!

CRANBERRY NUT BREAD

"Cranberries" were one of the first native American fruits shipped to the Old World. Wild cranberries were cooked with honey or maple sugar by the Indians and sailors ate them at sea to prevent scurvy.

1/2 cup butter or margarine, at room temperature	1 8-ounce carton sour cream
1 cup sugar	1 teaspoon almond extract
2 eggs	1 cup pecans or walnuts, finely chopped
2 cups all-purpose flour	1-1/2 cups halved cranberries or 1 (16-ounce) can whole cranberry sauce
1/2 teaspoon salt	
1 teaspoon baking powder	
1 teaspoon soda	1/4 cup Rum (optional, but good)

Blend butter and sugar together in a mixing bowl. Add unbeaten eggs, one at a time on medium speed of mixer. Reduce speed, and add sifted dry ingredients alternately with sour cream. Add flavoring and nuts. Pour half of batter into a greased and floured 10" tube pan. Spread cranberries or sauce over the batter; carefully spoon the remaining batter over the cranberries. Bake at 350 degrees for 50 to 60 minutes or until bread tests done. Cool in pan for about 5 minutes, then remove to cool completely. Add Glaze if desired.

Glaze:	1 Tablespoon warm water
1/4 cup powdered sugar	1/2 teaspoon almond extract

Mix well and drizzle over cranberry bread.

GEORGIA PEACH BREAD

3 cups sliced fresh peaches
6 Tablespoons sugar
2 cups all-purpose flour
1 teaspoon baking powder
1 teaspoon soda
1/4 teaspoon salt

1 teaspoon ground cinnamon
1-1/2 cups sugar
1/2 cup shortening or butter
2 eggs
1 cup finely chopped pecans
1 teaspoon vanilla extract

A moist bread good for breakfast with cream cheese or used as sandwiches with cream cheese filling for a luncheon. Place peaches and 6 tablespoons sugar in container of electric blender; process until pureed (should yield about 2-1/4 cups). Combine flour, baking powder, soda, salt, and cinnamon; set aside. Cream shortening; gradually add sugar, beating well. Add eggs, one at a time, beating well after each addition. Alternately add dry ingredients and peach puree to creamed mixture, beginning and ending with dry ingredients. Stir in chopped nuts and vanilla. Pour batter into greased, floured 9x5x3" loafpan. Bake at 350 degrees for 1 hour or until toothpick inserted in center comes out clean. Cool in pan 10 minutes; remove from pan and cool completely.

IRISH SODA BREAD

Excellent served with New England boiled dinner, Irish beef brisket or sliced and spread with hot mustard for ham sandwiches.

1-1/2 cups unsifted all-purpose
    flour
3 cups unsifted whole wheat
    flour
1-1/2 teaspoons baking powder
1-1/2 teaspoons baking soda

1 teaspoon salt
3 Tablespoons sugar
1 Tablespoon caraway seeds
1 cup dark seedless raisins,
    separated
2-1/4 cups buttermilk

Combine both flours; measure out 4 cups of the mixture and retain remainder. Add 4 cups flour to baking powder, soda, salt, sugar, and caraway seeds. Stir in raisins. Add buttermilk all at once and stir with fork. Using flour from remaining mixture, flour a kneading surface well and knead dough for 5 minutes (it usually takes all of the leftover flour to get a good consistency). Grease and flour the center of a cookie sheet; form dough into ball and place on cookie sheet. Cut an "X" into top of ball 1/2" deep with a sharp knife. Bake at 375 degrees for 45 to 55 minutes or until it sounds hollow when tapped on bottom. (Loaf usually spreads to about 12" diameter.)

NOTE: Irish Soda Bread was first brought to New England in the 1800's by the Irish settlers. Irish Soda Bread has become a popular St. Patrick's Day delight. It is a cross between a biscuit and a coffee cake.

LEMON BREAD

A marvelously fresh-tasting light bread. It's even good as a dessert or toasted for breakfast. Freezes beautifully.

1 cup sugar
1/3 cup butter, melted
1 teaspoon lemon extract
1/4 cup fresh lemon juice
2 eggs
1-1/2 cups all-purpose flour, unsifted
1 teaspoon baking powder

1 teaspoon salt
1/2 cup milk
grated rind of 1 large lemon
1/2 cup chopped pecans
Topping:
1/2 cup powdered sugar
1/4 cup fresh lemon juice

At least 24 hours before serving, preheat oven to 350 degrees. Combine sugar, butter, lemon extract and juice. Beat in eggs, one at a time, until smooth. Sift dry ingredients and stir in alternately with milk. Add lemon rind and pecans. Pour into buttered 8" loaf pan and bake for 1 hour or until toothpick inserted in center comes out clean. Dissolve powdered sugar in lemon juice over low heat. Remove bread from oven, pierce top in several places with sharp knife blade or thin fork tines. Pour on topping. Cook in pan 1 hour. Remove from pan, wrap in foil, and allow to stand 24 hours before cutting. Will keep 2 to 3 months in refrigerator.

BOURBON PECAN BREAD

A lovely gift bread, similar to pound cake. Makes two loaves, one for the baker and one to use as a gift to a hostess or friend.

3/4 cup raisins
1/3 cup bourbon
1-1/4 sticks butter/margarine, softened
6 eggs, separated

1-1/2 cups sugar
2-1/4 cups flour
1-1/4 teaspoons vanilla
1 cup coarsely broken pecans

Soak raisins in bourbon for 2 hours; drain, reserving bourbon. If necessary add enough bourbon to make 1/3 cup. Generously grease two 8-1/2x4-1/2x3" loaf pans; line bottoms with greased waxed paper. Preheat oven to 350 degrees. Cream butter and 1/2 cup sugar until fluffy. Add egg yolks, one at a time, beating well. Add flour in thirds, alternating with bourbon, and mix until blended. Stir in raisins, vanilla, and pecans. In a large bowl with clean beaters, beat egg whites until soft peaks form when beater is raised; gradually beat in remaining cup of sugar and beat until stiff. Gently fold egg whites into batter. Turn batter into prepared loafpans and bake for 1 hour or until done. Makes 2 loaves.

ORANGE NUT BREAD

Chunks of homemade orange-peel preserves flavor this bread; leftover preserves are superb with toast or muffins.

2-1/4 cups all-purpose flour
3/4 cup granulated sugar
1 Tablespoon fresh-grated orange rind
2-1/4 teaspoons baking powder
3/4 teaspoon salt
1/4 teaspoon baking soda
1 cup drained orange-peel preserves, finely chopped

3/4 cup mixed candied fruit
2 Tablespoons solid vegetable shortening (at room temperature)
3/4 cup plus 2 Tablespoons freshly squeezed orange juice
1 large egg
1 cup chopped walnuts or pecans

Twenty-four hours ahead of serving, grease and flour a 9x5x3" loafpan. Heat oven to 350 degrees. In large bowl, mix flour, sugar, orange rind, baking powder, salt and baking soda. Add preserves and candied fruit and toss until thoroughly coated with flour mixture. Add shortening, 3/4 cup orange juice, and egg; stir until all ingredients are moistened. If batter is too thick, stir in remaining 2 tablespoons orange juice. Stir in nuts and spoon batter evenly into prepared pan. Bake 1 hour or until cake tester inserted in center of pan comes out clean. Put pan on wire rack to cool for 5 minutes. Turn cake out onto rack. When completely cool, wrap in aluminum foil and allow to stand overnight at room temperature.

STRAWBERRY NUT BREAD

1 cup butter
1/4 teaspoon lemon extract
1-1/2 cups sugar
1 teaspoon vanilla
1/4 teaspoon lemon extract
4 eggs
3 cups sifted plain flour
1 teaspoon salt
1/2 teaspoon baking soda

1 teaspoon cream of tartar
1 cup strawberry preserves
1/2 cup sour cream
1 cup walnuts/pecans
Strawberry Butter:
10-ounce package frozen strawberries
1 cup softened butter
1 cup sifted confectioners sugar

Cream butter, lemon extract, sugar, vanilla and lemon extract together until fluffy. Add eggs one at a time and beat after each addition. Sift flour, salt, baking soda and cream of tartar together in separate bowl. Combine strawberry preserves, sour cream, and pecans in separate bowl. Alternately add dry ingredients and preserves mixture to creamed ingredients. Grease and flour two loafpans. Divide batter between pans and bake 50 to 55 minutes at 350 degrees or until loaves test done. Cool 10 minutes in pans; turn out and serve with butter or strawberry butter.

To make strawberry butter, combine ingredients in blender container; cover and blend until completely smooth. Makes 2-1/2 cups. Serve on warm strawberry bread.

ZUCCHINI BREAD

4 eggs
2 cups sugar
1 cup vegetable oil
3-1/2 cups all-purpose flour
1-1/2 teaspoons baking powder
1-1/2 teaspoons baking soda
2 teaspoons cinnamon
1 teaspoon salt
1 cup chopped pecans
2 cups grated zucchini, skin and all

2 teaspoons vanilla
1 cup white or dark raisins
1 cup crushed pineapple,
  drained, or 2 Tablespoons
  grated lemon peel
1 Tablespoon lemon juice
1 cup chopped walnuts/pecans
  may be substituted for
  raisins and pineapple

Prepare zucchini and set aside. Rinse and drain raisins and mix with 2 tablespoons flour. Sift remaining flour with soda, salt, baking powder, and cinnamon. Beat eggs until light and fluffy. Gradually add sugar and oil. Blend in dry ingredients, adding alternately with grated zucchini. When thoroughly blended, stir in raisins, pineapple, and nuts (or raisins, lemon peel, and nuts). Add flavorings. Pour into two greased, floured 9x5x3" loafpans. Bake at 350 degrees for 55 minutes or until top springs back when lightly touched. Cool in pans about 10 minutes before turning out on wire racks to cool. Freezes well.

SOURDOUGH

The story goes that sourdough, or fermented dough baked without yeast, came to San Francisco along with the '49ers during the Gold Rush. The miners brought their sourdough starter with them along with Mexican tools and mining methods. When gold made the area rich, along came the European immigrants and fine bakers. One was Isadore Boudin who in 1849 established the first sourdough bakery, the French Bakery, on what is now Grant Avenue in San Francisco.

Sourdough was a very important part of a miner's life. The Forty-Niners toted their containers of sourdough starter from claim site to claim site. At night, the miner would protect his sourdough from the temperatures by curling up with it in his bedroll.

Sourdough is much older than the American West, however. It is thought that the Egyptians 5,000 years ago discovered the secret of making sourdough bread. It is said that an Egyptian noticed some flour he had left out in the open had become wet and bubbles had formed. When he used it to bake bread, the loaf had a light texture and a tangy taste.

We can quickly figure out that airborne yeast or the kind of bacteria which forms in sour milk fell into the open container of flour and water. This is precisely what is called a sourdough starter, flour, water, and micro-organisms are the essential ingredients for a starter.

(Continued)

There are three ways to obtain a starter. You can mix ingredients together and make your own, you can purchase a starter mix from health food stores, or you can receive a gift of starter from a friend or family.

Sourdough feeds on the flour and water and it grows and multiplies until it reaches a point of stabilizing. While it grows, it produces carbon dioxide gas, and this gas is what is trapped in the dough and causes the bread to rise.

The micro-organisms also convert carbohydrates in the wheat kernel into a clear yellow liquid called hooch which collects on the top of the starter. This is alcoholic, and Alaskan Indians and miners used to drink it. But hooch is not recommended for this purpose.

If at any time the layer of hooch gets more than 1/4" of the total starter, stir well and throw half of the starter away.

Replenish with enough flour and water mixed together to arrive at the original consistency and volume. Your starter, once stabilized, should be stored on the bottom shelf of your refrigerator. It is most active at 85 degrees, and as the temperature drops it becomes less active. However, should you store it above 85 degrees, it runs the risk of dying. Temperatures around 95 degrees and above will kill it.

If you wish your starter to provide a more robust twang to baked goods, simply let it rest longer than the recommended proofing period, or you can store it on a cool cupboard shelf instead of the refrigerator. For a milder flavor, shorten the proofing period or increase the amount of sugar called for in the recipe by 1 tablespoon.

Not planning to use your starter for awhile? Just freeze it, but let it slowly come to room temperature before baking (allow it to thaw in the refrigerator).

Gold miners used to keep a crock of sourdough with them, and as the years passed some starters were valued quite highly and were passed down through generations. From your basic starter you can create a batter which is made into whatever bread product you like, pancakes, biscuits, loaf bread, or cakes.

BEA'S SOURDOUGH BREAD

1 cup sourdough starter
1/2 cup warm water
1 package yeast

4 Tablespoons oil
2-1/2 to 3 cups flour (self-rising)
dash of salt

Mix dough and allow to rise, covered, for 1-1/2 hours. Work dough until very firm. Makes two large or four small loaves. Allow to rise in a warm place until dough reaches top of pans. Shape into loaves and bake at 350 degrees for 20 to 30 minutes.

SOURDOUGH STARTER

1 package active dry yeast
1/2 cup warm water
2 cups warm water

2 cups flour, sifted
1 Tablespoon sugar

Dissolve yeast in 1/2 cup warm water in a large bowl; let stand for 10 minutes. Stir in remaining ingredients with a wooden spoon until smooth. Cover loosely and let stand at room temperature for 5 to 10 days; stir down 2 to 3 times a day. Time to ferment will depend on the room temperature. When ready, starter will have a yeasty sourdough smell. Place in a covered container and refrigerate until ready to use. Do not use a metal container to store. Use a wooden or plastic spoon to stir. Makes 2 cups starter.

To Keep Starter Going:
1 cup sourdough starter
3/4 cup water

3/4 cup flour
1 teaspoon sugar

Stir all ingredients together and allow to stand at room temperature until bubbly and well fermented (at least 1 day). Refrigerate. If not used within 10 days, stir in a teaspoon of sugar.

NOTE: You can keep a small portion of the starter, almost indefinitely in a container in the refrigerator. It will save time the next time you decide to bake. It was sourdough that won the West. In the Gold Rush days, a sour dough starter was a precious resource, passed from friend to friend and family to family. A special gift to a new bride was a jar of sourdough starter.

SAN FRANCISCO SOURDOUGH BREAD

1 cup flour
1 cup water
1 Tablespoon sugar
1 cake or package yeast
1-1/2 cups warm water

6 cups flour
2 teaspoons sugar
1/2 teaspoon baking soda
1/2 teaspoon salt

If you have no starter or can not get one from a friend, use the first four ingredients to make one. Combine 1 cup flour, 1 cup water, 1 tablespoon sugar and yeast in a small bowl. Let stand in a warm place 2-3 days until fermented.
To make the bread:

Combine starter with 1-1/2 cups warm water, 4 cups flour, 1/2 teaspoon salt and remaining 2 teaspoons sugar. Stir vigorously for 3 minutes. Place in a greased bowl, cover, let rise until dough has doubled in size. In another bowl, mix baking soda and 1 cup of flour; stir into risen dough. Place dough on floured surface and work remaining 1 cup flour in until dough is smooth. Divide dough in half; shape into 2 oblong loaves. Place on a lightly greased cookie sheet that has been sprinkled lightly with white cornmeal. Let rise until loaves have doubled. Brush with water; score tops diagonally with a sharp knife. Bake at 400 degrees for 40 to 45 minutes.

"HERMAN" STARTER

The flavor of this starter evolves as it ages — mildly sweet when young, more like sourdough when older. No one seems to know exactly how the "Herman" starter got its name. What is "Herman"? It's a cultured dough you add to new dough to give it distinctive flavor and texture it wouldn't otherwise have.

CARE AND FEEDING OF "HERMAN": Unlike other starters that require constant feeding, stirring and using, this one doesn't make a slave of you. "Herman" only needs replenishing after you use it (if not used within 14 days, simply put "Herman" in the freezer until you are ready to bake). Immediately after use, feed "Herman" as follows: stir or whisk in 1 cup flour, 1 cup milk, and 1/2 cup sugar (mixture need not be completely smooth). Wait 24 hours before freezing again. Cover tightly to freeze. Thaw "Herman" at room temperature until bubbly before reusing, as freezing slows fermentation.

2 cups flour	**1 teaspoon salt**
3 Tablespoons sugar	**2 cups warm (105 to 115 degree)**
1 envelope active dry yeast	**water**

In a large bowl, mix flour, sugar, yeast, and salt. Gradually stir in water; beat or whisk until smooth. Cover with towel and set in warm (80 to 85 degree) draft-free place, the kitchen or other warm room in summer, or in cold weather on top of insulated furnace or radiator (on a buffer such as a folded heavy towel or pillow). Stir two or three times a day for about 3 days or until starter is bubbly and produces a yeasty aroma. Transfer to larger bowl, large jar, or plastic container. Cover partially (tilt lid or punch holes in plastic cover); refrigerate. Makes about 1-1/2 to 2 cups starter, depending on thickness. Because of room conditions, "Herman's" age, or other variables, starter can be creamy or as thick as dough.

Care of Sourdough Starter or "Herman Starter"

1. Never store sourdough starters in metal. Crockery is ideal. You may use a refrigerator container.
2. Keep starter refrigerated. It will keep indefinitely if used regularly. Some cooks have starters that have been in use for close to 100 years.
3. When you replenish the starter, let it stand at room temperature until it bubbles, then refrigerate.
4. If you do not use the starter at least once a week or every 10 days, freshen it by pouring off half the starter and adding equal amount of warm water and flour or, in case of some starters, milk, flour and sugar.
5. Never cap a jar of starter tightly. Allow room for the starter to expand and "work".
6. Never add leftover batter to any starter recipes.
7. Let starter reach room temperature before using.
8. Starter recipes are interchangeable.
9. The older the starter the better the results will be. It improves with age.
10. If you are using a bread recipe that is leavened only with a starter, it is all right to "fudge" a bit. Simply add an envelope of active dry yeast dissolved in 1/4 cup of warm water to the sponge. The recipe will require a bit more flour. You can work this out as you go along.

NOTE: Sourdough bread recipes may be used for Herman also.

"HERMAN" COFFEE CAKE

1 cup flour
1/2 cup sugar
1 teaspoon baking powder
1/4 teaspoon baking soda
1/4 teaspoon salt
1 cup "Herman" starter
1/3 cup oil
1 egg

1/2 cup raisins
1/4 cup chopped nuts
Topping:
1/2 cup packed brown sugar
1-1/2 teaspoons flour
1-1/2 teaspoons cinnamon
1-1/2 teaspoons granulated sugar
2 Tablespoons butter/margarine

Prepare topping by mixing brown granulated sugar. Cut in butter, warmed to room temperature, until crumbly. Set aside.

Combine flour, sugar, baking powder, baking soda and salt in a large bowl. Add starter, oil, egg, raisins, and nuts; stir to mix well. Spread in greased, floured 8" or 9" square pan; sprinkle with topping. Bake in preheated 350 degree oven for 30 to 35 minutes or until browned and pick inserted in center comes out clean. Cool slightly in pan on rack, then cut in squares. Best served warm. Makes 9 servings.

NOTE: Original "Herman" or "Friendship" coffee cake recipe was doubled and baked in a 13x9x2" pan for 45 minutes.

Per serving, using walnuts: 347 calories, 4 grams protein, 53 grams carbohydrate, 13 grams fat, 36 milligrams cholesterol (using butter) or 28 milligrams cholesterol (using margarine), 279 milligrams sodium.

ANADAMA BREAD

1 cup self-rising meal
1 cup milk, scalded
1 cup boiling water
3 Tablespoons shortening

5 cups plain flour
1/2 cup molasses
2 packages dry yeast
1/2 cup lukewarm water

An old wives tale relates how a sea captain had a very lazy wife who hated to cook. Every night the poor cold captain came home only to have her set before him a big bowl of cornmeal mush. One night when he was extremely tired, he flew into a rage upon seeing the mush yet again. "Ana," he shouted, "damn, 'ave had enough of this!" He rushed into the kitchen and started throwing other ingredients into the mush. Then he popped it into the oven and behold! Out came a delicious bread. The recipe has since been improved, but it is still known as Ana-dam-a bread.

Stir cornmeal slowly into hot milk and water. Add shortening and molasses. Let stand until lukewarm. Sprinkle yeast in lukewarm water and stir until dissolved. Alternately stir yeast water and flour into cornmeal mixture. Turn out on lightly floured board and knead until smooth and elastic, using more flour to control stickiness. Place in greased bowl, turn once to bring greased side up. Cover and allow to rise in warm place until doubled in bulk. Knead down and divide dough into two equal parts. Shape each part into a loaf. Place in loaf pans and allow to rise again. Bake at 375 degrees for 45 to 50 minutes. This can also be baked in small cans or one-pound coffee can.

BATTER BREAD — SALLY LUNN

Early settlers brought this recipe with them from England. It is legendarily attributed to the English girl who sold bread on the street calling "Sol et Lune" from the French for sun and moon because the tops of the buns were golden and the bottoms white. In the colonies, it became "Sally Lunn," a bread baked in a mold rather than as buns. In some parts of the country it is a breakfast favorite. Good Sally Lunn must be baked like a cake and is as good toasted the day after it is baked as when it is fresh from the oven. Serve hot and spread with butter or margarine or toast slices and serve with jelly or jam.

BASIC SALLY LUNN BREAD

1 package dry yeast	2 eggs
1/4 cup warm water	1 teaspoon salt
2 Tablespoons soft butter	3-1/2 cups flour
1/2 cup sugar	1 cup warm milk

Soften yeast in warm water. Cream butter and sugar in a mixing bowl; beat in eggs and salt, stir in 1-1/2 cups flour, and beat vigorously. Cover and let rise in a warm place until doubled in bulk (about 1 hour). Stir down batter and spoon evenly into greased tube or bundt pan. Cover and allow to rise again until doubled (30 to 45 minutes). Bake in preheated 350 degree oven for 10 minutes; increase temperature to 375 degrees and continue baking for another 20 minutes. Remove from pan.

CINNAMON BUTTER

1 stick butter, softened	1 teaspoon ground cinnamon
2/3 cup honey	1/4 teaspoon vanilla
pinch of salt	

Beat butter in a mixer; slowly add honey, salt, cinnamon and vanilla. Use on pancakes, toast, waffles, doughnuts, etc. Keeps in refrigerator up to 3 weeks.

STRAWBERRY BUTTER

1/4 cup (1/2 stick) butter, at room temperature	1/4 cup strawberries, crushed
1-1/4 cups powdered sugar	1/2 teaspoon vanilla
	pinch of salt

Cream butter with sugar in medium bowl. Blend in strawberries, vanilla, and salt. Cover and refrigerate at least 2 hours. Bring to room temperature before serving.

LEMON SALLY LUNN BREAD

The flavor of this tall, ring-shaped loaf is enhanced with the tartness of grated lemon peel and the rich toasty flavor of crunchy pecans which cover the bread. Attractive enough for any occasion, the mild flavor makes an ideal complement to lunch and dinner menus.

2 Tablespoons vegetable shortening	1 package active dry yeast
3/4 cup chopped pecans	1/4 cup warm water
3/4 cup scalded milk	3 cups all-purpose flour
2/3 cup butter/margarine, melted	3/4 cup enriched cornmeal
1/4 cup sugar	3 eggs
1 teaspoon salt	1 Tablespoon grated lemon peel

Generously grease 9-cup ring mold or 9-cup bundt pan with shortening; coat pan with nuts. Combine milk, butter, sugar and salt in large mixing bowl, stirring until butter melts; cool about 5 minutes or until lukewarm. Dissolve yeast in warm water. Add dissolved yeast, 2 cups flour, cornmeal, eggs and lemon peel to lukewarm milk mixture, mixing at low speed with electric mixer about 30 seconds or until ingredients are blended. Continue mixing at medium speed 2 to 3 minutes or until smooth; stir in remaining flour, mixing well. Cover; let rise in warm place 1 to 1-1/2 hours or until doubled in size. Stir down batter; spoon evenly into prepared pan. Let rise in warm place about 45 minutes or until top of batter is even with top edge of pan. Bake at 350 degrees for 45 to 50 minutes or until golden brown. Loosen edges of bread from sides of pan; remove from pan and cool 10 minutes before slicing. Serve hot with butter and jam if desired. Makes 1 loaf.

EASTER BREAD

1/2 cup sugar	4 cups flour
1/4 pound butter/margarine	1 teaspoon grated lemon rind
1 whole egg	1 teaspoon salt
2 egg yolks	3/4 cup raisins
1 cup scalded milk, cooled	1 package dry yeast

Dissolve 1 package dry yeast in 1/4 cup lukewarm water. Cream butter, add sugar and eggs; mix well. Mix in lemon rind and salt. Sift in flour, then add the yeast mixture and milk all at one time and mix with a spoon until dough will not cling to spoon. Lastly, work in raisins and let dough rise until double in size. Then turn out on floured board and knead. Form round loaf or make a twist by sectioning dough into three pieces and braiding to form loaf. Grease pans. Bake at 350 degrees for about 30 minutes or until nicely browned.

CINNAMON ROLLS DIPPED IN BUTTER

Easy to make and great for a crowd!

2-3/4 to 3-1/2 cups unsifted flour, divided
1/3 cup sugar
1 teaspoon salt
1 package active dry yeast
3/4 cup milk
1/4 cup water
5 Tablespoons butter
3 eggs, at room temperature
1/4 cup sugar
3/4 teaspoon cinnamon
2 Tablespoons butter, melted

In a large mixing bowl, thoroughly stir 1 cup flour, 1/3 cup sugar, salt and undissolved yeast together. Heat milk, water, and 5 tablespoons butter in a saucepan over low heat until liquids are very warm (120 to 130 degrees); butter does not need to melt. Gradually add to dry ingredients and beat 2 minutes at medium speed of electric mixer, scraping bowl occasionally. Add eggs and 1/2 cup flour. Beat at high speed another 2 minutes, scraping bowl occasionally. Stir in enough additional flour to make a stiff batter. Cover and allow to rise in a warm, draft-free place until doubled (about 50 minutes). Stir batter down. Grease 2-1/2x1-1/4" muffin pans and fill about half full with batter. Cover and allow to rise again until doubled (about 45 minutes). Bake in preheated 375 degree oven for 25 minutes.

Stir remaining 1/4 cup sugar and cinnamon together. Remove rolls from pans; dip rolls in melted butter then in sugar mixture. Serve warm. Makes 18 rolls.

DILL BREAD

1 package dry yeast
1/4 cup warm water
1 cup cottage cheese, small curd
    or 1 cup sour cream
2 Tablespoons sugar
1 Tablespoon butter
1 teaspoon salt
1 Tablespoon instant onion
    flakes or 2 Tablespoons
    minced onion
2 teaspoons dill seed
1/4 teaspoon soda
1 egg, slightly beaten
2-1/4 cups flour
coarse salt, if desired to add to
    top of loaf, after baking

Soften yeast in warm water. Combine cottage cheese (heat to lukewarm), sugar, butter, salt, onion, dill seed, soda, egg, and softened yeast. Add flour to form a stiff dough, beating well after each addition. Cover and let rise in a warm place until light and double in size (50 to 60 minutes). Stir dough down. Dough is sticky, so oil hands before handling dough. Turn into a well-greased 8" round casserole and let rise 30 to 40 minutes. Brush with soft butter and sprinkle with salt. Bake at 350 degrees for 40 to 50 minutes. Good with slices of cold ham. Makes one round 8" loaf.

CARDAMOM CHRISTMAS BREAD

Pungent cardamom, one of Scandinavia's contributions to the flavor of Christmas, gives distinctive flavor to this fruit and nut filled bread.

5-1/2 cups all-purpose flour	1 teaspoon salt
2 envelopes active dry yeast	1-1/2 teaspoons ground cardamom
1/2 cup milk	3 eggs
1/2 cup water	1 cup raisins
1/2 cup (1 stick) butter/margarine	1 cup candied citron
1/3 cup sugar	1 cup slivered almonds

Dissolve dry yeast and 1/2 teaspoon sugar in 1/2 cup warm water. Measure 2 cups flour into large bowl of electric mixer; stir in yeast mixture. Heat milk, butter, remaining sugar, salt, and cardamom in a small saucepan until warm; add warm liquid to flour-yeast mixture and beat at medium speed of electric mixer for 2 minutes (300 strokes with a wooden spoon by hand). Add eggs and beat until well blended.

Add 1 more cup flour and beat 3 minutes at medium speed of electric mixer or 300 strokes by hand. Stir in raisins, citron and half the almonds. Add remaining flour to make a stiff dough. Turn dough out onto lightly floured pastry cloth or board. Knead 8 to 10 minutes, or until dough is soft. Turn into a large greased bowl, turning to coat all sides. Allow to rise in warm place, away from drafts, 1-1/2 hours or until double in bulk.

Punch down dough and let rest 10 minutes. Divide dough in half; then divide each half into 3 equal pieces. Roll each piece into a 15" strip. Weave 3 strips into a braid on a greased large cookie sheet, folding ends under. Brush with melted butter/margarine. Repeat shaping with remaining dough.

Allow to rise in a warm, draft-free place for 45 minutes or until double. Sprinkle with remaining almonds. Bake in 350 degree oven 35 to 40 minutes, or until golden brown. Cool on cookie sheet on wire rack 10 minutes. Loosen braids from cookie sheet with a sharp knife. Cool completely.

GERMAN CHRISTMAS STOLLEN

On Christmas Eve, breads of many kinds appear on festive tables. Such breads are also often given as gifts. All contain white flour, yeast, milk, butter, eggs, and sugar. The spices, dried fruits and candied peels which make the breads so good to eat represent the gifts which the Wise Men brought from the East to Bethlehem. It is the flavorings, toppings and fillings that make the difference from country to country.

The shapes of the breads are numerous. German Stollen is baked in a bread pan, its shape is symbolic of the Infant Jesus wrapped in swaddling clothes.

(Continued)

STOLLEN, like our traditional fruit cake, improves with age. It will keep 4 to 5 months properly wrapped with hot butter which is brushed on top of freshly baked loaf to seal in freshness. The actual origin of stollen, like so many food traditions, is lost in the aromatic haze of history.

The old German folk tale of the First Stollen tells about the First Christmas when shepherds, seeing the Star in the East, left their primitive dirt ovens where simple loaves of dough were baking to rush to where the Savior was born. Upon return, they expected to find burned, ruined loaves. Instead the loaves were perfect, as if blessed by the Christ child. From then on each Christ's birthday is celebrated with the stollen loaf, which has been added to through the years to make a sweet pastry traditionally served with coffee and/or sweet wine.

GERMAN CHRISTMAS STOLLEN

1-1/4 cups diced, mixed candied
   fruit
1 cup seedless raisins
1/2 cup candied cherries, chopped
1/4 cup brandy
2 packages yeast
1/2 cup honey
1/2 cup warm milk
1 cup sour cream at room
   temperature

2 teaspoons lemon juice
2 teaspoons vanilla
1 teaspoon salt
3 eggs, lightly beaten
1-1/2 cups butter
6 to 7 cups flour
1/2 cup melted butter
1 cup blanched, slivered almonds
1 Tablespoon lemon rind
confectioners sugar

Combine fruits and raisins; pour brandy over and marinate overnight. Mix yeast with warm milk and honey. Add sour cream, salt, lemon juice and vanilla. Stir in eggs, 1-1/2 cups butter and lemon rind. Add flour to make medium dough. Knead, adding enough flour to make dough smooth and elastic. Cover, greased; allow to rise. Knead fruits and almonds into dough just until evenly distributed. You may need to add more flour if dough becomes sticky. Cut dough in half. Roll each piece out to 9x12", folding each over like a parker house roll. Press edges together. Brush with melted butter, let rise until nearly double. Bake at 375 degrees about 45 minutes, covering last 15 to 20 minutes preventing edges from burning. Brush again with butter. Cool. Sift confectioners sugar over top of stollen or decorate. Wrap in foil and refrigerate or freeze. Will keep months in refrigerator. The sour cream makes the stollen richer, more moist and longer-keeping. Makes 2 large stollens.

HOME BAKED WHITE BREAD

So delicious and easy it's unbelievable!

8 cups all-purpose flour, divided
3 Tablespoons plus 1/2 teaspoon sugar, divided
2 packages (1/4 ounce each) dry yeast

2 cups milk
4 Tablespoons butter or margarine, divided
1 Tablespoon salt

Grease two 9x5" loaf pans; grease large bowl; set aside. Into another large mixing bowl, place 4 cups of flour, 3 tablespoons of sugar and the salt; set aside.

In a small bowl, stir together yeast, 1/2 teaspoon sugar and 3/4 cup of warm water; (105 to 115 degrees), set aside for 5 minutes until foamy and all the yeast is dissolved.

In a small saucepan over low heat, heat milk and 3 tablespoons butter until very warm (120 to 130 degrees). (Butter or margarine does not need to melt).

Into the bowl with flour mixture, with electric mixer at low speed, gradually beat yeast and milk mixtures into dry ingredients until well-blended. With wooden spoon, stir in remaining 3-1/2 to 4 cups flour until soft dough forms.

On a lightly floured surface, with hands floured, knead dough until smooth and elastic, about 10 minutes, kneading in remaining 1/2 cup flour if necessary to prevent sticking. Shape dough into a ball and place in greased bowl, turning dough to coat. Cover with a clean dish towel; let rise in a warm place until it is doubled, about 1 hour.

Punch down dough, divide dough in half, shape into 9" loaves, place into prepared pans, cover and let rise in a warm place until doubled, about 1 hour.

Preheat oven to 425 degrees. Melt the remaining 1 tablespoon of butter and brush on top of loaves. Place loaves in oven and bake 25 to 30 minutes, until browned and sound hollow when tapped on bottom. Remove from oven and place pans to cool on rack.

Delicious served warm with butter, jelly or jam or preserves!

Preparation time:

Mixing time 20 minutes; Rising time 2 hours; Baking time 30 minutes. Ready to serve in 3-1/2 hours!

HOT CROSS BUNS

Hot cross buns, warm and raisin-filled, remind us of Easter. Their earliest beginning was in Greek and Roman times, and the currant-filled buns symbolized the sun, bisected by a cross into four seasons. The buns bearing the cross later became associated with Easter and were sold only on Good Friday. Folk superstition from the Middle Ages embued rare virtues to hot cross buns baked and eaten on Good Friday; their distinctive cross would supposedly ward off any evil (in those days, Good Friday was considered the Devil's day and this very unlucky!).

(Continued)

Good Friday bread hung over the chimney place insured that all bread baked thereafter would be perfect. Good friends could preserve their friendship by breaking their bread within the doors of the Church on Good Friday and keeping the halves. Hot cross buns baked on this day were thought to have magical powers that would ease stomach problems, avoid shipwrecks, and generally drive away bad luck.

In England long ago on Good Friday morning, English wives were doing one of two things, either rushing around the kitchen baking hot cross buns, or looking for a street vendor chanting, "One a penny, two a penny, hot cross buns! If you have no daughters, give them to your sons."

HOT CROSS BUNS

1 cup milk	1 cup currants or raisins
1/2 cup granulated sugar	1/2 cup chopped mixed candied
1/2 teaspoon salt	fruit
1/2 cup butter/margarine	2 Tablespoons melted
1/2 cup warm water (105 to 115	butter/margarine
degrees)	Icing:
1 package active dry yeast	1-1/2 cups confectioners sugar,
2 eggs	sifted before measuring
5-1/4 cups unsifted all-purpose	1-1/2 Tablespoons milk
flour	

In small saucepan, heat milk just until bubbles form around edge of pan; remove from heat. Add granulated sugar, salt, and 1/2 cup butter, stirring until butter is melted. Cool to lukewarm (a drop sprinkled on wrist will not feel warm).

If possible, check temperature of warm water with thermometer. Sprinkle yeast over water in large bowl, stirring until dissolved. Stir in milk mixture. Add eggs and 2 cups flour; beat with electric beater until dough is smooth. Add remaining flour, currants, and candied fruit with wooden spoon; mix with hand until dough leaves side of bowl.

Place in lightly greased large bowl, turning to bring up greased side. Cover with towels and allow to rise in a warm draft-free place (85 degrees) until double in volume (about 1-1/2 hours).

To shape, turn dough onto lightly floured pastry cloth and, using palms of hands, shape dough into a roll 15" long. Cut roll crosswise into 15 pieces; with fingertips, shape each piece into a ball (tuck edges underneath to make a smooth top).

Arrange 1/2" apart in greased 13x9x2" baking pan. Cover with towel and let rise again until double in bulk (about 1-1/2 hours).

(Continued)

Preheat oven to 375 degrees. Carefully cut a cross 1/4" deep on top of each bun, using a very sharp knife or razor blade. Brush with melted butter and bake 25 to 30 minutes, or until golden brown.

Remove rolls to rack to cool for 10 minutes. Make icing by combining confectioners sugar and milk. With tip of spoon or pastry tube with #10 tip, drizzle a cross on each bun. Makes 15.

MORAVIAN SUGAR CAKE

The Moravians, a pious Germanic people who founded Salem, North Carolina, in 1766, were gifted cooks. An Easter favorite, still baked in the giant wood-fired oven in Old Salem's restored bakery, is Moravian Sugar Cake, a spongy, light coffee cake with pools of cream, brown sugar and cinnamon on top.

1/2 pound potatoes, peeled
1 package active dry yeast
1/4 cup warm water
3/4 cup lightly salted butter and
   lard, mixed
1 cup granulated sugar minus
   one Tablespoon
2 large eggs
1 cup warm potato water

2 teaspoons salt
5 to 7 cups all-purpose flour
2 Tablespoons lightly salted
   butter, cut up
1 cup dark brown sugar, firmly
   packed to measure
1 teaspoon ground cinnamon
1/2 cup light cream

Cook potatoes in water to cover. Drain when tender, reserving 1 cup water. Mash potatoes and measure 1 cup to use in recipe. Mix yeast with the 1/4 cup warm water and let stand 2 minutes. In a large bowl, beat 3/4 cup butter and lard with granulated sugar until creamy; beat in eggs one at a time. Mix in mashed potatoes, reserved potato water, salt and yeast mixture. Gradually add flour to make soft, sticky dough. Cover bowl with damp towel, let rise in warm place until double in bulk, 2 to 3 hours. Grease two 13x9x2" pans. Punch down dough and pat half in each of prepared pans. Cover with damp towel; let rise again until double in volume–1-1/2 hours. Heat oven to 400 degrees; with a sharp knife, punch small holes in top dough and insert bits of butter. Sprinkle with brown sugar and cinnamon. Dribble cream over top. Bake 20 to 25 minutes, or until brown. Let cool in pan. Cake reheats well. Makes 2.

LEMON CHEESE BABKA

(This will become a family favorite. Freeze one for later.)

1 envelope active dry yeast
1/4 cup sugar
1/4 cup very warm water
3-1/2 to 4 cups unsifted
    all-purpose flour
3/4 teaspoon salt
2 teaspoons grated lemon rind
2 eggs plus 2 egg yolks
1/3 cup warm milk
6 Tablespoons (3/4) stick
    softened butter/margarine
Cheese Filling:
8 ounces cream cheese

1/2 cup cottage cheese
1 egg yolk
1/4 cup sugar
1 teaspoon grated lemon rind
Crumb Topping:
1/3 cup chopped nuts
3 Tablespoons flour
3 Tablespoons butter, softened
3 Tablespoons sugar
1/4 teaspoon ground cinnamon
1/2 cup raisins
10X confectioners sugar

Sprinkle yeast and 1/2 teaspoon of the sugar over very warm water (should feel comfortably warm when dropped on wrist) in a 1-cup measure and stir to dissolve. Let stand until bubbly, about 10 minutes.

Combine 2 cups flour, salt, lemon rind and remaining sugar in large bowl; make a well in the middle. Beat eggs and egg yolks in a small bowl just enough to mix. Pour eggs, yeast mixture and warm milk into well, then stir liquids into flour until smooth. Beat well.

Add softened butter gradually, beating well. Stir in 1 more cup of flour. Beat until dough leaves side of bowl. Turn dough onto lightly floured surface; knead until smooth and elastic (about 10 minutes). Place dough in a buttered bowl, turning to bring the buttered side up; cover and allow to rise in a warm place, away from drafts, 1-1/2 to 2 hours until doubled in volume.

While dough is rising, make Cheese Filling: beat cream cheese and cottage cheese in small bowl with electric mixer until smooth; beat in egg yolk and sugar; stir in lemon rind.

Make crumb topping: combine nuts, flour, butter, sugar, and cinnamon in small bowl. Grease two 8-1/2" layer pans.

When dough has doubled, punch down; knead in raisins; divide dough into four equal parts; press two parts into bottoms and up about 1/2" on sides of each layer pan; spread each with about 1 cup of the cheese filling.

Shape remaining dough into 8" circles; place on top of cheese filling. Press spoon handle into dough around edges to seal. Sprinkle half the crumb topping over each Babka. Let rise in warm place until dough reaches top of pans (about 1 hour).

Bake in moderate oven (350 degrees) for 40 minutes or until cakes sound hollow when tapped. Turn out onto wire rack to cool (place foil loosely over crumb topping; invert onto rack, turn right side up). Allow to cool at least 30 minutes before serving. Sprinkle with 10X sugar.

PARKER HOUSE ROLLS

Parker house rolls were developed in the kitchen of a famous old Boston hotel soon after it opened in 1855. These tender yeast rolls were called "Pocketbook" rolls because each round of dough, brushed with butter and folded before rising, resembles a small purse.

1/2 cup sugar	2 cups water
2 teaspoons salt	1 cup butter or margarine
2 packages active dry yeast	1 egg
about 6-1/2 cups all-purpose flour	

Early in the day about 3-1/2 hours before serving start to make these delicious rolls. In a large bowl, combine sugar, salt, yeast, and 2-1/4 cups flour. In a 2-quart saucepan over low heat, heat water and 1/2 cup butter or margarine until very warm (120 to 130 degrees). Butter or margarine does not need to melt completely. With mixer at low speed, gradually beat liquid into dry ingredients just until blended; beat in egg, Increase speed to medium; beat 2 minutes, occasionally scraping bowl with rubber spatula. Beat in 1 cup flour to make a thick batter. Continue beating about 2 minutes, scraping bowl often. With a wooden spoon, stir in 2-3/4 cups flour to make a soft dough.

Turn dough onto a well-floured surface and knead until smooth and elastic, about 10 minutes, working in more flour while kneading (about 1/2 cup). Shape dough into a ball and place in a greased large bowl. Turn the dough over so that the top is greased. Cover with a towel; let rise in a warm place (80 to 85 degrees), away from draft, until doubled, about 1 hour. Dough is doubled when two fingers pressed lightly into dough leaves a dent.

Punch down dough. Turn dough onto lightly floured surface; cover with a bowl or towel and let rest for about 15 minutes for easier shaping.

Grease a 17-1/4"x11-1/2" baking pan lightly with butter. In a small saucepan over low heat, melt remaining 1/2 cup butter or margarine.

On lightly floured surface with floured rolling pin, roll dough to 1/2" thickness. Cut dough into rounds with a 3" cookie cutter. Brush rounds lightly with melted butter; fold over in half. Arrange folded dough in rows in pan, each nearly touching the other. Knead trimmings together; reroll and cut until all dough has been used, making about 36 rolls. Brush tops of rolls with remaining butter. Cover pan with towel and let rise in warm place until doubled, about 40 minutes. Preheat oven to 425 degrees. Bake rolls 18 to 20 minutes until browned. Serve with plenty of butter. With the aroma of baking bread every one will come running. You may not need the rest of the meal.

POTECA

Originating in Europe, Poteca is a sour cream-yeast coffee cake filled with luscious walnuts.

1 cup dairy sour cream	4 egg yolks
1/4 cup milk	1/2 cup (1 stick) unsalted
3/4 cup sugar	butter/margarine, softened
1 teaspoon salt	1/4 cup honey, warmed
2 envelopes active dry yeast	Walnut filling:
1 teaspoon sugar	1 pound shelled walnuts
1/2 cup very warm water	4 egg whites at room temperature
5-1/2 to 6 cups sifted all-purpose	3/4 cup sugar
flour	

Combine sour cream, milk, 3/4 cup sugar and salt in a medium-size saucepan. Heat slowly, stirring constantly, just until mixture begins to bubble and sugar dissolves; cool in large bowl.

Sprinkle yeast and 1 teaspoon sugar into very warm water in a 1-cup measure ("very warm" should feel comfortably warm when dropped on wrist). Stir to dissolve. Let stand until bubbly, about 10 minutes.

Stir yeast into cooled sour cream mixture; beat in 3 cups of flour until very smooth. Cover bowl with clean towel and allow dough to rise in a warm place away from drafts for one hour or until double in bulk; beat mixture down.

Beat egg yolks in a medium-sized bowl until well blended; beat in very soft butter until smooth.

Beat egg-butter mixture and enough of the remaining flour into yeast mixture to make a soft dough. Turn out onto lightly floured surface and knead 10 minutes or until dough is smooth and elastic.

Place dough in a buttered large bowl; turn to bring buttered side up. Cover and allow to rise in a warm place, away from drafts, for 1 hour or until doubled in volume. Punch dough down, knead a few times, and allow to rest for five minutes. Chop nuts very finely (if you wish, reserve 1/4 cup for garnish). Beat eggs enough to mix; add sugar and mix well. Add walnuts to egg-sugar mixture.

Divide dough in half; roll one half on lightly floured surface to a 26x10" rectangle. Spread half the walnut filling over dough, leaving 1/4" margins. Roll up jelly roll fashion, starting with one of the short ends. Pinch to seal seam; turn ends under, pinching to enclose filling. Place seam side down on greased cookie sheet. Repeat with remaining dough. Cover both cakes and allow to rise in a warm place away from drafts for 1 hour or until almost doubled in volume.

Bake at 350 degrees for 35 minutes or until cakes are golden. Cool on wire racks. Brush cakes with warmed honey; sprinkle with chopped walnuts.

SWEET ROLLS FROM HERREN'S

1 cup milk	4 cups flour, sifted
1/4 cup butter	Cinnamon-sugar mixture:
1/4 cup sugar	2 cups sugar
1-1/2 teaspoons salt	4 Tablespoons cinnamon
2 packages yeast	1/2 to 1 cup melted butter
1/4 cup warm water	

Let milk come to a boil in heavy saucepan. Add butter, sugar and salt. Cool. Soften yeast in water and stir into first mixture. Add flour, about half at a time, and beat well. Turn out onto a floured board, allow to sit for 15 minutes, then knead until smooth.

Place dough in a buttered bowl, cover with a cloth and let rise until double in size. Roll out dough on a floured board to about 1/4" thick and cut into rough 8" squares. Work with one square at a time. Brush melted butter and sprinkle cinnamon and sugar mixture generously over entire surface. Starting at one side of square, roll up into tube. Continue rolling tube back and forth until it is 12" to 16" long. Cut tube into wheels approximately 1/2" wide and place flat in pan that has been brushed with melted butter and sprinkled thoroughly with cinnamon and sugar mixture.

NOTE: Recipe makes 60 to 80 sweet rolls, so use three or four 6 to 8" aluminum pans. This will allow you to stagger cooking during your dinner or save to bake for breakfast.

Place sweet rolls in pans so that they touch, but don't overpack. Brush tops with butter and sprinkle mixture generously over entire surface. Let stand at room temperature for one hour.

Sweet rolls are now ready for baking at 350 degrees for 18 to 20 minutes. Bake now or cover with aluminum foil and refrigerate. Allow 30 minutes to bring back to room temperature when removing from refrigerator.

NOTE: This dough, minus the cinnamon and sugar mixture, is the same that Herren's uses for Parker House rolls. Save one 8" square of dough and serve both types of rolls with dinner. Cut the 8" square into 1-1/2" pieces. Pull pieces, dip in melted butter, fold over and place in buttered pan 1/2" apart. Let stand at room temperature for one hour, then bake for 15 minutes at 350 degrees.

If you have ever been to HERREN'S in Atlanta and eaten these, you will want to make these over and over.

LOVE FEAST BUNS

The love feast or agape is a religious custom dating back to early Christian days. No love feast is complete without the symbolic breaking of bread among the congregation. The Moravians, who settled in the New World in Pennsylvania and South Carolina, celebrated this rite using traditional flat yeast buns now known as Love Feast Buns. In early times the buns were prepared in the Brothers' House in Old Salem, but in 1774 a community bakery was established because some people felt it improper for young women to go to the single Brothers' House.

2 packages active dry yeast	1 egg
1 cup warm water (105 to 115 degrees)	1/2 cup warm mashed potatoes
	1-1/2 teaspoons salt
1 cup sugar	4-1/4 to 4-3/4 cups sifted flour
1/4 cup butter	cream or melted butter
1/4 cup shortening	

Soften yeast in warm water. Cream sugar, butter, and shortening. Beat in egg, potatoes, and salt. Add softened yeast to make a soft dough.

Turn onto lightly floured board and knead until smooth and elastic. Place in a greased bowl, turning once to grease top. Cover and let rise in a warm (85 degrees) place until doubled in bulk, about 1-1/2 to 2 hours. Turn onto lightly floured board; cut into 8 or 16 equal portions and shape into balls. Place 3" apart on a greased baking sheet. Cover and let rise again until double in bulk, about 45 minutes to 1 hour. Bake in moderate oven (375 degrees) for 20 to 25 minutes for large buns, 15 minutes for medium-sized buns, or until done. Remove from oven and brush tops lightly with cream or melted butter.

BASIC SWEET BREAD

1 package active dry yeast	1/4 cup sugar
1/4 cup warm water (105 to 115 degrees)	1/2 teaspoon salt
	1 egg
1/4 cup lukewarm milk, scalded and cooled	1/4 cup shortening
	2-1/4 to 2-1/2 cups plain flour

In a mixing bowl, dissolve yeast in warm water. Stir in milk, sugar, salt, egg, shortening, and half the flour. Mix with spoon until smooth. Add enough remaining flour to handle easily; mix with hand or spoon. Turn onto lightly floured board; knead until smooth and elastic, about 5 minutes. Place dough in greased bowl, rounding and turning to grease all sides.

Cover dough and allow to rise in a warm, draft-free place (85 degrees) until double (about 1-1/2 hours) to test for rising, stick 2 fingers in dough. If holes remain but top stays smooth, dough is ready. Punch down and divide dough for desired rolls or coffee cakes. Shape, allow to rise, and bake as directed for individual recipe.

CINNAMON ROLLS

basic sweet dough recipe
2 Tablespoons soft
  butter/margarine
1/4 cup sugar
2 teaspoons cinnamon
Creamy White Glaze:
1 Tablespoon water or milk or
  1-1/2 Tablespoons light cream
1 cup confectioners sugar
1/2 teaspoon vanilla

Butterscotch Variation:
1/2 cup butter/margarine, melted
1/2 cup brown sugar (packed)
1/2 cup pecan halves
Frosted Orange Variation:
3 Tablespoons soft
  butter/margarine
1 Tablespoon grated orange peel
2 Tablespoons orange juice
1-1/2 cups confectioners sugar
(mix all ingredients until smooth)

Prepare basic sweet bread recipe (page 135) according to directions. On lightly floured board, roll dough into a rectangle 15x9". Spread with butter and sprinkle with a mixture of the sugar and cinnamon. Beginning at the long side, roll up tightly as for jelly roll. Seal well by pinching edges of roll together. Stretch roll slightly to make even. Cut into 15 slices; place slices a little apart in greased muffin cups.

Cover and allow to rise until double in bulk (about 45 minutes). Heat oven to 375 degrees. Bake rolls 25 to 30 minutes.

Prepare glaze, mixing all ingredients until of spreading consistency. When rolls are done, remove from oven and frost while warm. Makes 15 rolls.

BUTTERSCOTCH VARIATION: Follow recipe above, but before placing slices in pan, coat bottom of baking pan with mixture of butter, brown sugar, and pecans. Place rolls in pan and bake at 375 degrees for 25 to 30 minutes. Immediately turn upside down on tray; let pan stay over rolls a minute so butterscotch mixture will run down over rolls.

FROSTED ORANGE ROLLS: Substitute half the creamy orange frosting for sugar-cinnamon mixture and spread over dough before rolling. After baking, remove rolls from pan and frost with remaining frosting.

SUGAR CRISPS

basic sweet dough recipe
melted butter/margarine

1 cup sugar
1 cup finely chopped pecans

Roll dough on a lightly floured board into a rectangle 18x9". Brush with melted butter. Mix sugar and pecans; sprinkle dough with half the mixture. Beginning at long side, roll up as for jelly roll; cut into 1" slices. Roll and flatten each piece of dough into 4" circle, using remaining sugar-nut mixture to dust board. Place circles on greased baking sheet. Cover; let rise until double, about 30 minutes. Heat oven to 375 degrees; bake for 10 minutes. Makes 18 rolls.

FRUIT ROLLS

(Fruit-filled buns similar to traditional Bohemian kolaches.)

basic sweet dough recipe	1 Tablespoon grated lemon peel
1/2 pound (1 cup) prunes	1 Tablespoon lemon juice
4 ounces (3/4 cup) dried apricots	melted butter/margarine
1/4 teaspoon allspice	confectioners sugar
1/2 cup sugar	

Prepare dough according to directions. For filling, simmer prunes and apricots (for 30 minutes or until tender) in enough water to cover. Drain fruit and chop finely; stir in allspice, sugar, lemon peel, and lemon juice. Divide dough into 24 pieces. Shape each piece into round ball and place 2" apart on a greased baking sheet. Using fingers of both hands, make a depression in each ball by pushing outward toward the edge, leaving a 1/2" ridge around outside. Fill with 1 tablespoon prune-apricot filling. Allow to rise about 30 minutes.

Preheat oven to 375 degrees. Bake rolls 15 to 18 minutes. Brush lightly with melted butter or margarine and dust lightly with confectioners sugar. Makes 24 rolls.

SWEDISH TEA RING

basic sweet dough recipe	Creamy White Glaze:
2 Tablespoons soft butter/margarine	1 Tablespoon water or milk or
1/2 cup brown sugar, packed	1-1/2 Tablespoons light cream
2 teaspoons cinnamon	1 cup confectioners sugar
1/2 cup raisins	1/2 teaspoon vanilla

Roll dough on lightly floured board into a 15x9" rectangle; spread with butter. Stir sugar, cinnamon, and raisins together and sprinkle mixture over dough. Beginning at long side, roll up tightly as for jelly roll. Seal well by pinching edge of roll. Stretch roll slightly to make even, then place sealed edge down in ring on lightly greased baking sheet. Pinch ends together. With scissors, make cuts 2/3 of the way through ring at 1" intervals. Turn each section on its side and allow to rise until double, about 45 minutes. Heat oven to 375 degrees; bake 25 to 30 minutes. Make creamy white glaze by stirring ingredients together until of spreading consistency. While warm, frost ring with creamy white glaze, and if desired, decorate with nuts and cherries.

BEST EVER BANANA NUT BREAD

1 cup butter or margarine	1 teaspoon salt
2 cups sugar	3-1/2 cups flour, sifted
2 teaspoons vanilla	2 teaspoons baking soda
2 teaspoons lemon juice	2 teaspoons baking powder
4 eggs	1 cup sour cream
2 cups bananas, mashed	1 cup chopped nuts

Cream butter and sugar until light and fluffy. Add vanilla and lemon juice. Add eggs one at a time beating well after each. Add mashed bananas. Sift together salt, flour, soda and baking powder. Add this to banana mixture alternately with sour cream. Fold in nuts. Pour into 3 greased and floured 8x2" loaf pans or 2 standard size loaf pans. Bake in a 350 degree oven for 50 to 55 minutes.

Freezes well. A loaf, wrapped in festive paper and tied with a pretty bow, makes a wonderful gift.

MAYONNAISE ROLLS

1 cup self-rising flour	2 Tablespoons mayonnaise
1/2 cup buttermilk	

Combine all ingredients, blending well. Drop by teaspoonsful onto lightly greased cookie sheet. Bake at 425 degrees for 10 to 12 minutes. Yields 8 to 10 rolls.

SOUR CREAM COFFEE CAKE

The lightest and loveliest of coffee cakes, the secret is in the proportions of the ingredients, and cake flour is a must.

1/2 pound softened butter	1 teaspoon baking powder
2 cups sugar	1/4 teaspoon salt
2 eggs	1/2 cup chopped pecans or
1/2 teaspoon vanilla	walnuts
1 cup sour cream	2 Tablespoons dark brown sugar
1-3/4 cups sifted cake flour	1-1/2 teaspoons cinnamon

Preheat oven to 350 degrees. Generously butter a 10" tube pan. Cream butter and sugar together in a large mixing bowl. Add eggs, one at a time, beating well after each addition; add vanilla and sour cream. Sift cake flour, baking powder, and salt together; stir into sour cream mixture. Combine nuts, brown sugar, and cinnamon. Spoon half of batter into tube pan. Sprinkle with half of nut mixture. Cover with remaining batter, then remaining nut mixture. Bake 60 minutes. Cool in pan on rack. When completely cool, carefully remove cake from pan so that it can be displayed topping end up on a cake plate.

JEWISH COFFEE CAKE

1 pound butter/margarine
2 cups sugar
4 eggs
2 teaspoons vanilla
4 cups plain flour
2 teaspoons baking powder
2 teaspoons baking soda

1 pint sour cream
juice & grated rind of 1 lemon
3 standard or 4 small loaf pans
1 heaping cup light brown sugar
1 cup nuts
1 teaspoon cinnamon

Cream butter and granulated sugar together. Add eggs one at a time, mixing well after each. Add vanilla. Sift baking soda, flour, and baking powder; add to creamed mixture. One at a time, fold in gently the sour cream, lemon rind, lemon juice. Divide half of the batter between 3 standard pans or 4 loaf pans.

Mix together the light brown sugar, nuts, and cinnamon. Swirl half of the sugar/nut mixture into batter in pans; add remaining batter, then swirl in remaining sugar/nut mixture. Bake at 350 degrees for 35 to 45 minutes until toothpick inserted in center comes out clean.

MATZO BALLS

2 eggs, separated
1/2 cup Matzo meal

1/2 teaspoon salt

Beat yolks and whites separately. Beat whites until almost stiff, then fold egg yolks into whites. Add salt and Matzo meal while folding. Stir until smooth. Refrigerate or set aside for about 30 minutes. Form into small balls by rolling in palms of hands (dampen palms with cold water). Drop into gently boiling clear chicken broth. Allow to boil slowly (covered) for 20 to 25 minutes.

ANGEL BISCUITS

5 cups flour
1 cup crisco
3 teaspoons baking powder
1 teaspoon salt
1 teaspoon soda
2 Tablespoons sugar

1 package dry yeast
2 Tablespoons sugar
1 package dry yeast
2 Tablespoons very warm water
2 cups buttermilk
melted butter

Dissolve yeast in warm water. Sift dry ingredients into large bowl; cut in shortening with pastry blender. Add buttermilk and yeast mixture; stir until thoroughly moistened. Turn dough out onto a floured board and knead 1 to 2 minutes (no rising time is required). Roll dough out to 1/2" thickness; cut with 2" biscuit cutter. Place biscuits on ungreased baking sheet and prick tops with fork. Bake at 325 degrees until golden and firm on top (15 to 18 minutes). Serve warm.

TENNESSEE BEATEN BISCUITS

4 cups sifted flour	1/2 cup Crisco or lard
2 teaspoons sugar	1 cup milk
1 teaspoon salt	

A southern favorite from way back, these are the only biscuits that are properly served cold. Recipes and methods of beating may vary, but there are still cooks who can turn out good beaten biscuits to serve with country ham and chicken salad.

Sift flour, sugar, and salt together. Cut in Crisco until mixture resembles coarse cornmeal; stir in milk (use just enough milk to make a stiff dough). Turn dough out onto lightly floured surface and knead or beat with a wooden spoon until dough blisters (about 30 minutes). Roll dough about 1/2" thick and cut biscuits out with a floured 1-1/2" cutter. Prick with fork and place on baking sheet. Bake at 350 degrees about 30 minutes or until delicately browned.

SPOON BREAD

2 cups milk	1 teaspoon sugar
4 egg yolks	1/2 teaspoon baking powder
1 cup white cornmeal	1/2 teaspoon salt
1/4 cup butter	4 egg whites

This is the "queen" of cornbreads. It is light and fluffy as a dream, and so delicate that it must be ladled onto your plate and eaten, dripping with butter, with a spoon. Most spoon bread is made with white cornmeal, but yellow meal is acceptable. It must never be made ahead of time, and must be served straight from the oven.

Thoroughly grease a 2-quart casserole. Scald milk in top of double boiler. Beat egg yolks until thick and lemon-colored; set aside. When milk is scalded, add cornmeal very gradually, stirring constantly until mixture thickens and becomes smooth. Remove double-boiler top from simmering water. Quickly and thoroughly blend cornmeal mixture into beaten egg yolks; add butter, baking powder, sugar, and salt. Using clean beater, beat egg whites until rounded peaks are formed. Spread egg yolk mixture over beaten egg whites and gently fold together. Turn into casserole and bake at 375 degrees for 30 to 40 minutes or until toothpick comes out clean when inserted in center. Serve at once with plenty of butter/margarine. Makes 6 to 8 servings.

VIRGINIA "MOST UNUSUAL" SPOON BREAD

Though the Indians introduced this to the colonists as breakfast food, its evolution is one of Virginia's great contributions. This version has cheddar cheese, garlic and bits of crisp bacon.

3/4 cup yellow cornmeal
1-1/2 cups cold water
2 cups shredded sharp cheddar
  cheese
1-1/2 cups cooked corn kernels
  (3-4 ears)
1/4 cup (1/2 stick) butter, room
  temperature

2 garlic cloves, minced
1/2 teaspoon salt
1 cup milk
4 egg yolks
1/2 pound bacon, fried, drained
  and crumbled
4 egg whites, stiffly beaten

Preheat oven to 325 degrees. Grease 1-1/2 quart souffle dish or casserole. Combine cornmeal and water in 3-quart saucepan. Bring to a boil over medium heat, stirring constantly, and cook until thickened (about a minute). Remove from heat; stir in cheese, corn, butter, garlic and salt. Add yolks and bacon and mix thoroughly. Carefully fold egg whites into batter and pour into prepared dish, smoothing top with spatula. Bake about 60 minutes or until knife inserted in center comes out clean and dry. Serve hot, spooned into individual dishes.

CARROT BREAD

3 eggs, well beaten
1 cup oil
2 cups all-purpose flour
1-1/2 cups sugar
2 teaspoons baking soda
2 teaspoons cinnamon
1/2 teaspoon salt
2 cups grated carrots

1/2 cup flaked coconut
1/2 cup chopped pecans
1/2 cup white raisins (optional)
1/2 cup chopped maraschino
  cherries (optional)
2 teaspoons vanilla extract
2 cups grated raw carrots

Preheat oven to 350 degrees. Sift flour, sugar, baking powder, soda, cinnamon, and salt together in a large bowl. Combine eggs, oil, and milk, then add to flour mixture. Mix just until thoroughly combined. Stir in remaining ingredients. Pour batter into greased 9x5x3" loaf pan and bake 50 to 55 minutes. Cool slightly and remove from pan. When cold, wrap and store in refrigerator. Makes one loaf.

CZECHOSLOVAKIAN VANOCKA

This magnificent bread brings many compliments and has a story as interesting as the bread itself. Legend says the bottom layer represents the stable where the Christ child was born; the second layer represents the manger and swaddling clothes; and the third layer is the Christ child himself. The varied colors of fruit represent the races of mankind.

2 packages yeast
1/4 cup warm water
2 eggs
1 egg, separated
6 Tablespoons honey
1/2 cup butter
1 cup milk
1/2 teaspoon salt
2 teaspoons grated lemon peel

4-1/2 to 5-1/2 cups unbleached
   flour
1/2 cup each light and dark raisins
3/4 cup blanched, slivered almonds
1/4 cup chopped candied cherries
Lemon glaze:
1 cup confectioners sugar
2 teaspoons lemon juice
2 teaspoons milk

Stir yeast, honey, warm water together. Beat eggs and egg yolk in large bowl. Heat butter and milk until warm; add to eggs. Blend in salt, lemon peel and yeast mixture. Gradually add flour to make soft dough. Mix in fruit and nuts; knead until smooth. Let rise until double and divide dough in halves. Divide one half into 4 pieces, 18" long. Braid these four. Place on greased baking sheet. Divide remaining dough as follows: take 2/3 of dough, divide into 3 pieces, 16" long. Braid and place atop first braid. Divide rest into two 14" strands, twist together and place on top. Cover with towel, let rise to double. Beat remaining egg white until light and brush over top. Bake at 350 degrees for 35 to 40 minutes until golden brown and loaf sounds hollow when thumped. (It may be necessary to cover Vanocka with foil during last 15 minutes to prevent overbrowning.) Transfer Vanocka to rack and allow to cool slightly. Spread with Lemon Glaze while still warm and decorate with pecan halves and red candied cherries. Makes a very large loaf.

Under the Big Oaks

THE AUGUSTA NATIONAL

The clubhouse of the world famous Augusta National Golf Club, home of The Masters, originally was constructed by Dennis Redmond in the 1850's. Shortly after, Fruitland Nurseries was established on the property. Redmond, editor of The Southern Cultivator, sold both the house and the 200 acre nursery to Louis E. Berckmans. His son Prosper J.A. Berckmans, an internationally known horticulturist, developed one of the largest nurseries in the South and also became a successful landscape architect.

In 1931, the recently established Augusta National Golf Club purchased Fruitland for a course to be designed by Bobby Jones and Alister Mackenzie. The Augusta National Invitational, which began in 1934, grew into golf's most prestigious tournament, The Masters.

Eggs, Cheese, Pasta and Rice

COMPANY EGGS
WITH BRANDIED CREAM SAUCE

6 eggs
salt and pepper
2 Tablespoons rich cream

2-1/2 Tablespoons butter
1 can crab meat
1 cup sharp cheese, grated

Beat eggs in mixer until light and creamy; add cream, salt, and pepper. Melt butter in frying pan. When butter begins to sizzle, pour eggs in. Stir into large chunks, stirring often enough to keep the eggs from scorching. Cook eggs slowly. Just before eggs are done, sprinkle crab meat and cheese over them, but don't mix completely. Turn out on hot platter and pour Brandied Cream Sauce over; serve immediately.

Brandied Cream Sauce:
2 Tablespoons butter, melted
2 Tablespoons flour
3/4 cup evaporated milk, heated

1/4 cup chicken broth, heated
2 Tablespoons brandy
salt

Melt butter and stir in flour, cooking until bubbly. Gradually add heated evaporated milk and chicken broth, stirring constantly until sauce thickens. Add brandy and season to taste.

DEVILED HAM STUFFED EGGS AU GRATIN

Filling:
6 hard-cooked eggs
1/4 cup butter/margarine, melted
1/2 teaspoon Worcestershire sauce
1/4 teaspoon prepared mustard
2-1/2 ounce can deviled ham
3 green onions, finely chopped
    (include some tops)
4 springs parsley, finely chopped
salt and pepper

Sauce:
1/4 cup butter/margarine
1/4 cup flour
2 cups milk
2 teaspoons chopped chives
1 teaspoon salt
1/4 teaspoon white pepper
1 cup grated Cheddar cheese
1/4 cup bread crumbs

Preheat oven to 325 degrees. Cut eggs in half lengthwise. Remove yolks and set whites aside. In a small bowl, combine yolks, melted butter, Worcestershire sauce and mustard; mash until smooth. Stir in deviled ham, green onions, parsley, salt and pepper to taste. Evenly spoon some mixture into each egg white. Arrange in 9" square buttered casserole.

Melt butter or margarine and stir in flour with whisk until smooth. Continue stirring, gradually pouring in the milk. Add chives, salt and pepper. Cook for 5 minutes, stirring constantly; pour over eggs. Sprinkle with cheese and top with crumbs. Bake 25 to 30 minutes. Makes 6 to 8 servings. Very good for a brunch.

CHEESE QUICHE

Crust:
1-1/2 cups flour
1/2 teaspoon salt

1 teaspoon sugar
1/2 cup salad oil (unsaturated)
2 Tablespoons milk

Place flour in mixing bowl. In a separate container, combine oil, milk, sugar, and salt and twirl vigorously with fork. Pour over flour and blend with fork and fingers. Pat over bottom and up side of pan, crimping edges. Bake 3 minutes at 350 degrees. Remove from oven.

Filling:
1-1/2 cups shredded Swiss cheese
1/2 cup shredded mozzarella
  cheese

1 cup shredded Cheddar cheese
3 eggs
1/4 teaspoon salt
1/4 teaspoon mustard

Mix cheeses and place in 8" pie crust. Beat eggs and add enough milk to make 1-1/2 cups liquid. Add salt and mustard. Slowly pour over cheese. Bake at 375 degrees for 45 minutes or until center is firm and top is golden brown.

SHRIMP-ARTICHOKE QUICHE

10" pie crust (see previous recipe)
  lined in pan
1 can medium-sized deveined
  shrimp
1 can artichoke hearts, cut up
4 ounces Swiss cheese, grated
1 tall can evaporated milk

1/2 cup fresh milk
4 eggs, beaten
1/2 teaspoon salt
1/4 teaspoon white pepper
1 teaspoon onion flakes
fresh nutmeg

Before filling, bake pie crust for 3 minutes. Arrange shrimp and artichokes on bottom of crust. Mix grated cheese, evaporated milk, fresh milk, eggs, salt and white pepper and pour over shrimp. Sprinkle onion flakes over top and lightly grind fresh nutmeg over top. Bake at 375 degrees for 45 minutes.

DEVILED EGGS AND SHRIMP

8 eggs, hard-cooked
1/3 cup mayonnaise
1/4 teaspoon dry mustard
1/2 teaspoon salt
1/2 teaspoon curry powder
1/2 teaspoon paprika

Sauce:
1 (10-3/4 ounce) can cream of
  shrimp soup
1 (10-3/4 ounce) can cream of
  chicken soup
1/2 cup Cheddar cheese, grated
1 cup soft bread crumbs, buttered
1/2 pound cleaned shrimp

Cut eggs lengthwise, remove yolks. Mash yolks and cream with seasonings. Fill egg whites with the yolk mixture. Arrange in a greased 13x9" baking dish.

Blend soups; add cheese and cook over low heat until cheese melts. Stir until smooth. Add shrimp and pour over eggs. Sprinkle with crumbs, dot with more butter and bake at 350 degrees for 25 to 30 minutes. Serves 6 to 8.

CHEESE AND FRUIT FOR DESSERT

Fresh fruits and cheeses make a refreshing, no-fuss dessert there's always room for, even after the most elaborate meal. Leftovers are never a problem! Tips for putting together a perfect food partnership:

Selecting Cheese and Fruits:

Choose three or more cheeses, varying in flavor from mild to sharp, in texture from firm to creamy, and in shape. Cut some chunks, some in slices, and leave others in balls, wedges, or bars. Choose several fresh fruits in season.

Serving Basics:

For best flavor, remove cheese from refrigerator about one hour ahead of time. While cheese is still cold, cut to desired shape. Arrange on a cheese board or tray, cover with plastic wrap and allow to stand at room temperature until ready to eat. (Cream cheese or Neufchatel should remain refrigerated until served.) Wash and prepare fruits as desired, then arrange in a basket or bowl or on a platter. Set out plates, small knives, and napkins. Complete with a basket of unsalted crackers or plain breadsticks and glasses of favorite beverage.

Delightful Combinations:

* Sharp Cheddar, provolone, cream cheese with green grapes, pears, straw-berries
* Fontina, Edam, bleu cheese with papayas, tangelos, apples
* Port du Salut, Brie, Stilton with apples, bananas, kiwi fruit
* Swiss, Gouda, French double creme with pears, honeydew melon, oranges
* Guyere, Tilsit, Gorgonzola with tangerines, pineapple, pears
* Samsoe, Camembert, Monterey Jack with bananas, red grapes, persimmons

BAKED SOUTHERN GRITS

1 teaspoon salt	1 cup milk
4 cups water	4 eggs, slightly beaten
1 cup hominy grits	1/2 cup shredded Cheddar cheese
1/2 cup butter/margarine	

Add salt to water and bring to a boil. Stir in grits slowly, keeping water at a brisk boil. Cover and cook slowly for 1 hour or until grits are soft, stirring occasionally. Remove from heat and stir in butter and milk. Cool to lukewarm; beat in eggs and turn into greased 2-quart casserole. Bake at 350 degrees for 1 hour or until knife inserted in center comes out clean. Ten minutes before dish is done, sprinkle cheese on top and bake until golden brown. Makes 6 servings.

NOTE: 1 to 1-1/2 cups shredded Cheddar cheese may be stirred in before baking; you may also like 1/4 teaspoon cayenne pepper stirred in before baking.

GARLIC CHEESE GRITS

4 cups water
1/2 teaspoon salt
1 cup regular uncooked grits
1/2 cup butter/margarine
6-ounce roll process cheese food
  with garlic

8 ounces shredded Cheddar
  cheese
2 Tablespoons Worcestershire
  sauce
1/2 teaspoon garlic salt
paprika (optional)

Combine water and salt in a medium saucepan and bring to a boil. Add grits, cover, and reduce heat to low. Cook until thickened (5 to 10 minutes), stirring occasionally. Remove from heat and add margarine, garlic cheese, Cheddar cheese, Worcestershire sauce, and garlic salt. Stir until cheese melts then pour mixture into a greased 1-1/2 quart casserole. Sprinkle with paprika and bake at 350 degrees for 15 to 20 minutes. Yields 6 servings.

AMERICAN CHEESE PIE

1/2 cup butter
1-1/4 cup sugar
1 Tablespoon flour
1/2 teaspoon vanilla

1/2 cup milk
3/4 cup grated American cheese
2 whole eggs
2 egg yolks

Cream butter, sugar, flour and vanilla together. Add whole eggs and additional egg yolks. Beat until smooth, then fold in cheese. Mix in milk; cook in unbaked pie shell in 400 degree oven until thick and brown (about 25 to 30 minutes).

CHEESE PINWHEELS

A melt-in-your mouth, perennial favorite.

2-1/2 cups flour
1 cup butter, softened
1 cup sour cream
seasoned salt to taste

3 cups (12 ounces) shredded
  sharp Cheddar cheese
paprika

Combine flour, butter, and sour cream in a bowl, mixing well. Divide into 4 equal parts, wrapping each in plastic film. Refrigerate until firm.

Using a floured pastry cloth and wax paper on top of the dough, roll portions out into 6x12" rectangles. Sprinkle each with seasoned salt and 3/4 cup of shredded cheese. Starting with the long side toward you, roll up each portion in jelly-roll fashion. Seal edges and ends by pressing together. Wrap in plastic film and refrigerate until baking time.

Preheat oven to 350 degrees. Using a sharp knife, cut rolls, seam-side down, into 1" thick slices and place on ungreased cookie sheets (about 12 to 15 per sheet). Sprinkle with paprika. Bake 25 to 30 minutes or until golden brown. Serve while warm.

NOTE: Unsliced rolls freeze beautifully for handy, last-minute appetizers. For those who enjoy a spicy snack, add a dash of Tabasco sauce to one portion before rolling out.

RAREBIT (RABBIT)

"Rarebit" is an ancient dish, but has been known by its present name for only about 200 years. The name is actually a culinary joke, when the hunter's bag was poor, a Welsh housewife cooked cheese instead of rabbit. Some cooks apparently began calling it "rarebit" because this sounded more refined.

1/2 cup milk or cream	1 egg, slightly beaten
2 cups (1/2-pound) cheese	1/2 teaspoon salt
2 Tablespoons butter	a sprinkle of cayenne

Heat milk and grated cheese in upper part of double boiler or blazer of chafing dish. When cheese is melted, add butter. Pour mixture over egg, then return to double boiler. Add seasoning. Cook until smooth and thick, stirring constantly. Serve at once over slices of toast or hot, crisp crackers.

WORLD'S EASIEST SOUFFLE

butter	1/3 cup milk, light cream or half
grated Parmesan cheese	and half
4 eggs	1/4 cup grated Parmesan cheese
4 ounces sharp Cheddar cheese,	1/2 teaspoon onion salt
cubed	1/2 teaspoon dry mustard
3 ounce package cream cheese,	
cubed	

Butter bottom and sides of a 1-quart souffle dish or casserole; dust with Parmesan cheese and set aside. Combine eggs, Cheddar cheese, cream cheese, milk, Parmesan cheese, onion salt, and dry mustard in order listed in a blender container. Cover and blend at medium speed for 30 seconds or until mixture is smooth. Blend on high for an additional 10 to 30 seconds. Pour mixture into pan and bake at 350 degrees for 25 to 30 minutes or until puffy and delicately browned.

Serve immediately. Serves 4 persons.

CHEESE WAFERS

2 cups all-purpose flour	8 ounces sharp Cheddar cheese,
1 teaspoon cayenne pepper	grated
1/2 teaspoon salt	2 cups toasted rice cereal or 2
2 sticks (1 cup) butter at room	cups chopped pecans
temperature	

Preheat oven to 350 degrees. Combine flour, cayenne, and salt in large bowl. Cut in butter until mixture resembles coarse meal. Mix in cheese, then fold in cereal or nuts. Form dough into 1" rounds. Place on ungreased baking sheets and flatten to 1-3/4" rounds, using back of fork. Bake until light brown (approximately 15 minutes). Cool on rack.

OPEN-FACE SANDWICHES
WITH WELSH RAREBIT SAUCE

4 English muffins, split, buttered, and toasted or 8 slices dark rye bread

1 pound thin-sliced, cooked ham or 8 slices Canadian bacon
4 slices tomatoes, sliced about 1/2" thick

Warm ham in oven (fry Canadian bacon). For each sandwich, place 1/4 pound ham or Canadian bacon on two slices of bread. Pour 1/2 cup Welsh Rarebit Sauce over each sandwich and top with tomato slice.

Welsh Rarebit Sauce:

2 Tablespoons butter/margarine
4 teaspoons flour
1/2 teaspoon dry mustard
dash of cayenne pepper
1/4 teaspoon salt
1/8 teaspoon paprika (hot)

2 eggs, slightly beaten
1/2 cup milk
3/4 cup half and half
4 cups (16 ounces) shredded sharp Cheddar cheese
1 Tablespoon Worcestershire sauce

Melt butter in a heavy saucepan over low heat; add flour, stirring until smooth. Cook about 2 minutes, stirring constantly. Combine beaten eggs, milk, and half and half. Gradually add to flour and butter mixture, stirring until mixture is thickened and well-blended, about 8 to 10 minutes. Stir in shredded cheese, salt, mustard, paprika and cayenne. Continue cooking at a very low heat until cheese melts, stirring often. Add Worcestershire, mixing well. Serve over open-face sandwiches or toast points.

JAN'S CHEESE STRATA
A Christmas Morning Favorite

6-8 slices buttered bread
1/2 to 1 pound bacon
2-1/2 cups diced cheese
4 eggs slightly beaten

2-1/2 cups milk
1 teaspoon salt
1/4 teaspoon mustard

Fry bacon crisply; drain on paper towel. Quarter each slice of bread. Layer bread, bacon, and cheese in an 8"x8" baking dish, ending with cheese. Mix remaining ingredients together and pour over top of cheese and bread layers. Cover and chill 6 to 8 hours or overnight.

About an hour before serving, preheat oven to 325 degrees. Bake strata for 45 minutes or until firm. Let stand a few minutes and cut into squares.

NOTE: Strata may be frozen after baking. Defrost before reheating.

SPECIAL LASAGNA

1/2 pound lasagna noodles
1 pound ground beef
1/2 cup chopped onion
3 cloves garlic, minced
1 Tablespoon olive oil
3 pounds tomatoes (6 to 7 large),
  peeled, seeded, and chopped
  or canned tomatoes, drained
  and chopped
1-1/2 teaspoons seasoned salt
2 Tablespoons chopped parsley
  (or 1 teaspoon dried)

1 teaspoon basil
1/2 teaspoon oregano
1/4 teaspoon freshly ground
  pepper
Bechamel Sauce
Ricotta Filling
Cheeses:
1-1/2 cups grated Parmesan cheese
4 ounces mozzarella cheese,
  sliced
4 ounces teleme cheese
butter

Cook lasagna noodles in boiling, salted water until "al dente," still firm to the bite. Drain and keep them in cold water until ready to use.

Saute ground beef, onion, and garlic in olive oil until meat is no longer pink. Add remaining ingredients and cook at a fast simmer until sauce is quite thick (about 30 to 40 minutes). Skim off fat. Preheat oven to 400 degrees.

In the following order, layer in a lightly greased 13x9" baking dish: A little meat sauce, half the noodles, half the remaining meat sauce, 1/2 cup Bechamel sauce, 1/2 cup Parmesan cheese, half the mozzarella, teleme, and ricotta filling; repeat layering, using remaining ingredients, ending with 1/2 cup Parmesan. Dot with butter. At this point the dish may be covered and refrigerated, if desired. From room temperature, bake at 400 degrees, uncovered, for 30 minutes or more, until bubbly. This dish freezes very well.

Bechamel Sauce:
1/2 cup butter
4 Tablespoons flour
1 cup milk
1 cup chicken broth

1 chicken bouillon cube
  (optional)
1/8 teaspoon salt

Melt butter, add flour and cook, stirring with a whisk, for one minute. Slowly add milk and chicken broth and bring to a boil, still using whisk. Taste and add chicken bouillon cube, if needed. Add salt.

Ricotta Filling:
1 egg
1/2 pound ricotta cheese
1/4 cup grated Parmesan cheese

1/8 teaspoon nutmeg (or less)
1/2 teaspoon salt

Beat egg in bowl, then add remaining ingredients and stir well with a fork.

CHEDDAR CHEESE LASAGNA

10 ounces lasagna noodles, cooked
meat mixture
sauce
1/2 pound sharp Cheddar cheese, grated

Place half the noodles in a 13x9" pan. Add a thick layer of the meat mixture, then a layer of sauce. Repeat layers, adding the rest of the noodles, meat mixture and sauce. Top with grated Cheddar cheese. Bake at 325 degrees for 20 minutes. Serves 6. (Can be made the day before and refrigerated, then baked when needed.)

Meat Mixture:

1 pound hamburger
1 Tablespoon oil
1 large onion, chopped
6 sprigs fresh parsley, chopped
1 clove garlic, chopped fine
3-1/2 cups whole peeled tomatoes, diced
8 ounces tomato paste
1 cup water
1 bay leaf, crushed
salt and pepper to taste

Heat oil in skillet. Add hamburger, onion, parsley, and garlic. Cook until meat is lightly browned. Add tomatoes, tomato paste, water, bay leaf, salt and pepper. Simmer, uncovered, for 45 minutes.

Sauce:

4 Tablespoons butter
1 medium onion, chopped fine
3 Tablespoons flour
2 cups milk
3 egg yolks, slightly beaten
1 cup grated Parmesan cheese
1 cup grated Cheddar cheese

Melt butter in small skillet. Saute onion, blend in flour. Heat milk in saucepan, add beaten egg yolks. Stir in onion mixture. Cook over medium heat until thickened, stirring constantly. Add Parmesan and Cheddar cheese. Stir thoroughly. Remove from heat.

CLIFF'S FAVORITE MACARONI AND CHEESE

(His favorite, now a family favorite)

7 ounces elbow macaroni
1 cup small-curd, cream-style cottage cheese
1 cup sour cream
2 eggs, slightly beaten
1/2 cup grated mozzarella cheese
1/2 cup grated swiss cheese
3/4 teaspoon salt
dash of pepper
8 ounces sharp American cheese, shredded (2 cups)
paprika
several cheese slices

Cook macaroni according to package directions; drain well. Combine cottage cheese, sour cream, egg, salt, and pepper. Add shredded cheese, mixing well. Stir in cooked macaroni. Place in a greased 9" square baking dish. Sprinkle with paprika and bake at 350 degrees for 45 minutes. Serves 6 to 8 persons. Good cold, cut in squares, as well as piping hot!

BAKED HUNGARIAN NOODLES

1/2 pound fine noodles
2 cups cream-style cottage cheese
2 cups sour cream
1/2 cup minced onion (green onions)
2 cloves garlic, minced
1 Tablespoon Worcestershire sauce
2 dashes Tabasco sauce

1 Tablespoon poppy seeds (optional)
1 teaspoon salt
freshly ground pepper to taste
paprika
1/2 cup shredded sharp cheese or freshly grated parmesan cheese

Cook noodles in boiling, salted water until tender. Drain. Combine the noodles with the remaining ingredients except the paprika and parmesan cheese. Approximately 30 minutes before serving, bake in buttered casseroles at 350 degrees until hot. Sprinkle with paprika and serve with Parmesan cheese. Serves 8 and may be made well in advance of serving.

An excellent company dish that leaves time for extras, when prepared in advance. If using grated cheese, add to top of casserole before baking.

NOTE: If desired, you may add 1/2 cup fresh finely chopped parsley for added taste and color.

MACARONI & CHEESE
WITH TOMATOES

4 Tablespoons butter
4 Tablespoons flour
2 cups milk
8 ounces sharp Cheddar cheese, grated
1/2 pound sliced American cheese, torn

1/3 cup grated Parmesan cheese
1/4 teaspoon white pepper
pinch of cayenne pepper
1 pound can plum tomatoes, drained and coarsely chopped
3/4 pound elbow macaroni, partially cooked

Melt butter in a saucepan, then add flour to make a paste. Add milk and cook, stirring constantly, until thickened. Stir in cheeses and pepper; simmer, stirring constantly, until cheeses are melted. Remove from heat. In a 9x13" baking pan, combine partially cooked macaroni, cheese mixture and chopped tomatoes. Bake in preheated 350 degree oven for 20 minutes or until bubbly.

PASTA SALAD

Salad:
1 pound fusilli, shell, or bow-tie pasta
1/2 green bell pepper, cut in thin strips
1/2 red bell pepper, cut in thin strips
1/2 red onion, cut in thin strips
1-1/2 Tablespoons oil
1/4 pound mushrooms, sliced
1 cup broccoli florets
2 small zucchini, cut in half lengthwise and sliced
12 fresh asparagus tips*
1 basket cherry tomatoes, cut in half
1 (6-ounce) jar marinated artichoke hearts, undrained
salt and freshly ground pepper to taste

Cook pasta until it is still firm to bite. In a large skillet, saute pepper and onion in oil. When peppers just begin to soften, add sliced mushrooms and stir-fry until slightly cooked. Remove to a large bowl. Stir-fry broccoli 1 to 2 minutes, adding another tablespoon of oil if necessary. Add zucchini and cook until tender but still crisp. Add to vegetables in bowl. Stir-fry asparagus tips, adding a touch more oil if necessary. As soon as they turn bright green, remove to bowl. Add cherry tomato halves and undrained artichoke hearts to bowl. Season with salt and freshly ground pepper to taste.

NOTE: If you happen to have any left-over salad, additional Parmesan cheese will freshen it.

*Chinese pea pods, sugar snap peas, or green beans make nice substitutes for asparagus.

Dressing:
1/2 cup parsley leaves
1 cup fresh (or 2 Tablespoons dried) basil leaves
2 cloves garlic
2 Tablespoons + 1/2 cup olive oil
1/2 cup red wine vinegar
1 Tablespoon dried oregano
1 teaspoon salt
1 teaspoon freshly ground pepper
1 to 2 teaspoons butter
1/3 to 1/2 cup pine nuts or toasted walnuts, chopped
1/2 cup freshly grated Parmesan cheese

Combine parsley, basil, garlic, and 2 teaspoons oil in food processor or blender until well-chopped. Combine 1/2 cup olive oil, wine vinegar, oregano, salt and pepper; add parsley mixture. Saute pine nuts in butter until brown; drain on paper towel. Combine pasta, vegetables, dressing, and Parmesan cheese. Toss gently but well. Correct seasoning and place in a handsome bowl or platter. Top with pine nuts and garnish with fresh basil leaves.

FOUR CHEESE SPAGHETTI

1 (12-ounce) package spaghetti
1-1/2 teaspoons all-purpose flour
3 Tablespoons melted
 butter/margarine
1 cup half and half
3/4 cup shredded provolone cheese
3/4 cup shredded Swiss cheese
3/4 cup shredded edam or gouda
 cheese
1/4 cup grated Parmesan cheese
1/2 teaspoon salt
1/8 teaspoon pepper
1 teaspoon dried (or 1 Tablespoon
 chopped fresh) basil

Cook spaghetti according to package directions; drain well, and keep warm. Stir flour into butter; cook over low heat, stirring constantly, until bubbly. Gradually add half and half; cook over low heat, stirring constantly, until smooth and thickened. Add cheese, salt, and pepper to white sauce; stir constantly until cheese melts. Pour cheese sauce over spaghetti, tossing to evenly coat spaghetti. Sprinkle with basil; serve immediately. Yields 6 to 8 servings.

ITALIAN SPAGHETTI SAUCE

1/2 cup olive oil
1-1/2 cups finely chopped onion
4 cloves garlic, finely chopped
1 pound ground beef
1/2 pound ground veal
1/2 pound sweet Italian sausage,
 cubed
3-1/2 cups Italian style tomatoes
2 (6-ounce) cans tomato paste
1 can tomato soup
1 cup water
1-1/2 cups dry red wine
1-1/2 teaspoons Worcestershire sauce
1 teaspoon salt
1 teaspoon sugar
1/2 teaspoon celery salt
1/2 teaspoon crushed red pepper
dash chili powder
dash ground cinnamon
dash fennel seed
dash oregano
3 bay leaves
4 whole allspice, crushed
3/4 cup green pepper, chopped
1/2 pound fresh mushrooms,
 sliced lengthwise through
 caps and stems
1 (4-ounce) jar pimientos,
 drained and chopped
1/2 cup stuffed olives, chopped

Heat the olive oil in a large skillet. Add the onion and garlic and cook until onion is tender, about 5 minutes. Add the beef, veal, and sausage. Brown well, stirring occasionally.

Meanwhile, combine in a large heavy saucepan or sauce pot, the remaining ingredients except mushrooms, olives and pimientos. Stir in the browned meat and onions. Simmer, uncovered, at least 4 hours, stirring occasionally, if necessary.

Add a little hot water as sauce thickens during cooking. Remove bay leaves. One-half hour before sauce is done, stir in mushrooms, olives and pimientos. Serve sauce over cooked spaghetti and top servings with grated Romano cheese. Makes about 4-1/2 pints of sauce.

This sauce, with its many ingredients, is well worth the time spent in preparation.

ITALIAN SPAGHETTI
WITH MEATBALLS AND SAUSAGE

Meatballs:
1-1/2 pounds ground beef
2 onions, minced
2 cloves garlic, minced
1/4 cup chopped parsley
1/2 cup grated Parmesan cheese
1/2 cup fine dry bread crumbs
1 egg, beaten

2 teaspoons salt
1/2 teaspoon pepper
1 bay leaf
1 teaspoon Italian seasoning
1/4 teaspoon oregano
1/4 teaspoon marjoram
1/4 teaspoon rosemary
2 Tablespoons olive oil

Mix ground beef, onion, garlic, parsley, Parmesan cheese, bread crumbs, egg, salt, pepper and herbs. You can add a little water, if mixture is too dry. Shape into meatballs and brown in olive oil before adding to the sauce. Meatballs can be frozen separately or added to the sauce and frozen.

Sauce:
2 onions, chopped
2 cloves garlic, minced
2 Tablespoons olive oil
1 pound hot or mild Italian
   sausage, cut into 2" pieces
3-1/2 cups tomatoes
1 cup water.
1 Tablespoon fresh basil, or 1
   teaspoon dried basil
1/4 cup chopped parsley
1/2 teaspoon crumbled thyme

2-1/2 teaspoons salt
1/4 teaspoon pepper
1/4 teaspoon crushed dried red
   pepper
1 (6-ounce) can tomato paste
2 (8-ounce) cans tomato sauce
1/4 teaspoon oregano
1/4 teaspoon marjoram
1/4 teaspoon rosemary
1 bay leaf
1 teaspoon Italian seasoning
12 ounces spaghetti, cooked

Brown Italian sausage and set aside. Saute onion and garlic in olive oil in large saucepan. Add tomatoes and water and bring to a boil. Simmer, uncovered, for 20 minutes, stirring occasionally. Add next 13 ingredients, the browned meatballs, the browned Italian sausage and simmer, uncovered, for 2 hours, stirring occasionally. Add more seasoning, if desired. Serve over hot spaghetti. Serves 8.

SPICY SHRIMP PIZZA

1 recipe pizza dough (see page 160)
1 cup coarsely grated Provolone
   cheese
1/2 cup coarsely grated Swiss cheese
1 large tomato, seeded and chopped
1 small green pepper, chopped
   (optional)

2 cups small cooked shrimp or
   medium shrimp, chopped
1/2 cup chopped green onions
1/2 teaspoon dried oregano
1/4 teaspoon black pepper
1/8 to 1/4 teaspoon ground red
   pepper

With oiled fingers, spread dough in 10" pizza pan. Place in pre-heated oven (425 degrees) and cook for 10 minutes. Remove crust from oven, spread with cheeses. Top with onions, green pepper, tomatoes, shrimp and seasonings. Bake on lowest rack of oven for about 20 minutes or until golden brown.

NOTE: 1 (10-ounce) can refrigerated pizza crust may be used.

CHICKEN SPAGHETTI

1-pound box Vermicelli
4 to 5-pound hen, cooked in 5
   cups water
4 cups celery, chopped
4 cloves garlic, minced
4 cups onions, chopped
1 cup green peppers, chopped
1 (2-ounce) can pimientos

2 Tablespoons chopped parsley
1 (6-ounce) can mushroom pieces
1 cup chicken broth
1 (10-3/4 ounce) can cream of
   mushroom soup
1/2 pound Cheddar cheese,
   shredded
Parmesan cheese

Cook chicken in water until tender. Remove from broth. Skin, debone and cut into bite-size pieces. Set aside. Strain the broth and save.

In a heavy saucepan, saute onions, garlic, celery and pepper until tender in chicken fat or margarine. When transparent, add pimiento, mushrooms, parsley, cup of chicken broth and cream of mushroom soup. Add chunks of chicken and mix all together thoroughly.

In another large saucepan, cook vermicelli, in water following directions on package. If desired, you may use the broth from cooking the chicken, adding the required amount of water. Drain into a large pan.

In large buttered casserole dish, alternate layers of sauce with vermicelli, ending with sauce. Add 1 tablespoon Worcestershire sauce to 1/2 cup of chicken broth and pour over the layered mixture. If using shredded Cheddar cheese, sprinkle on top and bake in a 350 degree oven for 30 to 50 minutes until slightly brown and bubbly. If using Parmesan cheese, bake and sprinkle cheese on top while hot before serving.

This may be prepared the day before and baked the day of serving.

CHICAGO-STYLE PIZZA
TOPPING AND SAUCE

1 recipe pizza dough (see page
   160)
1 (28-ounce) can Italian pear
   tomatoes, well drained and
   chopped
1 Tablespoon oregano

1 teaspoon sugar
1 pound Mozzarella cheese,
   thinly sliced
1 pound mild Italian sausage,
   broken up, cooked and drained
1/2 cup grated Parmesan cheese

For sauce, combine tomatoes, oregano and sugar. Set aside. Brush a 14", deep-dish pizza pan with 2 Tablespoons oil; sprinkle with cornmeal. Punch dough down; press in bottom of pan. Let rise about 30 minutes. Arrange cheese over dough. Place sausage over cheese. Spread with tomato sauce and sprinkle Parmesan cheese. Place pizza in a 500 degree oven. Immediately reduce heat to 450 degrees and bake 20 to 25 minutes or until cheese is melted and crust is golden.

PIZZA DOUGH

1 package yeast
1 teaspoon sugar
1 cup warm water
2 Tablespoons oil

1 teaspoon salt
2-1/2 cups flour
2 Tablespoons cornmeal

Dissolve yeast and sugar in warm water (115 to 120 degrees); let proof. Add oil, salt, and 2-1/2 cups flour to yeast. Beat 20 strokes (no rising necessary). With oiled fingers, spread in two greased 14" round pans or 1 cookie sheet and sprinkle with cornmeal. For thick crust let rise in warm (200 degree) oven for 5 to 10 minutes. Remove crust from oven and preheat oven to 425 degrees. Cook crust for 10 minutes. Remove from oven, spread with desired sauce, cheese and toppings. Cook 15 minutes at 425 degrees. For thin crust, spread dough in greased pans, spread with sauce, cheese and choice of toppings. Cook 20 to 25 minutes in 425 degree oven.

Sauce:
1 (15-ounce) can tomato sauce
1 large onion, chopped

1/8 teaspoon garlic powder
garlic salt to taste
pepper to taste

Combine tomato sauce, onion, garlic powder. Season with garlic salt, pepper.

Topping:
3/4 pound fresh mushrooms, sliced
   and sauteed in 2 Tablespoons
   butter
1 (3-1/2 ounce) package sliced
   pepperoni

1 pound hot bulk sausage (mild if
   prefer) cooked and well drained
2 Tablespoons dried oregano
1 pound Monterey Jack cheese,
   shredded
jalapeno slices, to taste

CHICKEN TETRAZZINI

2 (4-pound) stewing chickens
2 onions, sliced
4 ribs celery, finely chopped
3-1/2 teaspoons salt
1/2 pound Cheddar cheese, grated
1 (2-ounce) can pimientos, diced
   and drained

3 cups chicken stock
6 Tablespoons butter or margarine
6 Tablespoons flour
1/4 teaspoons pepper
3/4 cup half and half cream
1 (6-ounce) can sliced mushrooms
1-pound package spaghetti

Wash chickens. Remove all pin feathers and cut in pieces. Place in large saucepan and cover with water. Add 2 teaspoons salt to chicken. Cook covered, 3 to 4 hours or until tender. Cool chickens; remove skin and bones and cut meat into strips. Strain stock and save. In a skillet, saute onions and celery until tender in butter; remove with slotted spoon. Stir in flour, pepper and 1-1/2 teaspoons salt, cooking 3 to 4 minutes. Slowly stir in 3 cups hot chicken broth and half and half. Cook, stirring constantly, until smooth and thickened to prevent lumping. Drain pimientos and cut in small pieces. Drain mushrooms and add with pimientos and chicken to sauce. Set oven to 375 degrees. Cook spaghetti in boiling salted water until tender, then drain. Place spaghetti and chicken in alternate layers in casserole. Sprinkle top with grated cheese. Bake 25 minutes. Serves 12.

RICE

NOTE: An efficient way to prepare rice is to cook it beside other foods in the oven. Combine rice and boiling water (or other liquid, if desired) in a baking dish; stir. Then cover tightly and bake at 350 degrees for 25 to 30 minutes. For par-boiled rice, bake for 30 to 40 minutes; for brown rice, bake one hour.

GREEN RICE

1 cup raw long grain rice
1/3 cup bell pepper, finely
    chopped
2 Tablespoons fresh parsley,
    minced
1/2 cup green onions and tops,
    minced

2 Tablespoons cooking oil
3 teaspoons Worcestershire sauce
1/2 teaspoon salt
Dash of red pepper
2 cups chicken stock or canned
    broth

Mix all ingredients. Bake, with stirring, in a tightly covered 2 quart casserole at 350 degrees for 45 minutes or until rice is no longer soupy. Remove cover and toss with a fork as seasonings come to the top. Needs no gravy, but may be topped with Parmesan cheese. Serves 6 to 8.

GOURMET RICE AND DRESSING

Wild rice came to us from the Indians, for whom rice was the main source of carbohydrates. The Chippewa and Sioux fought many wars over ownership of the wild rice producing lakes.

1 package Uncle Ben's wild rice
4 slices bread
2 medium onions, chopped
4 to 5 ribs of celery
1 pound hot country sausage
1/2 pound fresh mushrooms
1/4 cup butter

1 Tablespoon poultry seasoning
2 Tablespoons sage
1 Tablespoon sweet basil
1 Tablespoon parsley
salt and pepper to taste
2 eggs

Cook rice as directed on package. Melt butter in fry pan. Saute mushrooms, onions, and celery. Cook sausage and let drain on paper towel. In a large bowl, combine the rice and sauteed mixture; add 4 crumbled slices of bread, poultry seasoning, sage, sweet basil, pepper, salt, and parsley; mix. Add slightly beaten eggs and pour into casserole dish or baking pan. Bake at 350 degrees for 30 minutes and serve as a buffet dish or as dressing.

RED RICE

1 cup long grain rice, cooked
2 medium bell peppers
2 medium onions
5 strips lean bacon (fried crisp)
1 can tomatoes

1 cup tomato sauce
1/2 teaspoon Tabasco
1 teaspoon Parmesan cheese
salt & pepper

Fry bacon and drain on a paper towel. Brown chopped onion and bell pepper in bacon drippings. Add tomatoes, sauce, Tabasco, and crumbled bacon. Pour in a greased casserole, sprinkle top with Parmesan cheese, and bake at 325 degrees for 30 minutes or until rice is dry enough to separate.

WILD RICE IN A CASSEROLE

1 cup wild rice, soaked overnight
1 (10-1/2 ounce) can consomme,
    undiluted
4 Tablespoons butter
3/4 pound mushrooms, sliced
1-1/2 cups finely chopped celery

1 bunch green onions, sliced
6-ounce can water chestnuts,
    drained and sliced (optional)
1/2 cup vermouth
butter

Rinse wild rice well and drain. Combine with consomme in a large sauce pan and simmer, covered, until liquid is absorbed (about 30 minutes). In a skillet, melt butter and saute vegetables until limp. Combine with cooked rice and place in a buttered, 2-quart casserole. Refrigerate until ready to use. When ready to heat, add vermouth and dot with butter. Bake, covered, in 350 degree oven for 30 to 40 minutes.

There are so many menus that wild rice complements!

Augusta Golf Party

THE AUGUSTA NATIONAL

The clubhouse of the world famous Augusta National Golf Club, home of The Masters, originally was constructed by Dennis Redmond in the 1850's. Shortly after, Fruitland Nurseries was established on the property. Redmond, editor of The Southern Cultivator, sold both the house and the 200 acre nursery to Louis E. Berckmans. His son Prosper J.A. Berckmans, an internationally known horticulturist, developed one of the largest nurseries in the South and also became a successful landscape architect.

In 1931, the recently established Augusta National Golf Club purchased Fruitland for a course to be designed by Bobby Jones and Alister Mackenzie. The Augusta National Invitational, which began in 1934, grew into golf's most prestigious tournament, The Masters.

Meats, Meat Casseroles and Sauces

Beef

WRANGLER'S BRISKET

4 pounds beef brisket	garlic salt
liquid smoke	onion salt
Worcestershire sauce	2 cups zippy barbecue sauce
celery salt	

Center heavy duty foil in a 13x9x2" baking pan. Place brisket in center of foil. Pour sauce over meat. Bring edges of foil together, double fold to seal tightly. Bake 3 hours or until meat is tender. Remove from oven. Carefully open foil; lift meat to heated serving platter. Pour sauce from foil into sauce dish, skim off excess fat, and serve with sliced meat. Serves 8 to 10.

Zippy Barbecue Sauce:

1 cup onion, finely chopped	1/4 cup Worcestershire sauce
2 cloves garlic, minced	1/3 cup brown sugar, firmly
1/4 cup vegetable oil	packed
2 Tablespoons chili powder	2 tablespoons prepared mustard
2 teaspoons cumin seed, crushed	1 Tablespoon celery seed, crushed
2 cups ketchup	2 Tablespoons butter
1 cup cider or white vinegar	1/2 Tablespoon A-1 Sauce
1/2 cup lemon juice	1/8 teaspoon cayenne pepper

Saute onion and garlic in oil in large saucepan until golden and tender, about 10 minutes. Stir in chili powder and cook 1 minute. Add remaining ingredients except butter; bring to boil. Reduce heat and simmer, uncovered, stirring often for 30 minutes. Remove from heat and stir in butter. Yields about 4-1/2 cups sauce.

BEEF A LA STROGANOFF

2-1/2 pounds lean beef, cut in strips	3/4 cup tomato juice
	2 cups water
1/2 cup butter or margarine	2/3 cup sherry
1-1/4 cups chopped onions	1/4 cup sour cream
2-1/4 cups sliced mushrooms	salt and pepper

Cut beef in 1/8" strips, 1-1/2" long. Roll beef in flour; saute in butter 5 minutes; add onions and cook until onions are soft. Add mushrooms; pour tomato juice, stock and sherry over meat. Season and simmer until meat is tender. Serve on buttered noodles and top with sour cream. Serves 4 to 6.

MOM'S CORNED BEEF WITH VEGETABLES

Corned beef hasn't any corn in it. It gets its name from the English, to whom "corn" meant any small particle, in this case the coarse salt they used for curing the meat. Cabbage was a rare and expensive delicacy on Roman tables. The Emperor Claudius hailed the combination of corned beef and cabbage as the best of all dishes!

1 4-5 pound corned beef brisket	2 Tablespoons brown sugar
1 clove garlic, peeled	1/4 teaspoon nutmeg
10 black peppercorns	1/8 teaspoon pepper
2 whole cloves	honey glaze
1 bay leaf	vegetables
1 medium onion, sliced	mustard sauce
4 Tablespoons prepared mustard	horseradish sauce

In a large kettle place corned beef brisket with onion and spices. Cover with water and cook over low heat for 3 hours, or until fork-tender. Let stand until cool. Remove form water.

Strain cooking liquid and save to cook vegetables, if desired. Meanwhile, make mustard glaze or honey glaze, whichever is desired.

Preheat oven to 350 degrees. Place brisket, fat side up, on rack over broiler pan. Glaze meat with 2 tablespoons of the prepared mustard. Brush on the chosen glaze and bake for 1 hour, brushing and turning every 15 minutes. Let set for 15 minutes before slicing, then slice very thin against the grain.

To serve: Slice brisket and arrange on a very large serving platter. With slotted spoon place cabbage wedges, carrots, and onions on platter. Drain potatoes in colander and return to saucepan. Toss with butter and sprinkle with parsley; place on platter. Serve brisket with either mustard sauce or horseradish sauce, or both for individual choice. Delicious with a good Irish Soda Bread!

Mustard Glaze:

2 Tablespoons prepared mustard	1/4 teaspoon nutmeg
2 Tablespoons brown sugar	1/8 teaspoon pepper

Mix all ingredients together and brush on corned beef brisket.

Honey Glaze:

1/3 cup catsup	2 Tablespoons mint jelly
2 Tablespoons red wine vinegar	1 Tablespoon butter or margarine
2 Tablespoons honey	1 Tablespoon prepared mustard

In a small saucepan over medium heat, combine all ingredients and heat to boiling. Stir constantly to prevent scorching. Spoon glaze over meat and bake, basting every 15 minutes, until well glazed.

(Continued)

Vegetables for Corned Beef Dinner:

12 new potatoes or 4 pounds
medium-sized boiling potatoes

2 pounds carrots

1 medium head green cabbage

corned beef cooking water, or
plain boiling water

1/2 cup butter or margarine

1/4 cup chopped parsley

Peel potatoes and carrots; cover with cold water. When corned beef is nearly ready to serve, cook potatoes and carrots, separately, in boiling water in 2 saucepans, 15 minutes or until fork tender. Drain and return to saucepans over low heat; toss vegetables to dry. Place on heated serving platter to keep warm.

Cut cabbage into 12 wedges. Soak in warm salted water in large bowl 1 minute; drain. Arrange, overlapping, in large skillet. Pour boiling water over cabbage to cover. Cover skillet, bring to boil, lower heat, and simmer 3 minutes. Remove cabbage and drain. Arrange on platter with potatoes and carrots. Heat butter and chopped parsley in small saucepan until bubbly. Pour over vegetables to coat well. Serve with corned beef with mustard sauce and horseradish sauce.

Mustard Sauce:

1/2 cup Dijon style prepared
mustard

1/2 cup lightly packed light
brown sugar

2 teaspoons dry mustard

3 Tablespoons red wine vinegar

1/4 cup salad oil

1/4 cup water

In a small bowl, with wire whisk, combine Dijon mustard and brown sugar to make a paste. Whisk in dry mustard, vinegar, oil and water. Place in small saucepan and bring to a boil. Remove from heat and keep warm. Serve with Corned Beef and Vegetable Platter.

Horseradish Sauce:

1 8-ounce container sour cream

2 Tablespoons prepared mustard

2 Tablespoons prepared
horseradish

Combine all ingredients in a glass or ceramic bowl. Cover with plastic wrap and refrigerate at least 2 hours to let flavors blend. Serve with Corned Beef and Vegetable Platter.

ROYAL MUSHROOM SAUCE

1/2 stick butter

1 cup chopped mushrooms or
canned stems and pieces

1/2 cup chopped green onion
with tops

2 Tablespoons snipped parsley

1 teaspoon cornstarch

1 teaspoon salt

black pepper to taste

1 cup red burgundy wine

1/2 cup water

Saute vegetables in butter until tender. Add water with cornstarch and seasonings. Add wine and heat just until thickened. Serve with roast or steak. Makes about 2 cups.

CINCINNATI FIVE-WAY CHILI

No one who loves to eat can visit Cincinnati without failing to eat and fall in love with this eccentric and delicious noodle dish — Five-Way Chili. It is thought to have been first cooked by Greek immigrants in the 1920s. It is unique to Southern Ohio, and is served in chili parlors. Nobody gives out the recipe: Every family has its own. Five-way Chili is a one-plate lunch and can easily be prepared in advance. It is fun to serve, and can be easily adjusted to your own taste. There is no WRONG way to make it! Hot, sweet, thick, thin, however you like it is right!

1 pound finely ground chuck (grind twice in a meat grinder)	1 (1/2-ounce) unsweetened chocolate, grated
2 medium onions, chopped fine	1/2 teaspoon turmeric
2 cloves garlic, minced	1/2 teaspoon marjoram
1 cup tomato sauce	1/2 teaspoon allspice
2 Tablespoons catsup	1/4 teaspoon nutmeg
1 cup water	1/2 teaspoon cinnamon
1 Tablespoon red wine vinegar	1/4 teaspoon ground cloves
1 Tablespoon chili powder	1/4 teaspoon mace
1 Tablespoon paprika	1/4 teaspoon ground coriander
1 teaspoon black pepper	1/4 teaspoon ground cardamom
1 teaspoon honey	1/2 dry bay leaf, crumbled
1/2 teaspoon ground cumin	1 teaspoon salt

Salt a large cast-iron skillet. Turn heat to medium and add meat, onions, and garlic. Cook until all meat is browned. Add tomato sauce, catsup, water and vinegar. As mixture begins to boil, add everything else. Adjust spices to taste, adding more salt if it needs perking up, turmeric and cumin for a sweatier chili flavor, cinnamon, cloves, and mace if you want it sweeter, cardamom for more bang, unsweetened chocolate for body.

Cover and simmer at very low heat for about 1 hour, stirring and tasting occasionally, adding tomato juice if it is getting too dry to ladle up easily.

Constructing the Chili:

8 ounces thick spaghetti, cooked	1 pound Wisconsin Cheddar
1 16-ounce can red kidney beans	cheese, grated fine, as fluffy
2 chopped onions	as possible

1. The bottom layer is always spaghetti, the thickest you can find. We found none that was thick enough, so we used perciatelli - long, thin macaroni - broke it into 4" lengths and boiled it in salted water to which 2 tablespoons olive oil were added. For a touch of swank, melt a stick of sweet butter into the just-cooked noodles before you dish them out.

You will need 2 to 3 ounces per serving. You want them soft enough to cut easily with a fork, but not so soft they lose their "oomph." Remember, they are the support layer for four other ingredients. Spread them out to cover the bottom of a small oval plate.

(Continued)

2. Next comes the chili. Ladle on enough to cover the noodles.

3. Next, kidney beans, one 16-ounce can. Wash, heat with 2 cups water, then drain. Don't season them or do anything fancy. They are here more for texture than taste. Spoon a sparse layer atop the chili.

4. Chopped onions. Spread them out, to taste, over the beans.

5. Quickly now, so it melts a bit, spread the grated cheese to cover everything. Don't skimp. Cheese should completely blanket the plate, enough so that you can pat it into a neat mound with your hands, just the way they do it in Cincinnati.

You may, if you desire, omit either the beans or onions, or both, for Four-Way, or Three-Way Chili.

We always serve Cincinnati Chili with bowls of oyster crackers, a couple of chili-and cheese-smothered wieners, called "coneys" in Cincinnati.

KIEV STYLE BEEF TENDERLOIN

2 pounds beef tenderloin	1 teaspoon prepared mustard
2 teaspoons grated onion	1/2 cup sour cream
1 pound mushrooms	salt and pepper
6 Tablespoons flour	1 teaspoon grated onion
1-1/2 cups beef broth	

Remove all fat and skin from meat. Cut in 1/2x2" strips. Sprinkle lightly with salt and pepper, let stand at room temperature for about 1 hour. Saute 2 teaspoons onion and mushrooms in 3 tablespoons butter until slightly browned. Sprinkle with flour and mix thoroughly. Add beef broth, mustard and sour cream; stir to blend. Bring to boil. Season sauce to taste with salt and pepper; simmer 10 minutes. Melt 3 tablespoons butter in skillet; quickly brown meat strips along with 1 teaspoon grated onion. Add meat to sauce. Cover, keep hot for 20 minutes to blend flavors. Do not boil or simmer. When ready to serve, heat quickly over direct heat. Serve over rice or noodles.

GREEK MEATBALLS

1 pound lean hamburger	2 Tablespoons mint leaf,
2 medium chopped onions	chopped fine
1 cup light brown bread crumbs,	1 lemon
crushed	2-1/2 cups water or 1 No. 2 can
1-1/2 cups olive oil	tomatoes
1 cup flour	salt and pepper to taste

Mix all ingredients except oil and flour. Add salt and pepper to taste and mix well. Take 1 tablespoon at a time and roll in flour, shaping into small balls. Shake off excess flour and fry in very hot olive oil, over medium flame, for 10 minutes or until brown on all sides. Transfer to large bowl or platter and keep warm until served. Sprinkle with juice of 1 lemon. Serve hot or cold. Serves 6.

MARINATED BEEF FONDUE

2 pounds sirloin, sirloin tips, or
   top round steak
3 Tablespoons lemon juice
3 Tablespoons vinegar
1/2 cup oil
1 medium onion, chopped
2 cloves garlic, minced

1 bay leaf
1 teaspoon dry mustard
1-1/2 teaspoons salt
1-1/4 teaspoons freshly ground
   pepper
1 cup butter
1 cup peanut oil

Cut meat into 1" cubes. Combine remaining ingredients, except butter and oil, and add to meat in a bowl. Cover tightly and refrigerate at least 8 hours, preferably overnight, stirring several times.

When ready to serve, place butter and peanut oil in a 1-quart fondue pot and heat to bubbling, either on top of stove or over fondue burner. Mound raw beef cubes on fondue or dinner plates for your guests to spear and cook in the pot. (Caution them not to eat directly from the hot fondue fork!) It is customary to serve an assortment of sauces. Since this recipe's marinade provides its own flavors, it is not a requisite, but Tarragon Mustard Cream is certainly good! Or Sunshine Fondue Meat Sauce.

Tarragon Mustard Cream:
2 Tablespoons butter, softened
2 Tablespoons Dijon mustard
1 Tablespoon red wine vinegar
1 teaspoon tarragon vinegar

1/3 cup sour cream
pinch of cayenne pepper
salt and coarsely ground pepper
   to taste
1/2 teaspoon tarragon leaves

With a whisk, cream together butter and mustard in the top of a double boiler, away from the heat. Blend in vinegars and then sour cream. Season with cayenne pepper, and salt and pepper to taste. Place over hot water and cook slowly, stirring. Do not allow to become too hot. Add tarragon leaves last.

Sunshine Fondue Meat Sauce:
1/2 cup butter
1/2 cup catsup
3/4 cup fresh orange juice
1/4 cup lemon juice
1/2 cup brown sugar

1 clove garlic, minced
1 Tablespoon soy sauce
1/2 teaspoon ginger
1 teaspoon cornstarch
1 Tablespoon cold water

Melt butter in small sauce pan over medium heat. Add catsup, orange juice, lemon juice, brown sugar, garlic, soy sauce, and ginger. Heat mixture, stirring until smooth. Combine cornstarch and water, mixing well. Remove sauce from heat and add cornstarch mixture. Stir well and return to heat. Simmer for 10 to 15 minutes. Serve as a dip for beef fondue. Makes approximately 2 cups.

FILLET OF BEEF STROGANOFF

1 teaspoon dry mustard
1 teaspoon Dijon wine mustard
1/2 cup cold water
pinch of sugar
2 Tablespoons flour
1/2 cup sour cream and 1/2 cup
  light cream
1/2 pound fresh mushrooms
2 Tablespoons butter
1/2 teaspoon salt
1/8 teaspoon freshly ground
  pepper

4 Tablespoons butter
1 Tablespoon oil
2 pounds beef tenderloin* cut in
  thin strips 2" long
salt and pepper
3 Tablespoons minced shallots
1 clove garlic, minced
1/2 cup strong beef stock
2 Tablespoons finely minced dill
  (or teaspoons dried dill)

In a small bowl, combine the 2 mustards with the water and sugar. Let the mixture stand for 30 minutes to develop flavor. Add the flour to the mustard mixture and blend well with a whisk. Add the sour cream and light cream and set aside.

Use only the mushroom caps and slice thinly. Melt 2 tablespoons of butter in a small skillet. When it is hot, add the mushrooms and season with salt and pepper. Cook over medium-high heat only until the butter separates from the mushrooms and becomes clear and golden. Immediately remove from heat and set aside.

Approximately 15 minutes before dinner is to be served, melt 4 tablespoons butter with 1 tablespoon oil in a wok or heavy 12" skillet. When very hot, saute the tenderloin strips, a few at a time, over very high heat. Do not crowd the pan. The strips should be browned but still a little rare inside. As each batch is done, remove meat from skillet and reserve, sprinkling with salt and pepper to taste.

Add the shallots and garlic to the wok or skillet and cook over medium heat until soft but not browned. Add beef stock and simmer to reduce by one-third. Add the cream-mustard mixture and stir with a whisk until the broth takes on a velvety appearance.

Add the mushrooms and dill and toss with all of the meat in the broth just to heat through. Taste and adjust seasoning, if necessary. Serve in a chafing dish with noodles or rice, a tossed green salad, and French peasant bread.

*Your butcher should be able to provide you with the tail of the tenderloin, a much less expensive cut of meat and yet just as tender and flavorful.

FLANK STEAK ORIENTAL

top quality flank steak, sufficient
for number of persons to be
served
garlic

salt and pepper
1/2 cup soy sauce
1/4 cup Worcestershire sauce
1/2 cup red wine

Rub steak with garlic, salt and pepper and place in shallow pan or bowl. Mix together remaining ingredients for marinade sauce and pour over meat; let stand for at least 5 hours. Cook as you would any steak. (This sauce is good on any kind of meat.)

VEAL AND PEPPERS

1 pound veal scallops (thin slices
of lean veal)
6 green peppers (long thin Italian
peppers if available)
3 large onions

2 cloves garlic
8 ounces Hunt's tomato sauce
1/2 can tomato paste
salt, pepper and oregano to taste

Slice veal and peppers into strips. Chop onions and saute; set aside. Saute peppers; set aside. Fry veal strips until brown. Sprinkle liberally with spices. Return onions and peppers to meat. Pour sauces over all and let simmer 15 minutes. Serve on loaves of Italian bread or over rice.

CUBED STEAKS AU POIVRE

4 beef cubed steaks
1-1/2 teaspoons coarsely ground
black pepper
1 teaspoon salt
3 Tablespoons margarine

1/3 cup water
1 teaspoon lemon juice
1/2 teaspoon Worcestershire sauce
1 medium tomato, sliced

Sprinkle steaks with pepper and salt. In 12" skillet over medium-high heat in hot margarine cook 2 cubed steaks at a time until browned on both sides, about 4 minutes. Arrange steaks on platter; keep warm.

Into pan drippings, over medium-high heat, stir water, lemon juice, and Worcestershire, stirring to loosen brown bits on bottom of skillet. Pour sauce over steaks on platter. Arrange tomato slices on platter with steaks. Serves 4; 275 calories per serving.

BEST LITTLE
CHICKEN-FRIED STEAK

2 pounds inside round steak, 1/2
  to 3/4" thick
flour for dredging

chicken-fried steak batter
chicken-fried steak gravy
chicken-fried steak biscuits

Have butcher tenderize or pound the steak thoroughly on both sides with meat-tenderizing mallet. Trim off all grizzle and fat. Cut into pieces 5 to 6" in diameter. Flour each piece thoroughly and shake off excess flour. Dip in steak batter and drain. Then flour again and shake off excess. Use deep fryer half-filled with vegetable oil. Preheat to 325 degrees. Cook meat 7 to 10 minutes or until golden brown. Serve with Chicken-Fried Steak Gravy and plenty of good biscuits.

Chicken-Fried Steak Batter:
3 Tablespoons sugar
1/2 teaspoon salt

1 whole egg, beaten
1 Tablespoon baking powder
2 cups milk

Mix the first four ingredients with half the milk and stir until smooth. Add remainder of milk and mix well.

Chicken-Fried Steak Gravy:
1 stick margarine
8 cups milk
1/2 cup cooking oil

1 cup flour
2 teaspoons salt
black pepper to taste

Melt margarine completely. Add milk and mix thoroughly. Bring to a boil. Blend flour into oil, then add to heated milk. Stir until smooth and thickened. Remove from heat. Add salt and pepper to taste.

BROOKOVER BEEF SAUCE

2 cloves garlic, minced
1 small onion, minced
3/4 teaspoon dry mustard
1 Tablespoon horseradish
1 Tablespoon mixed salad herbs
2 Tablespoons red wine vinegar
3 cups water
3/4 teaspoon salt

1 Tablespoon Worcestershire
2/3 cup butter
1/2 cup catsup
1/2 teaspoon Tabasco
2 teaspoons sugar
3/4 teaspoon chili powder
1/2 teaspoon freshly ground
    pepper

Combine all ingredients and cook slowly for an hour. Makes 3 cups of zesty, delicious sauce which can be used to baste beef while cooking or to dip slices of beef into heated sauce before serving.

STEAK STUFFING

Stuffing is thrifty and it adds Pizzazz. Stuffing can be a way to stretch meat. There is nothing at all new about stuffing steak; they were doing it back in the Gold Rush days in California. The specialty of some of San Francisco's finest food establishments (1880) was "Carpeting Steak", a thick cut of beef tenderloin stuffed with sauteed oysters. They didn't stuff a steak in order to save money, but to spend it. Neither beef tenderloin nor oysters cost today what they did during the Gold Rush days, but are still expensive. So stuffing a steak can stretch a good steak.

CARPETBAG STEAK

2 to 3 pounds top round steak, 2" thick, or porterhouse steak	1/2 teaspoon black pepper 1/2 teaspoon salt
2 pints oysters, well drained	3 Tablespoons fresh lemon juice
1/2 cup dry croutons	1/2 cup flour
2 Tablespoons chopped parsley	1/4 cup clarified butter
2 cloves garlic, pressed	1 cup oyster liquid
1/2 cup minced green onions	1 cup beef bouillon
3 Tablespoons butter, softened	

To stuff the steak, make a small cut with a boning knife in the center of the side without any fat cover. This is the inside of the steak. Do not cut a large opening, rather pivot the knife so as to enlarge the pocket inside the steak to within 1/2" of the outside edge, without enlarging the original opening more than a couple of inches.

Saute the oysters in 2 to 3 tablespoons butter until they are firm and plump. Remove from the pan and add croutons, parsley, garlic, onion, pepper, salt and lemon juice to pan juices, mixing well. Add sauteed oysters and stuff into pocket of steak, filling completely. Secure opening with 3 to 4 toothpicks and lace up with unwaxed dental floss or string.

Dust with flour and brown in butter. Add oyster liquid and beef bouillon to pan and cover. Bring to boil, then place in a 325 degree oven for 1-1/2 hours. Remove and let sit for 15 minutes before carving. Serve pan drippings separately.

Crab meat Stuffing can be substituted if oysters are not available or if crab meat is preferred.

Crab Meat Stuffing:

1/2 chopped onion	1/2 pound fresh or frozen crab meat
1 clove garlic, minced	
2 Tablespoons melted butter	1 Tablespoon Worcestershire sauce
4 ounce can sliced mushrooms	

Saute onion and garlic in butter until onion is tender. Add mushrooms, crab meat, and Worcestershire sauce; mix well. Stuff steak pocket.

COUNTRY-FRIED STEAK
WITH CREAM GRAVY

3 pound sirloin tip roast, sliced
  into 1/2" thick slices
1 to 2 Tablespoons salt
1 Tablespoon white vinegar
3 cups all-purpose flour

2 Tablespoons freshly ground
  pepper
vegetable oil for deep frying
cream gravy

Pound meat with spiked meat mallet to tenderize. Cut each slice crosswise into 3 pieces. Place in large bowl and cover with water. Mix in salt and vinegar. Marinate for 2 hours. Combine flour and pepper in plastic bag. Add meat (do not pat dry), 1 piece at a time, and shake to coat. Heat oil in deep fryer or deep large skillet over medium-high heat to 350 degrees. Add meat in batches (do not crowd) and fry until light brown, about 30 seconds per side. Drain on paper towels. Place meat on warm platter. Tent with foil. Serves 8 to 10.

Cream Gravy:

2 Tablespoons all-purpose flour
1/4 cup pan drippings
2 to 3 cups milk

1/4 teaspoon salt
1/4 teaspoon pepper
parsley sprigs

Pour off all but 2 tablespoons oil in skillet, leaving browned bits. Heat over medium heat. Add flour and stir 3 minutes, scraping up any browned bits. Remove from heat and gradually whisk in milk. Stir in salt and pepper. Whisk over medium heat until thickened, about 1 minute. Spoon over steaks. Garnish with parsley and serve.

CHINESE PEPPER STEAK

4 Tablespoons olive oil
1 teaspoon salt
1/2 teaspoon pepper
1 pound flank steak, cut in
  diagonal slivers
4 Tablespoons soy sauce
1/2 teaspoon sugar
2 cups bean sprouts
3 tomatoes, quartered

4 green peppers, chopped
  coarsely
1 clove garlic
1 Tablespoon cornstarch, mixed
  in 1/4 cup cold water until
  smooth
chopped scallions
cooked long grain rice

In heavy skillet directly over flame, heat oil with garlic, salt and black pepper. Add slivered steak. Brown 1 to 2 minutes. Add soy sauce and sugar, cover, and cook 2 minutes longer. Remove meat and keep warm. To pan juices add bean sprouts, tomatoes and green peppers. Cook 3 minutes longer. Add meat and cornstarch mixture. Cook until sauce is thickened. Sprinkle with chopped scallions and serve over rice.

TENDERLOIN DELUXE

3 pounds whole beef tenderloin
2 Tablespoons softened butter
1/4 cup chopped scallions
2 Tablespoons butter

2 Tablespoons soy sauce
1 teaspoon Dijon wine mustard
dash of ground pepper
3/4 cup dry sherry

The meat should sit at room temperature for 2 to 3 hours before roasting. Preheat oven to 400 degrees. Spread the tenderloin with the softened butter. Place on a rack in a shallow roasting pan and bake, uncovered, for 20 minutes. Meanwhile, saute the scallions in the remaining butter until tender. Add the soy sauce, mustard, and pepper. Stir in the sherry and heat just to boiling. When meat has baked 20 minutes, pour sauce over it and bake 20 to 25 minutes for medium-rare. Baste frequently. Remove from oven and let sit for 10 minutes; carve in 1" slices, overlapping them attractively on a warm platter lavished with parsley. Either feature the tenderloin in its own sauce or offer mushrooms in wine sauce and a Bearnaise sauce in separate gravy boats.

Mushrooms in Wine Sauce:
6 Tablespoons butter
1/2 pound mushrooms, sliced
2 medium onions, finely chopped
1 clove garlic, minced
2 Tablespoons chili sauce
1 Tablespoon Escoffier Diable
    Sauce (available in any
    specialty market)
1/2 teaspoon flour

pinch of dried marjoram
pinch of dried thyme
4 drops Tabasco sauce
2 dashes Worcestershire
5 ounces dry red wine
1 bouillon cube, dissolved in 1/4
    cup water
salt and freshly ground pepper to
    taste
minced parsley

Melt butter in a large skillet. Add mushrooms, onions, and garlic and saute until onions are soft. Add remaining ingredients and mix well. Barely simmer for about 10 minutes. Serve hot in a gravy boat with a sprinkling of minced parsley to compliment steak.

Bearnaise Sauce:
3 Tablespoons tarragon vinegar
1 teaspoon minced green onion
1/4 teaspoon coarsely ground
    black pepper
dash of dried whole tarragon

dash of dried whole chervil or
    parsley flakes
1 Tablespoon cold water
4 egg yolks
1/2 cup butter, softened
1 teaspoon minced fresh parsley
1/8 teaspoon salt

Combine first 5 ingredients in a small sauce pan; bring to a boil over medium heat. Reduce heat to low and simmer until half the liquid evaporates. Pour mixture through strainer, reserve liquid. Combine vinegar mixture and water. Beat egg yolks in top of a double boiler with wire whisk. Add vinegar mixture in a slow, steady stream. Bring water to boil (water in bottom should not touch top pan). Reduce heat to low; add butter, 2 tablespoons at a time, beating constantly until butter melts. Continue until smooth and thick. Remove from heat and stir in fresh parsley and salt. Serve over beef, poultry, or seafood. Yields approximately 1 cup.

LOBSTER-STUFFED
TENDERLOIN OF BEEF

4 to 6 pounds whole beef
    tenderloin
2 6-ounce frozen lobster tails
1 Tablespoon butter, melted
1-1/2 teaspoons lemon juice
6 slices bacon, partially cooked

1/2 cup chopped green onion
1/2 cup butter
1/2 cup dry white wine
1/8 teaspoon garlic salt
fluted whole mushrooms and
    watercress for garnish

Preheat oven to 425 degrees. Cut beef tenderloin lengthwise to within 1/2" of end and spread flat to butterfly, in effect doubling length of tenderloin. Place frozen lobster tails in boiling water to cover. Return water to boiling, reduce heat and simmer 5 to 6 minutes. Carefully remove lobster from shells. Cut lobster meat in half lengthwise and place halves end to end on beef. Combine the melted butter and lemon juice and drizzle on lobster. Close meat around lobster and tie roast together securely with string at 1" intervals. Place on rack in shallow roasting pan, roast approximately 40 minutes, until meat thermometer registers 140 degrees for rare, then lay bacon slices on top of roast and roast 5 minutes more. (If medium-rare meat is preferred, internal temperature should be 160 degrees; well-done, 170 degrees.)

Meanwhile, in saucepan, cook green onion in the remaining butter over very low heat until tender, stirring frequently. Stir in wine and garlic salt and heat through. To serve, slice roast and spoon wine sauce over it, garnishing platter, if desired, with fluted mushrooms and watercress. Serves 8.

Variation: Substitute 4 ounces of fresh crab meat for lobster, if desired.

APACHE BEEF STEW

2 pounds boneless beef stew, cut
    in 1-1/2" cubes
3 Tablespoons flour
1-1/2 teaspoons salt
3 Tablespoons lard or drippings

1 cup water
2 medium onions, sliced
1 Tablespoon chili powder
1 15-ounce can kidney beans

Mix together flour and salt; dredge beef cubes in seasoned flour. Brown cubes in hot lard or drippings. Add water, onions and chili powder. Cover tightly and cook slowly 2 hours or until meat is tender. Add beans and bring mixture back to a boil. Reduce heat and simmer 30 minutes longer until beans are heated through and flavors are blended. Serves 6 to 8.

ORIENTAL ROAST

3 to 5 pound chuck or brisket
   roast
slivers of garlic or onion
1 cup vinegar

2 cups strong black coffee
2 cups water
salt and pepper to taste

With a large knife cut slits completely through the meat. Insert slivers of garlic down into the slits. If you do not like garlic, use onions instead. Both may be used if desired. Pour vinegar over the meat and be sure it runs down into the slits with the garlic and onion. Refrigerate for 24 to 48 hours. When ready to cook, brown meat on all sides in oil in a large heavy iron pot (if possible) until meat is very brown, nearly burned. Pour coffee over meat. Add water and cover; simmer on top of stove 4 to 6 hours. Season with salt and pepper. If roast cooks too dry during cooking time, add hot water, not more than 1 cup at a time.

This roast falls apart at the touch of a fork and the yummy black gravy, on mashed potatoes, is heavenly. The gravy may be thickened or left as is. If you like more gravy, water may be added.

PEPPERED RIBEYE OF BEEF

1 5-pound ribeye of beef roast,
   trimmed
1/2 cup whole black peppercorns, coarsely ground
1/2 teaspoon ground cardamom
   seed

1 Tablespoon tomato paste
1 teaspoon paprika
1/2 teaspoon garlic powder
1 cup soy sauce
3/4 cup red wine vinegar
1 cup water

Place beef in 9x13" baking dish. Combine pepper and cardamom seed in small bowl. Firmly press pepper mixture into beef. Combine tomato paste, paprika and garlic powder in medium bowl. Stir in soy sauce and vinegar. Pour marinade over beef. Cover and refrigerate at least 6 hours, or overnight, basting occasionally.

Remove beef from refrigerator. Let stand in marinade at room temperature 1 hour. Preheat oven to 300 degrees. Remove beef from marinade using tongs and wrap in heavy-duty foil. Discard marinade. Transfer beef to shallow pan. Roast to desired doneness, about 2 hours for medium-rare.

Remove beef from baking pan. Degrease drippings. Combine 1 cup drippings with 1 cup water in small saucepan. Bring sauce to boil over medium-high heat. Unwrap beef and transfer to platter. Slice and serve immediately, passing sauce separately.

INVOLTINI UMIDO

2-1/2 pounds top round roast
1/4 pound prosciuto ham
2 celery stalks
1-1/2 tablespoons chopped
  parsley
freshly ground pepper to taste

3 cups plum tomatoes
1 medium onion
1 carrot
2 to 3 Tablespoons olive oil
salt to taste
1/2 cup white or red wine

Cut thin slices from roast and pound very thin. Cut into 4x4" pieces and save trimmings. Chop 1 stalk celery, 1 tablespoon parsley and meat trimmings together and add a twist of pepper, forming a paste. On each piece of beef, put a slice of prosciuto and 1 tablespoon of celery-meat paste. Roll slice up diagonally and fold in ends, fixing with a toothpick. Sieve tomatoes, mince onions and carrots with remaining celery and parsley. Brown vegetables in oil, then add meat and brown meat on all sides. Add salt, wine and tomatoes. Bring pan to a boil and simmer for 1 hour or until the sauce is reduced and the meat is tender.

SOUR CREAM MEAT LOAF

2 eggs
1 (8-ounce) carton dairy sour
  cream
1/4 cup milk
1/2 cup fine dry cornbread
  dressing mix (Pepperidge)
1/2 cup finely chopped green
  onions
2 Tablespoons snipped parsley

1 Tablespoon Worcestershire
  sauce
1 Tablespoon Dijon mustard
1/4 teaspoon salt
1/4 teaspoon pepper
1-1/2 pounds lean ground beef
1/2 pound sausage (Jimmy Dean)
1 (3/4-ounce) package brown
  gravy mix (Knorr)

In a large bowl combine eggs, 1/2 cup of sour cream, and milk; stir in bread crumbs, onion, parsley, Worcestershire sauce, mustard, salt, and pepper. Add beef and sausage; gently mix meat and seasonings thoroughly. Pat into a 9x5x3" loaf pan or shape into the same size loaf and place in a 12x7-1/2x2" baking dish. Bake, uncovered, in a 350 degree oven for about 1-1/4 hours or until a meat thermometer inserted in center of loaf registers 170 degrees. Let cool 10 minutes; remove from pan.

Meanwhile, for gravy, in a medium saucepan stir together the remaining sour cream and the dry gravy mix. Add water as called for on package. Cook according to package directions. Slice meat loaf and serve with mashed potatoes and gravy. Makes 6 to 8 servings. Leftover meat loaf makes super sandwiches, either cold or warmed.

CELESTE'S LEFTOVER BEEF-A-PLENTY

2 scallions, chopped
6 ounces fresh mushrooms, sliced
1 Tablespoon butter
1 pound leftover roast beef,
    sliced thin

10-1/2 ounce can dark beef gravy
10-1/2 ounce can mushroom gravy
16 ounce package noodles, cooked

Saute scallions and mushrooms in butter, in a large frying pan over medium heat. When they have cooked down sufficiently, add the sliced beef and stir-fry briefly, just enough to heat. Add both cans gravy. Stir, while heating, to serving temperature. Serve over noodles. This is so good, you may even want to make a roast specially for making this dish!

ALL-AMERICAN BEEF STEW

3 pounds well-trimmed beef
    round, cut into 1-1/2" cubes
1/2 cup seasoned flour (recipe
    follows)
1/3 cup vegetable oil
2 large onions, cut into wedges
4 medium-size carrots, cut into
    diagonal slices

1-1/4 pounds small red-skinned
    potatoes, quartered
3 ribs celery, cut in 1" lengths
4 cups beef broth
2 Tablespoons tomato paste
2 Tablespoons Dijon mustard
    (optional)
1/2 teaspoon salt
pepper to taste

Coat meat with seasoned flour and brown in hot oil (see Browning Secrets, below). Reduce heat to medium low. Drain off all but 1 tablespoon pan drippings. Add onions, carrots, potatoes and celery to pot. Cook about 5 minutes, stirring once or twice, until lightly browned. Add broth, tomato paste and mustard, stirring to scrape up browned bits. Bring to a boil. Return meat to pot. Reduce heat. Cover and simmer 1 hour, stirring once. Taste; add additional broth and salt and pepper if necessary. Cover and simmer 1 hour longer, stirring once or twice, until meat is tender and sauce is slightly thickened. Serves 8.

Seasoned-flour Secrets:

Coating meat with seasoned flour seals in juices and helps achieve a dark brown crustiness. The crusty bits left over from browning add flavor and color and thicken the stew. To make seasoned flour (enough to coat 3 pounds of meat):

1/2 cup all-purpose flour
1-1/2 teaspoons salt

1 teaspoon pepper

Mix all ingredients in a large bag or bowl. Shake or toss about half the meat pieces at a time until pieces are separated and evenly coated with seasoned flour. For large pieces of meat, such as chicken or turkey parts, or short ribs, coat only one or two pieces at a time, shaking bag or turning in bowl to coat all sides. Shake off excess flour into bag or bowl. Spread floured meat in a single layer on a sheet of waxed paper until time for cooking.

(Continued)

Browning Secrets:

Proper browning starts with the right pot. Use a 5 to 6 quart heavy, tightly lidded pot or Dutch oven (preferably not aluminum, unless it has a nonstick finish). Heat oil over medium-high heat. Be sure it is hot enough before adding the meat; it will look thin and rippling but not smoking.

Carefully add meat in a single layer with room between pieces. Too many pieces at a time lowers the temperature of the oil and prevents browning. Browning takes from 10 to 15 minutes per batch. Stir occasionally or turn pieces to brown on all sides. Remove each batch of browned meat to plate or bowl; reheat oil between batches.

Reheating Secrets:

Stews are even better the next day. Remove solidified fat from the top and start heating stew over low heat, stirring often. Add more liquid if needed. As stew warms and liquifies, increase heat to medium.

Flavor Secrets:

A few drops of lemon juice or red wine vinegar added during the last 15 minutes of cooking perks up the flavor of stew. Use fresh-ground pepper and fresh herbs whenever possible.

GRANDMA'S MEAT LOAF
(You can tell a good cook by her Meat Loaf)

8 ounces skinned and boned
   chicken breast
8 ounces boneless beef chuck
8 ounces boneless pork loin
3 ounces white bread, soaked in 6
   Tablespoons water
2 ounces bacon, chopped
2 ounces sausage
1 medium onion, chopped
1 large garlic clove
2 ounces fresh bread crumbs

2 eggs, beaten
1 Tablespoon minced fresh
   parsley
2 teaspoons salt
1/4 teaspoon freshly ground
   pepper
1/4 teaspoon dried marjoram,
   crumbled
all-purpose flour
1 egg, beaten, for glaze
1-1/2 cups water

Preheat over to 350 degrees. Grease roasting pan. Grind chicken, beef, pork, bread, bacon, sausage, onion and garlic through fine plate of meat grinder into large bowl. Mix in bread crumbs, 2 eggs, parsley, salt, pepper and marjoram. Shape into 9x5" loaf. Roll in flour, shaking off excess. Transfer to prepared pan. Brush with beaten egg. Pour in 1-1/2 cups water. Bake until juices run clear when meat loaf is pierced with skewer, basting occasionally and adding more water to pan if necessary, about 1-1/2 hours. Let stand at room temperature 10 minutes before serving. Serves 6.

BARBECUE VENISON

venison shoulder or leg   salt pork, sliced
meat tenderizer   basting sauce

Soak meat 6 to 8 hours or overnight. Penetrate meat with a fork. Add meat tenderizer several hours prior to cooking or overnight. Make several diagonal slices into meat and add slices of salt pork. Cook over slow charcoal fire until ready to eat. Baste with basting sauce frequently while venison is cooking.

Basting Sauce:
1 stick butter, melted   1 teaspoon liquid smoke
juice of 1 lemon   black pepper
1/2 cup vinegar

Mix all ingredients together and brush on venison frequently while meat is cooking.

FRIZZLED CHIPPED BEEF

1 large zucchini (about 1 pound)   2 cups milk
1 Tablespoon butter   1 8-ounce can water chestnuts,
1 3-ounce package smoked, sliced   drained and quartered
   beef   2 Tablespoons sherry
3 Tablespoons chopped onion   2 teaspoons Worcestershire sauce
1/2 pound fresh mushrooms,   4 ounces shredded Cheddar
   sliced   cheese
1 Tablespoon fresh lemon juice   6 tomato slices
3 Tablespoons butter   2 Tablespoons grated Parmesan
1/4 cup all-purpose flour   cheese
1 teaspoon dry mustard   chopped parsley

Cut zucchini into thirds crosswise; parboil in water for about 15 minutes, or until just tender. Set aside. In a large skillet melt 1 tablespoon butter. With scissors snip beef in small pieces into skillet. Cook and stir in butter until lightly frizzled. Add onion; cook and stir 1 minute. Add mushrooms and lemon juice. Cook and stir occasionally until mushrooms are slightly cooked. Meanwhile, prepare white sauce: In a 2-quart saucepan, melt 3 tablespoons butter. Add flour and mustard. Cook over low heat until mixture is smooth. Remove from heat. Stir in milk. Heat to boiling, stirring constantly. Boil and stir 1 minute. Remove from heat. Add frizzled beef mixture and water chestnuts. Mix well. Stir in sherry and Worcestershire sauce. Add Cheddar cheese and stir until cheese melts.

To assemble: Cut each third of zucchini lengthwise into 4 slices. Lay 2 slices in each of six 8-ounce buttered ramekins. Pour 1/2 cup of beef/cheese sauce over each portion. Place tomato slice on top of each portion. Bake in preheated 350 degree oven for 10 minutes. Sprinkle 1 teaspoon Parmesan cheese on top of each tomato slice and broil until lightly browned. Serve sprinkled with chopped parsley. Serves 6.

SUPREME BEEF CASSEROLE

1-1/2 pounds ground lean beef
1 teaspoon shortening or 2
  Tablespoons butter
1 medium onion, diced or 6 small
  green onions with tops
1 (1-ounce) can tomatoes
2 (8-ounce) cans tomato sauce
2 teaspoons salt
2 teaspoons sugar
2 garlic buds, crushed

1 (5-ounce) package broad
  noodles
1 cup grated cheese
1 cup sour cream
1 (3-ounce) package cream cheese
1 (6-ounce) can mushrooms,
  drained and chopped or 1/4
  pound fresh mushrooms,
  sliced

Brown beef in shortening, breaking up with fork. Drain off fat. Stir in tomatoes, tomato sauce, salt, pepper, sugar and garlic; add mushrooms. Simmer for 20 minutes. Meanwhile, cook noodles and drain. With a fork, blend sour cream, cream cheese and onions into noodles. Into a lightly greased 3-quart casserole, put 1/3 of meat mixture; then a layer of noodles, then 1/2 the grated cheese. Pour over this 1/2 of remaining meat mixture. Repeat layers with remaining noodles and cheese, then top with remaining meat mixture. Bake at 350 degrees for about 35 minutes. Serve with tossed salad and French bread. Serves 6 to 8.

SWEET AND SOUR MEATBALLS

Meatballs:
1 pound lean hamburger
1 egg
2 Tablespoons flour

1 teaspoon salt
dash pepper
1-1/2 Tablespoons chopped onion

Combine all ingredients and mix well. Form into small balls and fry in deep fat until brown. Drain and reserve.

Sauce:
1 teaspoon oil
1 cup canned soup stock
3 Tablespoons cornstarch
2 teaspoons soy sauce
1/2 cup water

2 Tablespoons plus 1 teaspoon
  vinegar
1/2 cup sugar
2 sliced onions
3 diced green peppers
2 cubed cucumbers

Boil together oil, soup stock, cornstarch (mix cornstarch with small amount of cold stock before adding to mixture), soy sauce, water, vinegar and sugar. Saute 2 onions and cucumbers, then add green peppers and cook a minute. Add to sauce. Last, add meatballs, bring to just below simmer and cook until meatballs are hot. Serve.

PORCUPINE MEATBALLS

1 pound lean ground meat
1/2 pound lean ground pork or
    veal
1 egg, beaten
1 teaspoon salt
1/8 teaspoon black pepper
1/4 teaspoon sage
1/3 cup uncooked long grain rice
1 teaspoon Worcestershire sauce
1 Tablespoon Crisco

1 small onion, finely chopped
butter
1 can (10-1/2 ounce) condensed
    tomato soup or 2 cans
    (8-ounce) tomato sauce (1
    with cheese and 1 with
    mushrooms)
2 cups water
cooked spaghetti or long grain
    rice

Brown chopped onion in small amount of butter. Combine ground meats, rice, onion, beaten egg and seasonings and mix thoroughly. Shape into balls about 1" in diameter. Heat shortening in a heavy skillet, add meatballs and brown well. Remove meatballs and set aside. Blend together tomato soup or tomato sauces, water and Worcestershire sauce. Pour into skillet, cooking over medium heat until mixture comes to a boil, about 3 minutes. Add meatballs to simmering sauce, spooning sauce over all. Return mixture to a boil, about 1 minute. Reduce heat and simmer 45 minutes, turning meatballs once or twice during cooking. Serve over cooked spaghetti or rice. Only a vegetable and a salad are needed to complete this meal.

Children are intrigued with these interesting looking meatballs, as after cooking the rice sticks out on all sides like the quills of a porcupine. Also makes an unusual cocktail meatball.

MEATBALL YUMMIES

1 pound ground beef
1/2 cup bread crumbs
1 egg
2 Tablespoons Prime Choice or
    Heinz 57 Sauce

2 Tablespoons oil
1/2 cup Prime Choice or Heinz 57
    Sauce
2 Tablespoons light brown sugar
2 Tablespoons margarine

Combine beef, bread crumbs, egg and 2 tablespoons sauce. Mix well and shape into 1" meatballs. Brown in oil in skillet. Drain fat from skillet. Combine rest of ingredients in skillet. Add meatballs and simmer, covered, for 15 minutes or until done. Yields 2 dozen meatballs.

PEPPER STEAK

1 Tablespoon Kitchen Bouquet
  sauce
1 Tablespoon molasses (Bead)
1-1/2 teaspoons Worcestershire
  sauce
1 Tablespoon cooking sherry
1-3/4 cups water
1/4 cup all-purpose flour or 2
  Tablespoons cornstarch
1/2 cup salad oil
3 Tablespoons soy sauce
1/4 teaspoon sugar

1 teaspoon salt
1-1/2 to 2 pounds flank or round
  steak, cut into 1/2" strips
2 green peppers, julienned
2 medium onions or 1 cup green
  scallions, white and some
  green
1 (6-ounce) can sliced mushrooms
1/4 teaspoon ground ginger
  (optional)
NOTE: Can use 1 red bell pepper
  and 1 green bell pepper

Trim excess fat from steak and cut into thin 1/2" strips. In a medium sized bowl, mix 1 tablespoon salad oil, soy sauce, sherry, sugar, and Kitchen Bouquet; add beef strips and set aside. Cut green peppers and onions into strips; saute in 2 tablespoons salad oil, stirring in hot oil until slightly brown and crisp; set aside. In a large skillet or saucepan, heat 5 tablespoons oil until very hot. Add steak mixture and stir fry until it loses its red color, 3 to 5 minutes. Add onion and peppers. Stir in flour. Add mushrooms, molasses and water. Simmer until thickened. Spoon into a deep serving platter. Sprinkle with finely chopped parsley, if desired. Serve at once with steamed white or brown or wild rice. This is delicious when served with snow peas or Chinese cabbage. A good dessert is gelatin or fruit pie.

CHINESE STEW

2 pounds stew beef, cut in small
  pieces
1 Tablespoon cooking oil
1-1/4 cups water
2 Tablespoons soy sauce

5 ounce can bamboo shoots,
  drained
1/8 teaspoon pepper
1 can condensed mushroom soup
1 small onion, sliced
5 cups green cabbage, chopped

Sprinkle meat with pepper; brown in hot oil in a skillet. Add soup, water, onions, and soy sauce. Cover and simmer for 1-1/2 hours or until meat is tender. Add cabbage and bamboo shoots, cover and simmer 10 minutes. Serve over hot rice.

CHOP "SOUPY"

1 pound round steak, cut in thin strips
2 Tablespoons salad oil
1-1/2 cups fresh mushrooms or 4-ounce can mushrooms
1-1/2 cups celery, diagonally cut

1 cup green pepper, cut in squares
1/2 cup Campbell's beef broth
2 Tablespoons soy sauce
2 Tablespoons cornstarch
1/2 cup water

Brown beef in oil; add vegetables, soup, and soy sauce. Cover and cook over low heat 20 minutes or until meat is tender. Stir occasionally. Blend cornstarch with water and stir into sauce. Cook, stirring, until thickened. Serve over rice.

VEAL SCALOPPINE

3 pounds veal or sirloin, sliced 1/4" thick
1/2 cup flour
1 cup freshly grated Parmesan cheese, divided
1 teaspoon salt
1/8 teaspoon pepper
2 teaspoons paprika
1 clove garlic
3 Tablespoons olive oil

1 6-ounce can sliced mushrooms or 1-1/3 cups sliced fresh mushrooms
1 beef bouillon cube or 1 cup canned bouillon
1/2 cup white wine
1 Tablespoon lemon juice
1/2 stick butter
1/4 to 1/2 cup chopped green pepper
parsley

Cut meat into 2" wide strips. Combine flour, 1/2 cup cheese, salt, pepper and paprika. Dredge meat in flour mixture and pound thoroughly. In a skillet, crush garlic; then add olive oil and meat. Brown meat and place in a baking dish. Drain mushrooms and reserve liquid. Add water to mushroom liquid to make 1 cup, heat to boiling, add bouillon cube, and dissolve. Remove from heat, add wine and lemon juice, and pour over meat. Bake at 350 degrees for 30 minutes. Saute green pepper and mushrooms in butter, pour over meat, and sprinkle with remaining Parmesan cheese. Bake 15 minutes longer. Garnish with parsley. Serve with buttered green noodles. Serves 8. May be frozen before or after the first baking.

TEENAGERS' DELIGHT

1 medium onion, chopped	2 Tablespoons oil
1 pound lean hamburger	1 teaspoon salt
1/2 teaspoon black pepper	1 teaspoon Worcestershire sauce
1 Tablespoon catsup	1 teaspoon mustard
1-1/2 cups chopped celery	10 ounce can tomato soup
1 teaspoon chili powder	1 teaspoon Italian seasoning

Cook onion in 2 Tablespoons oil until golden brown. Add hamburger, salt and pepper. Cook until meat is brown. Add Worcestershire sauce, catsup, mustard, chopped celery, tomato soup, chili powder, Italian seasoning and cover. Simmer for 30 minutes. Serve on rice or toasted buns.

CORNBREAD PIE

1 pound ground beef	1/4 teaspoon black pepper
1 large onion, chopped	1 Tablespoon chili powder
1 10-1/2 ounce can tomato soup	1 can whole kernel corn
1-1/2 cups water	1/2 cup chopped green peppers
1 teaspoon salt	

Combine ground beef and onion in a skillet and brown well. Add tomato soup, water, salt, pepper, chili powder, whole kernel corn, and green peppers. Mix well and allow to simmer 15 minutes. Turn into a greased casserole and top with cornbread. Bake at 350 degrees for 20 minutes.

Cornbread Topping:

3/4 cup corn meal	1 egg, well beaten
1 Tablespoon sugar	1/2 cup milk
1 Tablespoon flour	1 Tablespoon bacon drippings
1-1/2 teaspoons baking powder	

Sift corn meal, sugar, flour and baking powder together. Add well-beaten egg, milk, and bacon drippings. Turn onto beef mixture. Topping will probably sink, but it will rise again and cook crispy.

SWEET AND SOUR MEAT LOAF

Sauce:

1 (16-ounce) can stewed tomatoes	1/2 medium onion, minced
1/2 cup brown sugar	1/2 cup Pepperidge Farm
1/4 cup vinegar	cornbread dressing
1 teaspoon prepared mustard	2 Tablespoons prepared sauce
1/3 cup chopped green pepper	(recipe follows)
Meat Loaf:	1 teaspoon salt
2 pounds ground beef	1/2 teaspoon garlic salt
2 eggs, slightly beaten	1/2 teaspoon black pepper

(Continued)

Preheat oven to 350 degrees. Mix together sauce ingredients. Simmer until sugar dissolves. Combine meat ingredients and shape into a loaf. Place loaf in shallow pan. Pour 1/4 cup sauce over top of meat loaf. Bake, uncovered, for 1 hour. Heat remaining sauce and serve with meat. Serves 6.

CHANTILLY SAUCE

Chantilly is a picturesque little town located northeast of Paris, in the Ile de France region. The town is famous for the airy lace, now a precious collector's item, which the townspeople used to make with deft fingers as they sat in front of their little houses.

Something else, however, as airy and light as lace comes from Chantilly which is not made with bobbins but with a whisk! Legend says that whipped cream was served for the first time at a banquet at the castle in Chantilly in 1720, and, in true French fashion, the people commemorate to this day this delightful culinary creation. The French seldom refer to "whipped cream" . . . it is known as "Chantilly cream". Chantilly sauce, therefore, can only bear the name if it contains whipped cream.

7 ounces butter
3 egg yolks
2 Tablespoons water
pinch of salt

1 teaspoon lemon juice
few drops Worcestershire sauce
2 Tablespoons whipped cream

Melt butter, skim foam off with a spatula or small sieve. Allow to cool slightly and remove all milky residue.

In a top pan of a double boiler, beat the egg yolks with 2 tablespoons of water. Place over boiling water and whisk until eggs are creamy and thickened. Remove pan from double boiler. With a spoon, stir in lukewarm butter, season sauce with lemon juice, salt, and Worcestershire. Blend in whipped cream and serve with tender steak. Also delicious with lobster, other shellfish, and fish in general.

BEA'S BARBECUE SAUCE

1 quart red vinegar
1 pound margarine
14 ounces catsup
5 ounces Worcestershire sauce
12 ounces chili sauce
2 ounces onion salt
2 ounces garlic salt

1 ounce celery salt
1/4 bottle Tabasco sauce
8 Tablespoons lemon juice
  (4 lemons)
1 Tablespoon black pepper
1 Tablespoon salt

Combine all ingredients and simmer for about 3 hours. Pour into bottles. Makes approximately 1 gallon of sauce which keeps well and is good on chicken, pork, and beef.

MARTHA'S CITRUS AND HONEY BARBECUE SAUCE

(Good for Chicken or Pork)

1-1/2 teaspoon black pepper	2 cups beef or chicken broth
1 teaspoon salt	1-1/2 cups bottled chili sauce
1 teaspoon onion powder	1 cup honey
1 teaspoon garlic powder	5 Tablespoons fresh orange juice
1/2 teaspoon white pepper	2 Tablespoons fresh lemon juice
1/2 teaspoon ground red pepper	2 Tablespoons minced garlic
(preferably cayenne)	1 teaspoon hot pepper sauce
8 ounces sliced bacon, minced	1/4 cup unsalted butter
1-1/2 cups finely chopped onions	

Measure spices into a small bowl, mixing well. Fry bacon in a 2-quart saucepan over medium heat until crisp. Stir in onions. Cover and cook 8 to 10 minutes, stirring occasionally, until onions are dark brown but not burned. Stir in seasoning, mix and cook 1 minute. Add remaining ingredients except butter. Stir to mix. Reduce heat to low. Simmer uncovered 10 minutes, stirring often. Simmer 15 minutes longer for flavors to blend. Add butter and stir until butter melts. Remove from heat. Cool 30 minutes. Process in food processor or blender until bacon is finely chopped. Store in refrigerator in tightly sealed jars.

BORDELAISE SAUCE

2 Tablespoons butter/margarine	1/8 teaspoon salt
2 Tablespoons all-purpose flour	1/8 teaspoon coarsely ground
1 Tablespoon minced green onion	black pepper
1 Tablespoon chopped fresh	10-1/2 ounce can beef broth,
parsley	undiluted
1 bay leaf	3 Tablespoons dry red wine
1/4 teaspoon dried whole thyme	

Melt butter in a heavy saucepan over low heat; add flour, stirring until smooth. Cook 1 minute, stirring constantly. Stir in green onion, parsley, bay leaf, thyme, salt, and black pepper. Gradually add broth and wine; cook over medium-high heat, stirring constantly, until thickened and bubbly. Remove bay leaf. Serve over beef. Yields about 1-1/2 cups.

"The Arsenal" – Augusta College

AUGUSTA ARSENAL

Though its buildings are now converted into Augusta College, The Augusta Arsenal will always be indelibly engraved in the history of Augusta. The Arsenal dates back to 1819, when it was a small military outpost. At the end of the Revolution, old Ft. Augusta was only a heap of overgrown rubble, its military value was still important. As early as 1793, President Washington recommended establishing a federal arsenal in the town. The Arsenal came into being in 1816 near the Savannah River. Three years later in 1819, it was brought down by swamp fever and black fever. This caused it to be moved in 1826 to its location on Walton Way.

The Augusta Arsenal has the unique record of having munitions for use both for and against the United States. The Flag of the United States flew over the Augusta Arsenal until it was challenged just after January 19, 1861. At the beginning of the War between the States, the Arsenal was forced to surrender to the State of Georgia. It became one of the Confederacy's assets. Unlike Ft. Sumpter, no shots were fired here. Two former West Point classmates arranged the surrender through stiff diplomatic notes exchanged between Captain Arnold Elzey representing the Federal Government and Col. W. H. T. Walker representing the Governor of Georgia Joseph Brown. A single starred Georgia flag, a pure white banner with a large, red five-pointed star in the center was raised. Salutes were fired; one for the sovereignty of Georgia, five for the seceded State and 15 for the prospective Southern Confederacy. Tradition says that after the surrender, the Southern and Northern soldiers joined together for a friendly supper in the mess hall.

The Arsenal was enlarged the following year and used for the manufacture of cartridge percussion caps, grenades and other arms for the Confederacy. Some three million pounds of ammunition were provided for the confederate cause. After the defeat of the South, the confederate flag came down in turn, to be replaced once more by the United States flag. The government closed the Arsenal in 1955. Two years after closing, it became the Junior College of Augusta and now Augusta College.

Seafood

Crab
Finest Crab Casserole, 192
Meeting Street Crab Meat, 192
San Francisco Deviled Crab, 193
Golden Crab Puffs, 194
Crab Meat Stuffing for Baked Fish, 201
King Crab Royale, 204

Fish
Spirited Salmon Mousse
 with Avocado Sauce, 194
Baked Fresh Salmon, 195
Catfish Stew Riverbank Style, 199
Stuffed Red Snapper
 with Tomato Sauce, 200
Flounder Stuffed
 with Seafood Stuffing, 201
Fillet Marguerite, 202
Jan's Tuna Pie, 202
Broiled Fresh Salmon Steaks
 with Sour Cream Sauce, 203
Baked Salmon
 with Sour Cream Sauce, 205

Lobster
Lobster Newberg, 193

Shrimp
Shrimp Mull, 196
Shrimp and Wild Rice, 197
Hot Shrimp Salad, 198

Shrimp in Vinaigrette, 198
Shrimp Cocktail
 with Remoulade Sauce, 199
Shrimp Remoulade, 202
Sweet-Sour Shrimp, 203
Shrimp Creole, 204
Delicious Shrimp Casserole, 206

Seafood Casseroles
Seafood Casserole Supreme, 197
Karen's Seafood Casserole, 205

Oysters
Oysters "Johnny Reb", 200

Sauces
Avocado Sauce, 194
Cucumber Sauce, 195
Verde Sauce, 196
Remoulade Sauce, 202
Peppy Seafood Sauce, 206
Sharp Sauce, 206
Shrimp White Sauce, 206
Sweet and Sour Sauce, 207
Spirited Tartar Sauce, 207
Tomato Sauce, 200
Sour Cream Sauce, 205

Batter for Seafood
Tempura Batter, 195

FINEST CRAB CASSEROLE

2 cups medium white sauce
2 Tablespoons Worcestershire
    sauce
1 teaspoon hot pepper sauce
salt and lemon pepper to taste
4 Tablespoons butter or
    margarine, divided
1/2 green pepper, minced
1 cup celery, minced
1 large onion, minced
2 cloves garlic, minced
1/2 pound fresh mushrooms,
    sliced

1/4 cup dry sherry
juice of one lemon
2 pounds fresh lump crab meat
    (or shrimp)
1/2 cup fresh parsley, chopped
1 cup medium or sharp Cheddar
    cheese, grated
1 cup grated Parmesan cheese,
    divided
1 cup saltine crackers, crumbs,
    crushed
1-1/2 teaspoons paprika

Preheat oven to 350 degrees. Make white sauce using your own recipe and add to it the Worcestershire sauce, hot pepper sauce, salt, and pepper.

In a medium skillet, melt 2 tablespoons butter. Saute green peppers, celery, onion and garlic. Add this mixture to cream sauce. Add sherry, lemon juice, crab meat, parsley, Cheddar cheese and 1/2 cup Parmesan cheese to cream sauce. Mix thoroughly.

Spoon into casserole dish. Top with cracker crumbs. Sprinkle with remaining Parmesan cheese. Place in oven and bake for 30 to 40 minutes or until hot and bubbly.

MEETING STREET CRAB MEAT

1 pound cooked crab
4 teaspoons butter
4 teaspoons flour
1/2 pint cream or milk

2 teaspoons sherry
3/4 cup sharp cheese, grated
salt to taste
pepper to taste

Make cream sauce with butter, flour and the cream or milk; add salt, pepper and sherry. Remove from heat and add crab meat.

Pour into buttered casserole and sprinkle with grated cheese. Bake in preheated oven at 350 degrees for 20 to 30 minutes. Boiled shrimp may be used to stretch for company, along with the crab meat. Pour into pastry shells to serve.

LOBSTER NEWBERG

6 Tablespoons butter or
  margarine
2 Tablespoons flour
3 cups fresh or canned lobster
  meat, cooked and cut up
1/8 teaspoon nutmeg
dash paprika

1 teaspoon salt
3 Tablespoons sherry
3 egg yolks
2 cups light cream
toast points
buttered bread crumbs

In top of double boiler melt butter; stir in flour, lobster, nutmeg, paprika, salt, sherry. Beat yolks slightly; add cream and mix well. Slowly stir yolks into lobster mixture; cook over hot water, stirring, till just thickened. Serve at once on toast points, in patty shells, or in croustades. Or place in individual baking dishes. Top with buttered fresh bread crumbs; brown under broiler. Serves 6.

SAN FRANCISCO DEVILED CRAB

4 Tablespoons butter
1 Tablespoon vegetable oil
3/4 cup onion, finely chopped
1/2 cup celery, finely chopped
3 Tablespoons flour
1-1/2 cups milk
1 cup light cream
1-1/2 teaspoons dry mustard
1/8 teaspoon Tabasco sauce
1 teaspoon Worcestershire sauce

1/4 cup dry sherry
2 Tablespoons fresh lemon juice
2 Tablespoons fresh parsley,
  chopped
3 hard-boiled eggs, chopped
1 pound Dungeness crab meat,
  flaked
salt and white pepper to taste
1/2 cup Parmesan cheese, grated

In a large skillet combine 3 tablespoons butter and the oil and saute the onion and celery over low heat until soft, about 4 to 6 minutes. Add the flour, a tablespoon at a time, and cook, stirring constantly, for 3 to 4 minutes. Meanwhile, heat milk and cream in a small saucepan. Add the heated milk gradually to the onion mixture, stirring constantly.

In a small bowl combine the dry mustard, Tabasco, Worcestershire, sherry, lemon juice, and parsley. Add this mixture to the onion mixture in the skillet, stirring well. Bring to a simmer and stir until the sauce thickens, about 3 to 4 minutes. Add the chopped eggs and crab meat. Add salt and pepper to taste.

Divide the mixture between 6 buttered scallop shells or ramekins. Dot with the remaining butter and cover with the remaining cheese. Bake in a preheated 375 degree oven for 15 minutes or until they are lightly browned. Serves 6.

GOLDEN CRAB PUFFS

1 can (7-1/2 ounce) Alaskan King crab or 1 package (6 ounce) Alaskan King crab	2 Tablespoons green onion, chopped
1-1/2 cups buttermilk biscuit mix	1 egg, beaten
1/4 cup grated Parmesan cheese	1/3 cup water
	1/2 teaspoon Worcestershire sauce

Drain canned crab and slice, or defrost, drain and slice frozen crab. Combine biscuit mix, Parmesan cheese green onion and crab. Combine egg, water and Worcestershire sauce. Add to crab mixture, stirring just to blend. Drop by teaspoonfuls into 1-1/2" oil heated to 375 degrees. Fry until golden brown, turning once. Drain on paper towels. Serve hot with mustard dip, if desired. Makes 3 to 4 dozen.

May be prepared in advance and reheated in a 375 degree oven for about 8 minutes or until heated through.

Mustard Dip:

1/2 cup mayonnaise	1/2 teaspoon Worcestershire sauce
1/4 cup prepared mustard	3 to 4 drops Tabasco sauce

Combine all ingredients and serve as a dip. Makes 3/4 cup.

SPIRITED SALMON MOUSSE WITH AVOCADO SAUCE

1-1/2 Tablespoons unflavored gelatin	onion salt to taste
1/4 cup dry vermouth	celery salt to taste
1 cup hot sour cream (do not allow to boil)	salt and white pepper to taste
	1 cup heavy cream, whipped
2 cups cooked salmon (or a 1-pound can red sockeye salmon)	1/2 cup celery, finely chopped
	2 Tablespoons onion, minced
1/4 cup mayonnaise	1 Tablespoon parsley, finely chopped
1 Tablespoon lime or lemon juice	
2 teaspoons sherry	1 Tablespoon chives, finely chopped
1/2 teaspoon anchovy paste	cucumber and lime slices for garnish

Soften gelatin in vermouth. Dissolve in hot sour cream; cool. Bone and skin salmon. Add to sour cream mixture with mayonnaise, lime or lemon juice, sherry, anchovy paste, salts and pepper. Whirl briefly in electric blender, but do not puree. Refrigerate until mixture begins to congeal. Fold in whipped cream, celery, onion, parsley and chives. Adjust seasonings. Pour into a lightly greased, 5-cup ring or fish mold. Chill until firmly set. Serve with avocado sauce and garnish with very thin cucumber and lime slices.

Avocado Sauce:

2 ripe avocados	1 teaspoon salt
1 cup sour cream	chopped chives
1 Tablespoon lime juice	

Puree avocados, sour cream, lime juice, and salt in blender. Serve chilled with a sprinkling of chopped chives.

TEMPURA BATTER

1 cup flour
1/2 teaspoon baking powder
1/2 cup cornstarch

1/4 teaspoon baking soda
1 cup water
1 egg

Blend together dry ingredients with a whisk. Stir in 1 cup water, then egg. Beat until frothy.

BAKED FRESH SALMON

1 (4 to 6-pound) fresh whole
  salmon, boned
1/2 cup packaged herb-seasoned
  stuffing mix
1/2 cup cornbread stuffing mix
1/2 cup hot water
2 Tablespoons capers, drained
  and chopped
3 strips bacon, minced

2 Tablespoons chopped fresh
  parsley
1/2 cup onion, finely chopped
1/2 cup butter or margarine, melted
1/4 teaspoon finely ground white
  pepper
lemon slices
parsley sprigs
cucumber sauce (recipe follows)

Rinse and thoroughly dry the salmon, inside and out. In a 2-quart mixing bowl combine the stuffing mix, hot water, capers and chopped parsley. Toss lightly with a fork until mixture is moist and blended. Place the minced bacon in a heavy skillet and saute over medium heat for 4 to 6 minutes or until bacon is tender. Add onion and saute until bacon is crisp, stirring frequently. Add bacon, onion and pan drippings to the stuffing mixture. Toss lightly to combine. Brush the inside of the salmon with melted butter and sprinkle lightly with salt and pepper. Fill the cavity of the fish loosely with the stuffing mix. Skewer or sew the cavity shut.

Line a shallow baking dish or large pan with heavy foil. Place the fish in the pan and bake in preheated 425 degree oven for 25 minutes or until fish flakes easily when tested with a fork. Remove from oven and keep warm until ready to serve. When ready to serve, remove skin which will be easily done. Coat fish with cucumber sauce, garnish with lemon slices and parsley. Serve at once.

Cucumber Sauce:
2 cups sour cream at room
  temperature
1 Tablespoon onion, finely
  chopped
salt and pepper to taste

1 large cucumber, peeled, seeded
  and finely chopped
1-1/2 Tablespoons fresh lemon
  juice

Blend sour cream, onion, salt, pepper, cucumber and lemon juice. Adjust seasonings to taste.

SHRIMP MULL

2 quarts water	15 drops Tabasco sauce
2 cans (No. 2) tomatoes	1 bottle tomato catsup
1 can (No. 2) tomato soup	2 Tablespoons Worcestershire sauce
1/4 pound butter or margarine	1/4 teaspoon ground allspice
1 cup white bacon, diced	1/4 teaspoon curry powder
1 cup onion, chopped	5 pounds raw shrimp, peeled and
2 cloves garlic, sliced	deveined
1 whole lemon, sliced	1 cup sherry
1 cup celery, chopped	1/4 pound butter
1 teaspoon celery seed	cracker crumbs

Into a heavy kettle put 2 quarts water, canned tomatoes and tomato soup. Simmer. Melt butter in skillet and brown bacon and onion in it. Add to tomato mixture. Add all remaining ingredients except shrimp, sherry and 1/4 pound butter, and boil lightly for 2 hours. Add shrimp and simmer for 1 hour. Add 1 cup sherry and the remaining butter. Thicken with cracker crumbs. Serve with flaky dry rice. Serves 8 to 10.

VERDE SAUCE

2 Tablespoons fresh lemon juice	1 cup mayonnaise
1-1/2 cups spinach leaves, packed	1 cup sour cream
1/2 cup watercress, packed	1 teaspoon cream-style horseradish
8 to 10 sprigs parsley	1 Tablespoon finely minced
3 to 4 sprigs fresh chervil (optional)	parsley
6 sprigs fresh tarragon (or 1	1 Tablespoon finely chopped
teaspoon dried)	watercress

Bring 2 quarts water to a boil in a 3-quart sauce pan. Add spinach, 1/2 cup watercress, parsley, chervil, and tarragon; boil for 5 minutes. Remove from heat, strain, cool and press out all excess water. In a 2-quart bowl, combine mayonnaise, sour cream, and horseradish; set aside. Force cooled spinach mixture through a coarse strainer into a small bowl and add to mayonnaise mixture. Stir to blend well or mix in a blender for 2 to 3 minutes. Stir in minced parsley and chopped watercress; cover and refrigerate until time to serve. Sauce will hold for 3 to 6 hours in refrigerator. Makes 3 cups. Serve with cold poached salmon or trout.

TO BOIL SHRIMP BEFORE PEELING:

1-1/2 pounds shrimp	1/4 cup salt
1 quart water	

Wash shrimp. Place in boiling salted water. Cover and simmer for 3 to 5 minutes. Drain. Peel. Remove veins. Wash. Chill. Yields about 3/4 pound cooked shrimp.

(Continued)

TO BOIL AFTER PEELING:

1-1/2 pounds shrimp 2 Tablespoons salt
1 quart water

Peel shrimp, devein and wash. Place in boiling salted water. Cover and simmer for 3 to 5 minutes. Drain. Remove any particles of veins remaining. Chill. Yields about 3/4 pound cooked shrimp.

SHRIMP AND WILD RICE

1 cup cream of mushroom soup
2 Tablespoons green pepper, chopped
2 Tablespoons onion, chopped
2 Tablespoons butter, melted
2 Tablespoons lemon juice
1/2 teaspoon dry mustard

2 cups wild rice (7-ounce package Uncle Ben's), cooked
1-1/2 teaspoons Worcestershire sauce
1/4 teaspoon black pepper
1 cup Cheddar cheese, grated
1-1/2 pounds raw shrimp, peeled and deveined

Cook rice according to directions on package. Mix all of the ingredients, including cooked rice, thoroughly, with 1/2 cup of the cheese. Pour into a greased 2-1/2 quart buttered casserole dish. Sprinkle with remaining 1/2 cup cheese and bake in preheated 375 degree oven for 30 to 35 minutes. If mixture is too thick add a little milk at a time until mixture is of proper consistency. Serves 8 to 10. Frozen shrimp may be substituted, using 2 packages (12-ounce). Simmer frozen shrimp 2 minutes before adding to other ingredients.

SEAFOOD CASSEROLE SUPREME

1 cup long grain rice
1 pound fresh small shrimp, peeled and deveined
1 pound fresh crab meat
1 (4-ounce) can mushrooms, sliced
1/2 green pepper, finely chopped
1/2 cup onion, chopped
1 (4-ounce) jar pimientos, chopped
1 cup celery, chopped
1 (5-ounce) can water chestnuts, drained and sliced

1 cup mayonnaise
1/2 teaspoon salt
1 cup milk
1/4 teaspoon pepper
1 Tablespoon Worcestershire sauce
bread crumbs for garnish or 1/2 cup sliced almonds sauteed in 2 Tablespoons butter
1/2 cup grated Cheddar cheese

Preheat oven to 375 degrees. Cook rice. Boil shrimp for 3 to 5 minutes, until pink. Cool slightly. In a large bowl, mix shrimp, crab meat, mushrooms, green pepper, onion, pimientos, water chestnuts and celery. In a separate bowl, combine mayonnaise, salt, milk, pepper, Worcestershire sauce and cooked rice, mixing well. Combine mayonnaise mixture with shrimp-crab mixture, blending well. Place in a buttered 2-quart casserole. Sprinkle with bread crumbs and top with grated cheese or with toasted almonds and cheese. Bake for 30 minutes. May be held in a warm oven for 15 to 20 minutes. Also may be partially prepared ahead of time. Serves 8.

HOT SHRIMP SALAD

juice of 1 lemon
1 teaspoon salt
dash garlic powder
dash Tabasco sauce
1 teaspoon dry mustard
2 teaspoons Worcestershire sauce
2 pounds shrimp, cooked
1 cup celery, chopped
1 medium onion, chopped
1/2 cup green pepper, finely
    chopped

1 can (4-ounce) mushrooms
    chopped
1 can (8-ounce) water chestnuts,
    sliced
1/2 cup stuffed green olives,
    chopped fine
2 hard-cooked eggs, chopped
1 package (5-ounce) slivered
    almonds
buttered bread crumbs
paprika

Preheat oven to 350 degrees. Blend first 6 ingredients together in bowl. Fold in shrimp, vegetables, chopped eggs and nuts. Pour into a shallow 3-quart buttered casserole dish. Sprinkle buttered bread crumbs and paprika on top. Bake 30 minutes. Makes a good cold salad, also, either before or after baking. This recipe makes a good Seafood Salad by substituting 1 pound lump crab meat for 1 pound shrimp.

SHRIMP IN VINAIGRETTE

1 pound (14 to 18) fresh jumbo
    shrimp in shell
1-1/2 quarts water boiling in a
    large saucepan
2-1/4 teaspoons salt
3 Tablespoons vinegar
Vinaigrette:
2 Tablespoons Dijon mustard

1/2 Tablespoon minced shallot or
    scallions
2 to 3 Tablespoons lemon juice
    (fresh best)
1/4 teaspoon salt
1/2 cup olive oil or salad oil
freshly ground pepper
1/4 cup minced fresh parsley

Cook shrimp. If frozen, thaw in cold water until you can pull them apart from each other. Cook while still frozen. Drop shrimp into the boiling water, add the salt and vinegar. Bring rapidly back to boil and cook for about 2 minutes. They are done when bright pink and tightly curled. Test by eating one, if you have any doubts, but don't overcook them. Stir 1/3 cup of cold water to stop the cooking; let shrimp cool 15 minutes in their cooking liquid. While the shrimp is cooling, make the vinaigrette.

Whisk the mustard in a bowl with the shallot or scallion, lemon juice and salt; beat in oil by dribbles. Season to taste with pepper and more lemon and salt if needed.

Drain the shrimp and peel rapidly while still warm. Toss with the vinaigrette and parsley; toss several more times as they cool.

SHRIMP COCKTAIL
WITH REMOULADE SAUCE

A cocktail sauce should not overpower but heighten the delicate flavor of shrimp. The mayonnaise-based remoulade sauce fulfills this demand. Its name comes from the French verb "remoudre," which means to grind. To blend the flavors, the ingredients must be well pulverized.

shrimp
lettuce
cracked ice
3/4 cup mayonnaise
1/4 cup prepared mustard
1/2 clove garlic, pressed or 1/8 teaspoon garlic salt
1/4 cup minced onion
1/8 teaspoon sugar
salt and pepper to taste
1/2 teaspoon prepared horseradish
1/4 teaspoon celery seed
1 teaspoon Worcestershire
1 Tablespoon lemon juice
1 Tablespoon capers (optional)

Cook shrimp in boiling salted water until they are bright pink (2 to 5 minutes). Shell and devein shrimp, then chill. Arrange chilled shrimp in cocktail glasses on a bed of greens and cracked ice.

Make remoulade sauce by combining all ingredients and beating thoroughly with a wooden spoon. Garnish with capers, if desired, and serve over chilled shrimp. Makes enough sauce for six cocktails.

CATFISH STEW RIVERBANK STYLE

5 pounds of medium size catfish
3 pounds Irish potatoes
1 pound onions
1/2 pound fatback
2 teaspoons salt
1 teaspoon black pepper
pod or two of red hot peppers (optional)

Clean and dress catfish. Cut crosswise into 2" pieces. Peel and slice potatoes and onions. Slice fatback into 1/4" thick slices. If cooking on a riverbank, use a black iron spider pot, which has a flat bottom with legs and a tight-fitting lid. Put hot coals close under pot and get it hot enough to fry the fatback until all the grease is cooked out and the meat crisp. Remove meat from pot and reserve. Pour off part of the grease. Pull coals back so pot will not be quite so hot. Put layers of half the potatoes, half the onions and half the fish. Sprinkle some salt and pepper over each addition. Repeat layers. Put fried fatback on top; add the pods of hot pepper if desired. Put tight lid on pot and let simmer on low heat until potatoes are tender and fish flakes easily.

DO NOT STIR THIS POT AT ANY TIME. The onions, potatoes and fish produce their own liquid.

To serve, dip down deep into pot, but do not stir. Serve with hush puppies.

To cook on stove just be sure to use a heavy pot with a tight fitting lid and heat sufficient to fry fatback; but reduce heat when potatoes, onions and fish are added so that potatoes will not scorch.

OYSTERS "JOHNNY REB"

2 quarts oysters, drained
1/2 cup parsley, finely chopped
1/2 cup shallots, finely chopped
   (onion may be used)
salt and pepper to taste
Tabasco to taste
1 Tablespoon Worcestershire
   sauce

2 Tablespoons lemon juice
1/2 cup butter or margarine,
   melted
2 cups fine cracker crumbs
paprika
3/4 cup half and half cream

Place a layer of oysters in bottom of greased shallow 2-quart baking dish. Sprinkle with half of parsley, shallots, seasonings, lemon juice, butter and cracker crumbs. Make another layer of the same. Sprinkle with paprika. Just before baking, pour the half and half into evenly spaced holes, being very careful not to moisten crumb topping all over. Bake in preheated oven at 375 degrees for about 30 minutes or until firm. Serves 12 to 15.

STUFFED RED SNAPPER
WITH TOMATO SAUCE

1 large red snapper, cleaned,
   dried, salted and peppered
Stuffing:
8-ounce package Pepperidge
   Farm cornbread stuffing

1 to 1-1/2 pounds raw shrimp,
   cleaned and diced or 1 pound
   raw shrimp
1/2 pound crab meat

Prepare stuffing according to package directions. Add shrimp. Stuff snapper with dressing.

Sauce:
1/2 cup onion, chopped
1/2 cup celery, chopped
1/2 cup green pepper, chopped
oil or bacon drippings
32 ounces tomato sauce
6 ounces tomato paste

2 cups catsup (may use 2-1/2 cups)
salt to taste
pepper to taste
soy sauce to taste
1 teaspoon garlic salt
parsley

Preheat oven to 375 degrees. Brown onion, celery and green peppers in oil or bacon drippings. Add tomato sauce, tomato paste and catsup. Add seasonings and parsley last for color. Pour over stuffed snapper and bake for 45 minutes, basting occasionally. Serves 6 to 8. The sauce makes the fish, so be sure to prepare plenty.

CRAB MEAT STUFFING
FOR BAKED FISH

salmon, red snapper or other fish
of choice
1 cub crab meat, fresh or frozen,
picked for pieces of shell
1/2 cup sour cream
1/2 cup mayonnaise
1/2 cup onion or scallions, finely
chopped

1/2 cup celery, finely chopped
3 Tablespoons butter
1/2 cup cubed herb-seasoned
stuffing mix
salt to taste
pepper to taste

Saute onion and celery in the butter until tender. Remove from heat and add crab meat, sour cream, mayonnaise and stuffing mix. Toss to blend. Stuff fish and bake according to directions for fish of choice. Makes about 4 cups of stuffing.

FLOUNDER STUFFED
WITH SEAFOOD STUFFING

1 large or 2 small flounder
salt and pepper
8 Tablespoons butter or margarine
Stuffing:
1/2 cup green onions, chopped
1/2 cup celery, finely chopped
1/2 cup green pepper, finely
chopped or 1/4 cup red and
1/4 cup green
1 clove garlic, minced
1 Tablespoon all-purpose flour
1/2 cup dry wine or chicken
bouillon
1/2 cup milk

1/2 pound fresh shrimp, cooked,
peeled, deveined and
chopped
1/2 pound fresh or frozen crab
meat, drained and shredded
1/2 cup fresh bread crumbs or
saltine crackers, crushed
2 Tablespoons fresh parsley,
chopped
1 egg, beaten lightly
salt and pepper to taste
dash cayenne pepper
paprika
lemon juice

Clean flounder and make a pocket in side of fish. Season with salt. Saute onion, pepper, celery and garlic in 4 tablespoons butter or margarine until tender. Blend in flour. Add wine or chicken bouillon and milk; stir until thickened. Add shrimp, crab meat, bread crumbs, parsley and egg. Season with salt, pepper and cayenne pepper.

Stuff fish. Place in buttered baking pan. Cover with foil. Bake at 350 degrees for 25 minutes. Brush with remaining butter, sprinkle with paprika and lemon juice. Bake uncovered for 10 more minutes. Spoon pan juices over fish and serve.

NOTE: Four large flounder fillets or 8 small fillets may be used instead of a whole flounder. Place 1/4 or 1/8 of stuffing on each fillet and roll up and fasten with toothpicks. Then follow the directions above for stuffed fish.

FILLET MARGUERITE

1-1/2 pounds (4 or 5) fillets of
sole, red snapper, salmon
10 ounce can condensed cream of
shrimp soup

1/4 cup sherry or milk
2 Tablespoons butter
1/4 cup grated Parmesan cheese
paprika

Place fish fillets in greased crock pot. Combine soup and sherry or milk. Pour soup mixture over fillets. Dot with butter. Sprinkle Parmesan cheese and paprika over top. Cover and cook on low 3 to 4 hours or on high for 2 to 3 hours. If fish is frozen, cook on high for the first hour with vent open, then reduce heat to low.

JAN'S TUNA PIE

1 9" deep-dish pie crust
2 small cans tuna
4 eggs, beaten
1/2 cup milk
1 Tablespoon minced onion
1/8 teaspoon salt

1 Tablespoon lemon juice
8 ounces mozzarella cheese,
grated
1/2 cup Swiss cheese, grated
1/2 cup Cheddar cheese, grated

Drain tuna and flake into unbaked crust. Mix beaten eggs, milk, salt, pepper, onion and lemon juice. Pour over tuna. Cover with grated cheeses. Bake at 400 degrees for 12 minutes, then at 350 degrees for 20 to 30 minutes, until cheese browns.

Served with tossed salad and dessert, this makes a complete meal.

SHRIMP REMOULADE

1 quart salad oil
1 Tablespoon dry mustard
1 Tablespoon prepared mustard
2 Tablespoons paprika
2 Tablespoons horseradish
2 Tablespoon parsley, chopped
1 large bell pepper, finely
chopped
2 stalks celery, finely chopped

2 dill pickles, chopped
4 green onions, chopped
1/2 cup wine Tarragon vinegar
2 teaspoons Worcestershire sauce
1 teaspoon Tabasco sauce
2 Tablespoons salt
1 teaspoon sugar
4 pounds shrimp, boiled and
deveined

Gradually add oil to mustards, paprika and horseradish. Add other ingredients, except shrimp. Mix well. Place shrimp in sauce and cover. Refrigerate not less than 48 hours. Will keep for at least a week. Serves 12.

SWEET-SOUR SHRIMP

1/4 cup butter
1 green pepper cut in thin strips
1-1/2 cups celery, sliced
   diagonally
6 whole green onions, sliced
4 teaspoons cornstarch
2 cups orange juice

1 chicken bouillon cube
2 Tablespoons soy sauce
1/4 teaspoon salt
1/4 teaspoon ground ginger
1 pound shrimp, cleaned and
   cooked

Heat butter in skillet over high heat. Add green pepper, celery and green onions and cook 2 minutes, stirring constantly. (If one prefers less crunchy vegetables, they can be cooked at a lower temperature for 10 minutes.) Blend cornstarch with a small amount of orange juice until smooth; add to skillet with remaining orange juice, bouillon cube, soy sauce, salt and ginger. Cook, stirring constantly, until mixture thickens and comes to a boil and bouillon cube is dissolved. Add shrimp and heat. Serve over hot cooked rice. Serves 4.

BROILED FRESH SALMON STEAKS WITH SOUR CREAM SAUCE

4 to 6 salmon steaks, cut 1 to
   1-1/2" thick
mayonnaise
3 Tablespoons melted butter

1 Tablespoon lemon juice
salt and pepper
sour cream sauce (recipe follows)

Place foil over broiler rack and brush lightly with melted butter or margarine. Brush salmon steaks on each side with mayonnaise. Place on broiler rack. Broil under heat for 5 to 7 minutes on each side. Just before serving spoon sauce over each salmon steak. Serves 4 to 6. Serve with baked potato, tossed salad and French bread for a completely delicious meal.

Sour Cream Sauce:
1 cup sour cream
3 scallions, minced (or onion)
1 teaspoon fresh lemon juice

2 Tablespoons dill pickle, finely
   chopped

Blend sour cream, scallions (or onion), lemon juice and dill pickle together. May be heated (be careful not to boil), or served cold. Spoon over each salmon steak.

SHRIMP CREOLE

4 strips lean bacon
2 large onions, finely chopped
1 large green pepper, finely
    chopped (may use 1/2 red
    pepper and 1/2 green if desired)
2 small cans chopped mushrooms
4 ribs celery, finely chopped
2 cans (medium) pear tomatoes
1 clove garlic, minced
1 teaspoon black pepper
1/4 teaspoon cayenne pepper

salt to taste
1 teaspoon sweet paprika
1 Tablespoon sugar
2 Tablespoons Worcestershire sauce
1/2 cup tomato catsup
1 Tablespoon lemon juice
3 rounded Tablespoons flour
2 to 3 pounds peeled raw shrimp
2 Tablespoons sour cream
1/4 teaspoon Tabasco
1-1/2 cups long grain rice

Fry bacon and remove from skillet. Crumble and reserve. Add flour to drippings and brown, stirring constantly to made a dark roux. Add onions and fry slowly until well browned and are reduced to pulp. Add remainder of ingredients (including bacon), except shrimp, to the roux. Continue to cook slowly for at least 30 to 45 minutes. About 20 minutes before serving, add cleaned, deveined shrimp along with any liquid that has accumulated in the bowl. Simmer the mixture, stirring occasionally, for 3 to 5 minutes or until the shrimp are just cooked through. Stir in the sour cream and the Tabasco. Bring the mixture just to a simmer, stirring to keep from sticking. Add more seasonings if desired.

Serve with cooked rice or in a ring of rice made by: Cook rice according to directions on package. Butter a 1-1/2 quart ring mold generously, pack it firmly and evenly with the rice while the rice is still hot. Cover it tightly with foil The rice ring may be prepared in advance and warmed in the oven before serving. Invert a heated platter over the mold and invert the rice ring onto it.

Spoon the shrimp into the center and around the edge of rice ring and garnish with sprays of fresh parsley. This makes a festive party dish.

The Creole may be made 1 day in advance, kept covered and refrigerated. Reheat shrimp creole in a skillet over moderately low heat, stirring until it is heated through, but DO NOT BOIL!

KING CRAB ROYALE

2 packages (12-ounce) frozen
    split Alaskan King crab legs
    in the shell
1/4 cup butter, melted
1 Tablespoon lemon juice
1 teaspoon onion, grated

1 small clove garlic, crushed
1/4 teaspoon crushed tarragon
1/4 teaspoon salt
dash pepper
1 Tablespoon parsley, finely
    chopped

Defrost crab. Remove meat from shells and cut into bite-size pieces for easier serving. Return to shells. Combine remaining ingredients and brush over crab. Heat over hot coals or under the broiler, brushing occasionally with remaining butter sauce. Serves 6.

KAREN'S SEAFOOD CASSEROLE

1 cup shrimp, boiled, shelled and
  cleaned
13-ounce can crab meat
1/2 cup mayonnaise
1/2 cup cream of mushroom soup
3/4 cup chopped onions
3/4 cup chopped celery
4-ounce can mushrooms

1/2 cup chopped green pepper
  (optional)
1-1/2 cups cooked rice
1 teaspoon Worcestershire sauce
dash of Tabasco
salt and pepper to taste
bread crumbs
grated Cheddar cheese

Mix all ingredients together except bread crumbs and grated Cheddar cheese, and put in buttered casserole dish. Top with bread crumbs and grated Cheddar cheese. Bake at 350 degrees for 30 minutes, covered. Uncover and bake approximately 10 minutes longer. Let cool slightly before serving.

BAKED SALMON
WITH SOUR CREAM SAUCE

1 6 to 7-pound whole salmon
4 slices bacon

2 lemons, sliced

Cover salmon with bacon and lemon slices. Wrap in heavy duty foil and bake for 1 hour and 15 minutes, or until salmon flakes easily with a fork, in a 350 degree preheated oven. Do not overcook. Serves 10.

Sauce:

2 large onions, chopped
4 Tablespoons butter or
  margarine
1 cup dry sherry
2 cups Bechamel Sauce (recipe
  follows)

1 cup sour cream at room
  temperature
2 Tablespoons salmon juice from
  baking
1 Tablespoon fresh lemon juice
fresh parsley for garnish
lemon wedges for garnish

Saute onions in butter until soft. Add sherry and cook until liquid is absorbed. Add bechamel sauce and gently reheat. Just before serving add sour cream, salmon juice and lemon juice then adjust seasonings. Spoon over salmon. Garnish with parsley and lemon wedges.

Bechamel Sauce:

6 Tablespoons butter
5 Tablespoons flour

2-1/2 to 3 cups light cream

Melt butter in heavy saucepan. Stir in flour gradually and cook for 2 minutes without browning the flour. Add 2-1/2 to 3 cups light cream and cook until the sauce has a consistency of very thick cream.

DELICIOUS SHRIMP CASSEROLE

1-1/2 pounds shrimp
1 small onion, chopped
1 can mushroom soup (10-3/4 ounce)
dash garlic salt
3/4 cup grated Cheddar cheese

1/2 medium green pepper, sliced
1/2 cup sour cream
3/4 cup cooked rice
1 Tablespoon margarine
1/2 teaspoon lemon juice
salt and pepper to taste

Cook and clean shrimp. Saute onion in margarine. Make a sauce by mixing soup, lemon juice and seasonings together. Fold in shrimp and rice, then fold in sour cream. Pour into a 1-quart buttered baking dish. Sprinkle grated cheese on top. Parboil green pepper slices for 2 minutes, then use on top of casserole as a garnish. Bake at 325 degrees for about 30 minutes. Serve and ENJOY.

PEPPY SEAFOOD SAUCE

1/2 cup catsup
1/2 cup chili sauce
3 Tablespoons lemon juice
1 Tablespoon horseradish
1 teaspoon Worcestershire sauce

1 Tablespoon mayonnaise or salad dressing
1/2 teaspoon grated onion
3 drops Tabasco sauce
dash of pepper

Combine all ingredients; chill. Makes approximately 1-1/2 cups (6 servings).

SHARP SAUCE

2 egg yolks
2-1/2 teaspoons prepared mustard
1/2 teaspoon salt
1 Tablespoon dried dill

1/4 teaspoon pepper
1-1/2 teaspoon sugar
1/2 cup chilled salad oil
1 Tablespoon vinegar

Place egg yolks in a small bowl. Using an eggbeater or electric mixer, beat in mustard, salt, dill, pepper, and sugar until well blended. Add oil, 1 teaspoonful at a time, beating continuously. Beat in vinegar. Makes about 3/4 cup. Serve with cold cooked, cleaned shrimp or lobster chunks.

SHRIMP WHITE SAUCE

1/2 cup mayonnaise
1/2 sour cream
1/2 cup Durkee's salad dressing
2 Tablespoons creole mustard
2 Tablespoons sliced green onions

2 Tablespoons horseradish
2 Tablespoons Worcestershire sauce
juice of 1 lemon
hot pepper sauce
salt and pepper to taste

Combine all ingredients and refrigerate. Serve over cold or hot shrimp.

SWEET AND SOUR SAUCE

1/3 cup catsup	1 teaspoon prepared mustard
1/3 cup chili sauce	1/2 teaspoon Tabasco sauce
1/3 cup cider vinegar	1 Tablespoon lemon juice
1 cup dark brown sugar	3 Tablespoons butter/margarine
1 teaspoon Worcestershire sauce	2 Tablespoons chopped parsley
1/2 teaspoon garlic juice	

Combine all ingredients and heat until sugar dissolves; simmer 5 minutes. Serve warm with shrimp or smoked fish. Makes approximately 1-2/3 cups.

SPIRITED TARTAR SAUCE

1/4 cup mayonnaise	1 teaspoon grated fresh onion
1/4 cup sour cream	1/4 teaspoon Worcestershire sauce
1/4 cup sweet pickle relish, drained	dash of Tabasco sauce
	1 teaspoon fresh lemon juice
2 Tablespoons finely minced dill pickle	1/4 teaspoon cream-style horseradish (optional)

Combine all ingredients in a small mixing bowl and refrigerate for at least 1 hour. Sauce will keep in refrigerator for 3 to 5 days. Sour cream may be omitted and mayonnaise increased to 1/2 cup. Makes about 3/4 cup.

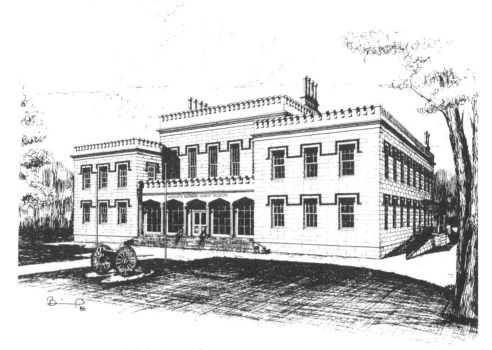

Old Academy of Richmond County Building - c. 1802

OLD RICHMOND ACADEMY

The Old Richmond Academy is a square structure of Tudor architecture, severed with crenelated parapets. It was made from hand-made stucco-covered brick and erected around 1800, the building housed the Academy founded in 1783. It was the oldest school of its kind in Georgia.

The original Academy was on the river bank. It was to this building George Washington visited when he was in Augusta. General LaFayette visited it also. It is the oldest institution for higher education of boys that has been in continuous existence under the same name and in the same place in the United States. It is erected upon crown lands confiscated after the Revolutionary War. In 1850 it was closed for repairs and reopened as a military hospital by the Confederate government.

Federal troops occupying Augusta used the building for military headquarters until 1867 when the trustees resumed control. It is now the home of the Augusta Museum, housing a variety of collections and exhibits on archeology, natural history, art, military history and railroads. It also was a library. The Academy of Richmond County is now on Russell St., having become a co-educational high school.

Pork and Ham

SPICY BARBECUED SPARERIBS

2 whole racks of ribs (5 to 6 pounds), cracked but not severed down the middle, all excess fat removed (1 pound serves one person as a main course or two as an appetizer when cut in half lengthwise, then into smaller rib sections) beer, water or chicken broth for basting Spicy Barbecue Sauce (recipe follows)

Prepare barbecue grill. If grill is adjustable, fix it so meat is 5 inches from the coals. If the grill is not adjustable, use soup cans filled with stones or some other make-shift arrangement to keep the meat at this distance. An 18-inch diameter grill will accommodate two racks of spareribs. Cover the grill rack with heavy-duty aluminum foil; turn up the edges to make a trough down the center to catch fat.

Put a single uncrowded layer of charcoal in the firebox, ignite and allow to reach to white ash stage, about 45 minutes. Scatter a handful of fresh charcoal over the hot coals; place the grill in position.

Place the two racks of ribs on the grill over the hot coal and cook, turning frequently, for about 45 minutes. Baste several times with beer, water, or chicken broth and remove fat with spoon or bulb baster as it accumulates in the foil trough. At the end of 45 minutes remove foil from grill.

Continue cooking the ribs on the bare grill until they are cooked through, about 45 minutes more. Keep turning and basting frequently with beer, water or broth. If the fire flares up because of fat drippings, lift the ribs off with tongs, baste well and return to the grill when flames die down. Do not spray the fire with water; that cools down the fire and scatters a lot of ashes.

Test for doneness by cutting into the thickest part of the meat. There should not be any pink color remaining. The outside of the ribs should be the color of dark mahogany.

Transfer the ribs to a cutting board and hack with a cleaver or knife into individual ribs. Brush generously with Spicy Barbecue Sauce. Return to the grill; turn ribs and brush second side and edges with sauce. Continue to cook, turning often and brushing with more sauce, until ribs are well-glazed, about 15 minutes longer. Serve immediately. Makes 6 servings as a main dish; 12 servings as appetizers.

SPICY BARBECUE SAUCE

3 Tablespoons vegetable oil (not olive oil)
1 extra-large onion, finely chopped (about 1-1/2 cups)
2 cloves garlic, finely chopped
1 cup catsup
1/2 cup wine vinegar

1/3 cup lemon juice
1/4 cup Worcestershire sauce
1/4 cup brown sugar
4 teaspoons chili powder
2 teaspoons ground celery seeds
1 teaspoon ground cumin

Heat the oil in a large heavy saucepan and saute the onion slowly until it is golden and tender. Add the garlic and cook one minute longer. Add catsup, vinegar, lemon juice, Worcestershire, sugar, chili powder, celery seeds and cumin; bring to boiling. Lower heat; simmer, uncovered, for 30 minutes.

CREOLE-STYLE PORK ROAST

1 Tablespoon butter/margarine
1/4 cup chopped green pepper
1/4 cup chopped onion
2 teaspoons Creole Seasoning
4-ounce can mushroom stems and pieces, drained

1/2 cup tomato paste
4 to 5 pound boneless pork loin roast, with string removed
2 Tablespoons all-purpose flour
1/4 to 1/2 teaspoon Creole Seasoning

Melt butter in a small saucepan; add green pepper, onion and 2 teaspoons Creole Seasoning. Cook until vegetables are tender; drain. Stir in mushrooms; blend in 1/4 cup of tomato paste. Unroll roast; spread vegetable mixture over surface of roast. Roll meat and tie securely with string. Place meat on rack in a shallow roasting pan. Roast at 325 degrees for 2-1/2 to 3 hours or until thermometer registers 170 degrees.

Remove meat to warm platter; keep warm. Skim and reserve fat from pan juices; measure juices. Add water to juices to measure 1-1/2 cups liquid. Return 2 tablespoons fat to roasting pan (add oil if necessary to make 2 tablespoons). Stir in flour, remaining Creole Seasoning and remaining tomato paste. Add juices. Cook and stir until bubbly. Garnish meat with fresh chili peppers, if desired. Slice roast crosswise, removing strings as meat is carved. Spoon some gravy over roast; serve remainder with rice. Serve 12 to 15.

CREOLE SEASONING

1/4 cup ground red pepper
3 Tablespoons salt
1 Tablespoon chili powder
1 Tablespoon paprika

1 Tablespoon ground coriander
1 Tablespoon pepper
2 teaspoons ground cloves
1-1/2 teaspoons garlic powder

Blend all ingredients. Store tightly covered in a cool place. Makes 3/4 cup.

This spunky hot pepper seasoning originated with South Louisiana cooks. Here's how to stir up your own supply to enliven roast and other meats. Try sprinkling 1/4 teaspoon on 4 servings of buttered vegetables; adding 3/4 to 1 teaspoon to 1/4 cup of mayonnaise for a zippy dressing, or sprinkling 1/4 teaspoon on each side of a 1-pound steak.

SAUCY LOIN OF PORK
WITH BAKED APPLES

4 to 6 pound boneless loin of
pork, rolled and tied
1 clove garlic, crushed
1/2 cup Dijon-style mustard
1/4 cup honey
1 Tablespoon lemon juice, (1/2
lemon)
1/2 teaspoon chopped fresh
marjoram or 1/4 teaspoon leaf
marjoram, crumbled
1/4 cup applejack or apple
brandy (may be omitted)

1 Tablespoon cider vinegar
dash liquid red-pepper seasoning
1/2 teaspoon freshly ground
pepper
6 to 8 red baking apples
4 to 5 Tablespoons unsalted
butter or margarine, softened
ground cinnamon
6 to 8 teaspoons brown sugar
charcoal

Wipe pork with damp paper toweling. Rub pork well with the garlic. Combine mustard, honey, lemon juice, marjoram, applejack, vinegar, red-pepper seasoning and pepper in a medium-size bowl; mix well.

Coat the pork with 1/2 cup of the mustard mixture. Let stand at room temperature, lightly covered, for 3 hours. Cover and reserve the remaining basting mixture.

Prepare the charcoal for grilling with a drip pan in the center under the grid, or preheat a gas unit with a drip pan. Place pork on grid or rotisserie. Cover the grill with the dome. Cook over high heat for 20 to 22 minutes per pound, basting often with the remaining mustard mixture, until a meat thermometer inserted in the thickest part of the meat registers 170 degrees. (If cooking over coals, replenish with new charcoal as needed.) Let the roast stand for 10 to 15 minutes before carving.

About 30 minutes before serving, place the apples (which have been cored with bottoms left intact, then rubbed with softened butter, sprinkled with cinnamon and 1 teaspoon brown sugar spooned into the cavities, then enclosed separately in a packet of heavy-duty aluminum foil) around the pork on the grill. Cook with the grill covered until tender, for about 25 to 30 minutes; the apples will give slightly when gently pressed.

To serve, remove the apples from the foil. Place upright on a serving dish. Make a cross with a sharp knife in the top of each apple, about 3/4" deep. Pour any liquid in the foil packets over the apples. Top each with 1 teaspoon of the softened butter.

This roast may be cooked in oven as well, and is equally delicious. If using oven start in hot oven 400 degrees for 10 minutes. Lower to slow oven, 325 degrees, and roast for 30 minutes per pound of meat (about 3 hours) or until meat thermometer registers 170 degrees.

TENDERLOIN OF PORK GLAZED
WITH HONEY AND THYME

1-1/2 to 2 pound pork tenderloin	2-1/2 Tablespoons honey
1 teaspoon minced shallots	2-1/2 Tablespoons red wine vinegar
1/2 teaspoon minced garlic	4 teaspoon vegetable oil
1/2 teaspoon fresh thyme leaves	3 cups brown stock
2 Tablespoons tomato paste	1-1/2 Tablespoons arrowroot
4 teaspoons Dijon mustard	Remove all fat and adjacent
1 teaspoon crushed black	membrane from pork. Keep
peppercorns	refrigerated until needed.

In small bowl, combine shallots, garlic, thyme, tomato paste, mustard and peppercorns; mix well to make a paste. Set aside until needed. Combine honey and vinegar. Set aside.

Heat oil in non-stick skillet over high heat. Pat tenderloin with paper towels to dry. Brown tenderloin on all sides in hot oil. Transfer meat to platter; set aside. Reduce heat under skillet to medium high. Add reserved tomato-mustard mixture. Cook, stirring constantly, until tomato is lightly caramelized and smells slightly sweet, about 30 to 40 seconds. Add reserved honey-vinegar mixture and stir well. The honey will begin to foam.

Slide reserved tenderloin back into skillet and baste with glaze, turning occasionally, until roast is completely coated. The glaze will be quite thick and should coat easily. Remove skillet from heat.

Place glazed tenderloin on a rack over a sheet pan or baking dish. Roast in preheated 375 degree oven for 20 to 25 minutes, until done. Tenderloin is done when internal temperature of meat reaches 150 degrees or juices run clear when meat is pierced with skewer.

Meanwhile, return skillet to heat and deglaze pan using brown stock. Bring to a simmer; reduce slightly. Dissolve arrowroot in a small amount of cold water. Stir into sauce to thicken slightly. Bring to boil and let simmer five minutes.

To serve, carve tenderloin on bias into thin slices. Arrange slices on warm plates. Coat with sauce. Serve immediately. Makes 8 5-ounce portions.

ROAST PORK TENDERLOIN
WITH CURRIED-FRUIT COMPOTE

2 Tablespoons Dijon mustard	4 or 5 fresh sage leaves, snipped,
1-3/4 pounds pork tenderloin	or 3/4 teaspoon dried sage
1/2 teaspoon salt	freshly ground pepper to taste
1/2 teaspoon minced garlic	Curried Fall-Fruit Compote
1/4 cup packaged plain bread	(recipe follows)
crumbs	

(Continued)

Heat oven to 450 degrees. Brush mustard over the meat and sprinkle with half the salt. Coat an 8" skillet with vegetable cooking spray; add garlic and cook over medium heat about 30 seconds. Add bread crumbs and sage; cook, stirring until crumbs begin to brown. Stir in remaining salt and pepper. Put half the crumbs in a roasting pan just large enough to hold the meat. Put roast on top; pat remaining crumbs around sides and top of meat. Roast in bottom third of oven 10 minutes. Reduce temperature to 325 degrees and roast 45 to 50 minutes longer until meat thermometer inserted in thickest part of roast registers 165 degrees. Remove roast from oven; before slicing, let stand in warm place for 10 minutes or until thermometer registers 170 degrees. Serve with Curried Fall-Fruit Compote. Makes 4 servings.

CURRIED FALL-FRUIT COMPOTE

1/3 cup chopped onion
4 Tablespoons beef or chicken
    broth
1 teaspoon curry powder
1/2 teaspoon ground cumin
1 pear, peeled, cored and chopped
1 Granny Smith apple, peeled,
    cored and chopped

1 Red Delicious apple, peeled,
    cored and chopped
2 dried apricots, cut up and
    soaked 20 minutes in 2
    Tablespoons apricot or other
    fruit-flavored brandy or
    orange juice
1/4 cup golden raisins.

In large saucepan over medium heat simmer onion in 2 tablespoons broth until limp. Add curry powder and cumin. Stir over medium-high heat about 15 seconds. Add remaining ingredients, including the brandy. Cover and cook over low heat 20 minutes until fruits are tender and flavors blended. Serve hot. Makes 4 servings.

PORK ROAST WITH PLUM SAUCE

Tips: The pork has more flavor if the roast has some bone. The butcher will cut meat off the bone then tie with roast for ease in serving. The plum sauce makes the difference and can be prepared ahead. Yields about 2 cups.

1 loin pork roast
1/2 teaspoon salt
1/2 teaspoon garlic salt
1 medium onion, chopped
2 Tablespoons butter
1 (6-ounce) can frozen lemonade
    concentrate

2/3 cup chili sauce
1 (12-ounce) jar plum preserves
1 Tablespoon soy sauce
2 teaspoons prepared mustard
1 teaspoon ginger

Prepare loin pork roast for roasting; season with salt and garlic salt. In a small saucepan saute onion in butter. Add remaining ingredients. Pour over pork. Allow 30 to 45 minutes per pound at a medium heat. Baste occasionally.

PORK ROAST WITH ROSY RED SAUCE
(A Heavenly Aroma)

1 3 to 4-pound, boned, pork loin roast
1/2 cup dry sherry
1/2 cup soy sauce
2 cloves garlic, minced
1 Tablespoon dry mustard
1 teaspoon ground ginger
1 teaspoon dried thyme, crushed
Sauce:
1 10-ounce jar currant jelly
2 Tablespoons sherry
1 Tablespoon soy sauce
1/4 cup dried currants (optional)

Place pork in a plastic bag along with sherry, soy sauce, garlic and spices. Securely tie or seal and let sit at room temperature for 2 to 3 hours, turning occasionally. Maybe marinated overnight in the refrigerator.

Preheat oven to 325 degrees. Place meat in a shallow baking pan, reserving the marinade. Roast, uncovered for 2-1/2 to 3 hours. Baste with reserved marinade during the last hour. Let roast sit 15 minutes before carving.

While the pork is roasting, make the sauce. Combine jelly with sherry, soy sauce and currants, if desired, in a small saucepan over medium heat. Simmer 2 minutes. Place in a sauceboat and serve with the roast at the table.

TANGY PORK ROAST WITH BEEF STUFFING

3 pounds boned pork loin, butterflied
Tangy Barbecue Sauce
1/2 pound ground sirloin
1 small onion, chopped
1 small clove garlic, minced
1/4 teaspoon salt
1/8 teaspoon pepper
1 cup fresh sliced mushrooms
1/4 cup fine dry breadcrumbs
1/4 cup grated Parmesan cheese

Pound meat into a 15x10" rectangle about 3/4". Brush top with 1/4 cup barbecue sauce. Combine ground sirloin, onion, garlic, salt, pepper and 1/4 cup barbecue sauce; spread evenly over roast. Press the mushrooms into ground beef. Sprinkle with breadcrumbs and cheese. Starting at the 10" side, roll up the meat and tie. Place on rack in a shallow roasting pan. Roast uncovered at 325 degrees for about 2-1/2 hours. Baste with additional barbecue sauce for last 15 to 20 minutes of roasting. Remove meat to serving platter. Cover with barbecue sauce. Serve with remaining sauce. Serves about 6 to 8.

Tangy Barbecue Sauce:
1 (14-ounce) bottle ketchup
1/2 cup chili sauce
1/3 cup wine vinegar
1/4 cup light brown sugar
2 Tablespoons lemon juice
1 clove garlic, minced
1/4 teaspoon pepper
2 Tablespoons Worcestershire sauce
2 Tablespoons mustard
2 Tablespoons vegetable oil
2 Tablespoons steak sauce
1 teaspoon dry mustard
1/4 teaspoon salt

Combine all ingredients; simmer for 30 to 50 minutes. Makes 2-2/3 cups. Store sauce in refrigerator until ready to use. Sauce may be made ahead and kept in the refrigerator.

LEMON SMOTHERED CHOPS

Sometimes we find an interesting way to cook from the "oldies that turn out to be the goldies," as does this one from the 1940s.

2 pounds pork or lamb chops, cut 1" thick	1 green pepper, cut in rings
2 unpeeled lemons, sliced	1 teaspoon salt
1 large onion, cut in rings	2 cups tomato juice
	butter or margarine

Place chops in large skillet with cover. Cover each chop with slices of lemon, onion and green pepper. Add the salt and pour tomato juice over all. Dot with butter or margarine.

Cover and cook on top of stove for 1-1/2 hours. Lift chops out, place on platter, being careful to keep the fruit and vegetable slices in place. Serves 6 to 8.

STUFFED CROWN ROAST OF PORK WITH MUSTARD SAUCE

16-rib crown roast with 2-1/2" cavity	1/2 cup raisins
salt and pepper	1/2 cup raw cranberries
thyme	4 tart apples, peeled and diced
Stuffing:	Mustard Sauce:
4 cups bread crumbs	4 Tablespoons flour
2/3 cup milk	4 Tablespoons fat from roast
1 cup minced onion	1 cup dry white wine
4 Tablespoons butter	3/4 cup chicken broth
1 pound pork sausage	3/4 cup water
1-1/2 cups chopped celery	2 cups heavy cream
	3 Tablespoons Dijon mustard

Have butcher trim, roll and tie roast. Sprinkle with salt, pepper and thyme. Place clean, empty 10-3/4 ounce soup can (label removed) in cavity. Cover ends of ribs with foil. Put in roasting pan and bake at 400 degrees for 20 minutes, then lower temperature to 325 degrees for 40 minutes.

Mix bread crumbs and milk. Saute onion in butter until soft. In a separate pan, break up and saute sausage. Drain off fat. Mix celery, raisins, cranberries and apples and saute 5 minutes with the onion. Combine with sausage and bread crumb mixture. Remove roast from oven, remove soup can and stuff cavity of roast. Place remaining stuffing in a baking dish. Return roast to oven and bake another hour.

To make mustard sauce, stir flour into hot fat with a wooden spoon. Cook slowly until well blended and bubbly. Add wine and reduce to 4 tablespoons. Add broth, water and cream; cook 5 minutes or until thickened. Stir mustard into sauce and serve warm. Serves 12 to 14 elegantly for a fancy occasion.

MUSTARD BARBECUE SAUCE

2 cups prepared mustard
1 cup mayonnaise
1/4 cup plus 2 Tablespoons catsup
2 Tablespoons sugar
2 Tablespoons Worcestershire
 sauce
1 teaspoon Kitchen Bouquet

1/2 teaspoon salt
1/2 teaspoon seasoned salt
1/4 teaspoon pepper
1/4 cup butter/margarine
1/2 cup water
1/4 teaspoon liquid smoke
 (optional)

Combine all ingredients in a saucepan, mixing well. Bring to a boil and reduce heat to medium. Cook, uncovered, for 10 minutes, stirring occasionally. Use to baste chicken, pork chops, or ribs when grilling. Yields about 5-1/3 cups.

DELUXE CROWN ROAST OF PORK
WITH SAGE DRESSING

Sage Dressing:
1 loaf white bread
1/2 pound fresh mushrooms,
 chopped
1/2 pound bulk lean pork sausage
1-1/2 sticks butter/margarine
2 large onions, peeled and
 chopped (about 2 cups)

6 medium celery ribs, diced
 (about 2 cups)
2 teaspoons dried sage leaves
2 teaspoons poultry seasoning, or
 to taste
salt and pepper to taste
1 cup chicken broth

Preheat oven to 200 degrees. Spread bread slices on a cookie sheet and place in oven to toast and dry out (about 15 minutes). Remove toast from oven and cool, then cut into half inch cubes and place in a large bowl.

In a large skillet over medium heat, saute pork sausage until brown, stirring to break up meat. Add sausage to bread in bowl. Drain fat from skillet, then melt a half stick of butter in the skillet. Add onions, celery and mushrooms; saute over low heat until barely tender but not browned. Add to bowl with sausage and bread.

Add sage, poultry seasoning, salt and pepper; toss to mix. Add chicken broth (more if needed) and remaining stick of butter (melted); toss thoroughly.

Roast:
7 to 8 pound crown roast of pork
salt and pepper to taste
1 teaspoon dried sage

1 teaspoon rosemary
2 cups dry white wine
sage dressing
lemon wedges (optional)

Preheat oven to 325 degrees. Rub roast, inside and out, with salt, pepper, sage and rosemary. Wrap aluminum foil around ends of bone to keep them from burning, then place a large ball of foil in center of roast. Place roast on rack in roasting pan. Pour about 1/3 cup wine over roast, then roast for 3 to 3-1/2 hours or until meat thermometer registers 165 degrees. During roasting, baste roast with about 1/4 cup wine every 30 minutes. Forty-five minutes before roast is finished, remove ball of foil from center of roast.

(Continued)

Pile sage dressing into opening and continue roasting. Any dressing not used for stuffing roast can be baked in a covered casserole for 45 minutes and served as a side dish.

Remove foil from ends of bone before serving. Garnish platter with lemon wedges, if desired. Serve with minted chunky applesauce or hot fruit compote.

NOTE: Have butcher trim, roll and tie roast.

DEVILED PORK CHOPS

butter or margarine	1/2 cup mayonnaise
1 medium red cooking apple, cut into wedges	1/3 cup soft bread crumbs
	1 Tablespoon chopped watercress
1 pound mushrooms, sliced	1 Tablespoon prepared mustard
1/4 teaspoon pepper	1/8 teaspoon paprika
salt	watercress sprigs for garnish
4 pork loin butterflied chops, each cut 1/2" thick	

About 45 minutes before serving: In a 12" skillet over medium heat, in 1 tablespoon hot butter or margarine, cook apple wedges about 5 to 7 minutes until apples are fork tender, turning once. Remove to large platter; keep warm.

In same skillet over medium heat, melt 3 tablespoons butter or margarine. Add mushrooms, pepper and 1/4 teaspoon salt; cook until mushrooms are tender, about 10 minutes, stirring occasionally. Remove mushrooms to platter with apple wedges; keep warm.

Preheat broiler if manufacturer directs. Place pork loin butterflied chops on rack in broiling pan; broil 10 minutes, turning pork chops once.

Meanwhile, in small bowl with fork mix mayonnaise, bread crumbs, chopped watercress, mustard, paprika and 1/4 teaspoon salt. When pork chops are done, spread mayonnaise mixture over chops; broil 1 minute longer or until topping is hot and bubbly.

To serve arrange pork chops on platter with apples and mushrooms. Garnish each chop with a watercress sprig. Makes 4 servings; 615 calories per serving.

HONEY-MUSTARD
STUFFED PORK CHOPS

Stuffing:

1/4 cup green onion, chopped	1/2 cup herb stuffing mix, mixed
1/4 cup chopped celery	according to package directions
1/4 cup chopped mushrooms	1/2 cup butter or margarine

Brown celery and onions in butter or margarine. When brown, add mushrooms and stuffing mix. Remove from heat.

(Continued)

Chops:
6 boneless loin pork chops
1 cup stuffing

2 Tablespoons spicy mustard
3 Tablespoons honey butter and
oil

Cut pockets in pork chops. Stuff each pocket. They will expand and hold a lot of stuffing. Secure pockets with toothpicks. Mix honey and mustard in a small bowl. Brown chops in oil and butter. Place chops in a baking dish (a glass dish for microwave). Coat both sides of browned chops with honey-mustard mixture. Add pan drippings, cover and bake in a preheated oven at 350 degrees for 40 minutes, or in microwave oven on medium high for 20 minutes, turning once. Serves 6.

CRUNCHY SAUSAGE CASSEROLE

1 6-ounce package long grain and
wild rice mix
1 pound bulk pork sausage
1 pound ground beef
1 large onion, chopped
1 8-ounce can sliced mushrooms,
drained

1 can (8-ounce) water chestnuts,
drained and sliced
3 Tablespoons soy sauce
1 package (2-3/4 ounce) sliced
almonds
lemon slice (optional)
parsley springs (optional)

Cook sausage, ground beef and onion over medium heat in a large skillet until meat is brown, stirring to crumble. Drain off drippings. Add rice, mushrooms, water chestnuts and soy sauce; stir well. Spoon into an ungreased 2-quart casserole. Cover and refrigerate overnight.
Remove from refrigerator and allow to sit at room temperature 30 minutes. Sprinkle almonds over top. Bake uncovered at 325 degrees for 50 minutes or until thoroughly heated. Garnish with lemon slice and parsley sprigs, if desired. Yield: 8 to 10 servings.
NOTE: Casserole may be baked without refrigeration, uncovered, for 20 minutes at 300 degrees.

PORK CHOPS PIQUANT

1 egg
3 Tablespoons water
4 pork chops
1 cup Ritz cracker crumbs
oil

4 Tablespoons Worcestershire
sauce
1 can cream of mushroom soup
dash of salt and pepper
4 slices Bermuda onion

Beat egg slightly with water; dip each pork chop into egg mixture. Dip into Ritz cracker crumbs. Brown lightly in small amount of oil in large skillet. Top with onion slices. Mix Worcestershire sauce with soup and spread over chops. Sprinkle with salt and pepper; add small amount of water. Cover and simmer for 45 minutes. Serves 4.

"PICKING PORK"

1 fresh pork ham, whole or
   shoulder or butt half (must
   be a fresh ham, not smoked
   or cured)

vinegar
seasoned pepper

Trim ham, leaving small amount of fat for flavor during the cooking. All skin and brine should be removed. Rub the fresh ham with a liberal amount of vinegar. Cover the ham completely with seasoned pepper, pressing the pepper into the sides so most of it will adhere. Wrap the ham in heavy-duty foil tightly. Place in a roasting pan and bake at 200 degrees overnight — at least 10 hours. When unwrapped, the pork should "fall apart" or shred when pulled with a fork. Place on a large serving platter on a buffet table and your guests will "pick" at it forever. Serve with your favorite barbecue sauce. Sounds too easy to be true or any good, but it is out of this world in flavor and taste! Great for sandwiches. Save the juices from the ham and cook rice in it for the best rice you will ever taste. Everybody will LOVE it.

FRIED COUNTRY HAM AND RED-EYE GRAVY

Fried Country Ham and Red-Eye Gravy is a favorite to any Rebel. All Rebels, regardless of their State of origin, will agree that nothing surpasses the flavor of a good country ham. The name red-eye comes from red eye-like beads of meat drippings that form when the water is added to them. Red-eye gravy is made from the residue left in the skillet about country or salt-cured ham has been fried. The fat is needed for the gravy, so do not trim it from the ham. The crusty bits that give the gravy its color and flavor will come from the lean of the ham and will stick to the skillet.

ham
milk to cover
1 cup water

2 Tablespoons black coffee
   (optional)
dash of pepper

Slice ham (preferably well-aged) into 1/2" steaks. Soak in milk overnight. The next morning, wipe ham with paper towels. Put enough ham fat into skillet (preferably cast iron) to keep ham from sticking. Add ham to moderately hot skillet and brown evenly on both sides. When done, remove to a hot platter.

Make red-eye gravy by adding 1 cup water and 2 tablespoons black coffee (optional) to hot ham drippings in skillet (do this step carefully to avoid splattering!). Cook, scraping pan to remove crusty bits, until mixture boils vigorously. Sprinkle in a dash of pepper and allow gravy to cook about 3 minutes more or until mixture is reduced by half to form red-eye gravy. Stir well and serve sizzling hot, along with grits, rice, beaten biscuits or Tara biscuits. RED-EYE DRESSING for garden salad: Cut ham slices very thin, about 1/16" thick or less. Prepare gravy as above except cook ham until crisp enough to crumble. With fingers protected with paper towels, crumble ham. Pour hot dressing over greens; toss and serve.

HEAVENLY HAM
WITH RAISIN SAUCE

10 to 12 pound ham	1/2 cup brown sugar
1 teaspoon mustard	1 Tablespoon flour
2 Tablespoons vinegar	2 Tablespoons lemon juice
1/4 teaspoon grated lemon rind	1-1/2 cups water
1/3 cup seedless raisins	pineapple rings

Wrap ham well in foil. Bake at 400 degrees for 16 minutes per pound.

Make raisin sauce, mixing brown sugar, mustard and flour first then adding remaining ingredients. Cook over low heat until thick, stirring constantly.

Thirty minutes before ham is done, pour off fat; spread with sauce and decorate with pineapple rings. Bake, uncovered, until done.

HONEY-GLAZED HAM

10 to 12 pound ham	3 (2") cinnamon sticks
2 cups apple juice or cider	1 cup honey
3/4 teaspoon whole allspice	1 teaspoon whole cloves
1 teaspoon whole cloves	paprika
1/2 teaspoon cracked ginger	

Place ham, fat side up, on rack in shallow pan. Insert meat thermometer in center, being careful not to touch the bone. Heat apple juice with allspice, ginger, cinnamon sticks and cloves. Bring to a boil; cover and boil five minutes. Remove from heat and brush a little of the mixture over the ham. Bake ham in slow oven (325 degrees) 1-1/2 to 2 hours, basting every 15 minutes with mixture.

Drizzle 1/2 cup honey over ham. Bake 30 minutes longer. Drizzle remaining honey over ham and cook until thermometer registers 160 degrees. Remove from oven and cool 30 minutes. Score fat and stud with additional cloves. Sprinkle with paprika. May be garnished with pickled peaches or crab apples.

TENNESSEE SUGAR CURED HAM
(Make Your Own)

1 pint salt	1 Tablespoon black pepper
4 Tablespoons dark brown sugar	

This mixture of ingredients is enough for one ham. Allow fresh ham to cool thoroughly. Mix well together the salt, sugar and pepper and pat on meat. Wrap in clean newspapers, then place the ham in a clean cloth sack. Old flour sacks are ideal if they can be found. Tie the sack securely and hang with shank end of ham down. Store in a cool place, allowing to cure for at least 4 to 6 months. Ham may be left for over a year if it is kept in a cool dry place.

BOURBON-BAKED HAM

Southern cooks believe that bourbon does something for ham that nothing else does. This recipe is a favorite from Kentucky.

1 mildly cured (10 to 12 pounds) ham with bone in	6 thick slices orange, unpeeled or 6 canned pineapple slices
	3/4 cup bourbon

Line a large roasting pan with heavy-duty aluminum foil, using enough to wrap ham completely. Place ham in pan, fat side down and cover with thick slices of unpeeled orange or canned pineapple slices. Pour bourbon over top of ham. Seal the foil tightly around the ham. Pour boiling water into the bottom of the pan to measure halfway up the outside of the ham. Cover roaster and bake in preheated oven at 350 degrees, allowing 18 minutes per pound.

Drain off water and remove ham from foil; turn fat side up. Discard fruit. Remove rind and excess fat, then with a sharp knife cut fat 1/2" deep in a diamond-shaped pattern and spread with bourbon glaze. Return ham to oven and bake about 25 minutes, or until the surface is nicely glazed. Serve cold, sliced thin. Serves 12 to 14.

MOLDED HAM MOUSSE

Ham mousse is a legacy from the bountiful plantation tables of the Colonial South. Use the leftover bits and pieces of a high-grade cooked, cured ham for this dish. This is one case in which leftover Smithfield ham can be used to good advantage. The blandness of the whipped cream will tame the very salty taste of the meat.

2 Tablespoons unflavored gelatin	2 Tablespoons finely chopped parsley
1/2 cup boiling water	1 cup heavy cream
2 cups finely ground cooked ham	leaf lettuce for garnish
2 teaspoons Dijon-style mustard	cold mustard sauce (optional)
4 teaspoons mayonnaise	crystallized pickles for garnish
1 Tablespoon freshly grated horseradish, or adjust to taste	(optional)
1/8 teaspoon Tabasco sauce	Tart Mustard Sauce

Dissolve gelatin in boiling water; set aside to cool.

Combine ham, mustard, mayonnaise, horseradish, Tabasco sauce and parsley in a medium-sized bowl. Stir in gelatin.

Whip cream until very stiff and fold into ham mixture.

Turn mixture into a 1-quart mold that has been rinsed in cold water (or use 6 individual molds). Chill a few hours, until firm. Unmold and garnish with leafy lettuce. Use a pastry tube to decorate with optional cold mustard sauce. Arrange optional sliced pickles around the mold.

RAISIN SAUCE FOR HAM

1/2 cup honey or 3/4 cup light
  brown sugar
1/2 cup water
1/2 cup raisins
1 Tablespoon butter

2 Tablespoons lemon juice
1 teaspoon Worcestershire sauce
1/4 teaspoon salt
2 teaspoons cornstarch
4 or 5 cloves

Simmer water, raisins, cloves, honey, butter, lemon juice and Worcestershire sauce until raisins are plump. Combine cornstarch with 1/4 cup water, salt and a dash of black pepper; add to raisin mixture gradually. Cook until clear, stirring constantly. Serve over baked ham.

YANKEE HAM LOAF
WITH MUSTARD SAUCE

The mustard sauce is a "must!" The beauty of this recipe is that everything can be prepared well ahead of time and frozen.

2 pounds lean ham
2 pounds lean pork
1-1/2 cups cracker crumbs, finely
  crushed
1/3 cup chopped onion
4 eggs, well beaten
1-1/4 teaspoons salt
2 cups milk
2 Tablespoons chopped parsley

Glaze:
1/2 pound brown sugar
1/2 cup cider vinegar
1-1/2 Tablespoons dry mustard
Mustard Sauce:
1/2 cup mayonnaise
1/2 cup sour cream
1/4 cup prepared mustard
1 Tablespoon chives, minced
2 Tablespoons horseradish
salt and lemon juice to taste

Have butcher grind pork and ham together. Add cracker crumbs and mix well. Add onion, eggs, salt, milk and parsley. Work all together until well blended. Shape into two loaves in bread pans and bake at 350 degrees for 30 minutes. While the loaves are baking, make glaze. Combine sugar, vinegar and mustard and boil one minute.

Remove ham loaves from oven, baste with glaze, then set pans on a metal tray to catch the drippings and bake one hour longer. If there is any glaze left, baste again after loaves have baked 30 minutes. Remove from pans while still warm. They can be used the same day or they may be cooled, wrapped and frozen. Serve with a zippy mustard sauce.

To make mustard sauce, mix all ingredients together and chill until ready to serve with ham.

An excellent way to make a gourmet meal out of leftovers. Also a very good way to use left over baked ham as well as being delicious!

FRESH PORK HAM
WITH ORIENTAL GRAVY

fresh pork ham
2 ribs celery, sliced
1 onion, sliced
1/4 cup soy sauce

salt and pepper to taste
1 can chinese vegetables
cornstarch

Place ham on rack with fat side up in broiler pan. Set oven at 200 to 250 degrees. Cook ham for 8 to 10 hours or until the knuckle wiggles easily. Remove skin and score fat. Increase oven temperature to 400 degrees and allow the fat to brown (this takes about 30 minutes). All ham to cool before slicing.

To make oriental sauce, pour off most of the fat from the broiler pan. Add water to brown drippings; stir well off the bottom of the pan. Add sliced celery and sliced onion; cook until tender. Season with salt and pepper and soy sauce. Thicken with cornstarch. Add a can of chinese vegetables and heat to boiling point (do not boil). Serve with meat over rice.

NOTE: This ham also makes excellent barbecue. Slice or chop meat as desired; salt, add barbecue sauce to cover. Return to oven to heat until sauce bubbles. Unless you tell someone your secret, they'll think you cooked the ham in the pits all day.

COLA-BASTED HAM

10 pound precooked (not cured
    or canned) ham
1 bottle (1 liter) cola
1 cup dark brown sugar, firmly
    packed

1 Tablespoon dry mustard
2 Tablespoons prepared sharp
    mustard
2 cups fine dry bread crumbs

Place ham, fat side down, in a shallow roasting pan. Pour cola into pan to 1/2 inch deep. Bake in preheated oven at 325 degrees for about 2 hours, until ham is tender when pierced with a fork, basting with the cola every 15 to 20 minutes. (If using a meat thermometer in thickest part of the meat, it will read 140 degrees when properly cooked.) Remove ham from pan and cool. Cut away rind and excess fat with a sharp knife. Score fat in a diamond pattern. Combine sugar, mustards, bread crumbs and enough cola to form a thick paste. Place ham on roasting rack in pan and pat all over with paste. Add remaining cola to bottom of pan. Turn oven up to 375 degrees and bake 45 minutes longer, basting every 10 to 15 minutes, until sugar-mustard paste has melted into a dark glaze. Let stand at room temperature 20 to 30 minutes before slicing. Serves 12 to 15.

SUGAR-CURED COUNTRY HAM

10 to 20 pound sugar cured ham, smokehouse style
1 quart Coca Cola
3 cups brown sugar
18 to 25 whole cloves or to taste
1 cup orange juice, pickled peach nectar, pineapple juice or apple cider
1 Tablespoon dry mustard
1/4 teaspoon ground cloves

Soak ham in cold water 24 to 36 hours. If ham is very salty, change the water every 12 hours. Scrub and trim ham to remove mold; rinse.

Place ham in large kettle of boiling water, skin side down. Reduce heat and simmer for 25 minutes per pound. Add Coca Cola and 1 cup brown sugar during the last 1-1/2 hours of cooking.

Remove ham from liquid, drain and clip off outer skin while still warm. Score fat and stud with whole cloves.

Bake at 400 degrees for 20 minutes, glazing with a mixture of 2 cups brown sugar, fruit juice, mustard and ground cloves. Cool. Serve sliced paper thin.

NOTE: The hock end may be cut away to use as a seasoning agent, if desired.

HOW TO COOK A COUNTRY HAM

ham
water
2 cups molasses or sugar
2 teaspoons whole peppercorns
1 teaspoon whole cloves
2 sticks cinnamon
1 cup vinegar
1/2 cup brown sugar
1 teaspoon dry mustard

It it's a sho' nuff Country Ham, scrub ham with a brush and scrape well. Let soak overnight or longer if the ham is very old and large. For a Talmadge, Old Virginia, or another ham of this type the soaking may be omitted. Drain off soaking water and place ham in a large kettle with skin side down. Cover with water. Add rest of ingredients, except brown sugar and dry mustard. Simmer until tender when pierced with a fork. Add water as necessary to keep ham covered. Allow about 20 to 30 minutes per pound for cooking time. When done, cool in broth until cold (usually overnight). Remove from water and remove rind and excess fat. Score ham diagonally about 1/2 inch deep in a diamond pattern. Mix sugar with mustard and rub over fat side of ham. Place on roasting pan rack, fat side up, and bake in a preheated 325 degree oven for about 35 to 40 minutes to glaze and brown.

A sugar cured ham is good cooked by this method, but does not take as long to cook.

GLAZES FOR HAM

Glazing a ham turns an everyday meat into a festive fare, and it's so easy to do! Simply cook your ham as usual. Thirty minutes before ham is ready, score surface in diamond shapes and baste ham with glaze mixture. Continue to baste about every 10 to 15 minutes.

BREAD-CRUMB GLAZE

3/4 cup dry white bread crumbs   3/4 cup light brown sugar
   (without crust)   whole cloves

Mix bread crumbs and brown sugar. Pat mixture over the fat side of a scored ham. Dot the center of each diamond with a whole clove.

CRANBERRY GLAZE

2 cups fresh cranberries   1 cup maple syrup

Cook cranberries in maple syrup until skins pop open. Process mixture in a blender or food processor until smooth. Spread over ham.

SPICY BROWN PINEAPPLE
HAM GLAZE

8 ounces Gulden's Spicy Brown   2/3 cup honey
   Mustard   1/2 teaspoon ground ginger
2 cans (8-1/4 ounce size) crushed
   pineapple in syrup
   (undrained)

Thoroughly combine all ingredients. Bring to a boil over medium heat and simmer 5 minutes, stirring occasionally. Makes 3 cups of glaze and is sufficient for an 8 pound ham.

Old Engine Company No.1 - Augusta, Georgia

ENGINE COMPANY NO. 1

Located on Ellis Street between 4th and 5th Streets, Engine Company No. 1 was completed in 1892 and was the first station constructed after Augusta began a salaried fire department. The original structure had a bell tower rising from the roof on the right side. This tower replaced "Big Steve," the fire bell at Green and 8th Streets. Starting in 1892, fire boxes were located in the downtown area. When the lever on one of these boxes was pulled, the signal sounded from the tower atop Engine Company No. 1. For a while after the station closed in 1954, the building was used by the Augusta Players as a rehearsal hall. It later became the Electrical Shop for the City of Augusta. In fact, the Christmas lights and decorations for the city were stored there. Since 1985, the building at 452 Ellis Street has been the offices of Cranston, Robertson and Whitehurst, architects.

Poultry and Game

ALMOND CHICKEN

2 frying-size chickens
2 Tablespoons sesame seed
1-1/2 cups chicken broth (2
　bouillon cubes with water)
3 Tablespoons soy sauce
1 5-ounce can bamboo shoots
　(drained)
1 3-ounce can drained mushrooms

salt to taste (usually 1 to 2
　teaspoons)
1 cup diced celery
3/4 cup green onions
1 cup bean sprouts
1 5-ounce can sliced water
　chestnuts
pimiento to garnish
3 Tablespoons sherry

Bone, shin, and cube chickens. Brown sesame seed in hot oiled skillet and add cubed chicken and stir-fry until meat turns white. Add chicken broth and bring to a boil. Thicken with cornstarch. Add soy sauce (to taste), bamboo shoots, drained mushrooms, and salt.

In another very hot oiled skillet with lid, stir-fry celery and green onions until celery is just tender. Add the celery and onions to first mixture and bean sprouts, water chestnuts, pimiento, and sherry. Heat to boiling point. Garnish with toasted almonds and/or pecan halves. Serve very hot over rice. Serves 6 to 8 people.

CREAMED CHICKEN
WITH CORNBREAD RING

Cornbread:

1 teaspoon poultry seasoning
1 cup plain corn meal
1 cup flour
1/4 cup sugar
1/2 teaspoon salt

4 teaspoons baking powder
1 egg
1 cup milk
1/4 cup vegetable oil

Preheat oven to 400 degrees. Sift dry ingredients. Add egg, milk and vegetable oil. Mix well. Pour batter into a buttered 8" ring mold. Bake at 400 degrees for 15 to 20 minutes. Turn out onto a serving platter. Fill center with creamed chicken.

Creamed Chicken:

1/3 cup butter
1/2 cup chopped onion
1/2 cup chopped celery
1/3 cup flour
1/2 teaspoon salt

1/4 teaspoon thyme
2 cups chicken broth
3/4 cup milk
1/4 teaspoon Worcestershire sauce
2 cups cooked and diced chicken

In a 3-quart saucepan, melt butter over low heat. Saute onion and celery until lightly browned. Add flour, salt and thyme. Stir well. Add chicken broth and milk; blend until smooth over medium heat. Season with Worcestershire and add diced chicken to sauce. Heat thoroughly. Pour into cornbread ring and serve immediately. Serves 8.

CHICKEN AND ARTICHOKE HEARTS

Chicken:
1-1/2 cups chicken broth
4 large whole chicken breasts

1 8-1/2-ounce can artichoke hearts
(not marinated), drained
2 Tablespoons butter
1 pound mushrooms, sliced

In a frying pan, bring chicken broth to a simmer and add chicken breasts in single layer. Cover and poach until tender — about 20 minutes. Lift from broth and cool, reserving 3/4 cup broth for sauce. Carefully remove skin and bones and place chicken in shallow baking dish. Cut artichoke hearts in half and arrange them over breasts in a frying pan. Over medium heat, melt butter in a frying pan and saute mushrooms lightly. Drain and spoon over chicken. (At this point the dish may be covered and refrigerated.)

Sauce:
1/4 cup butter
1/4 cup flour
1/4 teaspoon salt
1/4 teaspoon nutmeg
dash white pepper

3/4 cup light cream
2 Tablespoons sherry (optional)
1/2 cup freshly grated Parmesan
cheese or 1-1/2 cups mild
Cheddar cheese

Melt butter and add flour, salt, pepper and nutmeg, stirring for about 3 minutes or until smoothly blended. Gradually add reserved chicken broth and cream, stirring until thickened. Stir in sherry and Parmesan or Cheddar until cheese is melted and mixture is blended. (Cover and refrigerate if using later.) Preheat oven to 325 degrees.

Topping:
1/2 cup bread crumbs
1 Tablespoon butter
2 teaspoons minced parsley

2 Tablespoons minced green
onion tops
1/2 teaspoon thyme

Saute bread crumbs lightly in butter. Stir in parsley, green onion tops, and thyme.

When ready to serve, if necessary, warm sauce over low heat until it liquifies. Pour over chicken and sprinkle topping on. Bake chicken uncovered for 30 minutes. Do not overcook or sauce will separate. Serves 6 to 8.

ORANGE CHICKEN ELEGANTE

6 medium chicken breasts, boned
1 can cream of mushroom soup
3 ounce can mushrooms with
liquid

1 cup sour cream
1/2 cup orange juice
paprika

Place breasts in oblong baking dish. Combine sour cream, soup, and mushrooms with liquid. Blend in orange juice and pour mixture over chicken. Sprinkle with paprika. Cover with foil and bake at 350 degrees for about 1 hour (or until tender). Remove foil near end of cooking time to brown slightly. Serve over rice.

CHILLED CHICKEN BREASTS
IN GELATIN GLAZE

6 chicken breasts, boned and cut in half	3 to 4 slices lemon
4 cubes chicken bouillon	3 bay leaves
3 cups water	1 carrot, sliced
6 teaspoons leaf tarragon	2 stalks celery
2 Tablespoons instant onions	2 teaspoons salt
2 Tablespoons parsley	1/2 cup dry sherry
	unflavored gelatin

Bring the 3 cups water to a boil. Add slices of lemon, celery, carrot, bay leaves, bouillon cubes, and salt. Tie onion, tarragon leaves, and parsley in cheesecloth and add to boiling water. When above boils add chicken breasts; cover and simmer about 20 to 30 minutes until meat is tender. Add enough water to cover. Remove from fire and add 1/4 cup sherry and allow to cool in liquid until cool enough to handle. Pull off skin and chill.

Chill broth until fat rises to top, then skim off. Soften gelatin in 1/2 cup broth in a small saucepan. Heat, stirring constantly, until gelatin dissolves. Remove from heat and stir in remaining broth and 1/4 cup of dry sherry.

Place chicken breasts in a single layer on a wire rack set in a shallow pan. Measure 1/2 cup of the gelatin mixture; set cup in a small bowl of ice and water; chill just until as thick as unbeaten egg white. Brush over chicken breasts to coat. (Keep remaining gelatin at room temperature.)

Arrange a flower in gelatin on each chicken breast, using a carrot slice for blossom and a long strip of green onion top for stem and short pieces for leaves. Chill until firm. Measure out another 1/2 cup of the gelatin mixture and chill until thickened; brush over decorations on chicken; chill until firm. Chill remaining gelatin mixture; brush over chicken a third time to make a thick coating, then chill several hours.

When ready to serve, arrange chicken on a spinach-lined large platter. Garnish with cherry tomatoes cut to form flowers.

COQ AU VIN WITH NEW POTATOES

2 broiler-fryer (2-1/2 pound size), quartered	2 Tablespoons flour
6 slices bacon, diced	1 teaspoon salt
2 Tablespoons butter or margarine	dash of pepper
8 small white onions, peeled	1/4 teaspoon dried thyme leaves
8 small whole mushrooms	2 cups Burgundy
2/3 cup sliced green onion	1 cup canned chicken broth
1 clove garlic, crushed	8 small new potatoes, scrubbed
	chopped parsley

(Continued)

Wash chickens and pat dry with paper towels. In a 5 or 6 quart oval Dutch oven, over medium heat, saute bacon until crisp. Remove from Dutch oven; drain on paper towels. Add butter to bacon drippings; heat. In hot fat, brown chicken quarters well on all sides. Remove chicken when browned, and set aside. Pour off all but 2 tablespoons fat from Dutch oven. Add white onions, mushrooms, green onion and garlic to Dutch oven. Over low heat, cook, covered and stirring occasionally, 10 minutes. Remove from heat; stir in flour, salt, pepper and thyme. Gradually add Burgundy and chicken broth; bring mixture to boiling, stirring. Remove from heat. Add potatoes, chicken and bacon to Dutch oven; mix well. Cover Dutch oven and refrigerate overnight. The next day, about two hours before serving time, preheat oven to 400 degrees. Bake coq au vin, covered, about 1 hour and 50 minutes, or until chicken and potatoes are tender. Sprinkle with chopped parsley before serving. Makes 6 to 8 servings.

CHICKEN CURRY

3-1/2 to 4-1/2 pound chicken	1 clove garlic, finely diced
4 to 6 cups broth (save)	dash salt
5 medium onions chopped	dash black pepper
2 small celery stalks, sliced	1 Tablespoon curry powder
4 medium green peppers,	1 Tablespoon vinegar
coarsely chopped	1 Tablespoon sugar
1 small can pimientos, sliced	1 Tablespoon cornstarch
1 can mushrooms, sliced	

Boil chicken, saving 4 to 6 cups broth. Brown onions in chicken fat or 2 tablespoons butter. Add garlic, peppers and celery. Add 2 cups broth and let simmer until tender. Add rest of broth, chicken, pimientos and mushrooms, together with seasonings. Thicken with cornstarch and let come to a good boil. Serve on a bed of rice with chutney and condiments.

Serve Chicken Curry over steamed rice. Have bowls of condiments to serve on top of curry.

CHICKEN CHUTNEY

1 cup applesauce	1 teaspoon cinnamon
1/2 cup raisins	1 teaspoon nutmeg
1 small clove garlic, finely chopped	1/4 teaspoon Tabasco
1 small onion, finely chopped	dash cayenne pepper
1/2 cup vinegar	dash paprika
1/2 cup water	dash black pepper

Cook onions and garlic in vinegar and water, simmering until tender. Add seasonings, applesauce, and raisins; bring to a boil. Place in small bowl to serve with Chicken Curry.

Condiments that go well with Chicken Curry and Chicken Chutney, above, are: chopped onion, chopped celery, chopped green peppers, grated coconut, grated almonds, peanuts, raisins, melon. Serve with French bread and white wine.

MAMMY'S SHANTY CHICKEN SHORTCAKE

1/2 pint cream	1-1/2 teaspoons salt
1 cup milk	dash of black pepper
3/4 cup chicken fat (or butter)	2 ounces pimiento, chopped
1/8 pound butter, melted	4 ounces mushrooms, diced
1/2 cup flour	4 cups cooked, diced chicken

Heat cream and milk in double boiler. Add to this the chicken fat. Melt the 1/8 pound butter, slowly, add and blend the flour, salt, and dash of pepper. Add cream mixture. Stir in the pimiento, diced mushrooms and diced chicken. Heat thoroughly. Serve over hot bread slices, biscuits or cornbread squares. Makes 6 servings.

NOTE: This was a popular luncheon entree at the Old Mammy's Shanty Restaurant in Atlanta, Georgia.

COUNTRY CAPTAIN CHICKEN

The true originator of Country Captain is unknown. This combination of chicken, tomatoes, and curry is thought to have originated in India where it was prepared by the Country Captains, officers in the native Indian militia known as the Sepoys. Most likely, a Sepoy captain introduced this dish to the British, who brought it to America. The dish may have been brought to the port of Savannah by a mysterious captain of the spice trade, as Georgians claim, or it may have been the wild invention of a local cook desperately tired of fried chicken. However it originated, many cooks know this bold and pungent dish's appeal for an exciting menu.

1-1/2 cups all-purpose flour	2 cloves garlic, minced
salt	1 Tablespoon curry powder
freshly ground black pepper	2 10-ounce cans stewed tomatoes,
paprika	including liquid
2 frying chickens, cut in pieces	1 cup chopped peanuts or 1/2
6 Tablespoons margarine	pound toasted almonds
6 Tablespoons vegetable oil	1 cup golden raisins
2 large onions, chopped	4 cups steamed rice for
1 cup chopped green bell pepper	accompaniment

Combine flour, salt, and pepper in paper bag. Shake chicken pieces in the flour mixture until coated. Shake off excess flour. In a large saute pan, combine margarine and oil and heat until sizzling. Brown chicken on all sides over medium-high heat. Remove the chicken pieces, reduce heat to medium-low, and allow the fat to cool a little. Add onion, green pepper, and garlic to pan. Stir until the vegetables are soft, but not browned. Add curry powder and tomatoes; stir until blended. Return chicken to pan, cover, and cook over low heat 25 to 30 minutes, or until chicken is tender. Remove chicken pieces to platter and keep warm. Turn heat to high and reduce the liquid until thickened, stirring frequently. Taste and correct seasoning. Stir in raisins. Spoon sauce over chicken and serve with steamed rice. Top with toasted almonds or peanuts. Serves 8 to 10.

ITALIAN CHICKEN WITH TOMATO SAUCE

6 whole chicken breasts, skinned
and boned
2 eggs, beaten
1 cup Italian-style bread crumbs

1/4 cup oil or 2 Tablespoons oil
plus 2 Tablespoons butter
6 slices mozzarella cheese

Pound chicken breasts between waxed paper until thin. Dip chicken in egg and coat with bread crumbs. In large frying pan saute chicken in oil until browned. Top each chicken breast with slice of Mozzarella; cover and melt slightly. Serve with tomato sauce. Serves 12.

Tomato Sauce:
1 large onion, finely chopped
2 cloves garlic, finely chopped
1 Tablespoon butter
2 Tablespoons oil
1 (6-ounce) can tomato paste
1 (1-pound 13-ounce) can Italian
peeled tomatoes, mashed
2 bay leaves

4 Tablespoons parsley, finely
chopped
1/4 teaspoon oregano
1 small strips lemon peel, chopped
1/3 cup dry white wine
3/4 cup water
salt and pepper to taste
1 Tablespoon Worcestershire
sauce

Saute onion and garlic in butter and oil in frying pan until soft and transparent. Stir in tomato paste and cook 1 minute, stirring constantly. Add tomatoes, bay leaves, parsley, oregano, lemon peel, wine, water, salt and pepper. Simmer 1 hour, stirring occasionally. Stir in Worcestershire sauce. Serves 6.

CHICKEN BREASTS
IN SOUR CREAM-ALMOND SAUCE

4 to 6 whole chicken breasts,
halved, boned, and skinned
3 Tablespoons butter
2 Tablespoons onion, chopped
1 clove garlic, minced
1 Tablespoon tomato paste
2 Tablespoons all-purpose flour
1-1/2 cups chicken stock
3 Tablespoons dry sherry

2 Tablespoons almonds, shredded
1/2 teaspoon fresh tarragon
minced
salt and freshly ground pepper to
taste
3/4 cup sour cream at room
temperature
1/2 cup Gruyere cheese grated

Saute the chicken on both sides in butter, remove from skillet. Add onion and garlic, cook and stir for 2 to 3 minutes. Add tomato paste and flour to skillet, stir until blended and smooth. Gradually add the chicken stock and sherry, cook and stir until smooth and slightly thickened. Return chicken to skillet. Add almonds, tarragon, salt and pepper. Cover and simmer over low heat until tender or for about 30 minutes. Arrange chicken in a shallow casserole. Stir the sour cream into sauce and pour over chicken. Sprinkle with grated cheese and brown under broiler. Serve with rice or noodles. Serves 4 to 6.

CHICKEN JAMBALAYA

1-1/2 pounds hot Italian sausage, thickly sliced

12 chicken thighs (or other meaty portion), skinned

2 teaspoons salt

1/4 teaspoon cayenne pepper

3/4 cup vegetable oil

2 Tablespoons brown sugar

3 medium onions, chopped

5 stalks celery, chopped

2 large green bell peppers, cored, seeded, and chopped

4 cloves garlic, minced (about 1 tablespoon)

5 cups heated chicken stock

1 Tablespoon salt

1/4 teaspoon cayenne pepper

4 cups raw long-grain white rice

1 cup chopped fresh parsley

2 bunch green onions, chopped (about 1/2 cup, including green portion)

2 large ripe tomatoes, chopped, for garnish

In a 3 quart cooking pot with cover, or flameproof casserole, saute sausage over moderate heat. Remove with a slotted spoon and set aside. Brown chicken, a few pieces at a time, in fat remaining in the casserole. Sprinkle chicken pieces with 1 teaspoon salt and 1/8 teaspoon cayenne. Remove chicken pieces and set aside. Add oil to pan drippings and heat to nearly smoking. Add brown sugar and caramelize, stirring constantly. Turn off heat and immediately add chopped onions, celery, and green peppers. Stir to saute vegetables. Add garlic. Return heat to moderate, add stock, 1/2 tablespoon salt, 1/8 teaspoon cayenne, and rice; bring to a boil. Stir well, then add sausage and chicken. Do not stir again.

Cover casserole tightly and cook over low heat 40 to 50 minutes, or until rice has absorbed the liquid.

Fluff rice with a fork. Remove from heat and add parsley and green onions. Just before serving, fluff mixture again. Garnish with chopped tomatoes. Serves 12.

MRS. TERZIA'S PRIZE-WINNER CASSEROLE

6 Tablespoons fat

6 Tablespoons flour

1-1/2 teaspoons salt

dash of pepper

1/2 teaspoon celery salt

2 cups stock

1 cup evaporated milk, scalded

6 ounce can mushrooms

1/2 cup almonds, toasted

3 Tablespoons parsley, minced

2 Tablespoons cooking sherry

1/2 package medium noodles, cooked

2 cups chicken, diced

1/2 cup grated cheese

Make a cream sauce of fat, flour, salt, pepper, celery salt, stock and milk. Add mushrooms, almonds, parsley and sherry. Alternate layers of noodles, chicken, and sauce in buttered casserole. Cover with cheese and bake at 375 degrees for 20 to 30 minutes. Makes 6 to 8 servings.

MARINATED CHICKEN WINGS

1-1/2 to 2 pounds chicken wings   1 cup catsup
    (or other pieces if desired)   1/4 cup honey
1/4 cup lemon juice   1/4 cup soy sauce

Preheat oven to 275 degrees. Remove tips from wings; cut into two pieces. Combine remaining ingredients; pour over chicken and marinate several hours or overnight. Remove from marinade and place in a shallow baking pan. Bake at 275 degrees for about one hour. Serve hot.

SOUTHERN FRIED CHICKEN

2 (3-pound) frying chickens   1/2 teaspoon white pepper or
buttermilk   black
1/2 cup flour   2/3 cup butter or margarine
1-1/2 teaspoons salt   1 cup vegetable shortening

NOTE: Chicken may be soaked in 1 quart of cold water with 1 tablespoon salt added if desired instead of buttermilk.

Cut chickens into serving-size pieces. Place in bowl. Pour buttermilk over chicken to just cover. Cover bowl and place in refrigerator for one hour. Mix flour, salt and pepper in a paper bag. Drain chicken but do not wipe dry. Drop pieces of chicken into bag. Shake until all are well covered with flour. Melt butter and shortening in a large heavy skillet. Heat to 350 degrees. Fry chicken in fat until golden brown on all sides. Cook uncovered for 20 minutes, then cover and continue to cook for 20 minutes or until chicken is done. Serves 4 to 6.

NOTE: For the best fried chicken, always use fresh not frozen chicken from a good source and fry in a heavy skillet.

Gravy:
3 Tablespoons fat from pan   1 cup milk
2 Tablespoons all-purpose flour   salt and pepper to taste

Keep warm in 250 degree oven while making gravy.

Pour off fat from skillet, leaving brown bits; return 3 tablespoons fat to the pan. Add flour and cook, stirring and scraping brown bits from bottom, until lightly browned. Remove from heat; gradually stir in milk.

Return to heat; cook and stir until thickened. If too thick, add more milk. Season with salt and pepper. Serve with plenty of hot biscuits.

CHICKEN 'N SWISS EXTRAORDINAIRE

3 whole chicken breasts
1 teaspoon Accent
1/2 cup flour
1/2 to 1 whole stick butter or
    margarine

6 slices swiss cheese
1/2 pound mushrooms, sliced
2/3 cup white wine
1 teaspoon salt
1/4 teaspoon pepper

Bone and split chicken breasts with sharp knife. Place pieces of breast between wax paper and roll thin with a rolling pin. Shake salt, pepper, and Accent over meat. Dredge in flour; melt half stick of butter in skillet. Brown chicken breasts on both sides. Add butter when necessary. Place in broiler pan. After chicken is browned, put mushrooms in skillet and cook about 3 to 4 minutes. Add wine and simmer until sauce is slightly thickened. Spoon over breasts in broiler pan, reserving a pretty mushroom for each breast. Just before serving time place a slice of cheese over each breast. Decorate with mushroom and put back into oven just until cheese melts. Serve at once on buttered toast or as they come from the oven. Serves 3.

CHICKEN DIVAN

2-1/2 to 3 pound chicken or 6
    chicken breasts
1 pound bunch broccoli or 10
    ounce package frozen
    broccoli
10-3/4 ounce can cream of
    chicken soup, undiluted
1/2 cup mayonnaise
1 teaspoon lemon juice

8 ounce carton sour cream
1/2 cup fine dry bread crumbs
1/2 cup sharp cheese, grated
salt and pepper to taste
1/2 teaspoon curry powder
    (optional)
2 Tablespoons butter or
    margarine, melted

Boil chicken until tender. Remove chicken from bones, let cool. Set aside. Trim off large leaves of broccoli. Remove tough ends of lower stalks, wash thoroughly. Separate into spears. Cook broccoli until crisp-tender in small amount of water for about 10 minutes; drain and set aside. Butter casserole dish. Place broccoli on the bottom, then place chicken on top of broccoli. Pour sauce on top. Combine butter with bread crumbs, stirring well; sprinkle over top of casserole. Bake at 350 degrees for 20 minutes. Sprinkle cheese over top of casserole; return to oven for 5 minutes or until cheese melts. Serves 8.

Asparagus may be used instead of broccoli.

RICH'S MAGNOLIA ROOM CHICKEN PIE

1 4-pound chicken	1/2 Tablespoon salt
1 cup diced carrots	1/2 teaspoon pepper
1 cup small green peas	1 teaspoon monosodium
1/4 cup chicken fat	glutamate (M.S.G.)
1/4 cup flour	pastry for crust
1 quart chicken stock	

Boil chicken until tender, then strip meat from bones when cool. Cut into 1" pieces. Place layers of chicken and vegetables in individual casseroles, or use a casserole dish. Cover with sauce made with chicken fat, flour, chicken stock, and salt and pepper. Cover with pie pastry. Bake for 30 minutes at 400 degrees. Makes 4 individual casseroles, when divided.

CHICKEN 'N' DUMPLINGS

Just Like Grandma's

1 chicken	Dumplings:
2 carrots, sliced	2 cups flour
2 stalks celery with leaves, halved	1/2 teaspoon pepper
1 onion, quartered	1 teaspoon salt
salt and pepper to taste	1 beaten egg
water	1 Tablespoon shortening
butter	

Cook chicken with carrots, celery, onion, salt and pepper in water to cover until tender. Remove chicken. Strain broth and discard vegetables; add 2 tablespoons butter for each 5 cups broth. Set aside.

Cut flour, salt and pepper together with shortening like you would pie crust. Now put egg in a tea cup and fill rest of way with cold water. Combine flour, egg, shortening, salt and water.

Divide dough into three parts; roll each third very thin on a floured board or counter until it is so thin you can almost see through it. Let dough dry 20 minutes. While dough is drying, skin and debone chicken. Cut dough into strips or squares and drop into boiling broth a few at a time. Boil uncovered 10 minutes. Remove dumplings with a slotted spoon. Thicken broth with flour, if necessary, to make gravy. Return chicken and dumplings to gravy; heat through. Serves 4 to 6.

NOTE: These dumplings are good cut in strips and placed over a roasting hen last 30 minutes (or until brown). Makes a crisp tasty covering.

CHICKEN CACCIATORE

2 (2-1/2 to 3-pound) chickens
2 chicken bouillon cubes
1 large onion, quartered
1 large carrot, sliced
1 cup sliced celery with tops
6 Tablespoons minced parsley,
  divided
1 bay leaf
1-1/2 teaspoons thyme, divided
10 peppercorns
4 Tablespoons olive oil, divided
3/4 stick margarine, divided
1 pound fresh mushrooms, sliced
3 medium onions, chopped

3 large cloves garlic, minced
2 medium green peppers, seeded
  and cut into half inch squares
2 Tablespoons flour
16 ounce can Italian tomatoes
1 cup dry red wine
1 cup chicken stock
1/2 teaspoon salt
1 teaspoon sugar
2 cups freshly grated Parmesan
  cheese
16 ounce package spaghetti or
  vermicelli, cooked and
  drained

In a large kettle, place enough water to cover the chickens. Add bouillon cubes, onion, carrot, celery, 2 tablespoons parsley, bay leaf, 1 teaspoon thyme, and peppercorns. Bring the mixture to a simmer, add the chickens, cover, and simmer 45 minutes or until done. Cool, bone, and cube chickens. Strain the stock, cool, and skim fat. In a large frying pan, heat 2 tablespoons olive oil with 1/4 stick butter over medium heat. Add mushrooms and saute about 5 minutes or until slightly brown and juices evaporate. Remove from pan and set aside.

Add remaining oil and 1/4 stick butter to pan. Saute onions and garlic for about 5 minutes or until onions are wilted. Add green peppers and cook about 3 more minutes or until onions are golden. Sprinkle flour over onion mixture and stir until blended. Add tomatoes, breaking them with a fork. Stir in wine, stock, salt, remaining thyme, and sugar. Reduce heat and simmer for about 20 minutes, stirring often. Add mushrooms and 1 tablespoon parsley and continue simmering about 10 minutes or until sauce is thick. Place 1/2 the sauce in a shallow 3-quart baking dish, add the chicken, and cover with remaining sauce.

If making ahead, cover dish tightly with foil, and bake at 350 degrees for 30 minutes or 45 minutes if refrigerated. Remove foil and bake for 15 minutes. Sprinkle with 1 cup of the cheese and bake 15 minutes or until thoroughly heated.

Toss spaghetti with 1/4 stick melted butter and remaining parsley. Serve chicken with spaghetti and remaining cheese. Serves 8. Freezes well.

BRAISED ROCK CORNISH HENS

4 rock cornish hens, washed and dried

salt and pepper

1/4 cup salad oil

1/2 cup shallots or green onions, minced

2 Tablespoons melted butter or margarine

2 cups diced carrots

2 cups chopped celery

1/2 cup sherry or madeira wine

Wash hens and pat dry; sprinkle inside and outside with salt and pepper. Brown hens in oil on all sides in Dutch oven. Remove hens and set aside; discard drippings. Saute shallots in butter 1 minute, stirring occasionally. Add carrots, celery, and 1/2 teaspoon salt. Place hens, breast side up, over vegetables; add sherry or madeira. Cover and simmer 25 to 30 minutes or until hens are tender. Garnish as desired. Serves 4.

Or: Toss vegetables with 2 cups cooked wild rice. Heat through. Mound rice-vegetable mixture on platter and place hens around rice and vegetables. Very pretty and delicious, too.

STUFFED CORNISH HENS
WITH WINE SAUCE

1 (6-ounce) package seasoned long grain and wild rice mix

2-1/2 cups chicken broth

1/2 cup celery, chopped

1/2 cup green onions, sliced

2/3 cup water chestnuts, sliced

3-ounce can mushroom stems and pieces, drained

6 Tablespoons butter, melted

2 Tablespoons soy sauce

4 cornish hens

salt

melted butter

wine Sauce

1/2 pound fresh mushrooms, sliced

1/4 cup butter, melted

reserved pan drippings

3 Tablespoons dry white wine

2 Tablespoons green onions, sliced

Prepare rice according to package directions, substituting broth for water. Cool and add celery, onion, water chestnuts, mushrooms, butter and soy sauce. Toss lightly to mix. Sprinkle inside of hens with salt and stuff with rice mixture. Bake at 375 degrees for 50 to 60 minutes or until done. Baste frequently with melted butter. Reserve pan drippings for wine sauce. Serves 8.

To prepare wine sauce, saute mushrooms in butter and set aside. Combine pan drippings, wine and onions in small saucepan and cook over high heat until reduced by 1/2, about 10 minutes. Stir in mushrooms and serve over hens. Serves 4.

DOVE BREASTS STROGANOFF

12 to 18 dove breasts
1 medium onion, chopped
2 Tablespoons butter or
  margarine, melted
1 10-3/4-ounce can cream of
  celery soup, undiluted
1 4-ounce can mushrooms
1/2 cup Sauterne wine

1/2 teaspoon oregano
1/2 teaspoon rosemary
salt and pepper to taste
1 teaspoon bottled brown
  Bouquet sauce
1 cup commercial sour cream
cooked wild rice

Arrange meat in a large baking dish; do not crowd. Saute onion in butter. Add remaining ingredients except sour cream and rice. Pour mixture over meat. Cover dish lightly with foil. Bake at 325 degrees for 1 hour, turning occasionally. Add sour cream and stir into sauce. Bake, uncovered, an additional 20 minutes. When ready to serve spoon over wild rice. Serves 6 to 9.

DOVES IN A CROCK

18 doves
flour
salt
pepper

3 carrots, sliced
6 medium potatoes, quartered
1 onion, chopped
1 bell pepper, chopped

Flour, salt and pepper doves. Brown in oil in frying pan. Remove doves from oil. Pour out part of oil, leaving enough to make gravy. To the oil add flour, water, onions and bell pepper. Place doves in crock pot. Pour gravy over doves, then add potatoes and carrots. Cook on low 6 to 8 hours. Serves 6 to 8.

QUAILS WITH WILD RICE

10 quail
1-1/4 cups melted butter or
  margarine, divided
1-1/2 pounds chicken livers
2 large onions, chopped
1 green pepper, chopped

1 small can of mushrooms,
  chopped
2 cloves garlic, minced
2-1/2 cups cooked wild rice
2 cups chicken broth
1-1/2 cups port wine

Saute quail in 1/2 cup butter until brown. Place in baking dish; cover and bake at 325 degrees about 30 minutes. While quail are baking, saute livers, onion, pepper, mushrooms, and garlic in 3/4 cup butter. Do not let vegetables brown, but cook until transparent. Stir in rice, chicken broth, and wine. Spoon rice mixture into a 3-quart baking dish; cover and bake at 325 degrees about 20 minutes or until liquid is absorbed. Serve quail over rice. Serves 8 to 10.

TURKEY PIE

2 cups cubed, cooked turkey or
   chicken
1 cup carrots, sliced
1 cup onions, chopped
1/2 teaspoon thyme
1/4 cup butter or margarine

1 Tablespoon flour
1 cup cooked green beans
1 cup cubed potatoes
1/4 cup celery, sliced
1/8 teaspoon pepper
1 can cream of mushroom soup

Toss turkey or chicken with flour; set aside. In saucepan cook carrots, potatoes, onions and celery with thyme and pepper in butter until tender. Stir in soup, turkey mixture and green beans. Pour into 9" pastry-lined pie pan. Top with latticed top (1/2" wide strips). Bake at 350 degrees for 45 minutes or until crust is lightly browned. Makes 4-1/2 cups. Serves 4 to 5.

BROWN TURKEY GRAVY

Giblet Stock, 3 to 4 cups
2 Tablespoons plain flour
2 Tablespoons cornstarch
salt and pepper

water to giblet stock to make 3 to
   4 cups of liquid depending
   on desired thickness

Giblet Stock:

Place turkey giblets in a small saucepan and cover with water. Simmer for 1 hour; strain. Cool and cut liver and gizzard into small pieces and reserve for gravy, if desired.

When turkey is roasted, remove from pan. Remove as much fat as possible from the pan, reserving 1 tablespoon. Deglaze the pan with 1 cup of the giblet stock, scraping all the browned pieces from the bottom of the pan. Be sure to really deglaze the pan. Often, people are reluctant to scrape the bottom of the pan to release all the bits and pieces, but this is where most of the flavor comes from.

In a clean saucepan, add flour and reserved fat. Cook together for 1 to 2 minutes. Be sure the flour is thoroughly cooked before adding the liquid. Proper cooking at this stage will eliminate lumps in the final stage.

Add the cornstarch to a small amount of the liquid to mix well. Add remaining giblet stock and juices from the pan. Bring to a boil, reduce to a simmer and cook until thickened, stirring constantly to prevent lumps. Salt and pepper to taste. Add giblets, if desired.

NOTE: By using both flour and cornstarch, you get the best of both thickeners.

ROAST TURKEY WITH DRESSING
(And Gravy)

As wild turkeys were abundant in the New World, they were a very appropriate choice for the Pilgrim's first Thanksgiving dinner. Roasted and stuffed, sliced and stacked in a sandwich, or served cold with salad dressing and crisp vegetables, turkey is still an American favorite.

Allow 3/4 to 1 pound ready-to-cook weight for each serving. Fresh or frozen turkey is according to your preference. Most turkeys are sold frozen, regular or self-basting, and range from 8 to 24 pounds. Frozen turkeys should be bought at least 3 days before roasting to allow thawing time, since a 12-pound turkey takes 2 to 3 days to thaw in the refrigerator. Fresh turkey should be bought no more than 1 to 2 days before roasting.

Preparing the turkey:

Rinse thawed turkey. Dry thoroughly inside and out. Fill body and neck cavity loosely with Herb Stuffing (or recipe of your choice). Skewer neck skin to back of bird; twist wing tips under the bird so that they rest flat against the neck skin. Secure the legs under the bank of skin or the metal clamp or truss with kitchen string.

Roasting directions:

Follow packer's directions on label or proceed as follows: Heat over to 325 degrees. Place turkey, breast side up, on rack in a shallow pan. Do not add water or cover pan. Brush skin with melted butter or margarine, unless you are cooking a self-basting bird. If using roast meat thermometer, insert it into center of inside thigh muscle, or into thickest part of breast meat, making certain bulb does not touch bone. For 12-pound bird, roast 3-1/2 hours, basting frequently with pan drippings, or until thermometer registers 185 degrees. When bird is 2/3 done, cut the band of skin, or release legs from metal clamp, so heat can reach behind the thigh. To test for doneness, protect fingers with paper toweling and squeeze meaty part of the thigh (it should feel soft). Drumsticks should move up and down easily. Place turkey on heated platter; let stand 20 minutes for easier carving. When dinner is over carve the remaining meat from the turkey and wrap tightly in foil; refrigerate or freeze. Remove stuffing and refrigerate or freeze separately.

CORNBREAD DRESSING

5 cups cornbread
12 slices white bread, toasted (6 cups)
2 cups finely chopped celery
2 cups finely chopped onions
1/2 cup minced parsley (optional)

1/2 pound butter (if fowl isn't fat)
2 teaspoons salt
1/2 teaspoon black pepper
1 teaspoon sage (optional)
4 hard cooked eggs, chopped
giblets

Simmer gizzard, heart, and neck in a quart of water until tender. Add liver and cook a few more minutes until done. Cut all meat finely. Reserve for gravy. Saute celery and onions in butter until done; add seasonings, more or less than amounts suggested to suit your taste. Mix cornbread and toasted bread crumbs together. Combine all ingredients (sauteed seasonings, parsley, minced giblets, chopped eggs and bread mixture) together with sufficient liquor from the giblets to make a moist dressing. Stuff turkey or hen. Cook remaining dressing in baking pan until done in over 400 degrees (approximately 25 to 30 minutes).

OYSTER DRESSING

4 cups crumbled bread crumbs
4 cups crushed saltine crackers
1 onion, chopped
1/2 cup celery, chopped
1/4 cup butter, melted
turkey gizzard and liver finely chopped

1 pint oysters
1 egg, lightly beaten
2 Tablespoons chopped parsley
1 teaspoon salt
1/2 teaspoon black pepper
1/2 teaspoon thyme
1/4 teaspoon marjoram

Saute onion and celery in butter until transparent. Add liver and gizzard, cooking quickly for 3 to 4 minutes. Toss with bread and crackers. Strain oyster liquid through fine sieve if it is gritty, and bring to a boil. Add cleaned oysters. Simmer 3 minutes or until edges just curl. Skim out the oysters and cut into small pieces. Add to the bread. Mix in remaining ingredients and enough oyster liquid to moisten dressing. Season the cavity with salt and pepper; stuff very lightly using any leftover stuffing under the neck skin.

TURKEY DRESSING

1-1/2 cups white cornmeal
2 Tablespoons all-purpose flour
1-1/2 teaspoons sugar
1 teaspoon baking powder
1/4 teaspoon baking soda
1/4 teaspoon salt
1-1/4 cups buttermilk
2 eggs, beaten
1 Tablespoon vegetable oil
1 Tablespoon shortening or
    bacon drippings

2 stalks celery, diced
1-1/2 medium onions, grated
3-1/4 to 3-3/4 cups turkey or
    chicken broth, divided
1-1/4 cups herb-flavored stuffing
    mix
1 to 1-1/2 teaspoons rubbed sage
1 teaspoon white pepper
1/2 teaspoon garlic powder

Combine first six ingredients in large mixing bowl; add buttermilk, eggs, and oil, mixing well. Place 1 tablespoon shortening in a 10" cast-iron skillet, then place skillet in 450 degree oven for 3 to 4 minutes or until hot. Tilt pan to evenly distribute shortening; pour batter into pan. Bake at 350 degrees for 25 minutes. Cook; crumble cornbread into a large bowl. Cook celery and onion in 1/4 cup broth in a skillet until tender. Add celery mixture, remaining broth, and remaining ingredients to cornbread crumbs, adjusting broth for desired moistness. Mix well and spoon mixture into a lightly greased 12x8x2" baking dish. Bake at 350 degrees for 40 minutes. Yields 8 servings.

SAUSAGE DRESSING

1 loaf (1 pound) day-old bread,
    toasted and cubed
1 Tablespoon salt
1 teaspoon thyme
1 teaspoon pepper
1/2 teaspoon sage
1-1/2 cups minced onions

chopped liver and gizzard from
    turkey
1/2 cup butter or margarine
1 pound country style sausage
1/2 pound cooked ham, ground
1/2 cup minced celery
3 eggs
1/2 cup cream

Brown bread in 275 degree oven. Cube and place in a large bowl; add seasonings. Saute onions, liver and gizzard in butter for 10 minutes. Add sausage; simmer for 5 minutes. Add ham, celery, remove from heat. Add to bread and mix well. Lightly beat eggs and cream; add to mixture. Let cool completely. Season cavity with salt and pepper; stuff bird.

SUPREME SAUCE FOR CHICKEN

1 Tablespoon onion, finely
chopped
1/3 cup butter/margarine
1/3 cup all-purpose flour
1/2 teaspoon salt
1/8 teaspoon pepper

1 envelope or 1 teaspoon instant
chicken broth
2 cups milk
4 Tablespoons grated Parmesan
cheese
2 Tablespoons heavy cream

Saute onions in butter or margarine just until soft in a heavy sauce pan; stir in flour, salt, and pepper; cook, stirring constantly over low heat, just until mixture bubbles; add instant chicken broth.

Stir in milk slowly; continue cooking and stirring until sauce thickens and bubbles 3 minutes. Stir in cheese and cream. Keep warm over low heat. Makes about 2-1/2 cups.

Signer's Monument - Augusta, Georgia ©1991 Ray Baird

SIGNER'S MONUMENT

Georgia has three signers of the Declaration of Independence. They were George Walton, Lyman Hall and Button Gwinnett. If the Colonies had lost the Revolution, they surely would have been executed. This document was and is that immortal manifesto of Liberty. A 50 foot shaft of Stone Mountain granite was dedicated to them July 4, 1848. The bodies of George Walton and Dr. Lyman Hall are buried beneath the Signers Monument on Greene St. Button Gwinnett's body was to be re-interred here, but the exact spot of his grave has not so far been determined.

George Walton, born in Virginia, settled in Augusta, Georgia and was a Colonel in the Revolutionary Army. He was twice Governor of Georgia, Judge of Superior court and Chief Justice of Georgia. He was elected to Congress six times and served one term as United States Senator. He was wounded and captured by the British at Savannah.

Dr. Lyman Hall, born in Connecticut, was one of a group of ardent revolutionaries from Midway, Georgia, who helped lead Georgia into open rebellion in 1776. He represented Georgia in the Continental Congress.

Button Gwinnett, born in England, settled in Savannah before the Revolutionary War and was a magnetic and fiery figure in early days of the war. He was President of Georgia in March 1777. A quarrel with General Lachlan McIntosh, arising out of the ill-fated expedition to Florida, resulted in a duel in May, 1777, on the outskirts of Savannah. He was mortally wounded. The exact spot of his grave has not, so far been determined.

Vegetables, Vegetable Casseroles and Sauces

PARTY BEAN CASSEROLE

10-ounce package frozen
french-style green beans
10-ounce package frozen baby
lima beans
10-ounce package frozen small
peas
1-1/4 cups heavy cream
1-1/4 cups mayonnaise

3/4 cup grated Parmesan cheese
or 3/4 cup shredded Cheddar
cheese
1/8 teaspoon pepper
1/4 teaspoon salt
paprika
parsley

Preheat oven to 325 degrees. Cook vegetables in small amount of water just until thawed enough to be separated with a fork. Drain and cool. Whip the cream, fold in mayonnaise, cheese, salt and pepper. Butter a 2-quart casserole and add vegetables. Cover with cream mixture. Sprinkle with paprika and bake uncovered about 30 to 40 minutes or until browned and bubbly. May be prepared ahead and refrigerated until baking time.

ASPARAGUS, PETITE PEAS
AND MUSHROOM CASSEROLE

1 (15-ounce) can green asparagus
or 1-1/2 pounds fresh
asparagus
1 (16-ounce) can Lesueur Petite
Peas
1 can small mushrooms or 1/2
cup sliced fresh mushrooms
1 can cream of mushroom soup

1 small onion, grated (optional)
1 small jar pimientos, cut in
strips (optional)
1/8 teaspoon white pepper
3/4 cup (packed) grated sharp
cheese
1 cup soft white bread crumbs
2 Tablespoons melted butter

NOTE: 1 cup crushed potato chips may be substituted for buttered bread crumbs.

Wash and clean fresh asparagus, cut spears into approximately 2-1/2" lengths, cover with water, and cook until tender (about 10 minutes). Drain. Arrange asparagus around outer edges of a buttered casserole dish, stacking spears on top of each other. Drain peas and fill in center of casserole. Mix grated onion, mushrooms, cream of mushroom soup, grated cheese, pimiento strips and white pepper. Pour over asparagus and peas. Toss bread crumbs with butter and sprinkle on top of casserole (or use potato chips, if you prefer). Bake in 350 degree oven for about 30 minutes or until crumbs are brown. May be made ahead and refrigerated until ready to bake.

ARTICHOKE AND SPINACH CASSEROLE

2 (14-ounce) cans artichokes
2 (10-ounce) packages spinach
1 small bottle french dressing
Parmesan cheese
Cream Sauce:
3 Tablespoons all-purpose flour
3 Tablespoons butter/margarine

1-1/2 cups half and half or
  evaporated milk
1 (6-ounce) package cream
  cheese, cut into small bits
1 teaspoon salt
1/8 teaspoon white or black
  pepper

Drain artichokes and marinate in french dressing 4 to 5 hours. Cook spinach and drain well.

Melt butter in a heavy saucepan over low heat; add flour, stirring until smooth, and cook one minute, stirring constantly. Gradually add milk and cook over medium heat until thickened and bubbly; remove from heat and add softened cream cheese, stirring until cream cheese melts. Add salt and pepper.

Combine spinach and cream sauce. Place artichokes in bottom of casserole dish. Pour spinach and cream sauce mixture over artichokes. Sprinkle top generously with Parmesan cheese and cook at 350 degrees until bubbly and cheese is melted.

Even if you don't like spinach, you will love this recipe!

MAMA'S GREEN BEANS

3 pounds green beans
3 slices breakfast bacon

1 pint water
salt and pepper to taste

Fry bacon in black iron pot. Add green beans, water, salt and pepper. Cover and simmer one to two hours. The secret of this recipe is cooking in the black iron pot.

MARINATED STRING BEANS

1 can vertical pack string beans
2 small onions, cut in rings
1 small jar pimientos, slivered

Marinate:
1/2 cup vinegar
1/2 cup water
1/2 cup sugar
2 Tablespoons Wesson oil

Drain and wash beans. Prepare marinate, combining vinegar, water, sugar, and Wesson oil. Place beans, onions, and pimientos in a bowl, cover with marinate and allow to sit for 24 hours. Serve hot or cold.

RED BEANS & RICE
WITH HOPPING JOHN RELISH

1 pound red kidney beans
2 large onions, chopped
3 celery stalks with leaves,
   chopped
1 green bell pepper, chopped
3 garlic cloves, chopped
2 bay leaves
1 ham bone, hock, or leftover
   ham (about 2 cups of large

pieces or 2 cups sliced
   sausage)
4 teaspoons salt
1-1/2 teaspoons black pepper
1/2 teaspoon red pepper
1 teaspoon Tabasco
2 Tablespoons Worcestershire
   sauce

Cover beans with water and soak overnight in refrigerator; add more water if necessary to keep beans covered. Drain beans and put them in an iron dutch oven or heavy pot. Add remaining main ingredients with enough water to cover by about 2". Cook slowly for about two hours, stirring occasionally. Adjust seasoning to taste. Mash some of the beans to make gravy thicker and richer. Serve over rice with Hopping John Relish and cornbread. Freezes well. Serves 8.

Hopping John Relish:
1 tomato, chopped
1/2 onion, chopped

oil & vinegar Italian dressing

Combine tomato and onion and marinate in a little Italian dressing in refrigerator while beans cook. Serve in side dish for each person to use as a topping. Yields 1 cup.

BEANS AND BEETS IN VINAIGRETTE

2-1/2 pounds beets
1/2 cup balsamic vinegar
3/4 cup olive oil
1/2 cup minced scallions

1 teaspoon Dijon Mustard
2 pounds small tender green
   beans, whole

Cut off tops of beets and scrub with a soft brush. Cook unpeeled beets in boiling water in a medium saucepan until tender, about 30 minutes. Drain beets, run under cold water, remove skins and slice thin.

In a bowl, whisk 1/4 cup of vinegar with salt and pepper to taste. Add 1/4 cup of the oil on a stream, whisking until the dressing is emulsified. Add and mix well 1/2 teaspoon mustard. Stir in 2 tablespoons scallions. Add beets and toss the mixture well. Let beets marinate, covered and chill overnight.

Snap top of tip end from beans, leaving beans whole. Boil in a kettle of boiling salt water for about 10 minutes or until tender crisp. Drain and plunge into a bowl of ice and cold water to stop cooking. Drain beans again and pat dry.

(Continued)

Just before serving, whisk together the remaining 1/4 cup vinegar with salt and pepper to taste. Add the remaining 1/2 cup of oil in a stream, whisking and whisk the dressing until it is emulsified. Stir in the mustard and remaining scallions.

Arrange beets and beans (1/4 beets, 1/4 beans) in an attractive circle on platter. Brush the beans with dressing. Sprinkle the remaining 3 tablespoons of the scallions on top of beans and beets. Pass the remaining dressing in a small bowl. Makes 12 servings.

The beans may be prepared the day before and refrigerated in a covered bowl. This recipe may be halved and can be used as a vegetable or salad.

PICK-A-DILLY BEETS

1 can sliced beets, drained
1 onion (more if desired)
3 dill pickles, sliced
1/2 cup dill pickle juice

1/2 cup vinegar
3/4 cup sugar
1 teaspoon salt

Mix all ingredients. Chill for several hours to mellow before serving. These will keep in refrigerator for weeks. Serve as a pickle or as a side dish.

BROCCOLI-ONION CASSEROLE

1 to 1-1/2 pounds fresh broccoli,
cut into 1-1/2" pieces
3 small onions, sliced thinly
1 small can mushrooms (optional)
2 Tablespoons butter/margarine
3 Tablespoons all-purpose flour
1-1/2 cups milk
1 6-ounce package cream cheese,
cut into cubes

1/4 teaspoon salt
1/8 teaspoon white pepper
1/2 cup (2 ounces) shredded
processed sharp cheese
2 Tablespoons butter/margarine,
melted
1 cup toasted bread crumbs

Cook broccoli and onions in a small amount of boiling water for 3 to 4 minutes or until tender. Drain well. Melt 3 tablespoons of butter in a heavy saucepan over low heat; add flour, stirring until smooth. Cook 1 minute, stirring constantly. Gradually add milk; cook over medium heat until thickened and bubbly. Remove from heat; add cream cheese, stirring until melted. Stir in salt and pepper. Spoon broccoli, onion and mushrooms into lightly greased 1-1/2 quart casserole. Pour sauce over vegetables and top with grated cheese. Cover and bake at 350 degrees for 25 minutes. Uncover and sprinkle with toasted bread crumbs, dot with 2 tablespoons butter. Bake an additional 5 minutes or until golden brown. Serves 6 to 8.

SWISS ALPINE PIE

10" pastry shell, unbaked
1 package frozen broccoli, cooked
2 cups pre-cooked 1/2" ham cubes
2 cups shredded Swiss cheese
3 Tablespoons chopped onion

1-1/2 cups milk, scalded
3 eggs, slightly beaten
1/8 teaspoon salt
1/8 teaspoon pepper

Preheat oven to 450 degrees. Drain and chop broccoli. Layer broccoli, ham, cheese in pastry shell. Sprinkle onion over top. Stir milk into eggs; add seasonings and pour into pastry shell. Bake 10 minutes. Reduce heat to 325 degrees and bake another 30 to 35 minutes. Let stand a few minutes before serving.

CABBAGE DINNER

1 pound ground beef
1 small onion, minced
1 egg
1 teaspoon salt
1/4 teaspoon pepper
1/4 teaspoon oregano
1/2 cup bread crumbs
2 Tablespoons margarine

4 cups shredded cabbage
1 bell pepper, sliced
1 teaspoon salt
1/4 teaspoon pepper
4 raw potatoes, sliced
1 tomato, sliced
1/2 cup water

Mix first seven ingredients and form into small meatballs. In a heavy skillet, brown meatballs on all sides, drain on absorbent paper. In a 6-quart saucepan, melt margarine over low heat; add cabbage, bell pepper and half of the salt and pepper. Next add potatoes, arrange tomato slices on top, and sprinkle with remaining salt and pepper. Add water, then arrange meatballs on top of the vegetables. Cover tightly and steam over low heat for about 30 minutes or until potatoes are done. Do not stir while cooking.

COPPER PENNY CARROTS

2 pounds (16 to 18 medium)
  carrots
1 teaspoon sugar
green pepper slices (sweet)
1 medium onion
1 can tomato soup (10-1/2 ounce)
3/4 cup vinegar, white

1/2 cup vegetable or salad oil
1 cup sugar
1 teaspoon prepared mustard
1 teaspoon Worcestershire sauce
salt and pepper to taste
1/4 teaspoon of dill may be used,
  if desired

Cut carrots into slices and boil with sugar until tender. Drain and cool. Alternate layers of carrots with slices of green pepper and onion rings. Blend together well the tomato soup, vinegar, oil, and 1 cup sugar, mustard, Worcestershire sauce, and salt and pepper. Pour mixture over vegetables; refrigerate for 24 hours before serving. Keeps indefinitely.

CHEESY MUSTARD CAULIFLOWER

Cauliflower seeds were first brought to this country by a family of early Dutch settlers, and from that family monopoly our cauliflower industry grew. It wasn't until some time later, however, that Americans discovered the secret of undercooking cauliflower to enhance its unique flavor.

2 Tablespoons butter
1-1/2 cups sliced mushrooms
1 medium head cauliflower
3 cups water
1-1/2 teaspoons salt
3/4 cup mayonnaise

1 Tablespoon finely chopped onion
1 Tablespoon Dijon mustard
3/4 cup shredded sharp Cheddar
1/2 teaspoon horseradish

Trim leaves from cauliflower; leaving head whole, remove as much of core as possible by cutting a cone-shaped piece from bottom of head. Combine water and salt in 4-quart dutch oven; cook over high heat until water boils, about 4 minutes. Place cauliflower in boiling water, stem side down, and cook until water boils again (about 1 minute). Reduce heat to low and cook, uncovered, 5 minutes. Cover and simmer 10 to 15 minutes more or until cauliflower is tender (remember, don't overcook). Drain cauliflower in colander; return to dutch oven.

In a medium skillet, melt butter over medium heat. Add to this mushrooms and cook until tender about 4 minutes.

Combine mayonnaise, onion, mushrooms, horseradish, mustard and cheese in bowl; mix to blend. Spread mayonnaise mixture over cauliflower. Cook, covered, over low heat 5 minutes or until cheese melts. Transfer cauliflower to serving platter, using two pancake turners. Sprinkle with paprika and serve.

FRIED FRESH CORN

4 slices bacon
3 cups fresh corn, cut from cob, scraping cob to get corn milk out
1-1/4 cups water

1 Tablespoon sugar
1 teaspoon salt and 1/4 teaspoon white pepper
1 Tablespoon cornstarch
2 Tablespoons cold water

Fry bacon until crisp; drain, crumble and set aside. Drain all but 2 tablespoons drippings from skillet. Add corn, water, sugar and pepper. Bring to boil over medium heat. Cover and simmer for 20 to 25 minutes, stirring frequently to keep from burning. Combine cornstarch and 2 tablespoons cold water, stirring until smooth. Stir into corn mixture and boil for 1 to 2 minutes, stirring constantly. Top with crumbled bacon before serving. Makes 4 to 5 servings.

MRS. KITCHENS CORN PUDDING
(Best Ever)

1 can white creamed corn	salt to taste
1/4 cup chopped pimiento	3/4 cup extra sharp cheese, grated
1/2 cup finely chopped bell	1 stick margarine
pepper	1 hot green pepper, stripped of
1/2 cup finely chopped celery	seeds and finely cut
1 cup finely chopped onion	Topping:
2 eggs, beaten well	5 slices white bread, toasted
3/4 cup milk	1/2 stick margarine
3/4 cup sifted flour	1 cup sharp cheese
2 teaspoons black pepper	paprika

Melt but do not brown margarine. Add flour, stirring well. Add milk slowly and stir until smooth. Add grated sharp cheese, salt and pepper. Mixture will be thick enough to cut. Add beaten eggs, celery, pepper, onions, pimientos and corn. Pour into greased casserole and cook at 270 degrees for 1-1/2 hour. Make a topping by breaking toasted white bread into small pieces and placing on top of cooked casserole. Dot with margarine and sprinkle with cheese. Bake for an additional 15 minutes at 275 degrees. As you take the casserole from the oven, sprinkle with paprika and serve hot (leftovers freeze well).

EGGPLANT CASSEROLE

1 large eggplant	dash of black pepper
1 egg	20 Ritz crackers, crushed
1/2 cup cubed medium sharp	cheese slices
cheese	pat of butter
1/2 teaspoon salt	

Peel and cut up eggplant; boil in small amount of water on low heat until tender. Drain and mash; add cubed cheese, salt, pepper, egg and crushed Ritz crackers. Turn into buttered casserole. Top with sliced cheese to cover. Add butter pat and bake at 375 degrees for 20 to 30 minutes.

PEAS CONTINENTAL

2 Tablespoons butter	dash of pepper
1 (4-ounce) can sliced, drained	1/4 teaspoon nutmeg
mushrooms	1/8 teaspoon marjoram
1/4 cup minced onion	2 Tablespoons cooking sherry
1/4 teaspoon salt	2 cups drained hot peas

In a skillet, melt butter and saute mushrooms with onion until onion is tender. Add salt, pepper, nutmeg, marjoram and sherry. Toss with hot peas. Serves 4.

MOUSAKA (BAKED EGGPLANT)

1-1/2 pounds lean ground beef	2 cups tomato sauce
1 clove minced garlic	grated Romano or Parmesan
1/4 teaspoon pepper	cheese
1-1/2 teaspoons salt	Crema Sauce:
2 chopped onions	6 Tablespoons butter
1 teaspoon chopped parsley	6 Tablespoons flour
4 Tablespoons butter	3 cups milk
3 medium eggplants	4 to 6 egg yolks

Add garlic, salt and pepper to ground beef. Cook slowly until meat juices are absorbed. Add chopped onion, parsley and butter; brown well. Add tomato sauce; simmer until thickened (about 15 minutes). Slice eggplants, soak in salt water (15 minutes). Drain, squeeze slices gently to remove excess moisture, and brown in hot vegetable oil. Drain cooked slices on paper towel. Arrange layers of eggplant in a 9x13" baking pan, alternating with meat, topping with eggplant. Make crema sauce: melt butter, add flour, and stir until light brown; add milk gradually, stirring constantly until slightly thickened; slowly add slightly beaten egg yolks and cook over very low heat until thickened; season with salt and pepper to taste. Spread crema sauce over top of casserole, then sprinkle with grated cheese. Bake 30 minutes at 350 degrees. Makes 10 to 12 servings.

Recipe may be varied. For first variation, omit crema sauce. Instead, combine 4 well-beaten eggs with 2 cups milk and pour over top layer of eggplant; sprinkle with grated cheese and bake.

For second variation, sprinkle grated cheese over each layer of eggplant before covering with meat mixture.

FRIED OKRA

A True Southern Finger Food

2 pounds fresh okra	pepper
1 teaspoon cold water	cornmeal
3 large eggs, well-beaten	vegetable oil for deep frying
salt	

Remove tops and tips from okra and slice 1/2" thick. Add eggs to water. Dip okra slices a few at a time in egg mixture and roll in cornmeal to coat.

Fry in a heavy skillet in deep oil over medium heat (350 degrees on deep-fry thermometer) until golden brown, about 2 to 3 minutes. Keep the slices in single pieces. Try not to allow to lump together. Drain on a paper towel. Season with salt and pepper.

Some Southerners call this Georgia Popcorn. A true taste of the South.

"NOW FAMOUS" MUSHROOM CASSEROLE

12 slices day old white bread
with crusts removed
5 beaten eggs
2-1/2 cups milk
1 teaspoon salt
1/4 teaspoon pepper
1/2 teaspoon dry mustard
pinch red pepper

1/2 pound grated sharp Cheddar
cheese
1/2 cup melted butter
1 pound fresh mushrooms
2 teaspoons prepared mustard
2 teaspoons lemon juice
dash of Worcestershire sauce
can of cream of mushroom soup

Crumble half of the day-old bread into a 2 quart buttered baking dish. Mix eggs, milk, salt, pepper, dry mustard and red pepper. Pour half of mixture over bread and top with half of the grated cheese and 1/4 cup melted butter. Cut stems from caps and saute mushrooms in butter, a dash of Worcestershire sauce, mustard and lemon juice. Place the mushroom stems on top of casserole layers. Repeat all above layers, beginning with bread and ending with sauteed mushroom caps. Refrigerate 8 hours to 2 days. Prior to serving, top with 1 can cream of mushroom soup and bake 45 minutes at 350 degrees.

PATIO CHEESE POTATOES

4 large Idaho potatoes
3 Tablespoons butter/margarine
salt and pepper

minced parsley (or flakes)
1/2 cup sharp cheese, grated
1/2 cup cream

Peel and slice potatoes in strips as if for french fries. Line a casserole dish or oblong baking dish with heavy aluminum foil, leaving enough on sides to fold over and seal. Place potatoes in pan, dot with butter, sprinkle with salt, pepper, parsley and cheese. Pour cream over potatoes. Bring edges of foil over potatoes and seal. Place on cookie sheet and bake at 425 degrees for 40 to 50 minutes. A great side-dish for beef (steak, barbecue, etc.).

STUFFED ONIONS

8 onions of uniform size (at least
3" in diameter)
boiling salted water
Stuffing:
v-shaped cores of onions (see
preparation below)
1/4 pound butter
1/2 pound mushrooms, sliced
1 medium tomato, peeled and
chopped
1/2 cup reserved onion water
1 cup dry white wine
1/2 cup brown rice

1/2 cup freshly grated Parmesan
cheese
1/4 cup heavy cream (optional)
2 Tablespoons basil or 1
Tablespoon tarragon
1/4 teaspoon sage
1/4 teaspoon oregano
1/4 cup chopped fresh parsley
2 Tablespoons bread crumbs
salt and freshly ground pepper to
taste
dry white wine as needed

(Continued)

Preheat oven to 350 degrees. Cut top and bottom off onions and peel. Place bottom ends down and with sharp knife cut a cone-shaped core from top part of onions. Being careful to leave a 1/2" bottom in the shell, dig out centers of onions and reserve. Place onion shells in boiling salted water, and when water returns to boil, simmer, uncovered for 10 minutes or until just tender. Do not overcook, as onions must hold their shape. Remove from water and allow to drain upside down. Reserve liquid. Chop reserved onion cores. Melt butter and saute cores and mushrooms for 10 minutes. Add tomato, reserved onion water, 1 cup white wine and rice. Cover and simmer for 45 minutes or until rice is tender and most of liquid has been absorbed. Add cheese, cream, herbs, bread crumbs, salt and pepper, adjusting seasonings to taste. Stuff onion shells, place in a shallow baking dish to hold onions close together and pour in white wine to a depth of about 3/4". Bake for 20 minutes or until heated through.

CHEESE-STUFFED ONIONS

4 jumbo Vidalia onions
1 cup sharp Cheddar cheese,
    finely grated
1 cup fresh mushroom, finely
    chopped
1 cup sour cream
2 ounces cream cheese, softened

1 rounded Tablespoon
    mayonnaise
1-1/2 teaspoons prepared
    horseradish
4 strips bacon, cooked until crisp
1/2 teaspoon salt
pepper to taste

Remove outer layer of brown skin from onion. After removing stem core, place onions on stem ends (flat end of the onion). Using a small knife, scoop out about 1/3 of the onion making sure not to leave a hole in the bottom of the onion. If you do make a hole in the onion, use a separate piece of onion and place in bottom of onion as a patch. Place onions in a baking dish, and they are ready to stuff.

Grate cheese as finely as possible and set aside. Chop mushrooms and set aside until bacon is cooked. Cook bacon until crisp and reserve drippings. Saute mushrooms in the bacon drippings until soft.

In a mixing bowl, combine sour cream, softened cream cheese, mayonnaise, horseradish, salt and pepper, mixing well. Add cheese and sauteed mushrooms and combine well. Crumble 1 strip of bacon into the bottom of each onion, then fill to the top with stuffing mixture. Mound remaining stuffing on top of onions.

Place about 1/4 cup of water in bottom of casserole. Cover and cook for 1 hour at 350 degrees. Remove cover and bake for 15 minutes more or until browned. Makes 4 servings.

NOTE: Onions may be prepared at least a day ahead and stored in a tightly sealed container until ready to bake. An excellent dish to serve with beef. Any stuffing unable to get in onions, makes a delicious dressing for sliced tomatoes.

1830 HOPPIN JOHN

Contents are symbolic of good luck and happiness for the New Year. Black-eyed peas and hog jowls for good luck, rice for purity, rosemary for friendship, mustard for steadfastness, bourbon for happy hours with family and friends.

1 pound blackeyed peas	1 teaspoon dry mustard
1 pound bacon or 1 pound hog jowls	1 teaspoon rosemary
	1 teaspoon hot pepper sauce
water	salt to taste
1 cup chopped onion	1/2 cup good bourbon
1 to 2 cups cooked rice	

Soak peas in cold water overnight. Rinse and cook uncovered on low heat until soft. (Covering tends to cause the peas to "shell out" or the skins to separate from the pea.) Fry bacon until brown and crisp. Remove from the pan and saute onions in the bacon fat.

Combine all ingredients (except bourbon) in a large container. Stir once to mix the seasonings. Place in a large Crock or double boiler and steam for about 2 hours or until ingredients are well-seasoned and grease is absorbed.

When ready to serve, pour into a large warmed serving bowl. Add the "spirits" and stir with a fork. This is a good tasty dish without the bourbon also and may be enjoyed all year long. Serve with plenty of good cornbread or hot biscuits.

HOPPING JOHN

Hopping John was originally a native of the South Carolina. It is now relished throughout the South. It is well-known (but not why) that a dish of it eaten on New Year's Day brings luck all year. But for that matter, blackeyed peas are always lucky. A mixture of beans, rice and salt pork eaten on New Year's Day is supposed to guarantee good luck for the remaining 364 days. There are two theories for the origination of the name. One is that it came from an old custom that the children hopped once around the table before eating, to give them something to do and help them work off excess steam before dinner. The second is that it was named after the custom of inviting a guest to eat by saying, "Hop in John." It is delicious all year, not just for New Year's.

1 cup raw blackeyed peas	2 stalks celery, finely chopped
4 cups water	1 cup diced country ham or 1
2 teaspoons salt	pound meaty ham hocks
1 cup raw rice, long grain	cooked and boned
4 to 6 slices bacon, fried with 1 medium onion, chopped	

NOTE: Both bacon and ham may be used to make this dish especially good.

(Continued)

Garnishes: (if desired)

1 red ripe tomato, about 1/4
  pound, cored and chopped
1/4 pound sharp Cheddar cheese,
  finely grated

1 cup scallions, finely chopped
  with some of the green tops

Soak raw peas overnight in cold water. Drain and rinse. Cook in salt water until tender. Boil ham hocks until tender, cut meat in small pieces. Fry bacon until brown and crisp. Drain and cook onion in bacon drippings until tender. Place all ingredients in a double-boiler and cook for one hour or until the rice is thoroughly done and fluffy.

NOTE: If using garnishes, cook rice separately and place rice in the center of a serving platter. Spoon hot pea mixture including liquid over the rice and top with garnishes added by layers. Garnishes can be passed in individual bowls at the table.

TANGY BLACKEYED PEAS

2-1/2 cups water
2-3/4 teaspoons salt
2 packages (10-ounce each)
  blackeyed peas
1 teaspoon minced garlic
1 large firm tomato, chopped
  (1-1/4 cups)
1/2 cup thinly sliced green onions

1 large green bell pepper,
  chopped coarse
Dressing:
1/2 cup vegetable oil
1/4 cup red-wine vinegar
1 teaspoon Dijon mustard
dash black pepper
1/3 cup finely chopped fresh parsley

Bring water and 2 teaspoons salt to a boil in a medium-size saucepan. Add peas, cover and return to a boil. Reduce heat and simmer 30 minutes until just tender (do not allow to become mushy). Sprinkle garlic with the remaining 3/4 teaspoon salt and mash to a paste with the blade of a knife. Scrape into a medium-size bowl. Add oil, vinegar, mustard and pepper and beat with a fork to mix well. Drain peas and toss with the dressing. Add chopped tomato, green pepper and onions; toss again. Sprinkle with parsley. Serve warm or at room temperature. It can be made a day before serving and refrigerated. This seems to blend the seasonings. May be used as a vegetable or as a salad.

NOTE: 1) If desired, add about 2 teaspoons hot pepper, finely chopped (such as banana) or a dash of Tabasco. 2) A tablespoon of dehydrated parsley may be added to the dressing if fresh parsley is unavailable. The fresh parsley may be added to the dressing instead of sprinkling on top if desired. 3) A cup or 2 of diced ham makes a tasty addition. Also 1/2 cup crisp fried bacon.

PARTY POTATO CASSEROLE

1 (2-pound package) frozen hash
   potatoes
1/2 cup butter, melted
1 teaspoon salt
1/2 teaspoon black pepper
1/2 cup chopped onions

1 cup sour cream
1 (10-1/2 ounce) can cream of
   chicken soup
1 cup light cream or milk
8 ounces sharp Cheddar cheese,
   grated (2 cups packed)

NOTE: Fresh green onions may be used with part of the tops included as onions. Partially thaw potatoes. In a large bowl, mix potatoes, soup, sour cream, light cream, butter, cheese and chopped onions. Add salt and pepper to taste. Pour into a greased 9x13" casserole. Sprinkle the topping of your choice on the top. Bake at 350 degrees 1 to 1-1/4 hours, or until bubbly.

Topping:
Your choice of the following:
1 (2.8 ounce) can french fried
   onion rings

2 cups crushed potato chips
2 cups corn flakes
2 Tablespoons butter, melted

If using crushed potato chips or corn flakes, mix with butter; spread on top. NOTE: This casserole may be frozen. If desired, freeze with topping and add just before baking. If frozen, increase baking time to 1 hour at 350 degrees. May be made into two pans (9x9x2" pans), cooking one and freezing one.

SWEET POTATOES

Sweet potatoes are a traditional accompaniment to Thanksgiving turkey and may be sweetened with honey, maple syrup or brown sugar.

The sweet potato, a southern staple, is a thick sweet and nutritious root cooked and eaten as a vegetable. A tropical vine related to the morning glory with variously shaped leaves and purplish flowers, it is native to either Central (Mexico) or South America or the Polynesian Islands and is known to have grown in Virginia as early as 1648. The yam, on the other hand, is African or Chinese in origin and rarely grown in the United States. When slaves arrived in this country and first saw the sweet potato, they called it "nyami" (their native word for yam) and it was later shortened to "yam."

CANDIED SWEET POTATO SLICES

6 large sweet potatoes (about 3
   pounds)
water
salt

1/2 cup packed brown sugar
4 Tablespoons butter/margarine
   cut into small pieces

About 1-1/2 hours before serving, heat unpeeled sweet potatoes to boiling in a 4-quart saucepan over high heat with enough water to cover. Reduce heat to low, cover and simmer 25 to 30 minutes until potatoes are tender. Drain potatoes and allow to cool slightly until easy to handle.

(Continued)

Preheat oven to 375 degrees; grease 12x8" baking dish. Peel potatoes and cut into 1/4" slices. Arrange one third of potatoes in baking dish; lightly sprinkle with salt; then sprinkle with one third of brown sugar; dot with one third of butter or margarine. Repeat with remaining ingredients to form 3 layers in all.

Cover baking dish with foil; bake 30 minutes or until potatoes are heated through and sugar and butter are melted. Makes 8 accompaniment servings for ham, chicken or pork.

SWEET POTATO-PINEAPPLE CASSEROLE

6 sweet potatoes, baked or 2 large cans, drained and mashed
1 to 1-1/2 cups drained pineapple tidbits

3 to 4 Tablespoons butter, melted
1 teaspoon cinnamon
1/2 cup cream or half and half
marshmallows

Preheat oven to 375 degrees. Mix sweet potatoes, butter, cinnamon, and half and half. Mix thoroughly, beating until light and fluffy. Use more milk or fruit juice if needed. Fold in pineapple tidbits; place in buttered casserole and bake until heated thoroughly. Remove from oven and cover top with the marshmallows. Return to oven and allow to brown (it won't take long). Serves 6 to 8.

SWEET POTATO PARTY LOG

1-1/2 cups cooked sweet potatoes, mashed
1 cup granulated sugar
1/2 cup brown sugar
1/2 cup evaporated milk
2 Tablespoons corn syrup
dash of salt
1-1/2 cups shredded coconut

2 cups crushed cornflakes (or enough to make mixture of consistency to handle with hands)
1 (8-ounce) package cream cheese
1-1/2 cups powdered sugar
1 teaspoon vanilla
2 cups chopped nuts

Combine first 5 ingredients and cook over medium heat until very thick (about 10 minutes), stirring frequently. Remove from heat and allow to cool completely before proceeding. When cool, beat in mixer at high speed for several minutes to make smooth. Add coconut and cornflakes to the mixture until consistency is right to handle. Shape into 2 logs on waxed paper and allow to chill in refrigerator.

Blend cream cheese, powdered sugar and vanilla together. Spread on chilled logs as an icing. Roll in chopped nuts and refrigerate until time to serve to make slicing easier.

STUFFED SWEET POTATOES

6 sweet potatoes (1/2 pound each)	1/2 Tablespoon ground cardamon
1/4 cup butter	1/2 teaspoon salt
1/4 cup heavy cream	1/2 cup chopped black walnuts
2 Tablespoons honey	1/2 cup raisins
2 Tablespoons dark rum, if desired	1/2 cup chopped walnuts for topping before baking

Rub each potato with vegetable shortening. Bake 20 minutes. Prick with a fork. Continue baking for about 25 minutes. Cut off top 1/3 of each potato. Scrape pulp from tops into a mixing bowl. Scoop out center of each potato, leaving about 1/4" in the skin. Mash pulp, add butter, cream, honey, rum, cardamon and salt. Beat until fluffy. Add raisins and chopped walnuts. Stuff potato shells with the mixture. Sprinkle top of potatoes with some more chopped walnuts on top. Return to oven and bake in 350 degree oven for 20 to 25 minutes.

This makes Sweet Potatoes even better.

SPANAKOPITA
(SPINACH PIE)

2 pounds spinach	2 cups chopped feta cheese
10 prepared pastry sheets	7 eggs
1 medium onion, finely chopped	1/2 cup olive oil
3 Tablespoons butter	salt and pepper
3 Tablespoons olive oil for topping	

Clean and wash spinach thoroughly. Cut into 2" pieces. Drain, place in bowl and rub 1 tablespoon salt into spinach leaves with hands until all are well-covered. Allow spinach to stand 15 minutes. Drain well for 30 minutes. Brown onion lightly in hot olive oil. Beat eggs well and add eggs, cheese and onion to spinach in large bowl. Salt and pepper to taste. Mix olive oil and butter and brush a 9x13" pan lightly. Place 5 prepared pastry sheets into pan, brushing each sheet with butter. Spread with spinach mixture, then place 5 additional sheets on top. With sharp knife, cut through the top 5 sheets in three places. Bake in 375 degree oven for 50 minutes. Cut into squares and serve hot. Serves 15 persons.

SQUASH CASSEROLE

3 cups cooked, drained yellow
squash (1-1/2 pounds)
1 can cream of mushroom or
cream of chicken soup
undiluted
1 (8-ounce) carton sour cream
3 ounces pimientos drained and
sliced
1 (8-1/2 ounce) can water
chestnuts, sliced if desired

1 large onion, grated
1 carrot, grated
1 (8-ounce) package Pepperidge
Farm Herb Dressing mix
1/2 cup grated cheese, sharp
Cheddar
1 stick butter or margarine
salt to taste
pepper to taste

Cook squash in a small amount of water until tender. Drain well. Add to the squash the soup, sour cream, pimientos, water chestnuts, onion, carrot and cheese. Mix all together adding salt and pepper.

Melt butter, pour over stuffing mix and stir well. Using half of dressing mixture, place on bottom of a 13x9" casserole dish. Spoon squash mixture on top. Then cover with the rest of stuffing mix. Bake in oven at 350 degrees for 30 minutes or until bubbly.

NOTE: May be made up beforehand. Keep in refrigerator until ready to be cooked.

"IN CASE" CASSEROLE

Did your garden produce more squash than you can eat right now? Here's a good dish to make and freeze, then pull out when company shows up unexpectedly. It goes a long way and looks like you went to a lot of trouble.

2-1/2 pounds of squash (varieties
may be mixed)
3 onions, chopped
1 green bell pepper
1 red bell pepper
1 stick margarine

2 cups grated sharp cheese
1 cup Ritz crackers, crushed
1/2 cup vanilla wafers, crushed
2 well-beaten eggs
margarine
salt & pepper to taste

NOTE: Also good with crisp bacon bits or cubed ham cooked with vegetables.

In a deep saucepan, melt margarine and saute chopped onion and bell pepper (and bacon bits or ham cubes if desired). Add 1/4 cup water and sliced squash; cover and cook until squash is just tender. While squash is cooking, combine crushed crackers (Ritz and vanilla wafers) with well-beaten eggs. Stir squash several times to be sure it doesn't stick or cook dry. When squash mixture is tender, stir in the egg/cracker mixture. If it is too dry, a little milk may be added; if too wet, add more cracker crumbs. Stir in half of the grated cheese, then pour into a greased casserole dish. Top with the remaining grated cheese, dot with margarine. May be cooked now, refrigerated and cooked the next day, or frozen for later use. Just prior to serving, bake covered in a 350 degree oven until bubbly and cheese is a golden brown. This is a dish that gets better, too, when refrigerated and rewarmed.

CRANBERRY APPLE CASSEROLE

3 cups diced unpeeled apples
2 cups raw cranberries
1 teaspoon lemon juice
1 cup sugar
1/4 cup water
1/2 cup butter, melted

1-1/4 to 1-1/2 cups oatmeal (not instant)
1/2 cup brown sugar
1 cup chopped nuts
1/3 cup flour, plain
1 teaspoon cinnamon
1/2 teaspoon nutmeg

Mix apples, cranberries, sugar, lemon juice and water together. Pour into a greased 9-1/2x12-1/2" casserole dish. Mix butter, oatmeal, brown sugar, nuts, spices and flour together in a separate bowl; spoon over apple/cranberry mixture. Bake 45 minutes at 350 degrees. Excellent with ham, pork, chicken, or turkey.

May be used as a dessert over vanilla ice cream.

HOT FRUIT CASSEROLE

1 small can applesauce
1 can (16 ounce) sliced pears
1 can (16 ounce) cling peaches
1 can (15-1/2 ounce) pineapple chunks
1 can (16 ounce) apricot halves
2 (6 ounce) jars maraschino cherries

1 cup firmly packed brown sugar
1/4 cup butter or margarine
1/4 teaspoon ground cinnamon
1/8 teaspoon ground nutmeg
1/8 teaspoon salt
1 Tablespoon lemon juice

Mix spices together. Drain fruit and pat dry with paper towel or use a colander and allow fruit to sit awhile to dry. Place about half of the fruit in a casserole dish. Add half of the sugar mixed with spices over the fruit. Dot with butter, cover with half of the applesauce. Repeat the process, beginning with the fruit layer. Sprinkle top with lemon juice. Refrigerate several hours or overnight. Remove from refrigerator 15 minutes before baking. Bake at 325 degrees for 30 minutes. May be served hot or cold. Yields 8 to 10 servings. Delicious with ham or turkey. If desired, 1/3 teaspoon curry powder may be added to the spices.

HOT PINEAPPLE CASSEROLE

2 (15-1/2 ounce) cans chunk style pineapple
1 cup shredded sharp cheddar cheese
1/2 cup sugar

3 Tablespoons all-purpose flour
crushed buttery round cheese-flavored crackers (1/2 roll)
1/4 cup melted margarine

NOTE: cling peaches or apricots may be substituted for the pineapple

Drain pineapple and place in 2-quart casserole. Mix cheese, sugar, and flour and sprinkle over pineapple. Top with crushed cheese crackers and drizzle with margarine. Bake 20 minutes at 350 degrees. Make 6 to 8 servings. An excellent dish to serve with ham and pork.

CURRIED FRUIT CASSEROLE

1 pound can pear halves
1 pound cling peaches
1 pound can pineapple chunks or
   spears
1 pound can apricot halves
12 maraschino cherries

3/4 cup light brown sugar
3 teaspoons curry powder
1/3 cup butter or margarine
2/3 cup blanched slivered
   almonds

Prepare the day before. Drain all fruit. Add sugar and curry powder to melted butter. Arrange fruit and nuts in layers in a casserole; pour butter mixture over all. Bake at 325 degrees for 60 minutes. Refrigerate overnight and reheat at 350 degrees before serving. Yields 10 to 12 servings.

CURRIED FRUIT BAKE

1 pound can sliced peaches
1 pound can apricot halves
1 pound can chunk pineapple
1 pound white cherries, seeded
1 pound can apple sauce

1 cup raisins (optional)
1/3 cup butter
3/4 cup brown sugar
4 teaspoons curry powder
1 cup nuts

Drain all fruits. Melt butter in skillet and stir in brown sugar and applesauce. Add curry powder. Pour over remaining fruit and mix well. Pour into buttered casserole and bake until it bubbles through center. Remove from oven and top with nuts. Cover with tight lid and allow to cool to room temperature before serving. Prunes, bananas, and other fruits are good, too. Use any fruit you like.

ZESTY FRUIT COMPOTE

1 (16-ounce) can pears, sliced and
   drained
1 (8-ounce) can pineapple
   chunks, drained
1 (16-ounce) can cling peach
   slices, drained
1 (16-ounce) jar maraschino
   cherries, drained

1/2 cup brown sugar, firmly
   packed
8 Tablespoons butter
1-1/2 to 2 Tablespoons prepared
   mustard
1/3 cup toasted pecans, coarsely
   chopped

Preheat oven to 325 degrees. In a 12x8x2" baking dish, combine well drained fruit by layers. Set aside. In a small sauce pan, combine brown sugar, butter and mustard. Cook over medium heat, stirring constantly until smooth. Do not allow to burn. Pour over fruit and top with 1/3 cup coarsely chopped toasted pecans. Bake uncovered 20 minutes until thoroughly heated. Serve warm and top with a dollop of whipped cream if desired.

SWEET POTATO SOUFFLE

3 cups sweet potatoes, canned or
  fresh cooked
1 cup brown sugar, firmly packed
1 stick butter/margarine
1 egg
1/4 teaspoon salt
1/2 teaspoon cinnamon
1 teaspoon nutmeg

1/4 teaspoon allspice
1/2 teaspoon vanilla
1/4 teaspoon lemon juice
1/2 teaspoon orange juice
1/2 teaspoon grated orange rind
1/2 cup raisins (optional)
1/2 cup coconut (optional)
1/2 cup nut meats (optional)

Drain potatoes and run through potato ricer or mash thoroughly. Melt butter and mix with potatoes. Add other ingredients (except marshmallows) and mix well. Bake at 375 degrees for 20 to 30 minutes. Remove from oven and stir. Place marshmallows on top and return to oven to brown (it will not take long).

SWEET POTATO PUFFS ON PINEAPPLE RINGS

5 (2-1/2 pounds) medium sweet
  potatoes
1/4 cup orange juice
1 Tablespoon grated orange rind
1/4 cup dark brown sugar, firmly
  packed

2 Tablespoons butter/margarine,
  melted
3/4 teaspoon salt
1/8 teaspoon pepper
6 slices canned pineapple, well
  drained

Scrub sweet potatoes and cook in their jackets in a small amount of boiling water until tender (about 25 minutes). Peel and mash, adding orange juice and rind. Add more orange juice if needed to give potatoes a smooth consistency. Add sugar, butter, salt and pepper. Pile each pineapple slice with mashed potatoes and top potatoes with a small pat of butter. Place under medium broiler and heat until pineapple is warm and sweet potatoes are lightly browned. Serves 6.

SWEET POTATO BALLS

6 medium sweet potatoes
1/2 cup butter/margarine
1 cup brown sugar
1 cup chopped pecans or walnuts
2 cups crushed cornflakes

12 marshmallows
1/2 teaspoon salt
1 egg
1 Tablespoon water
2 Tablespoons grated orange rind

Boil sweet potatoes until tender; peel and mash. Mix well with butter, sugar, salt and nuts. Add grated orange rind. Form potato ball around marshmallows and dip into beaten egg which has been diluted with a tablespoon of water. Roll in crushed cornflakes. Bake at 350 degrees until brown. May be made ahead of time and refrigerated or frozen for later use. Makes 12 balls.

POTATO LATKES (PANCAKES) WITH ROSY APPLESAUCE

Potato Pancakes:
2 Tablespoons matzo meal
2 eggs
1 thinly sliced onion
1 teaspoon salt
2 Tablespoons parsley (optional)
3 cups diced raw potatoes

Rosy Applesauce:
3 pounds McIntosh apples or
   other tart red apples
3/4 cup sugar

Put all pancake ingredients except potatoes into a blender. Cover; using grate setting, blend about 20 seconds. With the motor on, remove cover and then add potatoes. As soon as the last piece of potato has been added, turn off the blender. Pour batter in buttered pan and cook on both sides until brown.

Make rosy applesauce. Wash apples, drain well; cut into quarters and core. In a large saucepan, combine apples in their skins with 1/2 cup cold water. Bring to boil and reduce heat; simmer, covered until soft (about 15 minutes). Using a medium-sized bowl, press apples through a colander to remove skins; and cooking liquid. (Unpared red apples add a faint pink tint to the applesauce and peel also adds flavor.) Add sugar and return to saucepan. Serve over pancakes.

GREEK SPINACH CHEESE PIE

2 packages frozen chopped
   spinach
6 eggs, well beaten
6 to 8 Tablespoons flour

1/2 pound brick cheese
1/2 pound American cheese
2 pounds fine-curd cottage cheese
1 stick margarine

Boil spinach until thawed; drain well. Melt margarine and add flour; stir until smooth. Mix eggs, spinach, margarine and flour, and cottage cheese. Cube cheeses and add to mixture. Stir well and place into buttered casserole. Bake at 350 degrees for 1 hour or until knife inserted in center comes out clean. Serves 10 to 12 persons.

RED BEANS, RICE DELUXE

1 pound red kidney beans
2 quarts water
2 medium yellow onions, peeled
and chopped (1 cup)
1 medium green pepper, chopped
2 stalks (1 cup) celery, minced
1/4 pound (1 cup) smoked ham,
minced
1 pound pepperoni, sliced

1/4 to 1/2 teaspoon cayenne
pepper
1/8 teaspoon black pepper
3 Tablespoons minced parsley
3 Tablespoons very thinly sliced
green onion tops
2-1/2 cups uncooked rice
1 clove garlic, minced

Place beans in large heavy kettle, add water to cover, and soak overnight. Next day, add onions, green pepper, celery, ham, pepperoni, salt, cayenne pepper, black pepper to beans and soaking water; bring to a boil over high heat. Lower heat so that liquid ripples gently, cover and simmer 2-1/2 hours. Uncover, stir well, turn heat to lowest point and cook uncovered 2-1/2 to 3 hours longer, stirring occasionally, until beans are very soft and mixture is about the consistency of chili.

Cook rice by directions on package.

Stir onion tops and minced garlic into beans; cook uncovered another ten minutes. Mix in parsley and cook additional ten minutes, stirring frequently. Serve rice and beans in separate bowls; let each person serve himself, spooning the beans over the rice. A tossed salad and cornbread compliment the beans.

PEAS ORIENTAL

3 (10-ounce) packages frozen
peas, cooked and drained
2 (16-ounce) cans water
chestnuts, drained and thinly
sliced
2 (20-ounce) cans bean sprouts,
drained

1 pound mushrooms, sauteed in
butter (canned stems and
pieces may be used)
2 (10-1/2 ounce) cans cream of
mushroom soup, beaten with
a fork
2 (3-1/2 ounce) cans French fried
onion rings

Mix all ingredients except onion rings with soup. Place in buttered casserole and bake at 350 degrees for 30 minutes. Top with onion rings and continue baking for additional 15 minutes. This delicious dish serves 12.

BEAN CASSEROLE

2 cans French style green beans, drained
1 can Lesueur peas, drained
1 can asparagus, drained
1 can water chestnuts, drained and sliced

2 cans cream of mushroom soup (undiluted)
1 large can French fried onion rings
1 package slivered almonds
3 or 4 hard-boiled eggs, sliced

Cut asparagus spears into thirds. Combine drained beans, peas, asparagus and water chestnuts with undiluted cream of mushroom soup. Place in 9x13" pan. Slice hard-boiled eggs on top and sprinkle with slivered almonds then French fried onion rings. Place in 350 degree oven and cook until warm and bubbly.

COWBOY POTATOES

6 large potatoes
4 Tablespoons bacon drippings
2 medium onions, chopped

salt and pepper to taste
grated Parmesan cheese

Peel potatoes and split in half lengthwise. Cut into thin half-rounds. Melt bacon drippings in a heavy skillet with cover. Add potatoes and chopped onions, season with salt and pepper, cover and cook 10 minutes. Potatoes should be tender but not completely browned. Uncover and brown potatoes on each side. Sprinkle with Parmesan cheese and serve hot. Serves 6 to 8 persons.

SAM'S FAVORITE
(TOMATOES & ARTICHOKES)

1 can whole tomatoes (2 lbs. 3 oz.)
14-ounce can artichoke hearts
1/2 cup onion, chopped
2 Tablespoons green onions, chopped

1/4 pound butter/margarine
1/2 teaspoon leaf basil
2 Tablespoons sugar
salt and pepper
Parmesan cheese

Drain tomatoes. Drain and cut artichoke hearts. Saute onions with green onions; add tomatoes and artichokes. Heat 2 to 3 minutes stirring gently. Season with sugar, basil, salt and pepper. Turn into casserole and top with cheese. Bake at 325 degrees for 10 to 15 minutes or until vegetables are heated through and bubbly.

YELLOW SQUASH CASSEROLE

2-1/2 pounds fresh yellow squash
1 small onion, minced
10-ounce can condensed cream of
chicken/mushroom soup
1 cup sour cream
1 cup seasoned Pepperidge Farm
croutons (herb and cheese),
crushed

1 cup coarsely grated sharp cheese
2 well-beaten eggs
2 Tablespoons butter/margarine
1 teaspoon salt
dash of black pepper

Cook squash and onion just until tender; drain. Combine soup, salt and pepper and butter in a small saucepan; heat until smooth and butter is melted. Add squash and onion to mixture. Add sour cream and grated cheese, mixing well. Fold well-beaten eggs into squash along with crushed croutons. Pour into greased 1-1/2 quart casserole and top with crumbs. Bake at 350 degrees for 30 minutes or until firm and nicely browned. Better if made a day before and baked just before serving. Do not add crumbs to top until ready to bake. Serves 6 to 8.

FRIED YELLOW SQUASH

2 or 3 medium squash
1 egg
3 Tablespoons water

1/2 cup flour
salt and pepper to taste
cooking oil

Wash and slice squash. Beat egg in medium bowl and add water, salt and pepper; stir. Add enough flour to make a sticky batter, mixing well. Add squash and stir to coat each piece. Fry in oil until golden brown and crispy. Serves 4 persons.

AUNT FANNY'S BAKED SQUASH

Aunt Fanny's Cabin (Smyrna, Georgia)

3 pounds yellow summer squash
1/2 cup chopped onion
1/2 cup cracker meal or bread
crumbs
2 eggs

1 stick butter
1 Tablespoon sugar
1 teaspoon salt
1/2 teaspoon black pepper

Wash and cut up squash. Boil until tender, drain thoroughly, then mash. Add all ingredients except 1/2 of butter to squash. Melt remaining butter. Pour mixture in baking dish, then spread melted butter over top and sprinkle with cracker meal or bread crumbs. Bake in oven for approximately one hour or until brown on top.

STUFFED YELLOW SQUASH

6 medium squash
1 medium onion, diced
3 slices bacon, fried crisp
salt and pepper to taste
4 Tablespoons Pepperidge Farm
 bread crumbs

1/4 green pepper, minced
2 Tablespoons butter
dash of garlic vinegar (2 to 3
 cloves of garlic in 1 pint of
 vinegar)

Saute diced onion and green pepper in butter for 5 minutes. Cook squash in salt water 10 to 15 minutes or until tender. Cool and cut each squash lengthwise; scoop out inside of each squash, leaving a thick shell. Add onion and pepper mixture to squash and mash well. Add crumbled bacon, salt and pepper, and a dash of garlic vinegar (this is made by adding 2 to 3 cloves of garlic to a pint of vinegar). Fill shells with mixture. Sprinkle with bread crumbs and dot with butter. Bake at 350 degrees for 20 minutes. Serves 6.

NOTE: Garlic vinegar will keep and age with time. It's great in salads!

SPAGHETTI SQUASH WITH MEAT SAUCE

1 medium-sized spaghetti squash
 (2-1/2 pounds)
4 Tablespoons butter
salt and freshly ground pepper to
 taste
Sauce:
1 Tablespoon olive oil
1 pound ground chuck
1 Tablespoon finely chopped garlic
1-1/2 cups finely chopped onion

salt and freshly ground pepper to
 taste
1/2 cup dry red wine
4 cups tomato paste
1/4 cup tomato paste
1 teaspoon dried marjoram
1 teaspoon dried oregano
1 teaspoon dried rosemary
1/8 teaspoon dried red pepper
 flakes

Squash Preparation:

Pierce squash in several places with tines of a fork. Place squash in a kettle and add cold water to cover. Bring to a boil; cover and simmer 30 minutes. Hold squash over a basin to catch all interior drippings and cut squash in half lengthwise. Using a heavy metal spoon, scrape out and discard the center section of each half, much as you would clean a cantaloupe half. Scoop and scrape out remainder of the squash leaving only the shells. Put the "spaghetti" strands into a skillet and add the butter, salt and pepper. Heat, tossing gently, until the strands are hot and coated with melted butter. Serve with meat sauce.

Meat Sauce:

Heat oil in a heavy skillet and add meat. Cook, chopping up meat with the sides of a heavy metal spoon to break up any lumps. When meat loses its raw, red look, add the garlic, onion, salt and a generous grinding of black pepper. Stir and cook about 1 minute. Add wine and cook until most of the liquid evaporates. Add tomatoes, tomato paste, marjoram, oregano, rosemary and pepper flakes. Cook 30 minutes. Serve with spaghetti squash or pasta. Serves 4 to 6 persons.

RATATOUILLE

1/2 teaspoon dried oregano, crumbled
1/2 teaspoon dried marjoram, crumbled
1/8 teaspoon dried sage, crumbled
salt and pepper to taste
1/2 cup (1 stick) butter, cut into 8 pieces
2 medium yellow onions, sliced coarsely
1/4 pound mushrooms, thickly sliced
5 green onions (white parts sliced, green tops finely chopped)
2 large garlic cloves, minced
2 yellow crooknecked squash, sliced 1/4" thick
2 small zucchini, sliced 1/4" thick
1 green bell pepper, seeded and cut into chunks
1 red bell pepper, seeded and cut into chunks
2 medium tomatoes, seeded and coarsely chopped
2 Tablespoons Worcestershire sauce
1 Tablespoon cornstarch
1/4 cup water
1 cup broccoli florets

Mix oregano, marjoram, sage, salt and pepper in a small bowl. Place 4 pieces of butter in Dutch oven. Top with onions, mushrooms, sliced onions, half of garlic, squash, zucchini, bell peppers, remaining garlic, tomatoes, Worcestershire sauce and remaining 4 pieces butter, sprinkling herb mixture between layers. Cook over high heat until vegetables begin sizzling, about 1 minute. Cover and cook 1 minute. Do not stir. Reduce heat to low and continue cooking 20 minutes without stirring. Dissolve cornstarch in water. Add cornstarch and broccoli to vegetables. Increase heat to medium. Stir ratatouille until thickened and broccoli is crisp-tender. Garnish with chopped green onion tops. Serve hot.

TOMATOES — FRUIT OR VEGETABLE?

In the eighteenth century, tomatoes were called "love apples;" they were not included in the diet, as they were considered poisonous. Tomatoes were being eaten by the Aztecs when the Spanish Conquistadors came upon them; the Spanish lads, believing the red fruit would give them greater powers as lovers, took the tomatoes back to Europe with them. The Italians recognized a good thing when they ate it and began using tomatoes in recipes almost immediately. As far back as the middle of the 16th century, the Italians were using tomatoes — and not just for spaghetti; but it took a long time for tomatoes to catch on in America because of the belief that they were poisonous. Robert Gibbon Johnson stood on the Salem County Courthouse steps and ate several tomatoes in front of a crowd gathered to watch him die. When he didn't succumb to the poison, the early settlers decided to give them a try.

Tomatoes may be the only vegetable to be given a hearing in front of the United States Supreme Court. In 1893, the Supreme Court declared the tomato to be a vegetable, not a fruit, although botanically it is a fruit. Americans have been enjoying them ever since!

BAKED STUFFED TOMATOES

6 medium-sized ripe tomatoes
3 cups Uncle Ben's Wild Rice,
    cooked
1 (10-ounce) can (or 1 package
    frozen) small peas
6 ounces prosciutto ham, cut in
    strips (chicken may be used)

salt
freshly ground pepper
3/4 cup olive oil
12 sprigs parsley, minced
juice of 2 lemons, strained

Slice bottom end off each tomato, leaving the stem end on to make a solid base. Scoop out pulp and seeds. Salt inside and turn upside down to drain.

Combine rice, peas and ham. Season with salt and pepper to taste. Add sufficient oil to moisten filling. Allow mixture to set so flavors can blend. Just before serving, mix in herbs and lemon juice, stirring well.

Fill each tomato shell and place in a baking dish; add a few tablespoons of water and bake at 350 degrees for about 12 minutes or until tomatoes are piping hot. Serve hot. Yields 6 servings.

BROILED TOMATOES WITH CHEESE

4 large tomatoes
1 teaspoon salt
1/2 teaspoon pepper

pinch of sugar
1/4 cup grated cheese

Cut tomatoes into 1/2" thick slices. Sprinkle with salt, pepper, sugar and grated cheese. Place in a shallow glass baking dish or pie plate and broil until cheese is melted and tomatoes are well heated (about 5 to 7 minutes). Serves 4.

FIRE AND ICE TOMATOES

6 large tomatoes, peeled and
    quartered
1 large green pepper, sliced in
    strips
1 red onion, sliced in strips
1 large cucumber, peeled and
    sliced
3/4 cup vinegar
1-1/2 teaspoon celery salt

1/2 teaspoon salt
4-1/2 teaspoons sugar
1/8 teaspoon pepper
1/2 teaspoon red pepper
1/4 cup cold water
1-1/2 teaspoons mustard seed or
    1-1/2 teaspoons prepared
    mustard

Reserve cucumbers and place all other vegetables in bowl. Prepare a dressing by combining all other ingredients in saucepan and boiling for 1 minute. Pour hot dressing over vegetables in bowl and allow to stand until cool. Just before serving, add cucumber. Arrange on platter. Serves 6 persons.

TURNIP GREENS

1/4 pound salt pork, diced
2 cups water
2 to 3 pounds turnip greens
2 turnip roots
salt and pepper to taste
1 Tablespoon bacon drippings or
to taste (optional)

3 slices crisp cooked bacon
(optional)
1/2 hardboiled egg, chopped
(optional)
vinegar or hot pepper sauce
(optional)

Cook salt pork in water for 30 minutes in covered saucepan. Wash greens carefully and add to water and pork. Bring greens to a boil, pour off water, then add new water to take out the bitterness. Cook greens until tender, then add chopped turnip roots and cook until roots are tender. Add salt, pepper, and bacon drippings if desired. Garnish with crisp bacon pieces and hardboiled egg. Serve with vinegar or hot pepper sauce.

SOUR CREAM DILL SAUCE

2-1/2 cups mayonnaise
1 cup sour cream
3 Tablespoons freshly grated
Parmesan cheese
3 Tablespoons chopped fresh dill
or 1 teaspoon dried dillweed
3 Tablespoons finely chopped onion

1 Tablespoon + 1 teaspoon cider
vinegar
1 Tablespoon freshly ground pepper
2 teaspoons fresh lemon juice
2 teaspoons Worcestershire sauce
2 cloves garlic, crushed

Combine all ingredients in processor or blender and mix well. Chill before serving. Makes about 4 cups.

SAUCES

One of the simplest and most versatile sauces is white sauce. This smooth, creamy sauce (also known as bechamel) is the basis for many creamed dishes as well as other sauces. By mastering this basic sauce, the creative cook can accomplish wonders.

A properly made roux is basic to the sauce: a mixture of butter and flour cooked together before the addition of milk. Cooking the flour first releases the starch (the thickening agent) and prevents a thin, floury-tasting sauce. Depending on its use, white sauce is usually made in one of three thicknesses: light, medium or heavy.

Preparation of a basic white sauce is quite simple; just follow the step-by-step procedure below!

1/4 cup butter
1/4 cup unsifted flour
1 teaspoon salt

1/8 teaspoon pepper
2 cups milk

(Continued)

In a heavy skillet or pan, heat butter until melted; remove from heat and add flour, salt and pepper, stirring constantly until smooth. Slowly add milk, stirring, and return to medium heat. Bring to a boil and cook 1 minute, stirring constantly. Makes about 2 cups of sauce of medium thickness.

FOR A THIN WHITE SAUCE, reduce butter and flour to 2 tablespoons each, following above directions. Use for soups.

FOR A THICK WHITE SAUCE, increase butter and flour to 6 tablespoons each, following above directions.

FOR AN EXTRA THICK WHITE SAUCE, increase butter and flour to 8 tablespoons each, following above directions. Use for a souffle base.

FOR FISH OR OTHER SEAFOOD, BROCCOLI, ASPARAGUS, add 1/2 teaspoon lemon juice and 1 tablespoon mayonnaise. Grated sharp cheese may also be added for a quick sauce.

CHEESE SAUCE

1 cup medium white sauce

4 ounces shredded sharp American cheese

Add cheese to warm white sauce; cook over low heat, stirring constantly, until cheese melts. Serve over poached eggs, poultry or vegetables. Yields 1-1/3 cups.

MORNAY SAUCE

1 egg yolk
2 Tablespoons whipping cream
1 cup thin white sauce
1 Tablespoon minced onion

2 Tablespoons shredded Swiss cheese
1/4 teaspoon salt
dash of white pepper

Beat egg yolk and whipping cream with a wire whisk; set aside. Combine warm white sauce and onion in a heavy saucepan. Cook over low heat, stirring constantly, 3 or 4 minutes until onion is tender. Gradually stir about one fourth of the hot mixture into the yolk mixture, stirring constantly. Add cheese to the sauce and cook, stirring constantly, until cheese melts. Stir in salt and pepper. Serve over poached eggs, seafood, or vegetables. Yields 1 cup.

WOODROW WILSON BOYHOOD HOME - AUGUSTA, GEORGIA

WOODROW WILSON HOME

The house located at Seventh and Telfair Streets was the home of T. Woodrow Wilson from 1858 to 1870. Young Wilson was two years old when his father Dr. Joseph R. Wilson accepted the call to be pastor of the First Presbyterian Church and moved the family to Augusta from Staunton, Virginia. "Tommy" (as he was called as a boy) spent his childhood days playing with his next door neighbor Joseph R. Lamar, who later became an associate justice of both the Georgia Supreme Court and the U.S. Supreme Court, and attending Joseph Derry's school. In his later writings, Woodrow Wilson recalled vivid memories of the excitement in Augusta when it was announced that Abraham Lincoln had been elected President. People ran through the streets shouting the news while small groups clustered to discuss their uncertain future. Years later, after he had achieved a successful law career and served as President of Princeton and Governor of New Jersey, Wilson was elected President of the United States. On his arrival in Washington, he was greeted by his former Augusta playmate, Associate Justice Lamar.

Something Sweet
Cakes, Candy and Cookies

ABBY'S FABULOUS CHOCOLATE CAKE

4 squares unsweetened chocolate
1/2 cup butter or margarine
1 cup water
2 cups sifted cake flour
1-1/4 teaspoons baking soda
1 teaspoon salt

2 eggs
1 cup (8-ounces) dairy sour cream
2 cups sugar
1-1/2 teaspoons vanilla
1 Tablespoon butter for topping
or Fluffy White Icing

Grease and flour lightly two 9" cake pans. Combine 3 squares of chocolate, 1/2 cup butter and water in top of double boiler; heat over simmering water until chocolate and butter are melted. Remove from heat and cool.

Sift flour, soda and salt into a large bowl. Beat eggs with sour cream until well blended; beat in sugar and vanilla; stir in cooled chocolate mixture. Beat into flour mixture, half at a time, just until smooth (batter will be thin). Pour into prepared pans and bake at 350 degrees for 40 minutes or until done. Cool in pans; loosen around edges with knife and turn out of pans.

Fill layers and frost top and sides of cake with Fluffy White Icing. Melt remaining square of chocolate with one tablespoon butter in a cup set in hot water; stir until smooth. Drizzle around edges of cake and down sides of cake.

Fluffy White Icing:
2 egg whites
3/4 cup sugar
1/2 teaspoon cream of tartar

dash of salt
2-1/2 teaspoons cold water
1 teaspoon vanilla

Combine egg whites, sugar, cream of tartar, salt and water in top of double boiler; beat until blended. Place over simmering water and cook, beating constantly with an electric or rotary beater, about 7 minutes, or until mixture stands in firm peaks; stir in vanilla. Spread between layers and on top and sides of cake.

JO'S RED VELVET CAKE

1/2 cup Crisco shortening
2 eggs
2-ounce bottle red food coloring
1 Tablespoon vanilla (correct
    amount)
2-1/2 cups cake flour

2 Tablespoons apple cider
    vinegar (correct amount)
1-1/2 cups sugar
2 Tablespoons cocoa
1 teaspoon salt
1 cup buttermilk
1-1/2 teaspoons soda

Preheat oven to 350 degrees. Cream shortening and sugar well. Add eggs. Make a paste of cocoa and coloring and add to sugar mixture. Mix salt and vanilla with buttermilk. Add alternately with flour. Mix soda and vinegar together and fold into the batter. Pour into 2 to 3 lightly greased and floured cake pans. Bake in a 350 degree oven for 30 minutes or until cake tester comes out clean.

(Continued)

Whipped Cream Icing:
3 Tablespoons flour
1 cup sweet milk

1 cup butter
1 teaspoon vanilla
1 cup powdered sugar

Make a stiff paste of the flour and milk. Cook over low heat until thick, stirring constantly so as not to allow to become scorched. Cool thoroughly. Cream butter in a bowl. Add sugar, beating about 4 minutes; creaming thoroughly. Blend with cooled flour mixture. Add vanilla and beat until it looks like whipped cream. Spread between layers and on top and sides of cake. You will think it won't work, but just keep beating. Makes a cake fit for a King. Excellent at Christmas and Valentine or any special occasion.

BLACK FOREST CAKE

1 (18.25-ounce) box Butter Recipe
    Fudge Cake Mix (Duncan
    Hines)
3 large eggs
1/2 cup butter or margarine
3/4 cup water

1 (21-ounce) can Sour Cherry Pie
    Filling
1 can Vanilla Frosting Mix with
    real butter
4 ounces cream cheese, softened
2 teaspoons fresh lemon juice

Preheat oven to 375 degrees. Grease and lightly flour two 9" cake pans. Soften butter to room temperature. Cream butter in mixing bowl with one egg until smooth. Add 1/3 cake mix and 1/3 of water. Mix well. Repeat procedure adding one egg, 1/3 of cake mixture, and 1/3 water until all has been used. Mix at medium speed for about 4 minutes or until batter is well mixed and smooth. Pour half of batter into each prepared pan. Bake for 23 to 28 minutes or until cake tester comes out clean. Cool in pan on rack for 15 minutes. Remove from pan and cool completely before frosting.

Frosting:

Beat cream cheese and lemon juice until smooth. Fold into vanilla frosting mix. Blend well. To frost cake, place one cake layer bottom side up on serving plate. Spoon about 1/2 cup of frosting in a 3" circle in the center of cake layer on the plate. Spoon one cup of frosting around the edge of the layer. Spoon 1/2 of the cherry pie filling between the icing circle and the solid ring of frosting around the edge. Top with the remaining cake layer bottom side up. Spoon the remaining frosting mixture on the edge of this layer making a circle of about 2" to 3" in diameter. Spoon the remaining cherry filling inside the circle, covering the top of cake. Chill. Refrigerate any leftover cake.

NOTE: Whipped cream may be used in place of cream cheese frosting. Sprinkle with curls made by shaving a chilled 4-ounce milk chocolate bar.

BEA'S DEVIL'S FOOD CAKE

1 cup butter
2 whole eggs
4 eggs, separated
3-ounces unsweetened chocolate,
   melted
1 teaspoon soda

3/4 cup sour milk or buttermilk
2 cups sugar
2-1/2 cups cake flour
pinch salt
1 teaspoon vanilla
Sea Foam Icing

Cream butter and sugar together thoroughly. Add 2 whole eggs and 4 egg yolks. Beat until light and fluffy. Set whites aside for icing. Add unsweetened chocolate. Sift together flour, soda and salt. Add dry ingredients alternately with sour milk or buttermilk. Bake in greased and floured layer cake pans for 25 to 30 minutes or until cake tests done.

Sea Foam Icing:
1 pound brown sugar
1 cup white sugar

1 cup water
4 egg whites
1 teaspoon vanilla

Mix sugars and water. Bring to a boil until it spins a good thread. Beat egg whites until stiff. Add boiling syrup a little at a time, beating constantly; beat until dull on top and thickened. Add vanilla. Do not make on a warm, wet day.

GERMAN CHOCOLATE CAKE

2 cups sugar
1 cup butter
1 cup buttermilk
4 egg yolks
2-1/2 cups sifted cake flour
1 teaspoon soda
1 teaspoon vanilla

1 package German sweet
   chocolate
1/2 cup boiling water
4 eggs whites
1/2 teaspoon salt
icing

Melt chocolate in boiling water, cool, cream butter and sugar until light and fluffy. Add egg yolks, one at a time and beat well after each addition. Add the melted chocolate and vanilla. Mix well. Sift together the salt, soda and flour; add alternately with milk to chocolate mixture, beating well until batter is smooth. Beat egg whites until stiff peaks are formed; fold into batter. Pour batter into three 9" layer cake pans that have been lined with waxed paper and greased and floured. Bake at 350 degrees for 35 minutes or until cake is done. Cool. Frost layer tops with Coconut Pecan Frosting. Then frost sides of cake with chocolate icing.

Coconut Pecan Frosting:
1-1/2 cups heavy cream or canned
   milk undiluted
1-1/3 cups sugar
3 slightly beaten egg yolks

1/2 cup butter
1 teaspoon vanilla
1-1/3 cups flaked coconut
1-1/3 cups chopped pecans

(Continued)

Combine heavy cream, sugar, egg yolks, butter and vanilla in saucepan. Cook, stirring constantly, over medium heat until mixture thickens (about 12 minutes). Stir in coconut and pecans. Put between layers and on top of cake.

Chocolate Icing:
3 squares semisweet chocolate
1/2 cup butter
1/3 cup heavy cream or canned milk, undiluted
1 pound powdered sugar
1 teaspoon vanilla

Melt chocolate and butter in a small saucepan over low heat. Stir in sugar, vanilla and cream; beat until smooth and spreadable. Add more cream if needed. Spread on sides of German Chocolate Cake.

DELUXE FRESH STRAWBERRY CAKE

2-1/2 cups sifted flour (plain)
2-1/2 teaspoons baking powder
1 cup (2 sticks) butter
2 cups sugar
1 (3-ounce) box Strawberry Jello
   (Wild Strawberry best)
4 eggs
1 cup whole milk
1 teaspoon vanilla
1/2 cup pureed strawberries

Preheat oven to 350 degrees. Grease and lightly flour three 9" cake pans. Sift flour and baking powder together. In the bowl of electric mixer, cream butter, sugar and Jello until well blended and fluffy. Add the eggs one at a time, beating well after each, then beat at medium speed until fluffy (about 2 minutes).

At low speed, beat in flour mixture alternately with milk. Add vanilla and strawberries. Beat one minute at medium speed. Pour batter into prepared pans and bake at 350 degrees for 25 to 30 minutes or until cake springs back when lightly pressed in the center of pan. Cool on wire racks. Remove cake from pans and frost with Cream Cheese Frosting and Strawberry Glaze. Place cake layer on cake plate, rolling the top of layer with tip of fingers to remove any remaining brown particles from the top of layer. Spread 1/3 of glaze on top, then spread with Cream Cheese Frosting. Follow this procedure with the second layer. Add the third layer, spread top with glaze, then frost the sides with the remaining Cream Cheese Frosting. Garnish with fresh whole strawberries.

Cream Cheese Frosting:
1/2 cup (1 stick) butter
8-ounce package cream cheese
1 pound (3-1/2 cups packed) confectioners' sugar
2 teaspoons vanilla

Cream butter, softened cream cheese and confectioners' sugar together, blending well. Add vanilla. Beat until creamy.

(Continued)

Strawberry Glaze:
3 cups fresh strawberries
1 cup sugar
1 Tablespoon lemon juice
1 Tablespoon cornstarch
a few drops red vegetable
coloring

This may be made the day before. Hull and crush the berries. Strain them first through a potato dicer, then through a fine sieve. Add the sugar, lemon juice, and cornstarch. (Mix cornstarch with sugar. This will aide in not forming lumps). Cook, stirring constantly over low heat until mixture is thick and transparent. Add red coloring. Cool until of spreading consistency. If made the day before, warm slightly to spread better.

NOTE: This is equally delicious when fresh peaches and Peach Jello is used instead of strawberries. An unbeatable summer special cake (or any time).

LUCILLE'S OLD FASHION COCONUT CAKE

(Time consuming, but well worth the effort)

1-1/2 cups butter or 1 cup butter
and 1/2 cup Crisco
1-1/2 cups milk
2 teaspoons vanilla
7 eggs
3 cups sugar
4-1/2 cups sifted flour
3 teaspoons baking powder
1/2 teaspoon salt
fresh grated coconut to sprinkle
on top and sides (about 2
cups)

Grease three 9" cake pans and line with wax paper. Lightly flour. Preheat oven to 350 degrees. Cream sugar and butter together until light and fluffy. Add eggs one at a time, beating after each. Sift together the flour and baking powder along with salt. Combine vanilla and milk. Add flour mixture and milk alternately to the creamed mixture, beginning and ending with flour. Divide the batter among the pans, shaking down to release air bubbles. Bake for 25 to 30 minutes or until cake tests done. Cool on a rack for 10 minutes. Then remove cake from pans, leaving waxed paper stuck to cake. Stack the layers on top of each other and cover with a light towel until completely cold. Take the layers apart, removing wax paper. Roll with fingers any remaining brown crumbs that remain on the cake, so none are left on the layers. Frost and store in the refrigerator for a day or two before serving. (Good Luck).

NOTE: This is a very old, old family recipe. The filling and icing will seep down into the cake, making the cake very moist and delicious!

Old Fashion Coconut Filling:
1 cup sugar
2 cups coconut milk or juice or 2
coconuts and sweet milk to
equal 2 cups
1/2 cup butter or margarine
2 cups grated fresh coconut or
frozen
1 teaspoon vanilla

(Continued)

Reserve 3 tablespoons for garnish. In a saucepan, combine sugar, coconut juice, and milk. Cook for about 10 minutes after the liquid has begun to boil. Reduce heat and add coconut, continue cooking more slowly until mixture changes color slightly, from a real white to an oyster white. Remove from heat, add butter and vanilla and stir well. Let filling cool to lukewarm. This filling will be thin. Place one layer of cake on cake plate, spread with layer of filling, topping with a layer of frosting if desired. Stack all layers this way. Use all the liquid. The cake will absorb the liquid and be very moist. Let cake stand for an hour or more before frosting with egg white frosting. Hold hand to catch coconut and cover frosting with grated coconut. The icing will seep down into the cake, making it very moist and delicious. The cake can be made the day before and frosted the next day.

Coconut Frosting:	1/2 teaspoon cream of tartar
2 egg whites	1 teaspoon vanilla
1-1/2 cups sugar	pinch salt
1/2 cup sweet milk	

Combine egg whites, sugar, milk and cream of tartar in top of double boiler. Cook, beating constantly until peaks stand. Remove, add vanilla and pinch of salt. Stir well. Frost cake. What a glorious cake! Well worth it!

NOTE: The flavor of fresh coconut milk can be approximated by heating 1-1/2 cups of flaked coconut with 1-1/3 cups of milk over low heat for about 3 minutes. Turn off heat, strain off milk. This will make about 1 cup of coconut milk.

LEMON-COCONUT CAKE

1 cup butter	3/4 cup milk
1-3/4 cups sugar	1/2 cup water
6 egg whites	1 teaspoon vanilla
3 cups sifted cake flour	Lemon Filling
3/4 teaspoon salt	Fluffy Frosting
4 teaspoons baking powder	

Cream the butter; gradually add sugar, creaming together until light and fluffy. Add the egg whites, two at a time, beating well after each addition. Sift together the cake flour, salt and baking powder. Combine milk, water, and vanilla. Add sifted dry ingredients to creamed mixture alternately with liquid, beginning and ending with dry ingredients. Beat smooth after each addition. Pour batter into two greased and floured 9" layer cake pans. Bake at 350 degrees for 30 to 35 minutes, or until cake tests done. Cool before frosting.

(Continued)

Lemon Filling: 1 teaspoon grated lemon peel
8 slightly beaten egg yolks   1/3 cup lemon juice
1-1/2 cups sugar   4 Tablespoons butter

Blend egg yolks with the sugar, lemon peel, juice, and butter. Cook over very low heat, stirring constantly, till very thick. Cool thoroughly. When cake has cooled, spread filling between layers.

Fluffy Frosting: 1/3 cup water
2 egg whites   1/8 teaspoon salt
1-1/2 cups sugar   1 teaspoon vanilla
2 teaspoons light corn syrup   shredded coconut

In top of double boiler, combine the egg whites with sugar, corn syrup, water and salt; beat well with rotary or electric beater. Place over, but not touching, boiling water. Cook about 7 minutes, beating constantly, until stiff peaks form. Remove from heat; add vanilla and beat 2 minutes longer. Frost cake and garnish with coconut.

LADY BALTIMORE CAKE

Owen Wister immortalized Charleston's Lady Baltimore Tea Room and its glamorous cake in his book, "Lady Baltimore," This cake is delicious. You can almost hear Owen Wister saying, "She brought me the cake, and I had my felicitous meeting with Lady Baltimore. O, my goodness! Did you ever taste it? It's all soft, and it's in layers, and it has nuts — but I can't write any more about it; my mouth waters too much."

1 cup butter   4 teaspoons baking powder
3 cups sugar   2 teaspoons vanilla
4 eggs   2 teaspoons almond extract
1 cup milk   1/2 cup water
3-1/2 cups cake flour   Frosting

Cream butter, add 2 cups sugar gradually and beat until mixture looks like whipped cream. Add eggs 1 at a time, beating well after each. Add 1 teaspoon vanilla and 1-1/2 teaspoons almond extract. Sift flour and baking powder together 3 times and add to creamed mixture alternately with milk, beginning and ending with flour. Pour into 3 greased and floured cake pans. Bake at 350 degrees, 30 to 35 minutes or until done. Cool; remove from pans and spread with hot glaze.

Shortly before cake is done, make glaze by combining remaining 1 cup sugar and 1/2 cup water in a saucepan. Stir over low heat until sugar is dissolved. Increase heat and bring mixture to boiling. Cover saucepan and boil gently 5 minutes. Uncover and continue cooking until mixture spins a thread. Remove from heat and stir in 1 teaspoon vanilla and 1/2 teaspoon almond extract. Spread over cake layers. Cool cake layers completely and frost with frosting.

(Continued)

Frosting:
2 cups sugar
2/3 cup water
2 egg whites, stiffly beaten
2 teaspoons corn syrup
2 cups seeded raisins, finely
  chopped
2 cups pecans or walnuts, finely
  chopped
12 dried light figs, finely chopped
2 teaspoons vanilla
1/2 teaspoon almond extract

Mix sugar, water and corn syrup in small saucepan; cook until mixture forms a firm ball in cold water. Pour gradually into stiffly beaten egg whites, beating constantly. Add raisins, nuts and figs (raisins and figs may be soaked overnight, if desired, in small amount of brandy or sherry). Add flavorings. Spread mixture between layers, on top and sides of cake. If desired, sides of cake may be iced with any good white seven-minute frosting.

HOLIDAY SPIRIT CAKE

1 cup butter
2 cups sifted granulated sugar
1 teaspoon vanilla
3-1/4 cups sifted all-purpose flour
3-1/2 teaspoons baking powder
3/4 teaspoon salt
1 cup milk
8 egg whites
Holiday Spirit frosting

All measurements are level. All ingredients at room temperature. Set oven to 375 degrees. Grease three 9" layer cake pans and line bottoms with waxed paper.

Cream butter; add sugar gradually and beat until fluffy. Add vanilla. Sift together dry ingredients; on medium speed of mixer add dry ingredients to butter mixture alternately with milk, beginning and ending with flour mixture. Separate eggs; keep yolks covered. Beat whites with mixer until they stand in glossy peaks, but are not dry; fold into batter with mixer on very low speed or by hand. Bake about 20 minutes or until done; cool on racks before frosting. After cake is frosted, cover with cake cover or loosely with foil; store in cool place to ripen several days before serving. Freezes well. If wrapped in vapor-proof wrapping it will keep indefinitely. This cake is delicious served as is, or try it with Seasoned Whipped Cream.

Holiday Spirit Frosting:
10 egg yolks
1-1/2 cups granulated sugar
1/2 teaspoon salt
1-1/2 stick butter or margarine (if
  using margarine at 1/8
  teaspoon butter flavoring)
1/2 cup whiskey
2 teaspoons vanilla
2 cups pear mincemeat (recipe
  follows)
1-1/2 cups of finely chopped
  pecans
1-1/2 cups Angel Flake coconut

(Continued)

Put egg yolks in top of large double boiler and beat slightly with rotary beater. Add sugar, salt and butter; cook over simmering water until thickened. Do not overcook or allow eggs to become scrambled in appearance. Remove from heat; add whiskey and vanilla. Beat mixture well with rotary beater; stir in pear mincemeat, nuts and coconut. Allow to cool. Spread frosting between layers and on top and sides of cake.

This Holiday Spirit Frosting also makes delicious pies and party tarts. Filling should be made several days ahead so it will mellow if being used for pies or tarts. For pie or tarts fill unbaked shells with filling. Top with mixture of 1/2 cup flour, 1/4 teaspoon salt, 1/4 cup light brown sugar and 3 tablespoons butter, mixed together with fingers. Sprinkle over pie and bake in 400 degree oven 35 minutes or until crust is golden brown. Serve warm with a scoop of vanilla ice cream or cold with seasoned whipped cream or as is.

Seasoned Whipped Cream:
1/2 pint whipping cream
1/4 cup sugar
1 Tablespoon whiskey
1 teaspoon vanilla

Whip to stand in peaks but not to butter consistency.

Pear Mincemeat:
4 quarts hard pears, ground
2 pounds seedless raisins, ground
2 whole lemons, ground
4 pounds sugar
1-1/2 teaspoons salt
3 teaspoons ground cinnamon
1 teaspoon each Allspice and cloves

Grind all the fruit and mix with rest of the ingredients. Cook in large thick pot until tender. Pour into hot sterilized jars and seal.

MRS. PERRY'S LEMON CHEESE CAKE

1 cup butter
2 cups sugar
1 teaspoon vanilla
3 cups cake flour
2 teaspoons baking powder
1 cup milk
1 teaspoon vanilla
4 eggs, separated (beat egg whites until stiff)
Lemon Filling and Icing

Cream butter and sugar well. Add beaten egg yolks. Sift flour and baking powder together and add flour mixture to creamed mixture alternately with milk, beginning and ending with flour. Add vanilla. Fold in beaten egg whites. Bake in three 9" layer cake pans which have been lightly greased and floured for 25 minutes at 375 degrees, or until cakes test done. Remove from pans; cool and ice.

Lemon Filling and Icing:
2 cups sugar
1 cup butter
4 whole eggs, beaten separately
dash salt
2 Tablespoons flour
5 lemons
grated rind of 1 lemon

Add flour to sugar, then add melted butter. Beat egg yolks until thick and creamy. Add lemon juice and grated rind to egg yolks. Add to the sugar mixture. Beat egg whites until very dry and add to sugar mixture. Cook until thick. Cool; spread between cool layers, on top and sides of cake.

CAROLE'S CARROT CAKE

2 cups sugar	2 teaspoons soda
1-1/2 cups salad oil	2 teaspoons cinnamon
4 eggs, well beaten	1 teaspoon salt
3 cups grated carrots	frosting
2 cups sifted all-purpose flour	

Mix sugar, oil and eggs and blend well. Add carrots and mix thoroughly. Add flour, soda, cinnamon and salt that have been sifted together. Mix and bake in two greased and floured 9" layer cake pans at 350 degrees, 30 to 40 minutes or until cake tests done. Cool and spread with frosting.

Frosting:	1 box powdered sugar
6 ounces cream cheese	2 teaspoons vanilla
1/2 stick butter	1/2 teaspoon salt

Soften cream cheese and butter. Cream well together. Add powdered sugar a small amount at a time, blending well. Add vanilla and salt. Spread between layers and on top and sides of cake.

MARDI GRAS PARTY CAKE

2/3 cup butterscotch morsels	1 cup sugar
1/4 cup water	1/4 cup firmly packed brown
2-1/4 cups sifted flour	sugar
1 teaspoon salt	1/2 cup Crisco
1 teaspoon soda	3 unbeaten eggs
1/2 teaspoon baking powder	1 cup buttermilk

Melt butterscotch morsels in water in saucepan. Cool. Sift flour, salt, soda and baking powder; set aside. Add sugar and brown sugar gradually to shortening, creaming well. Blend in eggs, beating well after each. Add butterscotch morsels, mix well. Add dry ingredients alternately with buttermilk, beginning and ending with dry ingredients. With mixer, using a low speed, blend well. Turn into two 9" layer pans, well greased and lightly floured on the bottom. Bake at 375 degrees for 30 to 35 minutes. Cool. Remove from pans and spread layers with Filling and Topping, or use filling between layers and frost top and sides with Sea Foam Frosting or Sea Foam Cream.

Filling and Topping:	1/3 cup butterscotch morsels
1/2 cup sugar	1 beaten egg yolk
1 Tablespoon cornstarch	2 Tablespoons butter
1/2 cup evaporated milk or half	1 cup shredded coconut
and half	1 cup chopped pecans
1/3 cup water	

Combine sugar and cornstarch in 2-quart saucepan. Stir in milk, water, butterscotch morsels and egg yolk. Cook over medium heat, stirring constantly until thick. Remove from heat and add butter, coconut and chopped pecans. Cool; spread between layers and on top of cake.

(Continued)

Sea Foam Frosting:
1/3 cup sugar
1/3 cup firmly packed brown
  sugar
1/3 cup water

1 Tablespoon corn syrup
1 egg white, beaten stiff
1/4 teaspoon cream of tartar
1 cup pecans, finely chopped

In a small saucepan combine the two sugars, water and corn syrup. Cook until a little syrup dropped in cold water forms a soft ball. Beat egg with cream of tartar until stiff peaks form. Add syrup to egg white in slow, steady stream beating constantly until thick enough to spread. Frost cake on top and sides, then sprinkle pecans over frosting.

Sea Foam Cream:
1 cup whipping cream
1/2 teaspoon vanilla

1/4 cup firmly packed light
  brown sugar

In a small mixing bowl, beat whipping cream until lightly foamy. Gradually add brown sugar, beating until it thickens. Frost sides and top edge of cake with Sea Foam Cream. Chill 1 hour before serving.

FOURTEEN CARROT GOLD CAKE
(King of the Carrot Cakes)

1-1/4 cups vegetable oil
2 cups sugar
2 cups less 2 Tablespoons
  all-purpose flour
2 teaspoons cinnamon
2 teaspoons baking powder
1 teaspoon baking soda

1 teaspoon salt
4 eggs
4 cups peeled and grated carrots
1 cup raisins
1 cup chopped pecans
Pecan Filling
Cream Cheese Frosting

Whisk oil and sugar together. Sift flour, cinnamon, baking powder, baking soda and salt together. Sift half the dry ingredients into sugar mixture and mix well. Sift in remaining dry ingredients alternately with eggs, mixing well after each addition. Stir in by hand carrots, raisins and pecans. Preheat oven to 350 degrees. Pour batter into greased and floured 10" tube pan and bake 70 minutes, or until cake tests done. Cool upright in pan. Invert onto serving plate and split into three layers. Spread pecan filling between layers and frost with cream cheese frosting.

Pecan Filling:
2 cups sugar
6 Tablespoons flour
1 teaspoon salt

2 cups heavy cream
1 cup unsalted butter
1-1/2 cups chopped pecans
1 Tablespoon vanilla

In heavy saucepan, combine sugar, flour and salt. Gradually stir in cream; work in butter. Cook over lowest heat, stirring constantly, until mixture simmers. Let simmer 20 to 30 minutes, stirring occasionally, until golden brown. Remove from heat. When lukewarm, add pecans and vanilla; cool completely, and spread between layers of cake.

(Continued)

Cream Cheese Frosting:
1 cup unsalted butter, softened
8 ounces cream cheese, softened
1 pound powdered sugar
1 teaspoon vanilla

With mixer cream butter; add cream cheese. Sift in powdered sugar; add vanilla and beat. Chill a bit if too soft to spread.

MRS. KITCHENS' CARAMEL CAKE

2-1/4 cups sifted cake flour
3-1/4 teaspoons baking powder
1 teaspoon salt
1-1/2 cups sugar
1/2 cup Crisco
1 cup milk
1/2 cup egg whites, unbeaten
1 teaspoon vanilla

Grease and flour two layer cake pans. Sift flour, baking powder and salt together. Cream sugar and Crisco until fluffy. Add flour and milk alternately; add unbeaten egg whites and vanilla and beat 2 minutes more. Pour into prepared pans. Bake at 350 degrees for 25 to 35 minutes. Fill and frost with either of the following Caramel Frostings or your favorite frosting.

Caramel Frosting No. 1:
1 pint whipping cream, warm (set
    on stove to warm)
3 cups sugar
1/2 pound country butter
1 teaspoon vanilla
1 cup sugar for caramelizing

Brown 1 cup sugar in an iron skillet or heavy pressure cooker on a fast burner. Add whipping cream and 3 cups sugar and cook to form a good soft ball. Immediately add 1/2 pound butter and 1 teaspoon vanilla. Place the pan in ice water and beat vigorously with wire beater or open spoon until the right consistency to spread. If, when cold all through, it is too hard, add 1 teaspoon of butter and continue beating. Should this fail, add 1 teaspoon cream. If it is too soft, return to burner and cook a little more. It gets easy, with practice, to tell just when to stop cooking.

Caramel Frosting No. 2:
4 cups sugar
1-1/4 cups half and half cream
2 sticks real butter
1 Tablespoon vanilla
pinch soda

Brown 1 cup sugar in a heavy skillet or pan on high heat, stirring constantly. Heat the 3 cups sugar and half and half together slowly, stirring well to avoid burning; add to the brown sugar mixture (it will bubble a lot). Cook over high heat and stir constantly until mixture reaches the soft ball stage; remove from heat and add a pinch of soda and the vanilla. Cool, beat until mixture reaches spreading consistency, then spread between layers and on top and sides of cake.

ITALIAN CREAM CAKE

1 stick butter
2 cups sugar
1/2 cup Crisco
5 egg yolks
2 cups flour
1 teaspoon soda

1 cup buttermilk
1 teaspoon vanilla
1 small can Angel flake coconut
1 cup chopped nuts
5 egg whites, stiffly beaten
Cream Cheese Frosting

Cream butter and shortening; add sugar and beat until mixture is smooth. Add egg yolks and beat well. Combine flour and soda; add to creamed mixture alternately with buttermilk. Stir in vanilla; add coconut and nuts. Fold in egg whites. Pour batter into three greased and floured 8" cake pans and bake at 350 degrees for 25 minutes or until cake tests done; cool. Frost with Cream Cheese Frosting.

Cream Cheese Frosting:
8 ounces cream cheese, softened
1/2 stick butter

1 box powdered sugar
1 teaspoon vanilla
chopped pecans (for garnish)

Beat cream cheese and butter until smooth. Add sugar and mix well. Add vanilla and beat until smooth. Spread on cake. Sprinkle top with chopped pecans.

SEVEN-UP CAKE

1 (18-1/4 ounce) package lemon
    supreme cake mix
1 (3-1/2 ounce) package Jello
    instant lemon pudding mix

3/4 cup oil
1 (12-ounce) can 7-Up
4 eggs
Pineapple Topping

Combine cake mix, pudding mix and oil; beat at medium speed until well blended. Add eggs, 1 at a time, beating after each addition. Add 7-Up; mix well. Pour batter into three greased and floured 9" cake pans. Bake at 350 degrees for 35 minutes or until cake springs back when lightly pressed. Cool in pans 10 minutes, then remove from pans and cool completely. Fill between layers and frost with Pineapple Topping.

Pineapple Topping:
1-1/2 cups sugar
2 whole eggs, beaten with fork
1 stick butter

1 (15-1/2 ounce) can crushed
    pineapple
1 (3-1/2 ounce) package flaked
    coconut

This frosting takes a long time to thicken, therefore it is recommended to begin making frosting once cakes are put in the oven. Combine the first four ingredients in a saucepan and cook over moderate heat until thickened. Add coconut and cool; then ice cake.

TATE'S WHITE CAKE
(Lithuanian)

1 cup Crisco	2 cups milk
2-3/4 cups sugar	2 teaspoons vanilla
4-1/2 cups cake flour	1/4 teaspoon almond extract
4 teaspoons baking powder	7 whites of large eggs
1 teaspoon salt	

Grease and flour two 10" tube pans. Cream shortening and sugar thoroughly until smooth and fluffy. Sift flour, measure, then sift flour, baking powder and salt together. Add flour mixture alternately with milk to creamed shortening. Beat well. Beat egg whites until stiff, but not dry. Add extracts and fold in egg whites. Pour into cake pans and bake at 350 degrees for 35 to 40 minutes.

Tate's Frosting:	dash of salt
1 stick butter	1/4 cup drained crushed
1-1/2 boxes powdered sugar	pineapple
1 teaspoon vanilla	1/4 cup coconut

Cream butter with one box sugar, gradually add milk and more sugar as needed for proper thickness. Add vanilla, salt, pineapple and coconut. Beat well. If too thin, add more sugar.

HELEN'S PINEAPPLE DELIGHT CAKE

1 package Butter Recipe Golden Cake Mix	4 eggs
1/2 cup oil	1 (11-ounce) can mandarin oranges with juice

Combine cake mix, mandarin oranges, eggs, and oil; beat two minutes at highest speed of mixer. Reduce speed to low and beat one minute longer. Pour batter into three greased and floured 9" round cake pans. Bake at 350 degrees for 20 to 25 minutes or until cake tests done. Cool in pans for 5 to 10 minutes; remove layers from pans and let cool completely. Spread with one of the following icings.

Icing No. 1:	1 large can crushed pineapple, drained (save juice)
1 (13-ounce) carton whipped topping	1 small package Jello Vanilla Instant Pudding

Combine all ingredients; beat 2 minutes at medium speed with electric mixer; let stand 5 minutes; add enough pineapple juice for spreading consistency. Spread mixture between layers and on top and sides of cake. Chill at least 2 hours before serving. Store in refrigerator.

Icing No. 2:	1 heaping Tablespoon sugar
1 (20-ounce) can crushed pineapple, undrained	8 ounces sour cream
1 (10-1/2-ounce) package Jello Cheesecake Filling Mix	9 ounces Cool Whip

(Continued)

Combine undrained pineapple, sugar, Cheesecake Filling Mix and sour cream and then fold in Cool Whip. Spread between layers and on top and sides of cake. Decorate with mandarin orange slices if desired. Refrigerate until ready to serve.

STARLIGHT DOUBLE-DELIGHT CAKE

2 (3-ounce) packages cream
    cheese
3/4 cup butter or Crisco
1/2 teaspoon vanilla
1/2 teaspoon peppermint extract
6 cups (1-1/2 pounds) sifted
    powdered sugar

1/4 cup hot water
4 squares chocolate, melted
2-1/4 cups sifted all-purpose flour
1-1/2 teaspoons soda
1 teaspoon salt
3 eggs
3/4 cup milk

Set oven at 350 degrees. Grease and flour two 9" round cake pans. All ingredients should be at room temperature. Cream cheese, butter, vanilla and peppermint extract until fluffy. Add half of powdered sugar to cream cheese mixture. Add hot water alternately with the rest of the sugar. Blend in the chocolate that has been melted. Reserve half of mixture (2 cups) as frosting for baked cake. Sift together the flour, soda and salt. Combine 1/4 cup butter and remaining chocolate-frosting mixture; mix thoroughly. Blend in eggs, one at a time, and beat for one minute. Add milk alternately with sifted dry ingredients to creamed mixture, beginning and ending with dry ingredients. Pour into prepared pans and bake for 30 to 35 minutes. Cool; frost with reserved frosting mixture.

JAPANESE FRUIT CAKE

Neither Japanese or a fruit cake, this long-time Southern favorite combines alternating spice and white layers with filling and boiled frosting topping. As to the name, it is believed it was first published in 1895 in a cookbook issued by the Women's Committee of the Cotton States Exposition in Atlanta. It had been contributed by an American woman who had lived in the Orient.

1 cup butter or margarine,
    softened
2 cups granulated sugar
4 eggs
3 cups cake flour
3 teaspoons baking powder
1/8 teaspoon salt
1 cup milk

1 teaspoon vanilla
1 teaspoon ground cinnamon
1 teaspoon ground cloves
1 teaspoon ground allspice
1/2 cup raisins chopped
1/2 cup pecans chopped
Lemon Coconut Filling
Lemon Frosting

(Continued)

Preheat oven to 350 degrees. Cream butter and add sugar gradually, beating until light and fluffy. Beat in eggs, one at a time. Sift together the flour, baking powder and salt. Add alternately with milk to the creamed mixture, beating well after each addition. Stir in the vanilla. Pour half of batter into two well greased and floured 9" cake pans. Add spices, raisins and nuts to the remaining batter and pour into two more prepared 9" cake pans. Bake all four layers for about 20 to 25 minutes, or until cake tests done and the cakes begin to shrink from sides of pans. Cool on racks in pans for 5 minutes; turn out and cool completely before filling and frosting.

Lemon Coconut Filling:	2 cups sugar
juice and finely grated rind of 2	1 cup boiling water
lemons	2 Tablespoons cornstarch
1 large coconut, grated	

Put all ingredients, except cornstarch, in saucepan; mix well and place over medium heat. When mixture begins to boil, add cornstarch, dissolved in 1/2 cup cold water, and cook mixture until it turns clear and will drop from a spoon. Cool and spread between layers of Japanese Fruit Cake.

Lemon Frosting:	1/8 teaspoon cream of tartar
2 egg whites	1/4 cup confectioners' sugar
1 cup granulated sugar	1 Tablespoon lemon juice
1-1/2 Tablespoons corn syrup	grated rind of 1 lemon

Place egg whites in medium size bowl of electric mixer. In small saucepan, dissolve granulated sugar in half a cup of water. Add the corn syrup and cream of tartar and cook, stirring constantly, until mixture is clear. Cook, without stirring, until syrup reaches soft ball stage (238 degrees on a candy thermometer).

Beat the egg whites until stiff. With mixer on low speed, pour in syrup in a steady stream. Beat for about 7 to 10 minutes. Add the confectioners' sugar and lemon juice and mix well. Spread on top and sides of filled layers. Sprinkle top with grated lemon rind.

NOTE: It is essential to use a candy thermometer for boiled icings such as this one.

LUCILLE'S JAPANESE FRUIT CAKE

1 cup butter	1 medium bottle cherries,
2 cups sugar	drained and chopped
4 eggs	1 teaspoon allspice
3 cups all-purpose flour	1 teaspoon cinnamon
1 teaspoon soda	1 cup chopped raisins
1/2 teaspoon salt	1 cup chopped nuts
1 cup buttermilk	Coconut Filling

(Continued)

Cream butter and sugar until light and fluffy. Add eggs one at a time, beating well after each. Combine flour, soda and salt with butter mixture alternately with buttermilk, beginning and ending with flour mixture. Divide batter with a little more than half in one part. Add chopped cherries to the larger part and mix well; add spices, raisins and nuts to the other part of the batter. Bake at 275 degrees in three layers for about 1-1/2 hours. Turn out on wire rack and cool. Starting with a spiced layer, put layers together with coconut filling, ending with second spiced layer. Spread filling on top of cake.

Coconut Filling:	1 cup hot water
1 package shredded or flaked	2 Tablespoons flour, rounded
coconut	2 large lemons, grated
2-1/2 cups sugar	

Combine all ingredients and cook until thick and glossy, but not too thick to spread. Fill between layers and spread on top of cake.

SOUR CREAM STRAWBERRY JAM CAKE

1 cup Crisco	2 cups self-rising flour
2 cups sugar	1 cup milk
4 eggs	1 teaspoon vanilla

Cream Crisco, sugar and eggs for 10 minutes on high speed. Add 1 cup flour and beat one minute on medium speed; add rest of flour and milk, beat 1 minute on medium speed. Add vanilla and mix well. Grease and flour four 9" cake pans. Bake at 350 degrees until done, about 25 minutes. Cool 5 minutes; remove from pans and cool completely.

Strawberry Frosting:	1 cup sour cream
strawberry jam	1 large container Cool Whip

Mix sour cream with Cool Whip. Frost layers and spoon strawberry jam on layers and top. Any jam may be used but freezer jam is best. Also, fruit pie fillings may be used. Fresh mashed strawberries, sweetened, is good between layers with sliced berries for decorations on top.

FROZEN STRAWBERRY JAM

4 cups (1 quart) fully ripe	3/4 cup water
strawberries (2 cups crushed)	1 package powdered fruit pectin
4 cups sugar	

Use only perfect, fully ripe berries. Crush berries or whiz in blender, 1 cup at a time, until finely chopped. Measure 2 cups crushed berries into bowl. Add sugar, blend thoroughly, and let stand for 10 minutes. Combine water and pectin in saucepan; bring to a boil, and boil for 1 minute, stirring constantly. Mix into fruit and continue stirring for 3 minutes. Ladle at once into 1/2 pint containers that have been scalded and drained. Cover and let stand at room temperature for 1 hour, then refrigerate until mixture jells, about 24 hours. Label, date, and freeze for up to 6 months.

Frozen red raspberries or blackberries may be used by increasing berries to 6 cups (1-1/2 quarts) to make 3 cups crushed berries, and increasing sugar to 5-1/4 cups.

J'S LANE CAKE

1 cup butter	3/4 teaspoon salt
2 cups sugar	1 cup milk
1 teaspoon vanilla	yellow food coloring
3-1/4 cups sifted all-purpose flour	8 egg whites
3-1/2 teaspoons baking powder	Frosting

Grease and lightly flour four 9" layer cake pans; line bottoms of pans with waxed paper and grease and flour again. Preheat oven to 375 degrees.

Cream butter in large mixing bowl until light and fluffy. Gradually add sugar, beating after each addition until light and fluffy. Add vanilla and beat until mixture is like whipped cream. Sift, then lightly spoon flour into measuring cup. Do not shake down or pack; level off with a knife. Sift measured flour with baking powder and salt three times. Add flour to creamed mixture alternately with milk, beginning and ending with flour, and blend after each addition until smooth. Add food coloring to batter.

Thoroughly wash and dry bowl and beaters before beating egg whites (even a speck of butter on beater or in bowl will prevent whites from becoming stiff). Beat egg whites until they stand in soft glossy points, but not dry. With large spoon or rubber spatula fold whites into batter. To do this, drop beaten egg whites on top of batter and with side of spoon cut down through batter to bottom of bowl; turn spoon and bring it up side of bowl, folding batter over whites. Do not press down on whites. Continue until whites are evenly distributed. Divide batter evenly among four pans and spread to sides with a spatula. Place pans on racks so that one pan is not directly beneath another. Bake 15 to 20 minutes or until done. Let pans stand on rack for 3 to 5 minutes, then carefully loosen around edges. Invert layers on racks, remove paper, and cool thoroughly before frosting.

Frosting:	1/2 cup bourbon whiskey
1-1/2 cups seedless raisins, chopped	1-1/2 cups chopped pecans
12 egg yolks	1-1/2 cups chopped candied red
1-3/4 cups sugar	cherries
1/2 teaspoon salt	1-1/2 cups grated coconut, fresh
3/4 cup butter	or frozen

Prepare fruits and nuts (may be done the day before). Put 12 egg yolks in top of double boiler and beat slightly with rotary beater. Add sugar, salt, and butter and cook over simmering water, stirring constantly, until sugar is dissolved and butter melts. Mixture will be slightly thickened. Do not over-cook or let egg yolks become scrambled in appearance. Mixture should be almost translucent. Remove from heat and add bourbon. Beat mixture 1 minute with rotary beater. Add raisins, nuts, cherries and coconut. Mix well. Spread between layers, on top and on sides of cake. After an hour, if any has dripped off plate, use knife to spread back on cake. Repeat if necessary. Cover cake loosely with foil and store in cool place several days to ripen. Cake will keep well for several weeks and freezes well.

KENTUCKY BLACKBERRY CAKE

(Old Fashion Jam Cake)

4 cups flour	2 cups blackberry jam
2 teaspoons ground allspice	1-1/2 cups buttermilk
2 teaspoons ground cloves	2 teaspoons baking soda
2 teaspoons ground cinnamon	1-1/2 cups raisins, cut in half
2 teaspoons ground nutmeg	(optional)
3 sticks butter, room temperature	1 cup pecans, chopped (optional)
2 cups sugar	Walnut Frosting or Fruit Frosting
6 eggs	

Preheat oven to 350 degrees. Sift flour and spices together. In another large bowl, cream the butter and sugar until fluffy. Beat eggs slightly and beat eggs and jam into butter mixture. Beat in flour mixture alternately with the buttermilk, into which the soda has been stirred. Begin and end with flour mixture. Stir in raisins and pecans. Pour batter into three buttered and floured 9" layer pans and bake for 35 minutes, or until cake tests done. Transfer the cake pans to racks and let cakes cool, then remove from pans and invert on racks. Frost with Walnut Frosting or Fruit Frosting.

NOTE: This makes a very large cake. Some people use it as a fruit cake at Christmas.

Walnut Frosting:	2 egg yolks
2 cups white sugar	1 cup coarsely chopped walnuts
2 cups brown sugar, firmly	1/2 teaspoon vanilla
1 stick butter	

In large saucepan, combine the sugars and light cream, butter, and egg yolks. Cook over moderate heat, stirring and washing down any sugar crystals which cling to the sides of pan with a brush dipped in cold water, until the sugar is dissolved. Bring mixture to a boil, stirring, and cook over moderate heat, continuing to stir as necessary, until it is thickened, about 10 minutes. Remove the pan from the heat and stir in walnuts and vanilla; then let frosting cool until of spreading consistency. With a metal spatula, spread frosting on cooled cake. Store in an airtight container.

Fruit Frosting:	2 cups evaporated milk
1-1/2 Tablespoons all-purpose	1-1/2 cups raisins
flour	1-1/2 cups chopped nuts
2 cups sugar	2 cups coconut

Mix flour and sugar, then add milk. Mix all ingredients together and cook until thick; set aside until cold. Spread between layers of cake and on top and sides of cake.

TENNESSEE STRAWBERRY JAM CAKE

1-1/2 cups butter	2 teaspoons cinnamon
2 cups sugar	2 teaspoons nutmeg
6 eggs	6 Tablespoons buttermilk
3-1/2 cups flour	2 cups strawberry jam
2 teaspoons soda	Caramel Icing or White Frosting
2 teaspoons allspice	

Sift all-purpose flour and measure; then sift again with soda and spices. Cream softened butter; add sugar slowly, beating until creamy. Add eggs, room temperature, one at a time. Beat well after each egg. Add flour mixture alternately with buttermilk, beginning and ending with flour; mix to blend well. Fold in strawberry jam. If berries are large, chop fine. Pour into four square 8" layer cake pans, 2" deep, which have been brushed on bottoms lightly with shortening or salad oil, and liners placed in pans; then brushed lightly over liners and pans with shortening or salad oil and floured well. Level batter with spatula, then drop pans several times from a height of 4". Bake in moderate oven, 375 degrees, about 30 to 40 minutes or until done. Cool on cake rack completely before icing with Caramel or White Frosting.

Caramel Icing:	
3/4 cup butter	2 teaspoons vanilla
1/2 cup cream	1/2 teaspoon salt
2 cups dark brown sugar	powdered sugar

Melt butter in 1/2 cup cream; while hot, stir in 2 cups dark brown sugar. Cool and stir in vanilla and salt and enough sifted powdered sugar to make spreading consistency. Spread between layers and over top and sides of cake.

White Frosting:	
3/4 cup sugar	3 egg whites
1 Tablespoon water	1/8 teaspoon salt
1/2 cup light corn syrup	1-1/2 teaspoons vanilla

Boil sugar, water and syrup until mixture spins a thread, about 10 minutes. Pour this hot syrup gradually over egg whites, which have been beaten to stiff peaks, beating constantly. Beat in salt and vanilla. Beat until mixture loses its shine and holds its shape. Frost cake, then spoon strawberry jam on top of cake for garnish.

MISS EFFIE'S FRUIT CAKE
(A Layer Fruit Cake)

1 cup butter	1 pound dates, chopped
2 cups sugar	1 pound currents
4 eggs, beaten separately	1/2 pound citron, finely chopped
4 cups all-purpose flour	1 small package figs, chopped
2 teaspoons baking powder	1/4 pound candied cherries
1 teaspoon cloves	(optional)
1 teaspoon cinnamon	1/4 pound candied pineapple,
1 teaspoon nutmeg	chopped (optional)
1/2 teaspoon allspice	Filling and Frosting
1 cup milk	

Cream together butter and sugar until light and fluffy. Add beaten egg yolks. Sift flour, baking powder and spices together and add to creamed mixture alternately with milk, beginning and ending with flour. Fold in beaten egg whites and fruits. Pour into 3 lightly greased and floured 9" cake pans. Bake at 275 degrees for about 35 to 40 minutes or until a wooden pick comes out clean. When cool, fill and frost with filling. Store for a few days in a cool place to ripen.

Filling and Frosting:	1 cup pecans, chopped
juice of 1 lemon	1 cup boiling water
juice of 1 orange	3 Tablespoons cornstarch,
1 coconut, grated, plus milk	dissolved in 1/4 cup cold
2 cups sugar	water

Combine lemon juice, orange juice, coconut, coconut milk, sugar and nuts in a saucepan and bring to a boil. Add the cornstarch mixture and cook until thickened. Spread between layers and on top and sides of cake.

IMPORTANT TIPS FOR TENDER DELICATE POUND CAKE

Use sifted cake flour and sifted confectioners' sugar for top quality. Unsifted cake flour and confectioners' sugar will produce acceptable results, but the texture will not be so uniform or tender as with sifting.

If you sift the sugar, you must sift the flour, too. Likewise, if you do not sift the sugar, do not sift the flour. Follow exact measurements as specified in recipes. Do not round off measurements.

For characteristic pound-cake flavor use butter. However, margarine may be used and will give acceptable but less distinctive flavor.

Stir flour gently into creamed mixture just until thoroughly incorporated. Do not over mix.

FLO'S APRICOT BRANDY POUND CAKE

large tube pan, well-greased and floured
2 sticks margarine
3 cups sugar
6 eggs
3 cups all-purpose flour
1/2 teaspoon salt
1/4 teaspoon soda
1 cup commercial sour cream
1/2 teaspoon lemon extract
1 teaspoon orange extract
1/4 teaspoon almond extract
1/2 teaspoon rum extract
1 teaspoon vanilla extract
1/2 cup apricot brandy

Cream margarine and sugar until light and fluffy. Add eggs, one at a time, beating well after each addition. Sift dry ingredients together and add to creamed mixture. Combine sour cream with extracts and brandy; add to cake batter and mix well. Bake in a large well-greased and floured tube pan (or a bundt pan and a loaf pan) at 325 degrees for 70 minutes. Let cool in pan before removing.

APPLE POUND CAKE

2 cups sugar
1-1/2 cups Crisco oil
3 large eggs
3 cups all-purpose flour
1 teaspoon baking soda
1 teaspoon salt
3 cups firm apples, diced
3/4 cup shredded coconut (optional)
2 teaspoons vanilla
1 cup chopped pecans
Brown Sugar Icing

Mix sugar and oil; add eggs and blend well. Combine flour, soda and salt. Add to oil mixture. Stir in apples, coconut, vanilla and nuts. Mix well and spoon into a greased and floured 9" tube pan. Bake at 325 degrees for 1 hour, 20 minutes or until cake tests done. Remove cake from oven and while still hot, pour icing over top. Leave cake in pan until completely cool.

Brown Sugar Icing:
1 stick butter
1/4 cup milk
1 cup brown sugar

Combine all ingredients together in a small heavy saucepan. Bring to a boil. Simmer for about 20 minutes. Then pour over hot cake. Leave in pan to cool.

MIKE'S FAVORITE BANANA POUND CAKE

1 box light brown sugar
1 cup white sugar
1 cup butter or margarine
1/2 cup Crisco
5 large eggs
3 cups all-purpose flour
1/2 teaspoon baking powder
1/2 teaspoon salt

1/2 teaspoon cinnamon
1 cup milk
3 large bananas, mashed
1 teaspoon vanilla
2 cups chopped pecans (optional)
Caramel Frosting or Cream
  Cheese Frosting

Cream sugars, Crisco and butter until light and fluffy. Add eggs one at a time, beating well after each addition. Sift dry ingredients together and add to batter, alternating with milk, beginning and ending with flour. Fold in mashed bananas and vanilla. If desired, add 1 cup of chopped pecans to batter. Pour into greased and floured tube cake pan. The second cup of chopped pecans may be added to top of cake batter before baking, pressing them down slightly. Bake in 325 degree oven for 1-1/2 hours or until done. Cool. May or may not be frosted with Caramel Frosting or Cream Cheese Frosting.

Caramel Frosting:
3/4 cup butter (1-1/2 sticks)
3/4 cup firmly packed brown
    sugar

6 Tablespoons evaporated milk
  or coffee cream
3-1/2 cups confectioners' sugar
1-1/2 teaspoons vanilla

Heat butter with brown sugar in a small saucepan over low heat until sugar is melted, stirring constantly. Blend in milk or cream; cool. Gradually beat in confectioners' sugar until of spreading consistency; add vanilla and spread on cooled cake.

Cream Cheese Frosting:
1 (8-ounce) package cream cheese
1/4 cup melted margarine
1 teaspoon vanilla extract

1 (1 pound) box powdered sugar
1/2 cup chopped pecans

Combine all ingredients and blend well. Spread over cooled cake.

BROWN SUGAR POUND CAKE

2 sticks butter (or half butter and
half margarine)
1 pound light brown sugar
1 cup white sugar
5 large eggs
3 cups all-purpose flour

1/2 teaspoon baking powder
1 cup milk
1 teaspoon maple flavoring
1/2 teaspoon vanilla extract
1 cup nuts, chopped fine and
dredged with flour

Cream together shortening and sugars. Add eggs, one at a time, blending well. Sift flour and baking powder together and add alternately with milk to creamed mixture, beginning and ending with flour. Add flavorings. Add chopped nuts (black walnuts or pecans) and fold in gently. Bake in a 350 degree oven for 1 hour, 25 minutes in a well-greased and floured tube cake pan. Do not open oven until last 5 minutes to test. Cool 10 to 15 minutes before removing from pan. When cake is completely cool may be frosted with Brown Sugar Icing.

NOTE: Nuts may be omitted and added to icing if desired. Toast nuts before adding.

Brown Sugar Icing:
1 stick butter or margarine
1 cup dark brown sugar

1/4 cup sweet milk
3/4 cup powdered sugar

Bring margarine, sugar, and milk to a boil and boil for 3 to 4 minutes. Remove from heat and add 3/4 cup powdered sugar. Beat until creamy and spread on cake, allowing to drip down sides.

BUTTERMILK POUND CAKE WITH LEMON GLAZE

3 cups sugar
1 cup Crisco
6 eggs, separated
1 teaspoon butter flavoring
1 teaspoon lemon extract
3 cups all-purpose flour

1/4 teaspoon soda
1/2 teaspoon salt
1 teaspoon baking powder
1 cup buttermilk
Lemon Glaze

Cream sugar and Crisco thoroughly. Add egg yolks, one at a time, beating well after each addition. Add butter and lemon flavorings. Sift together dry ingredients three times and add buttermilk and flour mixture alternately to egg mixture, beginning and ending with flour mixture. Fold in stiffly beaten egg whites. Bake in a well-greased and floured tube pan at 350 degrees for 50 to 60 minutes. Cool cake; then glaze with Lemon Glaze.

Lemon Glaze:
1 egg, beaten
2 Tablespoons flour
1/2 cup water

1 cup sugar
juice and rind of 2 lemons
1/2 stick butter

Combine ingredients in a saucepan and cook over medium heat until mixture is of a thin custard consistency. Pour over cooled cake.

BOURBON WALNUT POUND CAKE

2 cups finely chopped walnuts
1/2 cup bourbon
3-1/2 cups sifted all-purpose flour
1-1/2 teaspoons baking powder
1/2 teaspoon salt
1/2 teaspoon nutmeg
1/2 teaspoon cinnamon

1/4 teaspoon cloves
2 cups soft butter or margarine
2-1/2 cups sugar
8 eggs, well beaten
1 teaspoon vanilla extract
1/2 cup bourbon

Preheat oven to 350 degrees. Grease well and flour a 10" tube pan. In small bowl, combine walnuts and 1/2 cup bourbon; mix well; let stand. Sift together flour, baking powder, salt, and spices; set aside.

In large bowl of electric mixer, at medium speed, beat butter with sugar until light and fluffy. Add eggs, and vanilla; beat well, at high speed, occasionally scraping sides of bowl and guiding mixture into beaters with rubber scraper, for 4 minutes until the mixture is thick and fluffy. At low speed, gradually beat in flour mixture just until combined. Stir in bourbon-walnut mixture. Turn batter into prepared pan, spreading evenly. Bake 1 hour, 10 minutes, or until cake tester inserted in center comes out clean. Cool in pan on wire rack 15 minutes. Then turn out of pan; cool completely on wire rack. Soak cheesecloth in 1/2 cup bourbon. Wrap cake completely in cheesecloth, then in foil, and refrigerate for several days. To serve, slice thinly.

CHOCOLATE POUND CAKE

3 cups sugar
2 sticks butter or margarine
1/2 cup Crisco
5 eggs
3 cups all-purpose flour

1/2 cup cocoa
1 teaspoon baking powder
1 cup milk
1 teaspoon vanilla extract
Chocolate Frosting (optional)

Sift together flour, cocoa and baking powder; set aside. Cream sugar and shortening together; add eggs one at a time, beating well after each addition. Add flour mixture alternately with milk to mixture, beginning and ending with flour. Add vanilla. Pour batter into a greased and floured tube cake pan and bake at 325 degrees for 70 minutes or until done. May or may not be frosted with Chocolate Frosting, after cake has been completely cooled.

Chocolate Frosting:
2 squares semisweet chocolate
2 Tablespoons butter
2 cups powdered sugar

3 to 4 Tablespoons milk or cream
1 cup finely chopped pecans
(optional)

Melt chocolate and butter in small saucepan, stirring constantly. Remove from heat; stir in sugar and 3 to 4 tablespoons milk, stirring until frosting is of easy spreading consistency. Spread on cooled cake. If desired, spread top of iced cake with 1 cup finely chopped pecans.

CREAM CHEESE POUND CAKE

8 ounces cream cheese, softened
3 sticks margarine
3 cups sugar
6 eggs

1-1/2 teaspoons vanilla
3 cups cake flour
1-1/2 cups finely chopped pecans
(optional)

Cream together butter and softened cream cheese; gradually add sugar and beat until light and fluffy. Add eggs one at a time, beating well after each addition. Add flour and salt, stirring until well blended. Stir in vanilla and blend well. If desired, add 1 cup finely chopped pecans, reserving 1/2 cup for bottom of tube pan. Grease and flour bottom and sides and tube of 10" tube pan (evenly spread reserved 1/2 cup nuts over bottom of pan, if desired). Pour batter into prepared pan and bake at 325 degrees for 1-1/2 hours or until cake tests done. Cool in pan 10 minutes; remove from pan and cool completely on wire rack.

J'S FRESH COCONUT POUND CAKE

1 cup butter, softened
3 cups sugar
6 eggs
3 cups all-purpose flour
1/4 teaspoon soda
1/4 teaspoon salt

1 (8-ounce) carton commercial
sour cream
1 cup frozen coconut, thawed
1 teaspoon vanilla
1 teaspoon coconut extract

Cream butter; gradually add sugar, beating until mixture is light and fluffy. Add eggs, one at a time, beating well after each addition. Combine flour, soda, and salt; mix well. Add to creamed mixture alternately with sour cream, beginning and ending with flour mixture. Stir in coconut and flavorings. Pour batter into a greased and floured 10" tube pan and bake at 350 degrees for 1 hour, 15 minutes or until a wooden pick inserted in center comes out clean. Cool in pan 10 to 15 minutes; remove form pan and cool completely. Sift powdered sugar over top before serving or frost with icing.

NOTE: 1 teaspoon lemon extract or 1 teaspoon almond extract may be substituted for vanilla.

Icing:
1/2 cup vegetable shortening
1 (1 pound) box confectioners'
sugar

1/4 cup water
1/8 teaspoon salt
1 teaspoon vanilla or coconut
flavoring

Combine all ingredients in a large bowl of electric mixer. Mix on high speed until fluffy. Frost top and sides of cake.

LEMON JUICE POUND CAKE

3 cups flour
1 cup (2 sticks) real butter,
    softened
2-1/2 cups sugar
5 eggs, large
1/2 teaspoon baking soda

1/4 teaspoon salt
1 teaspoon vanilla extract
1 Tablespoon fresh lemon juice
2 teaspoons grated lemon rind
1 cup buttermilk

Preheat oven to 325 degrees. Lightly grease and flour a 10" tube cake pan (no smaller). Sift flour together with baking soda and salt; set aside. In a large bowl, cream the butter and sugar. Add eggs one at a time, beating well after each addition. Add the vanilla, lemon juice and grated lemon rind and blend well. Add dry ingredients and the buttermilk alternately, in three parts each, blending well after each addition. Spoon the batter into the prepared pan, spreading evenly.

Bake at 325 degrees for 65 to 80 minutes or until cake tester comes out clean. Let the cake cool in the pan on a wire rack for 10 minutes. Turn out to finish cooling top side up on the rack. While the cake is still warm, brush with glaze all over cake. Repeat this, waiting a few minutes between coats, until all the glaze is used up. When the glaze has been absorbed and the outside is no longer sticky, transfer cake to a serving platter.

Glaze:
3/4 cup water

1 cup sugar
3 Tablespoons fresh lemon juice

In a small heavy saucepan, combine water, sugar, and lemon juice. Bring to a boil and stir to dissolve the sugar. Lower the heat and simmer until it is reduced to 3/4 cup. Set aside.

ORANGE POUND CAKE

A delightful Summer Treat

2 cups flour
2 cups sugar
1 cup butter or 1 cup Crisco
5 large eggs

7 Tablespoons fresh orange juice
1 teaspoon vanilla extract
pinch salt

Preheat oven to 325 degrees. Lightly grease and flour a 10" tube cake pan. Cream butter or Crisco and sugar together. Add eggs one at a time, and beat well after each. Gently beat in flour and orange juice. Add vanilla. Pour into the prepared pan. Bake about 1 hour at 325 degrees or until tester comes out clean. Cool in pan for 10 minutes; turn out and place top side up. Pour or spoon glaze over warm cake. As cake cools, occasionally spoon glaze over the top and sides.

Orange Glaze:
2 cups confectioners' sugar

4 Tablespoons orange juice
1/2 stick butter

Combine all ingredients in a small heavy saucepan. Bring to boil. Simmer for about 10 minutes. Cool slightly.

PINEAPPLE JUICE POUND CAKE

2 cups sugar
1 cup Crisco
6 eggs
2 cups all-purpose flour

pinch of salt
4 Tablespoons pineapple juice
1 teaspoon vanilla

Cream Crisco and sugar, add eggs one at a time, beating well after each. Sift flour and salt together; add flour 2 tablespoons at a time to creamed mixture. Add pineapple juice and vanilla. Grease and lightly flour a tube cake pan. Pour batter into prepared cake pan and bake in a cold oven at 300 degrees for 1 hour before opening oven. Test cake for doneness (if wooden pick inserted into center of cake comes out clean, cake is done). Remove from oven and cool in pan for 10 minutes, then turn out on rack and cool completely. Cake may be glazed while still warm, or may be sprinkled with powdered sugar before serving.

GEORGIA PEACH POUND CAKE

1 cup butter or margarine,
  softened
3 cups granulated sugar
6 eggs, room temperature
3 cups all-purpose flour
1/4 teaspoon baking soda
1/4 teaspoon salt

1/2 cup sour cream, room
  temperature
2 cups finely chopped, peeled
  fresh peaches
1 teaspoon vanilla extract
1 teaspoon almond extract

Preheat oven to 350 degrees. Grease lightly and flour a 10" tube pan and set aside. Cream together butter or margarine and sugar until light and fluffy. Add eggs, one at a time, beating well after each addition. Combine flour, soda and salt in a separate bowl; set aside. Mix sour cream and peaches together. Fold dry ingredients into creamed mixture alternately with sour cream and peaches, beginning and ending with dry ingredients. Stir in vanilla and almond extract.

Pour batter into prepared pan and bake for 75 to 80 minutes or until cake tests done. Remove to a wire rack to cool. Sift powdered confectioners' sugar on top of cake before serving.

NOTE: If peaches are unusually juicy, be sure to drain them.

PRALINE POUND CAKE

3-1/2 cups sifted all-purpose flour
1/2 teaspoon baking powder
2 sticks butter, softened
1/2 cup Crisco
1 pound light brown sugar
1 cup white sugar

6 eggs, room temperature
1 cup milk, room temperature
2 Tablespoons vanilla (no mistake)
Praline Frosting

Preheat oven to 325 degrees. Grease and lightly flour a 10" bundt pan. Sift flour and baking powder together.

Beat butter, Crisco and sugar in a large bowl with electric mixer at medium speed until smooth. Beat in eggs, one at a time, until mixture is fluffy. Add flour mixture 1/3 at a time alternately with milk just until blended. Add vanilla. Pour batter into prepared pan. Bake in preheated oven at 325 degrees for 1-1/2 hours, or until top springs back when lightly pressed with finger tips. Cool cake in pan on wire rack 15 minutes. Loosen around edge and tube with knife; remove cake from pan and cool completely. Frost with Praline Frosting.

Praline Frosting:
1 cup chopped pecans
1 stick butter

2 cups powdered sugar
4 to 5 Tablespoons half and half
1/4 teaspoon vanilla

Brown chopped pecans in butter in a heavy medium-sized saucepan, stirring constantly until butter is a golden brown. Let cool. Stir in powdered sugar with enough half and half or milk a tablespoon at a time so that the frosting is creamy. It will take about 4 to 5 tablespoons. Add vanilla. Spread on top of cake allowing frosting to drip down sides and in center of cake.

PINEAPPLE POUND CAKE

1/2 cup Crisco
1 cup butter (2 sticks)
2-3/4 cups sugar
6 eggs
3 cups all-purpose flour
1 teaspoon baking powder

1/4 cup milk
1 teaspoon vanilla
3/4 cups undrained crushed pineapple
Topping

Cream Crisco, butter and sugar until light and fluffy. Add eggs one at a time, beating thoroughly after each. Sift flour with baking powder; add to batter alternately with milk. Begin and end with flour. Add vanilla, stir in crushed pineapple with juice and blend well. Pour into a well-greased and lightly floured 10" tube pan. Bake at 325 degrees for 1 hour, 20 minutes or until top springs back when touched lightly. Remove from pan and pour topping over hot cake.

Topping:
1/4 cup butter (1/2 stick)

1-1/2 cups powdered sugar
1 cup drained crushed pineapple

Combine all ingredients in a saucepan; bring to a boil and pour over cake while hot.

OLD SOUTH GEORGIA
SOUR CREAM POUND CAKE

2 sticks butter, at room temperature
3 cups Vanilla Sugar
1 cup sour cream
6 eggs, at room temperature, separated

3-1/4 cups sifted all-purpose flour
1/4 teaspoon soda
1 teaspoon vanilla
1/2 teaspoon lemon extract
1 teaspoon butter flavoring, optional

Cream butter well. Gradually add sugar, a little at a time, beating constantly until the mixture looks like whipped cream. Add sour cream and beat well. Remove from mixer and continue beating by hand, alternating egg yolks, one at a time, with flour that has been sifted with soda. Add flavorings. Beat egg whites until almost stiff and fold into mixture. Pour into a well greased and floured bundt pan or tube pan which has been well greased and lined with waxed paper. Bake at 325 degrees for 1-1/2 to 2 hours. Do not open oven door for the first hour during baking. Let cake stand when done in the pan for 10 minutes before removing.

Vanilla Sugar: Add one vanilla bean to 5 pounds of sugar in a covered container. Shake or stir occasionally for several days for flavor to absorb. May be kept indefinitely.

MISS SUSIE'S SOUR CREAM POUND CAKE

2 sticks butter
3 cups sugar
3 cups sifted flour
1/4 teaspoon soda
1/4 teaspoon salt

6 egg yolks
1 cup sour cream
6 egg whites
1 teaspoon vanilla extract
1 teaspoon almond extract

Cream butter and sugar until light and fluffy. Add egg yolks one at a time, beating well after each. Sift flour three times with salt and add to creamed mixture 1/3 at a time, alternating with sour cream, to which soda has been added, beginning and ending with flour. Beat egg whites until they form a peak. Fold in cake batter, then add flavoring. Bake in preheated oven at 300 degrees for 1-1/2 hours. Powdered sugar may be sprinkled over top of cake before serving.

SEVEN-UP POUND CAKE
WITH LEMON CURD SAUCE

3 sticks butter or margarine, softened
3 cups sugar
5 eggs

3 cups flour
3/4 cups 7-Up at room temperature
Lemon Curd Sauce

(Continued)

Cream butter and sugar until light and fluffy. Add eggs, one at a time, beating well after each addition. Add flour and fold in the 7-Up. Pour into a greased and floured bundt pan, and bake at 325 degrees for 1-1/2 hours or until cake tests done.

Lemon Curd Sauce: juice of 6 lemons
2 cups sugar   6 eggs, beaten
1-1/2 sticks butter or margarine

In a saucepan, over medium heat, stir together sugar, butter, and lemon juice. Add eggs and continue stirring until sauce is thickened and is boiling softly.

FIVE-FLAVOR POUND CAKE

3 cups sugar   1 teaspoon coconut extract
1 cup butter, softened   1 teaspoon lemon extract
1/2 cup shortening   1 teaspoon rum extract
5 eggs   1 teaspoon vanilla extract
3 cups all-purpose flour, sifted   1 teaspoon butter flavoring
1/2 teaspoon baking powder   Coconut Glaze
1 cup milk

With mixer cream sugar, butter and shortening. Beat in eggs, one at a time. Slowly blend in flour and baking powder. Mix in milk, extracts and flavoring. Pour batter into greased 10" tube pan and bake at 325 degrees for 1-1/2 hours. Glaze while warm. May be prepared ahead or frozen. Serves 12.

Coconut Glaze: 1/2 teaspoon almond extract
1/2 teaspoon coconut extract   1/2 teaspoon butter flavoring
1/2 teaspoon lemon extract   1 cup sugar
1/2 teaspoon vanilla extract   1/2 cup water

Mix all ingredients in saucepan and heat to boiling. Remove from heat, cool, and spread over warm cake.

BLUE RIBBON POUND CAKE
(Best of the Best Pounds)

Read through the entire recipe first. These are the ingredients needed. Make no substitutions. All measurements are level. Assemble ingredients and let stand at room temperature one hour before mixing.

1 pound (2 cups) butter, real   1 teaspoon cream of tartar
3-1/2 cups sifted all-purpose flour   2 cups sifted confectioners' sugar
1/4 teaspoon soda   grated rind of 1/2 lemon
1/2 teaspoon ground mace   1 teaspoon lemon juice
3 cups granulated sugar   3 Tablespoons water
3 Tablespoons fresh lemon juice   4 candied cherries
1 Tablespoon vanilla extract   angelica or candied citron
10 eggs, separated   marzipan, if desired
1/4 teaspoon salt

(Continued)

Preheat oven to 300 degrees. Lightly grease and flour a 10" or 12" tube cake pan. Do not use flour from the 3-1/2 cups for cake; turn pan upside down to shake excess flour from pan.

Sift, then lightly spoon flour into measuring cup. Level top with a spatula. Place 3-1/2 cups sifted flour into sifter. (Do not use cake flour or self-rising). Add soda, mace and 1-1/2 cups granulated sugar. Sift into a large bowl. Cream butter until well blended. Add to flour mixture and mix well.

Stir 3 tablespoons lemon juice and 1 tablespoon vanilla into the unbeaten egg yolks. Add a small amount at a time to the butter mixture, blending well after each addition.

With electric mixer or rotary beater, beat the egg whites with 1/4 teaspoon salt until whites stand in glossy peaks, but not dry. Gradually add the remaining 1-1/2 cups granulated sugar, beating after each addition until all blends well. With a spoon or rubber spatula gently fold in 1 teaspoon cream of tartar. Drop beaten whites on to batter; fold in gently with hands or rubber spatula until whites are evenly distributed through the batter. Spoon batter into prepared pan, smoothing top with the back of spoon. Set pan down hard to remove any air bubbles. Bake about 2-1/4 hours. Cake is done when it shrinks from sides of pan and the surface springs back when pressed lightly with finger. Turn off heat and leave cake in the oven 30 minutes. Remove from oven and let stand in pan on rack 30 minutes. Loosen sides with spatula. Turn cake out on rack.

Glaze:

Sift 1/2 package or more confectioners' sugar. Measure 2 cups and place in a small bowl. Grate rind of 1/2 lemon. Add grated rind, 1 teaspoon lemon juice and 3 tablespoons water to sugar. Mix until smooth. Place rack holding cake on a sheet of wax paper. Pour glaze over cake, allowing it to run down sides and into center. Make sure top is covered. Halve the candied cherries; arrange on top of cake. Cut 24 small strips of angelica or candied citron. Insert 3 strips around each cherry half. Marzipan may be used if desired in place of cherries.

Cover the cake with a cake cover or loosely with foil. Store in a cool place. Stored this way, cake will keep for several weeks. If frozen, then wrapped well and stored in freezer, it will keep indefinitely. Good luck. A warm slice is pure delight. It's worth the effort to get an enormous, delicious cake that serves a lot of people and gets better, the older it gets. A fabulous Christmas cake. An excellent gift.

FLO'S BEST EVER POUND CAKE

1 pound butter (real)	8 eggs, separated
2-2/3 cups sugar	8 Tablespoons cream
3-1/2 cups plain flour	1 teaspoon vanilla

Beat egg whites with 6 tablespoons sugar until stiff; set aside. Cream butter and sugar. Add egg yolks two at a time. Add vanilla. Add flour alternately with 2 tablespoons cream, beginning and ending with flour. Fold in egg whites. Bake in greased and floured tube pan at 325 degrees for 1 hour, 15 minutes. Remove from oven and cool completely in pan before removing.

HALF POUND CAKE

2 cups sugar	2 cups all-purpose flour
2 sticks butter	1/2 teaspoon baking powder
5 eggs, well beaten	1/4 teaspoon salt
1 teaspoon vanilla	Orange Glaze

Cream butter and sugar. Add eggs and vanilla. Beat well. Add flour, baking powder and salt and mix until blended. Bake at 300 degrees for 1 hour or until cake tests done. Cool in pan until warm; while still warm, cover with Orange Glaze. Cool completely, then remove from pan.

Orange Glaze:	1/2 cup orange juice
1 cup sugar	1/2 stick butter

Boil all ingredients in saucepan for 2 minutes. Cool slightly and pour over warm cake.

MOTHER'S NO FAIL PLAIN POUND CAKE

2 sticks butter	Flavoring #1:
1 stick margarine	2 teaspoons vanilla
1 box powdered sugar, sifted	Flavoring #2:
6 eggs	1 teaspoon vanilla
3 cups cake flour, sifted	1 Tablespoon fresh lemon juice
3 Tablespoons milk	Flavoring #3:
pinch of salt	1 teaspoon vanilla
	1/2 teaspoon mace

In large bowl of mixer, beat butter until creamy. Gradually beat in sugar, beating well after each addition, until light and fluffy. Add salt. Alternate adding 2 eggs at a time, 1 cup flour, 1 tablespoon milk and flavorings; repeat three times. Do not over beat. Turn into well-greased and lightly floured tube cake pan. Bake in preheated oven at 300 degrees for 1-1/2 hours or until wooden pick inserted in center comes out clean. Cool in pan 5 minutes. Turn out on rack; cool completely. Glaze or sprinkle with Vanilla Confectioners' Sugar.

(Continued)

Glaze: 2 Tablespoons milk
1 cup sifted confectioners' sugar

Mix sifted confectioners' sugar with 2 tablespoons milk or other flavoring to make of consistency to glaze cake. Pour on top and allow to run down sides of cake.

Vanilla Confectioners' Sugar: 1 vanilla bean, split
2 cups confectioners' sugar

Split a vanilla bean. Bury in 2 cups confectioners' sugar; cover tightly. Let stand for at least 24 hours. Sift on cake before serving.

OLD FASHION POUND CAKE
(Queen of the Pound Cakes)

4 sticks (1 pound) real butter,   2 Tablespoons fresh lemon juice
   softened to room temperature   2 teaspoons pure vanilla extract
4 cups sugar   4 cups sifted cake flour
10 eggs, room temperature

Preheat oven to 325 degrees. Grease and lightly flour a 12-cup tube cake pan. Cream together butter and sugar, using a heavy-duty electric mixer. Add whole eggs one at a time with mixer running continuously at medium speed. Add lemon juice and vanilla. Then add sifted flour a little bit at a time. Pour thoroughly mixed batter into prepared pan. Bake at 325 degrees for 1-1/2 hours or until straw test comes out clean. Remove to a rack to cool about 30 minutes. A pound cake's true consistency is better if allowed one or two days to set up or "ripen". Pound cake usually disappears like it is going out of style. But it never does. A well baked pound cake in the old fashioned way can bring joy to everybody. It is delicious served by itself or made more so when served with fresh fruit. If there's any left over, there's nothing better than a slice toasted for breakfast.

VANILLA WAFER POUND CAKE

1 (12-ounce) box vanilla wafers   1/2 cup sweet milk
1 teaspoon vanilla extract   1 (7-ounce) package coconut
1 cup butter   1 cup pecans, chopped
2 cups sugar   3/4 cup raisins (optional)
6 eggs

If using raisins, plump in hot water for a few minutes, then drain thoroughly before adding to cake batter.

Grease and flour a tube cake pan. Crumble vanilla wafers very fine (like flour; a blender may be used). Cream butter and sugar. Add eggs one at a time, beating well after each. Add vanilla wafer crumbs to egg mixture alternately with milk. Add coconut, pecans, raisins (if desired) and vanilla. Mix well and spoon into prepared tube pan. Bake at 350 degrees for 1-1/2 hours or until cake tests done. Be sure cake is completely cooled before removing from pan.

WHIPPING CREAM POUND CAKE

1 cup (2 sticks) butter, softened
3 cups sugar
6 large eggs, room temperature
3 cups cake flour, sifted twice
1 cup (1/2 pint) heavy cream

2 teaspoons vanilla extract or 1
teaspoon vanilla extract, 1
teaspoon almond extract and
1 teaspoon lemon extract

Grease and flour a 10" bundt pan or tube cake pan. In a large bowl, with electric mixer, beat butter until fluffy. Add sugar and beat until well combined. Add eggs, one at a time, beating after each addition. Mix flour into the butter mixture alternately with cream, beating well after each addition. Beat about 5 full minutes. Add vanilla or seasoning of choice.

Pour batter into prepared pan. Set in a cold oven. Heat oven to 325 degrees. Bake 60 to 75 minutes or until a light golden brown. Cool cake in pan on wire rack for 10 minutes. Remove cake from pan and cool completely on wire rack.

ANGEL FOOD CAKE

(A Heavenly Morsel)

Two cities claim the origin of this cake: 1. A family from Atlantic City, New Jersey, moved to "a picturesque spot on the Hudson River" and opened a boarding house. There, one of the ladies of the family was given "a valuable receipt" by a friend who had received it from a lady in India. When the family returned to Atlantic City, the lady began to sell the cake, which was made with the greatest secrecy behind closed doors. Finally, an 1883 cookbook revealed the secret for the first time.

2. St. Louis, Missouri, claims the honor of inventing Angel Food Cake. Although the creator's name is lost to history, in the 1880's the cake was featured at the Hotel Beers. The hotel went so far as to advertise the cake's distinguished qualities in its catalog. The cake passed all taste tests and has become an all-American favorite.

1-1/2 cups superfine sugar
1 cup cake flour
1-1/2 cups egg whites (about 12)
1/4 teaspoon salt
1 teaspoon cream of tartar

1 Tablespoon fresh lemon juice
1-1/2 teaspoons vanilla or may
use 2 teaspoons vanilla with
1/4 teaspoon almond extract

Preheat oven to 350 degrees. Mix 1/2 cup of the sugar with the flour. Set aside the remaining cup of sugar. Sift the combined flour and sugar four times. In a large bowl, beat the egg whites, slowly at first, with a rotary or an electric beater, until they are moist and foamy. Sprinkle the salt, cream of tartar, lemon juice and vanilla over egg whites. Beat at high speed until mixture begins to form soft peaks, but is still moist. Sprinkle in reserved cup of sugar, 2 or 3 tablespoons at a time, beating at medium speed.

(Continued)

Sift one-quarter of the flour mixture over the egg whites and fold gently into the batter; follow the same procedure for the rest of the flour. Pour the mixture into an ungreased 10" tube pan and gently cut through the batter with a knife spatula to remove any air pockets. Bake for 45 to 50 minutes or until cake springs back when pressed gently. Remove from oven and turn pan upside down on wire rack. Let cake "hang" until cold, about 1-1/2 hours, before removing cake.

NOTES: Clean, dry and completely grease-free bowl, beaters, and tube pan are essential for the cake to rise correctly. Angel Food Cake may be frosted, glazed or served plain, accompanied by seasonal fresh fruit and whipped cream. To serve, pull wedges apart with two forks instead of using a knife.

APPLESAUCE CAKE SUPREME

3 cups sifted cake flour	2 cups seedless raisins
1 teaspoon salt	1 cup dates, chopped
2 eggs	1 cup pecans, chopped
1-1/4 teaspoons baking powder	3/4 cup shortening
1 teaspoon baking soda	1 cup sugar
1-1/2 teaspoons cloves	1-1/2 cups unsweetened
2-1/2 teaspoons cinnamon	applesauce
2 teaspoons allspice	1-2-3 Caramel Frosting

Sift dry ingredients together. Mix raisins, dates and pecans with flour mixture. Cream shortening, adding sugar gradually. Add eggs one at a time and beat well. Fold in applesauce. Add dry ingredients. Turn into a greased and floured 9" tube pan and bake at 350 degrees for 60 to 65 minutes. Allow to cool before turning out of pan. Frost with 1-2-3 Caramel Frosting.

1-2-3 Caramel Frosting:	1 Tablespoon all-purpose flour
1 cup light brown sugar, firmly	3 Tablespoons cream or milk
packed	1 teaspoon vanilla extract
2 Tablespoons butter or margarine	

Combine sugar, butter, flour and cream in a saucepan and cook over low heat, stirring constantly, until mixture boils. Continue stirring and cook for 1 minute. Remove from heat and add vanilla extract. Beat until of spreading consistency.

"BEE-BEE" JAM CAKE

1 cup butter or margarine	1 teaspoon cloves
2 cups sugar	1 teaspoon allspice
1 cup buttermilk	2 teaspoons cinnamon
1 teaspoon soda	1 Tablespoon vanilla or
4 egg yolks, beaten	1 teaspoon vanilla and
4 egg whites, beaten	1 teaspoon almond extracts
3 cups cake flour	1 cup blackberry preserves
1 teaspoon nutmeg	

(Continued)

Cream butter and sugar. Dissolve baking soda in buttermilk and add egg yolks. Sift flour and spices together three times. Add a little buttermilk and egg mixture to sugar mixture. Add flour mixture alternately with milk and egg mixture. Add vanilla, then blackberry preserves. Fold in beaten egg whites. Bake in tube pan (greased and floured) at 300 degrees for 15 minutes, then at 360 degrees for 30 minutes longer. Place on rack and cool. Red or black raspberry preserves may be used. Preserves with or without seeds may be used.

BUTTER CAKE

1 pound butter (real butter, not margarine)
1 pound English walnuts, chopped
1 pound raisins

2 cups sugar
4 cups flour
2 Tablespoons milk
6 eggs

Cream butter and sugar until light and fluffy. Add eggs one at a time, beating well after each. Add flour a small amount at a time; add milk. Fold in nuts and raisins. Pour into a large tube cake pan, or two small loaf pans that have been greased and floured. Bake in a slow oven 325 degrees for 1 to 2 hours, according to size of pan. Cool before removing from pan.

KENTUCKY BUTTER CAKE

1 cup butter, softened
2 cups sugar
4 eggs
1 cup buttermilk or sour milk
3 cups all-purpose flour

1 teaspoon baking powder
1 teaspoon salt
2 teaspoons vanilla extract
1/2 teaspoon soda
Butter Sauce

Grease bottom only of 10" tube pan. In a large mixer bowl, cream butter at high speed. Gradually add sugar and continue creaming until light and fluffy. Add eggs, one at a time, beating well after each addition. Add remaining ingredients except Butter Sauce. Blend at low speed, scraping bowl occasionally. Pour batter into prepared pan. Bake at 325 degrees for 60 to 65 minutes or until cake springs back when lightly touched. Prepare butter sauce. Prick top of cake with a fork or ice pick. Pour warm sauce over warm cake. Cool completely before removing from pan. If desired sprinkle with confectioners' sugar before serving.

Butter Sauce:
1 cup sugar
1 Tablespoon rum extract

1/4 cup water
1/2 cup butter

In small saucepan combine sugar, water and butter. Heat until butter is melted. Do not boil. Add rum flavoring. Pour over warm cake.

BLUE RIBBON CARROT CAKE

3 cups packed shredded carrots
1 Tablespoon lemon juice
1 20-ounce can crushed pineapple
   in pineapple juice, drained
3 cups unsifted all-purpose flour
1 cup white sugar
1 cup brown sugar, packed
2 teaspoons baking powder
2 teaspoons baking soda
1 teaspoon salt
2 teaspoons ground cinnamon
1/2 teaspoon ground cloves

1/2 teaspoon ground nutmeg
1/2 teaspoon ground allspice
1-1/2 cups vegetable oil
5 eggs
2 teaspoons vanilla
1 cup flaked coconut
1 cup walnuts, coarsely chopped
1 cup raisins, chopped
Lemon Cream Cheese Frosting or
   Caramel Icing or Buttermilk
   Glaze

Preheat oven to 350 degrees. Line bottom of 10" tube pan with wax paper ring. Grease and flour paper, sides and tube of pan.

Combine carrots and lemon juice in small bowl. Squeeze as much liquid as possible from pineapple. Combine flour, sugars, baking powder, baking soda, salt and spices in bowl. Beat in oil until blended. Mix in carrots. Beat in eggs one at a time. Stir in vanilla, coconut, walnuts, raisins and pineapple until well blended. Pour batter into prepared tube pan.

Bake in preheated moderate oven (350 degrees) for 1-1/2 hours or until wooden pick inserted in center of cake comes out clean and cake shrinks from side of pan. Cool cake in pan on wire rack 5 minutes. Remove cake from pan. Cool to room temperature on rack.

Frost top and sides of cake with Lemon Cream Cheese Frosting, Caramel Icing or Buttermilk Glaze. If using Buttermilk Glaze, put glaze on hot cake.

Lemon Cream Cheese Frosting:
1 (3-ounce) package cream
   cheese, softened

1/4 cup (1/2 stick) unsalted butter
1-1/2 cups confectioners' sugar, sifted
lemon juice

Beat together cream cheese and butter in bowl until smooth and fluffy. Add confectioners' sugar and beat until light and fluffy. Thin with lemon juice as necessary. (Pineapple juice may be substituted for lemon juice.)

Caramel Icing:
1 cup brown sugar
3 Tablespoons margarine
1 teaspoon vanilla

3 Tablespoon milk
1 (3-ounce) package cream cheese
powdered sugar

Cream margarine and brown sugar with cream cheese. Add vanilla and milk. Add enough powdered sugar to make icing of spreading consistency.

Buttermilk Glaze:
1 cup sugar
1/2 teaspoon soda
1/2 cup buttermilk

1/2 cup butter or margarine
1 Tablespoon corn syrup
1 teaspoon vanilla

In a small saucepan, combine sugar, soda, buttermilk, butter and corn syrup. Bring to a boil and cook 5 minutes, stirring occasionally. Remove from heat and stir in vanilla.

FRESH LEMON CHIFFON CAKE

A delightful and refreshing summer dessert

2-1/2 cups sifted cake flour
1 Tablespoon baking powder
1 teaspoon salt
1-1/2 cups sugar, divided
1/2 cup vegetable oil

5 egg yolks, beaten
3 Tablespoons grated lemon rind
3/4 cup fresh lemon juice
5 egg whites
1/2 teaspoon cream of tartar

Sift together twice the flour, baking powder, salt and 3/4 cup of sugar. Place in a mixing bowl. Beat vegetable oil, egg yolks, lemon juice and rind until smooth. Make a well in the center of flour mixture. Add egg yolk mixture and beat at high speed of the mixer for 5 minutes or until satiny smooth.

In a large bowl, beat egg whites (at room temperature) and cream of tartar until soft peaks form. Add the remaining 3/4 cup sugar, 2 tablespoons at a time, beating until stiff peaks form.

Pour egg yolk mixture in a thin, steady stream over entire surface of egg whites and gently fold whites into yolk mixture.

Pour batter into an ungreased 10" tube pan, spreading evenly with a spatula . Bake at 325 degrees until cake springs back when lightly touched. Invert pan; cool 40 minutes. Loosen cake from sides of pan using a narrow metal spatula; remove from pan. Place on cake plate; drizzle top with fresh lemon glaze. Serve plain or with a scoop of sherbert the same flavor as cake.

Glaze:
3 cups sifted powdered sugar
2 teaspoons grated lemon rind

3 to 4 Tablespoons fresh lemon juice

Combine all ingredients. Stir until mixture is smooth. Drizzle on top of cake.

NOTE: Fresh Orange juice and rind may be used in place of lemon.

FRIENDSHIP CAKE #1

(Made from a Cake Mix)

1 box yellow cake mix,
   (preferably Duncan Hines,
   plain)
1 box vanilla instant pudding
   mix (Jello)

4 large eggs
2/3 cup oil
1 cup pecans, chopped
2-1/3 cups brandied fruits,
   drained

Drain fruit and save juice for starter for other cakes. Mix the yellow cake mix, instant pudding mix, eggs and vegetable oil together until well mixed. Add fruits and pecans. Stir well and pour into greased and floured bundt cake pan. Bake at 325 degrees for 60 to 90 minutes or until cake tests done.

FRIENDSHIP CAKE #2
(From Scratch)

1 cup butter or margarine, melted	1/4 teaspoon ground nutmeg
1-3/4 cups sugar	2 eggs, large
3 cups all-purpose flour	2 cups drained brandied fruit
1 teaspoon baking soda	1 cup chopped pecans
1 teaspoon ground cinnamon	1/4 cup brandied fruit juice
1/2 teaspoon salt	powdered sugar (optional)
1/4 teaspoon ground cloves	

Combine butter and sugar in large bowl; beat well. Combine next 6 ingredients; add to butter mixture, beating well. Add eggs; beat well. Coarsely chop brandied fruit and stir into batter. Add chopped pecans and juice; mix well. Pour batter into a well greased and floured 10" bundt pan. Bake at 350 degrees for 1 hour. Cool in pan 10 minutes; remove from pan and cool completely on a wire rack. Sprinkle cake with powdered sugar, if desired.

BRANDIED FRUIT STARTER
(Friendship Cup)

1 cup pineapple tidbits	1-1/2 cups sugar
1 cup cling peach slices	1 (8-cup) glass jar (apothecary jar is
1 cup Maraschino cherries	excellent or a gallon glass jar
1 package dry yeast	with a wide mouth and lid)

Drain fruit well and pour all ingredients into the jar, stirring with a plastic spoon. Put top on jar loosely and allow to ferment on kitchen counter top or in a warm place for about 2 weeks. Stir with a plastic or wooden spoon several times the first day, then once a day. After seven days it is ready to use, but do not add more fruit for 2 weeks. Never let the contents of the jar get below 3 cups or the process will stop. Every 2 weeks, you may add one cup of drained canned fruit and one cup of sugar in order listed above. You must not add more often than every 2 weeks. But you may delay adding a day or two without disastrous results. When you have six cups of fruit, you may divide it into two portions with at least 3 cups in each jar. Divide just before adding fruit and sugar. Stir about every three days to help sugar dissolve, but do not refrigerate. The apothecary jars are just right because there is room for expansion since the lids move up a bit with pressure inside. Never put the lid on tightly or stir with a metal spoon, this stops the growth process.

This popular fruit is often called a "Friendship Cup". When the jar has been built up to six or more cups of fruit, the contents of the jar may be divided and a second started with at least 3 cups to give to someone who will be sharing your "Friendship". This fruit is delicious on pound cake or as a sauce for vanilla ice cream. I have also frozen the drained fruit and used later for cakes. The cakes make unusual Christmas gifts, as well as the "Friendship Jar of Fruit".

NOTE: Can be used as gifts, sauce for ice cream and as fruit in cakes.

FRESH FRUIT CAKE

2 sticks butter
2-1/3 cups sugar
5 eggs
1 teaspoon salt
1 teaspoon each lemon and
  vanilla extracts
3-1/3 cups cake flour
1/2 teaspoon baking powder

1/2 box white raisins
1 quart pecans, chopped
1 small can crushed pineapple,
  liquid included
1 (10-1/2 ounce) bottle
  maraschino cherries
other fruits, if desired

Boil raisins; pour off water and cool. Cream butter and sugar; add flavorings and eggs one at a time, beating well after each addition. Add salt and baking powder to flour and combine with the butter mixture, alternately with pineapple. (Reserve 1/2 cup of flour to dust over nuts and raisins.) Add nut and raisin mixture to cake batter, stirring only enough to mix thoroughly. Bake in greased and floured tube cake pan at 225 degrees until firm to touch, approximately 2-1/2 hours.

TWELFTH NIGHT CAKE

According to old English custom, if a single bean is concealed in the cake before baking, whoever finds the bean on his plate reigns over the 12th Night merrymaking.

1 cup unsalted butter (room
  temperature)
1 cup brown sugar
4 eggs
3 Tablespoons milk
1/3 cup brandy
3 cups sifted all-purpose flour
1 teaspoon baking soda
1/2 teaspoon allspice

1 teaspoon cinnamon
1 teaspoon ground coriander
1 cup raisins
1 cup currants
additional 1/2 cup flour
1/3 cup candied cherries or diced
  angelica
1-1/4 cups mixed candied peels
1/2 cup coarsely chopped nuts

In a large bowl, cream the butter and sugar until fluffy. Beat in the eggs, one at a time. Beat in the milk and brandy. In another bowl, toss the raisins and currants in the additional flour until they are evenly coated. Add these and the remaining fruits and nuts to the dough. Place the dough in a 2-quart, well-greased tube pan and bake at 250 degrees for about 1-1/4 hours, or until a toothpick inserted in the center comes out dry. Cool in the cake pan, then turn out onto a cake rack and ice, if desired, decorating with additional candied fruits.

VERY FAST FRUIT CAKE

1 package Duncan Hines Deluxe
   Spice Cake mix
1 small package instant Jello
   lemon pudding mix
2/3 cup apricot nectar
1/4 cup apricot brandy
1/2 cup cooking oil

4 eggs
1 cup white raisins
1 cup candied pineapple, cut in
   small pieces
1 cup pecans, chopped
apricot frosting

In a large mixing bowl beat for 2 minutes on medium speed cake mix, pudding mix, nectar, brandy and oil. Add eggs one at a time, beating well on medium speed after each addition. Fold in fruits, nuts and raisins. Turn into well greased and floured tube pan. Bake in preheated oven at 350 degrees about 55 minutes. After cake is cooled, frost with Apricot Frosting.

Apricot Frosting:
1 cup sifted powdered sugar

3 Tablespoons apricot brandy

Stir brandy into powdered sugar, a few drops at a time, until frosting is of spreading consistency. Spread over outside of cake.

BEST WHITE FRUIT CAKE

1/2 pound butter
1 cup white sugar
5 large eggs
3/4 pound glace cherries
1 pound glace pineapple

4 cups shelled pecans
1-3/4 cups flour
1/2 teaspoon baking powder
1/2 ounce each vanilla and lemon
   extracts

Cream butter. Add sugar gradually, creaming until fluffy. Add eggs which have been beaten with rotary beater; blend. Chop nuts and fruits and dredge with part of flour. Sift remaining flour with baking powder and fold in. Add flavorings and mix well. Add fruits and nuts. Pour into greased paper-lined small loaf pan or tube pan. Place in cold oven and bake at 250 degrees for 3 hours for tube pan, 2-1/2 hours for loaf pan. Store for at least 24 hours before slicing.

TUNNEL OF FUDGE CAKE

1-3/4 cups sugar
1-3/4 cups butter or margarine,
   softened
6 large eggs

2 cups confectioners' sugar
2-1/4 cups all-purpose flour
2 cups chopped walnuts
3/4 cup unsweetened cocoa

Grease and lightly flour a 12-cup or 10-cup tube cake pan. Heat oven to 350 degrees. In a large mixing bowl, cream sugar and butter or margarine until light and fluffy. Add eggs one at a time, beating well after each addition. Gradually add 2 cups confectioners' sugar, blending well. Lightly spoon flour into measuring cup; level off. Sift flour and cocoa together. Stir flour mixture into the creamed mixture by using a large mixing spoon or rubber spatula. Add chopped walnuts and blend well. Spoon batter into prepared pan, spreading evenly. Bake at 350 degrees for 60 to 65 minutes. Cool upright in pan on a wire rack for 1 hour; invert onto serving plate. Cool completely. Glaze.

(Continued)

Glaze:
3/4 cup confectioners' sugar
1/4 cup unsweetened cocoa

1-1/2 to 2 Tablespoons half and
half (whole milk may be
used)

In a small bowl, blend 3/4 cup confectioners' sugar, 1/4 cup cocoa and enough milk for desired drizzling consistency. Spoon over cake, allowing some to run down the sides of the cake. Store tightly covered.

NOTE: Nuts are essential for the success of this cake. This cake was originally made with a dry frosting mix that is no longer available. This recipe will produce the same tunnel of fudge surrounded by delicious chocolate cake. Since this cake will have a soft tunnel of fudge, an ordinary test for doneness cannot be used successfully. Accurate oven temperature and baking time is essential.

GRAHAM CRACKER FRUIT CAKE

2 cups seedless dark raisins
2 cups golden raisins, chopped
1 cup chopped pitted dates
1/2 cup halved candied cherries
2/3 cup slivered candied pineapple
1/4 cup diced citron
1/3 cup slivered orange or lemon
   peel

1 cup chopped walnuts
2 cups port wine
1 Tablespoon vanilla extract
1 cup soft butter
1 cup sugar
6 eggs
5 cups (1 package) graham
   cracker crumbs

In a large bowl mix all fruits, nuts and 1 cup wine; add vanilla. Place in tightly covered bowl and let stand for at least seven days. Preheat oven to 250 degrees. In large bowl, mix butter and sugar at medium speed until it is creamy. Beat in eggs two at a time. Fold in graham cracker crumbs alternately with fruit mixture, including any wine not absorbed by the fruit. Mix thoroughly. Pour into greased and floured bundt pan and one small loaf pan that has been lined with waxed paper. Bake three to 4 hours or until done. Cool cakes and remove from pans. Wrap cakes in cheesecloth that has been sprinkled liberally with wine. Wrap tightly in aluminum foil. Sprinkle once a week with wine. Store for at least 3 weeks.

HUMMINGBIRD CAKE
(Dr. Bird Cake)

3 cups flour
2 cups sugar
1 teaspoon salt
1 teaspoon cinnamon
1 teaspoon soda
3 eggs, beaten

1-1/2 cups vegetable oil
2 cups chopped bananas
1 (8-ounce) can crushed
   undrained pineapple
1 cup chopped pecans or almonds
1-1/2 teaspoons vanilla extract

(Continued)

Grease and lightly flour a 10" tube cake pan. Preheat oven to 350 degrees. Sift flour, sugar, cinnamon, salt and baking soda together. Mix well. Add eggs and oil, stirring until moistened, mixing well. Do not beat. Stir in bananas, pineapple, pecans and vanilla; mix with a large spoon, but do not beat. Pour batter into prepared cake pan. Bake 1 hour and 10 minutes or until done. The top will crack slightly on top. Cool in pan before removing.

May be iced with Cream Cheese Icing or French Vanilla Icing. Good even without icing.

NOTE: This batter may be baked in three greased and floured 9" round cake pans. Bake at 350 degrees for 25 to 30 minutes or until a wooden pick comes out clean when inserted in the center of layer. Cool in pans for 10 minutes; remove and ice with cream cheese icing. Sprinkle chopped pecans on top of iced cake. This makes a large and delicious layer cake.

Cream Cheese Icing:
1/2 cup butter, softened
1 (8-ounce) package cream
   cheese, softened
1 (1-pound) box confectioners'
   sugar
2 teaspoons fresh lemon juice
1 teaspoon vanilla extract
1/2 cup finely chopped pecans
   (optional)

Combine cream cheese and butter; beating until the mixture is smooth. Add powdered sugar and vanilla; beat until light and fluffy. Spread on cooled cake.

NOTE: If baked as tube cake, cut icing in half.

French Vanilla Icing:
1 cup milk
5 Tablespoons flour
1/2 pound butter or margarine,
   softened
1 cup sugar
1 teaspoon vanilla

In top of double boiler, stir flour and milk over boiling water until thick (custard consistency). Set aside to cool. In a medium mixing bowl, whip butter or margarine with sugar; add cooled milk and flour mixture and vanilla. Mix to blend.

TEXAS LEMON DATE NUT CAKE

1 pound butter (4 sticks)
1 pound sugar (2 cups)
1 pound chopped dates
1 pound pecans, coarsely chopped
6 large eggs, separated
2 ounces lemon extract
3 cups flour
1 teaspoon soda
1 Tablespoon water
1 10" tube cake pan, greased and
   lined with brown paper

(Continued)

Cream butter and sugar together well. Add egg yolks. Mix well. Dissolve soda in the tablespoon of water; add to sugar-egg mixture with extract. Add flour a third at a time, beating well to mix after each addition; about 3 to 4 minutes. Add dates and chopped pecans. In a separate bowl, beat egg whites until they form stiff peaks. Fold in to batter, mixing well until all white streaks are gone. Bake at 250 degrees for 2-3/4 hours in a tube cake pan that has been lined with brown paper. White raisins may be used in place of dates if desired. Cool in pan for about 30 minutes. Turn out and turn cake upright.

PECAN CHRISTMAS CAKE

2 cups butter, softened	1-1/2 cups golden seedless raisins
2 cups sugar	4 cups chopped pecans
6 eggs	3 cups all-purpose flour, divided
1 Tablespoon lemon juice	1/4 teaspoon salt
1 teaspoon grated lemon peel	1 teaspoon baking powder
1 Tablespoon vanilla extract	Glaze

Cream butter and sugar until light and fluffy. Add eggs one at a time, beating well after each addition. Stir in lemon juice, lemon peel and vanilla. Combine raisins, pecans and 1/4 cup flour. Combine remaining flour, salt and baking powder; fold into butter mixture alternately with nut mixture. Spoon batter into greased and floured 10" bundt pan. Bake at 300 degrees about 1 hour and 50 minutes. Cool slightly and remove from pan. Pour glaze over cake.

Glaze:	1/4 cup lemon juice
1/4 cup orange juice	1/4 cup sugar

Combine all ingredients; heat, stirring constantly, until sugar is dissolved. Pour over warm cake. Makes enough for one 10" cake.

PISTACHIO CAKE

1 package deluxe white cake mix	1 teaspoon almond extract
1 package pistachio pudding mix	4 eggs
3/4 cup cold water	1 cup chopped nuts (optional)
3/4 cup vegetable oil	Topping
1/4 teaspoon green food coloring	

Stir cake mix with pudding mix. Add water and oil to the mix; then add extract and food coloring. Add eggs, one at a time, using low speed of mixer and beat well after each addition. Beat 5 minutes. Grease a large tube cake pan and flour lightly. Pour batter into pan and bake at 350 degrees for 45 to 50 minutes. Pour either Topping No. 1 or Topping No. 2 over cake and return to oven for 5 minutes. Cool. Sprinkle cake with confectioners' sugar before serving. This cake freezes well.

NOTE: If desired, sprinkle top of batter with 1 cup of chopped nuts before baking.

(Continued)

Topping No. 1:
3 Tablespoon margarine, melted
1/3 cup water
2 cups confectioners' sugar
1/4 teaspoon almond extract

Mix all ingredients together and boil 1 minute. Cool and pour over cake.

Topping No. 2:
1 cup powdered sugar
1/4 cup milk
5 Tablespoon margarine
6-ounces semi-sweet chocolate
bits

Mix all ingredients together and boil 1 minute. Cool and pour over cake.

BETH'S RUM CAKE

2 sticks butter (not margarine)
1/2 cup Crisco
3 cups sugar
5 eggs
3 cups sifted all-purpose flour
1 teaspoon baking powder
1/4 teaspoon salt
1 cup milk
4 teaspoons rum flavoring
chopped nuts

Cream together butter, Crisco and sugar until light and fluffy. Add eggs, one at a time, beating after each addition. Sift dry ingredients together and add alternately with milk, beginning and ending with flour. Add flavoring last. Line bottom of greased and floured tube pan with waxed paper. Cover paper with chopped nuts. Pour batter into pan and bake at 325 degrees for 1 hour 25 minutes or until done.

NOTE: For one of the very best pound cakes, omit rum flavoring and add 1 teaspoon vanilla and 1 teaspoon almond extract.

RUM NUT CAKE

1 cup pecans, finely chopped
1 package Duncan Hines Butter
    Recipe Golden Cake Mix
1 (3-3/4 ounce) package Jello
    vanilla pudding mix
1/2 cup light rum or imitation
    rum flavoring
1/2 cup water
1/2 cup vegetable oil
4 eggs
Glaze

Grease with margarine and lightly flour a bundt pan. Sprinkle nuts evenly over bottom of pan. In large bowl toss together lightly cake mix and pudding mix, then add next 4 ingredients. Beat with electric or hand beater for 2 minutes. Pour carefully into bundt pan; do not disturb nuts more than necessary. Bake in 325 degree preheated oven for 50 to 60 minutes, until lightly firm to touch. Remove from oven and place on rack. Carefully insert silver knife around cake to loosen from pan and center tube. Pour hot glaze over cake at once and allow to stand 30 minutes. Invert on plate.

Glaze:
1 cup sugar
1/4 cup rum
1/4 cup water

Boil all ingredients in saucepan for 3 minutes and pour at once over hot cake. Distribute evenly while pouring.

SUNSHINE SPONGE CAKE

6 eggs, separated
3/4 teaspoon cream of tartar
1-1/2 cups sugar
1/2 cup water

1 teaspoon vanilla extract or 1/2
  teaspoon lemon and 1/2
  teaspoon almond extracts
1 cup cake flour
1/4 teaspoon salt
Butter Sauce

Preheat oven to 325 degrees. Beat egg whites with cream of tartar until stiff peaks form. Set aside. Bring sugar and water to a boil in a medium saucepan and cook until mixture reaches 234 degrees on a candy thermometer. Slowly, but in a steady stream, pour sugar syrup into egg whites, continuing to beat until cool, about 5 minutes. Beat egg yolks, add flavoring and fold into egg white mixture. Sift flour and salt together and fold into egg mixture, 1/3 cup at a time. Gently pour or spoon batter into an ungreased 10" tube pan and bake for 1 hour. Serves 8 to 10.

Serve with Butter Sauce or fresh sweetened fruit.

Butter Sauce:
2-1/2 cups sugar
2 cups water

1 stick butter (1/2 cup)
1 teaspoon vanilla extract
dash of salt

Combine ingredients and cook until mixture begins to thicken. Add 1 teaspoon vanilla and a dash of salt. Keep sauce warm. Pour over pieces of sponge cake when ready to serve.

SUGAR-PLUM CAKE

1 cup butter
4 eggs
2 cups sugar
1 teaspoon baking soda,
  dissolved in 1/2 cup
  buttermilk
3-1/2 cups all-purpose flour

1 box dates, cut in small pieces
1 pound candy orange slices, cut
  in small pieces
1 (3-1/2 ounce) can Angel Flake
  coconut
2 cups chopped pecans
Orange Glaze

Combine flour and salt; stir and set aside. Combine orange slices, dates, pecans and coconut; stir in 1/2 cup flour mixture. Set aside.

Cream butter; gradually add sugar, beating until light and fluffy and sugar is dissolved. Add eggs, one at a time, beating well after each addition. Combine buttermilk and soda, mixing well. Add remaining 3 cups flour mixture alternately with buttermilk to creamed mixture, beginning and ending with flour. Add candy mixture; stir until well blended.

Spoon batter into a greased and floured 10" tube pan. Bake at 300 degrees for 2 hours or until cake tests done. Remove from oven to wire rack. While cake is hot punch holes in top of cake, using a toothpick; spoon glaze over top of cake and let cake cool completely before removing from pan.

(Continued)

Orange Glaze: 2 cups powdered sugar
1 cup orange juice, fresh or frozen
Combine orange juice and powdered sugar. Spoon over hot cake.

CHEESECAKES

The basic cheesecake recipe was recorded by a Greek writer in 230 A.D. Athenaeus said, "Take cheese and pound it until smooth and pasty. Put cheese in a sieve. Add honey and flour. Heat in one mass, cool and serve."

George Washington was served a "cheesecake" in Philadelphia more than 200 years ago by an innkeeper's wife by taking some milk "gone badde" as described in her diary, eggs "to make thick," some soft cheese and honey. She spread it over a pan lined with pieces of "hardtack" — a flat, dry, cracker-like bread. She placed it on the hearth, not meaning to let the dessert get the least bit warm. It did, thickening with the time in which she had forgotten it. When she remembered it and went to serve it, full of embarrassment and apologies, Washington raved about how delicious it was. He begged her for another to take to Martha. She did and from those few ingredients and an accidental technique, she created "cheesecake."

Colonial wives used the fresh curd with spices and almonds or candied peels and lemon. They call them "chess pyes." Over the years more and varied recipes were brought to the New World by immigrants. The Italians favored a heavy-bodied cheese "pie" with almonds and citron topped with lattice pastry. Not until 1872 did cheesecake baking as we know it became popular and practical. William Lawrence developed a method to produce cream cheese in Chester, New York. Another New York dairyman created a fine cream cheese that was to become Philadelphia Brand Cream Cheese. These made the cheesecake an American Classic — one to remain a culinary favorite forever.

TIPS FOR CHEESECAKES

1. Use pan size specified in recipe. Cheesecakes can be made in pie pans but are best made in springform pans. They have a removable bottom and are 2" to 3" deep. The spring-lock on the side makes for easy removal and are most commonly used. They can be used for all kinds of cakes, tortes and other desserts.

2. Crusts may be varied according to your likes and dislikes and the flavors of the filling mixture. Shortbread cookies, graham crackers, Zwieback, vanilla or chocolate wafers, gingersnaps, or a sweet pastry all work well for sweet cheesecakes. For an additional variety, add toasted coconut, finely ground nuts or a dash of cinnamon may be added. For savory cheesecakes add zip to the crust with chili powder, dry mustard and sesame seeds.

3. Play it safe, when using a crumb crust, line the outside of the spring-form pan with foil to avoid having any butter or filling leak out.

4. Be sure cheese is at room temperature so that you will have a smooth mixture.

5. Bake cheesecakes in the center of the oven.

6. Test for doneness 5 to 10 minutes before the specified time given in the recipe.

7. After cooking, use a silver knife to loosen the cake from sides of pan as soon as the cake is removed from oven.

8. Do not "Peep" in the oven while baking for at least 1-1/4 hours. Cheesecakes don't take kindly to sudden changes in temperature. Allow cake to cool gradually and wait to reach room temperature before refrigerating it.

LINDY'S FAMOUS CHEESECAKE

1/4 cup soft butter
1 cup sifted all-purpose flour
1/4 cup sugar
1 egg yolk
1 teaspoon grated lemon peel
1/2 teaspoon vanilla
Glaze
Filling:
5 (8-ounce) packages cream
   cheese, softened

1-3/4 cups sugar
3 Tablespoon flour
1-1/2 teaspoons grated lemon peel
1-1/2 teaspoons grated orange
   peel
1/4 teaspoon vanilla extract
5 eggs
2 egg yolks
1/4 cup heavy cream

Combine flour, sugar, lemon peel and vanilla. Make a well in the center of mixture and add 1 egg yolk and butter; mix with fingertips until dough leaves side of bowl. Form a ball of the dough, wrap in wax paper and refrigerate about 1 hour. Preheat oven to 400 degrees. Grease bottom and sides of a 9" springform pan. On bottom of pan form half of dough into a ball. Place waxed paper on top; roll pastry to edge of pan. Remove paper. Bake 6 to 8 minutes; cool. Meanwhile, divide rest of dough into three parts. Roll each part into a strip 2-1/2" wide and about 10" long. Put together springform pan, with baked crust on bottom and fit strips to sides of pan, joining ends of strips to line inside completely. Trim dough so it comes only 3/4 way up side of pan. Refrigerate until ready to fill. Preheat oven to 450 degrees.

In a large bowl of mixer, combine cheese, sugar, flour, lemon and orange peel and vanilla. Beat at high speed until just blended. Beat in eggs and egg yolks, one at a time. Add cream, beating just until well blended. Pour into prepared pan. Bake 10 minutes. Reduce heat to 250 degrees and bake 80 minutes longer. Cool in pan on wire rack. Top with glaze of choice. Serves 16 to 20.

Strawberry Glaze:
1 cup crushed fresh strawberries
1 cup sugar

3 Tablespoon cornstarch
1/4 teaspoon red food coloring
1 quart fresh strawberries

(Continued)

Combine all ingredients in saucepan, except quart of berries. Cook until crystal clear and transparent in color. Wash and hull fresh berries, drain; arrange berries, point up, over cooled cheesecake and spoon glaze over strawberries and cake.

Cherry Glaze:
1 can sour red cherries
1/2 cup sugar
2 Tablespoons cornstarch
1 Tablespoon lemon juice
few drops red food coloring

Drain cherries, reserving liquid; set cherries aside until ready to use. In saucepan combine sugar and cornstarch; add cherry juice, stirring until mixture is smooth. Bring to a boil, stirring over medium heat; boil 1 minute or until mixture is thickened and translucent. Remove from heat; let cool slightly. Add lemon juice, cherries, and coloring. Cool thoroughly before spooning over top of cooled cake. Chill.

Pineapple Glaze:
2 Tablespoons sugar
4 teaspoons cornstarch
2 (8-1/2 ounce) cans crushed pineapple in heavy syrup, undrained
2 Tablespoons lemon juice
few drops yellow food coloring

In saucepan, combine sugar and cornstarch. Stir in remaining ingredients and bring to boil over medium heat, stirring constantly. Boil until thickened and translucent. Cool. Spread top of cheesecake with glaze. Refrigerate until well chilled.

CLANCY'S CHEESECAKE

1/4 cup (1/2 stick) butter, melted
1-1/2 cups graham cracker crumbs
3 Tablespoons sugar
1/2 teaspoon cinnamon
Filling:
3 (8-ounce) packages cream
   cheese, room temperature
1-1/4 cups sugar
6 eggs, separated
1 pint sour cream
1/3 cup all-purpose flour
2 teaspoons vanilla
grated rind of 1 lemon
juice of 1/2 lemon

Generously grease a 9" springform pan with butter. Place pan in center of a 12" square of aluminum foil and press foil up around side of pan. Combine graham cracker crumbs, sugar, cinnamon and melted butter in a small bowl until well blended. Press 3/4 cup of crumb mixture into bottom and sides of pan. Chill pan while making filling (reserve remaining crumb mixture for topping). Beat cream cheese in a large bowl at low speed until soft; gradually add sugar until light and fluffy. Beat in egg yolks, one at a time, until well blended. Stir in sour cream, flour, vanilla, lemon rind and juice until smooth. Beat egg whites until they hold stiff peaks. Fold whites into cheese mixture, souffle-fashion, until well blended. Pour into prepared pan. Bake in moderate oven 350 degrees 1 hour, 15 minutes or until top is golden brown; turn off oven heat and allow cake to cool in oven for 1 hour. Remove cake from oven and allow to cool on wire rack at room temperature. Sprinkle remaining crumbs on top. Chill overnight before serving. Dust with powdered sugar just before serving.

SOUR CREAM, CREAM CHEESE CAKE

1-3/4 cup graham cracker crumbs
(about thirty 2-1/2" square
crackers)
1/4 cup walnuts, chopped fine
1/2 teaspoon cinnamon
1/2 cup melted butter

Filling:
16 ounces cream cheese
1 cup sugar
2 teaspoons vanilla
3 cups sour cream
3 eggs

Mix together crumbs, walnuts, cinnamon and 1/2 cup melted butter; press into an ungreased springform pan. Reserve 3 tablespoons for topping. Soften cream cheese; mix together with sugar. Add eggs one at a time, beating well after each. Add sour cream and vanilla. Blend well. Pour into prepared crust; garnish with reserved crumb mixture. Bake 60 to 65 minutes or until filling has set. Place pan on rack to cool 15 minutes before running a thin knife around sides to loosen crust. Refrigerate until cool or overnight before removing from pan.

May be served plain or with a topping of your choice. Garnish with fresh strawberries, blueberries or strips of lemon and mint leaves.

NOTE: Pecans or almonds may be used in place of walnuts if desired.

ANNA'S CHEESECAKE SUPREME

Crust:
3/4 package graham crackers
2 Tablespoons butter, melted
2 Tablespoons sugar
Filling:
1/2 cup sugar
2 Tablespoons flour

1/4 teaspoon salt
3 (8-ounce) packages of cream
cheese, softened
1 teaspoon vanilla
4 eggs, separated
1 cup heavy cream

Roll crackers into fine crumbs and blend with melted butter and 2 tablespoons sugar. Press mixture into bottom and sides of a 9" springform pan. Blend together 1/2 cup sugar, flour, salt and cream cheese; add vanilla and egg yolks. Mix well. Add heavy cream and mix again. Fold in stiffly beaten egg whites. Pour into pan on top of crumbs and bake in 350 degree oven about 1-1/2 hours or until set in the middle. Cool before serving. Do not "peep" in oven while baking for at least 1-1/4 hours. Loosen around side of pan with a silver knife as soon as cake is removed from oven.

NOTE: A Zwieback Crust is delicious and may be made instead.

Zwieback Crust:
1-1/2 cups (4-ounce package)
     Zwieback toast, crushed
     (found in baby food section)

1/3 cup melted butter or
     margarine
2 Tablespoons sugar
1 teaspoon cinnamon (optional)

Mix crumbs with butter and sugar. Press into the bottom of up sides of a 10" springform pan which has been lightly greased. Chill.

FRANCES'S CHERRY CHEESECAKE

1 loaf style pound cake (Sara Lee
   or Merita) thinly sliced
3 (8-ounce) packages cream
   cheese at room temperature
1/2 pint sour cream
4 eggs, separated
1 cup sugar
2 Tablespoons flour

1 teaspoon vanilla
juice and grated rind of 1/2 lemon
1 large can sour pitted cherries
2 Tablespoons corn starch
red cake coloring (makes it
   prettier)
2/3 cup sugar

Line a springform pan with sliced pound cake; press pieces together so that they form a solid crust. Cream together cream cheese and sour cream; add slightly beaten egg yolks and sugar, blending well. Add flour and vanilla, then lemon juice and rind. Beat egg whites with 1/4 cup sugar until stiff. Fold into creamed mixture. Pour into prepared pan and bake in preheated oven at 275 degrees for 1 hour. Do not open oven during baking. After 1 hour, turn off oven and allow cake to cool in oven for another hour. Remove from oven and cool. Drain cherries. Dissolve cornstarch in cherry juice; add sugar and a few drops red coloring; bring to slow boil, stirring constantly, until mixture clears. Let cool. Spread on cake and place cherries on top. Refrigerate until thoroughly chilled.

CHOCOLATE CHEESECAKE

Crust:
1-1/4 cups graham cracker crumbs
2 Tablespoons sugar
3 Tablespoons melted butter
Filling:
1 cup sugar

1/4 cup cocoa
2 teaspoons vanilla
3 eggs
2 (8-ounce) packages cream
   cheese plus 1 (3-ounce)
   package

Heat oven to 350 degrees. Stir together crumbs and 2 tablespoons sugar; mix in melted butter well. Press mixture evenly in bottom of ungreased 9" springform pan. Bake 10 minutes; cool. Reduce oven temperature to 300 degrees. Beat cream cheese in large mixing bowl. Gradually add 1 cup sugar and cocoa, beating until fluffy. Add vanilla. Beat in eggs one at a time. Pour over crumb mixture. Bake until center is firm, about 1 hour. Cool to room temperature. Spread with topping and refrigerate at least 3 hours. Loosen edge of cheesecake with knife before removing side of pan.

Coconut Pecan Topping:
2 Tablespoons butter
1/3 cup light cream or evaporated
   milk
2 Tablespoons brown sugar

2 egg yolks
1/2 teaspoon vanilla
1/2 cup chopped pecans
1/2 cup flaked coconut

Cook butter, cream, sugar and egg yolks in small saucepan over low heat, stirring constantly, until thickened. Remove from heat and stir in vanilla, pecans and coconut. Cool. Spoon on top of cooled cheesecake. Refrigerate.

DELUXE CHOCOLATE CHEESECAKE

1/2 cup butter, melted
2 (8-1/2 ounce) packages
   chocolate wafer cookies
1/2 teaspoon cinnamon
Filling:
1 cup sugar
4 eggs
3 (8-ounce) packages of cream
   cheese, softened

16 ounces semi-sweet chocolate
1 teaspoon vanilla
2 Tablespoons cocoa
3 cups sour cream
1/4 cup butter, melted
semi-sweet chocolate
whipped cream

Preheat oven to 350 degrees. Crush chocolate wafers and mix with cinnamon and melted butter. Press crumbs firmly into a 9" springform pan; chill. Beat sugar and eggs until fluffy. Add cream cheese and beat until well mixed. Melt chocolate and add to egg mixture. Add vanilla, cocoa and sour cream, beating constantly. Add melted butter and mix well. Pour mixture into chilled crust and bake 45 minutes. Chill overnight. Before serving, pipe with whipped cream and grate semi-sweet chocolate over cream; or top with Cream Topping.

Cream Topping:
3 ounces cream cheese
1/2 cup whipping cream

1/4 cup confectioners' sugar
1 Tablespoon creme de cocoa
   (optional)

In a small electric mixer bowl, cream the cream cheese until soft. Gradually add whipping cream. Mix at high speed to the consistency of stiffly whipped cream. Blend in confectioners' sugar and creme de cocoa. Cover and chill until ready to use. Spread over cooled cake. Grate the semi-sweet chocolate over cream topping.

SWEET GEORGIA PEACH CHEESECAKE
(A Summer Delight)

Crust:
1-1/2 cups vanilla wafer crumbs
   or shortbread cookie crumbs

6 Tablespoons melted butter
1/2 cup finely chopped nuts

Combine all ingredients in a small bowl, mixing well. Press into the bottom and up sides of a 9" springform pan.

Filling:
2 pounds cream cheese, softened
   (four 8-ounce packages)
1-1/3 cups sugar
2 Tablespoons flour
1 teaspoon vanilla extract
1/2 teaspoon almond extract
2 Tablespoons peach brandy
1/4 teaspoon grated lemon peel
2 Tablespoons fresh pureed peaches
5 eggs

2 egg yolks
2 cups peeled, finely chopped
   fresh peaches, drained
Glaze:
2 to 3 peeled, thinly sliced peaches
1/2 cup peach preserved, heated
whipped cream
1 pound fresh peaches, sliced
2 teaspoons fresh lemon juice
2 Tablespoons confectioners'
   sugar

(Continued)

Beat softened cream cheese at medium speed until fluffy. Gradually add sugar; mix well. Scrape down sides of bowl and add flour, vanilla, lemon peel, almond extract, brandy and pureed peaches. Combine well. Add eggs one at a time, then egg yolks. Mix slowly along with pureed peaches. Pour filling into prepared pan. Bake at 500 degrees for 10 minutes. Turn oven down to 250 degrees and bake for about 60 to 90 minutes or until the center is firm to touch. Cool cake at room temperature for one hour. Place in refrigerator to chill.

After the cake has chilled, cover the top of cake with sliced peaches that have been tossed with 2 teaspoons of lemon juice and confectioners' sugar. Design; brush the top with warmed peach preserves. Before serving, ring the outer side with whipped cream, topping cream with slivered almonds, if desired. This is very rich, so it may be sliced in small portions.

SARAH'S COTTAGE-CHEESE CHEESECAKE

graham cracker crumbs
1 pound small curd cream style
    cottage cheese (use as dry as
    possible)
2 (8-ounce) packages cream
    cheese, softened

1-1/2 cups sugar
4 eggs, slightly beaten
1/3 cup cornstarch
2 Tablespoons lemon juice
1 teaspoon vanilla
1/2 cup butter, melted

Grease a 9" springform pan and dust with cracker crumbs. Sieve cottage cheese into large mixing bowl. Add cream cheese and beat at high speed until well blended and creamy. At high speed, blend in sugar then eggs; reduce speed to low and add cornstarch, lemon juice and vanilla. Beat until blended. Add melted butter and sour cream. Blend on low speed. Pour into prepared pan and bake in 325 degree oven about 1 hour and 10 minutes or until firm around the edges. Turn off oven. Let cake stand in the oven for 2 hours. Remove and cool on wire rack. Chill. Remove sides of pan and place on serving plate. This cheesecake freezes well. Serve plain or with fruit or choice of sauce.

COCA COLA CAKE

2 cups unsifted flour
2 cups sugar
2 sticks butter
1 cup Coca Cola
2 eggs, beaten
1/2 cup buttermilk

3 Tablespoons cocoa
1 teaspoon soda
1 teaspoon vanilla
1-1/2 cups small marshmallows
Icing

Sift flour and sugar into a mixing bowl. In a heavy saucepan, mix butter, oil, cocoa and Coca Cola and bring to a boiling point. Pour over dry ingredients, blending well. Dissolve baking soda in buttermilk just before adding to batter along with eggs and vanilla, mixing well. Add marshmallows. This will be a thin batter with marshmallows floating on top. Pour into a well-greased 9x13" pan. Bake 35 to 45 minutes at 350 degrees. Remove from oven and frost immediately. When cool, cut into squares and serve.

(Continued)

Icing:
1 stick butter
1 box powdered sugar
3 Tablespoons cocoa
1 cup chopped nuts
6 Tablespoons Coca Cola

Combine butter, Coca Cola, and cocoa and heat until boiling. Pour over powdered sugar and beat until smooth. Add nuts and spread on cake while cake is still hot.

MINIATURE FRUIT CAKES

1 stick butter
3/4 cups sugar
3 eggs, beaten
3/4 cups all-purpose flour
1/2 teaspoon baking powder
1/2 teaspoon salt
1/2 cup wine, rum or brandy
1/4 cup flour
1 pound dates, chopped
1 pound nuts, chopped
1 pound candied pineapple, chopped
3/4 pound candied cherries, chopped

Cream butter and sugar well; add beaten eggs and beat well. Sift together flour, baking powder and salt and add alternately with rum or brandy, beginning and ending with flour. Dredge chopped fruits and nuts with 1/4 cup flour and add to batter. Mix well. Pour into small baking cups and bake in 300 degree oven for 40 minutes.

SNICKER BAR CAKE SQUARES

1 package German Chocolate
  Cake mix
14 to 16 squares caramels
1 stick butter
3/4 cup to 1 cup chocolate chips
1/3 cup milk
1 cup chopped pecans
1 small can flaked coconut, optional

Melt caramels with butter and milk over low heat, stirring constantly to keep from scorching. Set aside. Prepare cake mix according to directions. Pour one-half of cake mix into a greased 9x13" pan. This is the crust. Bake it for 20 minutes at 350 degrees. Pour melted caramel mixture over baked crust. Sprinkle chocolate chips and nuts (plus optional coconut) over caramel mixture. Spread remaining batter over top. Bake 20 minutes at 350 degrees; then bake 10 minutes longer at 325 degrees. May be iced with Chocolate Icing, or served as is. Cut into squares when cold.

Chocolate Icing:
1 stick butter
1/3 cup milk
3-1/2 Tablespoons cocoa
dash salt
1 box powdered sugar
1 cup chopped nuts

Bring butter, milk, cocoa and salt to a boil over medium heat. Add sugar and nuts. Pour over cake while both are hot.

GRANDMA'S PINEAPPLE UPSIDE DOWN CAKE

It is said that Fannie Farmer made this cake famous. In her day it was a sensation — it still is!

1 can (1 pound, 4-ounce) Dole sliced pineapple in syrup
1/2 stick butter
2/3 cup firmly packed light brown sugar
maraschino cherries
1 cup unsifted all-purpose flour
1-1/2 teaspoons baking powder

1/2 teaspoon salt
3/4 cup sugar
1/2 cup milk
1/4 cup Crisco shortening
1 egg
1/4 teaspoon grated lemon rind
1 teaspoon lemon juice
1 teaspoon vanilla

Drain pineapple, reserving 2 tablespoons syrup. Melt butter in a heavy 10" ovenproof skillet. Stir in brown sugar and 2 tablespoons pineapple syrup; blend thoroughly. Remove from heat. Arrange pineapple slices in sugar mixture. Place a cherry in center of each slice. Combine flour, sugar, baking powder and salt in a large bowl. Add milk and Crisco; beat at high speed with electric mixer, 2 minutes. Add egg, lemon rind, lemon juice and vanilla; beat another 2 minutes. Pour over pineapple in skillet, spreading evenly. Bake in a 350 degree oven for 40 minutes, until cake tests done and is beginning to pull away from sides of skillet. Let cool in skillet for 5 minutes, then turn out on a serving plate. If any bits of pineapple stick to skillet, remove them with a spatula and replace them on top of cake. Serve warm or cold. Serves 8 to 10.

MISSISSIPPI MUD

2 cups sugar
1 cup butter
4 eggs
1-1/2 cups all-purpose flour
1/3 cup cocoa

3 teaspoons vanilla
1 cup nuts, chopped
1/4 teaspoon salt
6 ounces tiny marshmallows

Preheat oven to 350 degrees. Grease and flour a 9x13x2" cake pan; set aside. Cream butter and sugar together until light and fluffy. Beat in eggs, one at a time, beating well after each. Blend in vanilla. Combine flour and cocoa and add to creamed mixture, blending well. Fold in nuts. Spoon batter into prepared pan, spreading evenly. Bake until cake tests done, 30 to 40 minutes. Remove from oven and immediately cover top with miniature marshmallows and frost with chocolate frosting.

Chocolate Frosting:
1 stick butter
1 teaspoon vanilla
1 box powdered sugar

3 Tablespoons cocoa
1/2 cup evaporated milk
1 cup chopped pecans (optional)

Cream butter and vanilla; combine sugar and cocoa and gradually beat into butter mixture, alternating with milk. Continue beating until frosting is light and fluffy, 3 to 5 minutes. Spread over marshmallows on cake. Cool and cut into squares. If desired, sprinkle with additional marshmallows and chopped nuts.

GRANDMOTHER DEVAULT'S ORANGE CAKE

1/2 cup butter
1 cup sugar
1 cup ground seedless raisins
1 orange, peeled and ground
   coarsely
2 eggs, beaten separately

1 teaspoon soda, dissolved in 2/3
   cup buttermilk
2 cups all-purpose flour
juice of 1 orange
1 Tablespoon sugar
think orange slices
whipped cream

Cream butter and sugar until light and fluffy. Add raisins and orange, mixing well. Add 2 beaten egg yolks, mixing well to blend. Add flour and milk-soda mixture alternately. Fold in beaten egg whites. Pour into lightly greased and floured square or rectangular cake pan (12x2x8"). Bake at 350 degrees for 30 minutes. While cake is still hot and in the pan, pour over it the juice of 1 orange with 1 tablespoon sugar dissolved in it. Cool; cut into squares. Top squares with thinly sliced orange slices and a dollop of whipped cream. Cake is very moist. May be served hot.

CHOCOLATE CAKE WITH CHOCOLATE ICING

1 stick margarine
1/2 cup oil
1 cup water
2 cups sugar
1 teaspoon salt
2 cups all-purpose flour

1 teaspoon soda
3 Tablespoons cocoa
2 eggs, beaten
1/2 cup buttermilk
chocolate icing

Mix margarine, oil and water and bring to a boil. Remove from heat and add sugar, salt, flour, soda and cocoa. Mix well, then add eggs and buttermilk. Mix well, then spread in a shallow greased pan. Bake at 350 degrees for 20 minutes. While cake is baking, make icing. When cake tests done, remove from oven and spread icing on hot cake.

Chocolate Icing:
1 box powdered sugar
3 Tablespoons cocoa
1 teaspoon vanilla

1 stick margarine
6 Tablespoons cream or black
   coffee
1 cup chopped nuts

Mix all ingredients together well. Spread on cake while cake is still hot.

FRUITCAKE IN GRAPEFRUIT SHELLS

1 package instant yellow cake mix
1/2 cup applesauce
4 eggs, unbeaten
1 teaspoon salt
1 teaspoon orange extract
2 cups cut dates (about 1 lb.)

1/2 pound candied green
pineapple, cut in narrow
strips
1/2 pound whole red candied
cherries
4 cups walnut halves (1 lb.),
broken
1/2 cup flour

Empty cake mix into bowl; add applesauce, eggs, salt and extract. Beat 3 minutes until smooth and creamy. Combine fruits and nuts, mix well with flour. Stir into batter. Fill candied grapefruit shells almost full. Bake at 275 degrees about 2-1/4 hours. Cool thoroughly. Wrap cakes tightly in moisture-proof cellophane, pliofilm or aluminum foil; store in refrigerator or freezer until ready to use. (Cakes should be stored for 2 to 4 weeks before using to allow fruits to mellow and flavors to blend.) Makes enough to fill 6 large grapefruit shells.

NOTE: You may want to use your own favorite fruitcake recipe.

Grapefruit Shells:

Select large grapefruit of good shape and color. Cut in half, making zig-zag edge. Remove pulp, being careful to leave all the thick part of the peel and not to break the shell. Cover shells with cold, salted water; bring to boil, cook about 10 minutes. Drain off water. Repeat three or four times to remove bitter flavor from peel. Cool. Make a syrup with equal parts of sugar and water. Use enough syrup to float the fruit. Cook to medium thick syrup; let fruit stand in syrup at least 24 hours, turning several times. Return to heat and cook to very thick syrup; remove from syrup and cool. If shells are large, invert each over a small bowl to dry.

CARAMELS

1/2 pound butter/margarine
2 cups sugar
1/2 cup sifted flour

2 cups light corn syrup
2 (15-ounce) cans condensed milk
1 teaspoon vanilla

Melt butter in heavy saucepan; add corn syrup and sugar and boil for 5 minutes over medium heat, stirring constantly. Add 1-1/2 cans of condensed milk. Mix flour thoroughly with remaining 1/2 can of milk; add to syrup-sugar mixture. Cook until mixture darkens and forms a medium hard ball (240 degrees). Stir constantly or mixture will stick! Add vanilla and pour into buttered 9x13x2" pan. Allow to cool and cut into 1" pieces, using a sharp buttered knife.

CARAMEL APPLES

14 ounce bag caramels
2 Tablespoons water

5 medium apples
sticks or spoons

Melt caramels with water over very low heat, stirring occasionally, until smooth. Wash and dry apples. Dip apples into hot caramel, turning until covered. Place to harden on buttered, waxed paper. Cool.

CREAMY DELIGHT PRALINES

2 cups granulated sugar
1 cup light brown sugar
1 small can evaporated milk
1/2 cup milk or light cream
1/2 teaspoon salt

5 Tablespoons butter/margarine
4 Tablespoons light corn syrup
1 teaspoon vanilla flavoring
2 cups pecan halves

Mix all ingredients except flavoring and pecans in saucepan. Place over low heat and cook to 236 degrees (soft ball). Stir frequently during cooking to prevent sticking. Remove from heat and allow to stand five minutes without stirring. Add flavoring and beat until mixture loses its gloss. If candy appears to be curdling, the beating will clear it. Add pecans and drop candy from tablespoon in patties onto waxed paper. Let stand until cold.

NOTE: If mixture becomes too hard to drop, set pan in hot water to soften a bit.

STUFFED DATES

pecans   granulated sugar
bourbon   dates

Soak whole nuts in bourbon overnight. Stuff marinated nuts into dates and roll date in granulated sugar. Store in tight-fitting cake tin.

CHOCOLATE COVERED CHERRIES #1

2 pounds sifted confectioners'   12 ounces semi-sweet chocolate
   sugar   chips
2 sticks soft margarine/butter   1/2 block paraffin
1 teaspoon vanilla   4 medium jars maraschino
                               cherries

Mix butter until fluffy; add sugar and vanilla. Drain cherries well. Wrap about 1 teaspoon of the butter/sugar mix around cherries; allow to chill for 4 hours. Melt wax, a teaspoon of butter, and chocolate chips in double boiler. Dip cherries into chocolate mixture. Makes 85 to 100 chocolate covered cherries.

CHOCOLATE COVERED CHERRIES #2

2/3 cup butter/margarine   36 maraschino cherries,
2 cups marshmallow creme   well-drained and dried with
dash of salt   paper towels
1 teaspoon almond extract   12 ounces semi-sweet chocolate
4 cups sifted powdered sugar   morsels
                            1 block paraffin

Cream butter; beat in marshmallow creme, salt and almond extract. Add powdered sugar gradually, mixing well after each addition. Turn out and knead until smooth, working in extra powdered sugar if mixture becomes too sticky; refrigerate 1 hour. Wrap each cherry in marshmallow mixture, making sure to completely cover; refrigerate. Melt chocolate and paraffin in top of double boiler over hot, not boiling, water. Using toothpicks or cherry stems, dip cherries into melted chocolate, then place on waxed paper. Close the holes left by toothpicks with a dribble of hot chocolate. Refrigerate until chocolate hardens; store. Fondant will not liquify until cherries are removed from refrigeration for a day or so.

MARTHA WASHINGTON CREAMS

2 pounds sifted confectioners'
  sugar
1 stick butter/margarine
1 can condensed milk
1 teaspoon vanilla

1 pinch salt
1 can (1 cup) Angel Flake coconut
2 to 4 cups finely chopped pecans
12 ounces chocolate chips
1/3 cake paraffin

Melt butter slowly and add condensed milk. Stir in sugar and salt. Add coconut, pecans, and vanilla. Chill until mixture can be easily handled. Roll into balls, insert a toothpick and place in refrigerator or freezer until firm. Melt chocolate and paraffin together in top of double boiler. Remove candy from chocolate quickly and place on wax paper. Take a small number of balls from refrigerator at a time to prevent them from getting soft.

DATE NUT BALLS

2 sticks margarine/butter
16 ounces chopped dates
2 cups light brown sugar
1 can Angel Flake coconut

2 cups chopped nuts
4 cups Rice Krispies
confectioners sugar

Mix margarine, dates, brown sugar, and coconut; cook 6 minutes, stirring constantly. Remove from heat and add nuts and Rice Krispies. Shape into balls and roll in confectioners sugar.

NO-COOK DIVINITY

1 package fluffy white frosting
  mix
2/3 cup white corn syrup
1 teaspoon vanilla

1/2 cup boiling water
1 box powdered sugar
1 cup nuts

Combine frosting, syrup, vanilla and water. Beat on high until stiff peaks form. Transfer to large bowl and gradually blend in sugar. Continue beating with mixer until very thick. Add nuts and drop by teaspoonful onto waxed paper. Allow to stand 5 to 6 hours until dry, then turn and let the other side dry.

FOOLPROOF CHOCOLATE FUDGE

18 ounces semi-sweet chocolate
chips
1 can Eagle Brand Condensed
Milk (not evaporated milk)

dash of salt
1-1/2 teaspoons vanilla extract
1/4 cup chopped nuts, optional

In heavy saucepan, melt chips with condensed milk over low heat. Remove from heat and stir in remaining ingredients. Spread evenly into wax paper-lined 8" square pan. Chill 2 to 3 hours until firm. Turn fudge onto cutting board, peel off paper, and cut into squares. Store loosely covered at room temperature.

To cook in microwave:

Combine semi-sweet chocolate morsels and condensed milk in large glass measuring cup. Microwave on high for 3 minutes. Stir until morsels melt and mixture is smooth. Stir in walnuts and vanilla extract. Spread evenly into foil-lined 8" square pan and chill until firm (about 2 hours). Makes about 1-1/4 pounds of fudge.

MS. C'S FUDGE

4-1/2 cups sugar
15-1/2 ounces evaporated milk
3 cups semi-sweet chocolate chips

1 cup butter
2 cups chopped walnuts
1 Tablespoon vanilla extract

Butter a 9x13" baking pan. Combine sugar and evaporated milk in a large, heavy saucepan. Bring to a rolling boil, stirring constantly, and boil for 6 minutes. Remove from heat and quickly add remaining ingredients. Stir until chips are melted and pour into prepared pan. Yield: 4 pounds.

JUDY'S FUDGE RING

6-ounce package Nestles
semi-sweet chocolate morsels
6-ounce package Nestles
butterscotch morsels

1 can Eagle Brand condensed
milk
1 cup chopped pecans

Mix chocolate and butterscotch morsels with condensed milk and cook until thickened. On aluminum foil, arrange pecans in a round circle. Spoon fudge out onto pecans, and place the candy in refrigerator to cool until firm. When candy has hardened, flip out and over onto a plate and cut into pieces.

CLOUD-TOPPED
PEANUT BUTTER FUDGE

1 cup evaporated milk	1/2 cup firmly packed brown
2 cups sugar	sugar
1 teaspoon salt	6 measuring Tablespoons butter
1/4 cup butter	1/2 cup corn syrup
12 ounces Nestle peanut butter	2 cups sifted confectioners' sugar
morsels	1 cup walnuts, chopped

In heavy gauge saucepan, combine evaporated milk, sugar, salt and butter. Bring to a boil over moderate heat; boil 8 minutes, stirring constantly. Remove from heat and add Nestle peanut butter morsels. Stir until morsels melt and mixture is smooth. Spread into foil-lined 9" square pan and chill 30 minutes. In heavy gauge saucepan, combine brown sugar, butter and corn syrup; stir until smooth. Bring to a boil and remove from heat. Add confectioners' sugar and walnuts, stirring until well blended. Spread over peanut butter fudge layer. Chill until firm (about 2 hours). Makes about 3-1/4 pounds of fudge.

NO-COOK QUICK
PEANUT BUTTER FUDGE

1/3 cup margarine	1 teaspoon vanilla
1/2 cup corn syrup	4-1/2 cups sifted confectioners'
3/4 cup creamy or chunk style	sugar
peanut butter	3/4 cup chopped pecans
1/2 teaspoon salt	

Blend margarine, corn syrup, peanut butter, salt and vanilla in large mixing bowl. Stir in sifted confectioners' sugar gradually. Turn onto board and knead until well blended and smooth. Add nuts gradually, pressing and kneading into candy. Press out with hands or rolling pin into square 1/2" thick. Cut into serving pieces. Makes about 2 pounds of fudge.

MINTS

1 stick butter/margarine	1 box 4x sugar
2 Tablespoons Eagle Brand	3 or 4 drops oil of peppermint
condensed milk	food coloring

Creamy butter; add milk, sugar and peppermint. Roll and cut.

PULLED MINTS

2 cups sugar
2/3 cup water
1/4 teaspoon oil of peppermint

1/2 stick butter
pinch of salt

Combine sugar, water, butter, oil of peppermint and cook to 265 degrees. Pour on buttered marble. Pull like taffy candy. Cut off sections with scissors; store in air-tight container until creamy for several days.

WHITE CONFETTI FUDGE

1-1/2 pounds confectioners'
coating*
14 ounces Eagle Brand condensed
milk
1/8 teaspoon salt

1 teaspoon vanilla
1 cup chopped cherries
*Purchase in candy specialty
stores

*Melt confectioners' coating with condensed milk, remove from heat. Stir salt, vanilla and cherries. Spread evenly onto wax paper-lined 8" square pan and chill 2 to 3 hours until firm. Turn onto cutting board, peel paper off and cut into squares. Makes about 2-1/2 pounds.

KENTUCKY KERNELS

1/2 pound soft butter/margarine
2 boxes 10x sugar
1 cup finely chopped pecans

DIP: 5 squares bitter chocolate
1/3 cake paraffin

Soak nuts in enough bourbon to cover for at least 3 days. If allowed to sit in bourbon several weeks, nuts will absorb all the liquid. Mix nuts and 10x sugar and roll into very small balls. Melt bitter chocolate with paraffin; using a hat pin, dip balls into mixture.

PEANUT BRITTLE

3 cups granulated sugar
1/3 cup water
1 Tablespoon butter/margarine
2 teaspoon baking soda

3 cups white Karo syrup
3 cups raw shelled peanuts
1 teaspoon salt

Boil sugar, Karo and water until hot enough to spin a thread (300 degrees on candy thermometer). Add peanuts and stir constantly until mixture turns golden brown. Remove from heat, add salt and soda and pour onto a buttered pan to cool. Break into pieces.

POPCORN BALLS

2 cups sugar	1 teaspoon vinegar
1-1/2 cups water	1 teaspoon vanilla
1/2 teaspoon salt	5 quarts popped corn
1/2 cup light corn syrup	15 to 20 candy canes

Butter sides of saucepan. Combine sugar, water, salt, syrup and vinegar. Cook to hard ball stage (250 degrees). Stir in vanilla; slowly pour mixture over popped corn, stirring just to mix well. Butter hands lightly; shape popcorn into balls around the candy canes. Makes about 20 small or 15 large balls.

REESE PEANUT BUTTER CUPS

1-1/2 cups Graham cracker crumbs	1 box confectioners' sugar
	3/4 cup butter/margarine
1-1/3 cups peanut butter	18 ounces semi-sweet chocolate

Melt margarine and peanut butter in a large pan; add cracker crumbs and sugar. Mix well and roll into small balls. (Refrigerate for an hour or two to make them easier to handle.) Melt chocolate chips and paraffin in pan over low heat. Dip balls into mixture, one at a time on a toothpick. Place on wax paper to set.

ROCKY ROAD CANDY

8 ounce milk chocolate bar, broken in pieces	2 cups miniature marshmallows
	3/4 cup broken walnuts
6 ounces semi-sweet chocolate chips	

Melt chocolate over very low heat. Spread 1/3 of the melted chocolate in buttered or wax paper-lined 8" square pan. Add walnuts and marshmallows, pressing them into the chocolate. Cover with the remaining chocolate; spread to cover marshmallows. Refrigerate until firm but not hard. Cut into squares and return to refrigerator to chill thoroughly. Makes about 3 dozen squares.

STRAWBERRY FAKES

1 can condensed milk	1 package red sugar
3 3-ounce packages strawberry gelatin	1 package slivered almonds
	green food coloring
1 cup pecans, chopped	1/2 Tablespoon water
1 can Angel Flake coconut	

Blend together condensed milk, gelatin, pecans and coconut. Chill in refrigerator for 2 days. Roll dough into shape of strawberries. Roll "strawberries" into red sugar. Soak almond slivers in 2 drops green food coloring and 1/2 tablespoon water. Use green almond slivers for strawberry stems. Makes 2 to 3 dozen.

A COOKIE OR A KISS

A house should have a cookie jar,
For when it's half-past three
And children hurry home from
   school
As hungry as can be,
There's nothing quite so splendid
For filling children up
As spicy, fluffy ginger cakes
And sweet milk from a cup.

A house should have a mother,
Waiting with a hug
No matter what a boy brings
   home...
A puppy or a bug;
For children only loiter
When the bell rings to dismiss
If no one's home to greet them
With a cookie or a kiss.

BERLINER KRANSER
(CHRISTMAS WREATHS)

1/2 cup sugar
2-1/2 cups all-purpose flour
1 cup butter

2 egg yolks
2 teaspoons grated orange peel
1/4 teaspoon salt

Measure 1/2 cup sugar into a large bowl; add flour, butter, egg yolks, orange peel and salt. Beat at low speed, then increase to medium speed for 4 minutes. Roll teaspoons of dough into 6" ropes. To form wreaths, cross ropes. Brush with beaten egg white, then sprinkle with sugar. Press pieces of green and red cherries on each. Bake at 400 degrees for 10 to 12 minutes. Cool on cookie sheet. Makes 4-1/2 dozen cookies.

CHEESE DIAMONDS

Rich, tender fold-overs with a marvelous cream cheese filling

1 sweet dough recipe
1 package (8 ounces) cream
   cheese, softened
1/4 cup sugar
3 Tablespoons flour

1 egg yolk
1/2 teaspoon grated lemon peel
1 Tablespoon lemon juice
1/2 cup favorite jam
chopped nuts

Prepare dough for filling, beat cream cheese and sugar until light and fluffy. Stir in flour, egg yolk, lemon peel and juice. Roll dough on lightly floured board into a 15" square; cut into twenty-five 3" squares. Place on greased baking sheet; spoon 1 tablespoon cheese mixture in center of each square. Bring two diagonally opposite corners to the center of each square, overlapping corners slightly; pinch together. Cover and allow to rise until double (approximately 30 minutes). Preheat oven to 375 degrees. Bake 12 minutes. Heat jam separately until melted. Brush jam lightly over hot rolls and sprinkle with nuts. Makes 25 rolls.

CHRISTMAS BELLS

3 cups sifted flour
1 teaspoon cinnamon
1/2 teaspoon soda
1/2 teaspoon salt
1-1/4 cups firmly packed brown
    sugar

1 cup shortening
1/4 cup dark corn syrup
1 unbeaten egg
1 Tablespoon cream

Sift together flour, cinnamon, soda, salt...set aside. Cream together shortening and sugar, creaming well. Blend in dark corn syrup, unbeaten egg and cream, mixing well. Add dry ingredients and mix thoroughly. Roll out on a floured surface, using approximately 1/3 of the mixture at a time. Roll to 1/8" thickness and cut into 2-1/2" circles. Place on ungreased cookie sheet and spoon 1/2 teaspoon of nut filling into center of each circle. Shape into a "bell" by folding sides to meet over the filling. Make top of bell narrower than "clapper" end. Place half a maraschino cherry at the open end for a clapper. Bake at 350 degrees for 12 to 15 minutes.

Nut Filling:
1/3 cup brown sugar
1 Tablespoon butter

3 Tablespoons maraschino cherry
    juice
1-1/2 cups finely chopped pecans

Combine sugar, butter and cherry juice and mix well. Add finely chopped nuts.

CHRISTMAS COOKIES
(A FAVORITE)

3 cups all-purpose flour
1 teaspoon baking powder
3/4 teaspoon salt
1/2 cup Crisco

1-1/2 cups sugar
2 eggs
1-1/2 teaspoons vanilla
1 Tablespoon milk

Sift flour and measure; add baking powder and salt; sift again. Cream shortening and sugar together until light and fluffy. Add eggs one at a time, beating well after each. Stir in vanilla and milk. Add dry ingredients and mix until well blended. Wrap dough in wax paper and chill about two hours. On lightly floured board, roll out dough 1/8" thick; cut out in choice of shapes. Bake on greased cookie sheet at 375 degrees for 8 to 10 minutes. Cool thoroughly on rack. Frost cookies with Ornamental Frosting.

For Candy Cane Cookies: Make the dough as directed; before chilling, divide dough and add 1/2 teaspoon red food coloring to half of the mixture. After chilling, pinch pieces and roll into ropelike strips 6" long and 1/2" thick. Make canes, laying one red and one white strip together; starting in the middle, twist the two strips together to each end. Bend to resemble cane and bake as directed. Sprinkle hot canes with crushed peppermint candy.

CHOCOLATE COVERED CHERRY COOKIES

1/2 cup semi-sweet chocolate
chips
1/2 cup firmly packed light
brown sugar
1/2 cup sugar, white
1/4 cup butter or margarine,
softened

2 eggs, separated
1 cup all-purpose flour
1/2 teaspoon baking powder
1 (16 ounce) jar maraschino
cherries, well drained,
reserving juice
pecans, finely ground

Heat oven to 350 degrees. Melt 1/2 cup chocolate chips in a small saucepan over low heat, stirring constantly. In a small mixing bowl, cream sugars and margarine or butter until light and fluffy. Beat egg yolks. Add egg yolks and melted chips to the creamed mixture, mixing well. Lightly spoon flour into measuring cup, level off. Sift flour and baking powder together. Add to creamed mixture. Add 2 tablespoons cherry juice. Beat egg whites until stiff. Fold into batter.

Sprinkle nuts in the bottom of greased miniature muffin pans or miniature muffin paper cups placed in miniature pans. Add 1 teaspoon batter, then 1 cherry, topping with another teaspoon of batter. Bake at 350 degrees 10 to 14 minutes or until set. Remove, cool and frost with frosting. Makes 3 to 4 dozen cookies.

Frosting:
1/2 cup semi-sweet chocolate
chips

2 teaspoons butter or margarine
maraschino cherry juice

In a small saucepan, melt 1/2 cup chocolate chips and 2 teaspoons margarine or butter over low heat until smooth, stirring constantly. Add enough cherry juice until frosting is of desired dipping consistency. Beat until smooth. Dip cooled cookies into the frosting or spoon on top of cookies.

NOTE: These go like hot cakes. If any are left, they freeze well.

ORNAMENTAL FROSTING

1 egg white
1-1/4 cups sifted confectioners'
sugar

1/4 teaspoon vanilla
few drops of water
desired food coloring

Beat egg white until stiff but not dry; add sifted sugar and vanilla; blend well. Stir in a few drops of water until mixture is a good spreading consistency. To pipe through a decorating tube, add a little more sugar. Add food color desired to small quantities of the frosting, adding more sugar if needed.

Light brown frosting: blend in small amount of instant coffee or a little chocolate frosting.

Dark brown chocolate frosting: make the above recipe, using 1 cup sifted confectioners' sugar with 1/4 cup cocoa; add a few more drops of water to obtain spreading consistency.

CHUNKY CHOCOLATE PECAN COOKIES

2/3 cup butter or margarine at
   room temperature
2/3 cup sugar, granulated
1/2 cup dark brown sugar, packed
1 large egg
1 teaspoon vanilla
1-1/2 cups all-purpose flour

3 bars (3 ounces each) dark Swiss
   chocolate, chopped into 1/2"
   pieces or 9 ounces semisweet
   chocolate chunks (1-3/4 cups)
2/3 cups (3 ounces) coarsely
   chopped pecans

Preheat oven to 325 degrees. Lightly grease two 17x14" cookie sheets. In a large bowl of electric mixer, beat butter, sugars, egg and vanilla at medium speed until fluffy. Reduce mixer speed to low, add flour, increasing speed gradually and beat just until blended. Stir in chocolate and pecans. Drop by heaping tablespoons of dough 2-1/2" apart on the prepared cookie sheets. Bake one sheet at a time for 15 to 17 minutes or until edges are slightly brown and the tops look dry. Cool on a wire rack for about 5 minutes. Makes about 22 cookies.

RAISIN CHOCOLATE CHIP COOKIES

2 cups (4 sticks) margarine,
   softened
3/4 cup firmly packed brown
   sugar
3/4 cup granulated sugar
1 teaspoon vanilla
1 teaspoon water
2 medium size eggs

2-1/2 cups sifted, all-purpose flour
1 teaspoon baking powder
1/2 teaspoon salt
2 cups raisins
1 (12-ounce) package semisweet
   chocolate pieces
1/2 cup nuts, chopped (optional)

Beat softened margarine, brown and white sugars, vanilla, water and eggs in a large mixing bowl with electric mixer until creamy and thoroughly blended. By hand, stir in flour, baking soda and salt until well mixed. Stir in raisins and chocolate pieces, also nuts. Using a teaspoon, spoon dough by teaspoonfuls onto cookie sheets. Allow 1 to 1-1/2" between cookies for spreading. Bake in a moderate oven at 375 degrees for 8 minutes, or until cookies are nicely browned, depending on how crisp or well done you like them. Makes about 6 dozen cookies.

CRESCENTS NUT FINGERS

1/2 cup butter
1/2 cup powdered sugar
2 cups flour

1 teaspoon vanilla
1-1/2 cups nuts
1/4 teaspoon salt

Cream butter, add sugar, salt and vanilla. Add flour gradually. Add nuts and mix well. Place in refrigerator to chill thoroughly. Cut off small pieces and shape. Bake in very slow oven (200 degrees). Bake for 30 to 40 minutes. Roll in sifted powdered sugar.

COCOA-NUT BALLS

(A crisp, buttery, wonderful holiday cookie)

1 cup butter or margarine	1/4 cup Hershey's Cocoa
1/2 cup sugar	1/2 teaspoon salt
2 teaspoons vanilla	2 cups finely chopped pecans
2 cups sifted all-purpose flour	confectioners' sugar

Preheat oven to 325 degrees. Cream butter or margarine, sugar and vanilla together until fluffy. Sift flour, cocoa and salt together; add to creamed mixture, blending thoroughly. Add pecans and mix well. Shape into 1" balls and place on ungreased baking sheet. Bake approximately 20 minutes; do not brown. Cool, then roll in confectioners' sugar. Yield: about 6 dozen cookies.

CONFETTI COOKIES

1 cup butter	1 teaspoon soda
1 cup white sugar	1 cup coconut
1 cup brown sugar	1 cup gumdrops, cut fine (no
2 eggs, beaten	black)
2 cups oatmeal	2 teaspoons baking powder
2-1/2 cups plain flour, sifted	1 teaspoon vanilla

Cream butter and sugars well. Add eggs and blend well. Add dry ingredients and mix until smooth. Add coconut, oatmeal, gumdrops and vanilla last. Drop by spoonfuls on cookie sheet and bake in 400 degree oven until lightly brown. These cookies freeze well.

DIPPED COOKIES

2 sticks margarine, melted	1/2 cup peanut butter
1 box or bag graham cracker	1 box 4X sugar
crumbs	1 teaspoon vanilla
1 cup Angel Flake coconut	1/2 block paraffin
1 cup chopped nuts	1 large package chocolate chips

Mix all ingredients (except paraffin and chocolate chips) well, using hands. Shape into balls about the size of walnuts (squeeze hard). Melt 1/2 block of paraffin and 1 large package chocolate chips in top of double boiler. Dip balls in chocolate mixture and place on waxed paper. Store in air tight container. Cookies will keep 3 to 4 weeks and improve with age.

FORGOTTEN COOKIES

2 egg whites   6-ounce package chocolate chips
3/4 cup sugar   1 cup chopped nuts
1 teaspoon vanilla   pinch of salt

Separate eggs and beat whites until stiff. Continue beating as sugar is added until whites are thick and heavy. Add pinch of salt and vanilla. Fold in chocolate and nuts. Drop by teaspoons on two large cookie sheets. Place cookie sheets in oven preheated to 350 degrees. IMMEDIATELY turn off oven. Leave until the following morning. These cookies can be made at night, as they are not much trouble. No need to grease cookie sheets.

GINGERSNAPS

1-1/2 sticks butter   1 teaspoon cinnamon
1 cup sugar   1/2 teaspoon salt
1 egg   2 teaspoons soda
1/4 cup molasses   2-1/2 cups plain flour
1 Tablespoon ground ginger

Cream the butter and gradually add sugar. Beat until light. Beat in egg and molasses, then little by little blend in sifted dry ingredients. Form into small balls, roll in more granulated sugar and place on ungreased cookie sheet about 2" apart. Bake at 350 degrees for 10 to 12 minutes.

GUMDROP COOKIES

2-1/2 cups brown sugar   20 orange slice gum drops (chopped)
4 whole eggs, beaten   2 cups nuts
2 cups flour   1 teaspoon lemon extract

Add 1/2 flour to 1/2 cup sugar and mix. Add nuts and orange slices (chopped), eggs and add remainder of sugar and flour. Add extract. Pour into well-greased baking pan and bake in 250 degree oven for 50 to 60 minutes. Cut into small squares and dust with powdered sugar. Cookies are better 2 to 3 days after baking.

JAM POCKETS
(AUSTRIA)

1 (8-ounce) package cream cheese   1 cup margarine
1/4 teaspoon salt   2 cups sifted flour
3 Tablespoons sugar   apricot jam

Combine cream cheese, salt, sugar and margarine, creaming well. Work in flour. Chill several hours or overnight, then divide dough into thirds. Roll out one division at a time on a well-floured board to about 1/8" thick. Cut into 3" squares. Place 1/2 teaspoon apricot jam in center of each square, then fold corners to overlap in center, enclosing jam. Bake on greased cookie sheet at 350 degrees for about 16 to 18 minutes or until golden brown.

JITTERBUGS (YEE-ter-bugs)

(A cookie from Sweden)

1-1/2 cups sifted all-purpose flour
2 teaspoons baking powder
1/2 teaspoon salt
1/2 cup butter
3/4 cup sugar
1 unbeaten egg
2 Tablespoons light cream

1/2 teaspoon vanilla
Meringue:
1 egg white
1/8 teaspoon salt
2 Tablespoons sugar
1-1/2 teaspoons cinnamon

Make meringue, beating egg white and salt together until slight mounds form when beater is raised. Gradually add sugar and beat well after each addition. When meringue stands in stiff glossy peaks, add cinnamon and blend well. Spread on cookie dough before rolling up. For cookie dough, sift flour, baking powder and salt together. Cream butter and sugar together well, then add egg yolk, cream and vanilla. Beat well, then blend in dry ingredients gradually. Roll out on floured surface to a rectangle 16x9". Spread with meringue, leaving about 1" of dough uncovered along one edge. Cut crosswise into four strips. Roll each as for jelly roll, starting with 4" side and rolling toward uncovered edge. Chill for 30 minutes for easier handling. Cut into 1/4" slices and place on greased cookie sheet (dip knife in warm water occasionally for easier cutting). Bake at 400 degrees for 8 to 10 minutes until light brown. Remove from cookie sheet immediately.

LEMON JEWEL TEA COOKIES

1-2/3 cups all-purpose flour
1/3 cup powdered sugar
1 cup butter or margarine, softened
1 teaspoon vanilla
Filling:
1 egg, beaten
2/3 cup sugar

2 to 3 teaspoons grated lemon peel
1 teaspoon cornstarch
1/4 teaspoon salt
3 Tablespoons lemon juice
1 Tablespoon butter or margarine
powdered sugar to dust

Lightly spoon flour into measuring cup; level off. In a medium bowl, combine flour, sugar, margarine or butter and vanilla, blending well. Roll into a ball and chill well. Heat oven to 350 degrees. Shape dough into 1" balls. Place 2" apart on an ungreased cookie sheet. With thumb or forefinger, make an imprint in the center of each cookie. Bake 8 to 10 minutes until lightly browned. Cool.

In a medium saucepan, combine beaten egg, sugar, lemon juice, lemon peel, cornstarch, salt and butter. Cook over low heat, stirring constantly until smooth and thickened. Cool. Top each cookie with about 1/4 teaspoon of filling. Sprinkle with powdered sugar. Store in a single layer, loosely covered. Makes 3 dozen cookies.

JEFFERSON'S BACHELOR BUTTONS

2/3 cup butter or margarine
1-3/4 cups sugar
2 eggs, well beaten
1/2 teaspoon vanilla

3 cups flour
2 teaspoons baking powder
1/2 teaspoon salt
maraschino cherries (garnish)

Preheat oven to 425 degrees. Cream butter with sugar until light and fluffy. Stir in well-beaten eggs; add vanilla. Sift flour, salt and baking powder together, then stir into creamed mixture. Mix thoroughly. Drop by teaspoons onto greased cookie sheet. Garnish top of each "button" with half a cherry. Bake 8 to 10 minutes or until lightly browned. Makes about 3 dozen cookies.

LEMON MERINGUES

2 egg whites
3/4 cup sugar

1/4 teaspoon lemon juice
1/4 teaspoon grated lemon zest

Beat egg whites in a bowl until very stiff. Slowly beat in sugar. Mix in lemon juice and zest. Drop mounded teaspoonfuls of mixture onto cookie sheets lined with aluminum foil (or pipe out with a pastry bag). Place in a preheated 350 degree oven and immediately turn off heat. Leave in oven at least 6 hours or overnight. Do not open oven door during this time. Makes about 36 cookies.

LINZER COOKIES

2 cups sifted flour
1/2 cup powdered sugar
1/4 teaspoon baking soda
1/2 cup unsalted butter
1 egg yolk, slightly beaten

1/4 teaspoon vanilla
1/4 teaspoon grated lemon peel
1/4 cup sugar
1/4 cup finely chopped walnuts

Mix together nuts and granulated sugar and set aside for topping cookies. Into a large bowl sift together flour, powdered sugar and baking soda. Work unsalted butter into dry ingredients by pressing against bottom and sides of bowl with fork; chill and cut into small pieces. Gradually add to this, mixing with a fork after each addition, the egg yolk, vanilla and grated lemon peel. Gather dough into a ball and turn out onto a lightly floured surface. Work with hands, squeezing dough until well blended. Shape into very smooth ball (chill if too soft). Roll out 1/4" thick on lightly floured wax paper; cut out cookies, 1 round cookie and 1 scalloped cookie, using a thimble to cut a small hole in the scalloped cookie (after the cookie is placed on cookie sheet). Brush lightly with beaten egg and sprinkle nuts on the scalloped cookies. Bake 15 to 20 minutes until golden brown. Remove cookies very carefully from cookie sheet and cool. Top whole cookies with thick jam, then add scalloped cookie on top for a cookie sandwich. Sprinkle with confectioners' sugar. Makes 1-1/2 dozen.

OATMEAL-FRUITCAKE COOKIES

3/4 cup shortening	1 cup sifted all-purpose flour
1 cup brown sugar	1 teaspoon salt
1/2 cup granulated sugar	1/2 teaspoon soda
1 egg	3 cups oats
1/4 cup water	3/4 cups candied fruit

Beat first 6 ingredients until creamy. Sift dry ingredients and add to creamed mixture. Stir in oats and fruit. Drop by teaspoon onto greased cookie sheet. Bake at 350 degrees. Yields 5 dozen cookies.

MACADAMIA NUT COOKIES

The macadamia nut is luxurious in every sense. The crop flourishes in tropical climates of Hawaii, Australia and South America. The golden round nut has a rich and creamy flavor. It's buried inside an unusually hard shell, which explains why the nut is almost always sold ready to eat. The delicate meat spoils quickly making vacuum packing and home refrigeration necessary after opening.

3/4 cup unsalted butter, slightly softened	1/4 teaspoon salt
1/2 cup packed light brown sugar	3 Tablespoons sugar
8 ounces white chocolate	1 large egg
1-1/2 cups flour	1 teaspoon vanilla extract
3/4 teaspoon baking powder	1/2 cup coarsely chopped,
1/2 teaspoon baking soda	unsalted, macadamia nuts

Place butter in a heavy, medium sized saucepan over low heat and heat until butter boils and bubbles gently but steadily. DO NOT let butter burn; continue simmering uncovered for 4 to 5 minutes or until golden but not browned, stirring frequently. Be careful not to burn the butter. Immediately remove pan from heat and stir in brown sugar. Pour into a large mixing bowl and refrigerate 50 to 60 minutes until mixture is solid, but is not hard. Preheat oven to 350 degrees. Grease several baking sheets and set aside. Grate 3 ounces of the chocolate. Coarsely chop the remaining chocolate; set the two aside separately.

Thoroughly stir together flour, baking powder, baking soda and salt and set aside. Remove bowl from the refrigerator and beat cooled butter-brown sugar mixture until lightened. Add granulated sugar; beat until fluffy and smooth. Beat in egg and vanilla. Beat in dry ingredients. Add grated chocolate and half of the chopped chocolate and the nuts. Stir until well combined. Roll dough into generous 1-1/2" balls. Dip top of each ball in chopped white chocolate, pressing lightly to imbed some pieces in the dough. Space balls, chocolate-studded tops up, about 2-1/4" apart on baking sheets. Press down balls slightly by hand.

Place on center rack of oven and bake 9 to 10 minutes or until just tinged with brown. Be careful NOT TO OVERBAKE!! Remove from oven and let stand 4 to 5 minutes. Using a spatula, transfer cookie to a wire rack to cool. Store in an airtight container. Makes about 2 dozen 3" cookies. Well worth the trouble for extra special occasions!!

ORIENTAL GLAZED ALMOND COOKIES

1 cup butter or margarine, softened	1/2 teaspoon salt
	2 eggs, separated
1 cup sugar	1/2 teaspoon vanilla
2-2/3 cups sifted cake flour	1/2 teaspoon almond extract
1/2 teaspoon baking soda	4 dozen whole almonds

Cream butter; gradually add sugar, beating until light and fluffy. Add egg yolks and flavorings, beating well. Sift flour, baking powder and salt. Add to butter mixture, stirring well to mix. Shape dough into 1-inch balls and place 2 inches apart on a greased cookie sheet. Place an almond on top of each cookie and press down. Beat egg whites slightly and brush over cookies. Bake at 350 degrees for 13 minutes. Cool on rack. Makes 4 dozen cookies.

M&M COOKIES

1 cup shortening	2-1/4 cups sifted all-purpose flour
1 cup brown sugar	1 teaspoon baking soda
1/2 cup granulated sugar	1 teaspoon salt
2 eggs	1-1/2 cups M&M plain candy
2 teaspoons vanilla	

Cream shortening, sugars, eggs and vanilla together. Sift together the flour, soda and salt. Add dry ingredients gradually to creamed mixture. Stir in 1/2 cup of M&M candies, reserving remainder for decoration. Drop by teaspoons onto ungreased cookie sheet and bake at 375 degrees for 10 to 12 minutes

MOLASSES COOKIES

1 pound brown sugar	1 teaspoon salt
1/2 quart molasses	1 teaspoon soda
1/2 pint Crisco shortening	1/4 pint boiling water
2 teaspoons ginger	approximately 2 pounds plain
2 teaspoons cinnamon	flour, sifted
1/2 teaspoon cloves	

Mix all ingredients, adding flour last. Make a stiff dough, using about 2 pounds of flour. Roll very thin, cut and bake on greased cookie sheet at 350 degrees for about 8 minutes. Cool and store in tins.

NOTE: Although this recipe is at least 150 years old, it can be made today using the original proportions. The cookies are very crisp when first made, but become soft and mellow when stored in airtight cookie tins. The dough can also be used for gingerbread men. Unbaked dough can be covered and refrigerated for baking several days later. For less cookies, half the recipe.

PARLOR COOKIES

1 cup brown sugar
1 cup white sugar
1 cup butter
2 eggs
1 cup coconut
1 teaspoon vanilla

1 teaspoon soda
2 cups flour
1/2 teaspoon salt
1/2 teaspoon baking powder
2 cups branflakes
2 cups nuts

Cream brown sugar, white sugar and butter together. Add eggs, coconut and vanilla. Sift soda, flour, salt and baking powder together and add to creamed mixture. Add branflakes and nuts, mixing well. Form into small balls and place on ungreased baking sheet. Mash with fork, then bake at 375 degrees for 8 to 10 minutes. Yields 3 dozen cookies.

PEANUT BLOSSOMS

1-3/4 cups flour
1 teaspoon soda
1/2 teaspoon salt
1/2 cup sugar
1/2 c peanut butter
1 egg

2 Tablespoons milk
1 teaspoon vanilla
1/2 cup packed brown sugar
1/2 cup butter
chocolate kisses

Mix all ingredients together and roll into small balls. Roll in granulated sugar and bake at 350 degrees for 10 minutes. Top each cookie with a chocolate kiss while still warm.

PEPPERMINT CANDY CANE COOKIES

1 cup soft shortening (margarine)
1 cup sifted confectioners' sugar
1 egg
1-1/2 teaspoon almond extract
1 teaspoon vanilla
2-1/2 cups sifted plain flour

1 teaspoon salt
1/2 teaspoon red food coloring
1/2 cup crushed peppermint
   candy
1/2 cup confectioners' sugar (for
   sprinkle mixture)

Mix margarine, confectioner's sugar, egg, almond extract and vanilla together thoroughly. Sift flour and salt and stir into above mixture. Divide the dough into two parts. Into one half, blend the red food coloring. Shape into candy canes by rolling 1 teaspoon of dough into a strip about 4" long. Place one plain strip and one red strip side by side. Press lightly together and twist gently like a rope. Place on ungreased cookie sheet, curving top to form cane handle. Bake about 9 minutes at 375 degrees or until lightly browned. Remove from cookie sheet while warm and sprinkle with a mixture of crushed peppermint candy and confectioners' sugar. Makes about 4 dozen cookies.

PECAN BALLS

1 cup butter	2 cups pecans chopped fine
1/4 cup sugar	confectioners' sugar
2 cups sifted plain flour	granulated sugar

Cream margarine or butter, sugar and flour. Add pecans and mix well. Use 1 tablespoon of dough for each cookie and shape into balls. Bake at 300 degrees on an ungreased cookie sheet for about 45 minutes. Roll in a mixture of confectioner's sugar as soon as removed from the oven. Makes about 4 dozen cookies.

PEPPERMINT CANDY PUFFS

1 cup soft butter or margarine	Peppermint Fudge:
1/2 cup sifted confectioners' sugar	1/2 cup (1/4 lb.) crushed stick
1 teaspoon vanilla	peppermint candy
2-1/2 cups sifted all purpose flour	1/2 cup confectioners' sugar
1/2 cup walnuts or pecans (finely	1 ounce (2 Tablespoons) cream
chopped)	cheese
	1 teaspoon milk
	1/2 cup confectioners' sugar
	red food coloring

Cream butter, add 1/2 cup confectioners' sugar and vanilla, creaming well. Blend in sifted flour and walnuts, mixing thoroughly. Cover; prepare Peppermint Fudge filling.

Combine crushed candy and 1/2 cup sugar and set aside. Blend cream cheese and milk together until smooth and creamy. Add 1/2 cup plain confectioners' sugar gradually, then add 3 tablespoons of the candy-sugar mixture and one or two drops of red food coloring. Mix well.

Shape dough by round teaspoon into balls. Make a deep hole in center of each ball and fill with 1/4 teaspoon of filling. Reshape and seal. Place on ungreased cookie sheet and bake at 350 degrees for 12 to 15 minutes. Do not brown! While still warm, roll balls in remainder of peppermint-sugar mixture. Cool and reroll in candy mixture.

PECAN CRISPIES

1-1/2 cups butter	3-3/4 cups sifted all-purpose flour
18 Tablespoons brown sugar	3 teaspoons baking powder
18 Tablespoons granulated sugar	3/4 teaspoon soda
3 eggs	3/4 teaspoon salt
1-1/2 teaspoons vanilla	3 cups chopped pecans

Cream butter and sugars until light. Beat in egg and vanilla. Sift dry ingredients together, blend into creamed mixture. Stir in nuts. Drop from teaspoon on ungreased cookie sheet. Bake at 375 degrees for about 10 minutes. Cool cookies slightly before removing from pan. Makes 2-1/2 dozen.

RUM CAKE BALLS

1 cup chopped pecans
2 small packages vanilla wafers
(40 to 42)
2 Tablespoons white Karo syrup

2 Tablespoons cocoa
1/4 cup rum
1 cup powdered sugar

Crush vanilla wafers, add pecans and other ingredients. Roll into small balls. Let mixture set overnight in the refrigerator and roll in powdered sugar.

ROCKS

(A Grand Fruit Cookie)

1 stick butter
1/2 cup + 1 Tablespoon sugar
3 eggs
1-1/4 cups flour
1/4 teaspoon allspice
1/4 teaspoon salt
1/4 teaspoon cloves

1 teaspoon vanilla
1/4 cup whiskey
1/2 lb. pineapple (candied)
1/2 lb. cherries (candied)
1/4 teaspoon cinnamon
1 quart pecans

Cream butter and sugar until light and fluffy. Add eggs, one at a time, beating well after each addition. Add vanilla. Sift flour, salt, allspice, cloves and cinnamon together. Add whiskey to candied pineapple and cherries. Add to cake batter. Fold in nuts. Drop 2 teaspoons batter on greased cookie sheet. Bake at 250 to 300 degrees until brown. Store in tins. Will be hard at first but will soften after a few days.

SPANISH PECAN COOKIES

1/4 pound real butter
1/2 cup Crisco
2-1/4 cups powdered sugar
(unsifted)
1 Tablespoon vanilla

1 teaspoon cornstarch
1/4 teaspoon baking soda
4 ounces pecans (well-chopped)
powdered sugar for dipping

Cream together for 5 minutes on medium speed of an electric mixer butter and Crisco. Gradually beat in 2-1/4 cups unsifted powdered sugar, vanilla, cornstarch and baking soda. Add the pecans. Shape dough into 1" balls. Place on an ungreased cookie sheet about 1-1/2" apart. Bake at 325 degrees for 18 minutes exactly! Dip top of each cookie into a shallow bowl of powdered sugar. Makes 3-1/2 dozen cookies.

NOTE: The baking soda is the secret in making these delicious unusual cookies. It makes hollow centers during baking.

"TASSIE" PASTRY SHELLS

1 stick oleo
1 small package cream cheese

1 cup flour

Soften oleo and cream cheese to room temperature. Cream well and work in flour. Chill in refrigerator. Roll into walnut-size balls and place in center of small ungreased muffin cups. With fingers, push up and around sides and bottom of muffin cups to make shells (Yield: 18 shells). Fill with desired "Tassie" filling and bake according to directions for specific filling.

Variations: Orange Peel Pastry:

Add 1 teaspoon grated orange rind and 1/4 teaspoon grated lemon rind into the margarine/cream cheese mixture.

Cinnamon and Sugar Pastry:

Add 1 teaspoon cinnamon and 2 tablespoons sugar to the creaming.

APRICOT "TASSIE" PASTRY FILLING

1 cup drained mashed apricots
   (baby food works fine!)
1/2 cup sugar

2 Tablespoons orange juice or 2
   Tablespoons apricot brandy
pinch of salt

Use plain pastry shells. Combine apricots, sugar, orange juice (or apricot brandy) and salt. Cook over low heat until thick. Cool. Spoon into shells and bake 10 to 15 minutes at 400 degrees.

BANBURY "TASSIE" PASTRY FILLING

1/2 cup sugar
1/8 teaspoon salt
2 Tablespoons soft bread crumbs
2 Tablespoons chopped walnuts

1/2 cup chopped raisins
1 beaten egg
1 Tablespoon lemon juice
2 Tablespoons grated lemon rind

Use orange peel pastry. Combine sugar, salt, bread crumbs and chopped walnuts. Add raisins, egg, lemon juice and lemon rind. Mix well and spoon into pastry shells until not quite full. Bake 15 minutes at 400 degrees. Serve with or without whipped cream.

PECAN "TASSIE" PASTRY FILLING

chopped pecans
1 beaten egg
3/4 cup brown sugar (firmly
   packed)

1 Tablespoon melted butter
Pinch of salt
1 teaspoon vanilla

Use pastry with cinnamon and sugar added. Sprinkle bottom of tassies with chopped pecans. Bet egg and gradually add brown sugar, melted butter, salt and vanilla. Spoon mixture over tassies. Sprinkle tops with more chopped nuts and bake at 400 degrees for 15 to 17 minutes. Cool, then carefully remove from pans.

APPLE BROWNIES

2/3 cup soft butter or margarine
1-3/4 cups brown sugar
2 eggs
1 teaspoon vanilla
2 cups flour
2 teaspoon baking powder

1/4 teaspoon salt
1 cup chopped, peeled apples
1/3 cup chopped walnuts or
    pecans
1/3 cup raisins
Powdered sugar

Cream margarine and brown sugar. Add eggs and beat until well mixed. Add vanilla and mix again. Add sifted dry ingredients and beat until smooth. Add apples, raisins and walnuts. Stir gently with a strong spoon. Spread batter in a greased 9x13" pan and bake at 350 degrees for 30 to 35 minutes. Remove brownies from pan, cut and roll each one in sifted powdered sugar. Makes 1-1/2 dozen brownies.

PARTY APRICOT BARS

1 cup dried apricots
1 cup sifted all-purpose flour
1/3 cup granulated sugar
1/2 cup uncooked rolled oats
1/2 cup butter or margarine
1/3 cup sifted all-purpose flour

1/2 teaspoon double-acting
    baking powder
1/4 teaspoon salt
2 eggs, well beaten
1 cup brown sugar, packed
1 teaspoon almond extract
1 cup flaked coconut or nuts

Heat oven to 350 degrees. In saucepan, simmer apricots in water to cover for approximately 10 minutes; drain and cool. Meanwhile, combine 1 cup flour with granulated sugar and rolled oats. With pastry blender or two knives, cut in butter until mixture is crumbly. Press mixture evenly into greased 9x9x2" pan and bake 20 minutes. Meanwhile, cut apricots into small pieces. Sift 1/3 cup flour with baking powder and salt. Into well-beaten eggs, gradually blend brown sugar, then almond extract. Stir in flour mixture, coconut and apricots. Spread mixture carefully over hot baked lower layer, sprinkle with coconut and bake 30 minutes. Cool, then cut into bars. Makes 24 bars.

BUTTERSCOTCH SQUARES

2 cups sifted all-purpose flour
2 teaspoon double-acting baking
   powder
1 pound package brown sugar
1 cup flaked coconut

1/2 teaspoon salt
1/2 cup butter
2 eggs, unbeaten
1 cup coarse chopped nuts

Heat oven to 350 degrees. Sift flour with the baking powder and salt. In a pan over low heat, melt butter with sugar, stirring constantly. Turn into bowl, add eggs one at a time, beating well after each. Blend in flour mixture, then mix in coconut and nuts. Pour into a square pan 8x8x2" and bake 25 minutes or until done. Cut into squares. Very chewy and good.

FRUIT SALAD BARS

1/4 cup shortening
3/4 cup granulated sugar
2 eggs
1 teaspoon vanilla
1 can (8-1/2 ounce) crushed
   pineapple
1/2 cup mashed banana
2 cups sifted all-purpose flour
1-1/2 teaspoons baking powder
1 teaspoon salt

1/4 teaspoon nutmeg
1 cup coarsely chopped
   California walnuts
1 cup sliced pitted dates
Lemon Glaze:
1-1/2 Tablespoons melted butter
1-1/2 Tablespoons lemon juice
1 Tablespoon water
dash of salt
2 cups sifted powdered sugar

Cream shortening, sugar, eggs and vanilla together well. Drain pineapple well, pressing out all excess syrup with back of a spoon. Add drained pineapple and banana to creamed mixture. Resift flour with baking powder, salt and nutmeg. Stir into creamed mixture. Mix in walnuts and dates. Spread in greased 10x15x1" pan. Bake at 350 degrees for 25 to 30 minutes. Cool to lukewarm. Make lemon glaze by combining melted butter, lemon juice, water, salt and sifted powdered sugar. Blend until smooth and spread over cooled bars. Makes 3 dozen bars about 2-1/2x1-3/4".

FUDGE CUTS

2 squares (2 ounce) unsweetened
   chocolate
1/2 cup butter
1 cup sugar

2 eggs (well beaten)
1/2 cup sifted flour
1/4 teaspoon vanilla
1/2 cup chopped nuts

Melt chocolate and butter in top of double boiler. Remove and blend in sugar, then eggs. Add flour and salt. Stir well and add vanilla. Pour into 2 greased 8x8x2" pans and spread smooth. Sprinkle with nuts and bake at 400 degrees for 12 minutes. Cool and cut into squares.

JAN'S TOFFEE BARS

1/2 cup butter
1/2 cup light brown sugar
1 cup all-purpose flour
2 eggs
1 cup brown sugar
1/2 teaspoon vanilla

2 Tablespoons flour
1 teaspoon baking powder
pinch of salt
1 cup coconut
1 cup chopped walnuts or pecans
powdered sugar

Cream butter, sugar and flour. Press in a greased 8x9" square cake pan. Bake at 350 degrees for 10 minutes. Cool.

Filling:

Beat eggs and add brown sugar, vanilla, flour, baking powder and salt. Beat. Add coconut and nuts. Spread on crust and bake at 350 degrees for 25 minutes. Cut in squares and dip in or dust with powdered sugar.

This is a very rich cookie bar, a big favorite at Christmas time. The recipe may be doubled and then use a 9x13" pan.

JEWISH COOKIES

1 box light brown sugar
4 eggs
1 Tablespoon vanilla

1-1/2 cups flour
1-1/2 cups pecans, chopped finely

Mix sugar, eggs, vanilla, flour and pecans together well. Pour into greased, floured 9x12" pan and bake at 375 degrees for 30 to 40 minutes.

Frosting:
1/2 pound powdered sugar
1/2 stick butter or margarine

1 Tablespoon vanilla
1/4 teaspoon cinnamon

Melt butter in sauce pan, add powdered sugar, vanilla and cinnamon. Mix well. Spread on cookies while hot. Cut into bars.

LEMON CHEESE GOODY BARS

Crust:
1 (18-1/4 ounce) package yellow
    cake mix
1/2 cup butter or margarine,
    melted
1 egg, beaten

Topping:
1 (8 ounce) package cream
    cheese, softened
2 eggs, beaten
1 (1 pound) box confectioners'
    sugar
2 teaspoons fresh lemon juice
small amount grated lemon rind

Preheat oven to 350 degrees. Combine cake mix, margarine or butter and egg, mix well. Press into a 9x13" pan.

Combine cream cheese, eggs and sugar. Mix well. Add lemon juice and grated rind. Gently pour over crust. Bake 30 to 40 minutes. While hot, sprinkle with powdered sugar, cool and cut into small bars. Rich and delicious! Good to serve at a coffee. A lemon lover's delight.

SUNNY LEMON BARS

Crust:
1 cup butter or margarine
1/2 cup powdered sugar

1/2 teaspoon salt
2 cups all-purpose flour, unsifted

Heat oven to 350 degrees. Lightly spoon flour into measuring cup; level off. In a large bowl, combine the flour, 1/2 cup confectioners' sugar and butter at low speed with electric mixer until crumbly. Press the mixture evenly into the bottom of an ungreased 13x9" pan. Bake at 350 degrees for 20 to 30 minutes or until light golden brown. Watch closely so the crust does not burn.

Filling:
4 eggs, slightly beaten
1/4 cup flour
2 cups sugar

1/2 teaspoon baking powder
1/4 cup fresh lemon juice rind of
1 lemon, grated

Combine eggs, 1/2 cup flour, sugar and baking powder in a large bowl, blending well. Stir in lemon juice. Pour mixture over the warm crust. Return to oven and bake 25 to 30 minutes or until top is a light golden brown. Cool completely.

Glaze:
1 cup confectioners' sugar

2 to 3 Tablespoons fresh lemon juice or powdered sugar to dust bars when cool

In a small bowl, combine confectioners' sugar and enough lemon juice to achieve the desired glaze consistency. Blend until smooth. Spread over cooled filling. Cut into small bars. OR: Sprinkle with confectioners' sugar and cut into bars.

Serve alone or with fresh strawberries. Truly a taste of childhood from food cooked by our mothers!!

PECAN CHEWS

1 cup flour
2 Tablespoons white sugar
1/2 cup butter
1-1/2 cups brown sugar
1/2 cup chopped nuts

1/2 teaspoon salt
2 beaten eggs
2 Tablespoons flour
1 teaspoon vanilla
Bake in two steps:

Step 1: Mix cup flour, white sugar and butter. Mix well with your hands and pat into greased 8x13" pan. Bake 10 to 12 minutes at 350 degrees (longer if the pan is smaller).

Step 2: Mix brown sugar, pecans, salt, eggs, flour and vanilla together well. Pour over step 1 and bake for 20 minutes more at 350 degrees. Yields about 2-1/2 dozen.

REESE'S PEANUT BUTTER BARS

1 cup butter, softened
1-2/3 cups graham cracker crumbs
1 cup peanut butter (smooth or crunchy)

1 pound powdered sugar (2 to 2-1/3 cups)
1 (16 ounce) package semi-sweet chocolate bits (2 cups)

Combine butter, graham crackers and sugar by hand, combining well. Press entire mixture firmly into a 13x9" pan. Do not bake! Refrigerate at least 1 hour, preferably two. Melt 2 cups (16 ounce) package chocolate chips. Spread over cooled peanut butter mixture. Cool and cut into squares with a sharp knife, before the chocolate gets hard. Makes 3 to 4 dozen. Cut the squares small as these are very rich.

I'm sorry for people
Whoever they may be
Who live in a house
With no cookie jar.

Edgar A. Guest

GRANDMA'S GRAHAM CRACKER SQUARES

2 cups crushed graham crackers (23 squares)
1 cup chopped walnuts
1 cup chocolate chips

3 Tablespoons melted butter or margarine
1 teaspoon vanilla
1 can (14-ounce) Eagle Brand sweetened condensed milk

Mix the crushed cracker crumbs with walnuts, melted butter, vanilla and condensed milk together until well blended.

Grease a 9" round cake pan. Line with wax paper. Pour batter into the pan. Bake at 350 degrees for 20 to 25 minutes. Cool. Remove from pan the next day. Cut into strips, then cut across diagonally. Roll in powdered sugar.

Ezechiel Harris House - Augusta, Georgia

EZECHIEL HARRIS HOUSE

Ezechiel Harris, a planter and tobacco merchant, built a residence and a warehouse for tobacco inspection on 323-1/2 acres that he purchased west of Augusta in 1794. He divided the remainder of the land into lots and named the area Harrisburg. With an eye to taking advantage of the growing local economy, Harris offered lodgings to visiting planters and free ferry service across the Savannah for South Carolinians who used his warehouse. But his dream of financial success was dashed. Harris' opposition to the Yazoo Act, a land scheme in which a number of prominent Augustans were involved, and a quarrel with rival planters and merchants ended in his bankruptcy.

After the Civil War, textile factories were constructed along the nearby canal turning Harrisburg into a residential area for mill workers. In 1946, the Richmond County Historical Society purchased and restored the Harris House, which at the time was thought to be the "White House," scene of a Revolutionary battle. However, in 1975, research indicated that the house involved in the historic siege had been stone while the Harris House was grey frame and dated from about 1797. The land that Ezechiel Harris purchased in 1794 had been part of the 500 acre White House tract. In 1964, the Richmond County Historical Society deeded the property to the State of Georgia. It is now open to the public as a late eighteenth century residence.

"Just" Desserts and Pies

WHOLE APPLE DUMPLINGS

Crust:
2 cups sifted flour
2 teaspoons baking powder
1/2 teaspoon salt
1/3 cup shortening
1/3 cup butter
1/2 cup milk
Filling:
6 medium-sized, tart baking
 apples (about 2 pounds)
1/3 cup granulated sugar
1/2 cup light brown sugar, firmly
 packed
1 Tablespoon dark raisins
 (optional)
2 Tablespoons chopped walnuts
 (optional)
1 teaspoon cinnamon

4 Tablespoons lemon juice
3 Tablespoons butter
milk or cream
additional granulated sugar
Syrup:
1-1/2 cups brown sugar, firmly
 packed
3/4 cups water
2 Tablespoons butter
OPTIONAL TOPPINGS
Hard Sauce:
1/2 cup butter/margarine, softened
1 teaspoon vanilla extract
1-1/4 cups unsifted confectioners'
 sugar
Cream (choose one):
Cream, sweetened whipped
 cream, or vanilla ice cream

Peel and core apples. To prepare crust, sift flour, baking powder and salt together. Cut in shortening and butter with pastry blender until mixture resembles fine crumbs. Stir in milk. Knead 10 to 12 strokes on lightly floured board. Roll dough into a 14x21" rectangle. Cut into six 7" squares, using a fluted pastry cutter or sharp knife.

To prepare filling, center an apple on each crust square. Combine granulated and brown sugars and cinnamon. If desired, mix dark raisins and walnuts with the sugar mixture. Pour 2 teaspoons lemon juice over each apple. Sprinkle an equal amount of sugar mixture into cavity and over top of each apple. Dot each apple with 1-1/2 teaspoons butter. Moisten edges of pastry and bring four corners together over center of apple; seal edges completely. Arrange in a shallow baking dish, brush with milk or cream and sprinkle with a small amount of granulated sugar.

Place wrapped apples in refrigerator for 30 minutes or longer. Meanwhile, make the syrup by bringing brown sugar, water and butter to a boil over moderate heat. Boil gently for 5 minutes and remove from heat.

Preheat oven to 425 degrees. Brush apple dumplings with syrup and bake for 10 minutes. Reduce heat to 350 degrees and bake additional 30 minutes, basting every 10 minutes with syrup.

With broad spatula, remove dumplings to serving dishes. Serve dumplings hot or warm plain, topped with hard sauce or topped with your choice of cream, whipped cream or vanilla ice cream.

To make hard sauce, cream butter until it is light, using a portable electric beater. At low speed, add vanilla and confectioners' sugar and beat until smooth.

BOSTON CREAM PIE

This heavenly creation, also known as "Pudding-Cake Pie" was the product, so legend goes, of a rebellious Colonial cook tired of the ever-present fruit pies of the day.

Cake:
1/3 cup shortening
2/3 cup sugar
2 eggs
1 cup sifted cake flour
1 teaspoon baking powder
pinch of salt
1/2 cup milk
1/4 teaspoon butter flavoring
1/2 teaspoon vanilla extract
Cream Filling:
1/2 cup sugar
1/4 cup cornstarch
1/4 teaspoon salt
2 cups milk
4 egg yolks, slightly beaten
1/2 teaspoon vanilla extract
Chocolate Glaze:
2 Tablespoons butter/margarine
1-ounce square unsweetened
  chocolate
1 cup sifted powdered sugar
2 Tablespoons boiling water

Cream shortening; gradually add sugar, beating until light and fluffy. Add eggs one at a time, beating well after each addition. Combine flour, baking powder and salt; add to creamed mixture alternately with milk, beginning and ending with flour mixture. Stir in butter flavoring and vanilla. Pour batter into greased, floured 9" round cake pan. Bake at 325 degrees for 25 to 30 minutes or until a wooden pick inserted in center comes out clean. Cool in pan 10 minutes; remove from pan and cool completely.

Combine first 3 cream filling ingredients in a heavy saucepan. Gradually add milk and stir with a wire whisk until well blended. Cook over medium heat, stirring constantly, until mixture comes to a boil. Boil, stirring constantly, about 1 minute until thickened; remove from heat.

Gradually stir one-fourth of the hot mixture into egg yolks; add to remaining hot mixture, stirring constantly. Return to medium heat and bring to a boil, stirring constantly. Boil for 1 minute, stirring constantly until thickened and smooth. Stir in vanilla and cool. Makes about 2-1/2 cups.

Combine butter and chocolate in the top of a double boiler; bring water to a boil. Reduce heat to low and cook until chocolate melts. Cool slightly; add sugar and water and beat until smooth. Makes about 1 cup.

Split cake layer in half horizontally to make two layers. Spread cream filling between the layers, then spread the chocolate glaze over the top. Refrigerate pie until ready to serve. Yields about 10 servings.

PECAN BAKLAVA

14 pastry sheets
4 cups chopped pecans
1-1/4 cups sugar
1 teaspoon cinnamon
grated rind of one orange

1 cup butter/margarine
Syrup:
2 cups water
3 cups sugar
1 teaspoon lemon juice

Mix nuts, sugar, cinnamon and orange rind well. Melt butter and brush a 13x9" pan with butter. Place 2 pastry sheets in bottom of baking pan and allow ends to extend over the pan. Sprinkle heavily with nut mixture, then place two more pastry sheets on top. Brush with butter and sprinkle with nut mixture. Continue to alternate in this manner until all ingredients and pastry sheets are used, ending with 2 pastry sheets.

Brush top with remaining butter and trim edges with sharp knife. Cut through top with diagonal lines to form diamond shapes. Bake in 375 degree oven for one hour or until lightly browned, watching carefully so the Baklava will not burn.

Combine syrup ingredients (water, sugar and lemon juice) and boil for 10 minutes. While Baklava is still hot, cover with syrup. Serves 24.

OLD FASHION BLACKBERRY ROLL

2 cups all-purpose flour
2 Tablespoons sugar
1 teaspoon salt
8 ounces unsalted butter, chilled
    and cut into small pieces
1 egg, beaten

1/3 cup milk
2 pints fresh blackberries
3/4 cup sugar
2 Tablespoons unsalted butter,
    melted

In a medium size bowl, combine 1-1/2 pints of the blackberries and 1/2 cup sugar. Set aside to sweeten. Sift together the dry ingredients (flour, 2 tablespoons sugar and salt). Cut in 1/3 cup chilled butter. Add beaten egg and enough milk to make a soft dough. Mix lightly and turn out on a floured board and knead enough to bring dough together. Roll out into a 9x15" rectangle. Preheat oven to 450 degrees.

Brush dough with melted butter. Top dough with the sweetened blackberries. Dot with the remaining butter (chilled) and roll up as in a jelly roll. Place seam-side down in a buttered 9x13" baking dish. Cut several diagonal slits in the top side of roll. Sprinkle with the remaining sugar. Place the remaining blackberries around the roll. Bake 10 minutes. Carefully pour 1/2 cup hot water around the bottom of the roll. Lower the oven temperature to 350 degrees and bake 40 to 45 minutes or until the top is a golden brown. Remove from oven, slice and spoon juices on top. Serve with cream or vanilla ice cream.

NEW ORLEANS BREAD PUDDING

3 large eggs
1-1/4 cups sugar
1/2 teaspoon vanilla extract
1-1/4 teaspoons nutmeg
1-1/4 teaspoons cinnamon
1/4 cup unsalted butter, melted

2 ups milk
1/2 cup raisins
1/2 cup coarsely chopped pecans, toasted
5 cups very stale French or Italian bread cubes (with crusts on)

Grease a 9x5" loaf pan. In a large mixer bowl, beat eggs at high speed until extremely frothy and bubbles are the size of pinheads (about 3 minutes...a wire whisk takes about 6 minutes). Add sugar, vanilla, nutmeg, cinnamon and butter; beat at high speed until well blended. Beat in milk and stir in raisins and pecans. Place bread cubes in greased loaf pan. Pour egg mixture over bread and toss until bread is soaked. Allow to stand about 45 minutes, patting bread down into liquid occasionally. Place pan in preheated 350 degree oven. Immediately reduce temperature to 300 degrees and bake 40 minutes. Set oven for 425 degrees and bake pudding until well browned and puffy (15 to 20 minutes more).

To serve, place 1-1/2 tablespoons warm lemon sauce in each dessert dish, spoon in 1/2 cup hot bread pudding and top with 1/4 cup chantilly cream. May also be served with Louisiana Bourbon Sauce. Makes 8 servings.

Lemon Sauce:
1 lemon, halved
1/2 cup water
1/4 cup sugar

2 teaspoons cornstarch
1/4 cup water
1 teaspoon vanilla extract

Squeeze 2 tablespoons juice from lemon halves and place juice in 1-quart saucepan. Add lemon halves, water and sugar and bring to a boil. Stir in cornstarch dissolved in 1/4 cup water; add vanilla. Cook 1 minute over high heat, stirring constantly. Strain, squeezing sauce from lemon halves. Serve warm. Makes about 3/4 cup.

Chantilly Cream:
2/3 cup heavy or whipping cream
1 teaspoon vanilla extract
1 teaspoon brandy

1 teaspoon Grand Marnier
1/4 cup sugar
2 Tablespoons sour cream

Chill a medium bowl and beaters. Combine cream, vanilla and brandies in chilled bowl. Beat with electric mixer at medium speed for 1 minute. Add sugar and sour cream; beat at medium speed just until soft peaks form, about 3 minutes. Don't overbeat! Makes 2 cups.

Louisiana Bourbon Sauce:
8 Tablespoons sweet butter, cut in small pieces
2/3 cup quick dissolving sugar

1 egg
1 Tablespoon lemon juice
1/4 teaspoon nutmeg
1/4 to 1/2 cup bourbon

(Continued)

Place butter in upper part of double boiler; set over hot (not boiling) water to melt. Beat sugar into egg in a small bowl until mixture is blended and slightly thickened. When all butter has melted, stir in egg-sugar mixture and cook for 2 to 3 minutes, stirring constantly, over hot (not boiling) water. When sugar is all dissolved and sauce has slightly thickened, remove from hot water. Stir to cool for 3 to 4 minutes, then stir in lemon juice, nutmeg and bourbon to taste. Set aside and serve at room temperature over bread pudding.

CHARLOTTE RUSSE

"Charlotte Russe" probably got its name from Queen Charlotte of England, wife of George III. It is a Bavarian cram filling to which gelatin has been added. The custard is poured into a mold lined with lady fingers before being allowed to set. Charlotte Russe, as we know it, was created by Antonin Careme, the great and illustrious chef of the French kitchen (1784-1833), while he was chef of French diplomat/statesman Talleyrand.

Lady Fingers, divided	1/4 teaspoon salt
1/4 cup cold water	1 teaspoon vanilla
1 envelope unflavored gelatin	1 teaspoon fresh lemon juice
1 cup milk, scalded	1 pint whipping cream, whipped
4 egg yolks, beaten	Toppings:
1 cup sugar	fresh fruits (strawberries, etc.)

Soften gelatin in cold water; set aside. Scald milk in a saucepan (bring to the boiling point, but do not boil; a film will form on top). Dissolve salt and sugar in milk. Combine milk, sugar and gelatin in a saucepan; cook, stirring over medium heat until mixture comes to a boil. Pour a small amount of hot mixture into egg yolks, stirring quickly to blend. Add warmed yolks to milk mixture in saucepan, stirring to blend. Cook for 1 to 2 minutes. Chill until slightly thickened, then blend in vanilla and lemon juice. Cover with a plastic wrap or a lid to prevent skim from forming on top of mixture (this will also prevent lumping when you add the whipped cream).

Line the sides and bottom of a 6-cup mold or 9x5" loaf pan with lady fingers (a spring form pan is easy to unmold). Whip cream until stiff; fold into cooled mixture. Pour into lined mold and chill until firm. Unmold and top with fresh fruit or a fruit sauce.

Raspberry Sauce:	1/4 cup sugar
10 ounces frozen raspberries,	1-1/2 Tablespoons cornstarch
sweetened	

Combine raspberries and sugar in saucepan and bring to a boil; cook about 5 minutes. Put through a strainer, removing seeds. Add enough water to berry mixture to make 1-1/2 cups. Combine a small amount of mixture with cornstarch to soften. Stir into remaining raspberry mixture. Cook over low heat, stirring constantly until smooth and thickened, about 4 to 5 minutes. Cool and serve.

CHERRIES JUBILEE

Cook-at-the-table elegance is a snap with today's cookware. Cherries Jubilee is not only delicious but quite dramatic...you flame this chafing dish dessert with brandy right at the table as your guests watch!

2 cups pitted dark sweet cherries	1 Tablespoon butter
1/2 cup sugar	1/2 cup Blackberry brandy
2 Tablespoons cornstarch	1 quart vanilla ice cream cut into
1/4 teaspoon salt	6 to 8 slices
1/4 cup cold water	Pound cake, 6 to 8 slices
2 Tablespoons lemon juice	

Drain cherries and reserve. Heat drained cherry juice in a medium-size saucepan. Combine sugar, salt and cornstarch, adding a little water. Blend until smooth. Pour, stirring, into the hot cherry juice. Cook until the syrup is thickened. Stir in cherries, lemon juice and butter. Transfer to a chafing dish and keep hot over flame. When ready to serve, pour all but 1 tablespoon of brandy over cherry mixture. Do not stir. Warm the remaining tablespoon of brandy in a large metal ladle or spoon with a long handle. Carefully ignite the heated brandy and pour over the warm cherry mixture and all will ignite. Stir to blend brandy into sauce. Serve immediately over ice cream. Makes 2 cups of sauce.

NOTE: A piece of plain pound cake may be used in a serving dish, then ice cream and Cherries Jubilee sauce.

BRANDIED FRUIT FRITTERS

Brandied Fruit:	1 cup sugar
1 can apricots	1/2 teaspoon nutmeg
1 can sliced peaches	1 cup brandy
1 can chunk pineapple	confectioners' sugar
1 can purple plums	

Drain fruit well. Place in large glass jar. Dissolve sugar and nutmeg in brandy and pour over fruit. Allow to stand overnight (or longer). Just before making fritters, drain fruit well on a towel. Dip in batter and fry in hot oil at 375 degrees until golden brown. Drain on paper towel and sprinkle with confectioners' sugar.

Fritter Batter:	grated rind of lemon
1 cup all purpose flour	1 Tablespoon melted
1 teaspoon salt	butter/margarine
1/4 teaspoon ground nutmeg	1/2 cup water
2 eggs, separated	1/4 cup brandy
2 Tablespoons fresh lemon juice	

Sift flour with salt and nutmeg. Combine egg yolks with lemon juice, lemon rind and melted butter. Add water and brandy and blend well. Stir in flour mixture, beating until smooth. When ready to use, fold in egg whites beaten stiff but not dry. Makes about 1-1/2 cups batter.

CHOCOLATE MINT CUP CAKES

1 cup butter, softened	1 teaspoon peppermint flavoring
2 cups powdered sugar	vanilla wafers
4 squares unsweetened chocolate	chopped nuts
4 eggs	cool whip
2 teaspoons vanilla	maraschino cherries

Melt chocolate over low heat and add butter and sugar; beat together well. Add eggs, vanilla and peppermint flavoring. Mix well. Place a vanilla wafer in a cup cake paper; fill paper half full with chocolate mixture; sprinkle a few nuts on top. Freeze. To serve, top with cool whip and a cherry.

CHRISTMAS PLUM PUDDING

In England, the Christmas pudding is made moths before Christmas. Little silver favors...a button for a bachelor, thimble for a spinster, a ring to foretell a wedding, sixpence for coming riches...are wrapped in waxed paper and hidden in the batter. On Christmas day, brandy is poured on the pudding and set afire.

1/2 pound butter	1/2 pound sponge cake crumbs
1/2 pound sultanas	1/2 pound currants
1/2 pound raisins	1/4 pound shredded almonds
1/2 pound glazed cherries	1/4 pound sugar
2 ounces minced peel	2 teaspoons cake spice
4 eggs	small glass of stout or beer
small glass of brandy	pinch of salt

Cream butter and sugar; add eggs and all other ingredients. Put into well-greased bowls and tightly cover with waxed paper or cloth tied with string. Boil 10 hours, adding boiling water as necessary to the pans in which the bowls are placed. The longer the pudding is kept, the better it is!

NOTE: Other recipes call for suet and flour in place of the cake crumbs, but all require quantities of fruit, some alcohol and a long period of boiling or steaming, tightly covered.

ORANGE WHIP

2 envelopes plain gelatin	1 Tablespoon orange peel, grated
2 cups sugar	2 Tablespoons lemon peel, grated
dash of salt	3 Tablespoons lemon juice
4 egg yolks	2 cups orange sections
2-1/2 cups orange juice	2 cups cream, whipped

Thoroughly mix gelatin, sugar and salt in saucepan. Beat egg yolks and 1 cup of orange juice together; stir into gelatin mixture. Cook over medium heat, stirring constantly, until mixture comes to a boil. Remove from heat, stir in peels and remaining juices. Chill, stirring occasionally, until mixture mounds when dropped from a spoon. Fold in orange sections and whipped cream. Pour into a 2-quart mold and allow to set. An excellent light dessert that serves about 12.

MOLDED COCONUT DESSERT

1-1/2 teaspoons soft butter
2 cups fresh coconut, grated (1 medium)
4 teaspoons unflavored gelatin
1/4 cup cold water
1-1/2 cups coconut milk
3/4 cup sugar
1/4 teaspoon salt

1 cup heavy cream
1 teaspoon vanilla
10 to 12 whole large ripe strawberries
Mint Sprigs (fresh)
Brandied Fruit:
Figs or Prunes

Rub inside of a 6 cup mold with butter to coat evenly. Pat 1/2 of the coconut over the bottom and sides of the mold; set aside. Sift gelatin over cold water and allow to soak 5 minutes. Combine coconut milk, milk, sugar and salt in a saucepan and heat to a simmer. Remove from heat and stir in gelatin until dissolved. Chill the mixture in the refrigerator until thick and syrupy. Whip cream until just stiff, forming soft peaks. Fold into the gelatin mixture with the remaining coconut meat. Add vanilla, folding in gently, using light strokes. Turn into a mold (a melon mold is most attractive). Cover with plastic wrap or wax paper and refrigerate until firm. Unmold and serve with lemon sauce, garnished with strawberries or with Brandied figs or prunes. This is an excellent dessert for curries, chicken and pork dishes.

NOTE: If coconut milk is unavailable (canned or frozen) you may puree 1/4 cup dried, shredded coconut with 1 cup hot milk in a blender and strain.

Lemon Sauce:
1/2 teaspoon grated lemon rind
1/4 cup lemon juice
3/4 cup sugar
1 Tablespoon cornstarch

1/8 teaspoon salt
1/2 cup boiling water
2 egg yolks, beaten
1/4 cup white corn syrup
2 Tablespoons firm butter

Combine sugar, cornstarch and salt in a 2-quart saucepan and blend well. Stir in boiling water and cook over direct heat, stirring constantly, until sauce boils and thickens. Stir a small amount of the hot mixture into beaten egg yolks; stir warmed yolks into sauce, beating well. Add syrup and cook 5 minutes, stirring frequently. Remove from heat. Stir in butter, lemon juice and rind. Pour into a clean jar, cool and seal. Chill sauce until ready for use. Makes approximately 7/8 cup of sauce.

Brandied Figs or Prunes:
1 large can Kadota Figs, drained or 1 (12-ounce) package dried pitted prunes (2 cups) cooked

1/4 cup light brown sugar
1 Tablespoon lemon juice
1/4 teaspoon cinnamon
4 Tablespoons Brandy

Heat Brandy cinnamon, lemon juice and 1-1/4 cups fig or prune juice. Simmer for 3 to 5 minutes or until sugar has dissolved. Place fruit in a shallow dish; pour heated juice mixture over fruit. Allow fruit to cool in this flavoring before serving.

NOTE: If using Brandied Fruit with coconut dessert, unmold onto a shallow serving dish and surround with Brandied Fruit and mint sprigs. Pass remaining fruit and juice in a serving dish.

CREAM PUFFS

1 cup + 2 Tablespoons	1/2 teaspoon salt
all-purpose flour	4 eggs
1 cup water	Gloss Finish:
1/2 cup butter, cut into small pieces	1 egg yolk
1 teaspoon sugar	1 teaspoon milk or water

Sift flour onto a sheet of waxed paper. Combine water, butter, sugar and salt in a heavy saucepan; bring to a rapid boil. Using waxed paper as a funnel, pour the flour all at once into the boiling mixture. Cook the paste over low heat, beating it rapidly and vigorously with a wooden spoon until ingredients are thoroughly combined and the mixture cleanly leaves the sides of the pan and forms a ball. Remove pan from heat and beat in 4 eggs, one at a time, beating well either by hand or using a mixer after each addition. Allow the paste to cool before shaping it.

Cream puffs and similar simple shapes may be made with no more equipment than a spoon. Scoop up the desired amount of paste and using a rubber spatula or a finer, push it off in a high mound onto a lightly buttered baking sheet.

For a glossy finish, beat egg yolk with a teaspoon of milk or water and brush the cream puffs with the resulting mixture.

Bake puffs at 375 degrees for 20 minutes or until golden brown, light and dry. If necessary, prick the puffs with the top of a sharp knife and let them stand in a slack oven for 10 minutes to be sure the centers are quite dry. Cool puffs on a wire rack, split them in half and fill as desired. Sprinkle with sifted confectioners' sugar or ice them.

Pastry Cream:	4 egg yolks
1-1/2 cups milk	1/4 cup flour
1/2 cup sugar	2 teaspoons vanilla

Scald milk. Using a wire whisk, beat sugar and egg yolks together in a heavy saucepan until mixture is thick and creamy enough to form a ribbon on the batter when the whisk is withdrawn. Sift flour into the mixture, mixing just enough to blend. Stir in scalded milk very gradually until the batter is smooth. Cook mixture over low heat, stirring vigorously with a whisk until the boiling point is reached. Add vanilla and strain the cream through a fine sieve. As the cream cools, keep it stirred.

Chocolate Confectioners' Icing:	1 ounce unsweetened baking
2 cups confectioners' sugar	chocolate
	3 Tablespoons water

Sift confectioners' sugar into a bowl. Melt chocolate with water and add chocolate gradually to the sugar, beating constantly until icing is smooth and easy to spread. If desired, flavor with vanilla and beat well.

Variations:

Tiny puffs may be filled with melted cheese, sour cream with red or black caviar, lobster Newburg, or creamed crab. They may also be served cold with chicken salad.

GEORGIA PEACH DELIGHT

1-1/2 Tablespoons cornstarch
2 cups light cream, divided
4 large egg yolks, beaten
1/2 cup sugar
1 teaspoon vanilla extract
24 ladyfingers
1 cup peach preserves

4 Tablespoons Amaretto
3 Tablespoons peach brandy
24 coconut macaroons, coarsely
   crumbled (about 4 cups)
4 cups sliced fresh peaches
2 cups heavy cream, whipped
1/2 cup toasted, slivered almonds

Dissolve cornstarch in 1/4 cup of light cream. Combine beaten egg yolks with the cornstarch. In a heavy saucepan, heat the remaining light cream, being careful not to boil or scorch. Add sugar, stirring to dissolve. Pour 1 cup of the hot cream mixture into the egg yolks, stirring constantly. Return egg mixture to the saucepan. Continue to cook over medium heat, stirring constantly, until custard thickens and coats a metal spoon. About 5 to 10 minutes. Remove from heat and blend in the vanilla. Transfer custard to a bowl, cover with plastic wrap and let cool to room temperature.

Split the ladyfingers and fill with the peach preserves, sandwich like. Place half the ladyfingers in a crystal or decorative 8x4" deep serving bowl. Sprinkle with half the Amaretto and half the brandy. Cover with a layer of half the macaroons. Let stand for 30 minutes. Top with 2 cups sliced peaches. Cover with half the custard sauce. Repeat layers of the remaining ladyfingers, brandy, Amaretto, macaroons and peaches. Pour remaining custard sauce over top and cover with plastic wrap. Refrigerate until thoroughly chilled, about 2 hours. Just before serving, top with whipped cream and almonds. Best eaten day of preparation. Serves 12 to 14.

JELLYROLL

Jellyroll has long been a favorite dessert and intrigues all children. Although this spiral of delicate spongecake and jelly may look complicated to make, it really isn't. Once you've mastered the art of the jellyroll, try variations such as fruit filling, lemon-cheese filling, whipped cream, pudding or even ice cream.

4 eggs
3/4 teaspoon baking powder
1/4 teaspoon salt
3/4 cup sugar
3/4 cup all-purpose flour
1 teaspoon vanilla or lemon
   extract

powdered sugar
1 cup strawberry jelly (or desired
   flavor)
whipped cream (optional)
whole strawberries (optional)

Grease 15x10x1" jelly roll pan; line the pan with waxed paper, then grease and flour the waxed paper. Set aside.

(Continued)

Combine eggs, baking powder and salt and beat at high speed with an electric mixer until foamy. Gradually add sugar, beating until mixture is thick and lemon-colored. Fold in flour and lemon or vanilla extract. Spread batter evenly in prepared pan. Bake at 400 degrees for 10 to 12 minutes.

Sift powdered sugar in a 15x10" rectangle on a linen towel. When cake is done, immediately loosen from sides of pan and turn out on sugar. Peel off waxed paper. Starting at narrow end, roll up cake and towel together; cool on a wire rack, seam side down, for 10 minutes.

Unroll cake and remove towel. Spread cake with jelly and reroll. Place on serving plate, seam side down and allow to cool completely. Garnish with sifted powdered sugar or with whipped cream piped down the center spine and strawberries nested in the center of the whipped cream. Serves 8 to 10 persons.

Strawberry Jelly Roll Filling:

1 pint fresh strawberries	1-1/2 Tablespoons wild
1/2 cup sugar	strawberry gelatin
1-1/2 Tablespoons cornstarch	3 to 4 drops red food color
1/2 cup hot water	1 pint whipping cream, whipped
	and sweetened

Wash, drain and hull strawberries. Slice enough to make 1 cup. Set aside remaining berries. Mix sugar, gelatin and cornstarch together in a small saucepan; add hot water and cook over medium heat, stirring constantly until mixture comes to a boil. Reduce heat and boil gently 1 to 2 minutes. Remove from heat and pour into bowl. Add food coloring and cool mixture; add sliced strawberries.

Carefully unroll cake and spread with filling. Reroll cake and place open end down on serving platter. Chill well. Just before serving, ice cake roll with whipped cream and decorate with remaining strawberries. Serves 8 to 10 persons.

Lemon-Cheese Jelly Roll Filling:

3/4 cup sugar	2 egg yolks, lightly beaten
2 Tablespoons cornstarch	3 Tablespoons lemon juice
dash of salt	1 teaspoon butter/margarine
3/4 cup cold water	3 ounces cream cheese, softened
	2 Tablespoons whipping cream

Combine sugar, cornstarch and salt in a medium saucepan. Gradually add water, egg yolks and lemon juice. Stir until smooth and bring to a boil; cook, stirring constantly for 1 minute. Remove from heat and stir in butter. Cool mixture slightly.

Combine cream cheese and whipping cream, stirring until smooth; add to lemon mixture and beat until smooth. Makes about 1-1/4 cups. Spread on jelly roll cake and reroll, placing seam side down on cookie sheet.

Beat egg whites until soft peaks form. Gradually add 1/4 cup sugar, beating until stiff peaks form. Spread on sides and top of cake roll; bake at 400 degrees for 8 to 10 minutes or until lightly browned. Makes on 10" cake roll.

ENGLISH LEMON CURD

Curd is good to use in tart shells or as a pie filling. It is a great cake filling, delicious on pound cake, muffins, waffles...almost anything. It is an unusual treat served for breakfast on toast, scones, muffins, biscuits or croissants. Lemon curd keeps beautifully for weeks in a covered jar in the refrigerator for an elegant last-minute dessert. Little jars of curd with lids decorated with white paper doilies and ribbons or lemon leaves also make good gifts.

6 eggs	1/4 cup grated lemon peel
2 egg yolks	3/4 cup fresh lemon juice
2 cups sugar	1 cup (2 sticks) butter

Beat egg yolks and eggs in a small bowl with a fork or wire whisk. Grate lemon peel and squeeze juice. Combine lemon peel, lemon juice, butter and sugar in top pot of double boiler; set in bottom double boiler pot of hot water and stir until butter is melted. Add egg mixture to butter mixture and cook, stirring constantly until mixture is very thick and coats the back of the spoon well, about every 15 minutes. Press a piece of plastic wrap onto the surface of the curd to prevent a skin forming and refrigerate to cool.

Wash five 3/4-cup canning jars, lids and bands in hot soapy water. Rinse; leave jars in hot water. Place lids and bands in a saucepan of simmering water. Ladle curd into hot jars and place a slice of lemon on top. Seal jars and store in refrigerator several weeks.

LEMON DAINTY

A delicate crust will form on top of the pudding and it supplies its own sauce. Very fine. It is a very fine pudding cake...pretty, simple and refreshing.

3 Tablespoons butter	1/4 teaspoon salt
1 cup sugar	3 Tablespoons flour
4 egg yolks	1 cup milk
1/3 cup fresh lemon juice	4 egg whites
2 teaspoons grated lemon rind	1/3 cup toasted slivered almonds

Cream butter, add sugar gradually and continue to cream until light and fluffy. Add egg yolks and beat well. Add flour, lemon juice, rind and salt; mix well. Stir in milk, blend in 1/4 cup almonds. Beat egg whites until stiff and fold into mixture. Pour into 9x5" loaf baking dish; set dish in a pan of hot water and bake in 325 degree oven for 40 minutes. Turn thermostat to 350 degrees and bake until brown (about 10 minutes). Sprinkle with remaining almonds and serve either hot or cold. The baked pudding is a delicate sponge on top and yellow-gold sauce underneath. Served hot in winter with a dollop of whipped cream. It is gorgeous; chilled and served in shallow bowls with fresh berries, it's a lovely summer treat. Makes 8 servings.

PASTRY TARTS

2 cups flour
1/2 teaspoon salt

1/2 cup cold butter
5 Tablespoons cold water

Preheat oven to 425 degrees. Combine flour and salt in a bowl and cut in butter with a pastry blender until pieces are the size of small peas. Sprinkle water gradually over flour mixture, stirring with a fork and drawing flour into a ball. Add just enough water to hold mixture together and pull away from sides of bowl. Pat mixture into a ball and turn out onto a lightly floured board. Roll into a circle and cut shapes to fit small tart pans or muffin tins. Prick each shell with a fork and bake for 12 minutes. Cool and fill with your favorite filling.

OREO COOKIES
AND CREAM DELIGHT
(A new twist for an old favorite)

24 Oreo cookies, crushed
1/2 cup margarine, melted
1/2 gallon vanilla ice cream, softened
1 German chocolate bar, (4 ounces)
1/2 cup margarine
2/3 cup sugar

2/3 cup evaporated milk (5-ounce can)
1 teaspoon vanilla
1/8 teaspoon salt
1 (8-ounce) container, frozen whipped topping
chopped nuts (pecans or walnuts)

Crush cookies and sprinkle onto bottom of a 9x13" pan. Pour 1/2 cup melted margarine over the crumbs. Spread softened ice cream over the crumbs and freeze.

In a small saucepan, combine the chocolate bar, 1/2 cup margarine, sugar, milk, salt and vanilla. Boil for 4 minutes. Cool and pour over the top of ice cream. Top with the frozen whipped topping. Sprinkle with chopped nuts and freeze. Makes 10 to 12 servings.

NOTE: This one is a winner. Also a winner in it's own right is the chocolate sauce which is used in the dessert. It is well worth repeating to make and keep on hand for other desserts. A return to childhood for Oreo and ice cream!!

CLASSIC ENGLISH TRIFLE

Trifle is probably the best known of the British desserts and is a colorful addition to holiday dessert tables. Introduced to America by the British, it was a favorite dessert in Colonial Virginia. It was also known as TIPSY SQUIRE and TIPSY PARSON.

Custard Sauce, chilled:

3/4 cup sugar	3 egg yolks, beaten
1 Tablespoon cornstarch	1 teaspoon vanilla
1/4 teaspoon salt	1/4 teaspoon almond extract
2 cups half and half	

Combine sugar, cornstarch and salt in a heavy saucepan. Blend in half and half and cook, stirring constantly until hot. Pour about 1/3 of the mixture over eggs, stirring constantly. Stir into hot mixture and cook, stirring constantly, about 2 minutes or until mixture coats spoon and thickens. Stir in vanilla and almond extract and chill thoroughly.

Trifle:

2 dozen ladyfingers	1/4 cup brandy
12-ounce jar raspberry or strawberry jam or currant jelly	3/4 cup chopped candied fruits
	3 egg whites
	1/2 teaspoon vanilla
1/4 pound (1-1/4 cups) crumbled almond macaroons	2 Tablespoons sugar
	1/2 cup heavy cream whipped
3/4 cup cream or sweet sherry	

Split ladyfingers and spread bottom halves with preserves or jelly, using 1/2 cup. Put ladyfingers back together and stand them upright around the edge of a 2-quart glass or china serving bowl. Make a layer of ladyfingers over the bottom. Sprinkle 1/3 of the macaroon crumbs over the ladyfingers. Combine sherry and brandy; sprinkle 1/3 of the mixture over the crumbs; spoon 1/3 of remaining preserves over top; cover with 1/3 of chilled custard; sprinkle with 1/3 of the fruit. Repeat twice to make 3 layers.

Chill for several hours. Just before serving, beat egg whites and vanilla until white and foamy. Add sugar, a tablespoonful at a time and continue beating until stiff and glossy. Fold in whipped cream and spoon over trifle. Serve immediately. May be garnished with almonds, glaze cherries and angelica.

RIVIERA PEACHES

8 fresh or canned peach halves   1/3 cup red raspberry jelly
(drained, if canned)   1 pint pistachio ice cream

Place 2 peach halves in each sherbert glass. Melt raspberry jelly and pour over peaches. Refrigerate several hours. Just before serving, top with a scoop of ice cream. Serves 4.

Variation: Use bottled, brandied peaches and stir 1 tablespoon of the syrup into melted raspberry jelly OR use two tablespoons of brandy in melted jelly along with plain peaches.

TENNESSEE TRUFFLES

Sour Cream Chocolate Cake: 1/4 cup shortening
2 cups all-purpose flour   2 eggs
1 teaspoon salt   4 ounces unsweetened chocolate,
1-1/4 teaspoons soda   melted and cooled
1/2 teaspoon baking powder   1 cup water
3/4 cup dairy sour cream

Mix dry ingredients thoroughly. In a mixing bowl, cream sour cream and shortening; add eggs and mix well. Add melted chocolate, followed by dry ingredients alternated with water. Beat until smooth. Pour into miniature cupcake pans. Bake in a 350 degree oven for 10 to 15 minutes or until done, depending on size of cupcake (should be bitesize).

Remove from pans and cool. With an apple corer tool or paring knife, cut a plug out of each small cake and fill the cavity with buttercream frosting, then replace the plug.

Melt coating chocolate in top of double boiler and hold at 90 degrees. Dip each cake in melted chocolate, turning to coat well. Dry on wax paper.

Each truffle may be garnished while still soft with a candy flower or a pecan half. This is an especially good treat for teas, receptions, etc.

Buttercream Frosting: 2 teaspoons vanilla or 1 teaspoon
1/2 cup butter   orange extract
1/4 cup vegetable shortening   2 to 4 Tablespoons water
1 pound confectioners' sugar   12 ounces coating chocolate

Cream butter and shortening; add sugar and flavoring and cream again. Add water slowly until desired spreadable consistency. Beat 3 to 5 minutes.

PECAN TASSIES

1 cup butter, softened	3/4 cup light brown sugar firmly
6 ounces cream cheese, softened	packed
2 cups flour (sifted all-purpose)	1-1/2 cups chopped pecans
1/2 cup butter, softened	1 Tablespoon vanilla
1 egg, lightly beaten	1 cup chopped dates (optional)

In a large bowl, combine 1 cup butter, cream cheese and flour. Mix until well blended. Divide dough into 4 equal parts, then make 12 balls out of each part, all the same size (1"). Place the balls into ungreased miniature muffin pans. Using your thumb and forefinger, press each ball into its cup, working the dough evenly up the sides to the rim. Cream the remaining 1/2 cup butter with the sugar. Add beaten egg, pecans, vanilla and dates if using dates. Mix well. Divide the mixture among the unbaked shells, filling each completely.

Bake until golden brown, about 30 to 40 minutes. Cool on racks before removing the tarts from their pans. To remove, run a sharp knife around the edge and lift out. Sprinkle with powdered sugar before serving. These are lovely delicious tarts for a tea table, but they are a wonderfully easy dessert for large parties as well. They will keep several days before serving and may be frozen. Makes 48 miniature tassies or 24 larger size tassies.

WINE JELLY

(A Colonial Dessert Jelly)

2 cups sugar	juice of 3 lemons
2-2/3 cups cold water, divided	Whipped Cream Topping:
2 lemon rinds, cut into pieces	1 cup heavy cream, whipped,
3 envelopes plain gelatin	sweetened and lightly
2 cups cherry	flavored with almond extract
1 cup rum	

Soak gelatin in 2/3 cup cold water. Bring sugar and 2 cups cold water and lemon rind to a boil. Boil for 15 minutes. Pour hot mixture over the gelatin and stir until dissolved. Add remaining 2 cups water, sherry, rum and lemon juice. Pour into individual dessert cups or a 1-1/2 quart mold. Chill thoroughly. Serve topped with whipped cream and a maraschino cherry.

A delightful old fashioned dessert. Lovely for a luncheon or a very formal finish to a dinner party.

NOTE: A delicious change from whipped cream is a Creme Fraiche made by beating together, with electric mixer, 1/2 cup heavy cream and 1-1/2 tablespoons sugar until soft peaks form. Gently fold in 1/2 cup sour cream. Cover. Refrigerate until serving time.

VANILLA ICE CREAM CUSTARD

1 quart milk (half and half)	2 teaspoons vanilla
2 cups sugar	or
1/2 teaspoon salt	whole vanilla bean, split down
4 eggs	center and teaspoon vanilla
1 pint whipping cream	

Place milk, sugar, and salt in double boiler and heat over hot water. Beat eggs with electric mixer. Dip some of the hot milk mixture into the egg and stir well. Add egg mixture to hot milk, stirring constantly until custard coats the spoon. Let cool and add vanilla and whipping cream. Place in ice cream churn immediately. A quart of your favorite fruit will make delightful variations. Makes 1 gallon.

NOTE: If using vanilla bean, in a 2 quart saucepan, combine whipping cream with 6 tablespoons of sugar and vanilla bean. Slowly bring to a boil, stirring frequently. Remove from heat. Cover and let stand for 30 to 40 minutes to intensify flavor. Remove bean; using point of a paring knife, scrape vanilla grains from inside hull. With fingers rub off any cream or remaining vanilla grains and mix into cream. Then add to the cooled custard before placing in the ice cream churn.

ELEGANT STRAWBERRY CHEESECAKE TRIFLE

2 (8-ounce) cream cheese	1 angel food cake, torn into
2 cups confectioners' sugar	bite-size pieces (1 to 1-1/2"
1 cup dairy sour cream	cubes)
1/2 teaspoon vanilla or 1/4	2 quarts fresh strawberries,
teaspoon powdered vanilla	thinly sliced
1/4 teaspoon almond extract	3 Tablespoons sugar
1/2 pint whipping cream	3 Tablespoons Amaretto liqueur
1 teaspoon vanilla extract or 1/2	(optional) or 1 teaspoon
teaspoon powdered vanilla	almond extract
1 Tablespoon sugar	whole berries for garnish

In a large bowl, cream together cream cheese and sugar. Add sour cream, vanilla and almond extract. Set aside. In a small bowl, whip the cream, vanilla and sugar. Fold whipping cream into the cream cheese mixture. Add cake cubes, stirring gently, coating well. Slice the strawberries, then add the sugar and Amaretto; mix well. Layer into a trifle or clear glass bowl, starting with a layer of strawberries, then a layer of cake/cream cheese mixture. Continue layering, ending with strawberries. Cover with plastic wrap and chill well before serving. Garnish with whole strawberries and mint leaves, if desired. Tastes as wonderful as it looks.

NOTE: Blueberries or fresh sliced peaches may be used instead of strawberries.

GOURMET GINGERBREAD

2 eggs
3/4 cup brown sugar (light or
   dark)
3/4 cup light corn syrup
3/4 cup Crisco
2-1/2 cups plain flour
2 teaspoons baking soda
1/2 teaspoon baking powder
1/2 teaspoon cinnamon
1/2 teaspoon cloves

2 teaspoons ginger
1 cup boiling water
Topping:
1/2 cup melted margarine or butter
1 cup brown sugar
1/2 cup flour
2 teaspoons cinnamon
1 teaspoon grated lemon rind
2/3 cups chopped pecans or
   walnuts

Cream sugar and shortening together, mixing well. Add eggs and beat well. Add syrup and mix well. Sift together dry ingredients and fold in. Lastly, add boiling water and blend. Batter will be very thin. Pour batter into a 9x12" pan that has been lightly oiled and floured. Bake at 350 degrees for 30 minutes. While warm, spread with topping. Return to oven, cook until topping has melted and bubbles, about 5 to 7 minutes.

Five minutes before cooking time is up, mix all topping ingredients until thoroughly blended. Sprinkle on cake and cook for 5 to 7 minutes.

Gingerbread may be served plain or with one of the following sauces.

Whipped Cream Sauce:
1/2 pint whipping cream   1/2 teaspoon cinnamon
2 Tablespoons honey or 3
   Tablespoons confectioners
   sugar

Beat cream well in a mixing bowl until just before it holds a peak. Add honey and cinnamon and complete beating until it forms a peak. Chill. Makes 1 cup.

Lemon Sauce:
juice of 1-1/2 medium to large   3 egg yolks
   lemon   2 whole eggs
1 cup sugar   1-1/2 Tablespoons butter
1-1/2 heaping Tablespoons flour

Mix lemon juice and enough water to make 1-1/2 cups of liquid in a 2 cup measuring cup. Place the liquid in the top of a double boiler. Mix sugar and flour together and add to the lemon juice. Beat egg yolks and whole eggs and add to the mixture. Place the double boiler over high heat until water in the bottom comes to a boil, turn heat to a simmer. Stir lemon sauce to keep from forming lumps and until it becomes thick. When sauce is thick, remove from heat and add butter, stirring until melted.

OLD-FASHION
STRAWBERRY SHORTCAKE

The term "short" refers to the crisp texture of pastry made with a generous amount of shortening. European cooks were making shortcakes well before the colonization of America; and when the first settlers discovered the wealth of wild berries in their new homeland, they soon put them between rich shortcake layers. Today some people use sponge cake or butter cake for their berry cakes, but those are not genuine shortcakes.

4 cups sifted all-purpose flour	Filling and topping:
4 teaspoons baking powder	1 quart fresh, ripe strawberries
2/3 cup sugar	2 Tablespoons soft butter
1/2 cup butter	1-1/2 cups heavy cream
1/2 cup Crisco	2 Tablespoons sugar
2 large eggs, beaten	1/2 teaspoon vanilla
1-1/2 cups whole milk or	1/4 cup kirsh or light rum,
half-and-half	optional
1/2 teaspoon salt	

Sift flour with baking powder, salt, and 1/3 cup sugar. Cut butter into small chunks and blend into flour mixture with pastry cutter or two knives until mixture resembles coarse cornmeal. Beat eggs to mix well and stir in half-and-half (cream or milk may be substituted).

Drizzle liquid over flour and stir well. If there are still some dry ingredients left in the bowl, drizzle in a little more half-and-half, but just a small amount at a time. The dough should just hold together when pressed.

Turn mixture onto a lightly floured board and shape into a ball, pressing lightly (avoid handling the dough too much). Cut the ball in half with a sharp knife and shape into two smaller balls, using floured hands. Butter two 8" cake pans and press dough with floured fingers to fill the pans. Bake at 425 degrees in the middle of the oven for 12 minutes until medium golden in color.

Meanwhile, wash, dry, and hull strawberries. Slice berries into a small bowl and sprinkle with 1/3 cup sugar and kirsh (if desired).

Reserve several of the best-looking berries for the top. Let berries stand 30 minutes, stirring occasionally. Whip cream with 2 tablespoons sugar and 1/2 teaspoon vanilla until stiff.

When cakes are ready, turn out on wire racks and brush tops with soft butter, about one tablespoon for each top. Place one cake on a serving plate and top with half of the berrries and half whipped cream. Top with the second cake and spoon on remaining berries. Either spoon on whipped cream or serve it on the side. Decorate with whole berries. Cut into wedges and serve.

ELEGANT LEMON SOUFFLE

2 envelopes unflavored gelatin
1/2 cup cold water
6 large eggs
6 large egg yolks
1-1/2 cups sugar
1 cup fresh lemon juice
2 Tablespoons grated lemon peel
1-3/4 sticks unsalted butter, chilled and cut into small pieces

1 cup heavy cream (whipping)
2 dozen ladyfingers
1/2 cup heavy cream, sweetened and whipped (optional)
Thin lemon slice (optional)
Garnish:
   Fresh mint leaves
   Strawberries
   Raspberries

Dissolve gelatin in cold water. Whisk eggs and egg yolks in a heavy non-aluminum saucepan until foamy. Whisk in the sugar, then lemon juice. Mix in grated peel. Stir in gelatin mixture. Cook over low heat, stirring constantly until mixture thickens to consistency of heavy custard. About 10 minutes. Do not allow to boil. Remove from heat and stir in butter until melted. Transfer mixture to a bowl and cool until very thick, stirring occasionally, about 50 minutes.

Whip cream in a medium bowl to form soft peaks. Fold cream into lemon mixture just until combined. Butter the bottom of a 9" springform pan and line with ladyfingers. Stand ladyfingers up around the sides. Spoon souffle mixture into pan, cover with wax paper or plastic wrap. Refrigerate until set. About 4 hours or may be made the day before serving. Serve with fresh raspberry or strawberry sauce if desired.

Optional but beautiful; spoon dollops of sweetened whipped cream around outer edge, next to ladyfingers. Take a thin slice of lemon cut through the middle of the lemon and twist into an "S" shape. Place in the middle. Garnish with mint leaves and berries.

This is a rich dessert so small portions can be served.

DOUBLE CHOCOLATE SAUCE

6 ounce package semi-sweet chocolate morsels
2 ounces unsweetened chocolate, quartered
1 cup sifted powdered sugar

2/3 cup half-and-half
1/2 cup light corn syrup
2 Tablespoons butter
1/2 teaspoon salt
1 Tablespoon vanilla extract

Place chocolate in container of electric blender. Combine next 5 ingredients in medium saucepan and cook over medium heat until bubbly. Pour sugar mixture over chocolate; add vanilla. Process mixture 1 minute or until smooth. Serve warm with fresh fruit. Yields 2 cups. Sauce is also delicious served warm over ice cream or cake.

BAKED ALASKA PIE

9" baked pie shell
16 marshmallows
1 Tablespoon water or canned
   pineapple juice
2 egg whites

1/4 cup granulated sugar
1/4 teaspoon salt
2 cups chilled fresh or frozen
   raspberries
1 quart vanilla ice cream

Refrigerate pie shell until well chilled. Preheat broiler for 10 minutes. Over low heat, heat marshmallows with water or juice, folding constantly, until marshmallows are melted. Beat whites until quite stiff; gradually add sugar and salt, beating until very stiff. Fold in marshmallow mixture. Sprinkle 1 cup of berries into pie shell. Fill with ice cream. Then sprinkle the rest of the berries onto ice cream. Top with meringue, covering the ice cream completely all the way around, out to the edge of the pie to seal in the ice cream (this helps to keep the ice cream firm). Broil several inches below heat until lightly browned. Serve at once. Strawberries and peaches can be used in place of the raspberries.

NOTE: This pie can be made ahead of time and frozen. To serve, remove from freezer about 45 minutes ahead of serving time, so it can be easily cut.

CREME DE MENTHE ICE CREAM PIE

5-1/2 Tablespoons butter
1 box (8-1/2 ounce) Nabisco
   Famous Chocolate Wafers
1/2 gallon vanilla ice cream,
   divided
5 Tablespoons green creme de
   menthe

1 (1-ounce) square unsweetened
   chocolate
2-1/2 Tablespoons water
1/4 cup sugar
1-1/2 Tablespoons butter
dash of salt
1/4 teaspoon vanilla

Melt butter. Crush chocolate wafers in a blender. Mix butter and crumbs; press into a 9" spring-form pan, covering bottom and then sides to 1-1/2" high. Freeze.

Allow ice cream to soften to foldable stage. Using a large bowl, swirl the creme de menthe with 6 cups of ice cream. Pour into crust and spread evenly. Return to freezer. Whip 2 cups ice cream and pour over creme de menthe mixture to form a smooth white layer and return to freezer.

Over low heat, melt chocolate in water. Add sugar and salt, cooking and stirring until sugar is melted and mixture is thickened. Remove from heat and add butter and vanilla. Cool slightly. Drizzle fudge sauce over top of pie and return to freezer for at least 3 hours. Serves 6 to 8 persons.

LEMON VOLCANO PIE

1/2 cup butter	1 quart vanilla or French vanilla
1/3 cup lemon juice	ice cream
2 Tablespoons lemon rind	baked 9" pie shell
1/4 teaspoon salt	3 egg whites
1-1/2 cups sugar	1/2 empty egg shell
2 eggs	brandy, warmed
3 egg yolks	

Melt butter in top of double boiler. Add juice, rind, salt and 1 cup of sugar. Beat 2 eggs and 3 yolks thoroughly; gradually stir into butter mixture. Cook over hot water, stirring constantly, until thick and smooth. Chill.

Allow ice cream to soften, then press half of the ice cream in the pie shell; freeze. Spread half the lemon filling over frozen pie; freeze. Repeat layers. Beat egg whites until foamy; add sugar gradually, continuing to beat until stiff. Spread meringue on frozen pie, sealing edges. Insert half an egg shell in center; freeze. Just before serving, brown in 475 degree oven (1 to 3 minutes). Fill egg shell with brandy and ignite. An extraordinary and beautiful dessert for 8 persons which tastes as good as it looks!

NOTE: A lemon or other citrus fruit heated in hot water will yield 2 tablespoons more juice than an unheated fruit.

MISSISSIPPI MUD PIE

1 (15-ounce) package chocolate cream-filled cookies, crushed	2 Tablespoons brandy or 2 Tablespoons Kahlua
5 Tablespoons butter/margarine, melted	1/2 cup plus 2 Tablespoons chopped pecans or toasted
1 pint chocolate ice cream, softened	almonds
1/2 teaspoon vanilla	2 Tablespoons chocolate syrup or
1 teaspoon instant coffee powder	Best In The World Chocolate
1 (12-ounce) carton frozen whipped topping, thawed and divided	Sauce
	cherries

Combine cookie crumbs and butter, mixing well. Press mixture firmly into a 10" pie plate and place in freezer. Combine ice cream, vanilla, coffee powder, 1 cup whipped topping, brandy and 1/2 cup chopped nuts; mix well. Spread evenly on chocolate crust, cover and freeze overnight. Spread remaining whipped topping on pie, drizzle chocolate syrup over the top and sprinkle with 2 tablespoons chopped nuts. Top with a cherry before serving.

NOTE: For a really spirited pie, use both brandy and Kahlua.

BEST IN THE WORLD CHOCOLATE SAUCE

1 (13-ounce) can evaporated milk
1 pound caramels
1 cup butter

1 (12-ounce) package semisweet chocolate chips or 12-ounce chocolate bar

Combine milk, caramels, butter and chocolate in top of double boiler. Stir until smooth and cook for 30 minutes, stirring frequently. Remove from heat and beat 3 minutes with electric mixer. Serve warm or refrigerate.

CHOCOLATE ANGEL PIE

3 egg whites
1/8 teaspoon salt
1/8 teaspoon cream of tartar
3/4 cup sugar
1/2 teaspoon vanilla
3/4 cup chopped pecans

Chocolate Filling:
1/4 pound sweet chocolate
3 Tablespoons strong black coffee
1 teaspoon vanilla
1 cup whipped cream

Add salt and cream of tartar to egg whites; beat until stiff but not dry. Gradually add in sugar; fold in vanilla and nuts. Spread in a 9" pie pan, building up the sides. Place in a cold oven and bake for 55 minutes at 300 degrees. When cold, cover with chocolate filling made as follows: melt chocolate and blend well with coffee; add vanilla and cool; fold in whipped cream. Refrigerate pie for 2 to 3 hours. Just before serving, decorate with whipped cream.

MISS ANNA'S FROZEN GERMAN CHOCOLATE PIE

1 chocolate pie shell
1 (4-ounce) sweet German chocolate bar
1/3 cup milk
1 (3-ounce) package cream cheese, softened

1 Tablespoon sugar
1 (8-ounce) carton frozen Le Creme topping, softened
1/2 cup chopped pecans

Melt chocolate with 2 tablespoons milk in a small sauce pan over low heat. Add cream cheese to melted chocolate, stirring to mix well. Add remaining milk and 1 tablespoon sugar; cool. When cool, fold in Le Creme topping, mix well and freeze. To serve, garnish with a dollop of whipped cream of Le Creme, chocolate curls and a maraschino cherry or chopped nuts. Preparation time for freezing approximately 10 minutes. So very quick and easy! It takes about 10 minutes to prepare. Then it can be frozen and taken out before serving time.

TENNESSEE FABULOUS FUDGE PIE

1 cup sugar
1/8 teaspoon salt
2 eggs, beaten
1/2 cup butter/margarine
2 squares chocolate or 7
   Tablespoons cocoa

1/4 cup plain flour
1 teaspoon vanilla
1/2 cup chopped nuts (pecans,
   walnuts or hickory nuts)
ice cream or whipped cream

Melt butter and chocolate in double boiler; pour into mixing bowl and cool. Mix sugar, salt and beaten eggs together and add to butter and chocolate. Add flour and vanilla, beating until smooth. Add nuts and pour mixture into slightly greased glass pie pan. Bake for about 35 minutes at 300 degrees. Allow pie to set for two hours before serving. Serve with whipped cream or vanilla ice cream. Freezes well.

CHOCOLATE VELVET PIE

2 teaspoons softened butter/
   margarine
2 Tablespoons dry bread crumbs
8 (8-ounce) squares semisweet
   chocolate (save one for
   garnish)

3 Tablespoons hot water
7 eggs, separated
1/8 teaspoon salt
2/3 cup sugar, divided
1-1/2 teaspoons vanilla
2 cups whipped cream, divided

Coat a 9" pie plate generously with butter; sprinkle with bread crumbs to cover evenly; set aside. Combine seven squares of chocolate with hot water and melt over barely simmering water. Cover and allow to stand over low heat until chocolate has melted. Remove from heat and stir chocolate rapidly until smooth. Beat egg whites with salt until foamy and double in volume (be sure beater and bowl are perfectly clean). Add 1/3 cup sugar, one tablespoon at a time, beating well after each addition until sugar is dissolved (to test, rub a bit between your thumb and index finger; the sample should be smooth, not grainy). Continue beating until whites are smooth and form stiff peaks. Beat egg yolks in a large bowl until lemon colored. Gradually beat in remaining sugar and continue beating until thick. Add vanilla and gradually beat in melted chocolate, scraping sides of bowl often to make sure ingredients are well blended.

Stir 1/4 of the beaten egg whites into the chocolate mixture until smooth; then gently fold in remainder until mixture has a uniform color, with no light or dark streaks. Pour half of the mixture into prepared pie plate, spreading top to smooth (mixture should come just even with the rim of the pie plate). Bake at 350 degrees for 20 minutes; remove from oven and cool on a wire rack for two hours. As it cools, it sinks in the center to form a shell.

(Continued)

While shell is baking, quickly but gently fold 2/3 cup of whipped cream into remaining chocolate mixture, blending until no streaks of white remain. Cover bowl and refrigerate. When shell has cooled, fill with chocolate mixture, swirling the top with the back of a spoon. Drop dollops of whipped cream from a spoon to form a decorative border around edges of pie. Chill until ready to serve.

Just before serving, make chocolate curls for a garnish: hold remaining square of chocolate in your hand for a minute to warm slightly, then slowly but firmly draw the blade of a vegetable parer across the flat surface of the block, allowing curls to drop onto a plate. Make large and small curls. If the kitchen is hot, curls may need to be chilled a few minutes to firm. To pick up each curl, pass a toothpick or one tine of a fork through the hollow center. Gently drop chocolate curls in place on whipped cream border. Serves eight persons.

APPLE CRUNCH PIE

Crust:
1-1/2 cups flour
2 teaspoons sugar
1 teaspoon salt
1/3 cup oil
2 Tablespoons milk
Filling:
2/3 cup sugar
1/4 cups flour
1 teaspoon cinnamon

4 cups sliced cooking apples
(canned apple slices may be
used)
1/2 cup sour cream
Topping:
1 cup crushed cornflakes
1/3 cup flour
1/3 cup brown sugar
1/2 teaspoon cinnamon
1/2 teaspoon nutmeg
1/4 cup butter/margarine,
softened

To make crust, combine flour, sugar, salt, oil and milk in a medium size bowl and mix well. Pat into an ungreased 9" pie pan. Combine sugar, flour, cinnamon, apple slices and sour cream in a large bowl and mix well; spoon into unbaked crust. Combine crushed cornflakes, flour, brown sugar, cinnamon, nutmeg and butter in a small bowl, mixing well. Sprinkle over apples. Bake at 375 degrees for 40 to 45 minutes or until topping is a golden brown and apples are tender. Serve with vanilla ice cream if desired.

CRUNCHY CARAMEL APPLE PIE

1 (9") unbaked pastry shell
6 cups peeled tart apple slices
1/2 cup flour
1/3 cup brown sugar, packed
1/2 teaspoon cinnamon
1/2 cup chopped pecans

1/3 cup butter or margarine
3 Caramel Wrapples sheets or 16
   square caramels
1 stick butter or margarine
1/3 cup milk

If using caramels, melt with butter and milk over low heat, stirring constantly to keep from scorching. Set aside. Place half of the apple slices in the pastry shell. Top with 2 caramel sheets or 1/2 of melted caramels. Spoon caramel over the remaining apples and top with the last caramel sheet or last of caramel mixture, covering the top. Combine flour, sugar, cinnamon and nuts. Cut in margarine until mixture resembles coarse crumbs. Sprinkle over caramel. Bake at 375 degrees for 40 to 45 minutes or until apples are tender. Cool and serve or serve hot.

HARVEST APPLE PIE

1/2 cup sugar
1/2 cup brown sugar, firmly
   packed
1/4 cup flour
1/2 teaspoon cinnamon
1/4 teaspoon nutmeg
1/8 teaspoon salt
1/4 cup butter/margarine

6 to 8 medium-sized tart apples,
   peeled, cored and sliced (6
   cups)
2 teaspoons lemon juice
1 unbaked (9") cheese pastry shell
1/4 cup heavy cream
Cinnamon Ice Cream

Mix sugars, flour, cinnamon, nutmeg and salt together in a small bowl; cut in butter or margarine. Place apples in a large bowl and sprinkle with lemon juice; add 1-1/2 cups sugar mixture and toss gently to coat apples evenly. Arrange apples in pastry shell and sprinkle with remaining 1/2 cup sugar mixture. Bake at 450 degrees for 10 minutes; reduce heat to 350 degrees and continue baking 25 more minutes or until apples are just tender. Carefully pour cream over apples and bake 10 minutes longer. Serve warm with slices of cheddar cheese, plain or with Cinnamon Ice Cream.

Cheese Pastry Shell: plain pastry recipe
1/2 cup grated cheddar cheese

Cut in cheese with shortening called for in a plain pastry recipe.

Cinnamon Ice Cream: 1/2 cup sugar
1 quart vanilla ice cream, softened   1 Tablespoon ground cinnamon

Combine all ingredients in a large mixing bowl, blending well. Freeze until firm. Serve by large rounded spoon on apple pie. Makes a delicious added extra to apple pie.

APPLE WALNUT SOUR CREAM PIE

Crust:
1-3/4 cups flour
1/4 cup sugar
1 teaspoon cinnamon
1 teaspoon salt
5 ounces butter
4 Tablespoons water (or as needed)
Filling:
1-1/2 cups sour cream
1 large egg
1 cup sugar
1/2 cup flour

1/4 teaspoon vanilla
1/4 teaspoon salt
2-1/2 pounds tart apples (Granny
Smith or McIntosh), peeled
and cored
8 ounces unsalted butter
1 cup flour
2/3 cup white sugar
2/3 cup light brown sugar
1 Tablespoon cinnamon
1/2 teaspoon salt
2 cups walnuts, chopped

To make crust, combine flour, sugar, cinnamon and salt in a large bowl. Chop butter into dry ingredients with a pastry cutter until all is added (do not mix with hands). After all butter is added, pour enough water into mixture to bind dough together. Lightly grease two 9" pie pans. Roll dough out to 1/4" thick; place in pie pans, crimping edges. Bake at 325 degrees for 10 minutes; cool at room temperature.

Combine egg and sugar with sour cream in a large bowl and whip until blended. Add the 1/2 cup flour, vanilla and 1/4 teaspoon salt. Sliced peeled, cored apples into thin slices; add apples to mixture and toss. Fill prepared baked pie shells with mixture.

Cut butter into pea-size chunks. Combine 1 cup flour, 2/3 cup white sugar, 2/3 cup brown sugar, cinnamon, salt and walnuts in a large bowl. Add butter pieces to the dry ingredients and mix together. Place on top of apple mixture and bake pies in a 325 degree oven for 1 hour. Cool before cutting.

BANANA CREAM PIE

3/4 cup sugar
1/3 cup cornstarch
2-1/2 cups milk and 3/4 cup half
and half
5 egg yolks, slightly beaten
3 Tablespoons unsalted butter

3 teaspoons vanilla
2 large ripe bananas
1 fully baked 9" pie shell
1-1/2 cups heavy cream
1 ripe banana, sliced, for garnish
(optional)

Stir 1/2 cup sugar and cornstarch together in heavy-bottomed 2-quart saucepan. Stir in milk and half and half. Cook, stirring over medium-low heat, until thickened and bubbly (about 3 minutes). Remove from heat. Slowly stir 1 cup hot mixture into yolks in a small bowl. Stir yolk mixture back into saucepan and return saucepan to medium-low heat. Bring to a slow boil, stirring constantly. Cook, stirring, another 3 minutes; mixture will be thick. Remove from heat and stir in butter and 2 teaspoons of vanilla. Place plastic wrap directly on surface and allow to cool 15 minutes.

(Continued)

Slice one banana over bottom of crust; mash remaining banana in a small bowl. Gently stir mashed banana into pie filling mixture. Pour over sliced banana. Place plastic wrap directly over filling and refrigerate at least 4 hours.

To serve, beat heavy cream with remaining 1/4 cup sugar and 1 teaspoon vanilla until stiff. Remove plastic wrap from pie and spread whipped cream decoratively over filling. Garnish with banana slices, if you wish. This pie is best eaten the day made.

CHERRY PIE SUPREME

This pie combines two all-time American favorites — cherry pie and cheesecake. They are subtly mingled to make an applause winning pie. It is an elegant combination.

9" unbaked pie shell	1/2 cup sugar
1 (1 pound, 5 ounce) can Cherry	2 eggs
Pie Filling	1/2 teaspoon vanilla
4 (3-ounce) packages cream	1 cup dairy sour cream
cheese, softened	

Preheat oven to 425 degrees. Prepare pie shell. Spread half of cherry pie filling in bottom and set remainder aside. Bake shell 15 minutes or until crust is golden. Remove from oven and reduce oven temperature to 350 degrees.

Meanwhile, using a small bowl and a portable electric mixer, beat cheese with sugar, eggs and vanilla until smooth. Pour over hot cherry pie filling and bake 25 minutes (filling will be slightly soft in center). Cool completely on wire rack. To serve, spoon sour cream around edge of pie. Fill center with remaining cherry pie filling. Makes 8 servings.

Variation: Change to Blueberry Pie Supreme by substituting 1 can blueberry pie filling for cherry pie filling.

BLACKBERRY PIE

2 pie crusts, 9" size	1 to 1-1/2 Tablespoons lemon juice
6 cups fresh blackberries	1/4 teaspoon salt
1 cup sugar	1 Tablespoon butter/margarine
1/4 cups all-purpose flour or 1-1/2	1 egg white, beaten to blend
Tablespoons flour and 1-1/2	1 Tablespoon sugar
Tablespoons cornstarch	2 Tablespoons blackberry brandy

Line a 9" pie pan with one pastry; brush bottom of crust with some of egg white. Combine berries, sugar, flour, lemon juice and salt in a bowl; toss well. Spoon berry mixture into pastry-lined pie plate. Dot mixture with butter. Roll out remaining pastry to 1/8" thick and cut into ten strips 1/2 " wide. Arrange strips in lattice design over pie and trim edges; seal and flute. Brush lattice with remaining egg white and sprinkle with 1 tablespoon sugar. Bake at 350 degrees for 50 to 55 minutes. (Cover the edges with foil to keep the edges from overbrowning, if necessary).

(Continued)

If desired, the pie may be covered with a complete crust instead of lattice strips. Serve either cold or hot. A scoop of ice cream may be added. This recipe may also be used for cobbler, using a single crust (spoon berry mixture into deep casserole dish and top with one crust).
NOTE: For a truly delicious pie, add 2 tablespoons of a good blackberry flavored brandy to the berries when combining with sugar and flour mixture.

FRESH PEACH COBBLER WITH COOKIE CRUST

2-1/2 pounds fresh peaches,
    peeled and sliced (5 cups)
1/2 cup sugar
2 Tablespoons cornstarch
1/2 teaspoon ground cinnamon
1/2 teaspoon almond extract
1/2 cup light corn syrup
1 (17-ounce) package refrigerator
    sugar cookie dough

Place peaches in a 8x8x2" baking dish. In a small bowl, stir together, cornstarch and cinnamon. Gradually stir in corn syrup and almond extract until smooth. Pour over peaches and stir until peaches are well coated. Slice cookie dough into 1/4" slices. Arrange slices in rows on top of peach mixture. Bake at 350 degrees for one hour or until golden brown. Cool. If desired, top with ice cream. Makes 8 servings.

FRESH PEACH PIE

5 cups fresh, firm peaches, sliced
1 Tablespoon lemon juice
1-1/3 cups sugar
3 Tablespoons cornstarch
1 (3-ounce) package peach or
    apricot Jello
1-1/3 cups peach juice
1/4 teaspoon almond flavoring
dash salt
1 (8-ounce) package cream
    cheese, softened
2 to 3 Tablespoons milk or coffee
    cream
2 teaspoons lemon juice
1 cup heavy cream
2 teaspoons sugar
1 deep-dish pie shell, baked and
    cooled

Peel and slice enough peaches to make 5 cups. Sprinkle peaches with lemon juice and sugar, cover and allow to stand for one hour. Drain juice from peaches. If juice doesn't measure 1-1/3 cups, mash a ripe, soft peach to get amount needed. If you have more than 1-1/3 cups juice, bring to a boil and reduce to 1-1/2 cups juice. Mix gelatin and cornstarch together well; add peach juice. Cook, stirring constantly, over medium heat until a thickened, translucent amber and will flake off spoon (about 3 to 4 minutes). Remove from heat, add almond flavoring and allow to cool but not set.

Meanwhile, mix softened cream cheese with lemon juice and milk, beating until fluffy. Spread over bottoms and up sides of cooled pie crust. Fold drained sliced peaches into cooled juice and gelatin mixture; spoon into crust. Chill until ready to serve.

To serve, whip heavy cream with 2 teaspoons sugar and top pie. To garnish, add an extra slice of peach or sprinkle with nutmeg. Pies will keep in refrigerator for a day or two. The cream cheese on bottom and sides of crust keep it from getting soggy.

FRESH PEACH PARFAIT PIE

1 cup sifted plain flour
1/4 teaspoon salt
1/4 cup light brown sugar
1/2 cup margarine
1/2 cup chopped nuts (almonds
   or pecans)
Filling:
1 (3-ounce) package lemon Jello

1-1/4 cups boiling water
1 pint (2 cups) vanilla ice cream,
   softened
1/2 teaspoon almond extract
2 cups fresh peaches, sliced
1 cup heavy cream, whipped for
   topped

Mix flour, salt and brown sugar. Cut in margarine then mix in nuts. Spread into a 9" pie pan and bake in a 400 degree oven for about 10 to 15 minutes or until light brown in color. Remove and stir immediately. Then press with back of a spoon on bottom and sides of pie pan. Cool.

In a large bowl, combine lemon Jello and boiling water, stir to dissolve Jello. Cool and set aside only until it reaches a syrupy stage. Stir in softened vanilla ice cream. Blend in almond extract. Fold in sliced peaches. Spoon into crust. Chill at least 2 hours or until firm. Remove from refrigerator a few minutes before serving. Top with whipped cream and a slice of peach.

PEACH PIE

Crust:
1-1/2 cups flour
1/4 teaspoon salt
1/4 teaspoon sugar
6 Tablespoons butter, chilled
2 Tablespoons vegetable
   shortening
4 to 5 Tablespoons ice water
Filling:
5 cups peaches, peeled and sliced
1 teaspoon almond extract
1 cup sugar
3/4 cup dark brown sugar
1/4 cup flour
1/4 teaspoon salt

2 Tablespoons lemon juice
3 Tablespoons butter
1 teaspoon ground cinnamon
1 teaspoon ground nutmeg
1 Tablespoon grated orange rind
Topping:
1/4 cup dark brown sugar
2 Tablespoons flour
2 Tablespoons butter
1/2 teaspoon ground cinnamon
Cream:
1 cup whipping cream
1 Tablespoon orange liqueur
1 teaspoon grated orange rind

For crust, mix flour, salt and sugar. Cut in butter and shortening. Gradually add ice water until moist. Knead one minute. Divide into two balls and refrigerate one hour. Roll out one ball for 9" pie pan. Prebake bottom crust for 10 minutes at 350 degrees.

Combine peaches, almond extract, sugars, flour, salt and lemon juice. Allow to stand 5 minutes; drain and reserve liquid. Turn into pie shell and sprinkle with butter, cinnamon, nutmeg and orange rind. Add enough reserved liquid to cover fruit. Top with lattice crust formed from second ball of pastry.

(Continued)

For topping, mix brown sugar, flour, butter and cinnamon until crumbly. Spoon lightly into lattice holes. Bake at 400 degrees for 40 minutes on making sheet. Baste with juices that run over and any remaining reserved liquid until crust is glazed. Just before serving, beat cream, orange liqueur and orange rind until stiff. Serve over pie. Serves 8.

BERRY DAIRY PIE

Crust:
1 cup all-purpose flour
1/2 cup butter, softened
1/2 cup coarsely chopped nuts
    (pecans or walnuts)
1/4 cup light brown sugar
Filling:
4 ounces cream cheese, softened
3/4 cup confectioners' sugar

1 cup whipping cream
Topping:
1 pound frozen strawberries,
    thawed (reserve juice)
1 cup juice from strawberries
1 (3-ounce) package strawberry
    Jello, preferably Wild
    Strawberry

Mix flour, butter, nuts and brown sugar together until well blended. Press into the bottom and sides of a 9" pie pan. Bake in a preheated oven 350 degrees until light brown, about 8 minutes (slightly under bake). Cool on wire rack.

Put softened cream cheese and confectioners' sugar in a bowl. Blend together until smooth. Whip cream until it forms peaks. Fold whipped cream into the cheese mixture and spread over the cooled crust. Refrigerate. Heat the juice (1 cup) to a boiling point and pour over the Jello in the mixing bowl. Stir until dissolved. Add thawed berries. Cool to room temperature, then gently spoon over pie filling. Refrigerate overnight. Serve each slice of pie with a tablespoon of whipped cream and a fresh strawberry with a stem on.

"J's" FRESH STRAWBERRY PIE
(Lowell Inn)

Shell:
2 cups plain flour
1 cup Crisco
1 teaspoon salt
2 Tablespoons cold water
Filling:
1 cup crushed fresh strawberries
1 cup sugar

2 Tablespoons plain flour or 1
    Tablespoon flour and 1
    Tablespoon cornstarch (This
    gives you the best of both)
fresh whole strawberries to fill a
    9" pie shell
red food coloring
pinch of salt

Sift flour and cut in shortening. Combine salt and water. Add to flour mixture, stirring quickly until a soft dough is formed. Roll on a floured board to 1/4" thickness and to fit a 10" pie plate. Bake at 425 degrees for 15 minutes or until golden brown.

(Continued)

Wash and hull all strawberries before you start to make the syrup so they can be well drained on a paper towel before placing in the baked pie shell. This helps prevent a soggy crust. Crush 1 cup of berries (small berries, slightly green and pieces). A blender is very good for this. Mix flour, sugar, salt and cornstarch if using, blending well. In a heavy bottom saucepan, combine crushed strawberries and the flour mixture, stirring well to blend. Place over medium heat, cook stirring constantly to prevent scorching. Cook until mixture flakes off spoon and is a crystal clear transparent color. Remove from heat and add a few drops of red food coloring.

Fill pie shell with clean whole strawberries. Spoon the berry syrup over the strawberries in the shell. Chill in the refrigerator before serving. A ring of whipped cream may be placed around the pie near the crust. Spoon a dollop of whipped cream in the center of the pie and top with a whole strawberry with leaves on. You will never taste a better pie or see a more perfect picture.

NOTE: If strawberries lack flavor, add 2 tablespoons wild strawberry Jello. Mix with sugar and flour, before cooking. You may add anyway, for added flavor.

STRAWBERRY CHEESECAKE PIE "EXTRAORDINAIRE"

Of the strawberry it was written (some 300 years ago): "Doubtless, God could have made a better berry but, doubtless, God never did." Even today, strawberries rate as a perennial favorite.

Crust:
1 package graham crackers, crumbled
1/4 cups melted butter
Cheesecake Filling:
2 (8-ounce) packages cream cheese, softened
3/4 cup sugar
2 teaspoons fresh lemon juice
1/2 teaspoon vanilla
3 eggs
Sour Cream Topping:

8 ounces sour cream
1/2 cup sugar
1/2 teaspoon vanilla
Strawberry Topping:
1-1/2 Tablespoons cornstarch
1-1/2 Tablespoons wild strawberry gelatin
1/2 cup hot water
1/2 cup sugar
3 to 4 drops red food coloring
1 pint fresh, sliced strawberries

Mix melted butter and graham cracker crumbs together and shape to fit a 10" pie plate. Combine the softened cream cheese and sugar; beat until smooth. Add eggs, one at a time, beating well after each addition. Add vanilla and mix well. Pour into unbaked graham cracker crust and bake 30 minutes at 350 degrees. Allow to cool.

Mix sour cream, sugar and vanilla together and pour on top of the cheese cake. Bake 15 minutes at 350 degrees; allow to cool. Mix cornstarch, gelatin and sugar. Gradually add hot water, stirring constantly to prevent lumping. Add food coloring and cook over medium heat until thickened. Cool. Add sliced strawberries and spread over the cheesecake. Chill until ready to serve.

FRESH BLUEBERRY PIE

9-5/8" pie shell
1 (8-ounce) package cream
   cheese, softened
2 to 3 Tablespoons milk or coffee
   cream
2 teaspoons lemon juice
4 cups fresh blueberries, washed
   and drained

3/4 cup sugar
2 Tablespoons cornstarch
1/4 cup water
1 teaspoon lemon juice
1 cup heavy cream
2 teaspoons sugar

Bake pie shell and cool. Meanwhile, beat softened cream cheese until fluffy, adding milk a tablespoon at a time. Add 2 teaspoons lemon juice; beat well. Spread cream cheese mixture on bottom and sides of baked pie shell. Fill shell with 3 cups blueberries.

Mash 1 cup blueberries. Stir sugar and cornstarch together in a 2-quart saucepan. Gradually stir in water until smooth; add mashed blueberries and one teaspoon lemon juice. Over medium heat, stirring constantly, cook until thickened and boiling. Boil one minute; pour cooked mixture over the berries in the baked shell. Chill thoroughly before serving. Top with heavy cream whipped with 2 teaspoons sugar.

CAROLE'S PECAN PIE

3 eggs
1 cup sugar
1/2 cup corn syrup or 1 cup Mrs.
   Butterworth's syrup with butter

1/2 cup melted butter
1 cup pecans (chopped or halves)
9" unbaked pastry shell

Preheat oven to 375 degrees. Beat eggs slightly, using a 2-quart bowl. Stir in sugar, syrup and melted butter. Stir in pecans. Pour into unbaked pastry shell and bake near center of oven at 375 degrees for 35 to 40 minutes, or until filling is slightly firm.

MYSTERY PECAN PIE

An unusual and delightfully luscious nut pie layered with creamy cheesecake.

1 (8-ounce) package cream
   cheese, softened
1/3 cup plus 1/4 cup sugar
1/4 teaspoon salt
2 teaspoons vanilla

4 eggs
9" or 10" unbaked pie shell
1-1/4 cups chopped pecans
1 cup light corn syrup

Combine cream cheese, 1/3 cup sugar, salt, 1 teaspoon vanilla and 1 egg. Pour into pastry shell. Sprinkle with pecans. Combine remaining eggs, sugar, vanilla and syrup; pour over pecans. Bake at 375 degrees for 35 to 40 minutes until center is firm. Makes 6 to 8 generous servings or 10 smaller servings.

RICH'S MAGNOLIA ROOM PECAN PIE

This recipe was given out as a favor at a Georgia Medical Auxiliary State Meeting years ago in Atlanta at their downtown store.

3 whole large eggs	1/2 cups sugar
2 Tablespoons butter	1-1/2 cups dark corn syrup
2 Tablespoons flour	1-1/2 cups broken pecan halves
1/4 teaspoon vanilla	1 unbaked 8" pie shell
1/8 teaspoon salt	

Beat eggs, blend in melted butter, flour, vanilla, salt, sugar and syrup. Sprinkle nuts over bottom of unbaked pastry shell. Gently pour over the syrup mixture and bake in a hot oven 425 degrees for 10 minutes. Reduce heat to a slow oven (325 degrees) and bake about 40 minutes. Serves 6. Serve plain or with ice cream or for an extra special touch, with a dollop of Chantilly Cream.

Chantilly Cream:	1 teaspoon grand marnier
2/3 cup heavy cream	1/4 cup sugar
1 teaspoon vanilla	2 Tablespoons sour cream
1 teaspoon brandy	

Combine cream, vanilla, brandy and grand marnier and chill. Beat at medium speed for about 1 minute. Add sugar and sour cream. Beat at medium speed, until soft peaks form, about 3 minutes. Do not over beat.

PRALINE PECAN PIE

This is an elegant pecan pie and well worth the effort for special occasions.

1 (9") baked pastry shell	1/4 teaspoon salt
Praline Layer:	1 cup sour cream
1 stick butter or margarine	3/4 stick butter
16 square caramels	4 eggs, separated, room temperature
1/3 cup milk	1 teaspoon vanilla
Cream Layer:	1-1/2 cups chopped pecans
1 Tablespoon unflavored gelatin	1/2 cup sugar
1/4 cup cold water	1 cup whipping cream
3/4 cup light brown sugar	1/4 cup powdered sugar

Bake pie shell and set aside. Melt 3 tablespoons butter in a heavy small skillet. Add pecans and stir until lightly browned. Remove with slotted spoon and drain on paper towels. Melt caramels with butter and milk over low heat, stirring constantly to keep from scorching. Spoon into baked pie shell. Top with 1 cup of the toasted pecans.

Sprinkle gelatin over water in a small bowl. Let mixture stand 5 minutes to soften. Set bowl in a pan of simmering water and stir until gelatin is completely dissolved. Combine brown sugar, gelatin and salt in top of a double boiler. Add sour cream, 3 tablespoons of butter and beaten egg yolks. Set over hot water and stir until mixture thickens slightly and coats back of spoon, about 8 minutes. Remove from heat. Blend in vanilla. Refrigerate until mixture is thickened and mounds slightly when stirred, about 45 minutes.

(Continued)

With an electric mixer, beat egg whites to soft peaks in a large bowl. Gradually add 1/2 cup sugar and beat until stiff but not dry. Gently fold whites into sour cream mixture and spoon over the praline layer in crust. Cover and refrigerate until the sour cream mixture is set about 1 hour and 30 minutes. Beat whipping cream together with powdered sugar. Fold in the remaining 1/2 cup of toasted pecans. Mound onto pie. Cut into slices and serve.

WALNUT PIE

The English walnut trees of northern California are strong and majestic, thousands of them darkly defining the rivers and streams that wind their way through the golden foothills. Indians propagated the fine-flavored nut which has become one of California's most valuable industries. Walnut pie is a delicious testimony.

3 eggs	1/4 teaspoon salt
1/2 cup firmly packed brown	1 teaspoon vanilla
sugar	1 cup broken English walnuts or
1 cup light corn syrup	walnut halves
1/4 cup butter, melted	9" unbaked pastry shell
1 teaspoon cinnamon	

Preheat oven to 375 degrees. In a medium-sized bowl, beat the eggs and blend well with the brown sugar, corn syrup, melted butter, cinnamon, salt and vanilla (in that order). Stir in the nuts; pour mixture into the unbaked pastry shell.

Place pie on the lowest shelf of the oven. Bake 50 minutes or until filling jiggles only slightly when the dish is gently shaken. Cool pie on a wire rack at least 2 hours before cutting. The pie is at its best made a day ahead and refrigerated. It is every bit as good as pecan pie.

THE "LOWLY" PEANUT

Africans regarded the peanut as one of the plants possessing a soul, cultivated them extensively and brought them to the North American continent when they came here as slaves. The Southern synonym for peanut, "goober," comes from "nguba," the Congolese word for peanut used by Africans. In most European countries, the peanut is known as "cacahuete" from the Mexican word "cacahuatl."

PEANUT BUTTER CREAM CHEESE PIE

2 (3-ounce) packages cream
  cheese, softened
3/4 cup sifted powdered sugar
1/2 cup peanut butter
2 Tablespoons milk
1 Tablespoon vanilla
1 (8-ounce) carton non-dairy
  whipped topping, thawed

9" Graham cracker crust or
  Vanilla Wafer Crust
Garnish:
coarsely shopped peanuts
chocolate sauce
caramel sauce
whipped cream

Beat cream cheese and sugar together in a small mixing bowl until light and fluffy. Add peanut butter, vanilla and milk; beat until smooth and creamy. Fold whipped topping into peanut butter mixture. Turn mixture into prepared crust and chill 5 to 6 hours or overnight. Garnish top with whipped cream, topping with chopped peanuts and sauce of your choice.

Vanilla Wafer Crust:
25 vanilla wafers, crushed

1/2 cup finely chopped unsalted
  peanuts (without skins)
1/4 cup butter, melted

Combine vanilla wafers, peanuts and butter. Press into a 9" or 10" pie pan. Bake on 350 degrees for 15 minutes. Cool.

HEAVENLY PEANUT BUTTER PIE

Pecan Crust:
1-1/2 cups pecans, or peanuts
  toasted and finely chopped
1/2 cup sugar
1/4 cup clarified butter
1/4 teaspoon cinnamon
Or Cracker Crust:
1 cup graham cracker crumbs
  (about 9 double crackers)
1/4 cup firmly packed light
  brown sugar

1/4 cup (1/2 stick) butter, melted
Filling:
1-1/2 cups whipping cream
1-1/4 cups powdered sugar
1 Tablespoon vanilla
1 (8-ounce) package cream
  cheese, room temperature
1 cup creamy peanut butter
2 Tablespoons clarified butter
Chocolate Fudge Topping

Choose one of the optional crusts. For the nut crust, mix all ingredients in 9" metal pie pan; press into bottom and sides. Freeze crust until ready to use. For graham cracker crust, combine crumbs, brown sugar and 1/4 cup butter. Press into bottom and halfway up sides of 9" springform pan.

Make filling as follows. Using electric mixer and a large bowl, beat cream with 1/4 cup powdered sugar and vanilla to stiff peaks. Beat remaining cup of powdered sugar, cream cheese, peanut butter and clarified butter in another large bowl until fluffy. Fold in half of the whipped cream (refrigerate the remaining cream). Spoon filling into crust, cover and refrigerate until firm (about 2 hours). Garnish pie and chill for at least 6 hours before serving.

(Continued)

Chocolate Fudge Topping:
1 (14-ounce) can sweetened
condensed milk

2 (1-ounce) squares unsweetened
or semisweet chocolate
1 Tablespoon vanilla extract
2 Tablespoons butter

Combine milk and chocolate and cook over low heat until chocolate melts and mixture thickens. Add vanilla and butter. Blend well. Spoon into a jar and store in refrigerator until ready to serve pie. When ready to serve pie, warm slightly (do not have warm enough to melt the filling). Spoon over pie, leaving a 1" border. Re-heat the reserved cream briefly if necessary. Spoon around the border. Sprinkle the chopped peanuts over the whipped cream and serve.

ANGEL PIE

You will get superlative comments when you serve this. No one will guess what makes it so good.

3 egg whites
1 cup sugar
1 teaspoon almond extract
12 crushed saltines or Ritz
crackers
12 dates, chopped
1 cup chopped pecans

Vanilla Ice Cream
Or Whipped Cream Topping:
1/4 pint heavy cream
1/4 cup confectioners' sugar
1/2 teaspoon vanilla
chocolate, grated

Make a stiff meringue of egg whites, sugar and almond extract. Fold in crushed saltines, dates and pecans. Pour into pie pan and bake at 350 degrees for about 25 to 30 minutes. Cool. Cover with whipped cream or a scoop of vanilla ice cream on each slice. Especially good if ice cream is flamed with rum extract.

NOTE: This pie is also called Macaroon Pie, but is does not have macaroon in it even though it tastes like it does. It goes by another name — Georgia Cracker Pie.

OL' BUTTERMILK PIE

1 (9") baked pie shell
1 cup sugar
1/4 cup flour
1/8 teaspoon salt
1/4 level teaspoon soda
1 whole egg

3 eggs, separated
2 cups buttermilk
1 Tablespoon butter
grated rind and juice of one
lemon
3 Tablespoons sugar for meringue

Add soda to buttermilk. In top of double boiler, mix sugar, flour and salt well. Beat whole egg, egg yolks and buttermilk together; stir into sugar/flour mixture and cook over boiling water until smooth and thickened. Cool slightly and add butter and lemon juice. Pour into shell. Top with meringue and bake until lightly browned, about 5 minutes.

For meringue, beat egg whites with 1/8 teaspoon salt until frothy, then gradually add sugar (1 tablespoon for each egg white) and beat until stiff. Pile lightly on pie and bake in 350 degree oven until browned, about 12 to 15 minutes.

CHESS PIE

1-1/2 cups sugar
1 Tablespoon all-purpose flour
1 Tablespoon unsifted cornmeal
pinch of salt
3 eggs

1 stick butter/margarine, melted
2 cups whole milk
1-1/2 teaspoons vinegar
1 Tablespoon vanilla
1 prepared pie crust

In a large bowl, combine sugar, flour, cornmeal and salt. Add eggs one at a time, beating well after each addition. Gradually add melted butter, milk, vinegar and vanilla. Mix well and pour into baked pie crust. Bake at 350 degrees for 40 to 45 minutes or until firm in the middle. The meal rises to the top and forms a crust. May be served plain or with whipped cream and berries.

CHARLESTON CHESS PIE

The rich lemon flavor of Chess Pie makes a perfect finale to any meal.

1 cup sugar
3 Tablespoons cornstarch
6 eggs
2/3 cup lemon juice

5 Tablespoons butter, melted and
  cooled
3 teaspoons grated lemon rind
1 (9") pie shell, unbaked

Preheat oven to 325 degrees. Combine sugar and cornstarch together in a large bowl. Add eggs, one at a time, beating well after each addition. Blend in the lemon juice and butter. Stir in lemon rind. Pour mixture into the pie shell. Bake pie until puffed and golden and a thin knife inserted into the pie about 1" from the edge comes out clean (about 50 minutes). Cool completely on a wire rack.

DELUXE CREAM CHEESE PIE

pastry for 9" pie
8-ounces cream cheese
1/2 cup sugar
2 Tablespoons flour

3 eggs
1/3 cup milk
1 teaspoon vanilla

Line a 9" pie pan with pastry and chill. While preparing filling, preheat oven to 350 degrees. Beat cream cheese until soft. Gradually add sugar and continue beating until smooth. Stir in flour and unbeaten eggs, beating thoroughly. Add milk and vanilla and beat until all traces of cheese disappear. At this point, filling should be liquid. Pour into unbaked pie shell; bake for 40 minutes or until firm and delicately brown (when done, a knife tip inserted in center will come out dry). Cool pie and spoon on your favorite glaze.

BLUEBERRY GLAZE FOR CHEESE PIE

1 package frozen blueberries
1 teaspoon cornstarch
1 Tablespoon water

1 teaspoon lemon juice
1 teaspoon grated lemon rind

Heat frozen blueberries over low heat until the syrup liquifies. In a little bowl, stir cornstarch and water into a smooth paste. Add to blueberries along with lemon juice and grated rind. Cook, stirring constantly, until syrup is clear, bubbly and slightly thick. Cool, then spoon over cheese pie and chill several hours before serving.

CHERRY GLAZE FOR CHEESE PIE

1 (1 pound, 6 ounce) can tart red
   or Queen Anne cherries
   (water-packed)
1 Tablespoon cornstarch

1/4 cup sugar
1/4 teaspoon almond extract
4 to 5 drops red food color

Drain red cherries and pour 1 cup cherry juice into a saucepan. Mix in cornstarch and sugar. Cook, stirring constantly, until sauce is clear and bubbly. Remove from heat, add almond extract, a few drops red coloring and cherries. Cool, spoon over cheese pie and chill several hours before serving.

PEACH GLAZE FOR CHEESE PIE

1 (1 pound) can sliced cling
   peaches

2 teaspoons cornstarch
1/4 teaspoon almond extract

Drain peaches, saving syrup. Measure 3/4 cup peach syrup into a saucepan and stir in cornstarch until smooth. Cook over medium heat, stirring constantly, until clear and bubbly. Remove from heat and stir in peach slices gently. Flavor with almond extract. Cool; spoon over cheese pie and chill for several hours before serving.

PINEAPPLE GLAZE FOR CHEESE PIE

1 (1 pound, 4 ounce) can crushed
   pineapple
1 Tablespoon cornstarch

1 Tablespoon sugar
1/2 teaspoon vanilla
a few drops yellow food coloring

Drain pineapple thoroughly and put 1 cup syrup into a saucepan; mix in cornstarch and sugar until smooth. Cook, stirring constantly, until bubbly. Remove from heat, add yellow food coloring, crushed pineapple and vanilla. Cool; spoon over cheese pie and chill several hours before serving.

SAVANNAH EGG CUSTARD PIE

3 eggs
3/4 cup granulated sugar
1 level Tablespoon flour
1 Tablespoon vanilla

1 Tablespoon butter, melted
2 cups milk
1/4 teaspoon nutmeg

Whip eggs with electric mixer or rotary beater. Add sugar, flour, nutmeg, vanilla and milk. Mix thoroughly and add melted butter. Pour into 9" pie shell and bake at 350 degrees for 35 minutes.

FRESH COCONUT PIE

9" pastry shell, baked
3/4 cup sugar
3 Tablespoons cornstarch
1/8 teaspoon salt
2 cups milk
3 egg yolks
3/4 teaspoon vanilla

1/4 teaspoon almond extract
2 cups finely grated fresh
  coconut or 1 (7-ounce)
  package flaked coconut
1 cup whipping cream
2 Tablespoons confectioners'
  sugar

In a double boiler, combine sugar, cornstarch and salt; slowly add milk and heat over medium heat, stirring constantly, until thick. Cover and cook 15 minutes more, stirring often.

Beat egg yolks slightly. Add 1/2 cup of hot custard mixture to egg yolks; then return egg mixture to custard in double boiler. Cook two minutes longer, stirring constantly. Remove from heat and stir in flavorings and coconut. Pour into a bowl, cover and cool to room temperature, about 1 hour. Refrigerate until well chilled. Pour custard into pastry shell. Top with cream which has been whipped with confectioners' sugar. Refrigerate. Yields 6 to 8 servings.

MULBERRY PLANTATION LEMON CREAM PIE

A little hard work, but so, so good and sure to bring lots of raves!

4 egg whites, room temperature
1/2 teaspoon cream of tartar
1 cup sugar
4 egg yolks
2/3 cup sugar

1/3 cup lemon juice
2 teaspoons grated lemon rind
2 cups heavy cream
2 Tablespoons sugar

Beat egg whites until fluffy. Add cream of tartar and beat until they start to stiffen. Add 1 cup of sugar gradually, about 2 tablespoons at a time and continue beating until meringue is glossy and stiff enough to hold shape. Spread on lightly buttered 9" pie pan, making outside rim higher than middle. (It takes a lot of beating for meringue crust, but small additions of sugar with plenty of beating between are the secret of perfect meringue. Meringue may be made day before, if desired).

(Continued

Bake meringue in a 275 degree oven for 1-1/4 hours. Meringue will puff and then crack; as it cools, the center will sink somewhat. Cool thoroughly, but not in refrigerator.

While meringue is cooking, beat yolks until thick and lemon colored. Beat in 2/3 cup sugar, lemon juice and rind. Cook in double boiler about 15 to 20 minutes until thick. Cool. Whip 1 cup heavy cream, then fold whipped cream into lemon mixture, blending thoroughly. Fill center of meringue with mixture and chill 8 to 16 hours in refrigerator. When ready to serve, cover top with a cup of cream whipped with 1 tablespoon of sugar.

LEMON CLOUD PIE

Crust:
1 cup flour
1/2 teaspoon salt
1/3 cup shortening
1 egg, slightly beaten
1 teaspoon lemon rind, grated
1 teaspoon lemon juice
Filling:
3/4 cup sugar
1/4 cup cornstarch
1 cup water
1 lemon rind, grated
1/3 cup lemon juice
2 egg yolks
4 ounces cream cheese, softened
2 egg whites
1/4 cup sugar
whipped cream

Combine flour and salt. Cut in shortening with pastry blender. Combine egg, rind and juice. Add to flour mixture and press into 9" pie pan. Bake 12 to 15 minutes.

Combine sugar and cornstarch. Add water, rind, lemon juice and egg yolks. Cook over medium heat until thickened. Add cream cheese. Cool. Beat egg whites until soft peaks form. Add sugar and continue beating until stiff. Fold into filling mixture. Pour into crust. Serve with whipped cream.

LEMON MERINGUE PIE #1

Egg yolks are the only thickener in the filling of this rich pie. Watch carefully to determine when to remove custard from heat; yolks must be cooked enough so custard will firm when cooled, but not cooked too much or custard will curdle. The consistency of this pie, in comparison with traditional lemon meringue pie, will be more pudding-like and not as firm.

1 Tablespoon grated lemon rind
3/4 cup freshly squeezed lemon
    juice, strained (about 6 lemons)
1/4 cup water
2 cups sugar
6 Tablespoons unsalted butter
7 egg yolks
1 whole egg
4 egg whites (remaining whites can
    be frozen for other recipes)
pinch of salt
9" pie shell, fully baked

(Continued)

Combine lemon rind and juice, water, 1-1/2 cups sugar, butter, egg yolks and whole egg in top of double boiler. Place over barely simmering water (water should not touch bottom of boiler insert). Cook, stirring with whisk, until thickened (15 to 20 minutes). Mixture should be thick enough to coat a metal spoon and be consistency of unbeaten egg whites.

Remove top of double boiler from hot water; stir custard for 1 minute. Pour custard into pie shell. Press plastic wrap directly onto surface of custard. Refrigerate 3 hours or until set. Beat egg whites and salt in large bowl using medium mixer speed until soft peaks form. Add remaining 1/2 cup sugar, 2 tablespoons at a time, beating until fairly stiff, shiny peaks form. Decoratively spread meringue over lemon filling; make sure meringue touches crust all around pie to prevent "weeping." Brown meringue in preheated 425 degree oven for 3 to 5 minutes, turning pie occasionally for even browning. For easy cutting, dip sharp, thin-bladed knife into water before each cut.

LEMON MERINGUE PIE #2

Second only to apple pie as our country's favorite — lemon pie — piled high with meringue is a refreshing tart, sweet way to end a meal. We do not know who first made it, but we know that the lemons were introduced to our country by the Spanish explorers when they brought the seeds to Florida.

1-1/2 cups sugar	1/2 teaspoon grated lemon peel
3 Tablespoons cornstarch	1/3 cup fresh lemon juice
3 Tablespoons all-purpose flour	9" baked pie crust
dash of salt	3 egg whites
1-1/2 cups hot water	1 teaspoon lemon juice
3 slightly beaten egg yolks	6 Tablespoons sugar
2 Tablespoons butter	

Mix first four ingredients in a saucepan. Gradually stir in hot water and quickly bring to a boil, stirring constantly. Reduce heat and continue cooking and stirring 8 more minutes. Stir small amount of hot mixture into egg yolks, then return yolks to hot mixture. Bring to boiling and cook 4 minutes, stirring constantly. Add butter and lemon peel. Slowly stir in 1/3 cup lemon juice. Pour into cooled pastry shell and cool to room temperature.

Beat egg whites with 1 teaspoon lemon juice until soft peaks form. Gradually add 6 tablespoons of sugar, beating until stiff peaks form and sugar has dissolved. Spread meringue over cooled filling, sealing meringue to edges of crust all around to prevent shrinking. Bake at 350 degrees for 12 to 15 minutes until peaks are golden brown; cool thoroughly before serving.

LEMON SOUR CREAM PIE

So good you may never eat plain lemon pie again.

9" baked pie crust	1/4 cup butter
1 cup sugar	1 cup sour cream
3 Tablespoons cornstarch	Meringue:
1 cup milk	3 egg whites, room temperature
3 egg yolks, beaten	1/4 teaspoon cream of tartar
1/4 cup lemon juice	1/3 cup sugar
1 Tablespoon grated lemon rind	

Combine sugar, cornstarch and salt in small saucepan; stir in milk. Cook over medium heat, stirring constantly until thick (about 15 minutes). Remove from heat; stir 1/4 cup hot mixture gradually into beaten egg yolks. Pour egg mixture into saucepan, stirring constantly. Cook and stir over medium heat for 2 minutes; stir in butter, lemon peel and juice. Cool 20 minutes.

Stir in sour cream. Pour into prepared pie shell. Beat egg whites and cream of tartar in small bowl on low speed until foamy. Beat on high speed, gradually adding 1/3 cup sugar; beat until stiff but not dry. Spread over filling, sealing to edge of pastry. Heat oven to 350 degrees.

Bake pie until meringue begins to brown (about 20 minutes). Cool completely on wire rack, then refrigerate until served. Serves 6.

HUGH'S KEY LIME PIE

9" pastry shell, baked	1/2 teaspoon freshly grated lime
1 cup sugar	peel
3 Tablespoons flour	1 Tablespoon butter
3 Tablespoons cornstarch	3 Tablespoons sugar
1/4 teaspoon salt	1/8 teaspoon cream of tartar
2 cups boiling water	4 egg whites (the extra egg yolk
3 egg yolks	may be added to the filling if
1/4 cup freshly squeezed juice	desired)
from Key limes or Persian	
limes (bottled Key lime juice	
may be used)	

Preheat oven to 400 degrees. Blend sugar, flour, cornstarch and salt in top of double boiler. Add hot water, mixing well. Cook over simmering water, whisking frequently for 10 minutes. Remove from heat. Beat egg yolks slightly; add 1/4 cup of custard to yolks and blend. Combine remaining egg yolk mixture with custard and return to heat. Cook slowly for 2 minutes. Add lime juice, lime peel and butter. Remove from heat and stir until butter melts.

Beat egg whites until they begin to hold their shape. Continue beating and gradually add sugar and cream of tartar. Beat until stiff peaks are formed. Fold in about a cup of meringue into the custard mixture. Pour into the baked pastry shell. Top with remaining meringue, sealing to edges. Bake at 400 degrees until barely brown (about 5 minutes). Cool before serving. Refrigerate leftovers.

SOUTH FLORIDA LIME PIE

1-1/2 cups graham cracker crumbs
2 Tablespoons sugar
6 Tablespoons melted unsalted
  butter
1 Tablespoon gelatin
4 Tablespoons water
4 eggs, separated

1/4 cup sugar
1/2 cup lime juice (about 6 limes)
1 (14-ounce) sweetened
  condensed milk
zest of 1 lime, grated
pinch of salt
whipped cream for decoration

To make crust, combine graham cracker crumbs, sugar and melted butter. Press into a buttered 9" pie plate and chill 15 minutes. Bake in a preheated 325 degree oven for 15 minutes. Set aside to cool completely before filling. In a heavy saucepan, dissolve gelatin in cold water and carefully melt in a double boiler or over hot water. In a bowl over a saucepan of warm water, beat egg yolks with 3 tablespoons sugar. Gradually add 1/4 cup lime juice. When mixture forms a heavy ribbon when dripped from a spoon, drizzle in gelatin. Beat well to blend and dissolve completely. Remove mixture from over warm water and beat in remaining lime juice, condensed milk and lime zest.

In another bowl, beat egg whites until foamy. Add salt and continue beating until they form soft peaks. Sprinkle with remaining tablespoon sugar and continue to beat for 30 additional seconds. Fold one-third of the beaten whites into egg yolk mixture. Pile remaining whites on top and fold in completely. Mound filling into prepared, baked pastry shell. Decorate with swirls of whipped cream. Yields one 9" pie.

DIVINE FLORIDA KEY LIME PIE

Meringue Shell:
4 egg whites

1/4 teaspoon cream of tartar
1 cup sugar

Preheat oven to 275 degrees. Generously butter a 9" pie plate. In a small mixing bowl, beat egg whites and cream of tartar until foamy. Beat in sugar very slowly, 1 tablespoon at a time, until it is stiff and glossy, about 10 minutes. Pile the meringue into the pie plate, pushing up around the sides. Bake 1 hour. Turn off the oven, leaving pie shell in the oven with the door closed for 1 hour. Remove from oven and let cool.

Filling:
4 egg yolks
1/4 teaspoon salt
1/2 cup sugar
1/3 cup fresh lime juice (2 to 3 limes)

1 cup chilled whipping cream
1 Tablespoon grated fresh lime
  peel
whipped cream and lime peel for
  garnish

Beat egg yolks until light and lemon colored. Stir in salt, sugar and lime juice. Cook over medium heat, stirring constantly, until mixture thickens, about 5 minutes. Cool completely. In a chilled bowl, beat cream until stiff. Fold in filling mixture and grated peel. Pile into the meringue shell and chill for at least 4 hours. Garnish with whipped cream and lime peel twists. Serves 8.

NOTE: Key Lime Juice can be bought in gourmet stores.

GRANDMOTHER DeVAULT'S MINCEMEAT
(Over a century old and still one of the best)

2-1/2 cups apples, chopped and peeled
2-1/2 cups brown sugar, firmly packed
1-1/2 cups apple cider
1 cup raisins
1/2 cup mixed candied fruit, finely chopped
1/2 cup currents
1 cup pecans, chopped
1/2 cup candied orange and lemon peel, finely chopped
1/2 cup vinegar
1/2 cup molasses
1/2 cup citron, finely chopped
1-1/2 teaspoons grated lemon rind
2 Tablespoons lemon juice
1-1/2 teaspoons ground cinnamon
1-1/2 teaspoons ground nutmeg
1-1/2 teaspoons ground cloves
1 teaspoon ground mace
3/4 teaspoon salt
3/4 teaspoon pepper
1-1/2 pounds cooked lean beef, minced
1-1/2 pounds cooked pork loin, minced
1/2 cup rum or a good brandy

Combine all ingredients except meats in large Dutch oven. Stir well. Cook over medium heat 15 minutes. Add beef and pork; cook 15 minutes longer, then simmer 1-1/2 hours over low heat, stirring occasionally. Spoon into sterilized pint jars, seal and store in cool place.

NOTE: Mincemeat, as we enjoy it today, has a unique history dating back for several centuries. Europeans were thought to have first made it, as a way to preserve meat. Fruits, spices and sugar were added to meat and the mixture stored in crocks for use in the winter. Over the centuries the meat content of mincemeat was reduced, but mincemeat was and still is associated with holiday feasting. Today, mincemeat pie is regarded as a traditional Christmas dessert. It can be used in cakes, puddings, cookies and tarts.

OLD-FASHION PUMPKIN PIE

What moistens the lip,
And what brightens the eye,
What calls back the past
Like rich pumpkin pie?
John Greenleaf Whitter

Pumpkin pie reminds us of Thanksgiving and the early English settlers when the Indians introduced it to the colonists. The pumpkin goes back to primitive times in Mexico and long before the white man arrived in the New World the pumpkin made its way north. The Pilgrims grew it and depended heavily upon it for food. The Indians taught the white man how to cook it in many forms...with meat, fish and vegetables, added to sour, or ground into meal. But it was the settlers who learned to make the desserts from classic pie to cake to souffle.

(Continued)

The pilgrims first made a primitive sort of pie by slicing off the top of a pumpkin, scooping out the seeds and filling the cavity with milk, honey and herbs. They baked it in hot ashes as long as seven hours, then ate the bubbling filling with a spoon. As the pies improved and crust was introduced, they became a basic element in the New England diet. During pumpkin season, the pies were eaten for breakfast, lunch and dinner. What are the holidays without a pumpkin pie?

OLD-FASHION PUMPKIN PIE

9" pastry shell
1-3/4 cups canned pumpkin
1 cup sugar
1/2 teaspoon salt
1/2 teaspoon cinnamon
1/2 teaspoon ginger
1/4 teaspoon nutmeg
1-2/3 cups undiluted evaporated
    milk

2 beaten eggs
whipped cream
chopped nuts
Optional Hard Sauce:
1/4 cup butter/margarine
3/4 cup confectioners' sugar
1 Tablespoon brandy
1/4 teaspoon vanilla

Combine pumpkin, sugar, salt, cinnamon, ginger, nutmeg, evaporated milk and eggs and beat until smooth. Pour into pastry shell. Bake at 425 degrees for 15 minutes, then reduce heat to 350 degrees and bake 35 minutes longer or until set. Cool and top with whipped cream and chopped nuts or hard sauce.

To make hard sauce, beat softened butter/margarine with a mixer at medium speed until light and fluffy. Gradually beat in confectioners' sugar, brandy and vanilla, blending until smooth and creamy.

FROZEN PRALINE PUMPKIN PIE
(Extra Special Thanksgiving Pie)

1 pint butter pecan ice cream,
    softened
1 cup cooked pumpkin
3/4 cup brown sugar
dash of salt
1/2 teaspoon pumpkin pie spice

1 teaspoon vanilla
1 cup heavy cream, whipped
1 Tablespoon heavy cream
2 Tablespoons brown sugar
2 Tablespoons butter
1/2 cup pecans, chopped

Spoon ice cream into bottom and sides of a 9" pie pan. Freeze. Combine pumpkin, 3/4 cup brown sugar, salt, pumpkin pie spice and vanilla. Fold in whipped cream. Spoon into frozen ice cream shell. Freeze. Combine cream, brown sugar and butter in a saucepan. Heat to boiling. Cook one minute; then stir in pecans. Cool to lukewarm. Spoon pecan mixture in a ring on top of pie. Freeze at least three hours before serving. Yield 8 servings.

SOUR CREAM PUMPKIN PIE

1 cup sugar
1/4 teaspoon salt
1/2 teaspoon ground ginger
1 teaspoon ground cinnamon
1/4 teaspoon ground nutmeg

1/4 teaspoon ground cloves
1 (16-ounce) can pumpkin
1 (8-ounce) carton sour cream
3 eggs, separated
9" unbaked pastry shell

Combine sugar, salt and spices. Add pumpkin and sour cream, stirring well. Beat egg yolks until thick and lemon colored; stir into pumpkin mixture. Beat egg whites (warmed to room temperature) until stiff peaks form; fold into pumpkin mixture. Pour into pastry shell. Bake at 450 degrees for 10 minutes; reduce heat to 350 degrees and bake 55 minutes or until set. Yields one 9" pie.

FAMILY'S MINCEMEAT

This recipe, more that 100 years old, makes a fine pie. It is also great served on toast, served warm over vanilla ice cream, or spread with peanut butter on a sandwich. The batch needs to be started well in advance of the holidays because the various ingredients need at least six weeks to blend and mellow.

3 cups water
1-1/2 pounds beef stew meat, cubed
3/4 teaspoon salt
3-1/2 pounds Granny Smith apples
1/2 medium unpeeled lemon, seeded
2 cups sugar
1 cup raisins
3/4 cup light molasses

1/2 cup cider vinegar
1-1/4 teaspoons cinnamon
1-1/4 teaspoons freshly grated nutmeg
1 cup brewed coffee or 1 teaspoon instant coffee powder
1/2 teaspoon salt
1/4 teaspoon ground cloves
1/3 cup brandy
1/4 teaspoon coarsely ground pepper

Core apples and cut into 1" pieces; set aside. Cut lemon into 3/4" pieces and remove seeds. Set aside. Combine water, beef and salt in large, heavy saucepan or Dutch oven medium-high heat. Bring to boil, skimming foam from surface. Reduce heat, cover and simmer until meat is tender (1-1/2 hours).

Remove meat with slotted spoon and cool slightly. Reserve 3/4 cup cooking liquid. Coarsely grind meat in batches in processor using on/off turns (or use food mill). Transfer to another heavy large saucepan or Dutch oven. Coarsely grind apples in batches in processor using on/off turns. Add to meat. Finely grind lemon in processor using on/off turns and add to meat. Mix in reserved liquid and remaining ingredients except brandy and pepper. Simmer over low heat until very thick but not dry, stirring frequently (about 1 hour).

Remove from heat and stir in brandy and pepper. Transfer mincemeat to airtight containers. Cover and cool to room temperature. Refrigerate at least six weeks. Yields about 10-3/4 cups mincemeat, enough for several delicious pies.

WALNUT CRUNCH PUMPKIN PIE

9" pastry shell
1 (16-ounce) can pumpkin
1 (13-ounce) can evaporated milk
2 eggs
3/4 cup packed brown sugar
1-1/2 teaspoons ground cinnamon
1/2 teaspoon salt
1/2 teaspoon ground ginger

1/2 teaspoon ground nutmeg
Walnut Topping:
1 cup California walnuts,
  chopped
3/4 cup packed brown sugar
4 Tablespoons butter/margarine,
  melted
1/4 cup whipping cream, whipped

About three hours before serving time, preheat oven to 400 degrees. Using a large bowl with mixer at medium speed, beat pumpkin with evaporated milk, eggs, brown sugar and spices until well mixed. Place pastry-lined pie plate on oven rack; pour in pumpkin mixture. Bake 40 minutes or until knife inserted 1" from edge comes out clean. Cool pie.

Preheat broiler. In a small bowl, combine walnuts, 3/4 cup brown sugar and melted butter, mixing well with a fork. Spoon topping evenly over pie. Broil pie about 5" to 7" from source of heat for about 3 minutes or until topping is golden and sugar is dissolved. Cool pie on wire rack. Garnish pie with whipped cream. Makes 10 servings.

BASIC PIE CRUST

1-1/2 cups flour
3/4 teaspoon salt

2/3 cup vegetable shortening
3 Tablespoons cold water

Preheat oven to 450 degrees. Sift flour and salt together into a mixing bowl. Remove 1/4 cup of flour mixture to a small bowl. Using a pastry cutter or knives, cut shortening into first bowl until the size of small peas. With a fork, combine cold water and reserved 1/4 cup of flour until a smooth paste. Stir into shortening and flour, combining well.

Because this is a very tender pastry, use a pastry cloth and rolling pin cover. Roll out to 1/8" thickness to line a 9" glass pie plate (there will be some excess). Be careful not to over-stretch the dough, since this can cause shrinkage while baking.

Fold dough in half, then half again, to transfer to pie plate. Unfold and gently press into dish, crimping edges of pastry securely to rim. Press out any air bubbles under pastry. For pre-baked shell, use a table fork to prick throughout, including sides; bake 8 to 10 minutes until very lightly browned and cool on rack.

CHEDDAR CHEESE PASTRY

1 cup all-purpose flour
1/2 teaspoon salt
1/3 cup shortening

1/4 cup (1-ounce) shredded sharp
   cheddar cheese
2 to 3 Tablespoons water

Combine flour and salt; cut in shortening with pastry blender until mixture resembles coarse meal. Stir in cheese. Sprinkle cold water evenly over surface and stir with a fork until all dry ingredients are moistened. Shape dough into a ball. Roll out dough on a floured surface; cut dough to cover top of a deep-dish 9" pie plate. Makes one 9" crust.

SCOTCH PIE CRUST

5 cups flour
1 pound Crisco shortening
2 teaspoons salt

1 egg
2 Tablespoons vinegar
water

Add egg and vinegar together in a mixing cup; fill to 8-ounce level with water and set aside. Combine flour, Crisco and salt. Pour in 8-ounces of liquid and mix. Makes 8 crusts and freezes well in pie pan or dough ball.

NEVER FAIL PIE CRUST

This recipe also makes lovely, light tart crusts.

1 Tablespoon white vinegar or
   lemon juice
1 egg, beaten
5 Tablespoons water

1 teaspoon salt
3 cups flour
1 cup + 2 Tablespoons vegetable
   shortening

Combine vinegar and egg in a bowl. Blend well, then add water and salt; set aside. Place flour in a large bowl. Cut the shortening into the flour until small balls form. Add the liquid ingredients. Mix well. Divide dough into 3 equal portions. Roll each portion out on a floured board or between sheets of waxed paper and transfer to individual pie plates. If you need only one crust, tightly wrap remaining pastry and freeze for later use. Makes two 9" pastry shells.

MERINGUE CRUST

3 egg whites, room temperature
1-1/2 cups sugar
1/4 cup boiling water

1-1/2 teaspoons distilled white
   vinegar
1-1/2 teaspoons vanilla

Preheat oven to 450 degrees. Combine egg whites, sugar, boiling water, vinegar and vanilla in a large bowl. Beat with electric mixer at high speed until mixture forms stiff peaks (about 10 minutes), scraping down sides of bowl with rubber spatula as necessary. Spoon mixture into 9" pie plate, building up sides to form a rim. Place crust in preheated oven on lower rack. Turn off heat and leave in oven four hours or overnight; do not open oven door.

FOOLPROOF MERINGUE

3 egg whites
dash of salt

1 (7-ounce) jar marshmallow
creme

There is a way to make meringues practically foolproof; it's a secret ingredient you may already have in your kitchen. Marshmallow creme, made with real egg whites, is the perfect addition to meringue because it makes the mixture more stable so that it can be beaten to fullest volume without fear of overbeating and having the meringue "fall." Simply beat egg whites with a pinch of salt until they form soft peaks, then add a jar of marshmallow creme and continue beating until stiff peaks form. Since the marshmallow creme provides all the sweetness necessary for meringue, there's no need for the tedious addition of sugar spoonful by spoonful as frequently specified in meringue recipes.

NEVER-FAIL MERINGUE

1 Tablespoon cornstarch
2 Tablespoons cold water
1/2 cup boiling water
3 egg whites

6 Tablespoons sugar
1 teaspoon vanilla
pinch of salt

Blend cornstarch and water in a saucepan. Add boiling water and cook, stirring until clear and thickened. Let stand until completely cold. Beat the egg whites with an electric beater at high speed; add sugar, salt and vanilla. Gradually beat in cold cornstarch mixture; turn mixer to high speed and beat well. Spread meringue over cooled pie filling and bake at 350 degrees for about 10 minutes. This meringue cuts beautifully and is never sticky.

Original Medical College of Georgia   ©1991 Ray Baird

GARDEN CENTER
(OLD MEDICAL COLLEGE)

In 1828, the Georgia Assembly authorized the Medical Institute of Georgia. Dr. Milton Antony, who had worked diligently to improve medical standards and training, was among the first faculty. His two colleagues were Dr. Ignatius P. Garvin and Dr. Lewis Ford. Charles Cluskey was selected to design a building for the Medical College of Georgia as it became known in 1833. The facility completed two years later at the corner of Telfair and Sixth Streets is of classic style utilizing six large Doric columns to support the pediment. Dr. Antony, who died in 1839 during a fever epidemic, is buried to the left of the entrance walk.

In 1913, the Medical College moved to the former Tuttle-Newton Home (Orphan Asylum) on Thirteenth Street. For a time, the old building was used for extra classrooms by the Academy of Richmond Academy located next door. Later, the Council of Garden Clubs of Augusta purchased the structure and is used for flower shows, receptions, meetings, dances, and exhibitions.

A Little Bit Extra

OLD-TIME GRAPE CATSUP

This was usually made with wild grapes such as "Bullices" or Muscadines and the "Fox Grapes". However you may use the cultivated Blue Concord Grapes.

4 pounds grapes, Blue Concord or wild varieties	2 teaspoons ground allspice 2 Tablespoons ground cinnamon
2 cups vinegar	2 pounds sugar
2 teaspoons ground cloves	

Wash grapes and remove stems. Place grapes in a pan and steam without water until soft. Press fruit through a sieve, pushing most of the fruit through but removing the seeds. Add remaining ingredients and simmer mixture for 20 minutes or until thick. Pour into hot, sterilized jars and seal.

NELL'S CHILI SAUCE

4 quarts chopped tomatoes (8 pounds)	2 Tablespoons salt 1 cup sugar

1 cup each red and green bell
   peppers, chopped and seeded
   (3 peppers of each color)
	1 teaspoon ground cinnamon
	1 Tablespoon white mustard seed
	1 Tablespoon whole allspice

1 small hot pepper, seeded and minced	1 Tablespoon whole cloves 1 quart cider vinegar
2-1/2 cups chopped onions	

Tie whole spices in a cheesecloth bag. Drain all vegetables and combine with salt and sugar in a large kettle. Add vinegar, cinnamon, and spice bag; cook, uncovered, over medium heat for about 2-1/2 to 3 hours or until quite thick, stirring often. Remove spice bag and pour sauce at once into hot, clean preserve jars. Adjust jar covers as recommended by the manufacturer. This sauce is excellent served with meats or as a side condiment with beans, field peas, etc.

APPLE CHUTNEY

5 cups thinly sliced apples	1/2 cup lime juice
3 cups sugar	1/2 cup golden seedless raisins
1-1/2 cups vinegar	3 ounces crystallized ginger,
2 cloves garlic, minced	chopped
3 Tablespoons Worcestershire sauce	1 cup chopped onions
1 cup finely chopped apples	3/4 cup diced watermelon rind
1/2 cup dry red wine	pickle

Cover sliced apples with brine (2 tablespoons salt to one quart water) and soak for about 36 hours. Drain apples. Mix sugar, vinegar, garlic, and Worcestershire sauce and heat to boiling. Add drained apple slices and simmer until apples are fairly clear. Remove apples from syrup and set aside. To the syrup, add all other ingredients except watermelon pickle. Cook until mixture is fairly thick. Add cooked sliced apples and watermelon pickle and bring back to boiling. Pour boiling hot into half-pint fruit jars and seal immediately. Makes 6 half-pints.

CRANBERRY CHUTNEY

Long before the white man's arrival in America, the native Indians crushed cranberries with dried venison and fat, and formed the mixture into little cakes and called their concoction pemmican. The recipe was shared with the colonists and was served at the first Thanksgiving. Cranberries were shipped to Europe in 1550, but the first record of commercial cranberry cultivation was in Cape Cod, Massachusetts in 1816.

2 cups fresh cranberries
2/3 cup brown sugar
1 large orange, peeled, pit
   removed, and cut into 1/4"
   slices
1/2 cup golden raisins, chopped
1 medium tart apple, pared,
   cored, and coarsely chopped

1/2 cup raspberry vinegar (apple
   if raspberry not available)
1/4 cup water
1/8 teaspoon ground nutmeg
1/8 teaspoon ground ginger
1/8 teaspoon dry mustard
1/8 teaspoon ground allspice
1 Tablespoon brandy or rum
   (optional)

Using a heavy medium-sized saucepan, place in all ingredients. Stir until well blended. Heat over medium-high heat to boiling. Reduce heat to low; simmer and stir, watching carefully so it will not burn. Cook until thickened (about 45 minutes). Store in refrigerator. May be placed in hot sterilized pint or 1/2 pint jars, sealed and stored in a cool place. Good for gift giving.

May be used as a sauce when served warm or at room temperature with pork, ham, chicken or turkey. Also may be used as an appetizer. Spread a generous layer of the chutney over a wheel of Brie. Bake at 350 degrees for 10 minutes until the cheese is soft, but not runny. Serve with slices of crusty French Bread.

NOTE: Ingredients may be doubled if more is desired and used as gifts for special times.

BEST EVER CHUNKY CHUTNEY

4 large tart apples, peeled, cored
   and diced (about 6 cups)
3 large firm pears, peeled, cored
   and diced (about 4 cups)
3 oranges, peeled, seeded and
   diced
grated rind of 2 oranges
3 large lemons, sliced paper thin
3 large onions, peeled and diced
3 large garlic cloves, peeled and
   minced
2 (8 ounce) boxes pitted dates, diced

3/4 cup raisins
1 cup cider vinegar
1 cup orange or apple juice
1/2 cup dry white wine
1/2 cup honey
2 teaspoons coarsely ground
   black pepper
1/2 teaspoon nutmeg
1/2 teaspoon ginger
1/2 teaspoon cloves
1/2 teaspoon salt
1/4 teaspoon chili powder

Combine all ingredients in large heavy saucepan or Dutch oven. Bring to a boil, stirring constantly. Simmer until fruit is tender and mixture is thick, stirring occasionally. Pour into hot sterilized jars and seal. Makes about 10 cups. Good with curry.

MANGO CHUTNEY

Probably about as close to Major Grey's as you will ever get.

6 pounds of fruit (firm mangos and a few apricots cut like shoe string potatoes)
1 pound white raisins, chopped in half
1 pound currents
1/2 medium size lemon, seeded and chopped (with peel)
1/4 pound fresh ginger, finely chopped (about 4 tablespoons) or more to your taste
1/4 pound citron, cut in fine slivers
4 cloves garlic, chopped fine
3 red peppers (chili), chopped or 1/4 teaspoon ground red pepper
2 pounds sugar
1/8 cup salt
1 quart cider vinegar
1/2 teaspoon cinnamon
1/2 teaspoon allspice
1/2 teaspoon ground cloves
1/2 teaspoon nutmeg
2 medium onions, minced

Wash, peel, cut and slice mangos and apricots. Place in a large stainless-steel or non-reactive pot. Add all the remaining ingredients. Stir well, cover loosely and let stand several hours or overnight. Set the pot over medium heat and bring to a boil. Adjust heat to maintain a vigorous simmer. Cook, stirring often so as not to scorch. Cook until mango and onion pieces are translucent and the chutney has thickened. (If the chutney threatens to really stick before this point is reached, add a few spoonfuls of water and continue cooking.) When chutney is sufficiently thick, remove from heat and taste for tartness and degree of hotness. If desired add, a little more vinegar sugar or hot pepper. Ladle the boiling hot chutney into, hot clean and sterilized pint or half pint canning leaving about 1/4" space at the top of the jars. (Will make about 3 to 4 pints.) Seal the jars and plan to let the chutney rest undisturbed for a few weeks so that its many flavors can blend and balance. Label and store in a cool place. This makes excellent gifts, when using a pint or half pint jars. Add a pretty bow and a card.

PEACH CHUTNEY
A Delicious Old Recipe

4 pounds peaches
4-1/2 cups sugar
8 peach kernels, shredded
1/2 teaspoon ground cloves
1/4 pound raisins
1/4 pound preserved ginger
1/4 pound almonds
1/4 pound English walnuts
1 orange

Do not peal peaches; cut into quarters and weigh. Add sugar and peach kernels. Heat mixture slowly on back of stove. When thoroughly hot and juicy, draw to the front and cook for one hour, stirring frequently. Add cloves and cook five minutes longer. Add raisins, ginger, almonds, walnuts, and juice of one orange during last half hour of cooking. Yields 4 pints. Seal, processing in a water bath, and store in a dark, cool place.

CRANBERRY WINE JELLY

This is perfect at Christmas time as well as Thanksgiving. It is a tart jelly and a perfect gift. It is good with meats and breads as well.

7 cups sugar
3 cups cranberry juice
1/4 teaspoon ground cinnamon

1/4 teaspoon ground cloves
1 cup port wine
6 ounces liquid fruit pectin

Combine first 4 ingredients in a Dutch oven. Bring mixture to a boil, stirring to dissolve sugar. Boil 1 minute, stirring frequently. Remove from heat; stir in wine and pectin, then skim off foam with a metal spoon. Quickly pour jelly into sterilized jars, leaving 1/2" headspace. Cover at once with a 1/8" layer of paraffin. Cover with lids. Yields 7 cups.

PEPPER JELLY

Many Southerners keep Pepper Sauce on their tables and put a dash of it on everything they eat. Pepper jelly is piquant but more refined and is seen, green or red colored, on top of cream cheese spread on saltines. It is also excellent with country ham, or green beans or with cooked dried peas. It can be made as mild or as hot as your tastes dictates by varying the amount of hot pepper or Tabasco.

Hot Version:
1/2 cup seeded hot red peppers
1/2 cup seeded hot green peppers
1 medium onion, quartered pep

1-1/2 cups vinegar
5-1/2 cups sugar
1 bottle liquid pectin
red or green food color (optional)

Place pepper, onion and vinegar in food processor. Process until very fine. Measure sugar and pour into six-quart pot. Add pepper, onion, and vinegar to pot and allow to come to a boil. Boil for one minute, then remove from stove and cool for five minutes. Stir in pectin and food color and ladle into jars. Shake jars to keep peppers mixed. Cool. Makes four pints.

Mild Version:
1-1/2 cups chopped red or green
   bell pepper
1-1/2 cups cider vinegar

6-1/2 cups sugar
25 shakes Tabasco (optional)
1 bottle liquid pectin
red or green food color (optional)

Combine first three ingredients (four, if you wish a hot jelly) and bring to a full boil over high heat. Remove from heat and set aside for 20 minutes Return to heat and bring back to a full rolling boil; boil for 2 minutes. Remove from heat, add liquid pectin and a few drops of food color. Stir, skim and pour into hot sterilized jars. Cover with a thin layer of paraffin. Makes 8 to 10-1/2 pints.

NOTE: This recipe makes a lovely clear jelly. If you like both mild and hot, one way to remember which is which is to leave the food color out of the one with no "heat," use green food color for one mildly hot, and use red for your "scorcher". Little decorated jars make Christmas gifts which will be much appreciated.

OLIVE CHERRIES

1-1/2 pounds dark sweet cherries
   with stems, about 4 cups
1-1/2 cups distilled white vinegar

1-1/2 cups water
1-1/2 teaspoons salt

Pierce each cherry with sterilized needle to prevent bursting and shrinking. Heat remaining ingredients just to boiling. Pack cherries into hot, sterilized jars, leaving 1/2" headspace. Cover with syrup, wipe top of jar to remove any splashed syrup, and seal. Process in boiling water bath for 10 minutes. Place on towels to cool. Before storing, check to be sure jars sealed properly. Makes 3 pints.

NOTE: Olive cherries are good served with baked ham, pork, or poultry...or in martinis.

MARINATED OLIVES

3 (6 ounce) cans of pitted ripe
   jumbo olives (4-1/2 to 5 cups)
1 cup (4-1/2 ounces) blanched
   whole almonds
2 large lemons, cut into 12 slices

4-1/2 teaspoons coriander seed
1-1/4 cups dry white wine
1 cup water
1/4 cup olive or salad oil

Stuff the pitted ripe olives with whole almonds. Place lemon slices around sides of three decorative pint containers. Place 1/3 of the stuffed olives in each pint jar. Crush the coriander using a mortar and pestle; add 1-1/2 teaspoons of the coriander seed to each jar. In a screw-top jar, shake together the wine, water and oil. Pour over olives in containers. Store in refrigerator for 2 weeks before using. Makes three 2-cup containers which can be used as gifts. The olives are good served with salads, dips or as appetizers. Store in refrigerator up to 6 months.

FLO'S PEAR HONEY

Make a lot; it will disappear fast

1 quart ground pears (about 8
   cups)
1 lemon ground with pears
1 bottle of maraschino cherries,
   drained and coarsely
   chopped (optional)

1 (20 ounce) can crushed
   pineapple
6 cups sugar

Mix pears ground with lemon and pineapple and cook over medium heat until pears are tender. Add sugar and continue until mixture is thick. Stir often, taking care not to scorch. Pour into sterilized jars and seal.

PEAR MINCEMEAT

Since this mincemeat does not contain meat or suet, it is simple to prepare. Use for pies or tarts, as topping for ice cream, pudding, or poached fruit or even as an accompaniment for roast meats.

2 pounds firm pears, peeled, cored and coarsely chopped (4 cups)

1 green apple, peeled, cored and coarsely chopped (1 cup)

2 Tablespoons grated lemon rind

1/3 cup grated orange rind

1/4 cup lemon juice

1/2 cup orange juice

1 cup golden raisins

1/2 cup currants

1/2 cup firmly packed light brown sugar

1 teaspoon ground cinnamon

1 teaspoon ground nutmeg

1/4 teaspoon ground ginger

1/4 teaspoon salt

1/4 cup walnuts, coarsely chopped

1/4 cup brandy

Combine pears, apple, lemon rind, orange rind, lemon juice, orange juice, raisins, currants, sugar, cinnamon, nutmeg, ginger and salt in a large, heavy sauce pan. Bring to boiling. Lower heat, cover and simmer 45 minutes, stirring occasionally. Uncover and cook 30 to 40 minutes longer, stirring occasionally, until very thick.

Add nuts and brandy to mincemeat mixture; cook 5 minutes. Immediately ladle into clean, hot canning jars, leaving 1/2" headspace. Wipe jar rims and threads clean with a damp cloth. Place lids on jars and screw bands on firmly. Process in boiling water bath 10 minutes (water should cover jars by 1 to 2 "). Before storing, check seals on jars and allow to cool. Store in cool, dark place. Jars may be decorated with ribbons or gingham "caps".

NOTE: Mincemeat may be stored in the refrigerator, unprocessed, in covered, airtight jars with tight-fitting lids.

SPICED CARROT STICKS

5 pounds medium carrots	4 Tablespoons mustard seed
3 cups sugar	1 Tablespoon pickling salt
3-1/2 cups vinegar (5% acid	2 cinnamon sticks (3" long)
strength)	12 whole cloves
3 cups water	12 whole allspice

Pare carrots; cut into 4" strips. Place carrots in a large saucepan with enough salted water to cover. Cook seven minutes or until tender. Drain.

Combine sugar, vinegar, water, mustard seed and salt in saucepan. Bring to boiling; simmer 20 minutes. Pack carrots into six hot, sterilized pint jars. Place a 1" piece of cinnamon in each jar along with two whole cloves and two allspice. Pour boiling liquid over carrots, filling jar to within 1/4" from the top. Wipe tops of jars, seal and process in boiling water bath for 10 minutes (begin processing time when water in the canner returns to boiling). Remove jars to cool on wire racks 12 to 24 hours. Before storing, check jars to be sure they are properly sealed.

DISAPPEARING PICKLES

12 pickling cucumbers	1/2 cup salt
4 large onions	1-1/4 teaspoons tumeric
4 cups sugar	1-1/4 teaspoons celery salt
4 cups apple cider vinegar	1-1/4 teaspoons mustard seed

Slice cucumbers and onions in 1/4" slices. Layer cucumbers and onions in a 1 gallon jar. Combine sugar, cider vinegar, salt, tumeric, celery salt and mustard seed. Pour over cucumbers and onions. Refrigerate. Enjoy after 1 week. It is difficult to wait a whole week before tasting these crisp and delicious bread and butter pickles. Once you do, watch how quickly they disappear.

OLD-FASHIONED PICKLED BEETS

3 pounds beets (12 to 15 beets),
  tops removed
1 Tablespoon cider vinegar
1 cup water
1 cup cider vinegar
1 cup sugar
1 teaspoon mustard seed

1 stick cinnamon
2 whole cloves
1/2 teaspoon salt
1/4 teaspoon whole allspice
1/2 pound boiling onions, thinly
  sliced

In boiling salted water to cover, cook beets with 1 tablespoon vinegar until tender (35 to 45 minutes). Drain and peel skin from beets. Combine water, vinegar, sugar, mustard seed, cinnamon stick, cloves, salt and allspice in a medium-size sauce pan. Heat to boiling; reduce heat and simmer uncovered 15 minutes. Makes 2 quarts.

Pack sliced cooked beets and onions into hot jars, leaving 1/2" headspace. Cover with boiling syrup, wipe jar top to remove any splashed syrup, and seal. Process in boiling water bath 15 minutes. Set jars on towels to cool. Before storing, check to be sure jars sealed correctly.

PICKLED CUCUMBER STRIPS

7 pounds cucumber strips
2 gallons water
3 cups lime
5 pounds sugar

5 pints white vinegar
1 teaspoon oil of cloves
1 teaspoon oil of cinnamon
1 teaspoon mace

Use outside of large cucumbers, even those that have turned yellow, to make cucumber strips. Dissolve lime in water. Soak cucumber strips in lime water for 24 hours. Change water and rinse strips. Soak in clear water four hours, changing water every hour.

Make syrup of sugar, vinegar and spices. Bring to a boil, pour over cucumber strips, and soak overnight. Next morning, boil for 1 hour then seal in hot jars.

SWEET CUCUMBER PICKLES

7 pounds cucumbers, sliced
  crosswise
2 cups pickling lime
2 gallons water

2 quarts vinegar
4-1/2 pounds sugar
1 Tablespoon salt
pickling spice to taste

Mix 2 cups pickling lime to 2 gallons of water and soak cucumber slices 24 hours in lime water. Rinse in 3 different cold waters, then soak an additional 3 hours in ice and water. Remove from water. Make a syrup by combining vinegar, sugar and salt. Pour syrup over cucumbers and allow to sit overnight. Add pickling spice to taste, then boil mixture for 35 minutes. Put pickles in hot, sterilized jars, wipe jar mouth and seal.

GRANDMOTHER DeVAULT'S PEACH PICKLES

(Takes a while to make but worth every day required to do so)

6 pounds peaches, small
3 pounds sugar
1 pint vinegar
1 or 2 pieces loose cinnamon

spice bag containing 1/2 box
mixed spices
a few cloves

Mix sugar and vinegar and bring to boiling point. Add spice bag, cloves and cinnamon. Place peeled peaches in a stone jar and pour the boiling mixture over them. Keep jar loosely covered with a cloth. Each morning for seven days, pour this liquid off, bring to a boiling point, and pour back over the peaches. On the seventh day, cook the peaches in the liquid until tender and put them in clean, hot glass jars and seal.

If your children are like we were as children, you will not end up with a "full recipe". They will "snitch" a few a day, until they are sealed in jars on the 7th day and stored.

ORANGE PEEL PRESERVES

4 large naval oranges
2 cups granulated sugar

water to cover
2 cups water

Wash oranges, cut peel into 6 or 8 segments and remove. Cut peel into very thin slivers (eat the oranges). Place orange peel in a medium-sized saucepan. Add water to cover and bring to a boil over high heat. Boil 5 minutes; drain and discard water. Add sugar and 2 cups water; bring to a boil over moderately high heat and cook 30 to 45 minutes, stirring frequently, until thick and syrupy. Pack into a bowl or jar, cover and refrigerate until ready to use.

SPICED PINEAPPLE

(Very tasty and easy to make a good dish to keep in the refrigerator)

2 cans (1 pound, 4 ounce)
   pineapple chunks or spears,
   undrained
1/2 cup cider vinegar
24 whole cloves
1/2 cup sugar

peel of 2 lemons, cut in strips
   with vegetable peeler
6 sticks (3") cinnamon
1 small jar of Maraschino
   cherries, well-drained,
   (optional) for color

Mix all ingredients and store in refrigerator for two weeks in a covered container to develop flavor. Keeps well, and improves with time. It will be the hit of covered-dish dinners, holiday buffets, etc., and the liquid from the pineapple makes a delicious addition to hot tea.

M.K.'S PICKLED SQUASH

1 gallon small squash slices
8 medium onions, sliced
1/2 cup salt
5 cups sugar

5 cups vinegar
1/2 teaspoon celery seeds
1 Tablespoon mustard seeds
chopped red pepper

Cover squash, onions and salt with ice water for 3 hours. Bring sugar, vinegar, celery seed and mustard seed to a boil. Drain vegetables and drop into syrup mixture. Bring back to a boil, put in hot sterilized jars, and seal.

ICED GREEN TOMATOES

7 pounds green tomatoes (or
   cucumbers)
2 gallons water
3 cups powdered lime (plain yard
   lime)
5 pounds sugar
3 pints vinegar

1 teaspoon ground cloves
1 teaspoon ginger
1 teaspoon allspice
1 teaspoon celery seed
1 teaspoon mace
1 teaspoon cinnamon

Soak sliced tomatoes or cucumbers in lime water for 24 hours. Drain. Soak in fresh water for four hours, changing water every 30 minutes. Drain well. Make a syrup of sugar and vinegar; add spices. Bring syrup to a boil and pour over tomatoes; allow to stand overnight. Next morning, boil for an hour or until tomatoes are clear. Seal in jars while hot. Makes approximately 7 pints.

GREEN TOMATO AND ARTICHOKE PICKLES

Vegetables:
2 quarts cucumbers, thinly sliced
2 quarts small cucumbers
2 quarts onions, thinly sliced
2 quarts green tomatoes, thinly
   sliced
2 heads cabbage, shredded
8 bell peppers, sliced
2 quarts artichokes*
2 to 3 hot peppers
2 cups salt

2 gallons water
Dressing:
1 Tablespoon tumeric
1 cup flour
5 cups sugar
2 gallons vinegar
1 teaspoon black pepper
few white mustard seeds
few celery seeds
5 Tablespoons ground mustard

Slice all vegetables the day before you make the pickle. Make a brine of the salt and water. Soak vegetables overnight in the brine. Next morning, let the vegetables and brine come to a boil. Drain off the brine. Mix all dry ingredients together in a large kettle. Stir in vinegar and bring to a boil, stirring constantly. Add vegetables and let boil a few minutes. Spoon into hot sterilized jars and seal.

*HINT: Artichokes are easy to clean...just wash them in the washing machine in cold water without soap.

WATERMELON PICKLES
(A Blue Ribbon Winner any time)

An indispensable side dish for early Colonial and Southern tables.

3 to 4 pounds watermelon rind, peeled and cubed in small pieces

1/4 cup of canning and pickling salt to each quart of water used to soak rind overnight

Syrup:

6 cups sugar

2-1/2 cups cider vinegar

2 cups water

1 Tablespoon cloves

1 Tablespoon allspice

2 sticks cinnamon

2 thumb size pieces of fresh ginger

1 thinly sliced lemon

1/3 cup maraschino cherry juice

12 to 15 maraschino cherries, quartered

2 drops red food coloring (optional)

In a large pan, let watermelon rind stand overnight in salt water. Drain rind and cover with fresh cold water in a large pan, bring to a boil, reduce heat and simmer until tender. Drain well, discarding water.

Make a syrup of the sugar, vinegar and water in a saucepan. Tie the spices loosely in a spice bag made of cheesecloth. Tie securely. Add to the vinegar mixture and bring to a boil, along with sliced lemon. Cook for about 5 minutes. Add watermelon rind to the syrup mixture. Bring to a boil. Remove the spice bag. Making sure the rind is covered, let stand at room temperature overnight. On the second day, drain the syrup into a large saucepan. Bring to a boil and pour over rind. Let stand at room temperature overnight. On the third day, repeat second day process. On the fourth day, put rind and syrup into a large kettle. Add cherry juice, cherries, and food coloring. Bring to a boil, reduce heat and simmer 10 to 15 minutes. Ladle rind and syrup into hot sterilized pint jars, leaving 1/2" top space. Seal and process in boiling water bath, 10 minutes. Makes 7 to 8 pints. How festive they are at Christmas time and what a treat. You may want to make some green as well by using green food coloring.

NOTE: In choosing watermelon for this recipe, it is better to select cut pieces so that you can get the ones with thick, firm rinds. It is possible to cover rind with water and refrigerate for a few days until you have accumulated enough to make the pickles.

BEET-HORSERADISH RELISH

1 carton (8 ounce) sour cream
2 to 4 Tablespoons prepared
    horseradish
2 Tablespoons red wine vinegar
2 teaspoons sugar
1/2 teaspoon dry mustard
1/4 teaspoon salt
1/8 teaspoon pepper
2 (16 ounce) cans beets, diced and
    drained (3 cups)

Stir first seven ingredients together. Fold in beets, cover and chill. Serve with roast, ham or poultry.

CRANBERRY RELISH

Marvelous as gifts as well as Christmas dinner

1 (16 ounce) package cranberries
2 cups sugar
1 cup water
1 cup orange juice
1 cup celery, chopped
1 medium eating apple, chopped
1 cup golden raisins
1 cup nuts, chopped
1 teaspoon ginger
1 teaspoon orange rind, grated

The day before you wish to serve, bring cranberries, sugar and water to a boil and simmer 15 minutes. Remove from heat and add remaining ingredients. Allow to sit overnight. Yields 7 cups and takes approximately 20 minutes to make.

MARTHA'S KRAUT RELISH

1 (10 ounce) can sauerkraut
1/2 cup sugar
4 Tablespoons vinegar
1/3 cup chopped celery
1/2 cup chopped bell pepper
1/2 cup chopped onion
1 small slivered carrot
1 (2 ounce) jar pimiento

Mix all ingredients together and let stand in refrigerator to chill thoroughly before serving. This is very good and will keep for some time.

PEAR RELISH

1 peck pears (8 quarts or 1/4
    bushel)
6 large green peppers
6 large onions
5 cups vinegar
1 Tablespoon tumeric
1 Tablespoon salt
1 Tablespoon allspice
2 pounds sugar

Grind all ingredients together and cook for 30 minutes. While mixture is hot, put into sterilized jars and seal.

VIDALIA ONION RELISH

2 large Vidalia onions, peeled
2 green bell peppers, seeded and cored
4 medium yellow crookneck squash

1 Tablespoon salt
3 cups sugar
2-1/2 cups cider vinegar
2 teaspoons tumeric
2 teaspoons celery seed

Grind or finely mince onions, peppers and squash. Place in large glass mixing bowl and stir in salt. Cover with cold water and place ice cubes on top. Allow to soak 2 hours, draining and rinsing with fresh cool water three times during soaking.

In the meantime, bring sugar, vinegar, tumeric and celery seed to a boil in a large enameled pot. Reduce heat and continue simmering for 5 minutes. While hot, stir in soaked and drained vegetables. Simmer an additional 10 minutes. While hot, pour into sterilized jars and seal. Process in a water bath for 10 minutes. Cool before storing. Makes 4 pints.

STRAWBERRY FREEZER JAM

1 quart fresh strawberries
4 cups sugar

2 Tablespoons lemon juice
1 (3 ounce) pouch liquid pectin

Wash and hull berries; crush to make 1-3/4 cups crushed berries (if measure is short, add water). Scald jelly jars with lids. Combine crushed strawberries and sugar in a large bowl, stirring to mix well. Let stand 10 minutes. In a separate small bowl, stir lemon juice into liquid pectin. Add to fruit mixture and stir for 3 minutes. Spoon jelly into prepared jars, leaving at least 1/2" room at top. Wipe edges to remove spills and cover with lids. Let stand at room temperature for 24 hours, then freeze until ready to use (a 2 weeks supply may be refrigerated). The fresh berry flavor remains in the jam.

VARIATIONS: To use this recipe for blackberry, red raspberry, or blueberry jam, start with 2 cups of crushed berries. Some of the seeds may be strained out before measuring.

FLO'S SILLY SALT

1 pound salt
1 ounce accent
1 Tablespoon dry mustard
1 teaspoon garlic powder
1 teaspoon cinnamon

1 teaspoon ground oregano
1/2 teaspoon nutmeg
1 teaspoon ginger
1 ounce celery salt
1 Tablespoon black pepper

Empty salt in dry bowl. Add other spices and mix thoroughly. Put into a large shaker to use to season poultry, fish or anything you want.

VINEGARS

Vinegars may range in flavor from sharp to soothingly mellow. The variety among vinegars is astonishing. The most common vinegar is distilled white vinegar which is made by distilling alcohol from grain. Because of its biting acidity and neutral flavor, it is best used for pickling. Malt vinegar has an aggressive tang. It is made from malted grain. Used by the English. Cider Vinegar is the favorite of most Americans. It can be used in salad dressings. It adds to the flavor of pork, chicken and beef by basting with 2 to 3 tablespoons. Rice vinegar is made from rice. The most ubiquitous, it has a rather mild, plain taste. It is used in Oriental cooking. The range of wine vinegars is staggering. The most familiar is the mellow flavorful red, best suited for salad dressings. The sharper and less complex white is reserved for cooking purposes.

Champagne vinegar is basically white-wine vinegar with a fancy and expensive name. Sherry vinegar is remarkably full-bodied with a slightly sweet edge. The King of all wine vinegars is Balsamic Vinegar. It is made in Italy by an age-old process in which fine wine vinegar is scented with herbs and allowed to barrel-age for a decade or longer. The rich sweet and sour taste of Balsamic vinegar lends flavor to salads, soups and vegetables. Italians even sprinkle it on fruits, especially with sugar on strawberries.

Vinegars may be flavored with raspberries, herbs, blueberries, shallots and garlic, and are available commercially. But they can be so easy to make also. Simply place three or four large sprigs of a fresh herb in a glass jar and cover with white-wine vinegar. Garlic and berry vinegars may be made the same way. Allow to steep for at least seven days before using.

HERB VINEGARS

Herb vinegars make tasty and thoughtful gifts. The ancient Egyptians and Greeks revered herbs, using them in their rituals as well as in making them the key ingredients in their cookery, medicine and cosmetics. The magic of herbs has been rediscovered today. Herb vinegars can appear forbidding in price and in packaging on the gourmet shop shelves. But they can be easily made and given as special gifts by attaching a handwritten label to the front of the bottle with the herb lore included on to a handcrafted gift tag around the bottle neck.

1. Select a container of your choice; a ceramic crock or glass jar with a top that fastens securely. The glass jar shows off the herbs inside beautifully. Many stores carry Italian-style bottles or elegant cleanlined ones in an assortment of sizes. They can be found at flea markets or antique shops.

2. When making herb vinegars, use all parts of the herbs, leaves, seeds and flowers. Many varieties can be found fresh in supermarkets or you can grow your own, but pick them after the morning dew has dried. Pick only the best leaves and flowers.

3. You can use cider, red wine or white wine vinegar, but you should always use the highest quality. Even the best herbs cannot hide the unsavory taste of poor-quality vinegar.

4. Fill the bottle or jar with the apportioned herbs and spices, pouring the chosen vinegar over them until the container is full. Tightly secure the cap. Set the jar to "brew" on a sunny window sill, turning it every few days, for about three weeks. Check the vinegar regularly to be sure it still covers the herbs, adding more as needed to keep herbs from drying out. Stored in a cool place, herb vinegars will keep for at least one year, whether or not they've been opened.

Basil

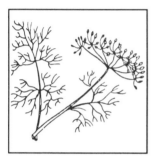

Dill

Thyme

Coriander

To the ancient Greeks, **Basil** was a curse, but Romans believed that a man who accepted basil from a woman would love her forever.

Garlic was revered by the ancient Egyptians. It was consumed by workers building the pyramids, in order to fend off illness.

Dill got its name from the Norse word dilla, meaning "to dull." Early American settlers referred to dill seeds as "meeting-house seeds" and chewed them to relieve hunger pangs that often erupted during long Sunday sermons.

Since ancient times, **Lavender** has been used in making soaps and perfumes, though during the Middle Ages its use was denounced as a shamefully luxurious experience.

To the ancient Greeks, **Thyme** was a symbol of bravery. In medieval Italy it was valued as a remedy for melancholy. And by the 17th century, many Europeans believed thyme soup to be a shyness cure.

From Roman to Tudor times, **Fennel** was considered a symbol of flattery. In medieval Europe, fresh fennel sprigs were stuffed into bedroom-door keyholes to ward off evil spirits that might disrupt sleep.

Flavorful **Coriander**, also known as cilantro or Chinese parsley, has a colorful past. The ancient

Garlic

Lavender

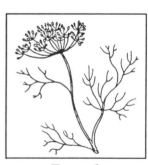

Fennel

Oregano

Rosemary

Bay Leaf

Chinese believed that anyone who ate coriander would enjoy immortality. In the Middle Ages in Europe and the Middle East, it was believed to have been an aphrodisiac. **Oregano** takes its name from the Greek word origanium, meaning "joy of the mountains." Ancient Greeks placed it on graves and believed that if it flowered it would ensure a happy afterlife to the deceased.

To the Greeks of lore, **Rosemary** was the herb of remembrance. In one legend, the Virgin Mary was said to drape her cloak to dry over the white-flowered rosemary bush, turning the flowers forever blue.

Though not botanically an herb, **Bay** has always been treated as such. In ancient Rome it was an emblem of glory and eternal prosperity.

BASIL GARLIC

Fill bottle or jar loosely with fresh basil sprigs, 4 or 5 cloves of peeled garlic. For a pleasing look, thread the garlic cloves onto a wooden skewer and insert in the bottle. Use white wine vinegar. Heavenly on tomatoes and in salads that include bitter greens.

DILL

Fill bottle or jar loosely to about 2/3 full with fresh dill. Use white wine vinegar. Wonderful in fish dishes and on green salads.

LAVENDER

1 or 2 large fresh lavender sprigs with flowers. Use white wine vinegar. The bittersweet rosemary-like taste of lavender adds a pleasing note to fruit salads.

RASPBERRY THYME

1 cup fresh raspberries, 1/3 cup sugar, 2 or 3 sprigs fresh thyme. Use red or white vinegar. Perfect for delicate green-leaf, cold-meat or vegetable salads.

SOUTHWEST

1 or 2 sprigs each fresh oregano and coriander, 3 or 4 large peeled garlic cloves, 1/2 thinly sliced lemon slice, 3 or 4 small dried red chili peppers, peppercorns. Use white wine vinegar. Gives punch to corn relishes or guacamole. Try as a marinade for pork or beef.

HERB OILS

Creating herb oils is equally as easy. Fill a jar or bottle with selected fresh herbs and spices. Cover them with a good quality vegetable oil or an olive oil of first quality. Cap the container snugly and put it in a warm place, not hot, for a couple of weeks before using. Your herb vinegars and oils can be as simple or as complex as your tastes. Combine the ingredients, keeping in mind that your favorite herbs and spices will make your favorite vinegars and oils. A few suggested combinations are:

Chinese Stir-Fry: **6 to 8 peeled garlic cloves**
6 to 8 small chili peppers   **6 slices fresh ginger**

Place all in a jar and cover with oil. Use in stir-fry dishes.

Italian: **8 to 10 small dried red chili**
30 fresh basil leaves   **peppers**

Place all in a jar and cover with oil. Use on pasta, in soups and for basting grilled vegetables.

Fennel Oil: **red and black pepper corns**
fennel leaves   **oil**
mustard seeds

Place all loosely in a jar. Fennel has subtle licorice like taste that makes it delicious on salads, in fish dishes or as a crudity dip.

Garlic: **1 bay leaf**
6 to 8 large peeled garlic cloves   **oil**

Place all in a jar. This is ideal for brushing on Italian and French bread when grilling. Also great for sauting vegetables or basting them for grilling.

Rosemary and Thyme: **a few black pepper corns**
sprigs of fresh rosemary   **3 to 4 large peeled garlic cloves**
sprigs of fresh thyme   **oil**

Loosely fill a jar or bottle with all ingredients. Superb as a marinade or as a basting sauce for lamb, chicken and fish. Splendid in pasta and sauces.

INDEX

RECIPE CONTRIBUTORS

1. Mrs. Flo Pursley (Norman B.)
2. Mrs. Helen Christman (Phillip)
3 Mrs. Josephine Engler
4. Mrs. Janice Pennington
5. Mrs. Carole Wright (Earl)
6. Mrs. Jan Steed Burk
7. Mrs. Jackie Scoggins (Henry)
8. Mrs. Jacqueline Wetherhorn
9. Mrs. Jeanette Steed (Wm. A.)
10. Miss Jessie Hall
11. Mrs. Carol Martin
12. Mrs. Melva Anderson (Gene)
13. Mrs. Wm. D. Morris
14. Mrs. Risa Newsome
15. Mrs. Jeania Walls
16. Mrs. Martha McGahee (O.O.)
17. Mr. Wayne Driggers
18. Mrs. Katherine Hammett (H.H., Jr.)
19. Mrs. Sandra Symonds
20. Mrs. Biddie Dugas
21. Mrs. Emma Roberts (S.M.)
22. Mrs. Sunshine Tedder
23. Mrs. Monnie R. Donald
24. Mrs. Lana Kimbrell
25. Mrs. Lillie Morris
26. Mrs. Dina Serandis
27. Mrs. Jane Barrett (Wm. H.)
28. Miss Sandra Scoggins
29. Mrs. Erona Hill
30. Mrs. Norma Reeves
31. Mrs. Jo Agostas (Wm. N.)
32. Mrs. William Alden
33. Dr. Henry Scoggins
34. Mrs. Fay Graham
35. Mrs. Harriette Spears
36. Mrs. Jane Armstrong
37. Mrs. Margaret Scheer
38. Mrs. Andrea Swift
39. Dr. Tom Scheer
40. Mrs. Shirley Wilson (Ronald)
41. Mrs. Nell Morris
42. Mrs. Jan Munn
43. Mrs. Dan Martin
44. Mrs. Nancy Moak (Robert)
45. Mrs. Debbie Tendor
46. Mrs. Suzanne Shapiro
47. Mrs. Anna Jo Turner
48. Mrs. Vonnie Poston
49. Mrs. Agnes Willingham
50. Mrs. Mary Kay Forbes
51. Miss Claire Pursley
52. Mrs. Louise Thigpen
53. Mrs. Ann Morris (W. W.)
54. Mrs. Sarah Murphy (Jennings)
55. Mrs. Anna Wall
56. Mrs. Frances Sideman
57. Mrs. Beth Kuhlke
58. Mrs. Lucy Lee
59. Mrs. Judy Ellis
60. Miss Alice Pursley
61. Mrs. Mary Gooding
62. Mrs. Nita Zachow
63. Mrs. Celeste Carswell (A.S.)
64. Mrs. Pearl Person
65. Mr. Jerry Pruitt
66. Sheila Swift
67. Andrew Swift
68. Elizabeth Swift
69. Mrs. Jean Waters
70. Mrs. Louise Hudson
71. Mrs. Linda Locke
72. Mrs. Cathy Shaffer
73. Josephine Steed
74. Mrs. Helen Maddox (Wm)
75. Mrs. Betty Jordan (Clarence)
76. Mrs. Anna Whitney (Charlie)
77. Mrs. Louise Sands
78. Mrs. Bea Hite
79. Mrs. Leah Quattlebaum
80. Dr. Evangeline Lane
81. Dr. Linda Clary
82. Mrs. Karen Sheppo (Michael)
83. Mrs. Tony Burk
84. Mrs. Connie Conrad
85. Mr. George Conrad
86. Mrs. Richard Terzia
87. Mrs. Margaret Johnson
88. Mrs. Ruth Ann Vericella
89. Mrs. Joan Puryear
90. Mrs. Lauren Burnett
91. Mrs. Bea Masengale
92. Mrs. Louise Callam
93. Mrs. Jane Wells
94. Mrs. Ann Galloway (Ronald)
95. Mrs. Mary K. Forbes
96. Mr. Ron Pittman
97. Mrs. Mary Frances Gray
98. Mrs. Amelia Cartledge
99. Mrs. Mary Conrad Allen
100. Mrs. Linda Conrad Miller
101. Mrs. Georgia Abraham
102. Mrs. Cherry Serpharin
103. Mrs. Eleanor Bolin
104. Mrs. Albert Hanger
105. Martha Blanchard
106. Udell Randolph
107. Mrs. Susan Jones
108. Mrs. Frank Steed
109. Mrs. Pan Vance
110. Mrs. Mary Kelly
111. Mrs. Judy Murphy
112. Mrs. Jean Baxley
113. Miss Jennie C. Steed

REORDER ADDITIONAL COPIES

AUGUSTA COOKS for COMPANY

Please send me _____ copies of
AUGUSTA COOKS for COMPANY $15.95 each _____
Georgia residents add 5% sales tax .96 each _____
Postage and handling 2.00 each _____
  Total Enclosed $ _____

Name _____

Address _____

City _____ State _____ Zip _____

*If shipping to multiple addresses, or enclosure card needed, please attach.

Please make checks payable to:
AUGUSTA COOKS for COMPANY

Send to:
Augusta Cooks for Company
P.O. Box 3231
Hill Station
Augusta, Georgia 30914-3231

Profits realized from the sale of *AUGUSTA COOKS for COMPANY* will be used for scholarship funds for Learning Disabled Youths and Teachers to Attend workshops on Learning Disabilities.

RAY BAIRD'S PRINTS

Lithographs of the original drawings by Augusta artist Ray Baird can now be ordered. Each painting has been reproduced at its original size as listed below and is printed on high-quality heavy stock.

The prints can be ordered individually for prices listed. The titles of each drawing can be found on the page behind each print within the cookbook, along with a short descriptive passage.

To order your prints, fill out the following order form or send the necessary information to:

Baird's Prints, Inc.
P.O. Box 211229
Martinez, Georgia 30917-1229
Telephone: 404-860-6570

Drawing	Size	B&W Color Print*	Hand Watercolored	Amount
1. Sacred Heart	14x17	$ N/A	$45.00	$
2. Old First Baptist Church	12x18	30.00	70.00	
3. St. Paul's Church	15x18	35.00	75.00	
4. First Presbyterian Church	15x18	35.00	75.00	
5. Augusta National	12x18	30.00	70.00	
6. Under the Big Oaks	12x18	30.00	70.00	
7. Augusta Golf Party	12x18	30.00	70.00	
8. The Arsenal-Augusta College	12x18	30.00	70.00	
9. Old Academy of Richmond County	12x18	30.00	70.00	
10. Old Engine Company No. 1	12x18	30.00	70.00	
11. Signer's Monument	12x18	30.00	70.00	
12. Woodrow Wilson Boyhood Home	12x18	30.00	70.00	
13. Ezechiel Harris House	12x18	30.00	70.00	
14. Old Medical College of Ga.	12x18	25.00	65.00	
Note Cards				

*Print only — not hand colored

Packaging		$1.00
Postage		$1.00
Georgia residents (5% tax)		$
	Total	$

❑ Check or Money order   ❑ Mastercard or VISA

Card number_____ Expiration date _____
    Bank number (Mastercard only) _____
Please allow 4 weeks for delivery

Name_____Date _____

Address _____

City_____State_____Zip_____